THE TAO OF SPYCRAFT

THE TAO OF SPYCRAFT

Intelligence Theory and Practice in Traditional China

Ralph D. Sawyer

with the collaboration of
Mei-chün Lee Sawyer

Westview Press
A Member of the Perseus Books Group

10014957 88

Copyright © 1998 by Ralph D. Sawyer

Published in 1998 in the United States of America by Westview Press, 5500 Central Avenue, Boulder, Colorado 80301-2877, and in the United Kingdom by Westview Press, 12 Hid's Copse Road, Cumnor Hill, Oxford OX2 9JJ

Library of Congress Cataloging-in-Publication Data
Sawyer, Ralph D.
  The Tao of spycraft : intelligence theory and practice in
traditional China / Ralph D. Sawyer, with collaboration of Mei-chün
Lee Sawyer.
     p. cm.
  Includes bibliographical references and index.
  ISBN 0-8133-3303-2
  1. Military intelligence—China—History. 2. Military
intelligence—China—History—Sources. 3. China—History, Military.
I. Sawyer, Mei-chün. II. Title.
UB251.C6S28 1998
327.1251—dc21   98-6521
                                                                                      CIP

The paper used in this publication meets the requirements of the American National Standard for Permanence of Paper for Printed Library Materials Z39.48-1984.

10   9   8   7   6   5   4   3   2   1

*In memory of those who courageously risked
their lives among the shadows,
only to be shunned and disdained
when peace arose*

Contents

Part 4
Theories of Evaluating and Intelligence

Part 5
Military Intelligence

Part 6
Prognostication, Divination, and Nonhuman Factors

Chronology of
Approximate Dynastic Periods

Dynastic Period	Years
Legendary Sage Emperors	2852–2255 B.C.
Hsia	2205–1766
Shang	1766–1045
Chou	
Western Chou	1045–770
Eastern Chou	770–256
Spring and Autumn	722–481
Warring States	403–221
Ch'in	221–207
Former Han (Western Han)	206 B.C.–A.D. 8
Later Han (Eastern Han)	23–220
Six Dynasties	222–589
Sui	589–618
T'ang	618–907
Five Dynasties	907–959
Sung	960–1126
Southern Sung	1127–1279
Yüan (Mongol)	1279–1368
Ming	1368–1644
Ch'ing (Manchu)	1644–1911

Preface

No nation has practiced the craft of intelligence or theorized about it more extensively than China, filling their military writings with discussions on concepts and techniques, littering their histories and popular literature with records of clandestine activities. Moreover, rather than diminishing in the present era of ostensible peace and harmony, these practices have instead proliferated, expanding to target business and industry equally with governments. However, despite Sun-tzu's *Art of War* being widely acknowledged as the first theoretical writing on agents and methods, and despite the presence of extensive chapters on these subjects in subsequent military texts, the history of intelligence and spycraft in China has never been seriously attempted. In fact, apart from Chu Feng-chia's late Ch'ing dynasty pastiche entitled *Chien Shu*, the secondary literature is virtually bereft of books devoted to the subject and the many journals devoted to China's history, whether in Chinese, Japanese, or Western languages, devoid of articles. Whereas in pre-twentieth-century China this absence might be attributable to the traditional disdain felt for military affairs in general and the "unrighteous" activity of spying in particular (not unlike the prejudice directed toward intelligence and spycraft in the West), it fails to explain the present lack of interest in China's achievements in the thorny field of intelligence over the millennia. The *Tao of Spycraft* therefore focuses upon the history and development of both overt intelligence theory and covert practices in China. Even though our subject matter is historically focused, since the PRC aggressively deploys thousands of agents of every type throughout the world who are ardently gathering commercial, industrial, and military intelligence, the materials included are not irrelevant to the present day.

Although based upon several years of extensive research in original Chinese materials and hopefully substantial in its conclusions, our study is designed to be accessible to anyone interested in things Chinese—whether history, intellectual developments, or military theory—as well as world military developments and the history of intelligence in general. We have perused in varying detail some fifty thousand pages of historical and theoretical writings and compiled hundreds of incidents of agent activities, some of great significance. Naturally most of them were minor, receiving only passing mention (as would be expected of secret operations—if known at all—especially when coupled with the prejudices of the literati writing the official histories toward such methods), but when assembled, they present a clear picture of unexpectedly intense intelligence activity. However, in a study of this type there is a temptation to see spies everywhere, to imagine significance in the least incident; therefore, as a counterbalance we have stressed episodes of apparent veracity and enough detail to subsequently assume a life of their own, to become part of the culture's common knowledge and thus a factor in its mindset and tendencies when conceptualizing and envisioning solutions to significant military and political problems.

Our focus throughout is on externally directed intelligence efforts, whether military or covert, rather then internal security—in other words, between the independent states during the ancient period, factions during periods of fragmentation, and China and its external enemies during the imperial period. Internal measures directed toward controlling the indigenous populace, while neither unimportant nor uninteresting, constitute a radically different orientation that may be studied in Richard Deacon's earlier book, the *Chinese Secret Service,* a popular, yet insightful work that emphasizes such matters and late intelligence history in China and even the PRC. (In concord with our overall military interest and to keep it distinct from our work on contemporary China, our study extends only up to the appearance of Westerners and the deployment of hot weapons, roughly synonymous with the Ming dynasty. [The famous novel known as *The Romance of the Three Kingdoms,* although apparently influential in establishing China's clandestine intelligence service prior to World War II, thus also falls outside the scope of our work.] However, contemporary Chinese practices have recently been addressed by Nicholas Eftimiades in *Chinese Intelligence Operations.*)

The sprawling nature of China's military and political history prompted a bifurcated organization rather than either a chronological progression or a topical examination. Since the formative period for intelligence activities falls into the ancient era, the initial section on antiquity examines the fundamental practices stimulated by the incessant conflict among the individual states as the Chou dynasty disintegrated, and the remainder of the book focuses on intelligence theory illustrated by cases from later history and chapters from the military texts. Whereas the theoretical materials from the latter are representative and comprehensive, the historical examples, especially less detailed ones from the twenty-five dynastic histories, could have been multiplied almost endlessly, easily doubling the length of the book. However, the most interesting and important cases, as well as all the basic practices and types of agents, fully evolve during the ancient period, essentially defining the field thereafter. Consequently, the earlier cases are disproportionately significant, as well as intrinsically more intriguing.

In order to provide as many original materials as possible, we have included extensive translations but refrained from summarizing and rephrasing them thereafter, assuming they will prove self-explanatory upon careful examination. Although this converts the book into something of a hybrid sourcebook, in intelligence work accuracy lies in details, which are best conveyed in their original form, as directly as possible, not grandiose schemes and charts. Moreover, since we hope this book will interest a wide audience, including sinologists, we have deliberately eschewed the employment of intelligence jargon while severely limiting the number of footnotes on translation matters, unlike in our *Military Methods*. However, three major topics— the theory of agents, evaluating men, and configurations of terrain— are extensively detailed so that the progression and ongoing reintegration of ideas across the sweep of centuries may be clearly seen by readers with corresponding interests.

The past decade has witnessed a great resurgence in Chinese interest in matters antique ranging from Confucian theory to the Taoist classics and military writings, spawning a vast horde of secondary works bent on applying ancient insights to every conceivable contemporary problem. One or two popular, poorly researched books touching on Chinese intelligence methods have even appeared, largely directed to business applications or developing esoteric tactics that will allow their readers to overcome others in even the most dire and unrealistic circumstances. These frequently cite passages and ideas from Sun-tzu and Han Fei-tzu—China's Machiavelli—but rarely explore substantial theory or historical practice. However, contemporary interest flourishes, and very much in accord with the centuries-long tradition of examining the past for knowledge and lessons, these traditional materials are reputedly once again being perused in the PRC's think tanks and spy schools for techniques, insights, and paradigms adaptable to China's quest for world domination, for forging a military and intelligence science with indigenous Chinese characteristics. Thus, while the *Tao of Spycraft* is strictly a historical study, it has contemporary relevance because the lessons that are being taught and mind-set instilled, whether in state-sponsored contexts or popular media, are mainly derived from China's centuries of intrigue.

As always it is a pleasure to acknowledge the efforts and cooperation of others in the development of this book. Thanks are due first of all to Professor Nathan Sivin for his illuminating ruminations on many subjects, not the least being *ch'i* and calendrical matters; next to Drs. Sean Sheehan and Rick Williams for overviews on covert medical matters; Brigadier General Karl Eikenberry for advice on military subjects; Professor Bruce Brooks, founder of the Warring States Project, for raising critical questions and generously sharing his knowledge on texts and dating; Howard Brewer and Guy Baer for insightful discussions over the years on intellectual and spiritual matters both Chinese and Japanese; H. Jeffrey Davis for fruitful conversations; Antoinette Loézere and Ed Swiniarski for intriguing narrations; Peter Kracht for his initial interest; Laura Parsons and Rob Williams for the courage to see it through; George Potter for valuable reference materials; and Max Gartenberg for his expertise in many matters. Happily, Lee T'ing-rong has again honored the book with his calligraphy. As in our previous works, while I am responsible for the primary research, translations, conceptions, and historical conclusions, Mei-chün collaborated in reading the later dynastic histories, reviewing secondary materials, discussing the translations, and generally scrutinizing the drafts, thereby making the book possible.

Finally, we would like to reiterate that this is a historical study based upon readily accessible materials and open, printed sources. None of our many clients, friends, relatives, or associates in the United States or Asia, including the PRC, provided any restricted materials whatsoever. Even though this project is in part an outgrowth of a paper presented at the Society for Military History's Sixty-third Annual Meeting sponsored by the CIA's Center for the Study of Intelligence in April 1996, there is no connection whatsoever with any intelligence agency in the United States or abroad. Moreover, although I have been a careful, hopefully astute, student of intelligence theory and methods over the years and our consulting practice has largely focused upon information and analysis, I have not been actively involved in any aspect of formal intelligence work on behalf of any government since the Vietnam era.

Ralph D. Sawyer

THE TAO OF SPYCRAFT

Part One

EARLY HISTORY

早 期 史 話

1

Early Records
and the First Spies

*D*ESPITE BEING COMMONLY PERCEIVED as long having been a
politically and culturally integrated state, China suffered almost incessant warfare and rampant political intrigue over the three millennia of its tenuous geopolitical existence. In consequence, as early as
the turbulent Spring and Autumn (722–481 B.C.) and Warring States
(403–221 B.C.) periods a body of military theory evolved that gradually
acquired canonical status centuries later. Remarkably, these ancient
tactical classics—famous works such as Sun-tzu's *Art of War* and Wu
Ch'i's *Wu-tzu*—retained their applicability through successive dynasties because military practices were essentially continuous until the
advent of hot weapons and contact with the West. Moreover, they
were studied not only by professional military men, but also by statesmen, bureaucrats, and philosophers, often in conjunction with the
records of battles and intrigues preserved in China's extensive historical writings.

The disproportionate influence of the early classics on subsequent
military theorizing, including the nature and objectives of China's intelligence activities over the past two millennia, should not be under-
estimated.[1] The assumptions and principles expounded by Sun-tzu,
China's earliest known theorist, largely defined the parameters and
categories that were vigorously followed thereafter, particularly in assessments of the enemy and the thrust of spycraft. Many of his conceptions may be traced into the T'ang, when they were particularly
expanded following the unrelenting strife and intrigue that had
marked the previous centuries of disunion, and then on through the
Sung into the Ming. In every case the authors embraced Sun-tzu's
principles and analysis but expanded the methodological details, cate-

gories of operatives, range of activities, types of mission, and psychology of recruitment, eventually emphasizing security and counterintelligence measures to frustrate increasingly numerous and effective
agents, both diplomatic and covert.

Chinese intelligence efforts have historically focused upon rulers
and powerful officials, economic factors, and military plans, capabilities, dispositions, and movements. The data collected were comparatively analyzed to determine probable intentions, develop a net assessment, and plot possible reactions. Clandestine operations naturally
evolved to gather secret information critical to "preparing against the
unforeseen," resulting in the employment of several types of agents,
methods of control, and techniques of analysis. Preserving secrecy became critical, necessitating efforts to prevent foreign agents from easily acquiring both open information and secret plans while stimulating counterintelligence activities to thwart and manipulate enemy
agents. Covert measures and psychological operations designed to disrupt the enemy's government, solidarity, and capabilities—including
conducting assassinations, sowing doubts and rumors, bribing and corrupting officials, and executing estrangement techniques—rapidly
multiplied even in the early period.

China's historical writings, while varied and voluminous, are unfortunately sketchy for the early Chou, Spring and Autumn, and Warring
States periods. However, the limited extant materials still provide a
fairly comprehensive picture of intrigue, machination, and ingenuity,
even though their terseness often requires imaginative interpretation
and their reliability has been questioned. Moreover, apart from their
fundamental value as chronological history, they subsequently assumed a life of their own, one validated by centuries of assiduous
study, eventually providing the basis for popular tales and a core of
general belief. Bolstered by Confucian reverence for antiquity, they
also came to function as compendiums of ancient practices and stories, the essence and foundation of a national mind-set that would delimit the very possibilities of conception and action. Eventually they
were viewed not just as benign portrayals of ancient times, but also as
virtual handbooks of covert practices, stealthy techniques, pernicious
concepts, and perverse methods that should be denied the unrighteous
and kept from the dangerous. Just as the military writings, they posed
a potential danger to the ruler, especially during periods of instability,
justifying stringent control measures. The paranoia that could result
is well illustrated by a T'ang dynasty incident prompted by the Turfan
forwarding a request ostensibly on behalf of a T'ang princess previously given to them in marriage for the core classics of Chinese civilization: the *Book of Odes, Li Chi, Tso Chuan,* and *Wen Hsüan.* In the

following memorial a high official vehemently opposed granting their request:

Your subject has heard that these barbarians are raiders who plague us while the classics are the essence of our state. We must be prepared against the passions of such barbarians. Since the classics contain timeless methods for governing, they cannot be loaned to other peoples. The *Tso Chuan* states: "The Shang did not plan against the Hsia, the Yi [barbarians] did not confuse the Hua [Chinese]." The way to resist their untamed hearts and be free of misfortune is to prepare.

In antiquity when King P'ing-tung visited the Han court seeking the *Shih Chi* and the writings of the philosophers, Emperor Ch'eng did not grant his request because the *Shih Chi* is replete with military strategies and the books of the philosophers with crafty techniques. So if the Han emperor was unwilling to show his own beloved relative these books on the conduct of warfare, how can we today hand over classics filled with such information to our nemesis, the Western barbarians?

Moreover, I have heard that by nature the Turfan are cruel and decisive, their emotions sensitive and sharp, and they excel in studying everything. If they penetrate the *Book of Documents*, they will certainly know how to conduct warfare. If they thoroughly understand the *Book of Odes*, they will know the martial. If their teachers probe deeply into the *Li Chi*, they will know about the monthly ordinances. When their experienced soldiers have penetrated the *Tso Chuan*, they will learn numerous deceptive methods and stratagems for employing troops. When they become thoroughly familiar with the literary pieces in the *Wen Hsüan*, they will know the regulations governing war dispatches. How will this differ from loaning weapons to the invaders and providing them with provisions?

I have heard that when the state of Lu embraced the *Chou Li*, Ch'i did not attack them. When Wu learned how to employ chariots, Ch'u's troops were exhausted in running for their lives.[2] The former preserved their state by maintaining the classics, the latter endangered their state by losing their tactics. Moreover, having been sent out in marriage, the princess has traveled a great distance to a foreign state where she should be embracing the rites of the Yi peoples, not turning around and seeking our outstanding books. According to my bumbling analysis, this is not really the princess's idea. I suspect that some defector is encouraging these teachings among them.

If your majesty is concerned about losing the affection of the Turfan and preserving the state's credibility so there is absolutely no other way, I suggest you eliminate the *Ch'un Ch'iu* [and *Tso Chuan*] because it was composed when the virtue of the Chou was already in decline, when the feudal lords were forcefully violating the constraints of rites and music, each going forth to engage in warfare. At that time prevarication was born, at that time change and deceit arose. There were cases of ministers summoning their rulers as well as seizing the awesomeness and name of hegemon. If you provide them with this book, it will be a source of misfortune to our state. In the *Tso Chuan* it states that [as his reward for valor] Yu-hsi requested certain minor privileges in court dress which, when granted, prompted Confucius to say: "Alas, why not give him more cities? Only names and vessels [of state] cannot be loaned to men."[3] These barbarians clearly covet expensive goods and disdain territory, so you can formally present them with silks and generously gift them with jades. Why must you grant what they seek and thereby increase their knowledge?[4]

The antecedent cited in which the emperor refused to provide the *Shih Chi* and other philosophical works even to his own uncle, the nominal king of a subsidiary Han fief, is similarly illuminating. First, it implies that nearly a century after its completion the *Shih Chi* was still largely retained in the court archives rather than generally circulated. Second, political works, including historical writings and the arguments of the philosophers, were seen as equally filled with insidious, potentially dangerous materials, viewed as veritable textbooks of plots and machinations, techniques and subterfuges. Thus, they were not granted to the king of P'ing-tung in 29 B.C. despite his royal lineage because General Wang Feng advised:

Some of the works of the philosophers are contrary to orthodox classical studies and criticize the Great Sages of antiquity, others illustrate ghosts and spirits and believe in oddities and curiosities. The *Shih Chi* contains the strategies of the Warring States, the horizontal and vertical alliances, tactical power and deception, the unorthodox measures employed by tacticians at the rise of the Han, Heavenly Offices, disasters, abnormalities, mountain passes and strategic points, and the topography of the realm, none of which should be in the hands of the feudal lords.[5]

These works, together with the military writings and *Twenty-five Dynastic Histories*, provide the basis for this study.

Yi Yin and Early History

Deliberately gathering information about one's enemies doubtlessly commenced with the earliest Neolithic conflicts, although short-term reconnaissance and direct line-of-sight observation, aided by conceal-ment and the advantage of height, would have been the only means available. Over the centuries the few military theorists and historians who contemplated the issues of intelligence gathering in China have often attributed the earliest known spy activities to King Shao-k'ang, said to have ruled the Hsia dynasty in the nineteenth century B.C., be-cause he apparently dispatched an agent to clandestinely observe his father's murderer while secretly developing the power base necessary to successfully restore Hsia rule, an event traditionally dated to 1875 B.C. The key historical reference, much cited thereafter, actually ap-pears in the *Tso Chuan*, embedded in Wu Tzu-hsü's futile attempt to persuade the king of Wu to exterminate their archenemy, the state of Yüeh under King Kou-chien, now that they had vanquished it. This single line runs, "Shao-k'ang employed Ju-ai to spy upon Chiao."[6]

By the end of the historical, though poorly documented, Hsia dy-nasty at least one famous figure is identified as a covert agent, while another was instrumental in subverting and overthrowing the Shang dynasty around 1045 B.C. According to Sun-tzu: "In antiquity, when the Shang arose, they had Yi Yin in the Hsia. When the Chou arose, they had Lü Ya (the T'ai Kung) in the Shang."[7] Sun-tzu's view apart, neither of them appears to have acted in the usual role of spies—that is, agents dispatched on clandestine missions—being instead "defec-tors," experts who had abandoned perverse governments to perform advisory roles for moral contenders. However, despite being volun-teers rather than recruited informants, they have still been considered "spies" *(chien)*, immediately suggesting the broad scope of the term *chien* in ancient China.[8]

Even though agents and observers had no doubt been plying their trade for centuries, Yi Yin eventually became recognized as China's first covert agent because Sun-tzu thus dubbed him so. However, the historical materials that purportedly chronicle ancient Chinese his-tory—particularly the *Shang Shu* (Book of Documents)—are devoid of any justification for Sun-tzu's ascription. Rather than some secretive, shadowy figure, in a motif much repeated thereafter these writings portray a recluse who righteously abandoned his pastoral obscurity and nominal allegiance to the tyrannical Hsia to guide a youthful ruler embarking upon the course of virtue and benevolence. In its earliest form the story simply located him on the periphery of the Hsia, but over the centuries it became more romanticized and explicit, eventually resulting in Mencius's definitive portrait in the middle Warring States period.

A chapter in the *Lü-shih Ch'un-ch'iu,* a late third century B.C. eclectic text, preserves the most dramatic account to be found among China's numerous historical writings. Not only does it integrate the image of a moral paragon with the deviousness of a seasoned spy; it also includes a painful cover story:

Because Emperor Chieh of the Hsia dynasty was immoral, brutal, perverse, stupid, and greedy, All under Heaven quaked in fear and were greatly troubled. However, reports of his deeds were contradictory and confused, so it was difficult for anyone to fathom the true situation. Availing himself of the emperor's awesomeness, the prime minister Kan Hsin was brusque and insulting to both the feudal lords and the common people. Because the worthy and outstanding ministers were all anxious and resentful, the emperor killed Kuan Lung-feng to stifle rebellious stirrings. The common masses, in consternation and confusion, all wished to emigrate elsewhere and, afraid to speak directly about the situation, lived in constant terror. Although the great ministers shared the same worries, they dared not cooperate to mount a revolt. Meanwhile Emperor Chieh increasingly regarded himself as a great worthy, boasted of his transgressions, and even viewed wrong as right. The imperial way was blocked and stopped, the populace in total collapse.

Terrified and troubled that the realm was not at peace, T'ang wanted Yi Yin to go and observe the mighty Hsia. However, he feared that Yi Yin would not be trusted, so he personally shot him with an arrow. Yi Yin then fled to the Hsia. After three years he reported back to T'ang at his enclave at Hao: "Earlier Chieh was befuddled and deluded by his consort Mo Hsi and now loves his two concubines from Min-shan, so he doesn't have any concern for the common people. The will of the people does not support him, upper and lower ranks detest each other. The hearts of the people are filled with resentment. They all say that Heaven fails to have pity on them, so the Hsia's mandate is over."

T'ang exclaimed: "What you have just said is much like a prophetic lament!" They then swore an oath together to evidence their determination to extinguish Hsia.

Yi Yin went again to observe the mighty Hsia, where he learned from Mo Hsi that "the previous night the emperor had dreamt there was a sun in the west and a sun in the east. When the two suns engaged in combat, the western sun emerged victorious and the eastern sun was vanquished." Yi Yin reported this to T'ang. Although the area was suffering from a severe drought, in order to keep faith with the oath he had sworn with Yi Yin, T'ang still mobilized their forces. Thereafter he ordered the army, after proceeding out from the east, to make their advance into Hsia territory from the west. Chieh fled even before their blades had clashed, but was pursued out to Ta-sha where he was finally killed.[9]

Remarkably, this episode already incorporates many crucial elements of spycraft. First, from the outset Yi Yin—whatever his wisdom and moral qualifications—was deliberately employed as a covert agent responsible for determining the true state of affairs in the Hsia, an enemy entity despite the Shang's own theoretical obligations toward their ruler. Second, he was given a plausible pretext for voluntarily allying himself with the perverse Chieh: a visible arrow wound (no doubt preceded by rumors and vivid, if inaccurate, accounts) emblematic of T'ang's hatred. Third, just as many rulers and innumerable officials throughout Chinese history, Chieh succumbed to sexual indulgence and the allure of beauty. Moreover, Mo Hsi, much dejected because new, foreign concubines were monopolizing the emperor's favors, acted as the archetypal slighted beauty in secretly revealing the king's frightening dream. (Throughout Chinese history many jealous consorts and concubines poisoned, stabbed, or otherwise murdered their unfaithful husbands and lovers, as well as betrayed their secrets, frustrated their plans, and thwarted their interests.) This information allowed King T'ang to exploit the ancient belief in the prophetic nature of dreams by enacting a scenario that actualized Chieh's secret fears. The advance of King T'ang's army from the west thus proved sufficient to trigger Chieh's terror and flight. Furthermore, Chieh's downfall was undoubtedly hastened because the hostile state of Min-shan had consciously exploited the debilitating power of women and sex. The two new concubines who so fascinated him were neither accidental acquisitions nor battlefield spoils, but instead were gifts deliberately presented by the minor state of Min-shan that lay in the barbarous area of northwest Szechwan, far beyond the central core area of Hsia-Shang culture, to debauch his mind and deflect further incursions. Finally, the importance of prophetic events, sayings, and phenomena may be seen in T'ang's reaction to Yi Yin's initial report, for he was apparently astounded that Yi's words echoed what was probably a common saying predicting such a downfall.

The enigmatic Yi Yin eventually garnered a hallowed place in Chinese history as one of the virtuous paragons cited by Confucian literati seeking to justify the employment of worthy men to China's

despotic rulers. He, the T'ai Kung, and a few other idealized figures became famous for having rescued their eras, not to mention monarchs,
while ever espousing the virtuous ways of Yao, Shun, Yü, and the
other semimythical Sage emperors of remote antiquity. They were inevitably portrayed as active, yet unsullied, pure, yet effective, and the
Shang Shu purportedly preserves Yi Yin's admonitory speeches charging the youthful ruler with the practice of virtue at the Shang dynasty's inception. However, it otherwise provides nothing more than a
sparse record of his activities, noting only that somewhat more than a
decade after he was summoned to King T'ang's court the Shang successfully overthrew the Hsia in a brief battle. (The preface to the
Shang Shu adds the comment that Yi Yin had been embarrassed to
serve under the Hsia and therefore returned to Hao, the site of T'ang's
domain.) He is further depicted as having continued as prime minister
under two or three of T'ang's successors, even temporarily deposing
one of them for a lack of virtue until restoring him to the throne following three years of enforced, isolated soul-searching.[10] However, the
Bamboo Annals, increasingly viewed by scholars as a somewhat reliable source for the period, offers a startlingly different conclusion to
this otherwise idealized story, stating that Yi Yin actually usurped the
throne and was eventually executed when the rightful king escaped
his confinement.[11]

Befitting his status as China's first recognized covert agent, Yi Yin's
historical image thus subsumes two different personae: a virtuous,
self-sacrificing minister, and the skilled spy who made the conquest
possible. The former was trumpeted by naive Confucians emphasizing
the idea that Virtue alone is sufficient to dominate the realm, the latter stressed by political realists in the late Warring States period. Although Yi Yin's name appears in a multitude of texts,[12] he was defini-
tively canonized as a paragon of virtue by Mencius when queried by a
disciple as to whether, as commonly suggested, Yi Yin had sought a
position under T'ang by becoming a cook rather than having been immediately recognized for his surpassing wisdom and virtue. (The
Huai-nan Tzu, a somewhat later work, notes that being troubled by
the realm being ungoverned, "Yi Yin harmonized the five flavors,
slung his cooking vessels over his back, and went forth." It adds that
"he went to Chieh five times, and also to T'ang five times, wanting to
make the turbid clear and the endangered tranquil."[13]) In reply, Mencius pedantically described Yi Yin as the epitome of righteousness: a
scholar fending for himself in the countryside, contentedly plowing
his fields while practicing the Tao of the ancient Sage emperors. No
amount of profit could coerce him into forsaking the path of righteousness, nothing cause him to commit the slightest transgression.
Thus, despite the misery wrought upon the empire by Chieh, he im-

perturbably declined the gifts accompanying T'ang's fervent invitations three times before finally deciding that the empire desperately required his services and responded to T'ang's fervent call, much besought and accordingly honored. Thereafter, in the Mencian account, he transformed King T'ang into a ruler morally qualified to rescue the world from Chieh's tyranny, no covert actions or secret missions ever being mentioned.[14]

Mencius's version may of course be seen as a hopeful projection of the process that rulers should undertake in humbly extending sincere invitations to moral exemplars (such as himself) to participate in their governments. However, the story persisted that after Yi Yin had failed to win T'ang's attention despite many audiences, he finally resorted to becoming his cook and thereby ingratiated himself sufficiently to gradually offer his persuasions. At the end of the Warring States period the brilliant but ill-fated Han Fei-tzu, often termed China's Machiavelli, in fact employed this story to illustrate the difficulty of achieving the objectives of persuasion: "In high antiquity T'ang was the most sagely, Yi Yin the most knowledgeable. But when the wisest persuaded the sagest, after seventy times he still had not been accepted. Only after personally carrying the cooking utensils and becoming a chef did they gradually become closer and more intimate and did T'ang fully realize his substance and employ him."[15]

Several centuries later Liu Shao, author of the incisive *Jen-wu Chih*, struck a balanced view: "Yi Yin's virtue was sufficient to sharpen their customs, his laws adequate to rectify All under Heaven, and his methods enough to plot the court's victory."[16] Moreover, even the *Chuang-tzu*, the penultimate Taoist classic, contains an interesting anecdote that unexpectedly illuminates Yi Yin's realistic methods and tactics. When he was about to invade the Hsia, T'ang asked Pu Sui how to proceed but was snubbed because such mundane, despicable topics did not fall within Pu's purview. After Kuang Wu similarly rebuffed him, he inquired about Yi Yin and was advised that Yi was "strong and able to endure insults." King T'ang then employed Yi Yin, they plotted a successful attack, and then T'ang sought to cede the empire to Kuang Wu, who disparagingly condemned the king for imagining he might be greedy enough to accept it, just as he had earlier thought him to be a brigand who would betray Chieh, his nominal lord.[17]

Chuang-tzu's anecdote implicitly raises the question of how defectors and traitors might be distinguished. From the dominant Confucian perspective, anyone who abandons a perverse ruler to support virtuous rebels claiming the Mandate of Heaven is a discerning defector, a hero rather than a traitor. Defectors are therefore ideologically and ethically motivated to opt for the victorious—and therefore, by de facto definition, the "moral"—side, while traitors are those who aban-

don the banner of righteousness or simply betray the eventual conqueror. Naturally, from a more cynical perspective, if involuntary
obligations imposed by birth in a land or under a particular ruler have
any legitimacy, they are all traitors. (Since defectors and traitors
played a monumental role throughout Chinese history, they will be
discussed in later sections.)

In sum, China's first spy thus has two faces—the first a moral
paragon and idealistic adviser, the second a realist highly versed in
subterfuge, skilled in disguising his intentions and motives, capable of
acting as an observer and strategist, clearly courageous in the face of
the enemy, and compellingly wise when confronted with tactical
problems. It is of course this second visage that the military writers,
popular legend, and many Legalist writings praise enthusiastically.

China's Second Spy: The T'ai Kung

Lü Shang, better known as the T'ai Kung, is a shadowy historical figure who reputedly played a crucial advisory role during the Chou's ascendancy, made the Shang conquest possible, and exercised a major
command role in the battles that accomplished it.[18] Apart from his
putative identification with the *Six Secret Teachings*—an extensive
work of military theory—the T'ai Kung has also been honored
throughout Chinese history as its first famous general, the progenitor
of strategic studies, and the state's martial patron.[19] However, his
identification as a "spy" no doubt results from his status as a defector,
someone who fled the oppressive conditions under the Shang court, after perhaps serving in some capacity, to wander about until finally being recognized in old age by King Wen for his sagacity. As the king's
most trusted adviser, he presumably furnished detailed information
about the Shang's strengths and weaknesses, as well as tactical information for the final assault that surprised the Shang by crossing the
frozen Yellow River to the south during January, thereby circumventing their westward pointing defenses.[20] However, if the *Six Secret
Teachings* actually preserves his essential thoughts, he may equally
well be viewed as the father of both tactics and spycraft, a role for
which he has been both praised and condemned.

The essential background to the T'ai Kung's achievements was the
archetypal battle between the forces of virtue, represented by the
Chou dynasty, and those of evil, personified by King Chou, the Shang's
perverse, debauched ruler. In a conflict reminiscent of T'ang's conquest of King Chieh of the Hsia, King Wen and his successor, King Wu,
developed a powerful state on the western periphery of Shang culture.
Although their policies were ostensibly based upon virtue and benevo-

lence, designed to attract both disaffected peoples and willing allies, their rise also encompassed the brutal conquest of numerous smaller states. From the systematic way in which they proceeded and their uninterrupted success, they clearly had well-developed, although now unknown, sources of information and certainly acquired further intelligence during their expansion from both captives and willing immigrants.

It has been suggested that the Chou easily developed alliances with nearby peoples, including disenchanted Hsia groups subjugated by the Shang, because of their agricultural heritage. In perpetuating the Hsia's agricultural offices and reflecting the spirit of their remote ancestor known as Hou Chi ("Lord of Millet"), the Chou had for many years dispatched advisers to instruct other states in basic farming practices and seasonally appropriate activities. Their efforts not only garnered them good will and respect, but also provided a perfect cover for aggressively seeking military and political intelligence, for acquiring a thorough knowledge of the inhabitants, customs, and terrain outside the Wei River valley.[21]

According to the *Yi Chou-shu*, when the center of Chou government was located in Feng, King Wu was kept informed about Shang's offenses and atrocities by spies *(tie)*. Determining their reports to be substantially credible, he advised the Duke of Chou about the contents, prompting the latter to comment that the time for attacking the tyrannical Shang ruler had arrived.[22] Furthermore, the late Warring States *Lü-shih Ch'un-ch'iu* even contains a dialogue showing how the king controlled his agents that, while definitely a fabrication, enjoyed credibility thereafter and added to the fund of ancient lore:

King Wu of the Chou deputed an agent to observe the state of Shang. The observer returned to the Chou capital and reported, "Shang is in chaos." The king questioned him, "To what degree?" The agent replied, "Sycophants and evil-doers overcome the good." The king replied, "It is not yet time."

The agent again went to Shang and then returned to report, "Their chaos has increased." The king asked, "To what extent?" The agent replied, "The worthy have fled." King Wu said, "It is not yet time."

Once again the agent went to observe conditions and reported back, "Their chaos has become extreme." King Wu inquired, "In what way?" The observer replied, "The common people do not dare criticize or express their resentment."

King Wu sighed and then hastened to inform the T'ai Kung, who commented: "When sycophants and evil-doers overcome the good it is termed 'extermination'; when the worthy flee it is called 'collapse'; and when the common people dare not criticize or express their resentment it is termed 'punishments conquering.' Their chaos is extreme, beyond control!"

The king therefore selected three hundred chariots and three thousand tiger warriors, and set the day with the feudal lords in the court for capturing the king of Shang.[23]

The Chou royal house also seems to have benefited from more reliable sources of information because many of its important members, including King Wen, had married Shang princesses. Furthermore, they were frequently compelled to pay homage and offer tribute to the Shang court, further exposing them to the political realities, coupled with opportunities for intelligence gathering, whether through observation or purchase. In this regard the Shang seem to have singularly failed, having blatantly ignored the Chou's growing threat because the ruler felt himself secure and well protected by the sanctions of Heaven, although he had earlier imprisoned King Wen for several years before releasing him in response to overly generous bribes. Even the *Han Fei-tzu* contains an episode portraying the Shang king's negligence in underestimating the dangers posed by King Wen's visible pursuit of righteousness:

Fei Chung attempted to persuade King Chieh: "The Lord of the West is a worthy so the hundred surnames are pleased with him and the feudal lords submit to him. You must execute him, for if you do not he will certainly be a source of misfortune for the Shang."

King Chou replied: "You are speaking of a righteous ruler. How can he be executed?" Fei Chung retorted: "A hat, even though worn through, must still be placed on the head; shoes, even though multicolored, must still tread upon the ground. Now the Lord of the West is a subject. He is cultivating righteousness so people incline toward him. If anyone will cause you misfortune, it will be him! Any person who does not employ his worthiness on behalf of his ruler must be executed. Moreover, where is the transgression in a ruler punishing his subject?"

King Chou replied: "Benevolence and righteousness are what rulers employ to encourage their subordinates. Now as the Lord of the West loves benevolence and righteousness, it is not possible to punish him." Fei Chung attempted to persuade him three times, then left the state.

However, perhaps the critical factor in the Chou's deliberate rise was the remoteness of the Wei River valley, situated in largely "barbarian" territory, whose isolation provided relative secrecy and deterred casual visitors. Under the T'ai Kung's guidance, King Wen was able to devise and implement the policies necessary to nurture the state's strength without attracting undue attention. The Chou thus managed to perfect themselves in the era's measures and technologies, and systematically develop policies, strategies, and even battlefield tactics not previously witnessed in Chinese history. In all, they required some seventeen years after the T'ai Kung commenced his advisory role to resolve the tactical problem of utilizing limited resources and restricted forces to attack a vastly superior, well-entrenched foe whose army probably outnumbered their entire population.

Unfortunately, even though the T'ai Kung has been accorded great respect for his apparent historical role, there is considerable controversy over his exact accomplishments, as well as centuries of Confucian revulsion over the possibility that military power and tactical measures were employed by the great moral paragons to achieve their conquest of the Shang. More significantly, there is a dearth of historical references to the T'ai Kung in the ancient sources that reputedly chronicle the period's major events, although the *Shih Chi* and *Yi Chou-shu* both provide supporting evidence. However, his biography in the former, well known for some two thousand years, established a lasting image:

> T'ai Kung Wang, properly named Lü Shang, was a native of the Eastern Sea area. One of his ancestors had served as a labor director and meritoriously assisted the legendary Yü in pacifying the flooding waters. In the interval between Emperor Shun and the Hsia dynasty he was therefore enfeoffed at Lü, or perhaps at Shen, and surnamed Chiang. During the Hsia and Shang dynasties some of the sons and grandsons of his collateral lines were enfeoffed at Lü and Shen, some were commoners, and Lü Shang—the T'ai Kung—was their descendant. His original surname was Chiang, but he was subsequently surnamed from his fief, so was called Lü Shang.
>
> Impoverished and in straits, Lü Shang was already old when, through fishing, he sought out King Wen, Lord of the West. The Lord of the West was about to go hunting and so divined about the prospects for success. What the diviner said was: "What you will obtain will be neither dragon nor serpent, neither tiger nor bear. What you will obtain is an assistant for a hegemon or king."
>
> Thereupon the Lord of the West went hunting and indeed encountered the T'ai Kung on the sunny side of the Wei River. After speaking with him, he was greatly pleased and said: "My former lord, the T'ai Kung, said, 'There should be a Sage who will come

to Chou, and Chou will thereby flourish.' Are you truly this Sage or not? My T'ai Kung looked out [*wang*] for you for a long time." Thus he called him T'ai Kung Wang, and returned together with him in his carriage, establishing him as strategist.

Someone has said: "The T'ai Kung had extensive learning, and once served King Chou of the Shang. King Chou lacked the Tao, so he left him. He traveled about exercising his persuasion on the various feudal lords but did not encounter anyone suitable, and in the end returned west with the Lord of the West."

Someone else has said: "Lü Shang was a retired scholar who had hidden himself on the seacoast. When the Lord of the West was confined at Yu-li, San-i Sheng and Hung Yao, having long known Lü Shang, summoned him. Lü Shang also said, 'I have heard that the Lord of the West is a Worthy and also excels at nurturing the old, so I guess I will go there.' The three men sought out beautiful women and rare objects on behalf of the Lord of the West, and presented them to the Shang king in order to ransom the Lord of the West. The Lord of the West was thereby able to go out and return to his state."[24]

Although the ways they say Lü Shang came to serve the Lord of the West differ, still the essential point is that he became strategist to Kings Wen and Wu. After the Lord of the West was extricated from Yu-li and returned to Chou, he secretly planned with Lü Shang and cultivated his Virtue in order to overturn Shang's government. The T'ai Kung's affairs were mostly concerned with military authority and unorthodox stratagems, so when later generations speak about armies and the Chou's secret tactical advantage of power, they all honor the T'ai Kung for making the fundamental plans.

The Lord of the West's government was equitable, even extending to settling the conflict between the Yü and Jui peoples. Thus the *Book of Odes* refers to the Lord of the West as King Wen once he received the Mandate of Heaven. He successfully attacked the states of Ch'ung, Mi-hsü, and Chüan-i, and constructed a great city at Feng. If All under Heaven were to be divided into thirds, two-thirds had already given their allegiance to the Chou. The T'ai Kung's plans and schemes occupied the major part.

When King Wen died, King Wu ascended the throne. In his ninth year, wanting to continue King Wen's task, he mounted a campaign in the east to observe whether the feudal lords would assemble or not. When the army set out, the T'ai Kung wielded the yellow battle ax in his left hand, and grasped the white pennon in his right, in order to swear the oath:

Ts'ang-ssu! Ts'ang-ssu!
Unite your masses of common people
With your boats and oars.
Those who arrive after will be beheaded.

Thereafter he went to Meng-chin. The number of feudal lords who assembled of their own accord was eight hundred. The feudal lords all said, "King Chou can be attacked." King Wu replied, "Not yet." He had the army return and made the Great Oath with the T'ai Kung.

After they had remained in Chou for two more years, King Chou of the Shang killed prince Pi-kan and imprisoned the Worthy Chi-tzu. King Wu, wanting to attack the Shang, performed divination with a turtle shell to observe the signs. They were not auspicious and violent wind and rain arose. The assembled dukes were all afraid, but the T'ai Kung stiffened them to support King Wu. King Wu then went forth.

In the eleventh year, the first month, on the day *chia-tzu* the king swore an oath at Mu-yeh and attacked King Chou of the Shang. The Shang army was completely defeated, so King Chou turned and ran off, and then ascended the Deer Tower. King Wu's forces pursued and beheaded King Chou. On the morrow King Wu was established at the altars: The dukes presented clear water, K'ang Shu-feng of Wei spread out a variegated mat, the T'ai Kung led the sacrificial animals, and the Scribe Yi chanted the prayers in order to announce to the spirits the punishment of King Chou's offenses. They distributed the money from the Deer Tower and gave out the grain in the Chü-ch'iao granary in order to relieve the impoverished people. They enfeoffed Pi-kan's grave and released Chi-tzu from imprisonment. They removed the nine cauldrons of authority, rectified the government of Chou, and began anew with All under Heaven. The T'ai Kung's plans occupied the major part.

Thereupon King Wu, having already pacified the Shang and become King of All under Heaven, enfeoffed the T'ai Kung at Ying-ch'iu in Ch'i. The T'ai Kung went east to his state, staying overnight on the road and traveling slowly. The innkeeper said: "I have heard it said that time is hard to get but easy to lose. Our guest sleeps extremely peacefully. Probably he is not going to return to his state." The T'ai Kung, overhearing it, got dressed that night and set out, reaching his state just before first light. The Marquis of Lai came out to attack, and fought with him for Ying-ch'iu, which bordered Lai. The people of Lai were Yi people who, taking advantage of the chaos under King Chou and the new settlement of the Chou dynasty, assumed Chou would be unable to assemble the distant quarters. For this reason they battled with the T'ai Kung for his state.

When the T'ai Kung reached Ch'i he rectified the government in accord with prevailing customs, simplified the Chou's forms of propriety, opened up the occupations of the merchants and artisans, and facilitated the realization of profits from fishing and salt. The people turned their allegiance to Ch'i in large numbers, and Ch'i thus became a great state.

When the youthful King Ch'eng ascended the Chou throne and the late King Wu's brothers Kuan Shu and Ts'ai Shu revolted, the Yi people in the Huai River valley again turned against the Chou. So King Ch'eng had Duke Chao K'ang issue a mandate to the T'ai Kung: "To the east as far as the sea, the west to the Yellow River, south to Mu-ling, and north to Wu-ti, thoroughly rectify and order the five marquis and nine earls." From this Ch'i was able to conduct a campaign of rectification to subdue the rebellious and become a great state. Its capital was Ying-ch'iu. Probably when the T'ai Kung died, he was more than a hundred years old.

The Grand Historian comments: "I went to Ch'i—from Lang-yeh, which belongs to Mt. T'ai, north to where it fronts the sea, embracing two thousand kilometers of fertile land. Its people are expansive, and many conceal their knowledge. It is their Heaven-given nature. Taking the T'ai Kung's Sageness in establishing his state, isn't it appropriate that Duke Huan flourished and cultivated good government and was thereby able to assemble the feudal lords in a covenant? Vast, vast, truly the style of a great state!"

Despite the lucidity of his biography and its frequent citation in various writings, over the centuries the T'ai Kung's reputation equally derived from the infamous book associated with his name, the *Six Secret Teachings*, which purportedly records his strategic advice and tactical instructions to Kings Wen and Wu in the mid-eleventh century B.C. (The present book unquestionably dates from the middle to late Warring States period; however, even today some traditionalists still believe it reflects the mature heritage of military studies found in the strong state of Ch'i and therefore preserves at least vestiges of the oldest strata of Chinese military thought.) Accordingly, the *Six Secret Teachings* would be the only Chinese military classic written to facilitate revolutionary activity because the Chou's aim was nothing less than a dynastic revolution. Paradoxically, Confucians throughout the imperial period excoriated the text because the T'ai Kung depicted therein vociferously insists upon exploiting every means available to achieve victory rather than confidently relying upon the benign power of Virtue. Critical measures therefore include feigning and dissembling to deceive the enemy and allay suspicions; using bribes, gifts, and other methods to induce disloyalty and cause chaos and consternation; and undertaking "civil warfare," a systematic, unorthodox program that stresses psychological techniques and covert methods to undermine and enervate the enemy, such as by distracting them and increasing their debauchery with musicians, wine, women, and fascinating rarities. Spies must be employed, complete secrecy is mandated, and once an engagement begins no constraints should ever be imposed on the fighters.

The *Six Secret Teachings* also analyzes numerous battle situations and formulates general principles to guide the commander's efforts to determine the most effective tactics based upon classifications of terrain, aspects of the enemy, and the relative strength of the forces. Intensive efforts to gather information must always be mounted because, in accord with the analytic thrust of Chinese military science, the enemy must be carefully evaluated and judgments weighed before a decision whether to attack or defend can be calculated. Among the numerous related topics are techniques for psychological warfare, procedures for probing and manipulating the enemy, ways to induce fear, and methods for deception. Because subterfuge and psychological ploys manipulate the enemy and thereby hasten their demise, confusion should be incited in the enemy's ranks, such as through disinformation. Furthermore, all weaknesses in an opposing general should be fully exploited and assaults directed toward undefended positions. No general should ever suffer a defeat from lack of training, preparation, or tactical intelligence.

Additional important issues found throughout the book concern military communications and the paramount need for secrecy, evaluation of the situation and decisive action when the moment arrives, various indications and cues for fathoming the enemy's situation, and the everyday basis for military skills and equipment. In addition, more than half the book is devoted to tactical principles, questions of command and control, the nature of leadership, and essential policies for the state. In sum, the work by which the T'ai Kung came to be known—one that has enjoyed numerous vernacular Chinese and Japanese translations in recent decades, as well as cartoon versions and abstracted applications for business endeavors—is a vast compendium of military science. Although certainly not China's first theoretical work, it founded the T'ai Kung's reputation for over two thousand years.

Tzu Kung

Along with Yi Yin and the T'ai Kung, Tzu Kung, who was active in the last decade of the sixth century B.C. and first decade of the fifth, is the third figure frequently identified as an early covert agent. A section of Confucius's biography in the *Shih Chi* briefly characterizes him with citations from the *Analects*, the famous composite writing embodying the Master's sayings, and purportedly preserves his successive discussions with the era's major feudal powers in his fervent quest to prevent Ch'i from exterminating the small state of Lu. Although almost certainly the product of later Warring States writers,[25] these dialogues may still reflect the essence of his arguments since he clearly persuaded several rulers to significantly alter their military plans, mostly to their regret.

Tzu Kung was prompted to undertake his mission when Confucius, openly ruing the imminent destruction of their ancestral state, sarcastically wondered why none of his disciples had been stirred to action. The *Shih Chi* unfolds the following events that probably occurred about 498 B.C. near the end of the Spring and Autumn period, right after Sun-tzu's strategies had made Wu powerful:

> Tuan Mu-hsi, known as Tzu Kung, was a native of the state of Wei. Thirty-one years younger than Confucius, he had a sharp tongue and spoke skillfully, prompting Confucius to frequently upbraid him for his argumentiveness. Confucius once asked him, "Who is superior, you or Yen Hui?" Tzu Kung replied: "How would I dare compare myself with Hui? When Hui hears one thing he knows ten; when I hear one thing, I know two."
>
> When Tzu Kung had completed his studies with Confucius, he asked, "What sort of man am I?" "You are a vessel," Confucius responded. "What sort of vessel?" "A jade vessel for sacrificial grains."[26]
>
> Ch'en Tzu-ch'in asked Tzu Kung, "With whom did Confucius study?" Tzu Kung replied: "The Tao of Kings Wen and Wu of the Chou dynasty has not yet totally fallen by the wayside, but is still present in men. The worthy recognize the important aspects, the unworthy the minor aspects. Thus everyone still retains the Tao of Kings Wen and Wu, so where would Confucius not learn? Why should he have had a constant teacher?"[27]
>
> Ch'en Tzu-ch'in further inquired: "When Confucius goes to a state, he invariably learns about its government. Does he seek it out, or is it given to him?" Tzu Kung replied: "The master acts

congenially and respectfully, and gains information through courtesy. Isn't his seeking thus different from other men?"[28]

Tzu Kung asked Confucius, "What do you think about being rich, yet not arrogant, or poor, yet not a sycophant?" Confucius replied: "It is acceptable. However, it is not as good as being poor, yet taking pleasure in the Tao, being rich, yet loving the true forms of behavior."[29]

T'ien Ch'ang, a high official in Ch'i, wanted to bring about chaos in his native state but was afraid of the four great families surnamed Kao, Kuo, Pao, and Ying. Therefore he shifted the forces under his control, intending to attack the state of Lu. Confucius, having heard about it, addressed his disciples: "Our ancestral graves are located in Lu, the state of our fathers and mothers. When the state is now thus endangered, why haven't any of you gone forth to take action?" Tzu Lu requested permission to go, but Confucius stopped him. Tzu Chang and Tzu Shih similarly requested permission to go, but Confucius would not grant it. Tzu Kung then asked to go and Confucius agreed.

Tzu Kung first went to Ch'i, where he spoke with T'ien Ch'ang: "Your lordship's attack on Lu is in error because it is a difficult state to attack. Its fortifications are narrow and low, its moats constricted and shallow, its ruler stupid and lacking in benevolence, and the ministers false and useless. Moreover, the officers and people detest military service. You cannot engage them in combat. It would be better for your majesty to attack Wu. Now Wu's walls are high and wide, the moats broad and deep, their armor stout and new, the officers carefully selected and well fed. Valuable vessels and elite troops are all gathered there. Moreover, Wu employs enlightened officials to preserve them. They would be easy to attack."

T'ien Ch'ang angrily flushed and said: "What you consider difficult everyone else takes as easy; what you consider easy everyone else believes to be difficult. What do you mean by instructing me in this fashion?"

Tzu Kung replied: "I have heard it said that one who suffers from internal difficulties should attack the strong, but one who suffers from external pressures should attack the weak. Now you are troubled about internal affairs. I have heard that your lordship has been enfeoffed three times unsuccessfully because some of the important ministers do not heed your words. Now if your lordship destroys Lu and thus broadens Ch'i, your victory will make the ruler arrogant. Destroying Lu will also cause the ministerial families [who command the armies] to be further honored, while your achievements will not rank among them. Therefore you will daily become further estranged from the ruler.

"When the ruler has become arrogant and the great ministers are free to pursue their desires, yet you seek to accomplish great deeds, it will be difficult. In general, when rulers become arrogant, they give free rein to their desires, but when ministers grow arrogant, they wrangle. For this reason differences will force you to defer to the ruler while you will have to struggle with the ministers. In such circumstances your position in Ch'i will be endangered. Thus I advised that it would be better to attack the state of Wu.

"If you attack Wu and fail to be victorious the people will perish outside while within the state the high ministers' positions will be empty. Then you will not have any powerful enemies within the ministerial ranks nor excesses in the people below. A solitary ruler will then govern Ch'i, and it will be your majesty."

T'ien Ch'ang said: "Excellent! However, I have already sent my forces forth against Lu, so withdrawing them now to send against Wu would cause the great ministers to be suspicious. What should I do?"

Tzu Kung replied: "Your lordship's forces should merely assume a position there without attacking. Meanwhile, I would like permission to go to Wu and persuade the ruler to rescue Lu by attacking Ch'i. You could then employ your army to respond to their offensive."

T'ien Ch'ang agreed and had Tzu Kung proceed south on his mission, where he gained audience with Fu-ch'ai, king of Wu. Tzu Kung said: "I have heard that a true king does not exterminate generations or a hegemon strengthen his enemies. A weight of a thousand tons can shift when but a few ounces are added. Right now the state of Ch'i, with its ten thousand chariots, and my own state of Lu, with its thousand, are struggling with Wu for supremacy.[30] I am afraid that you will be endangered by this conflict. However, rescuing Lu would result in a glorious name, attacking Ch'i would produce great profits. Nothing would be more advantageous than dispelling the worries of the feudal lords above the Ssu River and executing brutal Ch'i in order to bring about its subjugation to mighty Chin. Even the wise would have no doubts about the fame that would be achieved for preserving the lost state of Lu and actually putting strong Ch'i in straits."

Fu-ch'ai replied: "Excellent. Although we once engaged Yüeh in combat, isolated their forces, and then defeated them at K'uai-chi, the king of Yüeh has disciplined himself through enduring great suffering, nurtured his warriors, and harbors a burning intention to avenge himself.[31] Wait until we attack Yüeh, and then I will heed your words."

Tzu Kung said: "Yüeh's strength does not exceed Lu's, nor does Wu's might exceed Ch'i's. If you defer attacking Ch'i to strike Yüeh, Ch'i will have already pacified Lu. Moreover, your majesty was just now concerned with garnering a name for preserving the lost and continuing the extinguished, whereas attacking the small state of Yüeh while being frightened of mighty Ch'i is not courageous. Now the courageous never avoid hardship; the benevolent do not impoverish the straitened; the wise do not lose the moment; nor do kings extinguish generations—all just to establish their righteousness. Preserving Yüeh would display your benevolence to the feudal lords, while rescuing Lu by attacking Ch'i would impose your awesomeness on Chin. The feudal lords would then inevitably be compelled to lead each other to pay court to Wu, and hegemony will thus be achieved.

"Now your majesty must certainly hate Yüeh. I would like to go east for an audience with Kou-chien, king of Yüeh, to convince him to dispatch troops to support you. This will truly empty out Yüeh, although the image will be of following the other feudal lords in this concerted attack on Ch'i." Elated, the king of Wu then had Tzu Kung go to Yüeh.

Kou-chien, king of Yüeh, had the roads cleared, went to meet him in the suburbs, and thereafter personally escorted him to the guest house, where he asked, "How is it that such a great official has deigned to so dishonor himself with a visit to our uncivilized state?"

Tzu Kung replied: "I have just persuaded the king of Wu to rescue Lu by attacking Ch'i. He wants to do it but fears Yüeh and so said, 'Wait until I attack Yüeh, and then it will be possible.' Thus the destruction of Yüeh is therefore certain. Now to not have any intention to repay Wu [for permitting your survival] but yet cause them to have doubts is stupid. To be intent on taking revenge against others but let them know about it is disastrous. To allow the discovery of affairs that have not yet been initiated is dangerous. These three are great worries in undertaking affairs."

Kou-chien bowed twice and said: "Formerly I failed to calculate our strength, engaged Wu in combat, and ended up being in difficulty in K'uai-chi. The pain of this experience has penetrated my very bones. Day and night I have gritted my teeth and parched my mouth, seeking only to engage the king of Wu in a fatal struggle. This has been my wish."

Thereafter he further queried Tzu Kung, who advised: "The king of Wu is fierce and brutal, his ministers cannot withstand him. The state has been exhausted in frequent warfare, the officers and troops lack endurance, and the common people harbor resentment. The great ministers suffer from internal turmoil, and Wu Tzu-hsü has perished because of his direct remonstrance. Chancellor Po P'i controls affairs and accords with the ruler's excesses in order to preserve his own position.[32] This is the government of a doomed state. Now if your majesty were to send forth some troops to support their rescue of Lu, it would encourage their ambitions. Furthermore, if you were to send valuable treasures in order to assuage his heart and speak humbly in order to honor his court, it is certain that the king would attack Ch'i. If he engages in combat without being victorious, it would be your good fortune. If he proves victorious, then his army will certainly approach Chin. I would like to go north to have an audience with the duke of Chin and bring it about that he will attack Wu, for then Wu will inevitably be weakened. With its spirited soldiers all being spent in Ch'i and its heavy armor entangled in Chin, if your majesty exploits their exhaustion, Wu's extinction will be inevitable."

Kou-chien, being greatly pleased by these prospects, granted permission for Tzu Kung to see Chin and moreover sent him a hundred ounces of gold, a precious sword, and two superlative lances.[33] However, Tzu Kung did not accept them but went back to report to the king of Wu: "I respectfully reported your majesty's words to the king of Yüeh. Terrified, he said: 'I unfortunately lost my parents while still young and, failing to calculate our internal strength, attacked and thus offended the state of Wu. Our army was defeated and I was insulted, being isolated at K'uai-chi. The state was empty and overgrown with brambles, but through the great king's generosity we were able to survive and continue our ancestral sacrifices. Until I die I would never dare forget it, so what plots could I possibly entertain against the king of Wu?'"

Five days later Yüeh deputed the high official Wen Chung to bow before the king of Wu and say: "From the Eastern Sea where my lord Kou-chien has been established, I have been deputed to act as a minor emissary to inquire about your court. Now we happened to hear that your majesty intends to undertake great affairs, to execute the mighty and rescue the weak, put brutal Ch'i in difficulty and sustain the house of Chou. Yüeh requests permission to raise three thousand men from all over our state, and Kou-chien humbly requests the privilege of personally donning stout armor and bearing sharp weapons, of serving in the front where the arrows and points fly. Moreover, your humble servant offers some twenty thousand pounds of armor that our ancestors had stored away, including iron spears and glistening swords, in order to honor your army's officers."

The king of Wu, greatly pleased, informed Tzu Kung: "The king of Yüeh wants to personally accompany me in our attack upon Ch'i. Should I allow it?" Tzu Kung replied: "You should not. Now to empty out a ruler's state, to employ all his masses, and moreover have the ruler follow on would not be righteous. My lord should accept his monetary gifts, allow his forces to participate, but deny the presence of the ruler himself."

The king of Wu assented and declined Kou-chien's suggestion. Thereupon he mobilized troops from nine commanderies to attack Ch'i while Tzu Kung departed for Chin, where he spoke with the Lord of Chin: "I have heard it said that if plans are not first determined, it will be impossible to respond to exigencies; if the troops are not first ordered, it will be impossible to conquer the enemy. Now Ch'i and Wu are about to engage in battle. If Wu fails to be victorious, Yüeh will certainly cause disorder there. If they manage to conquer Ch'i, their troops will inevitably approach Chin."

The duke of Chin, seriously troubled, inquired, "What should we do?" Tzu Kung responded, "Prepare your weapons and rest your troops while awaiting them." The ruler agreed. Tzu Kung departed and went to Lu. The king of Wu indeed engaged Ch'i in battle at Ai-ling and inflicted a serious defeat. He captured the troops of seven generals and remained in the field, not returning to Wu but, as predicted, approaching Chin to confront them above Yellow Pool. When Wu and Chin fought for supremacy, Chin mounted an attack and severely defeated Wu's armies. The king of Yüeh learned of it, forded the Yangtze River, and suddenly attacked Wu, encamping seven kilometers from the capital. The king of Wu heard about these developments, abandoned Chin, returned to Wu, and engaged Yüeh in battle at Five Lakes. He failed to be victorious in three battles and could no longer defend the city gates. Yüeh's forces then surrounded the king's palace, killed King Fu-ch'ai, and executed Chancellor Po P'i. Three years after destroying Wu, Yüeh faced east and became recognized as hegemon. Thus once Tzu Kung ventured forth, he preserved Lu, brought chaos to Ch'i, destroyed Wu, and achieved hegemony for Yüeh. Tzu Kung's single mission caused the strategically powerful states to destroy each other, and within a decade each of the five states experienced significant changes.[34]

Tzu Kung loved real estate speculation and was able to profit from the material changes of the times. He enjoyed speaking about people's good points but was unable to conceal their errors. He frequently served as prime minister in Lu and Wei, and his family accumulated a fortune of one thousand ounces of gold. He finally died in Ch'i.

A modern reader puzzling through this lengthy biography might find Tzu Kung's reputation as an "agent" *(chien)* somewhat mystifying. Clearly he visited Ch'i as an overt spokesman for Lu. However, his subsequent visits, especially to Wu, which foolishly became persuaded to attack the strong state of Ch'i and eventually perished from its disregard of Wu Tzu-hsü's warning, were ostensibly to benefit the rulers he was addressing, not Lu, although they should have suspected that he was acting for Lu. Moreover, even though this was a period when diplomatic personnel frequently embarked on critical missions to save their states and acquire allies, the openness of the Warring States when peripatetic persuaders sought ready ears for their methods and strategies had not yet evolved. Tzu Kung simply acted on behalf of Lu to subvert the other states, exploiting existing conflicts and even internal dissensions, as in Ch'i. Therefore, although his work was largely overt, he has still been considered an "agent," and his activities should therefore be seen as both defining and reflecting the greater scope of the term's meaning throughout Chinese history. As the *Shih Chi* summarized, "Once Tzu Kung ventured forth, he preserved Lu, brought chaos to Ch'i, destroyed Wu, and achieved hegemony for Yüeh."

2

The Spring and Autumn Period

*T*HE FIRST PERIOD OF CHINESE HISTORY for which narrative materials become available, known as the Spring and Autumn period after the annals that chronicle it, is normally dated from 722 to 481 B.C. The terse *Ch'un Ch'iu* (Spring and Autumn Annals), traditionally said to have been personally edited by Confucius to reflect his moral approbation of political behavior during an increasingly turbulent period and serve as a handbook for future generations, becomes comprehensible only through its three classic commentaries, the famous *Tso Chuan* and the comparatively ignored *Kung Yang* and *Ku Liang*. Because all three were composed during the subsequent Warring States period, acrimonious controversy revolves around whether they accurately record Spring and Autumn history—the basic events having been distorted by later conceptions and reinterpreted to support politicized perspectives—or may be simply inaccurate. Although the veracity of events and relevance of interpretations clearly impinge upon the chronological accuracy of any intelligence history based upon them, irrespective of their fictional or substantial nature, the episodes and beliefs recorded in the *Tso Chuan* equally assumed a life of their own. Once penned, circulated, and assiduously studied, the stories and events became common knowledge, trusted and applied by subsequent generations, constantly revisited by military theorists and political writers throughout the imperial period.

Many of the entries in the *Tso Chuan*, although sometimes quite cryptic, provide crucial insights into the military history and political intrigues of the Spring and Autumn period, an era that saw several of the essentially feudal states originally established by the Chou dynasty after their conquest of the Shang in 1035 B.C. become increasingly powerful and independent. Regional rivalries arose; states, whether in pursuit of power or defensive integrity, invaded each other; and warfare expanded from chariot-centered battles largely conducted by the nobility, generally limited to some ten or twenty thousand combatants, to clashes between the massive infantry armies that supplemented vastly greater chariot forces. During the Spring and Autumn period survival suddenly became a question of economic and military preparedness, political acumen, effective central government, unwavering control of the masses, mobilization capability, strength and training of standing forces, and degree of professionalism. Acquiring knowledge about other states, whether friendly or hostile, grew critical because intentions had to be fathomed, preparations made, political actions initiated, and campaigns planned. The hundreds of incidents recorded in the *Tso Chuan* create a vivid portrait of these developments and provide a compelling picture that the individual states conscientiously gathered military and political intelligence, even though rarely depicting clandestine agents being employed on specific missions. Tangentially, these incidents also provide a record of many other aspects of intelligence operations; incorporate materials on evaluating men and motives; show the employment of covert measures to subvert, debilitate, and betray; portray the role of omens and divination; and illustrate how knowledge thus gained was deliberately exploited. In many ways the period was more complex than the Warring States era that followed—even though the latter is associated with the inception and development of political and philosophical doctrines—simply because many more states were struggling to survive and fighting for power, dramatically multiplying the number of potential alliances. In contrast, by the commencement of the Warring States period only seven significant states remained, virtually locked in an interminable death struggle.

Time and Communications

In the Spring and Autumn period cities were largely isolated, scattered about a rural countryside still marked by major woods and extensive marshes. Transportation and mounted communication were limited to ox-drawn carts and wagons, horse-drawn carriages, and military-style chariots. All three modes were equally constrained by the primitive road systems, which often became impassable quagmires after rain or snow, and somewhat impeded by the varying track widths found in different regions. Pack animals were also employed and mercantile goods increasingly circulated, particularly in areas with water transportation. However, the average person traveled, if at all, on his feet, while horses were not ridden for several more centuries, thereby precluding the establishment of the swift messenger services found in the imperial period, always remaining comparatively few and expensive throughout Chinese history.

These circumstances fundamentally affected the transmission of information and therefore its nature and relevance. A highly dedicated messenger proceeding on foot could perhaps achieve twenty miles per day for a sustained period and someone driving a fleet chariot easily double, but without prepositioned relay stations, a change of horses, and great urgency, the normal transmission of ordinary diplomatic and military information was severely constricted. However, the impact of these limitations was considerably ameliorated by the lengthy period needed to mobilize armies and advance them across similarly constricted terrain. Roads not being open thoroughfares, army columns would be strung out for miles, while innumerable logistical problems had to be solved and discipline maintained. For example, speakers in the *Tso Chuan* noted that approximately three months were required to respond to a military threat developing some two thousand kilometers away, to put forces on target from the date news was received, assuming the existence of a minimal standing force that might be rapidly provisioned and dispatched. When resisting an invader coming from some distance, the defenders would normally enjoy a preparation time of days or weeks based upon a sustained army advance of perhaps twelve miles per day compared with the slowest messenger's rate of twenty to forty and a normal transmission time for vital information between states of several days.[1]

Unlike later historical periods when, for example, messages are said to have been hidden in wax or rice balls—a development facilitated by the discovery and popularization of paper in the late Han dynasty—little information has been preserved about communication techniques. Apart from messages simply memorized by couriers and oral presentations extemporaneously composed, brush-written characters furnished the standard medium. Therefore the key questions simply become what materials could be written upon and how they might be protected from water since moisture would render the message illegible.

During the Spring and Autumn period two materials were widely employed: narrow, thin slats of wood—usually bamboo—and cloth, especially silk. The bamboo slips could be bound together with cords and rolled up when more than a couple of sentences were required. Cumbersome and bulky, they might serve adequately for diplomatic personnel and others unlikely to be searched or molested, but clearly not in doubtful circumstances or where robbers and brigands might attack, especially as captured information could prove valuable. Conversely, silk and other cloth materials might easily be written upon and easily concealed, whether under layers of clothing or in innocuous objects. (No doubt garment linings and undergarments frequently served to communicate clandestine messages, although there are no concrete references to it in this early period.) Hard objects, such as bowls, vessels, and wooden items, might also have messages written or inscribed upon them in relatively obscure places. However, because writing materials were limited in antiquity, great reliance was placed upon memory, and prodigious feats in this regard remain legion. Insofar as entire books were commonly memorized for study purposes and their subsequent recitation deemed flawless, lengthy diplomatic or military communiqués could be similarly treated. The difficulty—or more correctly, the fatal flaw—is that the messenger himself not only had to be physically present to verbalize his report, but also had to be in a conscious, unimpaired condition. Anyone suspected of conveying covert information could easily be detained, poisoned, or otherwise slain en route, the contents then irretrievably lost. In contrast, messages committed to writing existed independently of their originators or carriers and could be passed from person to person, forwarded innocuously, even unknowingly, without arousing suspicion, especially when buried among merchandise being plied by the itinerant traders increasingly common in the period.

Naturally such difficulties with communication means and modes not only restricted the range of possible covert activities, but also made the passing of information from clandestine sources to their consumers more difficult, often necessitating perilous face-to-face contact. An informant, traitor, or agent might have vital information but nothing at hand beyond a dining plate upon which to write. This conjures up imaginative scenes of people desperately trying to wedge bulky dishes or even valuable items into a dead drop outside a privy wall or burying them in a stable's straw for later retrieval where some bumpkin might suddenly stumble upon them! Although the advent of paper obviously facilitated clandestine communications, mere inconvenience and difficulty never deterred the truly determined, particularly when the fate of the state or vast rewards lay at stake.

Terminology and Agents

In an age that basically lacked organized intelligence staffs or distinctly defined functions, information had to be gathered from every available source. Particularly important would have been the relatively few travelers; emigrants, although low socioeconomic status would generally have precluded access to vital information; diplomatic missions, tasked with both specific evaluative missions and general observation; merchants; and defectors from among the military and nobility. The *Tso Chuan* depicts a wide range of intelligence activities, the practice of which can easily be followed down through the ages and will be again explored in the theoretical sections. Here selected examples from it and other writings that preserve materials from the period, such as the *Shih Chi* and *Kuo Yü*, are presented to minimally illustrate their range and breadth and thereby define the ground. The focus is solely upon historical episodes; theoretical issues, such as Sun-tzu's classification of secret agents, are considered separately.

Two Chinese characters that eventually became synonymous with "spy" or "covert agent" apparently first appeared in this period, and a number of more general terms—such as "looking at," "observing," and even "listening to"—are employed in ways and contexts that indicate their clandestine nature. Among the latter the term *sheng*,[2] pronounced *hsing* in its meaning of "to examine" or "observe," appears several times in the *Tso Chuan*,[3] with one instance of particular import: watching Prince Chien of Ch'u as part of a successful counterintelligence effort that will be described subsequently. *Shih*, another commonly seen character,[4] meaning "to look at" or "to see," found considerable applicability in describing reconnaissance activities. Finally, *kuan*,[5] a word that has essentially the basic meaning of "to see" or "observe," is also found in reconnaissance activities and occasionally covert settings. (Similarly, *t'ing*, to "listen," in certain contexts may indicate secret activity, although it was infrequently employed in this regard.) One or two other obscure characters also entail clandestine aspects, the main ones being *ssu* and *k'uei*, both shown.[6]

sheng	*shih*	*kuan*	*t'ing*

ssu	*k'uei*	*k'uei*

The first truly important character, *tie*,[7] is composed from the classifier or radical for "words" or "speech" and a right hand component for the foliage of a tree, prompting speculation (but no historical evidence) that it first referred to someone concealed in a tree covertly listening to or observing others:

words   foliage   *tie*/to spy

Although *tie* does not appear in the *Ch'un Ch'iu* itself, it functions both as a noun, referring to "spies," and a verb, meaning "to spy upon," in the *Tso Chuan*. In addition, *tie* also designates reconnaissance scouts inconspicuously observing the enemy, much like such ordinary terms as "observe," "watch," or even "investigate."

The first of seven usages in the *Tso Chuan* occurs in a passage chronicling events that occurred in 700 B.C.: "In invading Chiao, Ch'u's armies divided up to ford the P'ang River. The forces from Luo, wanting to attack, sent Po Chia to spy on them. Three times he went round their encampment, counting them."[8] Based upon this account, Po Chia obviously passed among Ch'u's forces in some sort of disguise in order to estimate their total numbers, part of the essential information needed for the process of assessing battlefield options under China's classic approach to warfare.

The next entry, for 666 B.C., sees the term being employed for a reconnaissance scout that Cheng dispatched to determine Ch'u's position after having successfully repelled their assault but remaining undecided about retreating themselves.[9] When Cheng's scout *(tie)* observed birds about Ch'u's encampment, in a very basic piece of military intelligence codified later, he concluded that it was empty, sufficient evidence to deduce that Ch'u's forces were in retreat. (The possibility that they had been deliberately feeding the birds to attract them seems not to have arisen.[10]) However, the nature of his report implies he did not actually enter the enemy encampment to verify his deduction and, although presumably making his observations early in the morning—the troops having dispersed during the night—offers no confirmatory indication of the equally important absence of cookfires.

(The records for 484 B.C. right at the end of the Spring and Autumn period similarly indicate a spy from Lu reported one night that Ch'i's forces had withdrawn following a disordered battlefield retreat at the end of the day.[11])

Records of the famous episode of approximately 635 B.C. that established Duke Wen of Chin's great credibility indicate that after he besieged the city of Yüan for three days and was visibly prepared to abandon the siege in accord with his earlier public proclamation, a spy *(tie)* came out and reported the city was about to fall. (Because sieges were difficult, expensive, and uncertain, employing subversives to both undermine the city's defenses and provide information about weak points in the fortifications, the defenders, and provisions was of paramount importance. This accounts for the presence of a Chin agent within Yüan.)

In the *Tso Chuan* the term *tie* also appears in Wu Tzu-hsü's diatribe (already mentioned in the section on early history) directed against granting a peace treaty to the just vanquished state of Yüeh, and again in a story related to Ch'u and Wu Tzu-hsü's difficulties. In the latter Ch'u's exiled former heir apparent, then dwelling in Cheng, foolishly agreed to assist Chin in assaulting Cheng's capital by mounting a coordinated internal response, even though he had been welcomed and well treated there.[12] In 477 B.C., needing to fix the exact date, Chin dispatched a covert agent, a *tie*, to Cheng, but this clandestine courier was caught in the first recorded example of Chinese counterintelligence because a staff member bitter over ill treatment had betrayed the heir apparent, resulting in the latter being secretly watched by local Cheng agents.[13]

Finally, an entry for 601 B.C. illustrates the working alliances that occurred between indigenous Chinese states and so-called barbarian steppe peoples even in antiquity. As the *Tso Chuan* concludes with a puzzling remark, it is worth quoting: "In the spring the White Ti and the state of Chin concluded a peace treaty, and in the summer they mounted a joint attack against Ch'in. Chin's forces captured a spy *(tie)* from Ch'in and executed him in Chiang's marketplace, but after six days he revived."[14] (Some commentators have suggested that the ill-fated spy was a Ch'in general, an appropriate choice for a military intelligence mission.[15]) Although long considered a dubious passage because of the bizarre conclusion, which no doubt stems from a corruption of the original text, it still provides important evidence of covert agents and countermeasures in the Spring and Autumn period.

Unfortunately the appearance of terms such as *tie* and *chien* in the *Tso Chuan* accounts for these early dates does not equate with their existence and use then because the *Tso Chuan* was compiled and edited

in the Warring States period—presumably from earlier, possibly contemporary records and oral recensions—by which time the character
tie had become commonplace. (Its appearance in the *Ch'un Ch'iu*,
clearly a close chronicle of early events, would be more conclusive.)
However, whatever the term, without doubt "covert agents" were employed and the concept of spying was already well developed in the
Spring and Autumn period.

A second character frequently found in the *Tso Chuan* and even the
Ch'un Ch'iu, hsien encompasses several meanings, only one of which
designates secret activities and would then be pronounced *chien*. Vi-
sually interesting, the character is composed of a radical or signifier
depicting the leaves of a traditional Chinese double door (or possibly a
gate around the outside) and essentially a pictograph of a half moon
between them:

door   moon   *hsien*/spy

Hsien's (*chien*'s) meaning evolved over the subsequent centuries,
with a variant character that substitutes the sun for the moon assuming most of the original senses:

door   sun   *chien*/spy

Both characters immediately suggest the moon or sun seen through
a crack between closed double doors, resulting in meanings such as
"crevice" and "the space between" and, by abstraction, "interval in
time." As a verb it came to signify "to estrange," "separate," or "put
space between," and thus designate the common, though covert, ac-

tivities of sowing dissension within the court, estranging rulers from their ministers, and besmirching successful generals and meritorious officials.[16] From this basic image also derives the extended usage of "peering into a crevice"—discerning the moon through the crack and otherwise learning what lies inside closed doors—and thus to spy on from without. Eventually *hsien,* the primary pronunciation of the character with moon, came to mean "leisure," "idleness," or "spare time," shedding the earlier meanings except in arcane language. However, perhaps in response to this shift an even more complex character evolved, redundantly placing the signifier for "eye" to the left of the original character:[17]

eye   *hsien*/space   *hsien*/to spy

Also pronounced *hsien,* meaning "to watch" or "spy on," it appears in the famous *Mencius.*

In some eighty occurrences of the original character *hsien* in the *Tso Chuan* (and virtually none in the other commentaries), only four unequivocally carry the meaning of "to spy on" or "secretly observe," two of which are particularly interesting. In the first, disaffected members among the nobility and extended royal family employed one member's cousin, a spurned concubine in the marquis of Ch'i's harem, to "spy on the marquis" with a promise of marriage if their rebellious plot should prove successful.[18] In the second case the minor state of Tun, subserviently dependent upon Ch'u for its continued existence, was compelled by the latter to clandestinely observe *(chien)* the nearby state of Ch'en in order to identify invasion opportunities. However, Ch'en's forces struck first by besieging Tun's capital.[19] Although the remaining two occurrences of *chien* are essentially matters of mounting observation, discreetly and unsuspected, the term became the common one for "spy" from the Warring States on, eventually coupled with such words as "turned," *fan,* and with *tie* to form compound words designating different types of agents from the Han dynasty onward.[20] In fact, its use became quite indiscriminate, with writers since the Sung even terming the merchant in the following episode a *chien:*

Duke Mu of Ch'in mobilized his army and was about to mount a sudden strike against Cheng. Chien Shu said: "You cannot. I have heard that to mount a surprise attack, the chariots should not travel over a hundred kilometers or the infantry march more than thirty kilometers in order that the plans not leak out. Moreover, in this way the ardor of the mailed soldiers will not have been exhausted, the foodstuffs and provisions not yet depleted, and the people not yet weakened and sickened. All of these are done so that their *ch'i* [spirit] will be at its highest and their strength flourishing when they confront the enemy and thus be awesome. Now you want to traverse several thousand kilometers and even cross through the territories of several feudal lords in order to launch a surprise attack. I do not see how it can succeed. My lord should rethink this plan." Duke Mu did not heed him, so Chien Shu saw the army off in his mourning clothes and wept for them.

While marching forward, the army passed by Chou and went east. A merchant from Cheng named Hsüan Kao, pretending it was the Earl of Cheng's order, feasted Ch'in's forces with twelve cattle. Ch'in's Three Armies were then afraid and muttered among themselves: "We have traveled several thousand kilometers in order to suddenly attack an enemy, but before we reach our objective they already know it. Their preparations will certainly be complete, so we will not be able to make a surprise attack." The army turned about and returned to Ch'in.[21]

This incident was subsequently cited as an example of clear thinking insofar as Hsüan Kao mounted a ruse that convincingly deceived an enemy that clearly did not have forward scouts reporting on the actual situation in Cheng.

Another character sometimes associated with the ancient period is *chan*, composed of the left and right components, respectively, of the radical or signifier for "prognostication" *(chan)* and that for "to see" *(chien)*:

prognosticate   to see   *chan*/to spy on

In at least one *Tso Chuan* passage it clearly means "to clandestinely observe,"[22] but the definitive use appears in the famous Warring States text on the nature, practice, and psychology of the rites or normative forms of behavior, the *li*, known as the *Li Chi*, in connection with a story about Tzu Han:

> When an armed guard at the east gate of Sung died, the City Magistrate, Tzu Han, entered his house and wept tears of grief. An agent from Chin, having secretly observed *[chan]* this, reported back to the marquis of Chin: "When an armed guard at the east gate of Sung died, the City Magistrate, Tzu Han, entered his house and wept tears of grief, which pleased the populace. It appears they probably cannot be attacked yet." When Confucius heard about this entire incident, he exclaimed: "Excellent, this spying upon a foreign state. The *Odes* state: 'Whenever the people experience mourning, he exerts every effort to assist them.' Even though this is only a minute matter for Chin, who under Heaven is capable of opposing them?"[23]

Diplomatic Missions

Diplomatic missions doubtlessly provided a major, comparatively reliable source of information about other states, even though important emissaries would probably have been denied extensive freedom. However, merely being present in a foreign state would immediately permit the emissaries to observe the general conditions, provide an opportunity to acquire information through conversations and bribery, and perhaps allow staff members and retainers to learn much from their counterparts and local servants. An early example of a deliberate evaluative mission occurred in 661 B.C.:

> In the winter Chung-sun Ch'iu went from Ch'i on a mission to observe Lu's difficulties [following the ruler's assassination]. After he returned, he reported, "Unless they get rid of Ch'ing Fu [the murderer], Lu's difficulties will never end."
> "How can he be eliminated?" the Duke asked.
> Chung-sun replied: "Since the difficulties are unending, he will perish by himself. Can you not wait for it?"
> "Can we seize Lu?" the duke inquired.
> Chung-sun Ch'iu replied: "We cannot. They still firmly adhere to the rites of Chou, the very foundation of a state. I have heard

that when a state is about to perish, only after the foundation has first been overturned will the leaves and branches follow. Since Lu has not yet abandoned the practice of the rites, it cannot yet be moved. My lord should concentrate upon bringing about tranquillity in Lu's difficulties and maintaining close relations with it. Being close to states that practice the rites, thereby reinforcing solidity, and keeping distant from the disaffected, thereby overturning confusion and chaos, are the practices of a hegemon."[24]

The dialogue suggests this mission was undertaken with a view to launching a punitive expedition to either extinguish or annex the state, and the emissary's reply reflects the parameters by which he judged the government's adherence to virtuous standards of behavior. The term employed to characterize his mission merits note: *hsing*, a variant pronunciation of the character *sheng*, meaning to investigate or observe, rather than *chien*, the character for acting as a clandestine agent.

A second example illustrates the criteria an astute observer might employ to evaluate the conditions in a subject state. Although the following episode is probably an imaginative reconstruction dating from the Warring States period, it is firmly rooted in historical events that took place in 603 B.C. when Duke Tan Hsiang apparently undertook a mission to ascertain the conditions in Sung. Upon his return he made a highly negative report based upon the contiguous state of Ch'en's disregard of proper diplomatic protocol and their neglect of agriculture and public works, fundamental activities that would have to be organized and administered by the state if it was to survive. Duke Ling, whose debauched demise is retold in this section of our study as well, was another sorry example of the myopic rulers who fervently destroyed the glorious heritage entrusted to them. The detailed criteria that Duke Tan systematically applied in making his political assessment, although illuminating in themselves, subsequently functioned as a virtual textbook example:

King Ting of Chou dispatched Duke Tan Hsing on a friendly mission of inquiry to Sung. Thereafter the duke requested permission from Ch'en to cross their state in order to visit Ch'u. Mars was visible in the early morning, but the roads were impassable due to heavy vegetation. The protocol officer did not appear at the border. The Director of Works did not inspect the roads, the marshes were not diked or the rivers bridged. The work of threshing was not yet finished. The roads lacked rows of border trees, newly reclaimed lands still had brush. The master of ceremonies did not

bring in the sacrificial meats; the attendant of guests did not provide a dwelling; the state lacked lodging places; the districts
lacked way stations. The people were about to erect a pleasure
tower for the Hsia clan. When Duke Tan reached the capital of
Ch'en, Duke Ling, K'ung Ning, and Yi Hsing-fu had gone to the
Hsia family's mansions garbed in rustic clothes, where they remained, so Duke Tan never interviewed them.

On his return to Chou the duke reported, "Unless Duke Ling of
Ch'en experiences a great awakening, his state will certainly perish." The king inquired why this should be so, to which Duke Tan
replied: "When *chen-chiao* is visible in the Heavens, the rainy
season is over. When *T'ien-ken* is visible, water begins to dry up;
when *pen* is seen, the season for shrubs and grass is at an end;
when *ssu* becomes visible, frost appears; when Mars is visible,
clear winds warn the people of oncoming cold.

"According to the instructions of the former kings, when the
rainy season ends, the roads should be cleared; when water dries
up, the dikes are completed; when the season for trees and grass is
ended, they are prepared for storage; when frost appears, winter
clothes are readied. When clear winds blow, the city's inner and
outer walls and its palaces are repaired. Thus the regulations of
the Hsia dynasty [employed even today] state, 'In the ninth month
clear the roads, in the tenth complete the bridges.' The seasonal
rescripts state: 'After harvesting, winnow the wheat. When the
year star is in the *ying* constellation, earth works are undertaken.
When mars is first seen, assemble under the directors of villages.'
This was the way the former kings bespread their Virtue throughout the realm without making fiscal expenditures. Now mars was
visible when I was in Ch'en, but the roads were almost blocked
with vegetation; the fields seem to have been abandoned; the
marshes were not yet banked; and the rivers lacked pontoon
bridges. They are neglecting the instructions of the former kings.

"The regulations of Chou include: 'Array rows of trees in order
to mark the roads, establish way stations in order to watch the
roads.' Cities had pastures in the outer suburbs, the borders had
permanent lookouts. Dried marshes provided tall grass, state gardens had trees and pools in order to prepare against disaster. All
the remaining land was planted in grain, and the people never
hung up their hoes. The fields did not have weeds. The people's
agricultural seasons were not interfered with, nor did the state
seek the people's labor. There was abundance without lack, ease
without exhaustion. The states were ordered, the districts disciplined. Now in the state of Ch'en the roads cannot be recognized,

the fields are covered with grass. Their grains, although mature, remain unharvested, while the people exhaust themselves in ease and pleasure. Thus they have abandoned the laws and regulations of the former kings.

"The Royal Offices of Chou state: 'When a high-ranking envoy from an enemy state arrives, the captain of the customs barrier informs the ruler about it. The director of guests greets him with his credentials. An usher guides them to the capital, a high minister comes forth to inquire after them at the suburbs. The city gatekeeper clears out the gate; the clan priest takes charge of the tablets; the director of villages assigns them a residence; the director of labor prepares the way; the minister of works checks the roads; the minister of justice suppresses evildoers; the master of marshes sees to the materials; the warden gathers firewood; the master of fire supervises the heating; the master of water supervises bathing water; the chief of provisions arrays the food; the chef prepares the rice; the stable master spreads the fodder; the mechanic attends to the carriages; and the hundred officials all attend to their affairs appropriately.' The guest enters as if going home, so all the members of his party embrace loving feelings.

"If a guest from an honored state arrives, all the representatives handling these affairs are increased by one grade and marked by augmented sincerity. When it is an officer of the king, all the office heads personally take charge of the affair and the chief chancellor oversees them. When the king conducts a tour of inspection and preservation [every twelve years], the ruler personally supervises.

"Now today, although I am not talented, I am still a collateral member of the Chou royal family and in accord with regal order was crossing Ch'en as an official guest, but none of the officials came forth. This is an insult to the office of our former kings. Their edict states: 'It is the Tao of Heaven to reward the good and punish the licentious. Therefore we have established states. Those who do not follow the precepts are dissolute, those who do not complete them are arrogant and licentious. Every one should preserve their foundations in order to receive Heaven's blessings.' Now Duke Ling of Ch'en has not thought about his role in continuing their line, has abandoned his consorts and concubines, and leads his ministers to assist in licentious relations with Hsia Chi. Ch'en's royal family is of the great surname Chi. To abandon regal robes and don a southern cap to go out, isn't this simply dissolute? So they have again offended against the laws of the former kings.

"The former kings exerted themselves to lead the people with Virtue, yet they still feared nearly committing transgressions. How can anyone who abandons their instructions and casts aside their regulations, insults their offices and contravenes their edicts, preserve their state? Dwelling amid four great states and yet lacking these four, how can Ch'en long endure?"

In the 601 B.C. year Duke Tan went to Ch'en; two years later Duke Ling was killed at the Hsia mansion; the following year the king of Ch'u exterminated Ch'en.

Agriculturally based societies such as China in the early sixth century B.C. were much subject to the vagaries of weather and climate and therefore relied for their very existence upon carefully prepared calendrical materials that included detailed instructions for initiating seasonally appropriate actions correlated with celestial phenomena. Failure to observe the admonitions and prohibitions, even without unexpected rains or drought, could result in crops damaged by frost in the spring or grains insufficiently mature for harvesting in the fall. Thus, in his report Tan Hsiang was very precise in describing Ch'en's failure to meet autumn's progressive responsibilities and therefore concluded that the government could not survive.[25]

The *Hsing-jen*

Theoreticians writing in the T'ang observed that the first administrative official operationally responsible for undertaking intelligence activities in China was the *Hsing-jen* of the Chou dynasty. A title composed of the characters for *hsing*, meaning "to travel" or "perform some action," and *jen*, "man" or "human being," the post and its duties seemed to have varied from state to state and the circumstances of the moment rather than systematically evolving over time. Every state that modeled on Chou bureaucratic organization employed *Hsing-jen*, sometimes several, and while ranking in power and prestige below the prime minister, they still resided at the apex of power, often as functionally significant as the early specialized ministers for war and works. As with many Chinese terms, no simple English equivalent suitably translates it in all its varied usages, but their primary responsibilities seem to have encompassed everything from simple messenger, in which case it was not a titled position, through diplomatic courier, protocol director, secretary of state, and foreign minister.

The *Chou Li* (Rites of Chou), an idealized reconstruction of Chou administrative offices and practices probably composed late in the

Warring States period, enumerates several critical responsibilities for both the Great *Hsing-jen* and Minor *Hsing-jen*:

The *Ta Hsing-jen* [Great *Hsing-jen*] administers the rites for important visitors and the formal ceremonies for major guests designed to gain the intimacy of the feudal lords. [Through his auspices], in the spring the king of Chou assembles the feudal lords at court to plan the affairs of the realm and in the autumn holds audiences to compare the achievements of the various states. In the summer he holds court to display the plans of the realm, and in winter convenes them in order to harmonize their thoughts. Seasonal assemblies are held in order to publicize the prohibitions applicable throughout the four quarters and audiences held in order to implement governmental measures throughout the realm.

From time to time [the *Ta Hsing-jen*] conducts friendly missions of inquiry to unite the feudal lords, at other times imperial audiences are employed to eliminate hidden evil among the feudal states. On an annual basis the *Ta Hsing-jen* makes inquiries among the feudal lords in order to fathom their intentions. Through him the king has sacrificial meats sent back to the feudal lords in order to invoke good fortune, deputes missions of congratulations in order to augment their happiness and missions of condolence in order to assist them during times of disaster. The *Ta Hsing-jen* discriminates among the edicts applicable to the feudal lords with the nine ceremonies and sets out the various ministerial ranks in order to unify the rites of the feudal states and attend to their honored guests.

The *Hsiao Hsing-jen* [Minor *Hsing-jen*] administers the rites of tribute for the submissive states and thus attends to the emissaries from the four quarters. He orders the feudal lords to submit their offerings in the spring and contribute their labor in the autumn. The king personally receives them and treats them according to their respective tributes. Whenever the feudal lords come to submit these tributes, the *Hsiao Hsing-jen* meets them at the border.

If a state is in mourning, the *Hsiao Hsing-jen* orders the other states to contribute to its funeral expenses. If a state suffers from famine, he orders them to distribute stores of grain as aid. If a state has suffered from military engagements, he orders the other states to provide material assistance. If a state enjoys some auspicious affair, he orders them to send presents in congratulation. If a state suffers some disaster, he orders the other states to condole with them in their grief. Now these five things, their causes, profits, and harm to the myriad people are all recorded in a book. The customs and ceremonies, government affairs, instructions, administrative measures, as well as adherence to and violation of instructions and prohibitions, are to make up another book. Those among the feudal lords who are contrary, perverse, brutal, chaotic, conceal hidden plots, or violate edicts are to compose one book; deaths and mourning, famines and impoverishment, another book; and health, happiness, harmony, and tranquillity, another book. Now all these five things should be discriminated by states in order to fulfill the king's mandate and thereby thoroughly know the causes and affairs throughout the realm.

Although the *Chou Li* elaborates a coherent vision of Chou government that was realized only in part, the *Hsing-jen* was clearly entrusted with supervising the major rites of state, an activity that obviously brought him into close contact with foreign dignitaries on a daily basis. Moreover, the *Hsiao Hsing-jen*'s responsibility for not only collecting basic information about all the activities occurring in the feudal states, but also seeing that it was properly recorded (and thus provide an objective basis for analyzing affairs and making judgments) indicates that apart from his basic role as an observant emissary, intelligence gathering was a dedicated function. Therefore, it might be concluded that China's first official staff position with intelligence responsibilities was the *Hsiao Hsing-jen*, operating within the purview of the *Ta Hsing-jen*.[26]

Records preserved in the *Ch'un Ch'iu* and *Tso Chuan*, while providing a more historically grounded portrait of *Hsing-jen* activities, essentially substantiate the claim that they should be considered not only China's first official covert agents, but also its first intelligence directors. However, their primary role was simply and probably originally that of a messenger, whether between states or enemies on a battlefield.[27] Accordingly, in such situations the title might be translated as "messenger" or "courier," although when deputed with full state sanctification "envoy," "emissary," or "ambassador" is more appropriate and even explicitly justified by the *Tso Chuan*. In fact, the *Kung Yang* commentary to the *Ch'un Ch'iu* emphasizes that one is termed a *Hsing-jen* only when acting on official business, not private concerns.[28] However, the three titles just mentioned imply discretionary powers within the parameters of a defined mission rather than a mere verbatim presentation of a message from a ruler or prime minister to foreign counterparts. Presumably the messenger would not only return with a reply or in the company of someone bearing a reply, but also carefully scrutinize the reactions of those receiving the message, note the situational context, and mark other relevant facts for subsequent analysis. In short, couriers and envoys did not simply convey messages with blind eyes and deaf ears.

Messengers were frequently employed preceding battles as part of the ancient ritual of issuing noble challenges and demands that the enemy surrender while no doubt undertaking a perceptive survey of their camp. For example, following the first day's clash at the battle of Yen-ling a messenger sent to pique Ch'u was evaluated as being fearful because his eyes kept moving, looking about apprehensively, prompting Ch'u to incorrectly deduce that Chin's forces would surreptitiously withdraw.[29] While the messenger, being in the midst of an enemy encampment, might naturally have been frightened, protocol should have dictated that he be returned unharmed, suggesting he was actually observing their preparations and evaluating their ability to sustain renewed combat.[30]

In their role as couriers and envoys several *Hsing-jen* were seized and even killed, implying the existence of clandestine aspects to their official roles, whatever the ostensible reasons for their detention. A number of nonfatal examples are also recorded, states such as Chin, Ch'u, or Ch'in detaining *Hsing-jen* and seizing those who violated their territory without permission while crossing to a third state.[31] Commenting on the *Ch'un Ch'iu* entry that "Ch'u seized Cheng's *Hsing-jen, Liang Hsiao,*" the *Tso Chuan* notes that Cheng had dispatched emissaries to announce a shift in allegiance from Ch'u to Chin, resulting in the envoys being detained, and adds that the *Ch'un Ch'iu* refers to them as *Hsing-jen* because they were official ambassadors. (Woeful were the prospects for bearers of such ill tidings!) After they were held for more than a year, Liang Hsiao and his companion finally persuaded Ch'u's ruler that he was only subverting Ch'u's purposes by frustrating their mission, thereby further estranging Cheng and allowing the remaining lords there a comparatively free hand.[32]

In another prominent incident the *Tso Chuan* explains that the "men of Chin seized the *Hsing-jen* from Wei, Shih Mai," because Wei, under Shih's leadership, had successfully mounted an attack on Ts'ao, Chin's client state, the year before. Although smoldering hatred triggered this precipitous action, of greater interest is the *Hsing-jen's* qualifications. Not just a faceless bureaucrat, he was an experienced commander and therefore doubtlessly seeking military information as well as fulfilling some innocuous cover mission.[33] Furthermore, Chin also detained a *Hsing-jen* from Lu who had been sent to investigate a skirmish between their people and those from the minor state of Chu.[34]

An unfortunate envoy from the peripheral southwestern state of Pa was seized and executed by border peoples in the minor state of Teng while en route there from Ch'u, eventually precipitating a battle between a Pa-Ch'u coalition force and Teng's army.[35] However, cases also arose in which *Hsing-jen* were the hapless victims of violence directed against them because of strife arising within their home states or some action in the greater diplomatic arena. For example, Ch'u seized and executed Ch'en's envoy even though "the guilt did not lie with the *Hsing-jen*."[36] A typical *Ch'un Ch'iu* entry for 501 B.C. that laconically states, "Ch'i seized Wei's *Hsing-jen*, Pei Kung-chieh, in order to invade Wei" is explicated by the *Tso Chuan:* "The marquis of Wei wanted to rescind his allegiance to Chin, but the great officers would not permit it. Therefore the marquis dispatched Pei Kung-chieh to Ch'i while privately advising the marquis of Ch'i to seize Pei in order to invade them. The marquis followed his suggestion and they subsequently concluded a covenant at Suo."[37] Whether the *Hsing-jen* unknowingly carried a written message to have himself seized is unclear but highly likely because travel between states was difficult, particularly for nonofficial travelers. Finally, the small state of Wei, having killed Wu's *Hsing-jen*, was terrified that powerful Wu would annihilate them and therefore plotted possible courses of action with their own *Hsing-jen*, thus preserving evidence of the latter's enlarged role in planning of military strategy.[38]

The *Ku Liang* defines the *Hsing-jen* as one "who assists in words between states,"[39] and in the simple role of courier he was expected to verbally deliver his message as dictated, without admixing his own views. In fact a court incident arose in the state of Chin when the prime minister designated Tzu Yün to undertake a mission over another *Hsing-jen*, the latter having been rejected because he often changed the words of communiqués to interject his own opinions.[40] However, *Hsing-jen* also acted as envoys with apparently wide discretionary powers, authorized to independently persuade and negotiate with officials in foreign states, and thus became, as the *Tso Chuan* comments, emissaries or ambassadors entrusted with diplomatic tasks.

That states apparently assumed foreign envoys bearing the title of *Hsing-jen* had hidden purposes may be gleaned from an incident in the autumn of 502 B.C. when Chin detained Sung's *Hsing-jen*. The *Tso Chuan* indicates that the envoy in question, Yüeh Hao-li, a minister in Sung, had advised the duke not to neglect the deputation of a submissive mission of allegiance to mighty Chin and was sent himself. Venturing into the state, he was met by Chao Chien, who grandly entertained him, prompting Yüeh to give him sixty willow shields as a present, despite his own steward's protests. Arriving at the capital, he was denounced by a Chin official for giving precedence to personal affairs, neglecting official state business, and delaying the execution of

his mission, thereby insulting two rulers, and was accordingly imprisoned. Superficially it appears he simply violated the protocol and procedures appropriate to his task, but more likely, given the internal
strife that would soon sunder Chin into three independent states, he
was probably suspected of providing aid to one of the factions, including weapons, whether on his own initiative or as part of a Sung effort
to politically undermine Chin.

Whether at home in his native state or abroad in the fulfillment of a
diplomatic mission, the *Hsing-jen* constantly interacted with foreign
officials and therefore had numerous opportunities to clandestinely
acquire information for the state. In fact, rulers routinely employed
their protocol chiefs to privately query visitors on mystifying actions
or behavior, thereby not only sparing everyone embarrassment, but
also establishing a convenient precedent and conducive context for
the secret exchange of information. For example, when an emissary
from Wei did not respond to the performance of the Odes as would be
expected, the *Hsing-jen* was instructed to personally question him.[41]

In their expanded roles, *Hsing-jen* also performed functions equivalent to a modern foreign secretary or secretary of state. While frequently defined by traditional commentaries as essentially chief of
protocol, an office mainly responsible for supervising the reception
and entertainment of foreign emissaries, in many cases they were
clearly charged with the task of acquiring knowledge about foreign
states, knowing their affairs, planning diplomatic and military strategy, and initiating actions, as indicated by the *Chou Li*. The position's
importance may be seen in three specific historical instances. First,
when the Duke of Shen departed from Wu after completing his military mission, he deputed his son to act as Wu's *Hsing-jen* and thus
control all its communications with foreign states.[42] Second, the historically famous Wu Tzu-hsü was appointed as *Hsing-jen* when he fled
to Wu, a post he retained throughout his career "so as to plot against
Ch'u." Although this vengeful plotting clearly was confined to the
court, he certainly consulted on state affairs in general and may also
have traveled, much as he did to Ch'i late in life, on missions he could
have subverted to this purpose had Ho-lü not also been in favor of an
aggressive, expansionist policy.[43] Yet until the rise of King Fu-ch'ai
and machinations of the traitor Po P'i, his influence and power were
unequaled as he plotted military actions with Sun-tzu.

Third, Tzu Yü, one of Confucius's most successful disciples, prominently served as *Hsing-jen* in Cheng, a state renowned for a government so effective that it flourished despite being surrounded by
mighty neighbors. In the *Analects* itself Tzu Yü is noted for his ability
to finalize or polish the drafts of communications with other states,
the commentators frequently citing a *Chou Li* definition of his du-

ties—"to oversee the rites connected with communicating with other states."[44] Moreover, in an appraisal of Cheng's strength a minister from Wei singled out the state's two *Hsing-jen*—Tzu Yü and Kung-sun Hui—for their comprehensive knowledge of other states, prompting the *Tso Chuan* to comment:

> Tzu Ch'an, in his administration of government, selected the capable and employed them; Feng Chien-tzu was capable of deciding major affairs; Tzu Ta-shu was handsome and refined; Kung-sun Hui was able to know about the activities of the four surrounding states, distinguish the clan and family names of the high officials, their positions, rank, and whether they were capable or not, and moreover was good at drafting orders. P'i Ch'en had planing ability that when exercised in the wilds was successful, but in the city was not.[45]
>
> Whenever Cheng had some pending matter with the feudal lords, Tzu Ch'an inquired about the actions of the surrounding states from Tzu Yü and moreover had him draft several versions of the edicts. Then he rode out into the countryside in a carriage with P'i Ch'en to decide whether the plans would work or not, and finally informed Feng Chien-tzu to have the decision rendered. When a decision was reached, he then entrusted it to Tzu Ta-shu to have it transmitted as a response to their honored guests. For this reason they rarely encountered failure.[46]

From this description Cheng's *Hsing-jen*, while nominally protocol directors, were clearly masters of foreign information, essentially state intelligence directors as detailed in the *Chou Li* definition of the *Hsiao Hsing-jen*'s duties. Tzu Yü's own fame derived from his superlative performance in executing foreign missions, handling visiting dignitaries, gathering and evaluating information, and planning state affairs, as befits a *Ta Hsing-jen*.[47]

The *Mu*, or Clandestine Shepherd

A *Han-shih Wai-chuan* passage asserts that an official called the *Mu*—a term meaning "shepherd"—should be established for the steppe and tribute regions and charged with intelligence gathering responsibilities:

> The king must establish two shepherds for each of the four quarters and depute them to secretly observe distant regions and oversee their masses. Whenever people in the distant quarters suffer

from hunger or cold without receiving clothing and food, there are criminal cases and lawsuits in which the charges are not equitably decided, or the worthy fail to be appointed to office, they should send reports back to the Son of Heaven. When their rulers come to pay homage at the court, after saluting and bringing them forward the Son of Heaven addresses them: "Alas, can it be that the instructions of our administration have not reached your domain? How can there be hungry and cold people who lack clothes and food, or criminal cases and lawsuits that have not been decided equitably, or worthies that remain unappointed?"

After the local ruler retires from the court, he will certainly consult with his ministers and high officials about this incident. When the people of those distant quarters hear about it, they will all acclaim: "He is truly the Son of Heaven. Although we live in a rustic corner, he sees us as if we were nearby. Although we live in darkness, he sees us clearly. How can he be deceived?" Thus the shepherds are the means by which to open the Son of Heaven's eyes to the four quarters and allow his perception to penetrate them.[48]

From this description it would appear that the shepherds or overseers functioned as central government observers deployed in a conscious, ostensibly benevolent attempt to rectify the administrative shortcomings of peripheral states. However, an examination of the classic works associated with the Spring and Autumn period—the *Ch'un Ch'iu* and *Tso Chuan*—reveals only one instance that asserts *Mu* are to be established for China's anciently delineated nine regions, essentially echoing a statement found in the "Cannons of Yao" in the *Shang Shu*.[49] In all other cases the term refers to shepherds, herders, fodder overseers (serving in the quartermaster corps), or cattle managers. Furthermore, even the lengthy *Chou Li*, while touching on the office some dozen times, contains only three passages that suggest a centrally deputed observer's role, but none that their activities would have a secret or clandestine character.[50] First, as one of the nine aspects or factors (such as "clans," "teachers," and the "Tao") by which the king gains and controls the people, the shepherd is said to "gain people with land" (whereas a "teacher gains people through his worthiness" and the "Confucian gains people through the Tao").[51] A second series of nine offices and aspects, such as rank and clothes, designed to rectify the states includes the establishment of *Mu*, understood by the commentators as "regional governors" but not necessarily so.[52] However, a third brief passage suggests they were intended to exercise some indefinite supervisory function over the states, especially when the king is about to make his tour of inspection, implying that they will provide the information necessary for the king's administrative judgments.[53] Yet the available material is so sparse, the references so minimal, that substantive conclusions beyond recognizing that something like the censors or independent inspectors of latter times that were turned against the state's own administrators, becoming an internal affair, were conceptually present in the Spring and Autumn era are unjustified.

Military Intelligence

Apart from information gained from diplomatic missions, spies, and defectors, the essential activities of military intelligence—observing the enemy and procuring the data necessary for evaluating threats and assessing intentions—were obviously carried out in the Spring and Autumn period and almost certainly in the Shang as well. Although structured approaches to information gathering awaited the military theorists of the Warring States and subsequent eras, basic practices were already being implemented for field armies. Moreover, events recorded in the *Tso Chuan* conclusively show that the individual states consciously and consistently acquired vital strategic and tactical information, enabling them to plan effectively and react adequately. A few examples are particularly telling.

In 706 B.C. the *Spring and Autumn Annals* laconically state that "in the summer the marquis of Ch'i and earl of Cheng went to Chi," but the *Tso Chuan* explains that they sought to mount a sudden attack against Chi. Much to their surprise and consternation, Chi already knew their intentions, evidence that it had been constantly gathering intelligence against its apparent friends.[54]

In 684 B.C. a high official of Lu went out to observe the coalition forces of Ch'i and Sung that had encamped near Lu's capital and then returned to make this report: "Sung's army is not well ordered and can be defeated. If Sung is defeated, Ch'i will certainly return home. I suggest we launch a sudden attack." Finding his proposal rejected, he personally led an assault on Sung's forces and defeated them, prompting Ch'i to withdraw as predicted.[55]

In 645 B.C. when Chin and Ch'in were about to engage in another of the numerous battles that would occur over the next century, Chin dispatched Han Chien to watch Ch'in's army. He advised, "Their army is fewer than ours, but their elite warriors are twice as many."[56]

China's first recorded active reconnaissance probe—a technique emphasized a century and a half later by the great tactician and general

know how they had compassion for the people. These three are the great constraints in the rites. Those who implement the rites will never be defeated.

"Now Ch'u suffers from numerous licentious punishments, so its high officials flee the country, die all about the four quarters, and act as strategists to the detriment of Ch'u. Since you haven't been able to remedy the situation, Ch'u is appropriately said to be incapable of employing them.

"During the turbulence caused by Tzu Yi, the Duke of Hsi fled to Chin. The men of Chin ensconced him in the rear of their martial chariots, where he acted as chief tactician. At the battle of Shao-chiao Chin was about to withdraw, but Duke Hsi said: 'Ch'u's forces lack substance and discipline and are easily shaken. If you beat all the drums in unison and press them at night, Ch'u's army will certainly withdraw.' The men of Chin followed his advice and Ch'u's army crumbled that night. Chin subsequently invaded Ts'ai; launched a surprise attack on Shen, capturing its ruler; and defeated the allied forces of Shen and Hsi at Sang-sui, capturing Shen Li before returning home. Accordingly Cheng dared not face south [toward Ch'u in allegiance] and Ch'u lost its power over the civilized central states, all due to Duke Hsi.

"When Yung-tzu's father and elder brother slandered him and neither the ruler nor high officials investigated, Yung-tzu fled to Chin. The men of Chin provided him with a metropolitan district and appointed him as a chief strategist. At the battle of P'eng-ch'en, when Chin and Ch'i encountered each other in the valley of Mi-chiao [in Sung], Chin was about to withdraw. However, Yung-tzu issued the following order to the army: 'The very young and old should return home, as well as solitary sons and the ill. When two men from a family have been impressed for combat, send one back. Select your best weapons and array the chariots. Feed the horses with grain and take breakfast while in your tents. After the army has deployed burn the encampment because tomorrow we shall engage in final combat.'[67] Those returning to Chin set off, and the prisoners from Ch'u were also released. During the night Ch'u's army collapsed. Chin then compelled the surrender of P'eng-ch'eng and restored it to Sung, taking Yü Shih back to Chin with them. Ch'u's loss of the Eastern Yi and the death of Tzu Hsin both resulted from Yung-tzu's efforts.

"Tzu Fan and the duke of Shen quarreled over the pernicious beauty Hsia Chi, resulting in the duke being harmed. The duke of Shen therefore fled to Chin, where the ruler assigned him the town of Hsing and made him chief of strategy. He successfully defended Chin against the Northern Ti and established diplomatic relations between Chin and Wu. Moreover he went on a mission to Wu, where he instructed the people how to rebel against the power of Ch'u. He taught them the martial arts related to chariot-eering, including driving, racing, and employing bows, as well as how to make swift invasions. Moreover, he had his son Ku Yung become *Hsing-jen* in Wu. Wu then attacked your subject state of Ch'ao, seized your district of Ho, conquered your city of Ts'e, and invaded your city of Chou-lai. Ch'u thus became exhausted racing about to preserve itself and continues to be troubled to this day, all because of the actions of the duke of Shen.

"During the rebellion of Jao-au royal clan, Duke Pen's son Pen Huang fled to Chin, where the ruler assigned him the city of Miao and he became a chief of planning. Early in the morning at the battle of Yen-ling Ch'u's forces pressed Chin's army and Chin was about to withdraw. However, Pen Huang, lord of Miao, advised: 'Ch'u's best regiments—those of the royal clan—compose the Center Army. If we fill in our wells, smash our cookstoves, and deploy to oppose them, and also have the forces under the Luan and Fan clans sloppily array their formations in order to lure the enemy forward, our two armies under the Chung-hang clan, in co-ordination with our Upper and New Armies, will certainly be able to vanquish the two Ch'u armies under the Mu clan. Then if we concentrate on the royal regiments from all four sides, we will certainly defeat them.' Chin's forces followed his counsel, and Ch'u's army was badly defeated. The king himself was wounded and the army exterminated. Tzu Fan died thereafter, Cheng re-volted, Wu began to flourish, and Ch'u lost the allegiance of the feudal lords, all because of Pen Huang's actions."

Tzu Mu assented, "These are all true."

Sheng-tzu then said: "At present there is an even more severe case than these. Wu Chü married into the family of Tzu Mou, so when Tzu Mou was accused of perversion and fled, the ruler and high officials all said his daughter and Wu Chü had in fact es-corted him away. Wu Chü was afraid and fled to Cheng, although constantly looking back and hoping for a reprieve. However, you have not made any plans in this regard, so he is now in Chin, where the ruler is about to grant him a district. If he should plot harm against Ch'u, wouldn't it be unfortunate?"

Tzu Mu, in fear, spoke to the king about restoring Wu Chü's po-sition and increasing his rank and emoluments. Sheng-tzu then sent Wu Chü's son to meet him upon his return.[68]

Two aspects in this extensive *Tso Chuan* account particularly merit noting. First, defectors from Ch'u found a ready refuge in Chin, its natural enemy, and in fact enjoyed not only a generous welcome, but also actual power in the state's administration and military command. Their insights apparently reversed the likely outcome of several battles, further evidence that they conveyed detailed military knowledge. (The damage incurred at the Battle of Yen-ling, mentioned in his discussion, was actually far more extensive, as will be evident from the detailed reprisal at the end of this chapter.) Second, the duke of Shen's defection, caused by complex intrigues that will be outlined subsequently, resulted in the initiation of diplomatic communications with the state of Wu and contributed to its rise as a significant power. (Even though Chin had been reasonably successful in its ongoing efforts to contain Ch'u, for various reasons it sought to develop a counterbalance to Ch'u's ascending might. In 584 B.C. the ruler was therefore happy to dispatch the duke of Shen—apparently at his own suggestion—with one hundred or more elite warriors and perhaps nine chariots to Wu for the express purpose of introducing the chariot and instructing them in land warfare tactics. Although his visit marked a military turning point and at least symbolically brought Wu into the realm of civilized states, Wu's growing strength clearly suggested the possibilities of such a mission. However, the direct military impact of the duke of Shen's chariot instructions was probably limited because naval and infantry forces continued to predominate.)

The duke of Shen's diplomatic mission marked two important developments: he was the first "guest adviser" to be honored in Wu, thereby initiating a practice that would later see Wu Tzu-hsü and Sun Wu entrusted with power, and his visit entangled Wu in an alliance with Chin, thereby ensuring its future enmity with Ch'u. Increasingly extensive clashes between Ch'u and Wu in fact commenced in 584 B.C. when Ch'u sought to occupy the region between them and Wu mounted a preemptive strike against Ch'u's client state of Hsü. Thereafter, over the next six decades battles occurred at least every few years as they both strove to dominate the region, with Wu emerging victorious from every significant encounter. These repeated defeats forced Ch'u to constantly reassess its military organization and methods, to rebuild and retrain its forces. As the decades passed, Wu commenced increasingly aggressive actions against Ch'u's cities, forcing them to undertake massive defensive preparations from 538 B.C. on, including the construction of city walls and other fortifications. Wu also benefited from Ch'u's brutal suppression of minority peoples and smaller states, readily exploiting their hatred and antagonism to acquire material support, local guides, and field intelligence.

The confluence of events that prompted the duke of Shen to flee Ch'u may be gleaned from several *Tso Chuan* narratives. Although he ran afoul of powerful government officials by opposing their interests and plans, the immediate cause of his departure was a conflict over one of the licentious beauties of ancient China, Hsia Chi. The duke of Shen had antagonized Tzu Chung when the latter requested two fiefs from the client states of Shen and Lü as a reward for his achievements following a siege of Sung's capital. Although the king of Ch'u consented, the duke of Shen immediately opposed it because the military taxes derived from those areas sustained the border defenses directed against the northern feudal lords now necessitated by their alliance with Ch'u. When the duke succeeded in persuading the king to rescind the grant, he invariably incurred Tzu Chung's undying enmity.[69]

A more notorious cause was the duke's entanglement with Hsia Chi, reputedly a highly promiscuous widow who caused "the deaths of three husbands, a ruler, her son, the extinction of her state, and the exile of two ministers."[70] She first appears in a remarkable scene (for a Confucian classic) of wanton excess in the court of Ch'en,[71] a minor state near Ch'u whose ruler and two ministerial cohorts not only had licentious relations with her, but also visibly wore her undergarments in court and otherwise blatantly flaunted them. This prompted a conscientious but foolish minister to remonstrate with Duke Ling, the ruler, but to his misfortune the latter not only failed to reform or embrace the path of exemplary virtue, but also informed the others of his upbraiding, prompting them to request permission to kill him. The *Tso Chuan* merely notes that the duke did not refuse, thus ensuring the moralist's demise.[72]

The next year Duke Ling was drinking at his paramour's house when he openly remarked that her son resembled one of the ministers, prompting the response that he also looked like the duke. This enraged her son, who killed the duke, but the ministers escaped and fled to Ch'u.[73] The following year the king of Ch'u invaded Ch'en, executed Hsia Chi's son for regicide, restored the two ministers, annexed Ch'en, and converted it into a district of Ch'u, although he later restored its independent status after enduring appropriate moral persuasion.[74] At the time the king himself had wanted to make Hsia Chi one of his concubines but was eventually dissuaded by the duke of Shen, who said: "You cannot. You summoned the other feudal lords in order to conduct campaign of rectification against the guilty. Now if you bring Hsia Chi into your palace, it will be because of avarice for her beauty. Avarice for beauty is licentiousness, and licentiousness is a great offense."[75] When the king reluctantly yielded, Tzu Fan sought to possess her, prompting the duke of Shen to similarly point out that she was the most cursed of women and exclaim: "Human life is truly difficult, how can one avoid death? However, there are many beautiful

he should wander among them. The ruler went and stared at them for a whole day, neglecting government affairs. Tzu Lu said to Confucius, "Now you may leave!"⁷⁸

Confucius remained hopeful and didn't depart until further incidents of governmental neglect, such as in the performance of the sacrifices, one of the two great affairs of state with war, became manifest. The *Analects* tersely records that the ruler remained away from the court for three days in a paragraph that countless millions memorized over the centuries: "The people of Ch'i presented female musicians and Chi Huan-tzu accepted them. For three days the ruler did not hold court and Confucius departed."⁷⁹ The fascination and appeal of beauty, subsequently decried by the Taoists for driving men mad, vividly clashed with Confucian puritanism. In the face of such allure even Confucius himself, despite significant accomplishments, was easily displaced, especially as Ch'i engaged in significant overkill, sending ten octets rather than just one or two, enthralling and overwhelming both Chi Huan-tzu and the duke of Lu. Later generations thus acquired an indelible image and assimilated a strong lesson on how to destroy governments and ministers through the lure of sex and beauty.

More than a century earlier an interesting incident between the peripheral state of Ch'in, just beginning to develop into a serious power, and the so-called barbarian Jung people illustrates the Chinese propensity to employ cultural weapons, including sophisticated women, to fascinate and thereby enervate those viewed as less civilized:

Having heard that Duke Mu of Ch'in was a worthy ruler, the king of the Jung nomadic peoples dispatched Yu Yü on a reconnaissance mission to Ch'in. Since his ancestors had been natives of the nearby state of Chin before fleeing into Jung territory, Yu Yü could speak Chin's language. When Duke Mu displayed his palaces and accumulated treasures to him, Yu Yü remarked, "If you had ghosts make all these, it surely exhausted their spirit; if you forced men to make them, it must have caused great suffering!"

Duke Mu, astounded by his reply, inquired: "The central states have structured their administrations on the *Book of Odes*, the *Book of Documents*, the rites and music, laws and measures, but still frequently experience turbulence. Now since the Jung and Yi peoples lack all these, what do you employ to govern? Isn't it difficult?"

Yu Yü laughingly replied: "This is why the central states are unsettled. Ever since the era when the sagacious Yellow Emperor fashioned the rites and music, laws and measures, and personally set the example but barely attained a minor degree of order, down through the present generation rulers have become increasingly arrogant and licentious. Superiors exploit the awesomeness of the laws and measures in order to upbraid and control those below them, while the people, totally exhausted, view their superiors with annoyance for failing to practice benevolence and righteousness. Thus superiors and inferiors compete in detesting each other and go on to murder and slay each other. This even results in the extinction of extended families, all through concepts such as the rites and music. However, the Jung and Yi are different. Superiors encompass purity and virtue in dealing with inferiors, while inferiors embrace loyalty and good faith in the affairs of their superiors. Governing the entire state is like controlling the body. Since the people do not perceive the means of control, it truly is the administration of a Sage."

Duke Mu thereupon withdrew to query his palace secretary: "I have heard that the presence of a Sage in a neighboring state is worrisome to its enemies. Since Yu Yü is a Worthy, we may be harmed. How should we handle this?"

The palace secretary replied: "The king of the Jung dwells in a rustic, isolated place so has never heard the sounds of the central states. You might try dispatching some female musicians in order to snatch away his will. You could also make some requests of Yu Yü in order to estrange him from the Jung, and retain him rather than sending him back so that he misses the appointed time to return. The king of the Jung will find this strange and certainly begin to doubt Yu Yü. When a gulf has developed between ruler and minister, we can then imprison him. Moreover, if the Jung king loves the music, he will invariably grow lax in government matters."[80]

Duke Mu assented. Therefore, after returning to the interview hall, he brought their mats close together, personally handed vessels of food to Yu Yü, and proceeded to interrogate him about the Jung's terrain, as well as the army's strategic power. After his queries had been fully satisfied, he had the palace secretary dispatch two octets of female musicians to the king of the Jung. When the latter received them, he was extremely pleased and therefore failed to shift their encampment at the end of the year.[81] Thereupon Duke Mu had Yu Yü returned. After arriving, he re-

monstrated with the king on several occasions but went unheeded. In addition, Duke Mu repeatedly had emissaries secretly
press Yu Yü until he finally abandoned the Jung and surrendered
to Ch'in. Duke Mu then treated him with all the courtesies due
an honored guest and queried him on the best deployments for attacking the Jung. Three years later, employing Yu Yü's strategy,
Duke Mu finally attacked the king of the Jung and eventually
added twelve new subsidiary states in territory that stretched a
thousand kilometers into the west, thereby becoming hegemon of
the Western Jung.[82]

Note that through their efforts to mesmerize the Jung ruler, Duke
Mu acquired a "local guide," one of Sun-tzu's five types of agents, converting an enemy agent—an observer—into a defector or turned agent.
Strangely, Yu Yü apparently was not perturbed about betraying the
Jung's strategic secrets even after growing up among them, eventually
responding to preferential treatment, despite his vaunted moral superiority. Ironically, Ch'in's employment of female musicians, viewed as
the essence of Chinese culture and a symbol of its material affluence,
was actually a case of a "semibarbarian" state simply wielding the enervating weapons of seductive decadence against a more robust, less
artifact burdened tribal people. (From the Chinese ethnocentrist perspective, each step away from the central states led only into less civilized, more unrighteous cultures. Accordingly, the sedentary, agriculturally bound central kingdom's subsequent policies to contain the
steppe peoples focused on employing the pernicious, debilitating effects of cultural weapons.)

The acquisition of power and influence by sexually beloved consorts
and concubines invariably provided a way for external forces to
achieve inimical purposes once the slightest disaffection became evident or the woman's or her son's position was vitally threatened. (Al-

Later ages were so struck by Duke Mu's story that it was incorporated in various forms in several eclectic works of the late Warring
States and Han periods, as well as the writings of such political
philosophers as Han Fei-tzu.[83] A version found in the *Lü-shih Ch'un-
ch'iu* embodies some interesting developments: "When Duke Mu dispatched two octets of female musicians and a skilled chef to them, the
king of the Jung was overjoyed and for this reason constantly ate and
drank day and night without interruption. Among his attendants
someone warned that Ch'in invaders would come, so he took up a
bow and shot him. When the invaders indeed arrived, the ruler was
sleeping drunkenly beside a wine jar, so the troops tied him up and
captured him alive."[84]

The acquisition of power and influence by sexually beloved consorts
and concubines invariably provided a way for external forces to
achieve inimical purposes once the slightest disaffection became evident or the woman's or her son's position was vitally threatened. (Al-

though stories abound throughout Chinese history of widespread human tragedy wrought by internal intrigues, they fall beyond the scope of our study, which focuses upon state-initiated covert actions rather than domestic politics.) Women also acquired power as a ruler's queen, empress, or mother, often to the detriment of state interests. A brief but telling example, much cited thereafter, appears in a *Tso Chuan* account of events following one of the many battles between the two powerful states of Chin and Ch'in. Chin's youthful ruler had been persuaded to attack Ch'in, despite his father's recent death—the body still lay uninterred—on the grounds that if "one releases an enemy even for a single day, the misfortune will extend for several generations." Despite his qualms, Chin's forces proved victorious, capturing three important commanders, who were brought back to the capital for execution. However, the ruler's mother—originally a princess of the enemy state of Ch'in—interceded on their behalf, craftily suggesting that "since they had caused enmity between two rulers, my father (the duke of Ch'in) would not be satiated even if he were to get hold of them and eat them. So why tarnish yourself by executing them? Why not have them returned to Ch'in and allow my father free expression of his will?"

Easily persuaded by his mother's words despite their obviousness, the duke assented and released them, to the great consternation of his chief commander, who, in scathingly rebuking him, expressed the timeless outrage of soldiers who find their sacrifices turned to naught for political reasons: "Our warriors, through brute strength, captured them on the plains of battle, yet in just a short while a woman has succeeded in releasing them. You have subverted the army's accomplishments and augmented the invader's enmity. We will certainly perish in no time!" Naturally the duke, realizing the enormity of his negligence, dispatched troops to recapture the three commanders, but the pursuers succeeded only in hearing a sarcastic retort as the former captives crossed the river. Rather than being executed, they were in fact warmly welcomed by the duke of Ch'in and lived to distinguish themselves in subsequent engagements with Chin.[85]

Bribes

When we extrapolate from the few important instances preserved in the *Tso Chuan* and other writings, we see that bribes were frequently employed in the Spring and Autumn period, whether to purchase information or alter the course of events by subverting important ministers. Moreover, their number and importance increased as the strife among the states intensified coincident with the decline of the Chou ruling house. As the peripheral states such as Ch'u, Wu, and eventually Yüeh grew in strength, alliance building among the original northern plains states became important and could reasonably be ensured by suborning the important ministerial families through generous treatment, both openly and covertly. One of the most famous cases in Chinese history unfolded in the upstart state of Wu in conjunction with Wu Tzu-hsü's campaign to guarantee Wu's mastery of the world by completely exterminating the just vanquished state of Yüeh. However, King Fu-ch'ai was persuaded by Po P'i—the Benedict Arnold whose name became synonymous with shortsighted, traitorous greed—to grant Yüeh leniency. Wu Tzu-hsü was betrayed and martyred by Po P'i's slanders, and his dramatic life story, initially portrayed in the *Shih Chi*, became the stuff of storytellers and playwrights down through the ages:

About 504 B.C. the state of Wu, employing the strategies of Wu Tzu-hsü and Sun Wu, had destroyed the strong state of Ch'u to the west, overawed Ch'i and Chin to the north, and forced the people of Yüeh in the south to act submissively. Four years later Confucius was made minister in Lu, and four years after that Wu attacked Yüeh. King Kou-chien of Yüeh mounted a counterattack and defeated Wu at Ku-su, injuring King Ho-lü's toe, so Wu withdrew its army. Ho-lü, who had developed an infection from his wound and was near death, addressed Heir Apparent Fu-ch'ai, "Will you ever forget that Kou-chien killed your father?" Fu-ch'ai replied, "I would not dare forget it." That evening Ho-lü died. Fu-ch'ai was then enthroned as king, appointed Po P'i as Grand Steward, and practiced warfare and archery.

Two years later he attacked Yüeh, defeating Yüeh at Fu-chiao. Kou-chien, king of Yüeh, with his remaining five thousand troops ensconced himself on the heights of K'uai-chi, and had the high official Wen Chung dispatched with generous gifts to seek peace through Wu's Grand Steward Po P'i, offering to subordinate their state as a menial subject to Wu. King Fu-ch'ai was about to give his assent when Wu Tzu-hsü remonstrated with him: "The king of Yüeh is capable of enduring great hardship. If your majesty does not exterminate him now, you will certainly regret it later." Instead of heeding his advice, the king of Wu employed Po P'i's plans and made peace with Yüeh.

Five years later the king of Wu heard that Duke Ching of Ch'i had died and that Ch'i's great ministers were contending for favor. Since the new ruler was weak, Fu-ch'ai mobilized Wu's army to go north and attack Ch'i. Wu Tzu-hsü remonstrated: "Kou-chien does not have two flavors in his food. He consoles the families of the dead and inquires about the ill because he wants to employ them. If this man doesn't die, he will inevitably cause disaster for Wu. Today Wu's possessing Yüeh is like a man having an acute illness in his abdomen. If your majesty does not make Yüeh his priority but instead focuses upon Ch'i, won't it truly be an error?" The king did not listen, but instead attacked Ch'i, greatly defeating their army at Ai-ling and going on to overawe the rulers of Tsou and Lu before returning. He increasingly distanced himself from Wu Tzu-hsü's plans.

Four years later when the king of Wu was about to go north to attack Ch'i, Kou-chien, employing Tzu-kung's strategy, led his masses to assist Wu while greatly augmenting the treasures that he had presented to Po P'i. Having already received bribes from Yüeh on several occasions, Grand Steward P'i's love and trust for Yüeh became ever greater, and day and night he spoke on Yüeh's behalf to the King of Wu. The king trusted and employed Po P'i's plans.

Wu Tzu-hsü remonstrated: "Now Yüeh is an abdominal illness. Today you trust their specious phrases and false behavior while coveting Ch'i. If you destroy Ch'i, it will be like gaining a rocky field, of no utility. Moreover the 'Announcement of P'an Keng' said: 'If there are those who overturn, overstep, or are disrespectful to my orders, then cut off their noses, utterly exterminate them. Ensure that they will not leave behind any posterity, do not allow their seed to be moved to this city.' This is how the Shang arose. I would like your majesty to abandon Ch'i and give priority to Yüeh. If you do not, you will experience immeasurable regret."

But the king did not listen, and sent Wu Tzu-hsü to Ch'i. When Tzu-hsü was about to return to Wu, he addressed his son: "I have remonstrated with the king several times, but the king has not employed my plans. I now perceive that Wu is lost. For you to perish together with Wu would be of no advantage." Then he entrusted his son to Pao Mu of Ch'i, and returned to report to Wu.

Wu's Grand Steward Po P'i had already had disagreements with Tzu-hsü, so he slandered him: "Tzu-hsü's character is hard and brutal, of little charity, suspicious and malevolent. I fear his enmity will cause great disaster. Previously your majesty wanted to attack Ch'i, but Tzu-hsü felt it was not possible. In the end your majesty attacked it with great success. Tzu-hsü was ashamed that his strategies had not been employed, so he reacted with rancor. Now that you are again about to attack Ch'i, Tzu-hsü alone opposes and strongly remonstrates against it. He obstructs and slanders those in authority and would rejoice if Wu should be defeated since his own plans would then prevail. Now your majesty is himself going forth, assembling the entire military force of the state in order to attack Ch'i. Because Tzu-hsü's remonstrances have not been heeded, he declines to participate and feigns illness and inability to travel. Your majesty must be prepared; for this to turn into a disaster would not be difficult.

"Moreover, I dispatched men to secretly observe him. When he was an emissary to Ch'i, he entrusted his son to the Pao clan of Ch'i. Now he is a minister who within has failed to attain his ambition and without relies on the feudal lords; who personally acted as the former king's minister for planning but now is not used. He is constantly discontented and resentful. I would like your majesty to plan for it early on."

The king of Wu said: "Not only do you speak about it, I also have doubted him." Then he had an emissary present Wu Tzu-hsü with the Shu-lü sword, saying, "You should use this to die."

Wu Tzu-hsü looked toward Heaven and sighed: "Alas! The slanderous minister Po P'i causes chaos, but the king turns around and executes me! I caused your father to become hegemon. When you had not yet been established as heir apparent and the various princes were contending for the designation, I engaged in a death struggle on your behalf with the former king. You almost were not established. When you gained the throne, you wanted to divide the state of Wu with me, but I wouldn't dare hope for it. Yet now you listen to the speeches of sycophants and thereby kill your elders."

Then he instructed his retainers: "You must plant my grave with catalpa trees in order that they may be used for coffins. And gouge out my eyes and suspend them above Wu's east gate so that I may see Yüeh's invaders enter and destroy Wu." Then he cut his throat and died. When the king of Wu heard about it, he was enraged and seized Tzu-hsü's corpse, stuffed it into a leather sack, and floated it out onto the Yangtze River. The people of Wu pitied him, so they erected a shrine above the river. Thereafter it was called "Mount Hsü."

When the king had executed Wu Tzu-hsü, he proceeded to attack Ch'i. The Pao clan of Ch'i assassinated their ruler Duke Tao and set up Yang Sheng. The king of Wu wanted to mount a punitive expedition against the brigands but was not victorious and abandoned it. Two years later he summoned the rulers of Lu and Wei to a meeting at T'ao-kao. The year after he convened a great meeting of the feudal lords in the north at Yellow Pool, forcing the Chou to come. Kou-chien, king of Yüeh, suddenly attacked, killing Wu's heir apparent and destroying his forces. When the king of Wu heard about it, he returned and had envoys arrange a truce with Yüeh with generous presents. Nine years thereafter Kou-chien went on to exterminate Wu, killing King Fu-ch'ai. He also executed the Grand Steward Po P'i because he had been disloyal to his ruler, accepted heavy bribes from external sources, and colluded with him.[86]

As the section on covert programs will show, Yüeh's conquest over Wu was not accidental, but was the result of careful planning, coupled with a focused effort to implement subversive measures, such as corrupting the king's confidant into becoming their minion. Po P'i's desire to eliminate his rival (despite Wu Tzu-hsü having introduced him when he arrived in exile), coupled with his greed, made him an ideal candidate for Yüeh's subversive efforts. Circumstantial developments were then easily twisted by Po P'i to Yüeh's advantage and Wu Tzu-hsü's fate sealed.

Assassins

Assassination was dramatically employed to eliminate both rivals and enemies, ensure the continued enjoyment of power, and adversely affect other states, as well as frequently resorted to in domestic intrigues and intracourt conflicts. The *Tso Chuan* notes the following incident for 626 B.C.:[87] "Tzu Tseng, a member of the royal family, fled Cheng and sought refuge in Sung. He liked to gather bird feathers to make hats. When the earl of Cheng heard about this, he was angered and dispatched a robber to lure him out of Sung and kill him in the border area between Sung and Ch'en." Although the *Tso Chuan* rationalizes that the glaring disparity between the man's actual dress and proper convention occasioned his death, the incident vividly illustrates the readiness of rulers to employ assassins outside state borders even for trivial reasons.[88]

A second example from the *Tso Chuan* shows how easily palace intrigues, even among minor nobles, spawned assassination attempts:

In the beginning Shu-sun Ch'eng-tzu wanted to establish Wu-shu to succeed him, but Kung-juo Mao strongly argued against it, saying that he should not. However, Ch'eng-tzu still designated him as his heir and then died. Kung-nan had a brigand shoot arrows at Wu-shu but was unable to kill him. As Kung-nan was Master of Horse, he dispatched Kung-juo to be steward of Hou township. After Wu-shu had been established, he ordered Hou Fan, Master of Horse in Hou, to kill Kung-juo but he failed. One of Wu-shu's grooms said: "If I wander through his court with a sword, Kung-juo will surely ask whose sword it might be. When I reply it is yours, he will certainly want to see it. I will feign awkwardness and grope for the end, and then I can kill him." He was employed as suggested. Kung-juo said, "Do you intend to treat me like the king of Wu?"[89] The groom then slew him.[90]

Probably the most famous episode, one romanticized in later legend and literature, was Ho-lü's employment of Chuan Chu (whose name became synonymous with assassins) to kill the king so that he could succeed him late in the sixth century B.C. The following retelling, from the *Wu Yüeh Ch'un-ch'iu,* commences with Ho-lü's resistance to Wu Tzu-hsü's growing influence over the king, forcing Wu Tzu-hsü to adopt a long-range plan:

King Liao knew that Wu Tzu-hsü wanted to mobilize the army to attack Ch'u and gain revenge for his father's and brother's deaths. Prince Kuang [Ho-lü], who was plotting King Liao's death, feared Wu might first become favored by the king and thus somehow thwart his plan. Therefore he calumnized Wu Tzu-hsü's plan: "This attack on Ch'u is designed solely to avenge his personal grievance rather than being in Wu's interest. My lord should not employ it."

Wu Tzu-hsü realized that Prince Kuang wanted to harm King Liao, so he said to himself, "Since this Kuang has subversive intentions, he cannot yet be persuaded to undertake external affairs." Then he went in to see King Liao and said, "I have heard that the feudal lords do not mobilize troops and attack other states for a common person."

King Liao asked, "Why do you say this?"

Wu Tzu-hsü replied: "The feudal lords exercise despotic government; it is not their intention to rescue the distressed and thereafter mobilize the army. At present your august majesty manipulates the state and controls its awesomeness. To mobilize the army for an ordinary fellow would not be righteous. Therefore I dare not act in accord with your majesty's edict." King Liao therefore ceased preparations for the attack, and Wu Tzu-hsü retired to farm in the wilds. However, he continued to seek out courageous individuals and recommend them to Prince Kuang, hoping thereby to curry favor with him. Thus the prince gained Chuan Chu.

Chuan Chu was a native of T'ang-yi. When Wu Tzu-hsü was fleeing from Ch'u to Wu, he happened to encounter him on the road when Chuan was about to fight with another man. When he attacked his enemy, his anger became as great as ten thousand men, so extreme it could not be withstood. However, as soon as he heard his wife's voice, he immediately returned home. Wu Tzu-hsü found this to be strange and therefore queried him about it: "How is it that, although your anger was overwhelming, as soon as you heard a woman's voice it broke? I would like to know if there is an explanation."

Chuan Chu said: "You have misclassified my behavior as simply that of a stupid fellow. How can you speak about it in such low terms? To humble oneself before a single man one must be able to stretch out over ten thousand."

Wu Tzu-hsü then examined his appearance: a blunt forehead with deep set eyes, a tiger's chest with a bear's back, fierce in coping with difficulties. Knowing that he was a courageous individual, he secretly allied himself to him, wanting to employ him later. Thus, when he chanced upon Prince Kuang's plot, Wu Tzu-hsü introduced him to the prince. After Kuang had admitted Chuan Chu as a retainer and treated him respectfully, he said to him, "Heaven has provided you to supplement my lost roots."

Chuan Chu replied: "When Yü-mei, the late king, died, King Liao established himself as the rightful heir. Why does your lordship want to harm him?"

Prince Kuang replied: "The previous ruler, Shou-meng, had four sons: the eldest, Chu-fan, my father; and then Yü-chi, Yü-mei, and Chi-cha. Chi-cha was morally exemplary, so when my father Chu-fan was about to die, he transmitted the throne to the next eldest of Shou-meng's sons, thinking that it would eventually devolve to Chi-cha. However, Chi-cha had been deputed on a mission to the feudal lords and was absent, unwilling to return. When Yü-mei died, the throne was vacant and Chi-cha should have been established. Otherwise, it should have been me, the eldest son of Chu-fan, so how is it that Liao came to be enthroned? My power was weak, inadequate to seize control of events. Without employing force, how may I now satisfy my ambitions? Even if I take the throne from Liao and Chi-cha returns from the east, he will not depose me."

Chuan Chu said: "Why not have some of the king's favored ministers leisurely speak about the former king's edict at the ruler's side in order to stimulate his thoughts? Arrange that he knows to whom the state will give their allegiance. Why must you personally prepare swordsmen and thereby damage the Virtue of the former king?"

Prince Kuang replied: "Liao has always been greedy and relies on strength. He knows the advantages of advancing but never considers withdrawing or yielding. For this reason I am seeking out similarly troubled men in order to unite our strength. I only wanted you to understand my righteousness."

Chuan Chu replied: "My lord's words have been extremely expressive. What do they imply for you, sir?"

Prince Kuang said: "Nothing. I was speaking about the altars of state. Ordinary men cannot undertake such affairs but only await Heaven's mandate."

Chuan Chu said, "I would like to receive your mandate."

Prince Kuang replied, "The time is not yet appropriate."

Chuan Chu said: "When one wants to kill his ruler, he must first find out what he loves. What is it that the king loves?"

Kuang replied, "He loves the taste of food."

Chuan Chu asked, "What flavors does he find delicious?"

Kuang replied, "He likes barbecued fish."

Chuan Chu then departed to Lake T'ai, where he studied how to barbecue fish for three months. When he had mastered its flavor, he sat back quietly and awaited Prince Kuang's orders.

In the spring of King Liao's thirteenth year, hoping to exploit Ch'u's mourning for their king by mounting an attack, the king dispatched Princes Kai-yü and Chu-yung in command of troops to besiege Ch'u's capital, and deputed Chi-cha as an ambassador to Chin, where he might observe the reactions of the feudal lords. Ch'u then sent forth some troops that cut off Wu's armies from the rear so that they were unable to return to Wu. Prince Kuang's heart then stirred.

Wu Tzu-hsü realized that Prince Kuang perceived that the vital moment for change had arrived, so he spoke with him: "Now that the king has attacked Ch'u and the fate of your two younger brothers and their troops is uncertain, Chuan Chu's actions are urgently required. The time will not come again and cannot be lost."

Accordingly the prince saw Chuan Chu: "Presently the king's two younger brothers are attacking Ch'u while Chi-cha has not yet returned from his mission. At this time, if we do not seek it, we will not gain anything. The moment cannot be lost. Moreover, I am the former king's direct descendant."

Chuan Chu said: "King Liao can be slain. His mother is old, his sons weak. His younger brothers have attacked Ch'u, but Ch'u has severed their rear. Now the state of Wu suffers from external difficulties while lacking stalwart ministers within. If I am not the man, who is?"

In the fourth month Prince Kuang secreted mailed warriors in ambush in a subterranean chamber, prepared a feast, and invited King Liao. Liao spoke plainly with his mother: "Prince Kuang has prepared a drinking feast for me. I do not expect any trouble, but what do you think?" His mother replied: "Kuang's temperament is hasty, and he constantly has an embarrassed, hateful countenance. You must be cautious."

King Liao then put on three layers of lamellar iron armor and had his personal bodyguards deployed along the road. All the way from the palace gate to Kuang's mansion, up the steps, and around his seat, all were the king's relatives. He had all those in attendance upon him stand, holding long spear-tipped halberds turned outward. When they were flushed with wine, Prince Kuang feigned having a foot pain and went into the subterranean chamber, where he had Chuan Chu place a dagger inside the barbecued fish and bring it in. When Chuan Chu reached King Liao he tore open the barbecued fish and pushed the dagger out. The attendants standing around the king immediately stabbed him in the chest with their halberds. Although his chest was split and shattered, Chuan Chu held the dagger firmly and stabbed King Liao, piercing through the armor and penetrating his back. With King Liao already dead the attendants slew Chuan Chu. All the officials in attendance moved about in confusion and Prince Kuang then attacked them with the mailed soldiers he had concealed in ambush, exterminating them all. The prince subsequently ascended the throne as King Ho-lü, enfeoffed Chuan Chu's son, and appointed him as a guest minister.[91]

The dramatic account concludes with the usurper symbolically offering to yield the throne to Chi-cha, who of course declines it, consistent with his previous posture in being unwilling to accept it instead of his older brothers or after their deaths. (Such "virtuous declinations," while ensuring temporary fame, frequently caused enormous political carnage in the Spring and Autumn and Warring States periods.) Further implications of Prince Kuang's actions included the surrender of the two Wu commanders to Ch'u, where they were subsequently rewarded for their treachery with fiefs in Ch'u's borderlands, and the murder of the former heir apparent by the infamous Ching K'o (whose mission is reprised in the assassination section).

Even though largely a case of resolving the internal issue of succession, this episode well illustrates not only a willingness to employ assassins, but also the preparation required, the importance of ferreting out the victim's desires and then exploiting them. Despite the prevalence of assassination throughout Chinese history, after Ssu-ma Ch'ien's definitive *Shih Chi* chapter the official histories never again sanctified such behavior with a dedicated biographical section. Individual biographies and the accounts of dynastic revolutions frequently mention covert murders, but rarely with the expansive detail that characterized the Spring and Autumn and subsequent Warring States periods when their employment was commonplace, thereby establishing a predisposition, a virtual mind-set for subsequent generations.

Strong-arm and Stealth Techniques

In 681 B.C. the state of Sung offered generous bribes to Ch'en if they would return a rebel who had fled there. Accordingly, "the men of Ch'en employed a woman to inebriate the rebel with wine and then thrust him into a leather sack made from rhinoceros hide. By the time they arrived in Sung, his hands and feet were both visible. He was subsequently executed and pickled."[92] The men of Ch'en thus employed two potent weapons in combination, women and wine, to throw the man off guard and capture him, being motivated by the promised rewards, even though they certainly knew he would be executed.

As a result of the complex factional struggles over Chin's regal succession in 620 B.C., Shih Hui—a high official with significant military experience—and others were compelled to take refuge in nearby Ch'in. Since Ch'in and Chin frequently clashed, his presence there was viewed as troubling, particularly when he began to provide intelligence and tactical advice:

> Because of its defeat at the battle of Ling-ku in 620 B.C., in the middle of winter, 615 B.C., Ch'in attacked Chin and seized Chi-ma. Chin's forces mounted a defense with Chao Tun in command of the Central Army and Hsi Ch'üeh in command of the Upper Army. After following Ch'in's force to Ho-ch'ü, Yü P'ien, assistant commander of the Upper Army, advised: "Ch'in cannot long endure. Let's deepen our moats, solidify the fortifications, encamp, and wait them out." They followed his suggestion.
>
> Ch'in's soldiers wanted to fight so the Earl of Ch'in asked Shih Hui, "How can we get them to fight?" He replied: "Chao Tun's recently appointed subordinate, Yü P'ien, certainly formulated this plan to exhaust our army. Chao has another staff member, an imperial relative named Ch'uan. He is spoiled and weak and lacks experience in military affairs, but loves courage, acts irrationally, and also hates it that Yü P'ien is acting as assistant commander of

the Upper Army. If you have some light troops strike him, it will be possible." The earl of Ch'in, throwing a jade disc into the Yellow River, prayed for victory to the river spirit.

On the fourth day of the twelfth month a Ch'in army suddenly mounted a fleeting attack on Chin's Upper Army. Chao Ch'uan, who pursued them but was unable to catch up, returned and angrily said: "We sack up provisions and wear armor solely to seek out the enemy. If we do not attack the enemy when they arrive, what are we waiting for?"

The provost said, "We are waiting for the right time."

Ch'uan replied: "I do not understand such plans. I am going out alone." Then he went forth with the troops under his command.

Huan-tzu said: "If Ch'in captures Ch'uan, it will be like getting one of our ministers. If Ch'in then returns home victorious, what shall we report to our ruler?" Then they all went forth to engage the enemy in battle, after which a mutual withdrawal occurred.[93]

Although Ch'in's forces eventually retreated that night after an inconclusive engagement, clearly Shih Hui understood Chin's command structure and how their personalities might be manipulated to achieve tactical objectives. Chin's officials therefore brooded over their misfortune:

The men of Chin were troubled by Ch'in's employment of Shih Hui, so in the summer of 614 B.C. the six cabinet ministers held a meeting at Chu-fu. Chao Hsüan-tzu said: "With Shih Hui in Ch'in and Chia Chi active among the Jung, difficult days have befallen us. What can we do about it?"

Chung-hang Huan-tzu said, "Please bring Chia Chi back because he is an expert in foreign affairs and previously distinguished himself in serving the state."

Hsi Ch'eng-tzu said: "Chia Chi is rebellious and his offense was great. He is not equal to Shih Hui, who can endure mean condition and has a sense of shame, who is complaisant and not offensive. He is wise enough to be employed and innocent of any offense."

They then dispatched Shou-yü to feign revolting from Chin with his fief of Wei in order to lure Shih Hui back. Moreover, they seized Shou-yü's wife and had him escape from Chin at night. He therefore sought refuge in Ch'in, where the earl allowed him to stay. While at court he deliberately stepped on Shih Hui's foot. When the earl of Ch'in deployed the army west of the Yellow River, forces from Wei were on the eastern side. Shou-yü said,

Ching. Lacking adequate information from other sources, the political elite, in the quest for reliable information on the advisability of courses of action, frequently turned to prognostication by turtle shell, divination by milfoil, the examination of natural phenomena, and cognizance of other unusual events. Pre-battle divination, routinely performed to decide whether to commit troops to an engagement, accounts for roughly one-fourth of the some sixty important prognostications recorded in the *Tso Chuan,* excluding the martial implications of the extensive accounts it preserves. (Marriage, sacrifices, children, moving of cities, and illness are the other common categories.) Because this tradition continued throughout Chinese history in an attempt to penetrate otherwise unfathomable events—despite strong voices raised in opposition—it will be examined more extensively in the final chapter. An example from 563 B.C., when a state's fate hung in the balance, illustrates this Spring and Autumn quest for military information:

In June Ch'u and Cheng attacked Sung and besieged its capital. The marquis of Wei sent a force to rescue Sung. Tzu Chan of Cheng said: "We must attack Wei; otherwise, we will not be supporting Ch'u. We have already offended Chin [by attacking its ally of Sung], so if we then offend Ch'u, how will the state survive?"

Tzu Ssu replied, "The state is exhausted."

Tzu Chan retorted: "If we offend two great states we will certainly perish. Isn't illness preferable to death?" The other high officials all concurred. Therefore Huang Erh led the army forth to invade Wei because of Ch'u's commands.

Wei's ruler performed divination by turtle shell to see if they should pursue this invading force and then presented the pattern to the late ruler's mother. She then inquired about the accompanying prognosticatory verses and was advised they read: "The omen is like a mountain height, there is a force that goes forth and suffers the loss of its stalwart leader." She then interpreted, "To lose the stalwart means that it will be advantageous to defend against the invaders. You should plan for it." The forces from Wei pursued Cheng's army and captured Huang Erh at Ch'ien-ch'iu.[101]

An incident somewhat more than two decades later, although evidencing strong belief in the veracity of such procedures, shows the importance of the charge and the offhand rejection of results that belie the tactical situation:

In 538 B.C. Wu attacked Ch'u. Yang Kai, prime minister of Ch'u, performed divination by turtle shell to inquire about the prospects, but the result was inauspicious. Tzu Yü, the Minister of War, said: "We have gained a position upstream from them, so how can it be inauspicious? Moreover, of old Ch'u's Minister of War made the charge before cracking the shell, so let me change it." He then ordered, "Even though I and my men perish, if the remainder of Ch'u's forces follow on may it be that we gain a great victory." The result was auspicious. They then engaged the enemy at Chang-an. The Minister of War died first, but the army sustained the effort and Ch'u severely defeated Wu's army, even capturing the king of Wu's command vessel.[102]

The Battle of Yen-ling

The battle of Yen-ling, which occurred in 574 B.C. and was previously mentioned in Sheng-tzu's review of Ch'u's numerous defectors, epitomizes the state of intelligence activities in the Spring and Autumn period and thus merits recounting to conclude the era's discussion:

> The duke of Chin was about to attack the state of Cheng, which had shifted its allegiance to Ch'u. Fan Wen-tzu remarked: "If I had my wish, all the feudal lords would rebel, for then Chin would truly arise. If only Cheng rebels, disaster will soon befall our state."
>
> Luan Shu replied, "In my time we cannot lose the allegiance of the feudal lords, so we must attack Cheng." Thereupon they mobilized the army. Luan Shu was in command of the Center Army and Fan Wen-tzu was his adjutant. Hsi Ch'i was in command of the Upper Army, with Hsün Yen as adjutant. Han Chüeh was in command of the Lower Army, while Hsi Chih was adjutant of the New Army. Hsün Ying was in charge of defense. Hsi Ch'ou went to Wei and then Ch'i to request forces, as did Luan Yen in Lu. Meng Hsien-tzu remarked, "They will be victorious."
>
> After Chin's four armies had set out, Cheng learned about the Chin force and deputed an emissary to inform Ch'u, accompanied by Yao Kou-erh, a high official. King Kung of Ch'u led his forces out to rescue Cheng, with the Minister of War, Tzu Fan, in command of the Center Army; the prime minister, Tzu Chung, in command of the Army of the Left; and the deputy minister, Tzu Hsü, in command of the Army of the Right. When they passed by the former state of Shen, Tzu Fan visited Shen Shu-shih, a retired Ch'u high minister, to inquire about his thoughts on the army.
>
> He replied: "Virtue, punishment, reverence, righteousness, the rites, and fidelity are the implements of warfare. Virtue is the

means to bespread beneficence, punishment to rectify, reverence to secure the spirits, righteousness to establish what is advantageous, the rites to accord with the seasons, and fidelity to preserve things. When the people's livelihood is abundant Virtue is upright, when employments are advantageous affairs are constrained. Government measures meet no opposition, whatever is sought is fully supplied, and everyone knows the proper measure. Thus the *Odes* state, 'Establish my people, let all be included.' For this reason the spirits send down good fortune and the seasons are free from disaster and harm.

"The people's lives were formerly fruitful and abundant, harmoniously they heeded the government. Everyone exhausted their strength to implement the ruler's commands and would die to supplement gaps in the line of battle. From this stems virtue in battle. However, internally Ch'u now casts away its people and externally severs connections with formerly close allies. It violates its alliances and eats its words. In acting, it contravenes the seasons and labors the populace to achieve its desires. The people no longer recognize fidelity; whether they advance or retreat, they commit offenses. When the people are anxious about their movements, who will die for the state? Exert yourself fully, but I will never see you again."

Yao Kou-erh returned to Cheng before Tzu Fan, whereupon Tzu Ssu inquired about his observations. He replied: "Ch'u's forces are advancing rapidly but in passing through constricted terrain are not well ordered. When an army moves quickly it has lost its resolve; when disordered, strength of formation is sacrificed. When their resolve is lost and formations sacrificed, how will they engage in battle? I fear that they cannot be employed."

When Chin's armies crossed the Yellow River in the fifth month they heard that Ch'u's forces were about to arrive. Fan Wen-tzu, who wanted to turn back, said: "If we pretend to flee from Ch'u we can extricate ourselves from the present misfortune. We obviously cannot bring the feudal lords together, so let us leave it to those who can. If we ministers unite in serving our ruler it will be enough." Luan Shu replied, "It is not possible."

In the sixth month Chin and Ch'u encountered each other at Yen-ling. Fan Wen-tzu did not want to engage the enemy, but Hsi Chih said: "At the battle of Han Duke Hui did not deploy his regiments in good order; in the engagement at Chi, Hsien Chen failed to fulfill his mission; and the army that went to Pi under Hsün Po was unable to return, all to Chin's disgrace. You also have personally witnessed these affairs of our former rulers. Now if we avoid Ch'u, it will only increase our shame!"

Fan Wen-tzu said: "Our former rulers fervently engaged in warfare because the Ti, Ch'u, Ch'i, and Ch'in were all strong. If Chin had not exerted all its strength, their sons and grandsons would have become weakened. Now that three powerful states have already submitted, Ch'u alone remains as an enemy. Only a Sage can be free from both internal and external worries. Since we are not Sages, if the state is externally at peace we will certainly have internal anxieties. Why not release Ch'u to provide us with an external source of fear?"

Early in the morning, on the last day of the lunar month, Ch'u deployed its forces close on Chin's encampment. Chin's officers were concerned, but Fan Wen-tzu's son raced in and said: "Fill in the wells, destroy the cookstoves, deploy our formations amid the encampment, and spread out the vertical rows. It is only a question of whether Heaven sustains us or Ch'u, so what is there to worry about?" Fan Wen-tzu seized a halberd and pursued him, shouting, "The state's preservation or destruction is a matter of Heaven. What does a kid know about it?"

Luan Shu said: "Ch'u's army is skittish, so if we solidify our fortifications and wait them out, within three days they will certainly withdraw. If we then suddenly attack their retreating forces, victory will be inevitable."

Hsi Chih countered: "Ch'u has six gaps that cannot be left unexploited. Its two ministers detest each other; the king's troops are fatigued; Cheng's formations are not well ordered; the Man tribal regiments cannot be deployed; and in deploying for combat, Ch'u has not avoided the most inauspicious lunar day. When in formation they are noisy, when uniting for deployment increasingly clamorous, every man looking behind him, no one having the will to fight. Since their veterans are not necessarily outstanding and they have offended the prohibitions of Heaven, we shall certainly conquer them."

When the king of Ch'u climbed up on a mobile observation tower in order to look out at Chin's armies, Tzu Chung had the grand counselor Po Chou-li [a defector from Chin] stand behind him. The king asked, "Why are they racing about to the left and right?" Po Chou-li replied, "They are summoning the army's officers."

"They are all assembling in the Center Army." "They are gathering to finalize the plans."

"They are raising a tent." "It is for respectfully performing divination before the ancestral rulers."

"They are striking the tent." "They are about to issue the orders."

"They are extremely noisy and dust is flying everywhere."
"They are filling in the wells, destroying their cookstoves and assuming formation."
"After mounting their chariots, the attendants, bearing their
weapons, have descended again." "It is to listen to the admonitory
oath."
"Will they fight?" "I still do not know."
"After remounting the chariots, the attendants have once more
descended." "This is for the battle prayer." Po Chou-li also advised the king about the duke of Chin's men.

Miao Pen-huang, a defector from Ch'u standing beside the duke
of Chin, similarly advised him about the king of Ch'u's forces.
The duke's attendants all said, "One of our natives, Po Chou-li, is
with the king of Ch'u and their forces are too great to oppose."
However, Miao Pen-huang said to the duke of Chin: "Ch'u's superior soldiers are found only in the royal clans composing the Center Army. I suggest that we divide up our elite warriors to launch
a sudden attack on their armies on the left and right flanks and
then our three remaining armies can concentrate upon the royal
troops. Without doubt we will severely defeat them."

The duke performed divination by milfoil to ascertain the
prospects. The Scribe observed: "It is auspicious. You have encountered the hexagram Fu, 'to return,' whose implications are 'a
southern state will shrink, there will be a shot, the king will be
hit in the eye.' When a state shrinks and its king is wounded, if
this doesn't mean defeat, what would?" The duke followed the indications.

There was a muddy stretch in front of their encampment, so all
the chariots separated off to the left and right to avoid it. Pu Yi
acted as the duke of Chin's driver, Luan Chen wielded the halberd
on the right; P'eng Ming acted as driver for the King of Ch'u, with
Pan Tang taking the position on the right. Shih Shou drove for the
earl of Cheng and T'ang Kou attended on the right. Fan Wen-tzu
and Luan Shu's troops advanced in parallel on either side of the
duke of Chin, but the duke's chariot became mired in the mud.
Luan Shu was about to convey the duke away in his own chariot
when Luan Chen, the duke's attendant on the right, shouted:
"Get away. When the state has entrusted you with great responsibility, how can you usurp that of others? Moreover, encroaching
upon another's official duties is impudence, neglecting your own
duties is negligence, and departing from your own unit is perversity. You cannot commit these three offenses." Then he raised up
the duke's chariot in order to extricate it from the mire.

The day before when Pan Tang and Yang Yu-chi had stacked breastplates on the ground to hold a shooting competition, each succeeded in shooting an arrow through seven layers of armor. Boastfully, they showed the results to the king: "Since you have two subjects so skilled as this, why worry about the coming engagement?" The king angrily retorted: "This is a disgrace to our state. Tomorrow morning your archery will be the skill that kills you."

Over in the Chin camp General Wei Ch'i dreamt that he had shot at the moon and hit it but on withdrawing became enmired himself. Having the dream interpreted, he was advised: "The sun represents the royal surname of Chi [the house of Chin], while those of different surnames [such as Ch'u] are the moon. That is certainly the king of Ch'u. You will shoot and hit him, but in withdrawing into the mire you will also die." When the battle was under way he hit the king in the eye with an arrow. The king then summoned Yang Yu-chi, gave him two arrows, and had him shoot Wei Ch'i, who was struck in the neck and fell prostrate on his quiver. Yang then took back the remaining arrow and reported the fulfillment of his mission.

Three times Hsi Chih encountered the king of Ch'u's clan troops, and each time when he saw the king, he removed his helmet and raced away like the wind. The king dispatched the Minister of Works to inquire after him and present a bow, saying: "In the fervency of our present engagement the man wearing red gaiters and leggings is a true gentleman. But since he runs off so quickly when he sees me, I wonder if he hasn't sustained some injury?"

When Hsi Chih saw the messenger, he doffed his helmet to receive the edict and then replied: "Your external servant, following his ruler in engaging in this matter of warfare, on account of your spiritual power has for some time now worn helmet and armor. I dare not bow in acknowledgment of your command but venture to advise it causes me uneasiness, this condescension of your ruler. Because of the activities of the moment, I can only salute you." He saluted three times and then withdrew.

Han Chüeh of Chin began to pursue the earl of Cheng so his driver said: "Let us quickly follow him because his driver is constantly looking about and obviously does not have his mind on the horses. We can overtake him." Han Chüeh replied, "I cannot insult another ruler." So they ceased their pursuit.

When Hsi Chih then pursued the earl of Cheng, his attendant on the right said, "Have some reconnaissance scouts[103] cut in front of him and I will mount the chariot from behind and bring him off as a captive." Hsi Chih replied, "Those who harm a ruler are punished," so he too desisted.

Shih Shou, driving the earl of Cheng's chariot, said, "Only because Duke Yi of Wei would not abandon his flag was he defeated at the battle of Ying." Then he took down the earl's pennon and stuffed it in his quiver. T'ang Kou, the attendant on the right, said to Shih Shou: "You must remain by the ruler's side. Since our defeat is horrendous, at this moment I am not as important as you. You should escape with the ruler and I will remain behind." Then he died in battle.

Ch'u's force were pressed onto constricted terrain, so Shu-shan Jan said to Yang Yu-chi, "Even though the ruler indicated otherwise, for the sake of the state you must shoot the enemy." So he shot an arrow and then shot again, and in both cases killed a soldier of Chin. Shu-shan Jan threw a man whom he had seized against a chariot, snapping the crossbar. Although Chin's troops then halted, they had already taken the king's son prisoner.

Luan Chen saw Tzu Chung's flag, so he appealed to the duke of Chin: "Ch'u's soldiers have advised me that is Tzu Chung's banner so that must be Tzu Chung. When I was formerly an emissary to Ch'u he inquired about the nature of Chin's courage. I replied, 'It is seen in masses of men well ordered.' He further asked what else, and I replied, 'In being tranquil.' This time, when our two states engaged in battle, we failed to dispatch a *hsing-jen*, so we cannot be said to have been well ordered. Now that the battle has commenced, I have had to eat my words, so this cannot be termed composure. Permit me to present him with some wine."

The duke of Chin consented, so he dispatched a *hsing-jen* with a flagon to invite Tzu Chung to drink. Advising Tzu Chung of his mission, he said: "As Luan Chen's ruler lacks capable men, he was ordered to drive and take up a spear and has not been able to attend to your troops. However, he has dispatched me bearing wine for you to drink."

Tzu Chung said: "This must be from the officer who once spoke with me in Ch'u. Do I not also recognize him?" He accepted the wine and drank it, dismissed the emissary, and then resumed beating the drums.

The battle had commenced at first light and was still raging when the stars became visible. That night Tzu Fan order Ch'u's officers to investigate the extent of the killed and wounded, supplement any deficiencies in troops and chariots, put the armor and weapons in good order, array the chariots and horses, prepare to eat at first light, and immediately obey all orders. Learning about this, the troops from Chin were uneasy, but Miao Pen-huang circulated about, saying, "Gather the chariots together, replace missing troops, tend to the horses and prepare your weapons, improve your formations and solidify your lines, eat in your tents and intensify your prayers because tomorrow we will again engage the enemy." Moreover he released the prisoners from Ch'u.

When the king of Ch'u in turn heard about these preparations, he summoned Tzu Fan to formulate their tactics, but the latter's attendant had given him wine to drink and Tzu Fan was too drunk to see the king. The king said, "When Heaven defeats us we cannot wait here." Then he withdrew during the night. Chin's forces entered their encampment and found three days' worth of provisions.[104]

This account of the battle of Yen-ling, the last of the *Tso Chuan's* well-known five great battles, while lengthy and evocative, actually provides virtually no information about the engagement itself beyond a few vignettes of ritual heroic acts (contrary to numerous Western scholars who have vigorously asserted that traditional Chinese values do not countenance such heroism and its writings are devoid of such accounts, unlike Greek heroic literature. The *Tso Chuan* narrative clearly depicts an encounter during the transitional period from chariot-centered conflict undertaken mainly by the noble class to mass-based infantry armies). The crucial tactical thrust was perceptively formulated by Miao Pen-huang, but the foundation, the possibility of mounting an effective assault rather than simply withdrawing, derived from Hsi Chih's conclusion that Ch'u's coalition was marked by dissension and fatigue, its forces too dispirited to fight effectively. However, both sides obviously employed agents and reconnaissance soldiers to gain information about the enemy prior to their confrontation and exploited extensive knowledge provided by defectors on either side. The stylized battle preparation would hardly have required a defector's explanation unless the king of Ch'u lacked battlefield experience, for Ch'u would certainly have followed similar practices. However, the value of defectors in providing key information—such as good troops being concentrated solely under the king of Ch'u—illustrates the main intelligence thrust at the end of the Spring and Autumn period.

The slow progression of events is also evident from this battle, for emissaries have the luxury of reaching out to allies for additional forces. Tzu Fan even managed to visit an old minister of Ch'u who reprised the essential foundations of military strength for him, all principles and values subsequently incorporated in Warring States military writings, but certainly grounded on Spring and Autumn experience.[105] The divination and dream accounts embedded in the narrative indicate how such information might have been interpreted and employed, as well as the fact that prophesied death would never deter military action. The deliberate release of prisoners to jangle the enemy with news of strong preparations, of resolve to fight, was a practice much discussed in later literature, but here already witnessed. (Alternatively, false information could have been scripted but would have required careful consideration of a myriad possibilities. Miao Penhuang, knowing that Ch'u's forces were already skittish, simply wanted to augment their fears.)

Finally, amid this portrait of military intelligence as practiced at the end of the Spring and Autumn period, the ill-fated Tzu Fan merits noting because his somewhat tragic fate was frequently employed to illustrate one principle or another in later centuries. Obviously a man who loved wine, he was (at least in Han Fei-tzu's subsequent account) deceived by his own steward, who insisted a proffered beverage wasn't wine. Since it is inconceivable that he wouldn't have recognized the taste of wine, once he partook of it all self-restraint must have vanished. Thus a valiant warrior and otherwise conscientious officer was doomed to suicide in the defeat's aftermath.

3

The Warring
States Period

*T*HE WARRING STATES PERIOD (403–221 B.C.), aptly named
because of the incessant warfare that plagued China throughout its
two centuries, saw the final demise of the old Chou nobility, the rise
of powerful despots, unimaginable social turbulence, and the disaffection and death of millions. The major states extant at the beginning of
the period—Ch'in, Ch'u, Han, Wei, Chao, Yen, Ch'i, and Yüeh—essentially battled each other into nonexistence, with Ch'in eventually
emerging from its advantageous position on the western fringes to
dominate all of China. As states and their entrenched nobility perished, the social structure underwent a major upheaval, creating a
pool of disfranchised individuals forced to seek employment through
knowledge and talent. Their availability proved opportune because the
period's insecurity compelled the surviving states to implement every
possible measure to strengthen themselves economically, politically,
and militarily. Political desperation fostered opportunity, giving rise to
professional bureaucrats, technocrats, political theorists, strategists,
and philosophers, all of whom roamed about the realm seeking a receptive ear. Although some important officials and members of the
nobility still defected or were exiled, their importance as intelligence
sources considerably diminished in comparison with the information
that might be easily elicited from professional advisers and peripatetic
persuaders such as Su Ch'in and Chang Yi, proponents of the Vertical
and Horizontal alliances, respectively, as well as major spies. However, prominent traitors, especially key generals, could still prove critical, often as much because they no longer served in an enemy state as
for the intelligence details they might provide.

Because the stakes had become higher and the fate of states often hung in the balance, covert practices not only were constantly employed, but also tended to be used in combination rather than singularly. Systematic subversion through bribes, disaffection through calumny, and estrangement through false accusations and rumors made up the main weapons. All three often proved surprisingly successful, no doubt being much facilitated by the emerging psychological and political analyses of court dynamics and human desire. Bribes invariably exploited ambition, internal discord, and the breakdown of ethical values, while palace jealousies were manipulated to doom states. Court cliques and powerful clans fought for power and influence, guaranteeing there would be no lack of easily identified potential subversives. Assassination surpassed its initial role as a final, desperate measure that spawned dire, often unexpected consequences, becoming an integral part of comprehensive approaches to covert warfare in states such as Ch'in.

In the military and political realms theoreticians began studying the lessons of human experience, formulating programs, and propounding systematic beliefs. Although military theorists naturally focused upon intelligence, spycraft, and covert operations, when pondering the nature of knowledge, historical experience, and political dynamics, many of the philosophical and political thinkers advanced fundamental insights and identified basic assumptions that quickly became essential to any analysis of intelligence practices. Great advances were witnessed in methods and procedures for evaluating men and armies, analyzing enemy behavior, assessing force levels, and targeting commanders. Moreover, Sun-tzu's classifications of terrain, while certainly reflecting knowledge accumulated over the preceding centuries and the classificatory impulse that produced regional theories embracing every aspect of flora and fauna, uniquely focused on the military impact of various characteristic features such as constricted and open areas. Since his topographical categories and their subsequent expansion will be discussed in the military intelligence section, it merely need be noted that the existence of difficult terrain—land that could slow, even entrap a force—now had to be recognized for purposes of both avoidance and exploitation. The astute commander therefore deployed reconnaissance patrols far ahead to prevent his own army from becoming entangled and plot measures to maneuver the enemy onto them, effectively creating a force multiplier, possibly even a killing ground such as seen at the famous battle of Ma-ling in the mid-fourth century.[1]

Agents and Intelligence

In accord with the rational character of Chinese military enterprises in part initiated by Sun-tzu's *Art of War*,[2] from the Warring States onward great emphasis was placed on analyzing enemy capabilities and intentions, determining the possibilities for victory, and then effectively employing the army by first confusing and debilitating the enemy. The Chinese practice of warfare attained its definitive style by the end of the period with the cavalry's initial use in supplementing massive infantry and chariot forces, the latter increasingly displaced from their earlier pivotal role. This analytical thrust required gathering information about the enemy, as well as oneself, preliminary to undertaking critical calculations. Apparently in accord with Sun-tzu's emphasis upon spycraft as the most efficient and necessary military activity, clandestine undertakings flourished. Instead of relying upon occasional diplomatic missions supplemented by dubious defectors, states dispatched agents and constructed foreign networks, generally through bribes and coercion. Although little information has been preserved about the nature of covert intelligence practices, their extensiveness at the end of the Warring States period may be seen in an oft-cited incident found in Wei Kung-tzu's biography in the *Shih Chi*:

> King Chao of Wei's youngest son, Prince Wu-chi of Wei, was the stepbrother of King An-li. When King Chao died and An-li ascended the throne, he enfeoffed his younger brother Wu-chi as Lord of Hsin-ling. About this time Fan Sui fled from Wei to Ch'in, becoming its prime minister. Because of Fan's hatred for Wei, he had Ch'in's troops surround Wei's capital of Ta-liang. They subsequently crushed Wei's army below Hua-yang and drove off Mang Mao.[3] King An-li and Prince Wu-chi agonized over these developments.
>
> Prince Wu-chi was benevolent and respectful to men of quality. Whether they were worthies or scoundrels, he treated them all courteously and deferentially, never presuming to be arrogant on account of his wealth and rank. Accordingly, warriors for thousands of kilometers around rushed to give their allegiance, and eventually he retained three thousand men on stipend. Because the feudal lords regarded the prince as a worthy man and knew he had numerous retainers, for some ten years they never dared plot against or attack Wei.
>
> One day when the prince and the king were gambling, word came from the north that signal fires marking a border invasion

had been seen. This was understood as indicating that Chao's forces had appeared at the border and were making an incursion. Putting the game aside, the king wanted to summon his high officials to formulate their tactics. The prince stopped him, saying: "It's not an invasion. The king of Chao is merely out hunting." He then returned to the game as before.

Being troubled, the king could not concentrate on their game. After a while word again came from the border reporting that the king of Chao was merely out hunting, not mounting an invasion. The king of Wei was astonished: "How did you know this?"

The prince replied: "Among my retainers are those who can deeply penetrate the king of Chao's secrets. Whatever the king is about to do, my retainers always report it to your servant. Thus I was able to know it." Thereafter, fearing the prince's ability and sagacity, King An-li did not dare entrust him with government affairs.[4]

Although Sun-tzu himself was active at the end of the Spring and Autumn period and his thoughts reflect the era's military practices, as a conceptual analysis the *Art of War* became influential only in the Warring States period when copies may have begun circulating and his teachings, through either his disciples or a family school, carefully studied. His characterization of spies, defined by their mode of action and objectives, has been widely acknowledged even by Western historians otherwise unfamiliar with China as history's first, and his chapter termed the earliest on spycraft. In "Employing Spies" Sun-tzu identified five categories that became the foundation for all subsequent Chinese thought upon the subject. Although they will be comprehensively discussed in the theoretical section on agents, they merit brief reprising here:

There are five types of spies to be employed: local spy, internal spy, turned spy or double agent, dead or expendable spy, and the living spy. When all five are employed together and no one knows their Tao, this is termed "spiritual methodology." They are a ruler's treasures.

Local spies—employ people from the local district.

Internal spies—employ their people who hold government positions.

Double agents—employ the enemy's spies.

Expendable spies—employ them to spread disinformation outside the state. Provide our expendable spies with false information and have them leak it to enemy agents.

Living spies—return with their reports.

Even though Sun-tzu's definition of "double agents" or "turned agents"—*fan chien*—is essentially the classical Western one, in common use from the Warring States on *fan chien* rarely meant "doubled agent," but instead someone recruited from the other side to act as an agent in place. Simply traitors to their states, rather than foreign agents who have been compromised and enlisted, they clearly fall into Sun-tzu's category of "internal agents," people who hold government positions or are otherwise close to the ruler and centers of power.

Su Ch'in

Even though his diplomatic missions were patently overt and he achieved his greatest fame for advocating the vertical alliance—successfully balking Ch'in's predatory attacks for some fifteen years—Su Ch'in has also been regarded as one of China's most successful and notorious agents. In fact, an *Art of War* text from the late Warring States period recovered in recent decades appends Su Ch'in's name to those of Yi Yin and Lü Ya as China's first spies, observing that "when Yen arose, Su Ch'in was in Ch'i." His counterfeit betrayal and flight from the state of Yen provide a dramatic example of subterfuge at its best, for through them he created a plausible motive for seeking revenge against the king of Yen and was therefore warmly welcomed in Ch'i, Yen's bitter enemy. Moreover, Su Ch'in not only achieved great fame in premodern China, but also continues to be a giant figure today as his story is retold in novels, comic books, TV programs, and movies.

Although his experiences and persuasions are recorded in several *Shih Chi* biographies and *Chan-kuo Ts'e* chapters, their reliability has been much questioned because they have apparently become admixed with romantic stories that evolved after his death. (In authoring the *Shih Chi*, Ssu-ma Ch'ien felt compelled to remark that Su Ch'in's biography was nebulous at best, and he further noted that many disparate elements had coalesced around Su Ch'in's name.) However, even though the dialogues and persuasions are almost certainly later fabrications, his activities are well recorded, and lost *Chan-kuo Ts'e* chapters that have recently resurfaced amplify the historical picture and provide further dialogues. The main difficulty therefore lies with the dates and range of Su Ch'in's activities, tentatively resolvable into the last decade of the fourth century and first two decades of the third century B.C., his death coming a year or two before 284 B.C., when Yüeh Yi led Yen's armies in a successful invasion of Ch'i.[5]

In Ssu-ma Ch'ien's narrative the critical point arrives when Su Ch'in plots to become a counterfeit exile:

The king of Yen's mother and Su Ch'in were involved in illicit relations. Even though the king knew about it, he treated him even more generously. Su Ch'in, afraid of being executed, suggested to the king, "If I remain here, I will not be able to make Yen a significant state, but if I were in Ch'i, I could certainly accomplish this objective."[6] The king concurred: "I consent to whatever you want to do."

Thereupon Su Ch'in feigned having committed an offense in Yen and fled to Ch'i where King Hsüan appointed him as a guest minister. When King Hsüan died, King Min ascended the throne.[7] Su Ch'in then persuaded King Min to make the burial extremely lavish in order to display his filiality and to undertake lofty palaces and large gardens to illuminate his Virtue, hoping to thereby enervate Ch'i and exhaust its resources to Yen's benefit.[8] When King Yi of Yen died, King Hui ascended the throne. Thereafter Ch'i's high officials competed with Su Ch'in for the ruler's favor and eventually had an assassin attack him. After fatally stabbing Su Ch'in, the assassin escaped. Even though the king dispatched men to catch the brigand, they failed.

Near death, Su Ch'in proposed to the king, "I am about to die, so if you have me torn apart by chariots in the marketplace as an exemplary punishment for causing turmoil in Ch'i on Yen's behalf, my assassin will certainly be caught." The king put his plan into effect and the assassin indeed came forth [to claim a reward], whereupon the king had him executed. When the people of Yen heard about Su Ch'in's violent death, they remarked, "How extreme was Ch'i's method for taking revenge on Su Ch'in." After his death Su Ch'in's actual mission completely leaked out, causing Ch'i to greatly fear and hate Yen when they learned about it.

The Grand Historian comments: "Su Ch'in and his two brothers became famous as peripatetic persuaders to the feudal lords. Their techniques emphasized shifts in authority, but after Su Ch'in was found to be a turned agent and executed, the world laughed at him and shunned the study of his methods. What people have said about Su Ch'in over the years varies greatly, even attributing to him unusual events from very different times. However, insofar as Su Ch'in rose from humble beginnings to unite the six states in a vertical alliance, his intelligence clearly surpassed that of ordinary men. Therefore I arrayed his actions and appended an introduction to his times in order that he not be tarnished solely by an evil name."[9]

Su Ch'in's remarkable biography raises the possibility that his reputation as a double agent for Yen was conceived solely on his deathbed as a final ploy to capture his assassin. However, when Ch'i employed him, they knew about his reputation among the feudal lords and his previous missions to create alliances in opposition to Ch'in, so Ch'i easily accepted his fabricated exile. Generations thereafter believed that he had truly betrayed Ch'i, just as his brother would subsequently. Moreover, the policy of exhausting a state through massive public undertakings was already part of current knowledge, having been a keystone in Wen Chung's systematic effort to undermine Wu at the end of the Spring and Autumn period.

The small but formidable state of Han essentially mimicked Su Ch'in's mid-fourth-century example by trying to generate unrest among the workers impressed for a massive, arduous canal project that it persuaded Ch'in to undertake. From antiquity, when the semimythical Yü exhausted himself in taming the floodwaters that perpetually inundated China, through the Spring and Autumn and into the Warring States periods, canals were undertaken on ever vaster scales, connecting rivers, lakes, and major streams. Multiuse, they immediately provided water for irrigation, as well as navigable waterways that might be negotiated by shallow draft boats either poled or pulled along from shore, thereby dramatically nurturing increased economic prosperity in the canal's vicinity. The *Shih Chi* therefore devotes a chapter to canals and China's ongoing struggle to control the Yellow River that coincidentally notes this covert attempt to exhaust Ch'in:

Hsi-men Pao diverted water from the Chang River to irrigate the district of Yeh and thereby enriched Wei's Ho-nei region. About this time the state of Han heard that Ch'in's ruler liked to initiate major undertakings. Therefore, in order to exhaust Ch'in and prevent them from launching an eastward attack, Han had the hydraulic specialist Cheng Kuo, in the capacity of a clandestine agent, persuade the king of Ch'in to chisel out a canal from the Ching River west of Mt. Chung westward to Hu pass, and also eastward around the northern mountains toward the Luo River, a total of some three hundred kilometers, in order to provide irrigation for the fields.

In the midst of its construction the king of Ch'in realized Cheng Kuo's true intentions and therefore wanted to execute him. However, Cheng Kuo said, "Initially I was a secret agent, but completing this canal will truly be to Ch'in's advantage!" The king of Ch'in, feeling this to be true, eventually had him complete it. When it was opened, the canal was employed to convey a flow of muddy water from the Ching River to irrigate several million acres of salt-laden land. Since the irrigation resulted in a yield of several bushels per acre, the territory within the pass was con-

verted into productive rice fields. Consequently, Ch'in never
again suffered from famine and was able to grow rich and strong,
subsequently uniting all the other feudal lords. They therefore
named the canal after its engineer, Cheng Kuo.[10]

Against a background of burgeoning economic prosperity stimulated by canal building, Cheng Kuo's advice would certainly have been
plausible, his own motive apparently being to enrich himself as its director. Moreover, this was an age when foreign advisers and technical
specialists were able to travel about seeking employment under the remaining feudal lords embroiled in the struggle for survival, frequently
by advocating the view that economic prosperity would provide the
foundation for military strength and political power. Ironically, Han's
subversive efforts significantly augmented Ch'in's economic base and
thereby substantially contributed to their own demise.

Military Intelligence

As the number of forces committed to the average campaign escalated
dramatically and battlefield success became vital to a state's very survival, greater resources and expertise had to be allotted to military affairs. As may be seen in the historical and theoretical writings of the
period, the importance of military intelligence grew correspondingly,
resulting in frequent admonitions to dispatch scouts, establish roving
patrols, and continuously watch the enemy. More intensive observation naturally provoked creative efforts in deception, including widely
implemented practices designed to mask numbers, misdirect attention, and conceal intent. Observational catalogs evolved that correlated visible phenomena with actual activities and projected probable
intent based upon battlefield behavior. Although largely focused upon
human intelligence, attempts were also made to capture enemy communications, interpret battlefield signals, and fathom early warning
systems. However, these and the critical issues of secrecy and counterintelligence are extensively discussed in Warring States military
writings; therefore, their analysis is best deferred to the theoretical
sections tracing the development of doctrine across periods. Here a
single example of a commander named Chao She astutely deceiving
enemy observers will illustrate the increased sophistication of coun-
terreconnaissance practices in the Warring States period.

Chao She became prominent in the state of Chao as an upright official who equalized and stabilized the taxes, thereby nurturing agricultural prosperity, and also brilliantly exercised military command responsibilities:

About 270 B.C., en route to attacking Han, Ch'in encamped at Yü-yü in Chao so the king of Chao summoned Lien P'o and asked, "Can we rescue the city of Yü-yü or not?"

Lien P'o replied: "The road is far, the passes narrow. Effecting a rescue will be difficult."

The king also summoned Yüeh Ch'eng and similarly queried him, only to receive an identical reply. He then summoned Chao She who answered: "The road is far and the passes narrow. It might be compared with two rats fighting in a cave. The more courageous general will emerge victorious."

The king therefore ordered Chao She to assume command of an army mobilized to rescue Yü-yü. When the army had ventured thirty kilometers from Han-tan, the capital, Chao She announced to his forces, "Anyone who presumes to advise upon military affairs will be put to death."

Ch'in's main army encamped west of Wu-an where the thunder of their drums and noise of their men shook the very roof tiles. Among Chao She's reconnaissance units was one soldier who admonished Chao to urgently undertake the rescue of Wu-an. Chao She immediately had him beheaded, then solidified the walls of his encampment and remained entrenched for twenty-eight days without advancing. Thereupon he again increased their height and augmented his fortifications. When enemy agents came from Ch'in, Chao She ensured that they were well fed and then sent them off. When these agents submitted their reports, Ch'in's commanding general was overjoyed: "After advancing only thirty kilometers they have stopped and merely increase their fortifications. Obviously Yü-yü is not Chao's objective."

However, immediately after sending off Ch'in's agents, Chao She had his troops roll up their armor and pursue them, arriving after a forced march of two days and one night. He then constructed a fortified camp but had his skilled archers stand off about fifty kilometers from Yü-yü. Just when they were completing their fortifications, Ch'in's forces learned about them and sped forth en masse.

An officer named Hsü Li requested permission to advise about military affairs, so Chao She gave permission for him to be brought in. Hsü Li said: "Ch'in never thought our army would reach here. They have rushed forth full of spirit, so you should deploy in depth in order to await them. Otherwise we will certainly be defeated."

Chao She responded, "I await your orders."

Hsü Li said, "Please proceed with my execution."

Chao She replied, "That can wait until later at Han-tan."

Hsü Li again requested permission to offer advice and said, "Whoever occupies the heights of the mountain to the north will be victorious, whoever arrives afterward will be defeated."

Chao She agreed and dispatched ten thousand men to race there. Ch'in forces subsequently arrived and fought with them for control of the mountain but were unable to ascend it. Chao She then released his remaining forces to suddenly strike them and thus inflicted a severe defeat on Ch'in's army. Ch'in disengaged from the conflict and fled, thereafter lifting their siege of Yü-yü and retreating back to their borders.[11]

Chao She's benign treatment of enemy spies—neither capturing nor killing them—not only is surprising for the time, but also assumes they had been detected by conscious effort. Through his actions he deliberately exploited them as *fan chien*, agents converted (and thus "doubled," even though unconsciously) to his own purposes. Numerous commanders followed his example in later dynasties, and theoreticians discussed the importance of manipulating foreign agents from the T'ang onward. Moreover, this incident—although chosen for its tactical employment of mountains—also appears as one of the historical illustrations selected for the Sung dynasty tactical compendium know as the *Hundred Unorthodox Strategies*, thereby ensuring it would thereafter be known to an even wider audience than simply literati studying the ancient histories.[12]

The role of the peripatetic persuaders already mentioned in disseminating military knowledge and exposing state secrets during the Warring States period merits closer scrutiny. Although they openly ventured from state to state, in the course of their travels and through discussions on statecraft and strategy with various officials and rulers, many of them—especially the more famous and those marked by noble birth, both of whom would have been well entertained by the powerful and rich—acquired a vast store of military knowledge. Depending upon their astuteness and observational skills, they might easily divulge a critical plan to another state after simply having deduced its existence. For example, the sort of force level information a ruler might obtain from peripatetic persuaders, itinerant strategists, and even mercenaries in the Warring States may be seen in the following summary developed from persuasions exercised by Chang Yi and Su Ch'in that are preserved in the *Chan-kuo Ts'e*. Whether their numbers were mere guesses, calculated estimates, or precise figures remains an important but unanswered question. Each state kept reasonably updated counts of their soldiers at both the central and local levels, while a general or two might always be found to carelessly discuss martial affairs. Alternatively, an experienced observer could certainly have estimated total strength with basic facts about unit size and the number of armies. Each of the stronger states could apparently field several hundred thousand troops at this time, although the composition and readiness of standing forces remain less clear. However, their force assessments for the major states extant in the mid-fourth century may be summarized as follows:

Wei—360,000 trained, mailed soldiers, plus perhaps a hundred thousand consigned to border defense; 1,000 or more chariots; 10,000 cavalry

Chao—100,000 trained, mailed troops; 1,000 chariots; 10,000 cavalry[13]

Han—200,000 trained, mailed troops; 100,000 additional on border duty

Ch'in—100,000 trained, mailed troops;[14] 1,000 chariots; 10,000 cavalry

Ch'i—300,000–400,000 trained, mailed troops

Ch'u—100,000 trained, mailed troops; 1,000 chariots[15]

The Warring States period also witnessed the development of "national combat profiles"—summary evaluations of an enemy's character and fighting potential, coupled with tactical principles for achieving victory—by such figures as Hsün-tzu and Wu Ch'i.[16] The *Wu-tzu*, a book identified with the great general Wu Ch'i that reflects early Warring States thought, preserves the following analyses:

Although Ch'i's battle array is dense in number, they are not solid. That of Ch'in is dispersed, with the soldiers preferring to fight individually. Ch'u's formations have good order, but they cannot long maintain their positions. Yen's formations are adept at defense, but they are not mobile. The battle arrays of the Three Chin are well controlled, but they prove useless.[17]

Now Ch'i's character is hard; their country prosperous; the ruler and ministers arrogant and extravagant and insulting to the common people. The government is expansive, but salaries are inequitable. Each formation is of two minds, with the front being heavy and the rear light. Thus while they are dense, they are not stable. The Tao for attacking them is to divide them into three, harrying and pursuing the left and right, coercing and following them, for then their formations can be destroyed.

Ch'in's character is strong; their land treacherous; and the government severe. Their rewards and punishments are believed in;

the people never yield but instead are all fiery and contentious. Thus they scatter and individually engage in combat. The Tao for attacking them is to first entice them with profits, for their soldiers are greedy and will abandon their generals to pursue them. Capitalizing on their misjudgment, you can hunt down their scattered ranks, establish ambushes, take advantage of the moment, and then their generals can be captured.

Ch'u's character is weak; their lands broad; their government troubling to the people and their populace weary. Thus while they are well ordered, they do not long maintain their positions. The Tao for attacking them is to suddenly strike and cause chaos in the encampments. First snatch away their spirit, lightly advancing and then quickly retreating, tiring and laboring them, never actually joining battle with them. Then their army can be defeated.

Yen's character is sincere and straightforward. Their people are careful; they love courage and righteousness, and rarely practice deception in their plans. Thus they will defend their positions but are not mobile. The Tao for attacking them is to strike and press them; insult them and put distance between you; then race and get behind them so that their upper ranks will be doubtful and their lower ranks fearful. Be cautious about your chariots and cavalry, avoid conflict on the open road, for then their general can be captured.

The Three Chin are central countries. Their character is harmonious and their government equitable. The populace is weary from battle but experienced in arms, and they have little regard for their generals. Salaries are meager, and as their officers have no commitment to fight to the death, they are ordered but useless. The Tao for attacking them is to press their formations, and when large numbers appear, oppose them. When they turn back, pursue them in order to wear them out. That then is the strategic configuration of force in these countries.[18]

No doubt observations such as these were common knowledge, formulated as a result of military experience, coupled with banter about the enemy. (A few such concrete observations have already been seen in the battlefield materials included in the Spring and Autumn section.) However, Wu Ch'i's assessments not only identify national traits derived from government practices, but also couple them with battlefield behavioral tendencies that, being predictable, can be exploited with appropriate tactics. Thus the practice of intelligence has already moved from simple observation to characterization and expectation, from mere reaction to analysis and exploitation. Once augmented with the details of concrete tactical situations, such profiles suggest plans for manipulating the enemy, for achieving Sun-tzu's critical objectives of debilitating them and achieving complete victory.

Hsün-tzu's well-known chapter on military affairs, much cited thereafter because it vigorously asserted the fundamental importance of righteousness and benevolence over mere military expediency (befitting good Confucian tradition), also contains a surprisingly realistic appraisal of warfare. Probably written by Hsün-tzu himself nearly two centuries after the *Wu-tzu*, several passages characterize three of the major states still extant late in the Warring States period:

The men of Ch'i esteem skillful attacks. When such skill results in killing one of the enemy, the soldier is rewarded with eight ounces of gold from the penalties imposed on others for battlefield failure, without any regard for whether the army itself proved victorious.[19] Accordingly, when the engagement is minor and the enemy inconsequential, Ch'i can still get by with them. But if the engagement is a major one and the enemy solid, they will disperse and scatter. Just like birds in flight, their formations can be disrupted and overturned at any moment. These are the troops of a lost state, none are weaker than they. It is almost as if they went into the marketplace to hire day laborers to engage in battle.

Wei's martial troops are selected according to standards that require them to sustain three sets of armor, be able to draw a twelve picul crossbow, carry fifty arrows in a quiver with a halberd hung on top, and when fully armored, bearing a sword, and carrying three days rations, race a hundred kilometers within a day.[20] Soldiers who meet these standards have their families exempted from labor duty and their land and household taxes remitted. However, when their skills decline with the passage of years, the benefits cannot be rescinded. Even changing the system would not be easy to fully implement. For this reason, although Wei's territory is vast, its tax revenues are invariably low. These are the soldiers of an endangered state.[21]

The men of Ch'in are sorely deprived in their ordinary lives, and the government employs them through cruelty and harshness. It brutalizes them through authority, grieves them with difficulty, tempts them with glory and rewards, and vanquishes them with corporeal punishment and fines. It ensures that the suppressed people cannot gain any benefits from the government except through combat.[22] It employs them out of their desperation, and acknowledges achievement only after they are successful in battle. Rewards compliment the degree of accomplishment. Thus someone who slays five of the enemy is placed in charge of

five families. Therefore, among these three states their troops
have long been the most numerous and strongest, and they have
expanded their territory greatly through conquest. The fact that
they have been victorious over the past four generations is not a
question of luck, but of methods.[23]

From a perspective that emphasized the virtually unopposable
strength of Virtue, Hsün-tzu was still compelled to conclude: "Ch'i's
skilled attacks are incapable of successfully countering Wei's martial
troops, but Wei's martial troops cannot counter Ch'in's elite warriors.
Ch'in's elite warriors could not have opposed the constrained and disciplined forces of the great hegemons Huan and Wen, while the constrained and disciplined forces of the great hegemons Huan and Wen
could never have been a match for the benevolence and righteousness
of Kings T'ang and Wu."

Although these two accounts were penned some two centuries
apart, they furnish evidence that working profiles were commonly developed for enemy states, no doubt the product of extensive military
experience buttressed by a pervasive theory of regionalism uniquely
ascribing physical and behavioral traits to different parts of the country. Clearly evolving from the concrete battlefield assessments witnessed in the Spring and Autumn period, they became significantly
more abstract, transcending the simple capability and intentions material furnished by defectors or through direct observation.

Finally, it should be noted that spies were not dispatched solely
against other states, but were also employed in border regions. For example, for many years General Li Mu of Chao was able to thwart
Hsiung-nu raiding parties through a combination of unorthodox tactics and refusing engagements, measures made possible through deploying numerous spies and thereby being well informed about the enemy's movements and intentions. No doubt information was also
acquired from various trading groups, local merchants, and disaffected
members of the steppe peoples. Furthermore, as in the case of Chao
She, a critical portion of his biography from the *Shih Chi* was similarly incorporated in the *Hundred Unorthodox Strategies* (as the historical incident in a chapter entitled "The Strong"), ensuring his experience would become a lesson for future leaders and commanders for
centuries thereafter.

Covert Practices

The Warring States period witnessed an amazing escalation in the employment of covert techniques designed to aggressively affect and sub-

vert other states. Not only did bribes continue to play a significant role, but also rumors and other methods were employed in combination to ensure their success. Most of the recorded efforts fall into the category of estrangement techniques, measures designed to foment dissension among important ministers, cause disaffection, and effect the dismissal of highly competent officials and generals. Because the strength of fighting armies rapidly increased, professional generals assumed an increasingly pivotal role; therefore, forcing a change in commander could reverse previous defeats, even result in complete victory, so extreme were the differences in strategic and operational abilities. However, as many commanders belatedly discovered, battlefield success also spawned court jealousies and created fertile ground for planting doubts in the ruler's mind that they represented a growing threat or might defect for greater glory and rewards.

The covert practice most widely employed in the Warring States was undoubtedly bribery, the limited materials preserved from the period recording a myriad instances. Without question bribery had been frequently employed in the Spring and Autumn but reached its apex in the Warring States because it proved the simplest, yet most effective approach amid the era's dire circumstances. As an adjunct to false rumors, bribery ensured that the loyal and courageous, the meritorious and wise, would be sufficiently disparaged to suffer exile or execution. The greater a man's achievements were, the more intense was the jealousy he aroused, greatly facilitating the identification of likely candidates to corrupt and suborn.

The conception and implementation of bribery as a systematic policy also played an essential and heretofore unnoticed role in Ch'in's dramatic consolidation of power during the final century of the Warring States period. Even though bribery could not win final victory, a task left to Ch'in's formidable warriors, it paved the way by undermining the formation of the antagonistic alliances that might have withstood them, thereby isolating the states for defeat in detail, and was also employed to persuade others to adopt policies of appeasement rather than undertake military preparations that "might be construed as provocative." According to a short reference found in the Ch'in Annals, about 237 B.C. the noted strategist Wei Liao-tzu advised the king to systematically employ bribes as a basic tool for weakening the other feudal states:

In comparison with Ch'in's vast borders, the feudal lords may be likened to rulers of provinces and districts. My only fear is that the feudal lords will form an alliance, will unite to do something unexpected. This is how Chih Po, Fu-ch'ai, and King Min perished. I suggest your Majesty not begrudge expending his wealth to bribe the great ministers and thereby confuse their plans. Without spending more than thirty thousand catties of gold, we can eliminate the feudal lords.

According to the *Shih Chi* account, the king followed his advice and also favored Wei Liao-tzu as an adviser.[24]

Li Ssu, who was then wielding the government's power, apparently undertook responsibility for implementing the plan:

He secretly dispatched strategists bearing gold and jewels to offer as presents as they wandered among the feudal lords exercising their persuasions. Famous officials in the courts of the feudal lords who might be tempted by material goods were to be entangled with abundant gifts; those unwilling to collaborate were to be assassinated with sharp swords. Whenever his plan to estrange the feudal lords from their ministers proved successful, the king of Ch'in would then have his expert generals follow up with attacks.[25]

Wei Liao-tzu was not the only voice advocating the aggressive use of bribes to achieve world domination. For example, slightly earlier the marquis of Ch'in suggested an ostentatious display of gifts amid sumptuous entertainments to buy off potential adversaries:

Officers from throughout the realm assembled in Chao in pursuit of the vertical alliance against Ch'in and wanted to attack it. Marquis Yin, then prime minister of Ch'in, said to the king: "My king, there is nothing to worry about. I request permission to force them to abandon their plans. The officers of the realm are assembling to attack Ch'in because they all want to be rich and honored, not because of any resentment against us. My king, observe your dogs. Some of them are lying down, others standing up; some are moving about, others staying still. Although they are not fighting among themselves, why is it that if you toss them a bone they will all jump up and snarl at each other? Because they have a will to fight."

Thereupon the ruler prepared to dispatch T'ang Chü, accompanied by female musicians and five thousand catties of gold, to dwell in Wu-an and drink with the members of the high assembly. There he was to inform the men of Han-tan [Chao's capital] that anyone who came to visit him would take away monetary gifts. Accordingly, those who had been plotting against Ch'in would not obtain anything from him, while those who came and received gifts would become his brothers. Marquis Yin further instructed him, "When you calculate the achievement for Ch'in, the ruler will not inquire about the gold, for if the gold is completely exhausted, the achievements will be many." The king moreover ordered men to follow on after T'ang Chü bearing an additional five thousand catties of gold. After T'ang Chü arrived at Wu-an and distributed the gold, before he had used up three thousand, the realm's officers were all fighting among themselves.[26]

Similar measures were employed to undermine the vertical alliance, the only hope the other states had to prevent Ch'in from annexing the entire known realm through piecemeal conquest of the remaining states. When the king of Ch'in asked whether he could seize the states east of the pass, Tun Jo replied:

"Han is the throat of the realm, while Wei is the stomach. If my lord will provide your servant with ten thousand pieces of gold, I will travel about listening to affairs in Han and Wei, and suborn their ministers. Then Han and Wei will become submissive to Ch'in. When Han and Wei are submissive, the conquest of the realm can be plotted."

The king of Ch'in replied, "Our state is impoverished, so I am afraid I am unable to provide it."

Tun Jo retorted: "The realm is never free of affairs. If it is not the Vertical Alliance, it will be the Horizontal Alliance. If the Horizontal Alliance succeeds, you will become emperor; if the Vertical Alliance is successful, the king of Ch'u will become king of the realm. If you achieve emperorship, All under Heaven will respectfully nurture Ch'in. If the king of Ch'u becomes king of the realm, even though you have ten thousand catties of gold, you will not be able to retain them."

Concurring, the king of Ch'in provided him with ten thousand catties of gold and dispatched him east to travel among the states of Han and Wei where he subsequently brought their generals and ministers under Ch'in's influence. Then Tun Jo went north to traverse Yen and Chao where he effected the death of General Li Mu. When the king of Ch'i visited Ch'in's court, the four other states had to follow, all because of Tun Jo's persuasion.[27]

Tun Jo thus turns out to be a clandestine agent par excellence who goes about subverting high officials, even though the survival of their states depended upon adopting a strong united front against Ch'in. But perhaps, if allowances are to be given, a political and military mind-set (or inexplicable miasma), such as witnessed in the early days of the German onslaught of World War II, overcame them.

Somewhat contradictorily, the extinction of Chao and death of Li Mu are also attributed to Wang Chien, the actual commanding general in the final confrontation with Chao. According to the *Chan-kuo Ts'e:*

> When Ch'in had Wang Chien attack Chao, Chao employed Li Mu and Ssu-ma Shang to command the defense. Li Mu's forces smashed and drove back Ch'in's army several times, killing a general named Huan Yi. Wang Chien, enraged by these developments, made generous gifts of gold to Chao's favored ministers such as Kuo K'ai, employing them as "turned agents" to say that Li Mu and Ssu-ma Shang wanted to betray Chao and join Ch'in to thereby receive generous fiefs from Ch'in.[28] The king of Chao, becoming suspicious, had Chao Ts'ung and Yen Ts'ui replace his generals. Thereafter he had Li Mu executed and exiled Ssu-ma Shang. Three months later Wang Chien extensively destroyed Chao's army through a fervent sudden strike, slayed Chao's commanding general, and captured both the king and General Yen Tsui. Thereafter Ch'in extinguished the state of Chao.[29]

The efficacy of these bribes in underpinning rumors designed to subvert Chao's commanding general is truly astounding. For a few pieces of gold Chao's ministers not only endangered the state, but also destroyed it, thus failing to learn from the well-known story of Po P'i and the state of Wu at the end of the Spring and Autumn period!

Rumors and Estrangement Techniques

The subsequent internecine strife between the two eastern states of Yen and Ch'i during the middle to late Warring States period contains an incident that well illustrates the effective use of spies to sow dissension and eliminate the capable. After pursuing a self-strengthening policy for many years, Yen finally took advantage of Ch'i's ill-advised assault on the smaller state of Sung to launch a massive attack in conjunction with several other states. Yüeh Yi, who apparently formulated Yen's political and military strategy and was the chief architect for the invasion plans, acted as commander in chief. As summarized in the various annals, the pinnacle of King Chao's rule then arrived:

> In 285 B.C. the state of Yen was flourishing and rich; the officers and troops took pleasure in military discipline and regarded war lightly. Then the king commissioned Yüeh Yi as general in chief

and planned an attack on Ch'i in unison with Ch'in, Ch'u, and the Three Chin states of Han, Wei, and Chao.

In 284 B.C. Ch'i's forces were defeated and King Min fled outside the state. Yen's army alone pursued the retreating forces to the north, penetrating the capital, Lin-tzu; seized all of Ch'i's treasures; and burned their palaces and ancestral temples. Only the cities of Liao, Chü, and Chi-mo did not surrender; all the others were subjugated by Yen within six months. Yüeh Yi was deputed to continue the campaign to pacify the remaining unsubmissive cities.[30]

Yüeh Yi's blitzkrieg tactics accorded with Sun-tzu's emphasis upon speed, mobility, and aggressive action. However, more cautious strategists criticized his rapid penetration into Ch'i's heartland as foolhardy,[31] and advocated conservative, presumably long-term views, thus sowing exploitable seeds of acrimony and dissension. Moreover, after the first year's stunning success, the two fortified cities that remained proved both resolute and impregnable, much in contrast to many among the seventy that had quickly crumbled. Yüeh Yi's calculated reluctance to dissipate the army's strength in a horrendous urban assault naturally provided fertile ground for political intrigue and the carping voices that vilified him:[32]

Three years passed, but still the cities had not submitted. Someone slandered Yüeh Yi to King Chao of Yen: "Yüeh Yi's wisdom and planning surpass other men. After he attacked Ch'i, within the space of a single breath he conquered more than seventy cities. Now only two cities have not surrendered. It isn't that his strength is unable to reduce them. The reason he hasn't attacked for three years is that he wants to avail himself on the army's awesomeness to force the people of Ch'i to submit, for then he will face south and become king. Now that the people of Ch'i have surrendered, the reason he hasn't yet initiated this plan is because his wife and children are in Yen. Moreover, in Ch'i there are many beautiful women; eventually he will also forget his wife and children. I would like your majesty to plan against it."[33]

Being wise, King Chao rebuked the accuser and had him beheaded, thereby temporarily silencing such accusations. However, his son, who succeeded him shortly thereafter, not only had previously quarreled with Yüeh Yi, but was also shortsighted and inexperienced, and thus fell prey to exactly the same innuendoes deliberately reinstigated by T'ien Tan—the popularly chosen commander in the holdout of Chi-mo—through intermediaries:[34]

In 279 B.C. it happened that King Chao died and his son was established as King Hui of Yen. When the latter had been heir-apparent, he had been displeased by Yüeh Yi. Therefore, when he ascended the throne and T'ien Tan learned of it, he released a double agent in Yen to say: "In Ch'i there are only two cities that have not surrendered. This being the case, I have heard that the reason that they were not taken earlier is that Yüeh Yi and the new king of Yen have had disagreements, so Yüeh Yi wants to unite his troops and remain in Ch'i, face south, and thus become king of Ch'i. The only thing that Ch'i fears is the disaster that would be brought about if some other general were to come."

When King Hui, having already been suspicious of Yüeh Yi, gained this information from the double agent, he dispatched Ch'i Chieh to replace him as commanding general and summoned Yüeh Yi back. Yüeh Yi knew that King Hui did not have good intentions in replacing him and, fearing execution, surrendered in the west to Chao. Chao enfeoffed Yüeh Yi at Kuan-chin with the title of Lord of Wang-chu, honoring and favoring him in order to frighten Yen and Ch'i.[35]

The new commander, being far less capable and overly self-confident, was soon tricked by T'ien Tan into believing that Chi-mo was about to surrender, only to be shocked when Ch'i's remaining forces mounted a ferocious night escape spearheaded by fire-oxen. T'ien Tan eventually succeeded in recapturing all of Ch'i's lost territory, causing the remorseful King Hui to beg Yüeh Yi to return to Yen, as much out of fear of his talent being exploited against Yen as the hope that he might again prove useful. However, Yüeh Yi wisely declined, and the destruction of Yen's mighty army became one of the most famous achievements of covert action preserved in the historical annals.[36] The *Shih Chi's* dramatic narrative, even as abridged here, also contains evidence of T'ien Tan's ready employment of agents to spread disinformation and thus manipulate the enemy into actions that would infuriate Tan's own men:

T'ien Tan ordered that whenever they ate, the people in the city should sacrifice to their ancestors in their courtyards. The birds flying about then all hovered and danced over the city, descending to eat. Yen's soldiers found it to be strange.

T'ien Tan then proclaimed, "A spirit has descended to instruct me." Afterward he said to the inhabitants, "There ought to be a spiritual man here who can act as my teacher." One soldier spoke up, "Can I act as your teacher?" Then he turned around and went away. T'ien Tan got up and had him returned, seated him in the eastern direction, and treated him as his teacher. The soldier said, "I tricked you; I am truly without ability." T'ien Tan said, "Do not speak!" Thereupon he made him his teacher. Every time he set forth any covenants or constraints, he would invariably attribute them to this spiritual teacher.

Subsequently he publicly announced: "The only thing I fear is that Yen's army might cut off the noses of our countrymen who have fallen captive and then parade them in front of us. If they then engaged us in battle, Chi-mo would be defeated!" Yen's soldiers heard about this and acted accordingly. When the city's inhabitants saw all the prisoners who had surrendered from Ch'i with their noses cut off, they were completely enraged and mounted a solid defense, fearing only that they might be captured.

Tan also let loose double agents who said: "The only thing that Yen's soldiers fear is that you will excavate the graves outside the city and disgrace our ancestors. This would turn our hearts cold." Yen's army thoroughly excavated the mounds and graves and burned the dead. Witnessing it from atop the city walls, the people of Chi-mo all cried and wept, and wanted to rush forth to engage in battle. Thus their anger increased tenfold.

T'ien Tan knew that the officers and troops could be employed in battle, so he personally took up the bar and spade used for building walls and shared the work with the officers and troops. His wife and concubines were enrolled in the ranks of five; he dispersed food and drink in order to feast all the officers. He ordered all the armored soldiers to conceal themselves and had the old, the weak, women, and children mount the walls. When he dispatched an emissary to arrange terms of surrender with Yen, the army all shouted, "Long life!"

T'ien Tan also gathered up the people's gold, accumulating a thousand ounces, and had Chi-mo's rich families send it out to Yen's generals, saying, "When Chi-mo surrenders, we hope that you will not plunder the homes of our clans or make prisoners of our wives and concubines, but let us be in peace." Yen's generals were overjoyed and agreed to it. From this Yen's army was increasingly lax.

Within the city T'ien Tan herded up more than one thousand cattle and then had red silken cloth decorated with five-colored dragon veins cover them. They tied naked blades to their horns and soaked the reeds bound to their tails in fat, igniting the ends. Before this they bored several tens of holes in the walls, and at night released the cattle with five thousand stalwart soldiers following in the rear. When their tails grew hot the cattle became enraged and raced into Yen's army.

Being the middle of the night, Yen's forces were greatly startled. The brightness of the burning torches on the cattle tails was dazzling. Wherever Yen's soldiers looked were dragon veins; anyone with whom the cattle collided died or was wounded. Availing themselves of the confusion, Ch'i's five thousand men, with gagged mouths, suddenly attacked, accompanied by a great drumming and clamor from within the city. The old and weak all made their bronze implements resound by striking them, the tumult moved Heaven and Earth. Terrified, Yen's defeated army ran off in turbulence and confusion. Ch'i's soldiers subsequently killed Yen's general Ch'i Chieh.

Ch'i's soldiers raced after the defeated and pursued those who fled. All the cities that they passed revolted against Yen and gave their allegiance back to T'ien Tan, so his troops constantly increased. Taking advantage of his victories and exploiting Yen's daily defeats and losses, T'ien Tan finally reached the region above the Yellow River. By then more than seventy Ch'i cities had been returned. Then he went to welcome King Hsiang at Chü, thereafter entering Lin-tzu where he submitted to the king's rule. King Hsiang enfeoffed T'ien Tan as Lord of An-p'ing.[37]

Although ruthless, T'ien Tan clearly understood what was necessary to reverse Ch'i's hopeless situation and rescue the state from oblivion. His systematic exploitation of the enemy's greed and gullibility through disinformation and feigned bribes (or rather an actual bribe for an ostensibly different purpose) disarmed the besiegers, encouraging the laxity that imminent victory often induces. In contrast, Yen's commanders apparently assumed they well understood the situation and never anticipated the possibility of unexpected change. They obviously lacked spies within the city and failed miserably in fathoming the enemy's activities, being easily misled by the birds and internal (even though termed "double") agents who provided them with prestructured data.

A second example of employing disinformation agents to effect the removal of a talented military commander and thereby achieve an overwhelming military victory with epoch-making consequences occurred less than two decades later. Once again Ch'in managed to subvert another state with but little effort, exterminating Chao's forces in a battle in which the total combatants from both sides reputedly approached the astounding figure of one million:[38]

For his great victory at Wu-an, King Hui of Chao awarded Chao She the title of Lord of Ma-fu and appointed Hsü Li as a state colonel. Chao She thus assumed the same rank as Lien P'o and Lin Hsiang-ju. Four years later King Hui died and his son was enthroned as King Hsiao. In his seventh year, 259 B.C., Chao and Ch'in were engaged in a stand-off at Ch'ang-p'ing. At this time Chao She had already died and Lin Hsiang-ju was seriously ill, so King Hsiao deputed Lien P'o to command the army in an assault upon Ch'in. However, Ch'in inflicted several defeats on Chao; therefore Lien P'o had his troops assume fortified positions and disengage from further hostilities. Several times Ch'in attempted to provoke Chao into combat, but Lien P'o was unwilling to engage them. However, King Hsiao believed Ch'in's agents in Chao who said, "The only thing that Ch'in fears would be the appointment of Chao Kua, Chao She's son, as commanding general."[39] The king thereupon designated Chao Kua to replace general Lien P'o.

Lin Hsiang-ju objected: "You are employing Kua solely because of his father's name, just like someone gluing the tuning stops but trying to play the lute. Kua only knows how to read his father's books; he doesn't have any idea how to effect battlefield segmentation and changes." Unheeding, the king formally commissioned Kua as commanding general.

From his youth Chao Kua had studied military theory and discussed military affairs and therefore felt that no one in the world could oppose him. Once when he argued tactics with his father, even his father was unable to stump him. However, when Chao She did not acclaim his son's excellence and his wife asked why, he replied: "The army is a field of death, yet Kua easily speaks about it. If our state never appoints Kua as a general, that will be the end of it; otherwise, if they insist he serve as a commander, the one responsible for destroying Chao's forces will certainly be Kua."

When Kua was about to depart to assume command, his mother submitted a letter to the king stating that he should not employ Kua as commanding general. When the king queried her as to the reason, she replied: "Formerly when I served his father, the general, those whom he personally presented food and drink and brought forward to dine were counted by tens, while his friends were numbered by the hundreds. Whatever the king or the royal house awarded him, he in turn presented to the officers and civil officials in the army. On the day he received his mandate of command, he no longer concerned himself with family affairs.

"Now Kua has just been appointed, but when he looked east in the court, none of the officers dared look up at him. He has stored away all the gold and silks your majesty presented to him in his house and daily concerns himself with real estate transactions. How could you imagine that he is at all like his father? Father and son are of different minds. I request that you do not to dispatch him into combat."

"Madam, cease your protestations. I have already decided," responded the king.

Kua's mother then said, "If you must employ him after all, if he fails will you exempt me from punishment?" The king agreed.

Once Chao Kua had replaced Lien P'o, he altered all the regulations and constraints, changed and dismissed the army's officers. When Pai Ch'i, Ch'in's commanding general, heard about it, he released his unorthodox troops in a feigned hasty retreat while also severing Chao's supply lines. Thereafter he cut their army into two and Chao's officers and troops became disaffected. After forty days the army was starving, so Chao Kua sent forth his elite forces and struck Ch'in himself. However, he was killed by Ch'in's archers and his army defeated, with some several hundred thousand troops subsequently surrendering. Ch'in then buried them all alive, so that Chao lost a total of some 450,000 men in these engagements. Because Chao Kua's mother had warned of Kua's inadequacy, the king remitted her punishment.[40]

Not only did the battle of Ch'ang-p'ing significantly weaken Chao; the losses it sustained were also the worst ever recorded in ancient Chinese history, even allowing for significant exaggeration despite recent archaeological discoveries that tend to confirm a massive toll at this battle. The logic of their surrender is unknown, as is the king's insistence on appointing Chao Kua in the face of dire warnings. According to his own biography, Pai Ch'i apparently felt the massiveness of Chao's forces presented a great danger and therefore took the opportunity to exterminate them. Chao Kua's name thus became synonymous with "armchair general," someone marked by book learning only, while Pai was condemned ever after for his unrighteous behavior in executing surrendered prisoners.[41]

Finally, although rumor spreading was one of the simplest and least traceable methods for undermining and besmirching, more sophisticated measures—such as forgeries and preprogrammed false accusations, further examples of which will be found in the covert section—were also employed. For example, even though the following episode arose as the outgrowth of one official's jealousy, it illustrates how contemporary beliefs might be exploited to frame an exemplary general:[42]

Tsou Chi, Lord of Ch'eng and prime minister of Ch'i, and T'ien Chi, General of the Army, were displeased with each other. Kung-sun Han addressed Tsou Chi: "Sire, why not plan an attack on Wei for the king? If we are victorious, then it will have been due to my lord's plans and you can receive the credit. If we engage in combat and are not victorious, if T'ien Chi has not advanced into battle and has not perished, you can wrangle an accusation of cowardice against him and have him executed."

Tsou Chi agreed, so he persuaded the king to have T'ien Chi attack Wei. In three engagements T'ien Chi emerged victorious three times, so Tsou Chi informed Kung-sun Han. Thereupon Kung-sun Han had a man take ten gold pieces to a diviner in the marketplace and inquire: "I am T'ien Chi's retainer. T'ien Chi engaged in battle three times and was victorious three times. His fame overawes All under Heaven. If he wants to undertake the great affair of usurping the throne, will it be equally auspicious or not?"

The diviner went out and had men detain the person who had requested the divination for T'ien Chi, and then attested to his words before the king. T'ien Chi subsequently fled.[43]

It seems incredible that Tsou Chi's simple ruse might have persuaded anyone that such a brilliant and successful general would have suddenly become so profoundly stupid as to blatantly initiate such inquiries. However, several of China's dynastic founders (including the Han and T'ang) availed themselves of—or manufactured—prophecies attesting to their "extraordinary" qualities and predestination. Had T'ien Chi actually ordered this public solicitation, it might well have been a sort of trial balloon to gauge the extent of potential adherents or a nucleus for deliberately stimulating rumors that could arouse public support.

Women, Sex, and Consorts

Perhaps because burgeoning economic prosperity afforded hedonistic practices and because debauching other states with female musicians was no longer viewed as a dramatic technique likely to have much impact, the practice seems to have largely ceased in the Warring States

period. Naturally women continued to be employed to seduce and befuddle powerful men—and men to influence consorts and dowagers—
but in a more circumscribed manner, without notoriety. Conversely,
exploiting the influence enjoyed by favored concubines and powerful
consorts seems to have evolved into a common technique, despite
their supposed isolation and remoteness. This is illustrated by a well-
known story about a rare white fox coat that coincidentally portrays
the tangled web of personal and political intrigue, as well as the perceptions and expectations, that characterized the Warring States period. Just at the start of the third century B.C. the Lord of Meng-ch'ang,
a member of Ch'i's ruling house, cultivated three thousand guests and
retainers of various skills, some notable, others disreputable:[44]

> In 299 B.C. King Min of Ch'i finally had the Lord of Meng-ch'ang
> return as ambassador to Ch'in where King Chao appointed him as
> prime minister. However, someone said to King Chao: "The Lord
> of Meng-ch'ang is worthy but is also a member of Ch'i's royal
> clan. If he now acts as prime minister in Ch'in, he will certainly
> put Ch'i first and Ch'in second, and then Ch'in will be imper-
> iled." King Chao therefore had the Lord of Meng-ch'ang seized
> and imprisoned, planning to kill him. However, the latter had
> someone visit the king's favorite concubine and entreat her to get
> him released. The concubine said, "I would like to have your mas-
> ter's white fox robe."
>   Meng-ch'ang once had a white fox robe worth a thousand cat-
> ties of gold, unlike any other in the world, that he had presented
> to King Chao when he entered Ch'in. Since there wasn't another
> one anywhere, Meng-ch'ang was worried and asked his retainers
> for advice, but no one could reply. Then the lowest ranking guest,
> someone with the ability of a sneak thief, said, "I can get the robe
> for you." That night, sneaking in like a dog, he entered the depths
> of the palace treasury and retrieved the robe that had been given
> to the king, which was in turn presented to the beloved concu-
> bine. She then spoke with King Chao on Meng-ch'ang's behalf and
> he was released.
>   He raced away but first changed his fief, name, and other as-
> pects of his identity in order to get through the pass. They reached
> the barrier at Han pass in the middle of the night. Meanwhile
> King Chao began to regret he had released Meng-ch'ang and
> sought him, only to discover he had already fled. Thereupon he
> dispatched men to race after, capture, and bring him back. The
> regulations of Ch'in forbade allowing guests out of the state until
> the roosters crowed in the morning. Meng-ch'ang was afraid his

pursuers would catch up, but one of the lowliest retainers was able to imitate a rooster's crowing. When he did so the roosters all crowed, so the gate was opened and they were allowed to pass through. In the time it would take to eat a meal the pursuit force arrived at the pass but were already too late because Meng-ch'ang had departed, so they returned. In the beginning when Meng-ch'ang had ranked these two men among his guests, all the others had been embarrassed. However, after they extricated him from Ch'in everyone acknowledged Meng-ch'ang's judgments.[45]

Because Meng-ch'ang and his party were ridiculed in the state of Chao, while returning to Ch'i, they angrily killed hundreds of their detractors. Hardly the behavior expected of someone characterized as a "worthy," it shows the power that private forces could brutally exercise in a tenuous age of chaos. Although later periods also witnessed powerful clans whose influence waxed and waned depending upon the strength of the central government, the Warring States clearly displayed an ethos of violence and its admiration, contrary to much verbiage about China's pacific heritage and pervasive deprecation of martial values.

Lord of Hsin-ling, Prince of Wei

Prince Wu-chi's biography, the first paragraphs of which have already been cited as evidence of the extensive covert intelligence operations mounted in the Warring States period, comprehensively illustrates a number of covert practices employed against one man.[46] Moreover, the significant impact of the bribery and exploitation of consorts clearly visible in it provided a lesson for subsequent ages. As background, it should be noted that the state of Wei had an aged, reclusive official named Hou Sheng who served as a watchman at the Yi Gate and in turn patronized a worthy named Chu Hai, who happened to be the town butcher. The prince made extraordinary efforts to cultivate a relationship with them and was rewarded, in turn, with a reputation for enduring their eccentricity simply to achieve it, one that Hou Sheng in fact had deliberately fostered. Even though the prince was hardly alone in such efforts, his skill in recognizing men of worth, in addition to simply being deferential to all such men, stands out. His behavior well accorded with the trends of an era that emphasized the cultivation of miscellaneous talents against the possibility of future use, although ideally these efforts were not supposed to be utilitarian in character, never deliberately undertaken to exploit the "recognized" at some critical moment.

By King An-li's twentieth year [257 B.C.] Ch'in forces had already destroyed Chao's armies at Ch'ang-p'ing and advanced to besiege Han-tan, Chao's capital. Prince Wu-chi's younger sister was the wife of the Lord of P'ing-yüan in Chao, so the Lord of P'ing-yüan sent several letters to the king of Wei and prince Wu-chi requesting that they dispatch a rescue force. The king of Wei deputed General Chin Pi, in command of a hundred thousand troops, to rescue Chao.[47] [Learning of this], the king of Ch'in dispatched an emissary to inform Wei that "our attack on Chao will succeed sooner or later, so if any of the feudal lords dare dispatch rescue forces, we will certainly redirect our forces to attack them first." The king of Wei fearfully sent an officer to stop Chin Pi and have the army ensconce itself at Yeh. Although termed "rescue forces," they actually assumed an indefinite posture and merely observed.

The Lord of P'ing-yüan continuously sent emissaries from Chao to Wei and deprecatingly said to the prince: "The reason I allied myself to your house through marriage was your great righteousness and ability to be troubled by other people's difficulties. In a few days Han-tan will have to surrender to Ch'in. If Wei's forces do not arrive in time, how will you ever be able to express your compassion for other people's difficulties? Moreover, even if you lightly abandon me to surrender to Ch'in, do you not care about your sister?"

Troubled by the situation, the prince asked the king to take action several times and also had his prominent guests and sophisticated persuaders ply the king with a myriad arguments. However, fearing Ch'in, the king would not heed them in the end. Prince Wu-chi, concluding that he would not gain his objective, calculated that he could not live and yet allow Chao to perish. Therefore he requested his retainers assist him and gathered a force of some hundred or more chariots, intent on going forth to confront Ch'in's forces and die with Chao. In departing he passed by Yi Gate where he saw Hou Sheng [the gatekeeper], and fully informed him about his intention to die before Ch'in's army. After a final salutation he prepared to depart. Hou Sheng said: "Make your best effort. I am unable to follow you."

After the prince had proceeded some kilometers he felt uneasy, thinking: "I treated Hou Sheng with the greatest respect and generosity. Everyone in the world knows this. Now I am about to die, yet Hou Sheng did not have a word to grace my departure. Do I have some shortcoming?" Thereupon he turned his chariot around and went to query him.

Hou Sheng laughed and said: "I knew you would return! Your name has been heard throughout the realm for delighting in men of talent, yet now that there is some difficulty, have you no other recourse but to go off and confront Ch'in's army? This may be compared to throwing meat to a hungry tiger. What will it accomplish? Among your guests you treated me very well, but when you departed I did not send you off. I knew you would hate it and return." The prince bowed twice and then asked him about possible tactics.

Hou Sheng, separating them off from the others, then secretly spoke with him: "I have heard that Chin Pi's military tally is always kept in the king's bedroom. Now the concubine Ju, being the most favored, goes in and out of his bedroom and has the ability to steal it. I have also heard that her father was slain and for three years she harbored enmity over it. From the king on down she sought to have someone avenge her, but no one succeeded. She cried before you because of it, and you dispatched one of you retainers to cut off the murderer's head which you then respectfully presented to her. She is willing to die for you, there is nothing she would decline, but has not yet had any opportunity. If you sincerely speak a word to her, she will certainly assent. Then you can get the tiger tally necessary to seize control of Chin Pi's forces, go north to rescue Chao, and force Ch'in in the west to withdraw. This is an attack worthy of a hegemon."

The prince followed his plot and requested Ju's aid, who indeed stole the tally of authority and gave it to the prince. The prince was about to depart, but Hou Sheng said: "When a general is in the field, for the benefit of the state there are orders from the ruler that he does not accept.[48] If you match the halves of the tally, but instead of turning the army over to you Chin Pi queries the king, affairs will turn precarious. My retainer, the butcher Chu Hai, can accompany you. He is a warrior of strength. If Chin Pi obeys, it will be excellent, but if he does not, you can have Chu attack him."

Hearing this the prince cried. Hou Sheng said: "Are you afraid of death? Is this why you shed tears?"

The prince replied: "Chin Pi is a courageous old general. If I go there, I am afraid he will not obey and I will certainly have to kill him. This is why I weep. How could I fear death?" Then he went and requested that Chu Hai accompany him.

Chu Hai laughed and said: "Although I am merely a butcher in the marketplace, you have personally honored me several times.

The reason I never expressed my thanks is that I have always felt minor rites to be useless. Now that you have some difficulty, this is the time when I might sacrifice my life in repayment." He therefore accompanied the prince.

Prince Wu-chi went to take leave of Hou Sheng. Hou Sheng said: "Although I am willing to follow you, I am too old. Let me give you several days' leave to travel, and on the day you reach Chin Pi's army I will face north and commit suicide in order to send you off." The prince then departed and went to Yeh where he forged the king's order to replace Chin Pi as commander. Chin Pi matched the halves of the tally but raising his hand said to the prince: "Right now I have command of some hundred thousand troops encamped here on the border. This is a great state responsibility. So how is it that you have come out here to replace me with a single chariot?"

Since Chin Pi was unwilling to obey, Chu Hai removed a forty-pound iron truncheon from his sleeve and slew him. The prince took command and then, when reviewing the army, announced: "If there are any fathers and sons present in the army, the father should return to Wei. If any brothers, the elder should return. Any solitary sons without brothers should also go back to nourish their parents." Accordingly he obtained a select force of some eighty thousand men, advanced the army, and attacked Ch'in. Ch'in lifted the siege and retreated, thereby rescuing Han-tan and preserving Chao.

As Wu-chi had forged the transfer order, he sent the army back under a subordinate commander but personally remained in Chao with a few attendants for some ten years, where he was well treated and attracted a local following. Fearing reprisals, he consistently rejected King An-li's entreaties to return—pleas prompted by unremitting Ch'in attacks that were eroding Wei's territory—until criticized by some worthies in Chao for failing to protect his own ancestral lands.

The prince returned to rescue Wei. When the king saw him they both wept. The king gave him the seals of supreme general and the prince took command of the army. In the king's thirtieth year [247 B.C.] the prince sent emissaries to the feudal lords who all dispatched rescue forces once they learned he had assumed command in Wei. Then in supreme command the prince led the soldiers of five states in defeating Ch'in's army out beyond the Yellow River and driving off Meng Ching, subsequently exploiting the victory to pursue Ch'in's forces back to Han pass. Ch'in withdrew within the pass and did not again venture east.

At this time the prince's awesomeness shook the realm, and retainers from the various feudal lords all submitted military texts to him which were collected under his name and commonly called *The Prince of Wei's Art of War.*[49] The king of Ch'in, worried about these developments, sent an agent to Wei with ten thousand catties of gold to seek out Chin Pi's former retainers and have them slander the prince before the king, saying: "The prince was in exile for ten years, yet now he is commanding general and the feudal lords all submit to him. The feudal lords have all heard of the prince of Wei but not the king of Wei. The prince also wants to take advantage of the moment to become king while the lords, fearing his might, jointly want to establish him."

Several times Ch'in sent turned agents[50] to ostensibly offer congratulations upon the prince soon becoming king. When the king heard these things every day, he could not help believing them and therefore eventually dispatched someone to replace the prince as supreme commander. The prince, knowing that he had again been maligned and cast aside, no longer attended court on the pretext of illness, instead drinking well into the night with his guests. When he revived from his inebriation he had many women brought in, and in this fashion drank and caroused night and day for four years. Eventually he died from alcoholism, and the king also died the same year.

When the king of Ch'in learned that the prince was dead, he had Meng Ching mount an attack on Wei that resulted in seizing twenty cities and establishing eastern commanderies for the first time. Thereafter Ch'in gradually gnawed away at Wei, eighteen years later [225 B.C.] making the king a prisoner and butchering Ta-liang.

This account of Wei's demise at the very end of the Warring States period, just three years before Ch'in finally unified the whole realm to establish the first imperial dynasty, contains a number of illuminating points. First of all, the king of Ch'in resorted to so-called *li-chien* (estrangement) techniques and, despite Wu-chi's enormous success in rescuing Wei, succeeded remarkably! (Whether this illustrates the skillful employment of estrangement methods in creating disaffection through slander and calumny or simply the stupidity of rulers is perhaps an open question. Rulers never learned from dramatic historical events such as the fatal dismissals of Lien Po and Yüeh Yi.) Second, the prince's assiduous cultivation of *shih*—gentlemen of the lowest noble rank—irrespective of their immediate worth bears noting because this was a period when men of any and every talent, including tacticians, murderers, and strong arms such as Chu Kai, might prove useful.[51] The prince received tactical advice from Hou Sheng, no doubt a student of history who knew the lessons and techniques of the past, while the earlier incident that caused the king uneasiness proved a well-constructed web of external connections.

The traditional method for controlling military power once a general had taken the field, for verifying that an order was genuine, may also be seen in this story. Tallies, usually of metal but sometimes of wood, were created in various shapes, such as a tiger, and appropriately inscribed so that the matching halves were still distinguishable. The commander retained one, the ruler another, with the authenticity of special communications being attested by the accompanying tally. (Naturally they were intended for extreme emergencies, being usable only once.) Assuming both parties properly safeguarded their respective halves, the method would prove secure. However, these precautions were easily circumvented when Wu-chi exploited the favored concubine who was already emotionally predisposed to cooperate with him. Thus the prince easily obtained the tally and made his escape through a gate guarded by the honored confidant who had suggested the plot. Unfortunately, his various actions obliged Hou Sheng to righteously die, which he did after ensuring the prince's success.

The term *hsien* appears throughout the account in several meanings, including "secretly," "agent," and "turned agent," although the latter is not synonymous with Sun-tzu's double agent. This single biography thus provides a portrait of spies infiltrating every aspect of statecraft, thereby dramatically affecting the outcome of Warring States political strife; the state of Ch'in virtually rolled up the other states, partly by aggressively subverting state governments through the stimulation of disaffection and by fomenting political wrangling among the remaining states.

Pivotal Role of Assassinations

During the Warring States period assassination continued to be actively employed by generals and rulers to swiftly resolve difficult situations, especially when confronted by disadvantageous battlefield odds. At the very end of the era Prince Tan of Yen, noting historical precedents of strong-arm measures coercing promised concessions that were subsequently honored, decided to employ an assassin against Ch'in to somehow forestall being vanquished by a massive Ch'in invasion force said to number several hundred thousand men. The account of the entire exploit, the longest in the *Shih Chi*'s chapter entitled "Assassins," so struck the Chinese mind that it remained famous ever after and the name of the warrior chosen for the task, Ching K'o, became synonymous with assassins. Significantly abridged, the *Shih Chi* depiction follows:[52]

> Ching K'o was a native of Wei, although his forebears had moved to Wei from Ch'i. He loved to read books and train in sword techniques. Traveling about to exercise his persuasion on the feudal lords, he finally arrived in the state of Yen. While staying there he was fond of drinking wine with two beloved friends, a lowly butcher and the lute player Kao Chien-li, so every day the three of them drank in the marketplace. As they became inebriated, Kao would play his lute and Ching would sing in accompaniment right in the market. Sometimes after singing they would weep, just as if no one were around.
>
> Although Ching K'o consorted with drunkards, he was profound and loved books. No matter which of the feudal lords he visited, he invariably associated with the worthy and with the leaders of powerful families. In Yen the reclusive scholar T'ien Kuang, recognizing he was not an ordinary man, similarly treated him generously.

The tale continues with Prince Tan's escape from his ill-treatment as a hostage in Ch'in, subsequent return to Yen, and decision to slay the king of Ch'in for both personal and state reasons. Having been introduced to Ching K'o through the auspices of T'ien Kuang (who then committed suicide), the prince interviewed Ching K'o:

> Prince Tan said: "At this moment the king of Ch'in is so beset by greed that his desires can never be satisfied. Unless he controls all the territory under Heaven and compels every king to become his subject, his ambitions will never be satiated. He has already taken the king of Han prisoner and integrated his territory, and has also raised and dispatched troops south to attack Ch'u in the south and encroach upon Chao in the north. General Wang Chien, in command of several hundred thousand troops, occupies Chang and Yeh, while general Li Hsin is proceeding out to T'ai-yüan and Yün-chung. Since Chao cannot withstand Ch'in, it will inevitably be annexed as a subjugated state. When it has become a subject of Ch'in, misfortune will reach Yen. Since Yen is small and weak

and has suffered several defeats in battle, I estimate that even mobilizing the entire state would prove inadequate to oppose them.
Because the other feudal lords have all submitted to Ch'in, no one
will dare join us.

I foolishly calculate that if I can find the most courageous warrior in the realm to serve as ambassador to Ch'in, we might inveigle the king with some great profit. Because the king of Ch'in is
greedy, circumstances could then be manipulated as desired and
the king coerced at knifepoint to restore all the territory of the
other feudal lords that he now occupies. It would be excellent if
the results were similar to Ts'ao Mei threatening Duke Huan of
Ch'i; however, failing that, he can still stab the king to death.[53]
With their great generals exercising independent command over
troops outside the state and chaos within it, the new ruler and his
ministers will certainly be suspicious of each other. In the interim
the feudal lords could reunite and certainly defeat Ch'in. Although this is my great desire, I do not know whom to entrust
with the responsibility. Perhaps you might ponder it a little."

After a long pause Ching K'o replied, "As this is a great affair of
state, while I have but little talent, I am afraid I would be unequal
to the task." The prince advanced, bowed his head before him,
and strongly entreated him not to refuse until Ching K'o finally
succumbed. Thereupon the prince honored him with an appointment as chief counselor and assigned him a superior mansion.
Every day the prince personally went to deferentially offer all the
delicacies of the greatest sacrificial feast, and separately sent over
unique objects, carriages, horses, and beautiful women to fulfill
his every desire and ply his intentions.

Time passed without Ching taking any action, until the prince finally pressed him and he revealed the plot's key, several objects that
would invariably draw the king of Ch'in's interest. It happened that a
disfavored Ch'in general had sought refuge with Prince Tan in Yen,
and despite Ch'in's menacing threats, the prince steadfastly refused to
be cowered into returning him to certain execution. Ching therefore
sought to have General Fan killed so that he might contritely present
his head and a map of Yen's border region as a pretext for calling upon
Ch'in. Although the prince righteously declined to have the general
killed, Ching personally went and persuaded General Fan that it provided the only way to avenge himself upon the villain who had exterminated his family. Even though the account to this point portrays the
prince as a man of great honor and courage, he not only arranged the
purchase of an extremely sharp dagger that was then quenched with

poison to ensure its effectiveness in case of a nonfatal blow, but he also "had it tried on men and found that if their clothes were stained by blood, they immediately died."

Following some additional delays, in a sorrowful scene worthy of the most tragic opera, Ching K'o and a bravado named Ch'in Wu-yang set out. Arriving in Ch'in, Ching arranged, through generous bribes, to be escorted into the court to submissively present the severed head and the map that was now wrapped around the poisoned dagger, leading to this melodramatic scene:

When the king of Ch'in heard about these developments he was greatly elated and, wearing his imperial robes, ordered the fullest ceremonies of state in granting an audience in the Hsien-yang Palace. To present the box containing General Fan's head and the map, Ching Ko and Ch'in Wu-yang respectively advanced. When they reached the dais, Ch'in Wu-yang blanched and shook with fear. As the assembled ministers thought his behavior strange, Ching K'o looked about and laughed at Wu-yang, then apologized to the king of Ch'in: "Because this uncouth fellow from the northern barbarian tribes has never before seen the Son of Heaven, he trembles with fear. I hope your august majesty will make some allowance for him so that we may fulfill our mission here."

The king of Ch'in, addressing Ching K'o, said, "Bring me the map Wu-yang is carrying." Ching K'o then took the map and formally offered it up to the king. The king opened the map and when it was fully unrolled the dagger became visible. Thereupon, seizing the king's sleeve with his left hand and grabbing the dagger with his right, Ching K'o thrust at the king. Before the blade struck his body the king had already recoiled and risen from his seat, tearing the sleeve Ching K'o had been holding.

The king tried to draw his sword, which, being long, remained stuck in the scabbard. Furthermore, because he was flustered the scabbard was hanging straight down, frustrating attempts to pull it out. Ching K'o pursued the king around a pillar on the dais. His attendants, in panic and confusion, all lost their heads. Moreover, Ch'in's regulations forbade any of those attending upon the king on the dais to wear any weapon whatsoever. Even though armed palace guards were stationed in the lower hall, unless summoned by the king they could not come forward into the upper chamber. In the urgency of the moment the king failed to summon these guards from below, so Ching K'o was free to pursue the king about. In his sudden panic, lacking anything else, the king struck him with his fists. At this moment the attending physician Hsia Wu-chü swung his medicine bag at Ching K'o, hitting him.

Meanwhile the king had been circling around a pillar, too panicked to know what to do, when his attendants shouted, "Get the sword to your back!" Doing so, he suddenly succeeded in drawing it and slashed at Ching K'o, severing his left thigh. As Ching K'o collapsed he cocked his arm and threw the dagger at the king, but missed and struck a bronze pillar instead. The king slashed Ching K'o again and again. Having suffered eight wounds and knowing he could not succeed, Ching K'o leaned back against the pillar and laughed. Sprawling out, he then cursed the king, saying: "The only reason I failed was because I wanted to extort an agreement from you to repay the heir apparent." Immediately thereafter attendants rushed forward and killed him.[54]

Naturally the attempted assassination only provoked the king of Ch'in to redouble his efforts to conquer Yen. The king of Yen, in a futile attempt to forestall the inevitable, had the heir apparent executed and his head presented to Ch'in after the latter's troops had forced them from their capital. But the gesture was of little avail as he was himself captured and his state exterminated five years later in 222 B.C.

Part Two

SPYCRAFT

用　間

4

Fundamental Thrust

*F*ROM ANTIQUITY CHINESE MILITARY THEORY emphasized rationality and control, calculation and planning. In the *Art of War*, perhaps written about the end of the Spring and Autumn period, Sun-tzu repeatedly stressed the necessity of avoiding all engagements not based upon extensive, detailed analyses of the strategic situation, tactical options, and military capabilities.[1] Detailed calculations were apparently performed in the ancestral temple in his era prior to mobilization for a campaign, with similar, more specific assessments being made by field commanders before actually engaging enemy forces.[2] Although undertaken in the ancestral temple, these calculations were not a form of divination but were based upon quantified estimates that systematically assigned numerical values to the strength of objectively examined aspects for both sides, perhaps employing a system of tally sticks.[3] In "Initial Estimations," the *Art of War*'s first chapter, Sun-tzu itemized the critical questions, thereby concretely defining the thrust of Chinese intelligence-gathering efforts thereafter: "When comparatively evaluating a situation through estimations, seeking out its true nature, ask: Which ruler has the Tao? Which general has greater ability? Who has gained the advantages of Heaven and Earth? Whose laws and orders are more thoroughly implemented? Whose forces are stronger? Whose officers and troops are better trained? Whose rewards and punishments are clearer? From these I will know victory and defeat."

Sun-tzu formulated some forty mutually defined, interrelated pairs that furnished the essential intelligence parameters grounding tactical analysis for the next twenty-five hundred years. Among them the major ones are Heaven-Earth, offense-defense, advance-retreat, and the unorthodox-orthodox. The comparative state of readiness can be deduced by reflecting upon such opposites as hunger-satiety, exhausted-rested, ordered-disordered, fearful-confident, cold-warm, wet-dry, and

lax-alert. Whenever the calculations or net assessment indicates that
the enemy holds a decided advantage, the general must either avoid
them, assume a defensive posture, or develop tactics that will convert
superiority into weakness, such as harassing the rested until they become exhausted:[4] "If it is not advantageous, do not move. If objectives
cannot be attained, do not employ the army. Unless endangered, do
not engage in warfare. The ruler cannot mobilize the army out of personal anger. The general cannot engage in battle because of personal
frustration. When it is advantageous, move; when not advantageous,
stop. Anger can revert to happiness, annoyance can revert to joy, but a
vanquished state cannot be revived, the dead cannot be brought back
to life."[5]

Therefore, only through analytic calculations based upon factual intelligence can the ruler decide whether to commit the state to military activities:

Before the engagement, one who determines in the ancestral temple that he will be victorious has found that the majority of factors are in his favor. Before the engagement one who determines
in the ancestral temple that he will not be victorious has found
few factors are in his favor.

If one who finds that the majority of factors favor him will be
victorious while one who has found few factors favor him will be
defeated, what about someone who finds no factors in his favor? If
I observe it from this perspective, victory and defeat will be apparent.[6]

Sun-tzu's thoughts, an expression of his belief that warfare is the
greatest affair of state, were echoed by virtually all the military writers thereafter, although frequently to little avail as rulers in the Warring States period and thereafter still insisted upon initiating
campaigns without careful analysis, frequently in the face of insurmountable odds. A chapter entitled "Temple Victory" in the *T'ai-pai
Yin-Ching*, the noted T'ang dynasty esoteric military text attributed to
Li Ch'uan, essentially reformulates Sun-tzu's analytic thrust with a
metaphysical vision:

Heaven esteems preserving the full and adhering to the patterns
of *yin* and *yang* and the four seasons. Earth esteems stabilizing
the precarious and observing the individuality of life and what is
appropriate to ordinary land. Men esteem constraint in affairs, the
harmonization of *yin* and *yang*, and the publication of seasonal
edicts. When affairs come they respond to them, when things

come they know them. All under Heaven fully express their loyalty and good faith and follow the government's orders. Thus it is said that "when the Tao of Heaven is free of disasters, you cannot come before them; when the Tao of Earth lacks calamities, you cannot take the lead; when human affairs have not suffered any losses, you cannot attack first."[7]

When the four seasons encroach upon each other; deluge and drought increase and recede; there is thunder in winter and frost in summer; and flying insects devour the fields, these are disasters of Heaven. When mountains collapse and rivers block up; when the fields do not produce harvests; water does not sink down to irrigate the land; the five grains remain unplanted; and the eight cereals do not mature, these are calamities of Earth. Heavy taxes and onerous government, high towers and deep pools; labor forces excessively mobilized; drunkenness, orgies, and licentiousness; loyal officials estranged and sycophants favored; soldiers exhausted and the army spent through prolonged employment, these are losses of the human realm.[8] Heavenly disasters are discerned above, calamities of Earth are observed below, and human loss witnessed all about.

Armies not modeled on Heaven should not act; those not patterned on Earth should not move; expeditions and attacks not in harmony with men should not be completed. Heaven must sanction the time, Earth make its resources available, and men define the plans. When the enemy is quiet observe their *yang* aspects [visible behavior], when they move investigate their *yin* [silent, hidden] side.[9] First observe their traces, thereafter know the enemy's mind.

What is termed a victorious army is victorious first and then seeks to engage in battle, whereas a defeated army first engages in battle and then seeks victory.[10] Thus Sun-tzu said: "Before the engagement one who determines in the ancestral temple that he will be victorious has found that the majority of factors are in his favor. Before the engagement one who determines in the ancestral temple that he will not be victorious has found few factors are in his favor. If one who finds that the majority of factors favor him will be victorious while one who has found few factors favor him will be defeated, what about someone who finds no factors in his favor? Observing it from this perspective, victory and defeat will be apparent."[11]

The idea of calculation, of accurately determining the possibilities of victory through thorough planning, naturally found expression in numerous writings apart from the military tradition. For example, the *Shuo Yüan* (a first-century B.C. syncretic text) states: "In undertaking an affair, the sage king invariably plans it carefully, scrutinizes it cautiously within the scope of his plans, and then confirms it through divination by the turtle and milfoil. The ordinary people dwelling in thatched huts are all concerned with his plans, those engaged in menial labors all exhaust their minds in the task. Thus the king may undertake ten thousand affairs, yet no factor will be left out or any plans fail."[12] The method of course requires balancing the tendencies of the moment with cognizance of their opposite: "Now whenever the wise undertake affairs, if they are full, they ponder excess; if peaceful, they contemplate danger; and if contorted, they consider the straight. For this reason in a hundred affairs they never sink into difficulty."[13] Another section reiterates: "Plans that precede affairs flourish, affairs that precede plans perish."[14]

Necessity for Intelligence and Agents

Because of the analytical nature of their approach to warfighting, virtually all the Chinese military writers addressed the need for an intelligence service to ferret out vital information unavailable from open sources and simple observation. For example, the *Ssu-ma Fa*, parts of which may predate Sun-tzu's *Art of War*, states: "In general, to wage war: employ spies against the distant; observe the near; act in accord with the seasons; take advantage of the enemy's resources; esteem good faith; abhor the doubtful."[15] The great general Wu Ch'i subsequently identified four vital points of warfare—*ch'i* (spirit), terrain, affairs, and strength—defining "affairs" in terms of successfully employing agents: "Being good at controlling clandestine operatives; with a few light troops harassing the enemy, causing them to scatter; and forcing rulers and ministers to feel mutual annoyance, higher and lower ranks to reproach each other, this is termed the vital point of affairs."[16] Clearly such agents did not just passively gather information, but also actively engaged in sowing dissension and undermining administrations.

Sun-tzu, widely known even in the West as the progenitor of spy-craft,[17] advanced a strong economic argument for deploying agents in the first paragraphs of his famous chapter "Employing Spies":

> When you send forth an army of a hundred thousand on a campaign, marching them out a thousand kilometers, the expenditures of the common people and the contributions of the feudal

house will be one thousand pieces of gold per day. Those inconvenienced and troubled both within and without the border, who are exhausted on the road or unable to pursue their agricultural work, will be seven hundred thousand families.

Armies remain locked in a standoff for years to fight for victory on a single day, yet generals begrudge bestowing ranks and emoluments of one hundred pieces of gold and therefore do not know the enemy's situation. This is the ultimate inhumanity. Such a person is not a general for the people, an assistant for a ruler, or the arbiter of victory.

Enlightened rulers and sagacious generals who are able to get intelligent spies will invariably attain great achievements. This is the essence of the military, what the Three Armies rely on to move.

Sun-tzu firmly believed that the successful management of warfare depended upon acquiring full knowledge of the enemy, for only upon such a basis can plans be formulated:

The prosecution of military affairs lies in according with and learning in detail the enemy's intentions. If one then focuses his strength toward the enemy, strikes a thousand kilometers away, and kills their general, it is termed "being skillful and capable in completing military affairs."

For this reason one who does not know the plans of the feudal lords cannot forge preparatory alliances. One who does not know the topography of mountains and forests, ravines and defiles, wetlands and marshes cannot maneuver the army. One who does not employ local guides will not secure advantages of terrain. One who does not know one of these four or five cannot command the army of a hegemon or a true king.[18]

Within the context of the vast commitments and expenditures required by warfare, Sun-tzu believed that wasting material and lives would be both stupid and inhumane because the ultimate intent of warfare should be to preserve one's own people while rapidly vanquishing the enemy. Thus, failing to gather any information that might facilitate victory could only be considered inhumane. However, for the past thousand years moral purists in China have condemned the book for its breaches of sincerity, righteousness, and trust, just as the first Westerners who eventually translated the text into French and later into English. (Remarkably, these early nonmilitary Western readers, being particularly appalled by the boldness of Sun-tzu's assertions, condemned the *Art of War* from a doctrinaire Christian perspective as a heathen work somehow typical of an inferior race, irrespective of their own covert traditions and practices.)

Details, such as the identity of key personnel and the assignment of responsibilities that might be exploited through contacts, hostages, and extortion, should not be neglected: "In general, as for the armies you want to strike, the cities you want to attack, and the men you want to assassinate, you must first know the names of the defensive commander, his assistants, staff, door guards, and attendants. You must have our spies search out and learn them all."[19]

When fully assembled, this information would furnish the means to "know the enemy," one-half of Sun-tzu's famous equation for victory:

If I know our troops can attack, but do not know the enemy cannot be attacked, it is only halfway to victory. If I know the enemy can be attacked, but do not realize our troops cannot attack, it is only halfway to victory.

Knowing that the enemy can be attacked, and knowing that our army can effect the attack, but not knowing the terrain is not suitable for combat, is only halfway to victory. Thus one who truly knows the army will never be deluded when he moves, never be impoverished when initiating an action.

Thus it is said if you know them and know yourself, your victory will not be imperiled. If you know Heaven and know Earth, your victory can be complete.[20]

Throughout the *Kuan-tzu,* an eclectic work traditionally attributed to the great Spring and Autumn governmental adviser Kuan Chung but largely composed during the middle to late Warring States period, "foreknowledge" is constantly emphasized:

Being ignorant about estimations and calculations but yet wanting to undertake military affairs is like wanting to cross over a dangerous river without a boat or oars.[21] . . .

When plans are not determined within the state but troops are dispatched across the borders, this is warfare that will prove self-defeating, attacks that will be self-destructive. Therefore, if one deploys the army but is unable to engage in combat, surrounds enemies but is unable to assault them, gains territory but is unable incorporate it—any one of these three can produce defeat. Therefore one who is not knowledgeable about the enemy's government cannot make plans against them. One who is not knowledgeable about the enemy's true situation cannot constrain them with agreements. One who is not knowledgeable about the enemy's generals cannot mobilize the army first; one who is not knowledgeable about the enemy's officers cannot deploy the army against them.[22]

Sun Pin, a brilliant descendant of Sun-tzu whose *Military Methods* was recently rediscovered after being lost for two thousand years, similarly emphasized the importance of knowledge gained through spy activities:

There are five aspects to constantly being victorious. One who obtains the ruler's sole authority will be victorious. One who knows the Tao will be victorious. One who gains the masses will be victorious. One whose left and right are in harmony will be victorious. One who analyzes the enemy and estimates the terrain will be victorious.
There are five aspects to constantly not being victorious. A general who is hampered by the ruler will not be victorious. One who does not know the Tao will not be victorious. A perverse general will not be victorious. One who does not use spies will not be victorious. One who does not gain the masses will not be victorious.[23]

The *Huai-nan Tzu*'s military discussion defined "tactical wisdom" in terms of clandestine intelligence gathering coupled with tactical command skills: "One who excels in employing secret agents [*chien tie*], investigating actions, and fathoming thought, establishing the obscure and setting ambushes, hiding and concealing his shape, and going forth where unexpected so that the enemy's troops never can succeed in defensive preparations is said to know the tactical balance of power."
The most successful military commander and thinker in the T'ang dynasty, which saw a sudden proliferation of military writings, was undoubtedly the great general Li Ching. Apart from the *Questions and Replies*, his views are preserved in a synthetic work reconstructed from scattered fragments entitled *Li Wei-kung Ping-fa*. Several lengthy passages are directed to the nature and importance of spy work, and the entire book stresses the importance of acquiring knowledge:

Now there are affairs which appear similar but whose strategic power differs, and those whose strategic power is identical but appearances differ. By according with the situation you can be completely successful with one movement, but if you strike when the situation is not conducive, your movements will certainly be defeated.

The measures for achieving decisive victory lie in investigating the opposing general's talent and abilities; analyzing the enemy's strengths and weaknesses; determining the configuration and strategic advantages of terrain; observing the advantages of the appropriate moment; and first being victorious, only thereafter engaging in combat and defending positions without losing them. This is termed the Tao for certain victory.[24]

The Sung dynasty *Unorthodox Strategies* summarized the thirteenth-century view in similar terms: "Whenever planning to conduct a major military expedition, you should first employ spies to determine the enemy's troop strength, emptiness or fullness, and movement and rest, and only thereafter mobilize the army. Great achievements can then be attained and you will always be victorious in combat. The *Art of War* states, 'There are no areas in which one does not employ spies.'"[25]

In the Ming, about the mid-sixteenth century, an unknown author strongly asserted:

Now any general who, assuming the mantle of authority over the Three Armies and controlling the fate of ten thousand men, confronts fierce enemies or pursues them into the wilds to engage in a standoff but does not know the enemy's situation is a blockhead. When two forces struggle to control each other, anyone who does not undertake spycraft techniques is a wild animal.

For this reason attacking other states through their ruler is more intelligent than attacking them yourself. Plotting against people through their ministers is more intelligent than plotting against them yourselves. Dispersing alliances and bringing allies together in conflict are more intelligent than engaging them in combat yourself.

It may be compared with the case of a tiger who eats men. Anyone who goes to pull its teeth ends up being eaten. Anyone who trusts it by feeding it meat also ends up being eaten. Whoever pursues it wielding halberds also ends up being eaten. Whoever attacks the tiger with stones are also all eaten. Therefore, you should have other people pull its teeth, not pull its teeth yourself; entrust other men to feed it with meat, not rely upon doing it yourself; have other men pursue the tiger with a halberd, not pursue it yourself. Conceal yourself when attacking a tiger with stones, and have other men confront its anger. In this fashion you attack others through their ruler, plot against men through their ministers, disperse their alliances, and instigate conflict among them. But without agents, how can you investigate their true nature, without spies how can you employ these techniques?[26]

Moreover, since the enemy also seeks information, he concluded that any failure to undertake similar actions is senseless at best:

Whenever two armies stand off against each other, it is not just we who plot against the enemy, but also the enemy who plots against us. To fail to gain accurate information about the enemy's situation but recklessly engage in battle is senseless. How can you then employ subtle changes to wrest victory? Now as for the enemy's situation, there are those aspects that can be learned through observation, and those that cannot be learned through observation. There are many methods, inexhaustible changes in such matters![27]

Stress on Human Agency

Sun-tzu, among the first to decry the widespread, traditional reliance upon spirits and prognostication, insisted upon confining intelligence efforts to the human realm: "The means by which enlightened rulers and sagacious generals moved and conquered others, that their achievements surpassed the masses, was advance knowledge. Advance knowledge cannot be gained from ghosts and spirits, inferred from phenomena, or projected from the measures of Heaven, but must be gained from men, for it is the knowledge of the enemy's true situation."[28]

This well-known passage has frequently been cited by Western historians unfamiliar with the vast corpus of Chinese military writings to conclude that Chinese intelligence theory was not only founded upon, but also strictly limited to human effort, in contradistinction to other lands and superstitious practices.[29] However, even though virtually all the tactical works stress human effort and deny the value of divination in fathoming the outcome of campaigns and battles, the prognosticatory tradition that originated in the Shang dynasty not only continued to flourish, but also vigorously evolved to encompass the interpretation of such diverse phenomena as sounds, clouds, weather, phases of the moon, natural omens, and the numerology of dates, producing numerous volumes devoted to arcane practices.

Commanders exhorted their men to ignore meteors, birds flying backward, and the sudden appearance of dense black clouds, but rulers and generals might still resort to nonhuman agencies in an attempt to predict favorable courses of action amid the confusion of military confrontations, as will be discussed in the final section on divination, prognostication, and countertrends.

5

Nature and Theory of Agents

*S*UN-TZU'S BRIEF CHAPTER "Employing Spies," being fundamental to all subsequent military thought about covert agents and their activities, merits presentation in itself before we dissect it and note a few historical commentaries and explications. The initial paragraphs presenting his justification for employing spies having just been cited, only the remaining two-thirds, which immediately analyze the types of agents, need be arrayed:

> There are five types of spies to be employed: local spies, internal spies, turned spies [double agents], dead [expendable] spies, and living spies. When all five are employed together and no one knows their Tao, this is termed "spiritual methodology." They are a ruler's treasures.
>
> Local spies—employ people from the local district.
>
> Internal spies—employ their people who hold government positions.
>
> Double agents—employ the enemy's spies.
>
> Expendable spies—are employed to spread disinformation outside the state. Provide our [expendable] spies [with false information] and have them leak it to enemy agents.
>
> Living spies—return with their reports.
>
> Thus of all the Three Armies' affairs no relationship is closer than with spies; no rewards are more generous than those given to spies; no affairs are more secret than those pertaining to spies.
>
> Unless someone has the wisdom of a Sage, he cannot use spies; unless he is benevolent and righteous, he cannot employ spies; unless he is subtle and perspicacious, he cannot perceive the sub-

stance in intelligence reports. It is subtle, subtle! There are no areas in which one does not employ spies.

If before the mission has begun it has already been exposed, the spy and those he informed should all be put to death.

In general, as for the armies you want to strike, the cities you want to attack, and the men you want to assassinate, you must first know the names of the defensive commander, his assistants, staff, door guards, and attendants. You must have our spies search out and learn them all.

You must search for enemy agents who have come to spy on us. Tempt them with profits, instruct and retain them. Thus double agents can be obtained and employed. Through knowledge gained from them you can recruit both local and internal spies. Through knowledge gained from them the expendable spy can spread his falsehoods, can be used to misinform the enemy. Through knowledge gained from them our living spies can be employed as times require.

The ruler must know these five aspects of espionage work. This knowledge inevitably depends on turned spies; therefore, you must be generous to double agents.

In antiquity, when the Yin [Shang] arose, they had Yi Chih [Yi Yin] in the Hsia. When the Chou arose, they had Lü Ya [the T'ai Kung] in the Yin. Thus enlightened rulers and sagacious generals who are able to get intelligent spies will invariably attain great achievements. This is the essence of the military, what the Three Armies rely on to move.

In his penultimate chapter Sun-tzu thus delineated the characteristics and functions of five categories of spies that founded all future theorizing. Even though the categories were gradually expanded over the years, essentially being subdivided, refined, and redefined until numbering some thirty-two in the Ming dynasty, the basic types remained unchanged. Even though Sun-tzu's definitions are generally clear, it should be noted that "local spies" refers not just to agents recruited in specific areas, but may also include anyone who temporarily resides outside their native habitant, such as emigrants, experienced travelers, and peripatetic "persuaders" who readily provide information about other states as an integral part of their persuasive efforts. Thus, as discussed in the section on early history, China's first spies—Yi Yin and the T'ai Kung—did not actually engage in clandestine spy work within a foreign state (a function performed by internal spies or living spies), but were essentially defectors. In this role, essentially in exile, they provided valuable general information about government officials and local configurations of terrain, thereby meriting the designation of "local spies" or "local guides."

Living spies were often talented individuals of exceptional perspicacity who could be dispatched to foreign states, sometimes in diplomatic guise, to observe and then report back. They normally comprised the greatest number of agents so as to provide the state with multiple means for acquiring data.

Double agents were spies dispatched by the enemy who had been detected and subsequently either converted to the state's cause or bribed. (Sun-tzu's definition eventually evolved to include enemy agents who were being unconsciously manipulated. Although such manipulation certainly was not unique to China, most traditions would not term such individuals "double agents" or "turned agents" given the absence of any volitional component. However, throughout Chinese history the process of converting or turning them to one's own use was the defining factor, not whether they were knowledgeable or participants.) Sun-tzu highly esteemed true double agents because they might provide extensive, detailed information about the enemy's internal situation:

You must search for enemy agents who have come to spy on us. Tempt them with profits, instruct and retain them. Thus double agents can be obtained and employed. Through knowledge gained from them you can recruit both local and internal spies. Through knowledge gained from them the expendable spy can spread his falsehoods, can be used to misinform the enemy. Through knowledge gained from them our living spies can be employed as times require.

The ruler must know these five aspects of espionage work. This knowledge inevitably depends on turned spies; therefore, you must be generous to double agents.

The prolific Li Ching also pondered the nature of spycraft at the start of the T'ang dynasty, concluding:

Can victory in warfare be sought in Heaven or Earth, or must it be accomplished through men? When we examine the ways the ancients historically employed spies, we find that their subtle techniques were not singular. Some spied on rulers, the ruler's close associates, capable officials, assistants, close neighbors, associates, and allies. Tzu Kung, Shih Liao, Ch'en Chen, Su Ch'in, Chang Yi, Fan Sui, and others all relied upon these techniques to achieve results.

There are five categories in the Tao of spycraft: Those who rely
on local connections to submerge themselves, observe and investigate, and then report on everything they have learned. Those
who take advantage of the enemy's closely trusted people to deliberately leak false information for transmission to them. Those
who rely upon their emissaries to twist affairs about and then return. Those worthy and talented individuals who are dispatched
to discover the enemy's inclinations and vacuities and return to
discuss them. And those who are accused of fabricated offenses so
that they might subtly leak out false reports and specious plans,
who then perish because of their reports to the enemy. Now these
five categories of spies all must be kept hidden and secret. Treat
them generously with rewards and keep them more than secret,
for then they can be employed.[1]

Obviously Li Ching's categories are closely based upon Sun-tzu, although with slight twists, such as the nature of so-called local spies or
connections—Sun-tzu's local guides; trusted personnel—internal
spies; emissaries—turned or double agents; selected worthies and talents—living spies; and entangled in offenses—dead agents.
    The *Ch'ang-tuan Ching*'s military section, dating from roughly the
first quarter of the eighth century, also discusses Sun-tzu's five agents
in a chapter that heavily quotes "Employing Spies" but illustrates the
categories with interesting historical examples:

The *Chou Li* states, "The one who circulates among the feudal
states and reports back on their spies is a 'turned agent.'"[2] The
T'ai Kung said, "When an agent snares words flying about, they
can be accumulated to compose a company of troops." From this
we know that the Tao for employing agents is not a momentary
affair. Thus there are five types of agents: local spies, internal
spies, double agents, living spies, and expendable spies. These five
types of agents all originated together, no one knows their Tao.
    Local spies—employ people from the local district.
    Internal spies—employ their people who hold government posi-
tions.
    Double agents—employ the enemy's agents.
    Living spies—return with their reports.
    Expendable spies—reemployed to spread disinformation outside
the state. Provide our [expendable] spies [with false information]
and have them leak to enemy agents.
    In the Han dynasty when Pan Chao, Protector for the Western
regions, was first appointed as chief of the regional generals, he

mobilized all the infantry and cavalry from the areas under his control—some twenty-five thousand—to attack the minor border state of Sha-ch'e. Sha-ch'e sought aid from the state of Kuei-tzu. The king of Kuei-tzu dispatched his General of the Left to mobilize troops from the states of Wen-su, Ku-mo, and Wei-t'ou, assembling some fifty thousand men to assist him. Pan Chao then summoned his subordinate commanders and the kings of Yü-t'ien and Su-leh and informed them: "Our troops are too few to be a match for the enemy, so it would be best to separate and disperse. The troops from Yü-t'ien should go east from here, I will return west. When you hear the sound of the drums in the middle of the night, have your troops set out." They all concurred. Thereafter he secretly arranged to have some captured prisoners escape and report his words to the king of Kuei-tzu. Overjoyed, the king had his General of the Left, in command of ten thousand cavalry, set off to intercept Pan Chao at the western border and the king of Wen-su, in command of eight thousand cavalry, intercept Yü-t'ien's forces at the eastern border. However, after conspicuously assigning their missions, Pan Chao secretly ordered his colonels, in command of picked troops and elite warriors, to race to Sha-ch'e encampment at the first cock's crow, whereupon they assaulted and overcame them. Although the defenders were terrified into running off, Chao's troops still killed some five thousand Hu tribesmen and eventually forced Sha-ch'e to surrender.

Furthermore, there is the case of Keng Yen conducting a punitive expedition against Chang Pu.[3] When Chang Pu, who had rebelled against the Han, heard about their approach, he had general Fei Yi deploy at Li-hsia and separately ordered troops to encamp at Chu-a. In addition, he established a line of several dozen fortified camps between T'ai-shan and Chung-ch'eng in preparation for Keng Yen.

Keng Yen crossed the Yellow River and advanced to attack Chu-a first. When seizing it, he deliberately left one corner of the encirclement open in order to allow some of their troops to flee back to their base at Chung-ch'eng. When the men there heard that Chu-a had already collapsed, they were terrified and fled, leaving behind a deserted shell. General Fei Yi split up his forces and dispatched his younger brother Fei Kan to defend Chü-li. When Keng Yen advanced, he first threatened Chü-li, loudly ordering the troops to cut down numerous trees to fill in the moat and build hillocks and thereby force its surrender within days. When Fe Yi learned that Keng Yen was about to assault Chü-li, he laid plans to go and rescue the city. Keng Yen then ordered everyone to repair their assault equipment, visibly planning to employ all their strength to assault Chü-li's fortifications in three days. However, he secretly left an opening in the siege so that a few soldiers from the city might escape, race back to Fei Yi, and report the time of Keng Yen's attack.

On the appointed day Fei Yi himself came forth to rescue Chü-li. Keng Yen happily addressed his staff generals: "The reason I had our assault equipment repaired was to entice Fei Yi to come here. His arrival is exactly what I wanted." Then, after splitting off three thousand men to maintain the effort at Chü-li, he personally led his elite units in ascending the surrounding hills and ridges. Thus, they were able to exploit the heights when engaging Fei Yi in battle and managed to severely defeat his army, killing Fei Yi himself. These are examples of employing local spies.

During the Chin dynasty Luo Shang, regional governor for Yi-chou, dispatched Wei Po to assault Li Hsiung, who held the city of P'i. After several pitched battles Li Hsiung summoned P'u T'ai, a native of Wu-tu; whipped him until he bled; and then had him falsely report to Luo Shang that he wanted to mount a treacherous response within the city, and would mark its initiation by setting a fire. Trusting him, Luo Shang sent forth all his elite soldiers and also dispatched Wei Po and other officers to follow to Pu T'ai's directions. Meanwhile, Li Hsiung had already dispatched Li Huan to establish an ambush along Luo Shang's route of approach. Pu T'ai then set some long ladders out against the walls and started a fire. When Wei Po saw the fire arise, his troops all competed with each other to climb their rungs. Pu T'ai also hauled up several hundred soldiers with ropes and killed them all. Li Hsiung then released the troops both from within the city and held in ambush outside to suddenly mount a two-pronged attack on the enemy. Striking from within and without, they extensively destroyed Luo Shang's army. Such is the power of employing internal agents.

Duke Wu of the state of Cheng wanted to attack the nomadic Hu peoples, so he first had his son take a Hu woman as his wife and then queried his ministers, saying: "I want to employ our army, whom might we attack?" Kuan Ch'i-ssu, a high official, replied, "The Hu can be attacked." Duke Wu angrily slew him, exclaiming: "The Hu are a brother state. How can you say we should attack them?" When the Hu heard about it, their ruler assumed Cheng regarded them as relatives and thus made no preparations against them. Cheng then launched a sudden attack that seized them all. This is the power of employing a dead agent.

Through bribery Ch'en P'ing released double agents amid Ch'u's army and caused Fan Tseng's estrangement when Hsiang Yü, the king of Ch'u, doubted his loyalty. This is the power of employing double agents.

Thus we know that among the intimates of the Three Armies, none are closer than spies; no rewards are more generous than given to spies; no affairs more secret than those pertaining to spies. Unless someone has the wisdom of a Sage, he cannot use spies. Unless he is secret and subtle, he cannot perceive the substance in intelligence reports.[4] This is the essence of the Three Armies, emphasized only by the wise and perspicacious.[5]

Although the chapter is organized around what might be termed "orthodox" definitions of agent categories, the actual terminology and examples are hardly what one would expect from Sun-tzu's definitions or the commentaries that coalesced around the *Art of War*. Perhaps this reflects the ignorance of an amateur writing on military matters; perhaps he had simply developed different conceptions of covert intelligence gathering. For example, the "local spies" found in his example are simply besieged soldiers who were tricked into becoming false prophets, disseminating pre-scripted information that would prompt desired enemy action. Some theorists would in fact term them "double" or "turned" agents because they were enemy personnel converted to one's own use, even though not originally spies. (In fact, the term "turned" agent in most of the historical works simply refers to such "others" being consciously employed to further covert causes, whether subversive or mere intelligence gathering.) Similarly, identifying P'u T'ai as an "internal agent" is rather skewed because he was clearly a counterfeit traitor or double agent who only appeared to be an internal agent from Luo Shang's perspective in the sense of already being present in Li Hsiung's camp and capable of undertaking a subversive, internal response coordinated with an external assault. (P'u T'ai's feigned betrayal of course also excludes him from the traditional definition of a turned or double agent—even though he would be so described today—not having been tempted from his original loyalties and assignment.) Kuan Ch'i-ssu in no way merits the designation of "expendable agent" because he was simply a sacrificial lamb, an essential part of a disinformation ploy to allay Hu suspicions. A foil for the duke's stratagem, he was never employed to spread disinformation or act in any covert capacity beyond the state's borders. However, the reference to Ch'en P'ing's double agents follows the more colloquial approach of the historical writings, for they may have actually been

double agents, but more likely were just agents sent in to spread disinformation, or perhaps local officials or staff members bribed to create
suspicion, and thus merely internal agents. Of all the theoretical writings based upon Sun-tzu's "Employing Spies," this chapter diverges
the most radically.

Li Ch'uan, writing in his *T'ai-pai Yin-ching* perhaps a half century
later, however, reverted to the old term of *hsing-jen*, which by this
time had evolved with the language and lost the early connotations associated with the Chou dynasty official previously examined, coming
to mean simply "traveler." He commences his chapter entitled
"*Hsing-jen*," which might be translated "Roving Agents," in Sun-tzu's
mode, condemning ignorance and any appeal to otherworldly sources,
then proceeds to examine what he considers the two fundamental
types of agents:

If the ruler selects a day to ascend the altar and appoint a commanding general; has the weapons and armor put into good order;
the troops venture forth to destroy the enemy's state, defeat the
enemy's army, kill the enemy's general, and take their people prisoner; transports provisions out ten thousand kilometers; and penetrates the enemy's borders, yet does not know the enemy's true
situation, this is the commanding general's error.

The enemy's true situation cannot be discerned among the stars
and constellations, or sought from ghosts and spirits, or acquired
through divination or prognostication, but can be sought among
men.[6] In antiquity when the Shang arose Yi Yin was a cook in the
Hsia; when the Chou arose, the T'ai Kung was a fisherman in the
Shang; when the Ch'in established imperial rule, Li Ssu was a
hunter in Shantung; when Han Kao-tsu ventured forth Han Hsin
was an exiled soldier from Ch'u; and Ts'ao Ts'ao found Hsün Huo,
Yüan Shao's cast-off minister. Ssu-ma T'an became emperor of
Chin because Chia Ch'ung had been entrusted with government
in Wei, while Wei itself arose because Ts'ui Hao had made Chin
his home. Thus through employing such men these seven rulers
became emperor over All under Heaven.

Now whenever worthy men flee a state, it must be because
sycophantic ministers control the ruler's authority. The true measure of things is then lost, the ruler's assistants form cliques, men
of little merit monopolize power, and scoundrels usurp the authority of state. For example, Ya Yi promiscuously served King
Chieh of the Hsia, Chung Hou immersed Chou of the Shang in licentiousness, and Yu Chan befuddled the second emperor of

Ch'in with his music. When its three benevolent advisers departed, the Shang became a wasteland; when the two elders gave their allegiance to Chou it became glorious. When Wu Tzu-hsü died, the state of Wu was lost. Fan Li lived and Yüeh became hegemon. Wu Yang entered the border and Ch'in was delighted; general Yüeh Yi departed and Yen was terrified.

When a general succeeds in securing the enemy's people, entrusts them with responsibility, and ferrets out the enemy's true situation, what worry will remain that he might not be victorious? Thus it is said that if you gather in their stalwarts the enemy's state will be overturned; if you snare their valiants the enemy's state will be empty. Truly, through stones from other mountains you can polish your own jade.

Now there are two employments for roving agents *[hsing-jen]*. First, we can capitalize upon the men dispatched by the enemy to observe our defects by offering them higher ranks and making their salaries more generous. Thereafter, investigate their words and compare them with actuality. If they prove accurate, you can then employ them; if specious, you can execute them. Employ them as "local guides."

Second, have our roving agents observe the enemy's ruler and ministers, attendants, and officials, noting who is worthy, who stupid. Among the ruler's intimates, those both inside and outside the palace, who is covetous, who incorruptible. Among his attendants and diplomatic personnel, who are perfected men, who menial men. Once we have acquired this knowledge, we can proceed to achieve our purpose.

Among those serving in the Three Armies, none are more important than spies. Among secrets within the Three Armies, none more secret than spies. When plots involving such spies have not yet been set into motion, anyone who leaks them, as well as those they inform, should all be executed. On the day when a plot is initiated, destroy the drafts, burn the copies, silence their mouths, and do not allow internal plans to leak out. Be just like a blackbird invisibly entering the heavy forest or a fish diving into the deepest pool without any trace. Remember that, despite his surpassing visual acuity, when Li Lou bent his head he couldn't discern the shape of things, and despite his acute hearing, when Shih Kuang tilted his ear downward he couldn't hear a sound. Subtle! Subtle, just like a swirl of fine dust arising. How can a drunken and sated general who must contend with force, yet lightly engages in battle, manage to discern the affairs of spies?

Li Ch'uan's "roving agents" would thus perform most of the functions of Sun-tzu's five categories, with an emphasis upon converting enemy spies into turned agents and using one's agents to gain a detailed knowledge of the enemy's staff and personalities preliminary to unspecified, but no doubt dramatic, actions.

By the late Ming the list of *chien*, normally understood as human agents, was expanded by an innovative military thinker, Chieh Hsüan, who regarded the employment of various techniques and the utilization of inanimate objects equally as "agents." Although this poses some problems for facile translation—requiring something like "agency through" or "clandestine action through"—his concept is clear and the range of activities comprehensive, amounting to some sixteen categories, prefaced and concluded with incisive remarks about employing covert agents under the definition for agent (*chien*) in the *Ping-fa Pai-yen:*

Definition: Those who enter among the enemy and implement unorthodox measures are termed "agents."

Original Text: Agents strike fear in the enemy's general staff, slay the enemy's beloved generals, and cause chaos in the enemy's estimates and strategies. The methods for employing agents include living, dead [expendable], written, civil, rumors, prophecy, songs, bribes, things, rank, the enemy, villagers [local guides], friends, women, goodwill, and awe.

Explanation: Spies *[tie]* who are dispatched and then return are living agents.

Those who enter enemy territory but do not return are dead [expendable] agents.[7]

Creating forged letters is clandestine written action.

Holding discussions that stupefy the enemy is clandestine civil action.

Sullying and contaminating the enemy's generals are clandestine action by rumor.

Creating prophetic verses that circulate among the people is clandestine action by prophecy.

Songs, such as used against Ch'u, to disperse the troops are clandestine action through song.

Using ten thousand ounces of gold to make bribes is clandestine action through bribery.

Sometimes seizing things, sometimes granting gifts, are clandestine action through things.

To promise rank and position is clandestine bribery through rank.

Allowing the enemy's agents to return and report is clandestine action though enemy agents.

To form connections with subordinates and partisan cliques with hamlets is clandestine action through local agents.

To influence people through their friends is clandestine action through friends.

Bribes that penetrate the women's quarters constitute clandestine action through women.

Exploiting personal friendship is clandestine action through goodwill.

Inflicting bodily harm to implement plans is clandestine action through awesomeness.

It is not that implementing clandestine activities is difficult, but employing men that is difficult. Therefore employing agents is more difficult than employing the army.

The author concludes with twelve examples and then notes: "Living and dead are the general names for agents. Employing them through benevolence or fear is subtle. Now enumerating the above twelve types of agents, distinguishing them as living or dead, and then completing the categorization by indicating whether they were employed through benevolence or fear are too complex to harmonize. Thus Sun-tzu's *Art of War* established a single chapter to distinguish the five types of agents." Although somewhat cryptic, his categories may easily be subsumed under Sun-tzu's five rubrics, many of them being local guides simply coupled with a more explicit listing of the means employed to entice or coerce cooperation among the enemy's people and thereby secure useful agents.

Shih Tzu-mei's Lectures on "Employing Spies"

In the middle of the Southern Sung dynasty Shih Tzu-mei penned a series of commentaries to the *Seven Military Classics* so extensive as to merit the title of lectures. Much studied and reprinted in both Japan and China over the centuries, they were the first work to treat the *Seven Military Classics* as canonical, remaining especially significant today because they show the continuity of military thought from Sun-tzu's *Art of War* through Li Ch'uan's T'ang dynasty *T'ai-pai Yin-Ching* and into his own work in the early thirteenth century. Moreover, several passages commenting on Sun-tzu's "Employing Spies" incorporate extensive, though unacknowledged, material from Li Ch'uan's chapter on roving agents. His views also embrace differing opinions from the Ten Commentaries edition of Sun-tzu's *Art of War,* as well as Li Ching's thoughts from *Questions and Replies,* sometimes citing the speakers, at other times merely co-opting their phrases and sentences. (The more important ones will be indicated with attributions in parentheses.) Although lengthy, because the interpretations and details are significant, the entire lecture on "Employing Spies" from his *Sun-tzu Chiang-yi* merits translating. Fortunately the lectures are mostly self-explanatory, so little additional commentary is required. Of particular interest are the examples interwoven among the explications, almost invariably from the ancient period. (Sun-tzu's original text, upon which he comments, appears in italic type.)

Employing Spies

T'ien Tan unleashed turned agents in Yen and Yen was indeed defeated. Ch'in had spies speak in Chao and Chao indeed surrendered. Spies being of such great use, Sun-tzu has a chapter called "Employing Spies."

Sun-tzu: *"When you send forth an army of a hundred thousand on a campaign, marching them out a thousand kilometers, the expenditures of the common people and the contributions of the feudal house will be one thousand catties of gold per day. Those inconvenienced and troubled both within and without the border, who are exhausted on the road or unable to pursue their agricultural work, will be seven hundred thousand families.*

Armies remain locked in a standoff for years to fight for victory on a single day, yet generals begrudge bestowing ranks and emoluments of one hundred pieces of gold and therefore do not know the enemy's situation. This is the ultimate inhumanity. Such a person is not a general for the people, an assistant for a ruler, or the arbiter of victory."

Mobilizing an army of a hundred thousand means the ultimate mass. Going forth a thousand kilometers means the farthest distance. When the ultimate mass was employed in a military campaign that took them the farthest distance possible and they calculated the transfer of supplies, what was expended and not recovered, what the royal family contributed above and the expenses of the common people below, each day they used a thousand catties of gold. Thus those bearing weapons were troublesomely employed in military service outside the state's borders, while grasses and grains were also onerously moved about within it. Along the roads delays could not be avoided.

The number of farmers who could not pursue their occupations amounted to seven hundred thousand families because in the ancient well-field system nine families farmed an equal number of plots, with the middle plot being the duke's share. If someone among the eight families personally farming these plots was impressed into the army, the remaining seven had to supply his clothes and food. Therefore, when a hundred thousand troops were mobilized, seven hundred thousand families were unable to concentrate upon their own affairs.[8] How can the immensely disruptive effect be fully described?

With the daily expenses of the army being so great, if the commanding general wanted to find a way to certain victory but begrudged expenditures for rank and salary or a hundred catties of gold to seek out the enemy's true situation, how could he achieve victory? Moreover, the ruler easily acquires things, but the enemy's true situation is especially difficult to know. If easily acquired things such as money and gold can be employed to gain elusive information, how can anyone be parsimonious and not give them in exchange?

Furthermore, maintaining a defensive posture for several years is extremely long, while victory or defeat may be decided on a single momentous day, so being incapable of employing agents to spy upon the enemy's situation would be the greatest inhumanity! Someone like this cannot be a general for men, an assistant for the ruler, or the master of victory. Accordingly, the *T'ai-pai Yin-ching* states: "The ruler selects a day to mount the dais and appoint the commanding general, they put the armor and weapons in order, and when all the troops are mounted they go forth to destroy other people's states and defeat their armies. They kill the enemy's generals and take their men prisoner. They transport provisions out ten thousand kilometers and traverse the enemy's terrain, but if they do not know the enemy's situation, it is not the ruler's error but the general's offense." If this is true, how can spies not be used!

Ch'en P'ing advised Han Kao-tsu that if he was willing to sacrifice several tens of thousands of catties of gold, he could send forth turned agents *[fan chien]* to estrange Ch'u's ruler from his ministers and cause doubts in his mind. Without any further questions Han Kao-tsu therefore gave forty thousand catties to Ch'en P'ing to freely employ as he might, and in the end he destroyed Ch'u through this method. Mencius said, "Those who work for wealth will not be benevolent."[9] The *Rescripts* state,

"When the general is not benevolent, the Three Armies will not be attached to him."[10]

Sun-tzu: "The means by which enlightened rulers and sagacious generals moved and conquered others, that their achievements surpassed the masses, was advance knowledge. Advance knowledge cannot be gained from ghosts and spirits, inferred from phenomena, or projected from the measures of Heaven, but must be gained from men, for it is the knowledge of the enemy's true situation."

The *T'ai-pai Yin-ching* states, "The enemy's situation cannot be sought for among the stars and constellations, or among ghosts and spirits, not through divination by turtle shell or milfoil stalks, but should be sought through men." Someone who knows this understands how the enlightened rulers and sagacious generals of old controlled their victories. Not one of them failed to base their efforts upon gaining knowledge of the enemy through human agents. Assuredly, if you do not know the enemy's situation, you will lack the means to realize great achievements. Similarly, if you are unable to use men, you will have no way to know the enemy's situation. If vital information about the enemy cannot be obtained, it will be difficult to determine the path to victory. Through relying upon men we can know the enemy's situation, so by employing spies we can fully know the enemy's advantageous and disadvantageous procedures and the appropriateness of their coming and going. This is why enlightened rulers and wise generals esteemed advance knowledge.

Now foreknowledge can be sought from ghosts and spirits, but the way of ghosts and spirits lacks form and shadow. Relying on men whose actions are submerged in the vacuous and nonexistent is hardly trustworthy. If we seek it in linked phenomena, the border for phenomenal associations lies in what has already passed. Since we cannot seek the future in the past, it is difficult to give it credence either.[11]

Some take affairs to be simply a matter of officers, with "officers" being understood as the worthy officials and Confucians who wear round hats and walk in square shoes. They are fully conversant about the Tao of the three realms of Heaven, Earth, and Man. Now if our foreknowledge is adequate to illuminate things, why imagize it with officers, a method inferior to the theory of phenomenal associations?

If we seek it through administrative order, although the traces and forms may be beautiful, they also cannot be believed. Then why not seek knowledge among men? Through employing agents we can know the enemy's advantages and disadvantages, movements and stopping, interior and exterior, vacuities and substantialities. Then since everything about the enemy will be known, why should we resort to ghosts and spirits? Therefore Li Ching said: "Why seek to gain military victory in Heaven and Earth? Victory lies in men completing their missions." Thus one who has advance knowledge knows the subtle and shadows, knows preservation and extinction. Someone who is enlightened about things that have not yet materialized, who knows the minuscule and makes decisions, employing them before things have rushed forward and sunk, can thus arise in an instant, the interstice of a thread.

Sun-tzu: "There are five types of spies to be employed: local spies, internal spies, turned spies [double agents], dead [expendable] spies, and living spies. When all five are employed together and no one knows their Tao, this is termed 'spiritual methodology.' They are a ruler's treasures."

Those who put on armor, grasp sharp weapons, and are first to break through the enemy's lines and mount their walls are men who dare to fight. Those who know the Tiger Secret Teaching and Leopard Strategy, who have mastered many methods and quick responses, excel at strategy. Those who understand riverboats and land wagons, the employment of cows and horses, excel at logistics. Those who precisely investigate the auspiciousness of natural phenomena and divine the implications of the wind's direction are diviners and prognosticators. We employ the courage of those who dare to fight, the wisdom of those who excel at planning, the labor of those who satisfy logistical needs, and the calculations of those who divine and prognosticate. As for those who spy out the enemy's closely held secrets, who ferret out their internal and external affairs, how can they not be treated as resources for spying?

Now spy activities are not singular. There are "local spies, internal spies, turned spies [double agents], dead [expendable] spies, and living spies. When all five are employed together and no one knows their Tao, this is termed 'spiritual methodology.' They are a ruler's treasures." Methodology is also technique. Rulers must regard these five as valuable treasures. The subtlety of those who excel in spy work cannot be fathomed. Rulers also must esteem those who excel at employing the vital points. When the employment of these five types of spies attains the point that "no one special, the way in which they all learn the enemy's affairs are one.

Sun-tzu: "Thus of all the Three Armies' affairs no relationship is closer than with spies; no rewards are more generous than those given to spies; no affairs are more secret than those pertaining to spies."

The methods for employing the military include the urgent and dilatory, light and heavy, hidden and visible. The urgent cannot be treated as dilatory, the heavy as light, or the hidden as visible. The urgency of spy work lies in weightiness and secrecy. Moreover, officers for supply, prognosticators, and strategists are all intimates of the ruler, but none are closer than spies. Those in the army who are first to ascend walls or penetrate enemy formations are rewarded, those who assault cities and force towns to surrender are enfeoffed, and those who seize battle flags from the enemy and kill their generals are also rewarded. All of them are rewarded generously, but none more so than spies. The Tao lies in what cannot be seen, affairs in what cannot be heard, victory in what cannot be known. In all these cases one wants secrecy, but nothing is more secret than spies. No one is more intimate than spies, for this is how the ruler treasures them. None are treated more generously than spies, for the ruler does not begrudge rank, salary, or a hundred ounces of gold. Spies are the most secret. This is why anyone who leaks out affairs before they are implemented are executed.

Sun-tzu: "Unless someone has the wisdom of a Sage, he cannot use spies; unless he is benevolent and righteous, he cannot employ spies; unless he is subtle and perspicacious, he cannot perceive the substance in intelligence reports. It is subtle, subtle! There are no areas in which one does not employ spies."

One who is not fully prepared in the Tao of spycraft is not qualified to control spies. One who does not keep their vital points secret is not qualified to know the true nature of spycraft. In spy work the most difficult aspect is knowing how to employ agents. The sagacity and wisdom of someone about to employ agents must surpass other men. When missions are assigned, agents must be governed with benevolence and righteousness. However, since human minds are difficult to fathom, without subtlety and mysteriousness of spirit how can anyone interpret the substance of their efforts?

Someone with sagacious wisdom can know men, so he can run spies. A righteous and benevolent controller can motivate men, so he can employ spies. Those who penetrate the subtle mysteries can exhaust their patterns, so they can grasp the subtlety of spy reports. Those who employ spies must plan before events begin to break in the enemy's state so that agents can be present when they actually unfold. Han Kao-tsu can be said to have penetrated the Tao for entrusting spies and known the vital points of spy work. He knew that Ch'in's generals could be corrupted and that Hsiang Yü could be estranged from his generals. Thus he employed agents with sagacious wisdom. He gave Ch'en P'ing a thousand catties of gold and used Shih-ch'i to subvert Ch'i. This was employing them with benevolence and righteousness. If Han Kao-tsu had not been so perspicacious, how could he have known the actual outcome? Although appearing similar these three cases are distinct, without spies they could not have been implemented.

Employing spies in this fashion is subtle, most subtle! There is no place men who cannot be fathomed are not employed. In the *Yin-ching*, the chapter on *hsing-jen* states: "Be just like a blackbird invisibly entering the heavy forest or a fish diving into the deepest pool without any trace. Remember that, despite his surpassing visual acuity, when Li Lou bent his head he couldn't discern the shape of things, and despite his acute hearing, when Shih Kuang tilted his ear downward, he couldn't hear a sound. Subtle! Subtle, just like a swirl of fine dust arising. How can a drunken and sated general who must contend with force, yet lightly engages in battle, manage to discern the affairs of spies?"

Sun-tzu: "If before the mission has begun it has already been exposed, the spy and those he informed should all be put to death."

There are no affairs more secret than spying. For spies you want secrecy, so apart from exceptional cases you cannot let anyone among the enemy know about them, nor can you let your own officers and troops know about them. If you do not let anyone among your own people know about them except in rare instances, then even your attendants and assistants cannot be allowed to learn of operations. Once they are no longer secret, such affairs will be widely disclosed. When affairs are disclosed and widely known, the plan will have to be abandoned. According to military law how should this be treated? It merits death.

Therefore, before spy work has been initiated, anyone who knows about the mission will have certainly learned it from our own spies. Thus the spy and all who were informed should be executed. In his *Hsing-jen* chapter Li Ch'uan said: "Among those serving in the Three Armies, none are more important than spies.

way they will know it is through double agents, double agents must be treated generously. Tu Yu says: "The double agent is the foundation of the five agents and the crux of spycraft." This is like saying: "Double agents are like the people's lives, the officers of the martial chariots, the martial cavalrymen, to all of whom one must be generous. Among men spies are the substance that cannot be slighted, among rulers the Tao that one does not dare disdain."

Sun-tzu: "In antiquity, when the Yin [Shang] arose, they had Yi Chih [Yi Yin] in the Hsia. When the Chou arose, they had Lü Ya [the T'ai Kung] in the Shang."

There are those who say that Sun-tzu's meaning is not that the T'ai Kung acted as a spy in the Shang and Chou. They claim that Sun-tzu's idea was that order gives birth to superior men, disorder to menial men. When the Shang was just arising, Yi Yin was still in the Hsia, so initially he was not one of the Shang's old ministers. The Hsia was unable to employ him, but the Shang used him, which is how they flourished. When the Chou first flourished, the T'ai Kung was still in the Shang, so initially he was not an old Chou minister either. The Shang was unable to use him, but the Chou employed him, which is how the Chou arose. King T'ang and King Wu were raised by benevolence and righteousness, Yi Yin and the T'ai Kung were assistants for kings. If these kings had their resources act as spies in order to achieve success, would later ages have praised them?

But if we investigate Sun-tzu's words to seek out his meaning, we find the two being discussed in the chapter entitled "Employing Spies," so they must have been acting as agents. That is certain. Now what the world terms "agents" certainly includes those who spied on their rulers, ministers, relatives, worthies, assistants, neighbors, and friends—not a one wasn't a spy. But if we go back to the original, ancient meaning for spies, it still would not be exhausted, for an agent knows the enemy's affairs. Sun-tzu earlier said that "advance knowledge cannot be gained from ghosts and spirits, inferred from phenomena, or projected from the measures of Heaven, but must be gained from men." To know the enemy's situation the ancients employed spies. If one only wants to know the enemy's situation, then Yi Yin and the T'ai Kung in the Hsia and Shang would certainly have had deep knowledge. So how does gaining intelligence this way differ from employing spies? [As the *Yin-ching* states]: "Probably when the Shang arose Yi Yin was a cook in the Hsia. When the Chou arose the T'ai Kung was a fisherman in Chou. When Ch'in assumed emperorship, Li Ssu was a hunter in Shantung. When Liu Pang became king of the Han, Han Hsin was merely an officer in Ch'u's army. When Ts'ao Ts'ao became hegemon, Hsün Huo was Yüan Shao's cast off minister. Ssu-ma T'an became emperor of Chin because Chia Ch'ung had been entrusted with government in Wei while Wei itself arose because Ts'ui Hao had made Chin his home." From this perspective Yi Yin in the Hsia and T'ai Kung in the Shang, even though not employed as spies, well knew the enemy's situation and thus performed the mission of early spies. So how could Sun-tzu not have spoken of their employment as spies!

Sun-tzu: "Thus enlightened rulers and sagacious generals who are able to get intelligent spies will invariably attain great achievements. This is the essence of the military, what the Three Armies rely on to move."

[Li Ching said:] "Water can float a boat, but it can also overturn the boat. Some use spies to be successful; others, relying on spies, are overturned and defeated." Truly. Yet Sun-tzu's thirteen chapters end with "Employing Spies" not because he slighted espionage but probably because he emphasized it. [Li Ching said:] "If one braids his hair and serves the ruler, maintains a proper countenance in court, is loyal and pure, trustworthy and completely sincere, even if someone were to excel in spy work, how could he be employed [to sow discord]?" But take the case of Ya-fu's estrangement in Ch'u. Wasn't he loyal? Wasn't he trustworthy? Yet through a single ploy mounted by Han agents he was unable to preserve himself, so how can it be said that spies are not worth employing! If you employ a spy but he proves incapable of being successful, it is not the spy's fault but yours because you didn't get the right man.

No doubt one must have surpassing ability to perform extraordinary tasks and thus realize greater achievements than ordinary men. Superior wisdom surpasses ordinary capability. Spying transcends human affairs. Spies must successfully undertake actions beyond the capability of other men. How can their achievements be compared with merely assaulting a city, occupying terrain, capturing an enemy's flag, or killing a general? Their greatness is incalculable, beyond words. At the least spies with superior wisdom must be like Yi Yin and the T'ai Kung, who established the Shang and created the Chou, amazing achievements!

The military's ultimate essence lies in spies. They are what the Three Armies rely upon to move and be employed, and without them cannot. Why? Spies can learn the enemy's vacuities and substantialities, their activities, and their internal and external affairs. Only after they have been successful can their desires be satisfied. The masses of the Three Armies rely on them to move. Formerly Li Su got Li Yu and took Wu Yüan-chi prisoner.[15] Kuang Pi got Kao Hui and destroyed Ssu-ming. Wasn't this relying on them and thereafter moving?

Expendable and Double Agents

The two categories of expendable and double or turned agents occasioned the most conceptual difficulty throughout Chinese history and therefore the most verbiage. Sun-tzu's original concept of expendable or "dead" agents—spies deliberately employed on missions likely to result in their deaths—became somewhat less precise over the centuries, eventually coming to encompass any agent who died in the performance of his mission. However, it also stimulated extensive discussions not just on the apparent righteousness of such actions, but also upon the applicability of the term. Although the question of whether the agent knew he was being sacrificed never arose—it was assumed that to be effective, he would not, although there were exceptions—the issue of intention was less clear. Some unfortunate individuals, such as Li Sheng and T'ang Chien, the two most famous expendable agents in Chinese history, were simply unfortunate victims of evolving circumstances, never having been dispatched on missions intended to threaten their lives. Li Sheng eventually knew Han Hsin's ruthless actions had fated him to death, but T'ang Chien never expected the consequences of Li Ching's aggressive exploitation of an otherwise unattainable opportunity. (No doubt enemy agents who had been deliberately deceived with false information and specious plans were equally surprised to find they were about to be executed for failure or collusion with the enemy.)

Without question the Spring and Autumn period already witnessed the conversion of enemy agents and diplomats, and the term "turned agent" is often employed in later commentaries discussing what should be simply "living spies." Surprisingly, the *Tso Chuan* even records a botched attempt to bribe and coerce a courier into betraying his mission and thus becoming a double agent. As his story includes many intriguing aspects, it provides an excellent example of early thought on missions and principles:

> Under siege by Ch'u forces, Sung dispatched Yüeh Ying-ch'i to the state of Chin to advise the extremity of their position and request their aid. The duke of Chin wanted to rescue them, but Po-tsung

advised against it: "The ancients had a saying, 'However long the whip, it will not reach the horse's belly.' Heaven is presently supporting Ch'u, so it is impossible for us to engage them in battle. Even with Chin's might, how can we contravene Heaven? Let us await the outcome." The duke therefore desisted in his plan and instead sent Chieh Yang on a mission to Sung to prevail upon them not to surrender by saying that "Chin, mobilizing all its forces, will shortly arrive."

En route to Sung's besieged capital Chieh Yang was captured in Cheng and forwarded to Ch'u's encampment outside the city. The prince of Ch'u, generously providing him with bribes, sought to have him reverse the contents of his message to Sung. At first he refused, but after three such entreaties consented. Ascending to the top of a mobile siege tower, he shouted out his original message to the people of Sung's capital, thereby fulfilling his mission. The prince of Ch'u, about to have him executed, sent a messenger to say: "Why did you make a promise and then violate it? It isn't I who lacks trustworthiness, but you that abandoned it. Hasten off to your punishment."

Chieh Yang replied however: "I have heard that righteousness consists in the ruler being able to administer orders and fidelity in a minister being able to execute commands. When faithfulness sustains righteousness in the implementation of such orders it is advantageous. When plans do not lose their advantage and thereby preserve the altars of state, this is a ruler for the people. Righteousness does not allow for two acts of faith, or faith for two commands. When your lordship bribed me, he failed to understand the essence of command. If I am willing to die without regret, how can I be bribed? The only reason I consented was to complete my mission. To die in the completion of his mission is a minister's joy. My ruler has a faithful minister, one who has gained his objective. Even if I die, what more could I seek?" The prince released him to return to Chin.[16]

The background to this incident oozes diplomatic intrigue and power diplomacy. Briefly, Ch'u invaded Sung in the ninth month of the preceding year (595 B.C.) after their provocateur—an official emissary ostensibly on a friendly mission to Ch'i—was captured while blatantly traversing Sung's territory without permission. This offense, which coincidentally illuminates the nature of state sovereignty and control in the Spring and Autumn period, compelled Sung to either boldly assert its independence by executing the agent or cower as a mere minion before mighty Ch'u, whose strength was expanding exponentially. Prompted by courage, righteousness, and the prospects of doom in either case, they chose to assert their independence and executed the emissary, who had, in fact, gone forth fully cognizant that it was designed to trigger exactly this response and was therefore in Sun-tzu's subsequent definition a "dead agent." However, in dispatching him, the ruler had promised to invade Sung to exact a horrendous revenge, thus showing that the entire sequence was pre-scripted, consisting of a stimulus, primary response, and secondary response or exploitative action designed to fabricate an excuse for Ch'u to subjugate the smaller, contiguous state of Sung and thereby at least nominally adhere to the ethical standards of the period.

Such sophisticated duplicity was hardly confined to Ch'u alone in the Spring and Autumn period, as Chin's actions in this very episode vividly illustrate. Although Chin never intended to undertake the military rescue of Sung, the duke still dispatched a messenger to encourage them to fervently resist their enemies, no doubt to thereby entangle Ch'u in a protracted conflict that would drain their resources, diminish their military capabilities, produce numerous casualties, and blunt their expanding influence into the northern plains. (He was perhaps oblivious to the possibility that Ch'u might enjoy much enhanced power once they conquered Sung and turned it into a client state.) The duke was too easily persuaded to desist in his plans to relieve Sung, and the historical records confirm no action was even attempted, the siege of Sung being resolved instead by the bold action of one man who crept into the chancellor's tent in the middle of their encampment one night and at knifepoint exacted a promise of release that Ch'u's ruler felt compelled to honor. Since Chieh Yang's original message was false, ironically Ch'u's coercion would have made it truthful, vividly illustrating the complexities of intrigue in this turbulent period.

When the fate of the Chinese empire following Ch'in's collapse was still uncertain, Liu Chi (Liu Pang), the eventual founder of the Han dynasty subsequently honored as Han Kao-tsu, benefited extensively from the clandestine work of Li Sheng, a headstrong Confucian remarkably capable of adapting himself to the momentary flux to realize great achievements. The circumstances that led to his tortured death suggest he was deliberately and unnecessarily sacrificed as a simple expedient by the ruthless Han Hsin, but his previous service, whereby he was prepared to subvert a city's defenses in conjunction with an externally mounted assault, and his subsequent reputation as a dead agent imply unrecorded dimensions to the story. His *Shih Chi* biography preserves the essentials:

> Li Sheng, whose personal name was Yi-chi, was a native of the town of Kao-yang in the district of Ch'en-liu. He loved to study,

but because his family was impoverished to the point of despair and he lacked any other means of livelihood, Li Sheng served as one of the lictors overseeing the village gates. Even then none of the Worthies or powerful men in the district dared employ him, while everyone termed him a foolish student.

When stalwarts such as Ch'en Sheng and Hsiang Liang initiated their revolts against the Ch'in dynasty, many of their generals came through Kao-yang en route to targeted areas. Li Sheng learned that these generals were all obsessed with trifles, loved detailed ceremony, and were too self-reliant to pay attention to portentous words, so he buried himself away. Subsequently he heard that troops under Kao-tsu's command had occupied Ch'en-liu's border and that one of their cavalrymen chanced to be a man of his own village. Han Kao-tsu had frequently queried him about the village's worthy and powerful men, so that when this officer returned to Kao-yang, Li Sheng intercepted him and said: "I have heard that, although Han Kao-tsu arrogantly disparages other people, he has conceived numerous far-reaching strategies. I would truly like to throw in with him but lack anyone to advance me. When you have an audience with Kao-tsu, say to him that 'in my village there is one Li Sheng, more than sixty years old and some six feet tall, whom everyone terms a foolish student. However, he asserts he is not foolish.'"

The cavalry officer said: "Kao-tsu does not like Confucians. Every time someone wearing a Confucian hat comes in, Kao-tsu grabs the hat off his head and urinates in it. When he speaks with people, he always swears loudly. He has never allowed any Confucian to expound on anything." Li Sheng said, "Merely tell him what I have said!"

The cavalry officer casually spoke to Kao-tsu just as Li Sheng had directed. When Kao-tsu reached Kao-yang's official hostel, he had men summon Li Sheng. When Li Sheng arrived and went into the hostel for his interview, Kao-tsu was just lounging on the bed, where two women were washing his feet. After entering, Li Sheng simply bowed low rather than formally prostrating himself and then asked: "Do you, sir, want to aid Ch'in in attacking the feudal lords? Or do you want to lead the feudal lords in destroying Ch'in?"

Kao-tsu cursed him: "Confucian dolt! Because All under Heaven have long endured the misery inflicted by Ch'in, the feudal lords are leading each other forth to attack it. How can you ask if I want to aid Ch'in in attacking the feudal lords?"

Li Sheng said, "If you are truly assembling followers to forge a righteous army that will execute perverse Ch'in, you should not interview your elders while lounging about!" Thereupon Kao-tsu ended the foot washing, arose, arrayed his clothes properly, and apologetically invited Li to take a seat of honor on the mat. Li Sheng then discussed the horizontal and vertical alliances that had developed during the Warring States period. Pleased, Kao-tsu presented something to eat to Li Sheng and then inquired, "How should I proceed?"

Li Sheng replied: "You have hastily assembled an untrained mass and gathered the remnants of chaotic forces, somewhat less than ten thousand men, yet want to advance directly into mighty Ch'in. This is termed 'tempting the tiger's jaws'! Now Ch'en-liu is the realm's focal location, situated on terrain that is open in all directions and traversable everywhere. Moreover, the city has accumulated large stores of grain. I am on good terms with the district magistrate and would like to be deputed to bring about its submission. If they prove unwilling to listen, you can then mobilize your army for an attack, while I will effect a response from within."

Accordingly Kao-tsu dispatched Li Sheng to proceed first and had his troops follow. They subsequently subjugated Ch'en-liu, so Kao-tsu granted Li Sheng the title of Lord of Kuang-yeh. Li Sheng then recommended his brother, Li Shang, to Kao-tsu, who entrusted him with command of several thousand men. Thereafter Li Shang accompanied Kao-tsu on his campaign to seize the southwest, while Li Sheng served as an adviser and was frequently deputed as an emissary to the feudal lords.

In the third year of the Han dynasty, autumn, Hsiang Yü attacked Kao-tsu's forces and seized Jung-yang, compelling the Han forces to escape to Pao-kung and Luo-yang. Hsiang Yü, king of Ch'u, on learning that Han Hsin had vanquished Chao and P'eng Yüeh had mounted several rebellions in Liang, divided his armies to rescue both Chao and Liang. Han Hsin was on the verge of attacking Ch'i in the east when Kao-tsu repeatedly encountered difficulty around Jung-yang and Ch'eng-kao. Kao-tsu therefore calculated that he should sacrifice the territory east of Ch'eng-kao and encamp in the Pao-kung and Luo-yang regions in order to resist Ch'u's forces under Hsiang Yü. Li Sheng then said: "I have heard it said that one who knows the Heaven of Heaven can achieve kingship, but one who does not know the Heaven of Heaven cannot achieve kingship. A true king takes the people as Heaven, but the people take food as Heaven. Now the realm has long been forwarding and transporting goods to the great storehouses at Ao-shan, and I have heard that extremely substantial amounts of grain are stored there. When Hsiang Yü captured Jung-yang, instead of stoutly defending the granary at Ao-shan he took his forces to the east, deputing some former convicts to guard Ch'eng-kao. In this way Heaven has provided resources for you. Now I dare to believe it will be a great error if we withdraw, thereby snatching opportunity away from ourselves, when Hsiang Yü may be so easily taken.

"Moreover, two valiant stalwarts cannot both be established. You and Hsiang Yü have long been locked in an indecisive stand-off, so the common people are vexed into movement and all within the four seas rocked and jangled. Farmers have abandoned their hoes and women their shuttles, while the hearts of All under Heaven remain unsettled. I suggest you urgently resume advancing your army to seize and appropriate Jung-yang. Then, by relying upon the grain stored at Ao-shan, securing the defiles of Ch'eng-hao, blocking the road to the T'ai-hang mountains, occupying the pass at Fei-hu, and defending the Yellow River ford at Pai-ma, you may show the feudal lords that you have effectively taken control of the realm's strategic dispositions. All under Heaven will then know where to give their allegiance.

"Now that Yen and Chao have already been pacified, only Ch'i has not submitted. T'ien Kuang presently occupies several hundred miles of Ch'i's old territory, and T'ien Hsien, in command of some two hundred thousand troops, is ensconced at Li-ch'eng. The mighty T'ien clan, backed by the sea and relying upon the obstacles posed by the Yellow and Chi Rivers, are encroaching upon Ch'u in the south. Their populace is highly changeable and crafty. Even if you dispatch an army several hundred thousand men strong, it will be months or years before they can be destroyed. I suggest you entrust me with the task of persuading the king of Ch'i to join you and thus become your eastern hedge."

"Excellent," Kao-tsu responded and then, in accord with his plan, retook the granary at Ao-shan, thereafter dispatching Li Sheng to exercise his persuasion upon the king of Ch'i.

"Does your majesty know to whom All under Heaven will give their allegiance?" Li Sheng asked of the king of Ch'i.

"No," replied the king.

"If your majesty were to know to whom All under Heaven will give their allegiance, you would be able to preserve your kingdom of Ch'i; if you do not know to whom All under Heaven will give their allegiance, you will be unable to retain your kingdom of Ch'i," said Li Sheng.

The king inquired, "To whom will All under Heaven give their allegiance?"

"To Han."

"Sir, how do you say that?"

Li Sheng replied: "Formerly, when Kao-tsu, king of Han, and Hsiang Yü, king of Ch'u, united their forces and ventured west to attack Ch'in, they agreed that whoever penetrated Hsien-yang first would become king. Kao-tsu advanced into Hsien-yang first, but Hsiang Yü abrogated the agreement by enfeoffing him as king of the Han area instead of Ch'in. Thereafter, when Kao-tsu heard that Hsiang Yü had shifted the Righteous Emperor out of Ch'u and then had him slain, he mobilized troops from Shu and Han to strike the three kings of Ch'in [set up by Hsiang Yü from the remnants of the Ch'in forces], went out through the pass, and gathered the soldiers of the realm to punish Hsiang Yü for his treatment of the Righteous Emperor and to reestablish the descendants of the feudal lords. Whenever he forced the submission of a city he enfeoffed a general, and whenever they gained material goods he divided them among his officers. Because he shared all the profits with All under Heaven, the powerful, valiant, worthy, and talented all take pleasure in being employed by him. Soldiers from the feudal lords are thus arriving from all directions, while boatload after boatload of grain is being shipped down from Shu and Han.

"Hsiang Yü now has a reputation for contravening agreements and the responsibility for slaying the Righteous Emperor. He never takes note of other people's achievements or forgets their offenses. When they prove victorious in battle the troops receive no rewards, when they capture a city no one is enfeoffed. Except for the members of his family, no one is entrusted with any responsibility. Whenever he has seals of authority carved for anyone, he holds them until the corners have been worn off, unable to award them. Whenever they assault a city and gain material goods he just accumulates them, unable to part with them as rewards. All under Heaven rebel against him, the worthy and talented revile him, and no one is willing to serve under him. That all the warriors of the realm will give their allegiance to Han Kao-tsu can be anticipated.

"Now Kao-tsu has exploited Shu and Han, pacified the three Ch'in, ventured beyond the Hsi-ho area, and gathered the soldiers from Shang-tang; proceeded down through Ching-ching and executed the Lord of Ch'eng-an; destroyed Northern Wei and occupied thirty-two cities. These are the soldiers of the legendary Ch'ih Yu, objectives accomplished through Heaven's beneficence rather than the strength of men. Since Kao-tsu has already availed himself of the grain supplies at Ao-shan, secured the ravines in

Ch'eng-hao, blocked the lower heights of the T'ai-hang mountains, defended the ford at Pai-ma, and occupied the pass at Fei-hu, the last to submit will be the first to suffer destruction. If your majesty quickly becomes among the first to submit to Kao-tsu, you will be able to preserve and retain Ch'i's altars, but if you do not submit to Kao-tsu, you will shortly be endangered and perish."

T'ien Kuang felt this to be true so he accepted Li Sheng's suggestions and desisted military preparations for the defense of Li-ch'eng, indulging himself in wine every day thereafter with Li Sheng.[17] Meanwhile, after suddenly retaking control of Han Hsin's forces, Kao-tsu appointed Han Hsin as chancellor and deputed him to attack Ch'i with idle troops from Chao. Han Hsin therefore led his new army to the east, but before he had forded the Yellow River at P'ing-yüan, he learned that Li Sheng had already persuaded Ch'i to submit and so wanted to stop his advance. K'uai T'ung, a sophist from Fan-yang, advised Han Hsin thus: "My general received an imperial summons to suddenly strike Ch'i, but Han Kao-tsu also secretly deputed an emissary to effect Ch'i's surrender. Has my general received an imperial edict to halt? So how can you not continue your campaign? Moreover, Li Sheng, a single officer, by bowing from his carriage and moving his three inches of tongue, has wrought the submission of more than seventy Ch'i cities, while my general, in command of seventy thousand troops, required more than a year to subjugate Chao's fifty plus cities. Is what you required several years to achieve, on the contrary, to be less than the success of a doltish Confucian?"

Han Hsin, feeling this to be true, therefore followed his original plan, forded the Yellow River, and suddenly struck Ch'i. T'ien Kuang, king of Ch'i, being informed about the arrival of Han troops, assumed Li Sheng had betrayed him and therefore said to him: "If you are able to stop this Han army, I will spare you; otherwise, I am going to boil you!" Li Sheng replied: "Undertaking momentous affairs is not a matter of fastidious circumspection, overflowing Virtue not a matter of courteous yielding. Your elder will never change his words just for you!"

The king of Ch'i then had Li Sheng boiled alive before leading his soldiers off to the east, where he was eventually defeated by Han Hsin.[18]

Li Sheng was thus a victim of Han Hsin's ambition coupled with Kao-tsu's probable duplicity or lack of confidence in Li's ability to successfully persuade the king of Ch'i to join them as an ally.

Another, somewhat earlier illustrative episode from the Warring States period finds a hapless courier being deliberately sacrificed (in accord with Sun-tzu's definition) to subvert an informant residing in another state. This dramatic measure—literally setting up the courier for detection—was apparently resorted to in the expectation that rumors alone would prove inadequate to implicate the defector:

> Ch'ang T'o fled to East Chou from West Chou and then fully informed them about West Chou's internal affairs. East Chou was elated, but West Chou was greatly angered. Feng Tan said to the ruler, "If my lord will provide me with thirty catties of gold, I can have him killed."
>
> Feng Tan then deputed an agent to take the gold and a secret letter to Chang T'o that instructed him: "You are advised that if the affair can be achieved, you must exert yourself to complete it; if it cannot be achieved, you should immediately flee back to West Chou. If the affair is prolonged and leaks out, it will cause your death."
>
> Shortly thereafter he dispatched an emissary to inform East Chou's border guards, "Tonight an evildoer will enter your state." The guards caught the agent and forwarded him to the ruler, who immediately had Ch'ang T'o executed.[19]

Despite being unqualified for any sort of covert activities and never having been dispatched on a clandestine mission, either with or without his conscious knowledge, T'ang Chien became the second famous "expendable agent" of Chinese history. The outlines of the episode that occurred just after the founding of the T'ang dynasty are found in the T'ang histories and the lengthy biography of General Li Ching, the probable author and chief spokesperson in the seventh Military Classic, the *Questions and Replies.* However, the story's importance may be seen from its employment as the illustration for Chapter 59 of the *Hundred Unorthodox Strategies,* "Advancing," whose tactical principle states: "Whenever engaging an enemy in battle, if you truly know that the enemy has a weakness that can be exploited to yield victory, you should quickly advance your army and pound it, for then you will always be victorious. A tactical principle states: 'Advance when you see it is possible.'" The story itself unfolds as follows:

> During the T'ang dynasty, when Li Ching was serving as commander in chief for the Ting-hsiang Circuit campaign army, he suddenly attacked and destroyed the Turks. Chieh-li, khan of the tribe, raced back to the protection of Mount T'ieh and dispatched

an ambassador to the T'ang court to acknowledge his offense and request that his state be allowed to submit in allegiance to the T'ang. The emperor dispatched Li Ching to accept their surrender.

Although the khan had visibly requested the privilege of visiting the imperial court, he still harbored doubts. Li Ching guessed his intentions. At this time the emperor summoned the Director of Rites, T'ang Chien, and dispatched him and others to officially condole with and placate the khan. Li Ching said to Chang Kung-chin, the Military Commissioner attached to his command: "With the arrival of imperial ambassadors, the Turks will certainly feel quite secure. If we were to have ten thousand cavalrymen, each carrying three days' rations, proceed via the Pai Road, we could suddenly attack them and certainly gain our objectives."

Chang Kung-chin said: "The emperor has already assented to their surrender. And what about the men who have gone out there?" Li Ching said: "The opportunity cannot be lost. This is the way Han Hsin destroyed Ch'i during the founding reign of the Han dynasty. As for men of T'ang Chien's advanced age, what is there to regret?" He supervised the soldiers in an urgent advance. When they had proceeded as far as Mount Yin, they encountered more than a thousand of the khan's perimeter defense troops, all of whom surrendered and joined Li's army.

When the khan received the T'ang's ambassadors he was greatly elated and neglected the army's supervision. Li Ching's vanguard took advantage of a heavy fog to advance within seven miles of the khan's command center before the khan first became aware of them. Before the Turkish formations could be deployed, Li Ching released his troops in an assault that resulted in killing more than ten thousand enemy soldiers. They also took more than a hundred thousand men and women prisoner, captured the khan's son Ku-luo-shih, and killed Princess Yi-ch'eng. The khan fled but was subsequently captured by Chang Pao-hsiang, the commander in chief of the Ta-t'ung Circuit campaign army, and sent back to the emperor. The T'ang thus enlarged its territory from Mount Yin north to the Gobi Desert.

T'ang Chien's fame was further enhanced among military readers when Emperor T'ai-tsung questioned his most successful and loyal general about his intentions and motives in so readily sacrificing the Director of Rites. As recorded in the *Questions and Replies*:

The T'ai-tsung said: "Formerly when T'ang Chien was an emissary to the T'u-chüeh [Turks], you availed yourself of the situation to attack and defeat them. People say you used T'ang Chien as an expendable spy. Up until now I have had doubts about this. What about it?"

Li Ching bowed twice and said: "T'ang Chien and I equally served your Majesty. I anticipated that T'ang Chien's proposals would certainly not be able to persuade them to quietly submit. Therefore I took the opportunity to follow up with our army and attack them. In order to eliminate a great danger I did not concern myself with a minor righteousness. Although people refer to T'ang Chien as an expendable spy, it was not my intention.

Li Ching's ruthlessness in consolidating the T'ang position prompted officials and the literati in his own age and thereafter to severely condemn him. However, from the perspective of many years of warfare and persistent external threats to the fledgling T'ang dynasty, he obviously calculated that sacrificing T'ang would be insignificant compared to the men and resources otherwise certain to be lost. That T'ang Chien became known as an "expendable spy" is one history's ironies because he was the epitome of the literati, well versed in ceremony and protocol, merely a symbolic choice to accept the khan's surrender on the emperor's behalf. Being a civil official rather than a military officer, his mission was initiated without covert intentions, becoming subversive only when opportunely and astutely exploited by Li Ching, who viewed him simply as an expendable diplomat.

Sun-tzu's definition of double or turned agents was premised upon them having originally been dispatched by an enemy state and subsequently turned around, whereas the contemporary Western idea of a double agent requires a conscious, if not always willing, choice. The Chinese concept came to entail the manipulation and exploitation of enemy personnel whether they had been active clandestine agents or not, whether they were consciously recruited or not. However, classic double agents continued to exist, as may be seen in this example from the Three Kingdoms period:

Tung Feng, de facto ruler of Su-ch'i city, together with his younger brother Wei-ch'ü, revolted after having previously surrendered to the government, so Chang Ni, the regional governor, executed him. However, as Tung's wife was the daughter of the king of the nearby mountainous state of Mao-niu, Chang Ni concocted a way to pardon her. Meanwhile Wei-ch'ü escaped across the western frontier.

Wei-ch'ü was hard, fierce, astute, and cruel, so all his subordinates were terrified of him. He deputed two of his close confidants to get information about Chang Ni on the pretext of wanting to surrender. However, Chang realized their true objectives, and by granting generous rewards converted them to double agents, thereafter planning with them how to assassinate Wei-ch'ü. When this was accomplished Wei-ch'ü's band all felt secure.[20]

Peripatetic persuaders sometimes seem to have consciously acted as double agents, even freelance triple agents, as the following example shows:

Eastern Chou wanted to plant its fields with rice, but Western Chou had blocked the river's flow. Eastern Chou found this disastrous, but Su-tzu asked the ruler, "May I be sent as an emissary to force them to provide the water?"

The ruler assented, so Su-tzu went to see Western Chou's ruler, to whom he said: "Your majesty's plan is in error. By cutting off the water you are enriching Eastern Chou because the people are now all planting wheat. If you want to harm them, nothing would be better than now letting the water flow and thereby distressing their plantings. Once you allow the river to flow through, Eastern Chou will certainly plant rice again. When they have sown the rice, you can again cut off their water. In this way you can force their populace to look toward you with raised heads, eager to receive your orders."

The ruler of Western Chou consented and subsequently let the river flow through. Su-tzu thus received payment from two states.[21]

Other Agents

Apart from the various categories of secret agent directly employed by states and armies to individually operate against their enemies, military staffs included a number of officers with designated intelligence, counterintelligence, and covert operations functions. Although they are rarely indicated in the extensive bureaucratic listings found in the twenty-five dynastic histories, their presence may be discerned in occasional military notes on command responsibilities and staffing. Fortunately a chapter entitled "The King's Wings" in the *Six Secret Teachings*, a product of the middle to late Warring States period, in detailing perhaps the earliest formal general staff in history stipulates many positions that clearly entail vital intelligence, psychological, and covert warfare responsibilities:

Chief of Planning, one: in charge of advising about secret plans for responding to sudden events; investigating Heaven so as to eliminate sudden change; exercising general supervision over all planning; and protecting and preserving the lives of the people.

Planning Officers, five: responsible for planning security and danger; anticipating the unforeseen; discussing performance and ability; making clear rewards and punishments; appointing officers; deciding the doubtful; and determining what is advisable and what is not.

Topographers, three: in charge of the army's disposition and strategic configuration of power when moving and stopped; information on strategic advantages and disadvantages; precipitous and easy passages, both near and far; and water and dry land, mountains and defiles, so as not to lose advantages of terrain.

Strategists, nine: responsible for discussing divergent views; analyzing the probable success or failure of various operations; selecting the weapons and training men in their use; and identifying those who violate the ordinances.

Secret Signals Officers, three: responsible for the pennants and drums, for clearly signaling to the eyes and ears; creating deceptive signs and seals; issuing false designations and orders; and stealthily and hastily moving back and forth, going in and out like spirits.

Officers of Authority, three: responsible for implementing the unorthodox and deceptive; establishing the different and the unusual, things that people do not recognize; and putting into effect inexhaustible transformations.

Ears and Eyes, seven: responsible for going about everywhere, listening to what people are saying; seeing the changes; and observing the officers in all four directions, and the army's true situation.

Feathers and Wings, four: responsible for flourishing the name and fame of the army; shaking distant lands with its image; and moving all within the four borders in order to weaken the enemy's spirit.

Roving Officers, eight: responsible for spying upon the enemy's licentiousness and observing their changes; manipulating their emotions; and observing the enemy's thoughts in order to act as spies.

Officers of Techniques, two: responsible for spreading slander and falsehoods and for calling upon ghosts and spirits in order to confuse the minds of the enemy's populace.

The large number of central staff devoted to deception, disinformation, observation, and similar functions out of a total of seventy-two clearly indicates the importance assigned to their functions in effecting victory.

"Selecting Officers," the second chapter in the military section of the *Ch'ang-tuan Ching*—a synthetic work written by Chao Jui in the T'ang dynasty that essentially interweaves selected passages from the classic writings on different topics, forming them into an extended discussion interspersed with the author's unifying comments—similarly enumerates the key staff members of any military command. The following obviously exercised military intelligence and spying functions:

Now whenever the king commands the army, he must carefully select courageous men and wise officers of all ranks, assign them duties in accord with their abilities, each based upon their individual strengths, to be his thighs [personal advisers] and wings [staff] in order to compete his awesome spirituality. Only thereafter will the myriad affairs be complete.

These include a chief of staff, five strategists, three astronomers, three topographers, nine tacticians, four quartermasters, four public relations officers, three signals officers for the drums and flags, four engineering officers, three tactical officers for unorthodox measures, seven ears and eyes [roving security agents], five claws and teeth [morale officers], four wings [psyops officers], eight roving officers [recon officers], two invocators [to call upon ghosts and spirits], two accountants, and two physicians.

The chapter continues with a discussion largely in the vein of Wu Ch'i's *Wu-tzu:* Select men of unusual motivation or physical skills, including those skilled in disputation and clever in speech, for grouping into cohesive units. Unmentioned in these two chapters but otherwise specified were the large numbers of scouts and reconnaissance patrols (discussed in the following section on Military Intelligence) that would be employed to observe the enemy and penetrate their camps whenever possible, responsible for secretly gathering information about disposition, conditions, plans, and tactics.

6

Operations and Control

WHILE MILITARY WRITERS ALL AGREED that spies were an integral part of intelligence gathering efforts, astute voices warned against relying upon them too extensively. The T'ang general Li Ching was particularly cautious, but in the conclusion to a passage previously cited about T'ang Chien, he expressed confidence that spies could not successfully penetrate a well-ordered court and estrange the ruler from truly loyal and capable ministers:

> According to Sun-tzu, employing spies is an inferior measure. I once prepared a discussion of this subject and at the end stated: "Water can float a boat, but it can also overturn the boat. Some use spies to be successful; others, relying on spies, are overturned and defeated."
>
> If one braids his hair and serves the ruler, maintains a proper countenance in court, is loyal and pure, trustworthy and completely sincere, even if someone excels at spying, how can he be employed to sow discord?[1]

Whereas Li Ching was somewhat oblivious to the impact of spy activities directed against court ministers and ruler, the Ming dynasty *T'ou-pi Fu-t'an* observed: "Now some spies simply watch the way the winds blow and transmit falsehoods, while others will be subject to enemy persecution and divulge your affairs to the enemy. These are intimately related to being overturned and defeated. Thus agents can be employed but cannot be exclusively relied upon. Employing them is wisdom; relying upon them is stupidity."[2]

Apart from discussing the types of spies and the importance of double agents, Sun-tzu's chapter identified two other critical points: controlling agents requires talent and character, while interpreting the data acquired demands wisdom and perspicacity:[3] "Unless someone has the wisdom of a Sage, he cannot use spies; unless he is benevolent and righteous, he cannot employ spies; unless he is subtle and perspicacious, he cannot perceive the substance in intelligence reports. It is subtle, subtle!"

Although personal integrity, righteousness, Virtue, and wisdom are considered prerequisites for understanding the spy and the data he retrieves, they are also essential to motivating men to the cause. Thus, for example, the *Three Strategies* states:

The *Army's Strategic Power* states: "One does not employ righteous officers with material wealth alone. Thus the righteous will not die for the malevolent. The wise will not make plans on behalf of an obtuse ruler."

The ruler cannot be without Virtue, for if he lacks Virtue his ministers will rebel. He cannot be without awesomeness, for if he lacks awesomeness he will lose his authority. A minister cannot be without virtue, for if he lacks virtue he has nothing with which to serve his ruler. He cannot be without awesomeness, for if he lacks awesomeness the state will be weak. If he is too awesome he himself will be overturned.

If your state's Virtue and strategic power are the same as those of the enemy, so that neither state has the means to overcome the other, then you must win the minds of the valiant, share likes and dislikes with the common people, and only thereafter attack the enemy in accord with changes in the balance of power. Thus without stratagems you have no means to resolve suspicions and settle doubts. Without rumor and the unorthodox you have no means to destroy evildoers and stop invaders. Without secret plans you have no means to be successful.[4]

Even though Chinese history provided many examples of brutal rulers and perverse states, such as Ch'in in the final stages of its conquest, successfully employing clandestine agents to disrupt their enemies and wrest a telling advantage, the military theorists generally persisted in their belief that righteous causes and moral leadership must underlie intelligence efforts. The famous but ill-fated Chu-ko Liang thus stated:

One who doesn't know the advantages of the nine configurations of terrain does not know the Tao for the nine changes. The *yin* and *yang* of Heaven, the configuration and names of Earth, the close associates of men—one who knows these three will dwell in their achievement. One who knows their officers knows the enemy; one who does not know their officers does not know the enemy. One who does not know the enemy will invariably be imperiled in every engagement. Thus for targets the army will suddenly strike, one must certainly know the ruler's attendants, the mind of the officers and troops. In the Tao for employing the five types of secret agents, they are what the army treats as most intimate, what the general is most generous to. Without Sagely wisdom one cannot employ them; unless one is a righteous worthy, one cannot dispatch them on missions. When the five categories of agents realize their appropriate nature, the populace of the state can be employed and the state can be long preserved.[5]

A chapter in the anonymous late Ming dynasty *Ts'ao-lu Ching-lüeh* further expanded the fundamental principles of spycraft with important insights regarding the management of agents and comparative evaluation of their material:

The *Military Rescripts* states: "The means by which enlightened rulers and worthy generals initiated actions, conquered others, and achieved success that surpassed the ordinary was advance knowledge." Advance knowledge of the enemy's true situation can be derived only from materials obtained by agents, so how can intelligence work be slighted?

Sun-tzu spoke in detail about the Tao for employing spies, what he referred to as "without subtlety and mystery being unable to realize the substantial employment of spies," so that especially in scrutinizing the essence, you must explicate the meaning. When the five types of agents are employed, you must invariably assemble all the data and probe for similarities. Thus for any single affair you cannot but multiply the number of agents employed in order to observe whether their words actually cohere or not, for only then will you begin to attain the truth.

When the five types of spies are kept ignorant about each other, and when your living spies, unaware of each other, also gather their information about various matters and forward it, each reporting what they have heard, you can begin to compare their commonalities and evaluate differences, ferreting out the true and false. Why is this? As soon as agents become aware of each other, they inevitably compare their findings and make them consistent, skillfully employing their craftiness, in turn deceiving you with their reports. Thus your agents should not be unified; only you should know who they are.

You should question them in detail and observe their sincerity, evaluating the data in accord with appropriate parameters in order to discern the most subtle points, thus being as vaporous as illusion, as secretive as ghostly spirits. Then, even though the enemy excel at bolting their doors, will they be able to conceal their true situation? By not proceeding in this manner, some employed spies to achieve success, but others relied on enemy spies to overturn their enemies, so how can agents be relied upon? As for managing them with benevolence and righteousness and stimulating them with heavy rewards, these hardly require mention.⁶

To facilitate gathering information and targeting individuals and objectives, preliminary steps to secure fundamental data—such as employing the eighty "travelers" described in the *Kuan-tzu*—should be undertaken: "Kuan Chung dispatched eighty warriors to wander about the four corners of the realm offering adornments, amusements, and delights for sale to the feudal lords in order to discern what the upper and lower ranks liked and valued and thereby select the dissolute and chaotic as priority targets for attack."⁷

As late as the mid-sixteenth century the *T'ou-pi Fu-t'an* pointed out:

If you want to learn the enemy's true situation through spies, you must first gain an understanding of their fundamentals—such as the price of goods, their customs and inclinations, their causes of happiness and anger—and fathom who among the upper and lower ranks are in harmony, who marked by acrimony. Only thereafter, in accord with slight openings, can you spy upon the ruler's close associates; through sycophants, estrange the loyal; through profits, control the disputatious; and through doubt, contrive dismissals. Cause their words to be deceptive, sow confusion in their actions and stopping, estrange the intimate, and disperse their alliances, all through the subtle work of employing agents.

Therefore, successfully mounting covert operations in enemy states requires first acquiring some knowledge of their situation. If you want to gain knowledge of the enemy's situation, you must not begrudge the expense of a thousand pieces of gold. To be parsimonious about a thousand pieces of gold and lose agents is to be defeated. To expend a thousand pieces and thereby learn the enemy's situation is to be victorious. This is the subtle crux of victory and defeat, it must be investigated!⁸

The importance of allocating adequate funds to acquire information, reiterated in the last paragraph, deserves note. Because of the risks undertaken by secret agents and the need for courage, determination, and self-control, all the military writers who pondered their employment emphasized two aspects: secrecy and generous rewards. As will be discussed in the section on counterintelligence, secrecy is paramount for any state that seeks to prevent the enemy from fathoming its plans and operations. However, the measures to be implemented with regard to running spy operations must be even more extreme. Thus Sun-tzu stated: "Of all the Three Armies' affairs no relationship is closer than with spies, no rewards are more generous than those given to spies, no affairs are more secret than those pertaining to spies. If before the mission has begun, it has already been exposed, the spy and those he informed should all be put to death."[9] Later, the *Wu-pei Chih-yao* asserted: "In employing the military, nothing is more important than using spies. The methods for employing spies are not singular, but the main point is to prevent people from fathoming them, the subtle essence is secrecy."

Sun-tzu was also the first to assert that spies could neither be recruited nor retained without strong material incentives, and he was followed by many others thereafter. Although the financial requirements for agents were frequently spoken of in isolation, the military sphere equally required courage and incentives, just as positions in the central government. Accordingly, both the military and philosophical writings developed a complex psychology of rewards and punishments during the Warring States period that fully explored the power of incentives to motivate and manipulate men. A chapter entitled "Administrative Distinctions" in the *Kuan-tzu* observes:

> The ruler does not begrudge gold and material wealth to the acute of hearing and sharp of eye. Thus a minor campaign occurring within one thousand kilometers is known about. The construction of substantial walls and the gathering of ten people will be espied within five days. A major campaign [by the feudal states] anywhere under Heaven will be known about within five days because the ruler disperses gold and material wealth in order to employ those who have acute hearing and sharp eyes. Thus one who excels at employing the military may lack ditches and ramparts because he has ears and eyes.

The value of clandestine information in reducing the state's military expenditures deserves note.

As for targeting individuals and manipulating agents, including enemy spies, Li Ching advised:

> If the enemy has spoiled favorites who are entrusted with confidential affairs, we should dispatch spies to bring them marvelous

curiosities, to debauch them with their desires, to accord with and entice them. If the enemy has important officials who have been deprived of power or whose ambitions are unsatisfied, we can inveigle them with generous profits to prevaricate against those close to the ruler, to pluck their true situation and learn it. If the enemy has those close to the ruler or attendants who are frequently boastful, who like to dispute about the advantages and disadvantages of things, we should have our spies pretend to warmly embrace them, to honor and praise them, and then generously provide them with marvelous gifts in order to ferret out their spies and convert them.

If the enemy dispatches emissaries with requests to us, we should detain their emissaries and have people constantly accompany them. They should act courteously and attend them congenially morning and night, taking good care of them, while we double and redouble their bribes and provide gifts that suit their tastes, constantly observing their countenances and words and investigating them. But early in the day and late at night we should see that they are always alone with our chosen attendants, and also dispatch men with acute hearing to conceal themselves in the double walls and listen to their leisure talk. When we have delayed their mission, they will fear being doubted and reprimanded by their governments, and will certainly discuss their true affairs among themselves. When we know their plans, we can dispatch them and use them for our purposes.[10]

Through such efforts double agents can easily be recruited, for they will have been forced into untenable positions in which their survival depends upon cooperating with the enemy rather than continuing to loyally serve their own state.

Although double agents have inordinate value, their employment entails the dilemma of reliability, ensuring they are neither false double agents nor expendable agents planted to spread disinformation by feigning a new loyalty. As the preceding passages already indicate, one method would be to compare the double agent's reports with those from other sources, increasing the credibility accorded them only after their veracity has been attested over time. Li Ching offered some suggestions for grappling with this problem and handling agents previously detained by the enemy who perhaps provided them with critical information or were seduced into their employment:

You should not heed the words of any agent who was captured by the enemy but later returned. However, if you do manage to receive true information through him, you can reverse your course and employ it. When you uncover an enemy agent, if you want to extinguish all trace of him, kill or imprison him. If you want to employ him as a double agent, treat him generously and then release him. This is the method for achieving certain victory, the essence of the military.[11]

In Li Ch'uan's estimation even so-called local guides—essentially defectors employed in an extended role—pose reliability problems and therefore require extensive measures to secure their loyalty and confirm the validity of their information:

Although deer naturally enter forests, one who does not employ local guides will find it difficult to realize advantages of terrain. Now employing local guides doesn't necessarily mean natives. Anyone familiar with the difficult and easy ground among the mountains and rivers, or with the enemy's vacuities and substantialities, can be entrusted with the task. Reward them generously to gain their willing allegiance, but be prepared to strictly guard against deception. Bestow offices and ranks upon them, enrich them with wealth and goods, and thereby cause them to have things they cherish. Match them with wives and children, and thereby cause them to have people they embrace. Thereafter, investigate their speech, examine their countenances, turn their words upside down, and if they are consistent throughout, from beginning to end, they can be employed.[12]

Li Ch'uan's policy was essentially a method of vetting spies rather than simply employing local guides on a temporary basis as the army advanced. His advice to ensure loyalty through nurturing both desires and ties of localized affection was unique among the military writers, as were his methods for querying and probing (which will be seen in the section on evaluating men). Clearly any men subject to such insightful handling were destined for future employment as spies and double agents.

Historically, many rulers fell victim to the machinations of trusted confidants who became enemy agents, often dismissing truly loyal and meritorious ministers at their behest. However, at least one ruler proved capable of fathoming false reports and employing generals, unlike numerous Spring and Autumn and Warring States failures, illustrating the knowledge necessary to successfully interpret events. His perspicacity in assessing agent reports was even cited by later generations:

Having gained permission to pass through the states of Han and Wei, a Ch'in army advanced to attack the state of Ch'i. King Wei of Ch'i had Chang-tzu assume command of the counterattack. After confronting Ch'in's army, both sides stood down and encamped. Meanwhile emissaries were dispatched back and forth a number of times. Then Chang-tzu changed their battle pennons and unit insignia [to match Ch'in's] in order to have his soldiers intermix with Ch'in's forces. An observer came back to the court and informed the king that Chang-tzu had gone over to Ch'in with all his troops.[13] King Wei made no reaction.

After the passage of some time another observer came and reported that Chang-tzu had surrendered with all his troops to Ch'in. The king made no reaction. After this happened a third time the chamberlain asked: "Using the same language, three different men have informed you that Chang-tzu has been defeated. Why have you not dispatched a general to suddenly attack him?"[14]

The king replied, "Since it is clear that he has not rebelled against me, why should I attack him?" After a while another report advised that Ch'i's forces had gained a great victory, Ch'in's army having been severely defeated. The king of Ch'in subsequently confessed his offense against Ch'i and bowed in acknowledgment as a barbarian subject. An attendant inquired how King Wei knew Chang-tzu had not deserted. He replied: "Chang-tzu's mother was unfaithful to his father, so his father killed and buried her beneath the stables. When I commissioned Chang-tzu as commanding general, I encouraged him by saying, 'If you return with all your forces, you will certainly be formidable enough to rebury her as the mother of the commanding general.' He replied: 'It is not that I am unable to rebury her. However, while still my father's wife, my mother proved unfaithful. Without instructing me otherwise he died. To formally rebury my mother would be to deceive my deceased father. Therefore I have not dared to undertake it.' How would a son who is unwilling to deceive his deceased father betray his living ruler while acting in the capacity of a high official?"[15]

Because King Wei understood Chang-tzu's character and believed in consistency of behavior—something that Han Fei-tzu subsequently proved could be highly misleading—he was able to correctly assess the incoming reports. Naturally he overlooked the possibility that fidelity to a ruler might not weigh so heavily as duty to a deceased father, even though this was an age when ministers and generals frequently betrayed their monarchs.

Identifying and Recruiting Agents

By any functional definition of morality the army is inherently an evil enterprise because it requires people to perform perverse, violent, and inhumane acts. This implies that either psychopaths must be coerced into directed action or good men somehow be motivated to abandon social and personal constraints to do what they would otherwise abhor and deem evil. Spy work naturally falls into this category, with some of the most successful spies even being comfortable in the least desirable circumstances, situations where so-called negative talents are best exploited. However, in general reliable spies can be found only among honorable, intelligent men and women, who must be persuaded to undertake what the Chinese literati always condemned as deceitful and dishonorable. The only solution thus resides in motivation and control, as Chieh Hsüan indicated in his meditations on the term "control" in the *Ping-fa Pai-yen:*[16]

Definition: To employ the greedy and deceitful is termed "control."
  Original Text: The military is not a good affair. The talents that are advantageous are exactly those that can harm it. The martial must kill, the courageous must hate, the wise must be deceitful, and strategists must exercise forbearance. The military cannot cast aside the martial, courageous, wise, or strategists, so it cannot abandon hatred, killing, deceit, and forbearance. Thus if those who excel in control employ these capabilities but eliminate the evil aspects, harvest the profits but impede the harms, then everything under Heaven will become a resource for the military. Enemies can be summoned, invaders pacified, brigands used, and the distant employed. It all lies in control, that's all.
  Explanation: If one simply gains their allegiance through material incentives but lacks deep plans and farsighted thoughts to control them, then the warriors of the Three Armies will either be arrogant or lax. Thus there are five ways to control them: First, Virtue, the armies of Emperors Yü and Yi. Second, public spirit, the armies of Kings T'ang and Wu. Third, righteousness, the armies of the hegemons Dukes Huan and Wen. Fourth, administration, the armies of Sun-tzu and Wu-tzu. Fifth, authority, the armies of Ssu-ma Yi and Ts'ao Ts'ao. Although their employment differs, they are still unified in being able to manipulate human talent.
  Moreover, there is control in the realm of the formless. The first is termed *ch'i:* When the ruler's *ch'i* is overflowing, the men

dare not have any rebellious intentions. Second, strategic power: When the army's strategic power is flourishing, the warriors dare not have any traitorous thoughts. These are matters of control found in a commander's complete achievement, not what just deep planning and foresighted thoughts are able to attain. Thus when the general's *ch'i* is not flourishing, he need not take command. When the army's strategic power is not flourishing, it need not be sent forth on campaign.

Even though Chieh Hsüan's general solution for the martial dilemma was control, his thoughts represent the final development of the tradition and perhaps an unfounded optimism. Somewhat earlier, much in the tradition of the *Wu-tzu* and the retainers found among powerful Warring States nobles, in the Sung dynasty Hsü Tung advocated recruiting men of every conceivable talent and employing them in accord with their skills, however despicable. Moreover, he made the remarkable point—astounding within the context of China's entrenched bureaucratic government and values of his era—that the normal method of selection and appointment, emphasizing the civil skills of language, literature, study, and disputation, automatically excluded men with martial talent and the courage to undertake and complete dangerous military missions:

In selecting men the present age focuses upon extensive learning and ignores specialized skills. This is not a good method. In contrast, the military finds it advantageous to employ men according to their strengths and weaknesses. Accordingly, those good at comforting others are not employed in the urgency of combat for fear that they will exhaust themselves but lack courage.[17] Those who excel in defense are not employed in mounting assaults for fear that they will be slow and not fierce. The crafty should not be employed in decisionmaking for fear that they will be indecisive. The recklessly courageous should not be employed in planning against the enemy for fear that they will regard them too lightly.

Employ the truly cruel in combat, the decisively courageous in assaults, and the profoundly resolute and stubborn-natured in occupying the passes and ravines. The petty-minded but greedy should not be employed in guarding stores and supplies. You can adopt the words of the wise and the adroitly decisive. The agile should be employed to entice a response from the enemy. The firm and strong-willed should be employed in the front. The fluent and loquacious should be employed to work as spies. Those good at filching things like rats and snatching things like dogs should be dispatched to steal the enemy's signals and investigate the enemy. Those who speak foully and curse a lot should be employed to slander, deprecate, and undermine the enemy. Those with unorthodox talents and unique knowledge should be employed to discuss future events. Those who have profound knowledge and are broad-minded should be employed to settle the masses. Those marked by surpassing strength and great power should be employed to open the way and cut through dense growth. Those who excel at erecting fortifications suitable to the terrain should be employed to measure trees and construct palisades.

Employ the timid and fearful in forwarding equipment. Employ the old and weak in preparing cookfires and wells. Those familiar with mountains and streams, who can select the advantages of high and low, streams and springs, should be employed to carefully investigate the terrain's configuration. Those who speak about portents and fabricate sayings, who excel at elucidating the mind of Heavenly ghosts and spirits, at invoking the mandate of Heaven, should be employed to raise a ruckus to delude the masses and thus move the enemy's hearts. Those who excel at selecting strategic configurations of terrain, the easy and difficult, who know both the major roads and minor bypaths for coming and going, should be employed to establish supply routes.

Those who use unorthodox language and loquacious discourse, who can inflate the vacuous and amplify greatness, should be employed to shake and flourish the army's awesomeness and virtue. Those whose ears and eyes are perceptive and sensitive, who can clandestinely investigate the enemy's true situation, should be employed to watch for villainy and artifice. The talented who are good at writing should be placed in charge of the documents and dispatches. Those knowledgeable about the sun, moon, five planets, blessings, and calamities should be made officers for calendrical matters. Those who excel at interpreting the auspiciousness and inauspiciousness of the winds and clouds should be made atmospheric officers. Those who understand the intricacies of portentous date calculation should be appointed officers in charge of selecting appropriate days for action. Those versed in prognostication by tortoise and milfoil should be made officers for divination. Even though these last four classes of officers all derive their prognostications from experience and embody predictions through *yin* and *yang*, they should be kept from confusing each other. Esteem any predictions in which they all concur.

There should also be at least twenty medical personnel, appropriately increased in accord with the army's numerical strength.

The number of veterinarians should be similarly calculated. When the commanding general weighs those with penetrating talents, he need determine only whether they can be employed in consultations or not. Thus, although there are both good and evil among the masses in our army, no one will ever be discarded. Since there will thus be no disaffection, when the army moves, it will achieve its objectives.[18]

Although relatively few personnel are entrusted with intelligence and covert operations, they clearly must have particularized skills that enable them to succeed in their missions.

Premised upon historical justifications, the *Ts'ui-wei Pei-cheng Lu* of the succeeding dynasty continued this thrust by encouraging a dynamic approach to ferreting out the unique talents necessary for spies and military professionals in a chapter entitled "Selecting Officers":

I once read in the thirteenth and last chapter of Sun-tzu's book that the wisest should be spies. "When the Shang arose, Yi Chih was in the Hsia. When the Chou arose, Lü Ya was in the Shang." Now the kings of the Shang and Chou assuredly were granted the Mandate of Heaven, for otherwise how could Yi Yin and the T'ai Kung have brought about the rise and fall of these states? Thus in the method for employing spies do not be troubled that bravos have not arrived, but the departure of bravos is sufficient cause for worry. Do not regard heroes failing to give their allegiance a matter of urgency for the army, but their departure to be a grave concern in the matter of close assistants. Even though the Hsia had not yet perished, once Yi Yin departed it succumbed. Even though the Chou had not yet arisen, when the T'ai Kung went there it flourished. Thus we know that the retention and departure of heroes and bravos determine the good or ill fortune of the empire and countries. Our present urgency must be upon this, and not on that.

Now famous mountains and great rivers are where superlative talents gather, while steep precipices and lofty mountain peaks are where the spirits descend. When the penultimate day arrives, somewhere in the mundane world there will certainly be eminent talents and outstanding fellows. However, their dreams have not yet taken form, nor have diviners yet discerned them, for they dwell among the poor and lowly, amid the common culture of the villages and lanes, or are hidden among the farmers, merchants, husbandry men, physicians, and prognosticators. Can you net them in through the examination system? They do not excel at the Confucian compositions needed to pass. Can you entice them with profits and salary? They do not follow the official routes to eminence. May they be found among the staff in military camps? They were not born amid fortifications and formations. The farmers of San-ch'eng T'ung-po, the wood merchants who gather firewood in Luo-yüan, the lofty recluses of Liu-an's distant peaks, the merchants of Yang-chien, and all others of this sort harbor dreams of outstanding accomplishments, but can they work together, will they be given a chance?

It is not that they do not want to be employed in the world, to exhaust their hard-won abilities, but that the upper ranks have no method for summoning them, while the lower ranks lack steps by which they can advance. Within the court there are no techniques for searching them out, while outside there are no doors by which they might enter. This is why the court must widely bring men in without being deterred by the distance. The Secretariat must exert itself in listening and gathering, not being put off by the earliness or lateness of the day. Circuit supervisors in the prefectures and districts must concentrate upon recommendations, neglecting neither the insignificant nor the lowly.

There are eight doors: First, "officeholders," referring to those buried in the lowest ranks, unable to shake themselves free. Second, "those without offices," normally found in rustic circumstances who are unable to advance themselves. Third, "later generations," the sons and grandsons of generals unable to distinguish themselves. Fourth, "bravos," leaders from around the rivers and lakes, the outstanding among the mountains.[19] Fifth, "tears from offenses," those who once offended the laws [in some minor way] and seek to escape from the criminal registry. Sixth, "criminals," whose talents and spirit surpass other men's, who carelessly offend the laws entailing corporal punishment. Seventh, "staff officers," who plot and plan and have long been buried in the regiments. Eighth, "minor clerks," who are hidden among the clerking staff and cannot become known.

The author goes on to detail the methods that might be employed to search out potentially useful men among the various corners of the ever shrinking Sung empire, such as listening to recommendations from among the various groups themselves, then testing candidates with appropriate positions to see if they can actually perform.

A second chapter somewhat later in the text, entitled "Bravos Make Spies,"[20] continues his theme by focusing upon recruiting courageous men for spy work. After opening with an identical passage about Yi Yin and the T'ai Kung, Hua Yüeh presses the argument for concentrating upon such men with further examples, no doubt because he was frustrated by the entrenched, appeasement-oriented literati currently monopolizing power.

Probably the retention or loss of the Mandate of Heaven is related to whether a state's heroes depart or remain. If you can bring in their heroes, enemy states will become impoverished by themselves. Only when the Ch'in dynasty truly lacked men could its adversaries begin to plan against it. Five times Yi Yin went to King T'ang, five times he went to King Chieh, and so acted as a minister to establish the state. Han Hsin was employed by the Han rather than Hsiang Yü, and Kao-tsu thus gained All under Heaven. Fen Juo-shui was not awarded a post by the Southern T'ang but by our Sung, enabling Emperor Yi to gain all of Chiang-nan. Probably when officers with heroic qualities are brought into the court or employed in the field, they can become loyal ministers and righteous warriors. But if they are left to the wilds, abandoned to the mountain forests, then they may become rebellious subjects and brigands. When we get them, we can realize the achievements of emperors and kings, while if the enemy gets them, they are capable of supplying effective, perverse plans.

In antiquity, sages and worthies concentrated upon seizing the minds of heroes; otherwise, assistants supplied by Heaven turned to become tools for others. Even though the Hsia had not yet perished, once Yi Yin departed it succumbed. Even though the Chou had not yet arisen, when the T'ai Kung went there it flourished. Isn't this frightening? From now on it would be appropriate to order two or three high-ranking ministers to circulate widely, to bring your generals into the Secretariat, and perspicaciously to issue invitations to gather the talented in, thereby keeping them from being banished to grassy wilds or neglected in suburban fields. When you select outstanding men, do not shy away from granting them strategic power or hesitate to assign them minor duties. Then you will see eminent men from Hsiang-huai, the bravos from among the rivers and lakes, the superlative swordsmen of Ch'u, the fishermen of the misty waves, rumors accumulating like the fog, and the courage of men banded together—all will be sought out and prepared for our selection. This is what is referred to as bravos becoming spies.

By the Southern Sung the T'ai Kung had again fallen from the lofty position accorded him by the T'ang, when he was honored as the martial patron, while an enervated Confucianism mouthed by an effete, self-serving literati largely dominated the court's political discussions and bureaucratic methods and objectives. The need for spies to penetrate the north, already lost to the Mongols, as well as the empire's fringe areas, was apparent, yet largely ignored in favor of ordinary reports forwarded by local and circulating government officials who had little incentive to identify trouble, to contravene the prevailing political climate.[21] One solution would have been to recruit more dynamic personnel for the government in general, and spies in particular, for whom many difficulties would loom. Although individual military commanders reportedly employed spies and reconnaissance personnel during this distressed period, there seems to have been no systematic effort to gather critical intelligence.

Finally, in the context of talent and agents the late Ming dynasty *Ping-fa Pai-yen* enjoys the distinction of being the only military text to advocate the recruitment and employment of women in clandestine operations. (Although the early historical writings are replete with examples of women in every covert role imaginable, there was no theorizing about their talents and suitable missions, no doubt because of traditional Confucian prejudices.) In this regard Chieh Hsüan's definition for women is illuminating:

Definition: Those who are able to act as intimate agents are termed "women."

Original Text: The great generals of antiquity sometimes relied on the pliancy of women. In civil matters they were employed to give pleasure to the enemy and amuse invaders, in the martial realm they were used to wage war and drive wagons. To realize opportunities, respond to tactical changes, overcome difficulty, and extricate forces from danger, they are always advantageous.

Explanation: Many of the ancient strategists relied upon female pliancy, even though it was not something that great generals were inclined to esteem. However, when commanding generals employed people it was like a physician prescribing medicine. Medicinal potions blend every sort of ingredient—animal, mineral and vegetable—nothing necessary ever being neglected. Since male villains and bravados are accepted in the army, how much more so should those who can penetrate deep secrets, search out hidden ambushes, or act skillfully as secret agents? How can you not concentrate on collecting and nurturing them in order to prepare against some unexpected need to dispatch them as part of your strategy? Furthermore, segmenting off the enemy's Army of the Right in order to buttress your own army's strategic power and relying on internal assistance in order to establish a meritorious name are what an intelligent, exceptional woman can accomplish. However, despite searching, few ancient examples are visible and discussing them in the context of history is blasphemous. Although I have explained the meaning and provided some examples below, speaking about such agents potentially harms them.

Examples: Wen Chung and Fan Li [in the state of Yüeh] secretly plotted and by introducing Hsi Shih and Cheng Tan turned the state of Wu into a fish pond. Marquis Ying employed an unorthodox scheme to steal the military tally of authority [through the ruler's favorite concubine] and thereby relieved the siege of Chao. Meng Ch'ang-chün presented a fur robe; Chang Yi offered bribes; Li K'o had his son intermarry with the Jung barbarians and thereby obtained experience in crossbow use that allowed the Han to extinguish the Jung. They all gained their power through female agents. Even if great generals do no rely upon them to stupefy their enemies, they must still be cautious and emphasize internal defenses against them.

China's covert practices, from ancient times through this very moment, have systematically employed and aggressively exploited women, as well as frequently adopted apparently feminine-oriented (passive) policies. However, apart from their role in debauching rivals and enemies, with the exception of this strong statement, their role in gathering information received only minimal, often grudging, recognition in the military texts. No doubt this reflects the literati's prejudice against military measures in general and clandestine practices in specific, as well as extreme embarrassment at the thought of employing women in such despicable endeavors, even though they were frequently married off for precisely such purposes and court intrigues often turned upon their effectiveness.

Operational Methods and Agent Control

With the flourishing of military thought in the T'ang dynasty and subsequent efforts in the Sung to compile the military classics and create integrated compendiums of tactical teachings, strategists began to address the question of how spies might be employed rather than simply categorizing and describing them. Although many martial writings contain materials on their functions within a military context (which will be seen in the chapters on military intelligence and topography that follow), only Hsü Tung seems to have pondered their nonmilitary utilization in two chapters of his *Hu-ling Ching,* "Employing Spies" and "Deceiving the Enemy." Commencing with his reflections on the *Hsing-jen* of the Chou dynasty, "Employing Spies" proceeds to delineate eight methods for employing covert agents.[22] Although the first two apply exclusively to military situations, several reflect fully developed counterintelligence practices that convert enemy agents to useful assets, whether knowingly or not, while the remainder are designed to acquire essential knowledge by subverting enemy officials:

The official described in the ancient *Rites of Chou* who traveled about the feudal states and reported back to the king on their plans was actually a spy.[23] Thus Sages have always valued the Tao of spycraft. If you would utilize the army to determine victory, you must also employ agents. If you use agents to fathom internal affairs, you must be secretive. Apart from the very wisest, who can attain this?

In general, a spy's activities depend upon the situation. There are eight basic techniques.

First, when your troops are locked in a standoff with the enemy at the border, pretend to be tired, in difficulty, and fearful. Clandestinely leak out word that you will generously provide gifts to the enemy's favorites so as to attain what you seek there. Next, dispatch emissaries with jade, silk, boys and girls, carriages, superlative horses, and subtle adornments to apparently seek a reconciliation. When you observe the enemy becoming arrogant and insulting, secretly select and dispatch elite troops by several routes, having them press their advance both early and late in order to exploit the enemy's laxity and negligence.

Second, when you capture enemy prisoners, leak false plans to them and secretly allow them to escape, thereby causing the enemy to trust in their validity. Since your actions will differ, you will thus be employing the enemy's soldiers as your agents.

Third, when enemy agents come to spy on you, pretend not to realize it, instead allowing them to acquire information about a fake plan. Thereafter unexpectedly attack their forces, thereby turning their agents around so that they speak as if they were your own.

Fourth, when enemy agents come, bribe them generously to compel them to betray their missions, thereby spying on the enemy while converting their agents into your own.

Fifth, when engaged in battle with the enemy, feign a minor defeat and urgently withdraw the army into a deep fortress, displaying a terrified countenance. Then select men whose speech is rustic and blunt, of little knowledge or thought, to act as emissaries to the enemy. Have them magnify and exaggerate your army's flourishing strength, causing the enemy to know that they are agents. They will certainly conclude that you are afraid since you have sent agents to speak boldly and spy upon them. After they have departed, mobilize your unorthodox troops to follow on with a surprise attack. This is employing visible agents as spies.

Sixth, when there are favorites in the enemy's court, have your confidants ply their families with gold and jewels so that they might clandestinely learn the enemy's secret affairs. This is employing court favorites as agents.

Seventh, to subvert the enemy's strategists, secretly bribe the ruler's confidants with gold and gifts to have them slander them in the court. Then appropriately respond to the slanders from outside the state, causing the ruler and his strategists to grow mutually suspicious, instigating them to ruin and harm each other. This is using slanderers as agents.

Eighth, seek out those that the enemy trusts with their affairs, copiously satisfy their desires, and then secretly ferret out information about the enemy's movements and rest, words and speech. This is employing local people as agents.

Accordingly, we know that agents are the critical essence of the military theorists. But without sagacious wisdom and moral worth, one cannot employ agents. Thus the Tao for employing agents lies in the subtle, secretive, clandestine, and submerged, all of which have long been stressed by the best generals.

The next chapter, "Deceiving the Enemy," continues Sun-tzu's thought on the critical importance of deceiving the enemy, a thrust that Hsü Tung envisioned as fundamental, as well as the reason for counterintelligence efforts. It expounds two techniques designed to spread disinformation through converting enemy personnel and victimizing false defectors:

Warfare is the Tao of deception. Even Heaven and Earth, ghosts and spirits cannot fathom the myriad changes of condensing and expanding. Thus there are two methods for deceiving the enemy.

When an enemy emissary comes to you, privately treat him as if he were a powerful minister, generously plying him with treasures and showing him great gifts. Converting his doubts with such manifest sincerity is the technique for tying up emissaries. When you have thus convinced him to believe you, when he has no further doubts, you can then delude him by apparently leaking state secrets. Contrary to the enemy's original intent, you will secretly entangle their estimations, yet they will never doubt their veracity. Then, in accord with the information thus passed on to the enemy's ruler, to encourage an internal response show that you are mobilizing troops at the time and place designated. But when the moment arrives, act unexpectedly, employing your elite troops to pound their vacuities and press them from outside. This is the first technique.

Select a courageous and daring officer as an attendant, then suddenly pretend to be angry and have him beaten with a bamboo whip until blood is visible. Afterward, secretly let him sneak away to the enemy. In addition, imprison his wife and children so that when he hears about it he will be angry and certainly transmit any secret affairs he formerly heard to the enemy, speaking about your attack at a certain place and time. You should then act as foretold at the right moment, but then secretly send forth elite troops to strike where unexpected. This is the second technique. These are both examples of employing the unorthodox to conquer, the essential Tao of the military. You can never be too knowledgeable about them!

The second case again shows how rulers might ruthlessly exploit their officers and revisits the question of volition and consciousness in the definition of "expendable agents" because Hsü Tung never implies any knowledge or willingness on the hapless victim's part, unlike Yao Li, King Ho-lü's second assassin, who may have been the inspiration for this method. According to Sun-tzu's terminology anyone so manipulated would certainly qualify as a "dead agent," someone provided with false information deliberately sacrificed in the ongoing effort to deceive the enemy, to gain a critical battlefield advantage through misdirection and false expectation. However, the first case is not simply a classic "turned agent"—someone who consciously chooses to work for the enemy—but rather a diplomat who becomes mesmerized by riches and profits, who is manipulated into readily believing whatever he apparently manages to learn, as well as might be told. This sort of conversion thus coheres with the broader definition that allows for duping enemy agents, for simply employing enemy agents without any shift in their allegiance or loyalties.

7

Secrecy and Countermeasures

CLIMATES IN WHICH SPIES PROLIFERATE naturally stimulate countermeasures to thwart their efforts. China proved no exception, with the military writers constantly warning of the urgent necessity for secrecy. Some states made it a matter of government policy. Astute generals required virtual silence, formlessness, and strict control in their encampments and when out on campaign to conceal their plans, strength, and preparations, as well as prevent dishonest practices, profiteering, and desertion. For example, within the context of strategic planning and tactical execution, the *Six Secret Teachings* advises:

> Strategic power is exercised in accord with the enemy's movements. Changes stem from the confrontation between the two armies. Unorthodox and orthodox tactics are produced from the inexhaustible resources of the mind. Thus the greatest affairs are not discussed and the employment of troops is not spoken about. Moreover, words that discuss ultimate affairs are not worth listening to. The employment of troops is not so definitive as to be visible. They go suddenly, they come suddenly. Only someone who can exercise sole control, without being governed by other men, is a military weapon.
>
> If your plans are heard about, the enemy will make counterplans. If you are perceived, they will plot against you. If you are known, they will put you in difficulty. If you are fathomed, they will endanger you.
>
> In military affairs nothing is more important than certain victory. In employing the army nothing is more important than ob-

scurity and silence. In movement nothing is more important than the unexpected. In planning nothing is more important than not being knowable.[1]

Sun-tzu, a prominent advocate of secrecy, advised making the army formless to preclude the enemy from fathoming intentions. An ignorant enemy being compelled to spread their defenses, vulnerable points are immediately created:

The pinnacle of military deployment approaches the formless. If it is formless then even the deepest spy cannot discern it or the wise make plans against it.[2] . . .

It is essential for a general to be tranquil and obscure, upright and self-disciplined, and able to stupefy the eyes and ears of the officers and troops, keeping them ignorant. He alters his management of affairs and changes his strategies to keep other people from recognizing them. He shifts his position and traverses indirect routes to keep other people from being able to anticipate him.[3] . . .

Thus if I determine the enemy's disposition of forces while I have no perceptible form, I can concentrate my forces while the enemy is fragmented. If we are concentrated into a single force while he is fragmented into ten, then we attack him with ten times his strength. Thus we are many and the enemy is few. If we can attack his few with our many, those whom we engage in battle will be severely constrained.

The location where we will engage the enemy must not become known to them. If it is not known, then the positions they must prepare to defend will be numerous. If the positions the enemy prepares to defend are numerous, then the forces we will engage will be few. Thus if they prepare to defend the front, to the rear there will be few men. If they defend the rear, in the front there will be few. If they prepare to defend the left flank, then on the right there will be few men. If they prepare to defend the right flank, then on the left there will be few men. If there is no position left undefended, then there will not be any place with more than a few. The few are the ones who prepare against others; the many are the ones who make others prepare against them.[4]

The later military classics echoed his concern, often in almost transcendent terms:

Control of the army is as secretive as the depths of Earth, as dark and obscure as the heights of Heaven, and is given birth from the nonexistent. Therefore it must be opened. The great is not frivolous, the small is not vast.[5]

The *Military Pronouncements* states: "For the general's plans one wants secrecy." When the general's plans are secret, treacherous impulses are thwarted. If the general's plans leak out, the army will not be able to effect a strategic disposition of power. If external agents spy out internal affairs, the disaster that will befall the army cannot be controlled.[6]

Even the military chapter of the Former Han, markedly Taoist *Huai-nan Tzu* espoused formlessness as the best defense against being fathomed:

Among the spiritual nothing is more honored than Heaven, among strategic power nothing more conducive than earth, among movements nothing more urgent than time, and among employments nothing more advantageous than man. Now these four are the trunk and branches of the army, but they must rely upon the Tao before they can be implemented and attain unified employment.

Now advantages of Earth overcome seasons of Heaven; skillful attacks overcome advantages of Earth; strategic power conquers men. Those who rely on Heaven can be confused, who rely on Earth can be constrained, who rely on time can be pressed, and who rely on men can be deluded. Now benevolence, courage, trust, and purity are attractive human attributes, but the courageous can be enticed, the benevolent can be seized, the trusting can be deceived, and the pure are easily plotted against. If the army's commander displays any one of these attributes, he will be captured. From this perspective it is clear that armies control victory through the patterns of the Tao, not through relying upon the talents of worthies. Only those without form cannot be ensnared. For this reason the Sage conceals himself in the originless so that his emotions cannot be perceived. He moves in the formless so that his deployments cannot be fathomed. Without tactics or appearance, he acts appropriately. Without name or shape, he changes and creates an image. Even among those with acute vision, who can spy out his nature?[7]

The late Ming dynasty *Ping-fa Pai-yen* even offered an operational definition of secrecy, examining the implications for personal behavior and demeanor:

Definition: Not to speak about anything to inappropriate persons is termed "secrecy."

Original Text: The affairs of one person are not leaked to a second person; what is to be implemented tomorrow is not leaked to anyone today. Carrying this to the minutest extreme, be careful not to leave even the space of a hair. When secrecy in meetings needs to be preserved, be wary about betraying the information in speech. When secrecy needs to be preserved in speech, be wary about betraying it in your demeanor.[8] When secrecy needs to be preserved in your demeanor, be wary about betraying it in your spirit and emotions. When secrecy needs to be preserved in your spirit and emotions, be wary about betraying it in your dreams and sleep. When you undertake an action, conceal the beginning; when you employ someone, gag his mouth. However, when something can be spoken about, you need not guard against being the first to reveal it so as to show other people that they are trusted. When such sincerity is extended over time, what is not secret will provide the means to establish the secrecy of what is.

Explanation: One who fills the role of general has a stomach and belly [chief of staff], thighs [assistants], ears and eyes [intelligence agents], claws and teeth [elite warriors, enforcers], hands and feet [messengers], and blood and pulse [various officers].[9] They are all parts of a single body. If I am secretive about all aspects of my single body, how does it differ from being secretive about myself? But among my officers and men there are those who understand affairs and those who do not; those who are circumspect in speech and those who are not; those with scintillating wisdom, those without it; those who compete for achievement, those who do not. If I fail to carefully select them and warily take precautions, others will gain control over my men and some may then turn and impede our affairs. How will this differ from divulging something myself? Thus one technique for secrecy is to keep secret what ought to be secret, but not that which need not be secret.

Example: One who acts as a general cannot dwell by himself when the army halts or move alone when on the march. Plans cannot come from him alone, actions cannot be undertaken solely by him. By being cautious about one's associates, it can be managed. To conduct secret affairs, first seek out reliable persons.

The *Yi Chou-shu* wisely advised against employing the loquacious because they may inadvertently leak plans, commenting that "disaster and good fortune lie in what is preserved in secrecy." However, the Han dynasty *Shuo Yüan* summarized much verbiage on security issues by simply saying, "If you do not want people to hear about something, nothing is better than not speaking of it,"[10] and added that "plans that leak out will lack achievement."[11] Accordingly, the *Six Secret Teachings* warned: "Those who are unguarded in their discussions can be clandestinely listened to."[12]

Apart from generally emphasizing secrecy in all activities, three concrete steps were widely implemented: strict constraints on movement, the employment of secret means of communication, and deceptive measures. Prior to embarking on a campaign and whenever the army was out in the field, airtight security had to be implemented, completely prohibiting the passage of unauthorized personnel and thwarting any attempts by the enemy to infiltrate spies among the troops disguised in appropriate uniforms. Sun-tzu stated, "On the day the government mobilizes the army, close the passes, destroy all tallies, and do not allow their emissaries to pass through."[13] Wei Liao-tzu added, "When itinerant persuaders and spies have no means to gain entrance, this is the technique for rectifying discussions."[14]

Since it is evident from the historical writings that spies still frequently gained access to military encampments and acquired vital information, the imposition of strict security measures became necessary. The *Ping-fa Pai-yen* encapsulated these concerns under the rubric of "caution":

Definition: Being careful in every aspect is termed "caution."

Original Text: There isn't a single moment when the army's employment is not dangerous; therefore, you need to be cautious at all times. Enter the army [to assume command] as if there were spies all about; when crossing the border, be as strict as when approaching battle. Whenever you obtain or seize something, make certain no harm is entailed; when you encounter natural obstacles of terrain, you must search about for villains. When emissaries approach from the enemy, ponder their plans, when you go forth, make calculations. Being cautious in advancing the army is the pinnacle of the Tao.

Explanation: When the ancients deployed their formations, they always consulted the Heavenly mansions and eight trigrams, so extreme was their caution. Thus they illuminated and reacted to everything about them. When the ancients advanced the army, they invariably had close, trusted associates act as their eyes and ears and burly relatives for their bodyguards. Moreover, they had wise and courageous men who were adept at handling the masses act as their "feathers and wings," so extensive was their caution.[15]

Within the army racing about on horses was prohibited, as was wild shouting and horseplay. Preventing them from wandering about was the height of caution. They quieted their voices and breath and undertook investigations in accord with affairs. Through investigations they realized the doubtful, through doubt they achieved preparation. Through preparation they could be employed, which is the height of caution. They made their concerns and contemplations numerous.

The establishment of laws gives birth to caution; sufficiency in material resources gives birth to caution; severity in commands gives birth to caution; numerous doubts give birth to caution. Thus caution depends upon laws, relies upon materials, is completed through commands, and arises from doubt.

Example: Caution, this one word, truly is the first essential in controlling the army and confronting the enemy. None of the great ministers or generals of antiquity ever violated it. Those who hope to imitate the achievements of antiquity's famous generals must first learn to emulate their caution.

The many Ch'in dynasty camp regulations apparently preserved in the *Wei Liao-tzu* underscore the strictness of the army's methods:

The Central, Left, Right, Forward, and Rear Armies all have their segmented terrain, each surrounded on all four sides by temporary walls, with no passage or communication among them permitted.

The general has his segmented terrain, the regimental commander has his segmented terrain, and the company commander has his segmented terrain. They should all construct ditches and sluices, and make the orders blocking communications explicit, so that it is impossible for someone who is not a member of the company of a hundred to pass through. If someone who is not a member of the company of a hundred enters, the commander should execute him. If he fails to execute him, he will share the offense with him.

Along the roads crisscrossing the encampment set up administrative posts every 120 paces. Measure the men and the terrain. The road posts should be within sight of each other. Prohibit crossing over the roads and clear them. If a soldier does not have a tally or token issued by a general or other commanding officer, he cannot pass through. Wood gatherers, fodder seekers, and animal herders all form and move in squads of five. If they are not moving in squads of five, they cannot cross through. If an officer does not have a token, if the soldiers are not in squads of five, the guards at the crossing gates should execute them. If anyone oversteps the demarcation lines, execute him. Thus if within the army no one contravenes orders or violates the prohibitions, then without there will not be any that are not caught.[16]

The Sung *Hu-ling Ching* advised two measures for camp security. First, observation towers should be erected some hundred paces outside the camp to watch for enemy activity and signal with flags to indicate the presence and direction of enemy movement. (They should also report force size, type, activity, and speed.[17]) Second, roving security patrols should be established from among the "courageous soldiers knowledgeable about the mountains, rivers, springs, and wells." Each patrol's movements should be confined to a designated area well outside the camp, and they must undertake responsibility for "seizing living spies dispatched by the enemy." To preclude the loss of vital information during interrogation should they be captured by enemy reconnaissance patrols, they were kept ignorant about their own troop dispositions and defensive measures.[18]

Whenever a campaign army penetrated enemy territory, these issues became even more acute, particularly if the area was unfamiliar and reconnaissance efforts less than effective. A primary concern would be anticipating and defending against sudden attacks masked by the terrain's configuration. "Defending Against the Enemy," another *Hu-ling Ching* chapter, expanded the tactics advanced by the *Six Secret Teachings* when a force was besieged or surrounded,[19] as well as the operational principles found in the *Ssu-ma Fa* and *Military Methods* governing deep penetration of enemy territory:

Whenever you have penetrated deep within the enemy's borders, if all is silent and you do not encounter a solitary person, in order to defend against ambushes you should not carelessly move about. You should carefully investigate the cloud formations in all four directions, feed the horses, encourage your warriors, have them assume a crouching defensive position, and wait. As soon as night falls you should deploy strong, courageous warriors as defensive forces all around outside the camp. You should also establish ambush forces with powerful crossbows and facile shields and array numerous drum sites. Beating the drums will signal a sudden perimeter assault.

If the enemy attacks the defensive forces, then the main camp should send forth light troops to support them. If they assault the main camp, then the defensive forces should attack them from all four sides while your main forces maintain a solid deployment, awaiting any changes that might arise. If the enemy retreats, you should pursue but not press them. The main camp can also follow on and advance further inland.

Naturally the use of scouts and reconnaissance forces (discussed subsequently) should never be neglected.

Communications

Communications being vital to the army's organization and mission, the *Ping-fa Pai-yen* pondered its nature and implications under the term "communications":

Definition: To transmit information where desired is termed "communication."

Original Text: When an army maneuvers without any method of communication, its segmented forces will not be able to recombine; its distant units will be unable to respond. Allowing forces to be obstructed and cut off is the Tao of defeat. However, if your communications are not secret, on the contrary they will become part of the enemy's calculations. Thus there are such things as the special golden signal banners, swift post horses, arrows symbolizing authority, and signal fires and smoke in order to report extremely urgent matters.

When two armies meet, you should establish clandestine watchwords. When a thousand kilometers apart, you should employ a simple letter, use unformed words, invisible writing, and even nonpaper strips. The messenger will not know about them, and if someone else obtains them there will not be any visible trace. It is spiritual, spiritual! If you are cut off by the enemy, your line of march severed far off where no one can reach, then you must communicate through subtle techniques.

Explanation: Communicating information is the army's most essential activity. However, every army's orders are different, so the main point is keeping the enemy from becoming aware of them while informing your own army. Although communication is the most secret activity, there are only three essentials: terseness, convenience, and astuteness. You should employ selected officers who are close confidants, who are courageous and daring, and specially train those who have agility and speed, whose minds are strong and bodies robust, several hundred or more, to be employed in going back and forth to ensure communications. Select these couriers and make their rewards generous. Be cautious about their missions, be diligent in their employment, for then your communications will be timely and responses rapid, with few failures.

Examples: Communication is a great achievement. The magnitude of its employment is seen in the signal mounds, its skill in the extremes of carrier pigeons.

Clearly by the end of the late Ming numerous methods of transport were available, including post horses, as were ingenious techniques such as invisible ink that are unfortunately little discussed in the military compendiums and can only be guessed at.

Generally speaking, secrecy might be achieved through verbal communications memorized and carried by messengers; codes, which seem not to have been much used in pre-Ch'ing China, although substitution charts or one-use pads could certainly have been created; prearranged secret systems of tallies or markers; various types of hidden messages, whether physically disguised or embedded in innocuous texts; and fragmented written communications. Verbal communications entrusted to reliable individuals were no doubt the most common, but also most readily compromised should the messenger be captured, killed, or simply bribed for his information. Since various types of symbolic tallies split in half were employed to signify power and confirm the authenticity of written communications—forged letters and documents having a long, effective history in China—it was a simple step to create more systematic sets that might unequivocally convey predetermined information.[20] Although simplistic and therefore limited in data capacity, something like the array described in the *Six Secret Teachings* may have been employed in the Warring States and thereafter:

The ruler and his generals have a system of secret tallies, altogether consisting of eight grades: for signifying a great victory over the enemy, one foot long; for destroying the enemy's army and killing their general, nine inches long; for forcing the surrender of the enemy's walls and capturing the town, eight inches long; for driving the enemy back and reporting deep penetration, seven inches long; for alerting the masses to prepare for stalwart defensive measures, six inches long; for requesting supplies and additional soldiers, five inches long; for signifying the army's defeat and the general's death, four inches long; for signifying the loss of all advantages and the army's surrender, three inches long.[21]

The T'ai Kung's measures for preserving the secrecy and validity of these tallies merit note: "Detain all those who bring in and present tallies, and if the information from the tally should leak out, execute all those who heard and told about it. These eight tallies, which only the ruler and general should secretly know, provide a technique for covert communication that will not allow outsiders to know the true situation. Accordingly even though the enemy have the wisdom of a sage, no one will comprehend their significance."[22] He also advocated the use of fragmented missives to convey more extensive information in relative security:

Whenever you have secret affairs and major considerations, letters should be employed rather than tallies. The ruler sends a letter to the general, the general uses a letter to query the ruler. The letters are composed in one unit, then divided. They are sent out in three parts, with only one person knowing the contents. "Divided" means it is separated into three parts. "Sent out in three parts, with only one person knowing" means there are three messengers, each carrying one part, and when the three are compared together, only then does one know the contents. This is referred to as a "secret letter." Even if the enemy have the wisdom of a Sage, they will not be able to recognize the contents.[23]

Of course the T'ai Kung assumed that only one of the messengers might be captured—which would of course render the other two parts useless even to the intended receiver—and that every nefarious measure would be employed to conceal the letter or the message itself, as mentioned in the introductory section.

In a section entitled "Tzu Yen" ("Verification Through Characters") the *Wu-ching Tsung-yao* cited an old method that essentially expanded the T'ai Kung's limited, length-based tallies:

According to the old methods, whenever some affair needed to be transmitted through documents that were passed back and forth, it was necessary to guard against leaks. If confidants were employed to transmit the information, not only did it labor them, but it was also necessary to take precautions against human emotions changing and rebelling. To issue orders or constrain the army there were forty items, each to be secretly designated by a single character. These were for requesting bows, arrows, swords, armor, spears and pennants, pots and screens, horses, clothes and grants, foodstuffs and provisions, grass and fodder, carts and oxen, boats, equipment for mounting sieges and defending against them, increasing the number of troops, shifting the encampment, advancing the army, withdrawing the army, and assuming a solid defensive position.

Also to report that the enemy had not yet been seen, had been seen arriving, that the enemy is numerous, few, an equal match, increasing their forces, shifting their encampment, advancing their army, withdrawing their army, or maintaining a solid defense. And to report having besieged the enemy's fortifications, lifted a siege against the enemy, being besieged by the enemy, the enemy lifting their siege, not being victorious in battle, winning a great victory, gaining a minor victory, the general and officers surrendering, the general and officers rebelling, the officers and troops falling ill, the regional commander being ill, and a significant conquest over the enemy.

All of them would be sequentially correlated with the individual characters of an old-style, forty-character poem selected because it was free of duplications. When the commanding general received his order to go forth and mount an attack or siege, he and his subordinate generals would each have a copy. When there was something to report or a reply to send, the appropriate character would be sought out in an ordinary letter or document and marked [with a solid circle]. When the report was acknowledged or the request granted, the same character would then be written or similarly found in a text and marked. If it was not granted, then it would be marked with an open circle. This kept the masses from understanding.

Essentially a one-time pad with a pre-scripted content, it represented one approach to encoding information. Assuming the forty items were strictly apportioned in standard sequence, the two parties would merely need to know the poem and silently recite it to themselves to determine the appropriate character. A simple variant, undiscussed here, would be to scramble the forty items before assigning them to a poem, thereby preventing anyone from guessing the contents even if they discovered the character and happened to know the poem. The transmission could be further concealed by burying the character at a predetermined position, thereby obviating any need to mark and thus draw attention to it. Fixed phrases or allusions could similarly be embodied within ordinary communications at specified count positions or appended to innocuous documents, such as a scenic scroll covered with poems. However, as David Kahn insightfully points out in his monumental work, until numeric codes (such as the nineteenth-century telegraphic code) were assigned to the individual characters, the nature of the writing system largely precluded ciphers.[24] Character substitution charts could of course be constructed—and no doubt were on a limited basis, especially for private, rather than official, use—but would invariably require cumbersome character substitution. Book codes would equally have been possible, indicating characters through page, line, and position numbers, but there doesn't seem to be any evidence for their use in either the historical writings or military texts.

Ordinary communications might also be couched in obscure language, written at length on paper, or conveyed by messenger unobtrusively, but the most critical form—the issuance and conveyance of battlefield commands to troops deployed in the field and the heat of battle—required the exact opposite: visibility and clarity. From antiquity China's forces were expertly directed by signal flags, drums, and gongs, and therefore early in the Spring and Autumn period had already long been capable of segmented and articulated action. Thus generals commanded rather than led, and were in fact expected to maintain control of the drums that signaled the type and speed of movement and the battle pennants that designated direction and the units that should respond to a command. To counteract the din of battle, writers from Sun-tzu on emphasized the need to multiply the drums and ensure they sounded in unison, compelling every soldier to respond. However, as their volume and clarity increased, the enemy's ability to hear and learn such commands equally benefited. A chapter entitled "Countering Leaks" in the Southern Sung *Ts'ui-wei Pei-cheng Lu* provides an overview of the problem and its solution:

I have heard that when we maintain security while the enemy leaks information, victory will always be ours. Conversely, when the enemy is secretive while we leak, victory will always be theirs. In recent years our border administration has truly been lax in this regard, and some nomadic peoples have completely adopted our army's flags and pennants, resulting in our own forces often being defeated through misperceiving nomadic units for our own. Moreover, some of these barbarian peoples are thoroughly familiar with our military organization, and our armies are constantly betraying themselves because their structure is not secret. Thus the methods for countering leaks should probably be discussed.

Now there are four methods for countering leaks. First, "summoning by signals." This refers to previously employing a green flag to direct generals and commanders, but now using green flags to summon officers and troops. Whereas formerly a white flag was employed to summon the commander in chief, now a white flag will be used to summon the divisional commanders.

Second, "flags and pennants." This refers to previously using green to signal the left flank, white the right flank, and now exchanging green and white to keep the enemy from learning the designations of my left and right armies. Whereas previously green was employed for the straight and black for the curved, now exchange the black and green to keep the enemy from knowing whether our strategic power will be deployed in straight or curved formations.

Third, "gongs and drums." Whereas the army formerly advanced to the sound of the drums and retreated to the gongs, on the contrary when the drums are now heard, it will halt. Where formerly it halted at the sound of the gongs, it will now advance to the gongs.

Fourth, "beacon fires." Whereas one torch previously signified enemy invaders and two torches a request for help, on the contrary one torch will now signal a request for help. Previously, whereas no smoke indicated the absence of incidents and smoke a warning, now on the contrary the presence of smoke will signify the absence of incidents. These are the ways to counter leaks.[25]

Whether these countermeasures would deceive the enemy or one's own troops more thoroughly may well have been problematic.

Concealment and Deception

Although the practice of deception was already prevalent in the Spring and Autumn period, to counter the increasingly effective and focused reconnaissance efforts found on Warring States battlefields and thereafter, military theorists strongly advocated its employment and commanders increasingly resorted to a wide variety of ruses, feints, and deceits. (The practice of deception is, of course, a hallmark of Chinese military thought, stemming in part from Sun-tzu's famous dictum that "warfare is the art of deception." However, to reduce Chinese warfare simply to an exercise in deception, as some uninformed Western writers have suggested, is absurd.[26]) A number of clever techniques became commonplace, stimulating a correspondingly increasing sophistication in observation methods and analysis to penetrate them. Moreover, because observers were restricted by the powers of the human eye and the vantage points they might secure, the deployment of spies also soared in the belief that plans clandestinely obtained would prove far more accurate than deductions derived from observations of partially obscured, not to mention aggressively deceitful, armies.

Given the difficulty of accurate observation, the first measure employed was concealment, whether through hiding a portion of the forces in another location, in ravines, inside tents, beneath clouds of dust or smoke, or even within deployments themselves. Its effective application may be seen in the events preliminary to Emperor Kao-tsu's famous encirclement by Hsiung-nu forces (whose resolution is more fully examined in the section on consorts):

When King Han Hsin revolted in the seventh year of the Former Han dynasty, Emperor Kao-tsu personally led the army forth to strike him. Reaching Ching-yang, Kao-tsu learned that Han Hsin was planning to attack his army in alliance with the Hsiung-nu. Enraged, the emperor dispatched emissaries to the Hsiung-nu. However, the Hsiung-nu concealed their stalwart warriors and stout horses and cattle so that all the emissaries saw were the old and weak, as well as emaciated livestock. Ten emissaries in a row came back to report that the Hsiung-nu would be easy to attack.

The emperor then had Liu Ching again go as ambassador to the Hsiung-nu, but when he returned he reported: "When two countries are about to engage in battle, they ought to diligently display their strengths [to overawe the enemy]. However, when I went out there, I saw nothing but emaciated livestock and the weak and old. This is certainly an example of wanting to display weakness while concealing troops in ambush in order to fight for advantage. I humbly believe that the Hsiung-nu cannot be attacked."

At this time the emperor's forces, more than three hundred thousand strong, had already crossed through Chü-chu and the soldiers were advancing. The emperor angrily cursed Ching, saying, "Son of the despicable Ch'i, you got your position through your tongue, yet you now wantonly use it to impede our army!" He then had him tied up and left at Kuang-wu and proceeded out.

When they reached P'ing-ch'eng, the Hsiung-nu indeed sent forth the unorthodox troops that surrounded the emperor at Pai-teng, and he only succeeded in escaping seven days later. When Emperor Kao-tsu reached Kuang-wu he pardoned Ching, saying: "I failed to heed your words and thus suffered the difficulty at P'ing-ch'eng. I previously sent out ten emissaries, all of whom had concluded they could be attacked." He then enfeoffed him with two thousand households as a lord within the pass and changed his title to Chien-hsin.[27]

In the ongoing confrontation between the Central Kingdom and the peripheral border peoples, just as in the earliest days of the Chou dynasty's decline, intelligence missions were largely carried out by official emissaries rather than indigenous spies. However, since the nature of these missions was transparent, measures to mislead and frustrate them could easily be mounted. For the highly mobile nomadic and seminomadic peoples it would have been a simple matter to divert their best warriors and livestock to less visible areas when apprised of an emissary's approach, particularly as diplomatic missions would have been burdened with extensive paraphernalia of office and probably relied on slow oxen to pull their supply wagons.

An early example of observational countermeasures dating to 555 B.C. embedded in a *Tso Chuan* account of a confrontation between Ch'i and Chin turns upon the opposite principle of manifesting apparent strength:

> The marquis of Ch'i ascended Mount Wu in order to observe Chin's army in the distance. However, Chin had ordered its commanders to establish outposts throughout the difficult terrain in the hills and marshes and even deploy regimental flags in areas where they would not emplace troops. Moreover, they had their chariots manned by real warriors on the left but dummies on the right,[28] set up large flags at the front of the chariot forces, and had other chariots, dragging brush, follow on. When the marquis of Ch'i saw this, he was afraid of their numerousness, abandoned the field, and returned to Ch'i.[29]

Another part of the same account, at first innocuous looking, when viewed in the context of Chin's actions indicates that the marquis of Ch'i was psychologically set up, primed to see or accept reports of great enemy strength. One of Chin's commanders deliberately provided his counterpart with the frightening news that the Chin coalition had granted Lu and Chü, each capable of fielding a thousand chariots, permission to join the effort and freely invade Ch'i. This fact was "sincerely" conveyed on the battlefield as if from one concerned officer to another, and therefore immediately advised to the marquis, who trembled at the prospect since the battle was already going poorly. (The marquis' lack of courage may have already been known to Chin, being much remarked by Ch'i's own forces, perhaps suggesting the possibility of literally frightening him off the battlefield.) This psychological preparation no doubt facilitated the execution of an extensive but still inherently simple deception that detailed observation by reconnaissance troops might otherwise have prevented. The clarity of the episode's lesson also prompted its selection as the historical example for the chapter entitled "Daylight" in the *Hundred Unorthodox Strategies*, abstracting and identifying it as an important lesson for later generations. The tactical principle illustrated there states: "Whenever engaging an enemy in battle during daylight, you must set out numerous flags and pennants to cause uncertainty about your forces. When you prevent the enemy from determining your troop strength, you will be victorious. A tactical principle from the *Art of War* states: 'In daylight battles make the flags and pennants numerous.'"

The story of Sun Pin's exploitation of P'ang Chüan's arrogance at the battle of Ma-ling some three centuries later provides another example of a simple but effective deception.[30] With P'ang's massive force in pursuit, Sun Pin created a facade of fear and desertion by hastily retreating while also dramatically reducing the number of cookfires every night. Since P'ang equated the number of fires with a corresponding troop presence, he concluded that Sun Pin's forces were rapidly dwindling and had little will to fight, making them easy prey. Thus P'ang was lured into rushing forward without adequate heavy forces and quickly massacred at a preestablished killing ground. From this China learned the trick of masking troop strength by manipulating the number of fires, making them more numerous to suggest larger armies and thereby deter attacks, or reducing them to lure the enemy forward.[31] Similarly, flags and pennons being essential for identifying and controlling the troops, as well as evidence of their degree of order or confusion (as discussed in the military intelligence section on evaluating enemy forces), Sun Pin himself advised that "spreading out the pennants and making the flags conspicuous are the means by which to cause doubt in the enemy" and "amid grasses and heavy vegetation one should employ visible pennants."[32] Naturally these techniques worked because signal flags and command pennants had to be positioned to be clearly visible at all times on every terrain.[33]

As a general tactical principle several writers advised multiplying the number of flags and drums or increasing their spacing when attacking an enemy to confuse the enemy's targeting and balk any estimates based upon them. For example, the *Six Secret Teachings* advises: "Change our flags and pennants several times and also change our uniforms. Then their army can be conquered.[34] Multiply the number of flags and pennants, and increase the number of gongs and drums.[35] In the daytime set up five colored pennants and flags. At night set out ten thousand fire-cloud torches, beat the thunder drums, strike the war drums and bells, and blow the sharp-sounding whistles."[36] Although primarily for communications purposes, Sun Pin himself stated: "In the daytime making the flags numerous and at night making the drums many are the way to send them off to battle. Rectifying the ranks and systematizing the pennants is the way to bind the formations together."[37]

Although innovative, effective, and amenable to categorization along general lines, the actual techniques employed to deceive enemies throughout China's military history are too numerous to consider here and must therefore be left for another book. However, a few examples, particularly those that became historically important through their inclusion in the *Hundred Unorthodox Strategies* and the military writings, coupled with a brief overview of the methods indicated in the theoretical classics, are merited. As with many concepts, Sun-tzu apparently enunciated the first tactics designed to exploit the impetus to deception: "Although you are capable, display incapability. When committed to employing your forces, feign inactivity. When your objective is nearby, make it appear as if distant; when far away, create the illusion of being nearby."[38]

In the massive work known as the *Six Secret Teachings* numerous suggestions for deceptively manipulating the enemy are interspersed throughout the sixty detailed chapters. For example, to resolve a difficult tactical situation, the T'ai Kung advised:

Make an outward display of confusion while actually being well ordered. Show an appearance of hunger while actually being well fed. Keep your sharp weapons within and show only dull and poor weapons outside. Have some troops come together, others split up; some assemble, others scatter. Make secret plans, keep your intentions secret. Raise the height of fortifications and conceal your elite troops. If the officers are silent, not making any sounds, the enemy will not know our preparations. Then if you want to take his western flank, attack the eastern one.[39]

The themes of secrecy and deception continued to be developed after the classical military writings. For example, Li Ch'uan's T'ang dynasty *T'ai-pai Yin-ching* integrates feints and deception with secrecy in an abstract, unified approach:

Those who excelled at employing the army could not have established themselves without trust and righteousness, achieved victory without *yin* and *yang*, realized advantages without the unorthodox and orthodox, or engaged in battle without deceit and subterfuge. Plans are concealed in the mind, but affairs are visible in external traces. One whose thoughts and visible expression are identical will be defeated, one whose thoughts and visible expression differ will be victorious.

Warfare is the Tao of deception. When capable, display incapability When about to employ the army, feign that you are not.[40] When your mind is filled with great plans, display only minor concerns. When your mind is planning to seize something, feign being about to give something away. Obscure the real, cast suspicion upon the doubtful. When the real and doubtful are not distinguishable, strength and weakness will be indeterminable. Be profound like the Mysterious Origin free of all images, be an abyss like the unfathomable depths of the sea. When you attain this, *yin* and *yang* can no longer be employed to calculate your intentions, ghosts and spirits will be unable to know them, techniques and measures will be unable to impoverish them, and methods of divination will be unable to fathom them, so how much more so mere enemy generals!

Now those who excelled in warfare achieved their victories in the clash of armies. The historical records are inadequate to attest to their plans, the form of their victories too insubstantial to be observed.[41] Those who can discuss tactics but not implement them harm a state, while those who can implement them but are unable to discuss them can be employed by the state. Thus it is said, "The highest plans are not spoken about, great military affairs are not discussed." It is subtle and mysterious!

Thus outstanding generals are able to penetrate the patterns of Heaven and Earth and fully prepare against the nature of the myriad things. They profit the greedy, thereby nurturing their desires, and are deferential to the strong, making them arrogant and boastful.[42] They estrange the intimate, causing them to become mutually disaffected. Men with insatiable desires will lack uprightness, the arrogant and boastful will neglect their defenses, and disaffected strategists will depart. King Wen of the Chou made generous gifts to the Shang and the Shang king was subsequently slain. King Kou-chien of Yüeh humbled himself before the state of Wu and King Fu-ch'ai of Wu was later exterminated. Han Kao-tsu became estranged from the kingdom of Ch'u, and Hsiang Yü, king of Ch'u, perished. Thus one subjugates the feudal lords with words and labors the feudal lords with plans.[43]

Those who excel in commanding the army attack what the enemy loves so that they must respond, and strike their vacuities so that the enemy must react.[44] They multiply their methods to coerce the enemy into dividing and create suspicious facades to force the enemy to prepare. When the enemy's response fails to be successful, they are compelled to divide their forces and defend their cities. If they are thus unable to unite their soldiers, we will be rested while they are labored; they will be few, while we are many. Now attacking the tired with the rested accords with martial principles; attacking the rested with the tired contravenes martial principles. Attacking the few with the many is the Tao for military victory; attacking the many with the few is the Tao for military defeat. Attacking the few with the many and assaulting the tired with the rested is the way to attain complete victory.

Now debilitating the enemy's spirit, seizing the general's mind,[45] exhausting the strength of their troops, and severing thousand kilometer supply routes do not lie in martial force but in the strategic power of deployments coupled with wise officers calculating the tactical imbalance of power. It is weak and soft! Roll it up, it won't fill the space of a sleeve. It is deep and secretive! Stretch it out, it will surpass the seas. A five-inch bolt can control the opening and closing of a door, a square inch of heart can change success to defeat. Thoroughly knowing all the aspects of the myriad things and thus never being imperiled, flexibly completing the myriad things without omitting any, according with Heaven and trusting men,[46] investigating the beginning and knowing the end, what worry is there that one's plans will not be followed?[47]

The first part of this lengthy passage thus opens with an assertion on the importance of being unfathomable, but the discussion then proceeds to link critical material from Sun-tzu in an integrated discussion that well illustrates how these concepts flow from one to another.

The *Hu-ling Ching*, composed during the Northern Sung period, advanced and expanded Sun-tzu's initial concept of misdirecting the enemy's perceptions in a chapter entitled "Far and Near" that equally evidences a thorough understanding of Li Ch'uan's *T'ai-pai Yin-ching*. The text explicates six tactical actions that exploit misdirections in the enemy's focus, including a nighttime river crossing made with bamboo rafts launched from upstream when the river's depth and current preclude direct fording and assault operations. Although largely an adaptation of the techniques for deceit found in Sun-tzu's thematic chapter "Initial Estimations," key passages merit scrutiny:

Warfare is the Tao of deception. Deception can make the empty appear full, the distant appear near, and the near appear distant. Thus there are six methods for employing the deception of the far and near. First, those who excel at attacking the enemy cause them to be alert to the front and then assault their rear, speak of the east then strike the west. They go forth where the enemy will not race, and race where the enemy does not expect. They lure them with profits, causing the settled to move, the rested to labor, and the sated to become hungry. They observe where they are unprepared and suddenly exploit it.[48]

These six all display objectives being nearby but gain victory far off. Such are the strategies of the unorthodox and orthodox. Sun-tzu said: "Armies engage in battle with the orthodox and gain victory through the unorthodox."[49] This is what he meant.

Another chapter in the *Hu-ling Ching* entitled "Five Differences," although ostensibly focusing upon differences in command style, explicates several deceptive techniques for countering a more powerful

enemy by exploiting their very superiority and consequent expectations, playing off normal perceptions and the "wisdom" of the common view:

> The T'ai Kung said: "One whose wisdom is the same as the
> masses is not a commander for the army, one whose skill is the
> same as the masses is not an artisan for the state. No movement
> is more spiritual than being unexpected, no victory greater than
> being unrecognized."[50] Sun-tzu said, "The strategic power of
> those who excel in warfare is sharply focused and their con-
> straints are precise."[51] "Leading" means to be different from the
> ordinary. For this reason those whose excel at employing the mili-
> tary act distinctively in five circumstances: The first is con-
> strained terrain; the second, lightness; the third, danger; the
> fourth, stupidity; and the fifth, fear.
>
> Exhausted roads and deep valleys, fatal and severed terrain, ru-
> ined fortifications and moats, places normally raced through, are
> ordinarily taken by the masses as constricted and to be avoided.
> However, on the contrary you should make your deployments in-
> ternally solid while externally manifesting an appearance of disor-
> der in order to entice the enemy. Internally you should be strict
> with your troops while externally appearing afraid in order to
> make the enemy arrogant. Then when they fail to recognize the
> true situation, oppress them with changes, assault them with
> troops. This is the Tao for utilizing constricted terrain.
>
> When they are numerous but you are few, your strength is ru-
> ined and supplies exhausted, and the power for victory lies with
> them, you should swear a blood oath with the warriors, strictly
> order generous rewards, and advance and retreat as if certain to
> die. Also select a small number of soldiers to suddenly mount a
> fierce defense against them. The enemy, being more numerous,
> will assume you are light, but lightness has its employment. Pass-
> ing through exhausted terrain on which the gate to life has been
> shut will convert lightness into decisiveness. This is the Tao for
> employing lightness.
>
> When a strong enemy mounts such a fervent attack that your
> soldiers are trembling, the masses will assume you are endan-
> gered, but you should not become agitated or chaotic. When you
> employ perilous conditions, your orders must be strict, your
> preparations thorough. Encourage the officers and troops with
> thoughts about the Will of Heaven; externally close off your ap-
> pearance; internally grasp the vital moment to covertly employ

unorthodox tactics in sending your troops forth. This is the Tao for employing danger.

When the enemy employs agents to spy upon you, pretend you do not realize it and receive them. When the enemy sends spies into your encampment, pretend you are unprepared, but establish ambushes to await their forces. The enemy will assume that you are stupid, but employing the method of apparent stupidity is, on the contrary, wise. This is the Tao for employing stupidity.

When you see the enemy's army approaching, retreat and concentrate behind defensive walls. When you see the enemy's emissaries approaching, speak deferentially and act dispirited, as if you hope to be reconciled with them. The masses will assume you are afraid. When utilizing fear you should withdraw and contract, establish ambushes, and then attack, employing unorthodox tactics to penetrate them. Act as if you want to be reconciled, move them with profits, and make them arrogant through your humility. This is the Tao for employing fear.

These five are contrary to the methods of the masses. When the masses assume you are constricted, employ their advantages. When they assume you are light, employ lightness to be decisive. When they assume you are endangered, utilize their [sense of] security. When they assume you are stupid, employ their wisdom. When they assume you are afraid, employ their courage. Thus the T'ai Kung said, "One who cannot extend and move [his troops about] cannot be spoken with about the unorthodox."[52] This is what he meant.

The inclusion of measures to thwart spies, treated as just one of many responses, provides further evidence that military forces were constantly employing agents to penetrate enemy encampments, no doubt in disguise either as merchants and other vendors or as members of the army itself. (A number of similar methods for exploiting enemy expectations arising from configurations of terrain, including examples from the *Hu-ling Ching*, will also be found in the section on military intelligence.)

The Northern Sung *Ts'ui-wei Pei-cheng Lu* advanced a method to deceive enemy spies by exploiting the reputation of armies and commanders:

I have heard that when a general is famous throughout the realm, shift the general, not the army. When an army is famous throughout the realm, shift the army, not the general. If a capable general whom the Three Armies heavily rely upon goes out one day to another encampment, enemy forces will secretly observe it and invariably exploit the rear. If elite troops that normally shake enemy states into submission one day go forth to some other area, enemy forces will certainly spy out this fissure and exploit it. Thus the army's secret method for shifting its generals is to not have the soldiers follow so as to make both armies heavy. Similarly, when you shift the army, the general does not accompany them so as to make them both complete.

On the day the troops set out, discard the mats and cookstoves so that neither the fires nor bedding leaves a trace. At first light set out and travel at night so that the dust will not arise. On the day when the general sets out, do not remove his official insignia from camp in order to stupefy the enemy's army, or lower the command pennants in order to keep our troops calm. Thus the general can be shifted without the army worrying about having lost their general, while the army may be shifted without the general being concerned about the loss of his army. These are termed "submerged changes."[53]

Again the techniques presuppose the presence of enemy agents in the encampment or their access to rumors and gossip.

By the late Ming period military contemplation of certain subjects such as the unorthodox and orthodox, secrecy, formlessness, and strategic power had become highly rarefied and abstract, no doubt in part because of the influence of such philosophical developments as Taoism, Buddhism, and Neoconfucianism over the nearly two thousand years since these subjects were first articulated by Sun-tzu. Conceptually important, their degree of realization in actual operations remains problematic, although there certainly was a general cognizance of the essential principles and a recognition of the need to be as deceitful and unfathomable as possible without creating impossibly complex plans and totally confusing one's own forces. The *Ping-fa Pai-yen,* a late Ming text composed by a loyalist leader and eventual recluse, ponders much of the corpus of Chinese military theory in the light of field practices and historical records. To provide an overview of what certainly must be considered the theoretical apex of the genre, several relevant definitions are translated here, while others will be found in the theoretical section on intelligence evaluation.

The technique of "according with" the enemy's expectations and desires requires first determining what they believe and want, then apparently conforming to them until the situation can be exploited:

Definition: When the enemy wants to take something and you yield it, it is termed "according with."

Original Text: In general, when going contrary to something merely solidifies it, it is better to accord with it in order to lead them to flaws. If the enemy wants to advance, be completely flexible and display weakness in order to induce an advance. If the enemy wants to withdraw, disperse and open an escape route for their retreat. If the enemy is relying upon a strong front, establish your own front lines far off, solidly assuming a defensive posture in order to observe their arrogance. If the enemy relies upon their awesomeness, be emptily respectful but substantially plan while awaiting their laxness. Draw them forward and cover them, release and capture them. Exploit their arrogance, capitalize on their laxity.

Explanation: Whenever you encounter a strong enemy, unless you have extensive wisdom and great courage, it is not possible to oppose them headlong and sever their forces. It is better to assume a solid defensive stance and refuse battle, waiting for their *ch'i* to decline. Deepen your moats and heighten your fortifications; conceal your sharp front and hide your arrows; endure taunts and curses without moving; accept insults without declining. Temporarily accord with the enemy's intentions, do not engage them in battle. Once some change develops, exploit any cracks and arise without waiting an instant. Then you can conquer the great with the small, the strong with the weak.

"According with" the enemy's assessment is but one technique in the panoply of misperception. Every commander should consistently mount efforts to mislead the enemy into making errors of judgment and undertake whatever actions might directly produce "misperceptions."

Definition: Causing the enemy's plans to be erroneous is referred to as "misperception."

Original Text: The essence of conquering an enemy is not only using your strength to control them, but also employing techniques that mislead them. Perhaps you will use your own methods to mislead them, perhaps exploit their misperceptions to impede them. Cause them to misperceive their basis of support, advantages, stupidity, and wisdom, and also misperceive ongoing changes. Provoke them with emptiness [feints], seize them with substantiality. If they are knowledgeable, cause them to be misled; when they are misled, you can be enlightened. Thus one who excels in military affairs misleads others and is not misled by others.[54]

Explanation: Misleading them with their own misperceptions accords with the natural tendencies of the situation. Misleading them in the absence of misperception is contrary to the tendencies of the situation. Even when the enemy doesn't have a perceptible crack that can be exploited, there are still techniques. For example, display weakness in order to mislead them about what they can rely on, manifest fear in order to mislead them about the advantages they enjoy. Show disorder in order to mislead their stupidity, manifest stupidity in order to obfuscate their wisdom. Show them you do not dare act in order to interfere with their tactical changes. When they nominally provoke you, act startled, when they employ substantial forces to seize terrain, display a sudden response. In all cases act as if your generals are incompetent and the army incapable. These are the methods of inner court officials, the Tao of pliancy.

Alternatively, destroy their solidity and thereby interfere with what they rely upon. Seize their riches in order to impede their realization of advantages. Employ the extremes of skill and artifice to mislead them in their stupidity, deepen your plans in order to obscure their wisdom. Employ intertwined attack and defense in order to confuse their tactical changes. When they nominally provoke you, exercise caution in the middle, when they employ substantial forces to seize terrain, occupy the strongpoints. In all these situations act as if neither your generals nor army can be matched by the enemy. This was the military strategy of the Yellow Emperor, the Tao of firmness.

The Tao of the Yellow Emperor, the Tao of Lao-tzu—sometimes being a dragon, others a snake—anyone who excels in employing the army must employ such methods.

Although the term "misperception" is active, conveying the sense of inducing a misperception or erroneous evaluation, it also includes the idea of actively impeding, misleading, or obstructing, so no single English word suffices to translate it, including "obfuscate," which has many appropriate connotations.

In defining a word best translated as "displays" (although "extensions" or "screens," depending upon the type and context, would also be possible), the *Ping-fa Pai-yen* similarly provides evidence that the technique of doubtful flags and screens was still practiced in the late Ming and ancient texts still assiduously studied, but now on a more abstract level, implemented through actual deployments rather than just flags themselves:

Definition: The establishment of multiple doubtful deployments is termed "displays."

Original Text: Ostentatiously flaunting one's capabilities to shake an enemy is an ordinary method; only when the substance is lacking does the term "display" apply. Thus only when something has not yet been realized should you trust to displays, only when insufficient do you thereby become full. Displays may be undertaken to cause doubt in the enemy. When you amplify your awesomeness to snatch away the enemy's morale and then employ unorthodox tactics to achieve victory, this is a case of empty fame attaining substantial employment, the skilled Tao of dwelling in weakness.

Explanation: When an army lacks substance but displays a facade, it is termed a "display." The method is to amplify what should be extended. When you blatantly flourish the army's actual awesomeness, it is termed a "substantial display." When you purely set out feigned deployments to incite doubt, it is termed a "vacuous display." Even so, substantial displays require rearguard actions to prevent the enemy from fervently and courageously mounting a sudden attack. Vacuous displays value concealed ambushes to prevent the enemy from leading you into a fierce engagement. Thus some displays result in victory by exploiting the enemy's fear, others their ignorance. When you have no alternative but to employ them, any victory achieved will be a matter of luck, not of normal methods. Those who excel in this method extend themselves externally but are constrained internally.

The concept essentially exploits Sun Pin's idea of confusing an enemy by setting out specious displays, especially when one is weak: "Set out artifice in order to cause doubt." The most spectacular example among those that Chieh Hsüan provides is Chao Yün blatantly opening his camp to make a vastly superior enemy afraid to attack since a fatal ambush had no doubt been prepared.

The foregoing measures, when abstractly extrapolated, may be theorized in terms of "shadows," a more all-encompassing, multidimensional form of "displays":

Definition: Being skilled in setting out doubtful formations is termed "shadows."

Original Text: In antiquity, when those who excelled in employing the military intended to do something, they would do something else in order to implement their actual intentions. This is an excellent method for destroying enemy armies, capturing generals, and forcing the submission of cities. When they did not intend to do something, they did it, thereby causing doubt in the enemy that they intended to do it. This similarly is a subtle way to destroy enemy armies, capture generals, and force the submission of cities. Thus doing something is shadowy, doing it without any intention to do it manifests shadows within shadows. Just as when two mirrors are hung opposite each other, profound and more profound!

Explanation: Men have straightforward principles, but military strategy does not. The sincere and trusting will not be able to comprehend a slippery enemy commander. Thus there are techniques for real and feigned assaults, methods for vacuous and substantial defenses. For battle there are unorthodox and orthodox tactics, including giving when you want to take, and taking when you want to give. When you want to capture something, you liberate it, when you want to liberate something, you capture it. Sometimes one acts contrary to this principle and actually seizes or gives, captures or liberates, all of which are termed "shadows within shadows." Thus shadows have shadows within them, but shadows also have reality within them. Within the real there are shadows, within the real there is reality. Thus reality and shadow complete each other, ever attaining the inexhaustible.

Examples: Chu-ko Liang wanted to seize Hsi-ch'uan but first blocked Sun Ch'üan's advancing to attack. T'ang T'ai-tsung was capable of pacifying the Turks, but he first humbly sought to make peace. Duke Wen of Chin wanted to engage in battle, but he first feigned a retreat at Ch'eng-p'u. Ch'in's army wanted to retreat, so it sought to engage the enemy in battle. In all these cases stretching out was taken as contracting and contracting as stretching out. How can the mind of the strategist be real and substantial like other men?

Although highly abstract and esoteric, battlefield practices of this sort represent the pinnacle of deception and the ultimate challenge to the mysteries of evaluation. Even though the conception appears more complex than Sun-tzu's feigned appearances, it essentially resolves into faking (but also sometimes actually performing) the opposite of an intended action to mislead the enemy, to cause misperceptions and thereby achieve one's real purpose. However, the language mirrors Li

Ching's discussion on the unorthodox and orthodox, as well as Sun-tzu's original passages on that topic, in Book I of the *Questions and Replies*. Moreover, it can be similarly conceptualized and phrased in terms of *yin*, the dark, passive polarity in the dynamic pairing of light and darkness, sun and moon, day and night:

Definition: Wisdom that cannot be perceived is termed "yin" [dark, obscure].

Original Text: When you employ *yang* [visible, overt measures] but others still are unable to fathom them, then *yang* is *yin* [dark, covert]. When you employ *yin* measures and others are even less able to fathom them, then *yin* measures are *yin*. Thus sometimes one borrows *yang* to implement *yin*, sometimes revolves *yin* to complete *yang*, neither of which differs from simply employing unorthodox measures and seizing subtle opportunities, using ambushes and sudden strikes.

Explanation: The myriad military tactics of antiquity can all be exhausted by a single word, *yin*. The talents of antique generals may similarly be encompassed by the single word *yin*. The wisest military calculations, if leaked out, will fail to achieve anything, whereas if preserved in secrecy, they will be effective. Allowing plans to become prominent invites misfortune, concealing them preserves the army intact. However, unorthodox and dangerous compounds and fiercely poisonous medicines such as bitter aconite or *ta-huang* are solely for striking diseases themselves. Thus if a disease's root is shallow but powerful medications are inappropriately employed to purge it, the life force may be harmed and original essence congealed to the detriment of the patient. *Yang* must be ameliorated with *yin*; through surpassing skill in *yin* achievements will be complete. *Yin* must be perversely contrary to *yang*; then, by reverting to *yang*, the Tao will be upright [orthodox].

After citing the *Yin-fu Ching* in the comments to his examples for "yin," the author concludes: "Without *yin*, how can the unorthodox aspects of calculations be successful? Without *yin* how can they be secret? The eye is a natural thief, the mind a natural robber." Although the language is enigmatic, the chapter simply focuses upon the ongoing battle between secrecy and perception, the contrast between things that, having form, are detectable and the invisible, which, being indiscernible, thwarts intelligence efforts. The chapter's insights depend upon the dynamic polar tension characterizing the opposition of *yin* and *yang* that underlies all phenomena in the traditional Chinese view and no doubt reflects Taoism's close interrelationship with Chinese military theory over the centuries.

Counterintelligence

The classic historical writings of the Spring and Autumn and Warring States periods preserve several accounts of early counterintelligence efforts mounted to thwart political and military observers seeking to assess the prospects for a successful military invasion. To thwart these enemy agents, whether clandestine or politically accredited, the visit had to be anticipated—no doubt reported by one's own spies—and the parameters by which a judgment would be rendered well understood. Generally speaking, until the middle of the Warring States period when disparate views began to arise, observers looked for a virtuous ruler, capable assistants, morally superior advisers, and economic prosperity among the people. A famous Spring and Autumn incident involved Yen-tzu, an astute Ch'i statesman around whom many disparate stories eventually coalesced in the Warring States period to make up the lengthy book attributed to him, the *Yen-tzu Ch'un-ch'iu*. (Reputedly a compilation of his remonstrances and advice, much of the material appears tenuous at best.) However, in the following episode his quick response successfully frustrated the enemy's attempt to insult them and thereby probe their moral excellence and administrative order. Although the original version appears in the *Tso Chuan* (and appears in several later compilations such as the *Hsin Hsü, Han-shih Wai-chuan,* and *Yen-tzu Ch'un-ch'iu* itself), a later version incorporated in the Sung dynasty *Hundred Unorthodox Strategies* is translated here because it provides evidence of the continuing importance of antique materials in the late Sung and subsequent centuries for military students who pondered the *Unorthodox Strategies* as a tactical handbook:

> During the Spring and Autumn period Duke P'ing of Chin wanted to attack the state of Ch'i, so he dispatched Fan Chao to observe Ch'i's government. At a feast in his honor Duke Ching of Ch'i presented him with a cup of wine, but Fan Chao asked to drink from the ruler's goblet. The duke ordered that his cup be brought to his guest. Fan Chao had already drunk from it when Yen Tzu seized the goblet and exchanged it for another cup. Later Fan Chao, pretending to be drunk, unhappily rose to dance. He asked the Music Master: "Can you perform the music of Ch'eng-chou

for me? I want to dance to it." The Music Master said, "Your ignorant servant is not familiar with it."

When Fan Chao went out Duke Ching said: "Chin is a great state. He came to observe our government. Now that you have angered this great state's emissary, what will we do?" Yen Tzu said, "I observed that Fan Chao was not ignorant of the proper forms of court behavior but sought to embarrass our state, so I did not comply." The Music Master said: "The music of Ch'eng-chou is the music of the Son of Heaven. Only the ruler of men can dance to it. Now Fan Chao, although a subject, wanted to dance to the music of the Son of Heaven. Therefore I did not perform it."

Fan Chao returned to Chin and reported to Duke P'ing: "Ch'i cannot yet be attacked. I tried to insult their ruler, but Yen Tzu realized it. I wanted to act contrary to their forms of court behavior, but the Music Master perceived it." Confucius subsequently said, "The saying 'to shatter an enemy a thousand miles off without going beyond the banquet hall' refers to Yen Tzu."

The tactical principle illustrated by this incident in the *Hundred Unorthodox Strategies* derives from Sun-tzu's *Art of War*: "If you attack the enemy just after they have formulated their strategy, it will ruin their plans and force them to submit. The *Art of War* states: 'The highest realization of warfare is to attack plans.'"

Even Ch'u, although regarded by the original Chou states as semi-barbaric, was similarly able to deter a planned Chin attack by thwarting its probe through an unexpected display of surpassing talent:

Ch'in wanted to attack Ch'u, so it dispatched an emissary to observe Ch'u's valuable treasures. Learning of his coming, the king of Ch'u summoned his prime minister Tzu Hsi and inquired: "Ch'in wants to inspect our valuable treasures. We have the famous Ho-shih jade and Sui-hou's pearl. Can we show them these?" Tzu His replied, "I do not know."

The king then summoned Chao Hsi-hsü and asked him the same thing. He replied: "They want to observe our state's attainments and losses and make plans against them. The state's valued treasures are its worthy ministers. Pearls and jewels are merely things for amusement, not the treasures that a state really esteems." The king then deputed Chao to prepare their response.

Chao Hsi-hsü deployed three hundred elite soldiers within the western gate. On the eastern side he constructed one mound, on the south four, and one in the west. When Ch'in's emissary arrived Chao said, "Honored guest, please assume a position in the east." He had prime minister Tzu Hsi stand in the south with Tzu Fang behind him, Tzu Kao in turn behind him, and Ssu-ma Tzu Fan behind him. Chao himself stood on the mound in the west and then called out: "Our guest wants to observe Ch'u's valued treasures. However, what Ch'u treasures is its worthy officials.

"To bring order to the people and ensure that the storehouses and granaries are full and settle the people in their positions are prime minister Tzu Hsi's responsibilities. To present appropriate offerings, undertake embassies to the feudal lords, mitigate difficulties of friction, bring states together in harmony, and keep us free from the worry of military affairs are Tzu Fang's responsibilities. To defend the borders and be careful about their definition so that we neither encroach on others nor other states encroach on us are Tzu Kao's responsibilities. To organize the armies and array the troops in order to oppose strong enemies, to take up the drumsticks and stir our million men to action so that they will all rush into boiling water or fire, stomp on naked blades, and die a thousand deaths without troubling about the difficulties of one's life, are Ssu-ma Tzu Fan's responsibilities. To embrace the bequeathed instructions of the hegemons and take hold of the winds of order and disorder, I am here. It only remains for your great state to observe us."

So frightened that he could not reply, the ambassador from Ch'in bowed and departed. He then returned to Ch'in and reported, "Ch'u has many worthy ministers so we cannot yet plot against them." Subsequently they did not attack. As the *Book of Odes* states, "With his splendid array of officers King Wen enjoyed tranquillity." This is what it means.[55]

A brief anecdote involving Chang Yi, the famous proponent of the so-called horizontal alliance that would submissively unite all the states under Ch'in, reveals he apparently had his own sources of information and was therefore able to counteract his opponents even though active in another state: "Chou Tsui was a partisan of Ch'i, while Ti Ch'iang advocated an alliance with Ch'u. Both of them wanted to harm Chang Yi's standing in Wei. Chang Yi heard about it and managed to have one of his people placed as a staff member to the king's protocol director to secretly observe audiences with the king, so they did not dare harm Chang Yi."[56]

As the military and political situation became more complex and intense in the Warring States period, the sort of highly visible observational missions undertaken by equally high-profile diplomats yielded to low-profile and totally clandestine efforts. Despite the most stringent measures to preserve secrecy, enemy agents often succeeded in penetrating them to gather information, bribe disaffected and greedy officials, or sow discord. They, and those already emplaced by the enemy, had to be detected and either eliminated or converted to one's own use, whether knowingly or not. As already examined, Sun-tzu discussed the need to recruit converted spies, valuing turned agents as the basis for all other efforts to penetrate the enemy, but with the benefit of another thousand years of experience General Li Ching of the T'ang dynasty provided perhaps the most succinct characterization of the situation's dynamics:

> Now while we employ agents to spy on other people, other people also use agents to spy on us. Our spies go forth secretly, theirs come forth secretly. The operative principle is that one must simply investigate reports with respect to possible motives and evaluate them comparatively, for then they will not be lost.
>
> If the enemy dispatches men to discover our vacuities and strengths, investigate our movement and rest, observe and learn our affairs and plans, and implement covert activities, we should feign being unaware of it, allowing them to continue, generously profiting them, and treating them well. House them and feast them, subtly inform them of false information and speak speciously of unreal affairs, both former and subsequent. What I need then will be what the enemy loses. Relying upon their spies, we will turn about and spy upon them.
>
> If they assume our vacuities are substantial and our substantialities vacuous, we can then take advantage of their exhaustion and seize their will. Now water can float a boat, but it can also overturn it. Although some use spies to be successful, others relying on them are overturned and defeated.[57]

At the end of the passage Li Ching pointedly raises the ultimate question in shadow work—how to ensure an agent's reliability—one already discussed, along with measures to evaluate and validate the content of reports, in the section on agent control.

Several military writers addressed the general question of how to evaluate men and motives, and in particular how to detect enemy agents and traitors from their behavior. The Northern Sung *Hu-ling Ching* includes a chapter entitled "Recognizing Villains" devoted to such evidence, together with responsive measures designed to gain control of the situation and in turn secretly exploit the opportunities thus presented:

When an emissary comes from the enemy whose eyes constantly move about, countenance frequently changes, and words are dissolute, he is an assassin.

When an enemy who is not yet distressed requests peace talks, it is a plot.

An enemy that speaks deferentially and presents generous gifts is trying to make you arrogant.

When they do not cease their plundering even though urgently dispatching emissaries, they are insulting you.

Those who provide generous gifts to your attendants want to ferret out your secret plans.

When their emissaries speak fluently, are skilled in disputation, and want to resolve tensions between your two states, they are about to mount a surprise attack when you are unprepared.

One whose emissaries speak brusquely and belligerently wants to deceive you.

When you encounter any of these seven forms of behavior in an enemy emissary, you should minutely investigate in order to seize and coerce them. Turn their plots against those who would plot against you. Feign arrogance toward those who would make you arrogant. Deal brusquely with those who insult you. Display false plans to those who seek to ferret out your plans. Respond by suddenly attacking those who hope to attack when you are unprepared. Execute those with desires. You cannot detain their emissaries for long because if they remain long, they will know your smallest affairs, in which case it would be better to kill them. For these reasons knowing the techniques of these seven villains is one of the foundations of military art and must therefore be investigated.

In conjunction with the methods for detecting and converting enemy agents to one's own use already presented in the theoretical sections on agents and turned agents, from the preceding passages it is clear that the military writers, and therefore military commanders, were compelled to actively ponder the problem of spies and undertake vigilant countermeasures.

A passage from the biography of the famous Sung general Yüeh Fei depicts the exploitation of a captured spy exactly as specified in the theoretical writings. At the time Yüeh Fei was pursuing the rebel leader Ts'ao Ch'eng, who was retreating before him in command of some one hundred thousand troops:

When Yüeh Fei advanced into Ho-chou they captured one of Ts'ao Ch'eng's spies and tied him up outside Yüeh Fei's tent. When

Yüeh came out from his tent the quartermaster advised: "Our provisions are exhausted, what should we do?" Yüeh Fei boldly replied, "We will temporarily return to Ch'a-ling." After that he looked at the spy as if he were very discouraged and walked heavily back into his tent. Thereafter he secretly ordered that the spy be allowed to escape.

The spy returned to Ts'ao Ch'eng's camp and reported these events. Greatly elated, Ts'ao Ch'eng decided to initiate his pursuit the next day. However, Yüeh Fei meanwhile ordered his officers and troops to eat early the next morning while still in their tents, after which they secretly raced out around the mountain and arrived before daybreak at T'ai-p'ing-ch'ang, where they destroyed Ts'ao's outlying camps. Ts'ao's forces then resisted by occupying the ravines, but Yüeh led his troop in a sudden, unexpected thrust that severely shattered the enemy.[58]

Han Shih-chung, another skilled Southern Sung general honored with a lengthy biography in the *History of the Sung,* also proved adept at manipulating the enemy's sources of information:

After having suffered a defeat, Li Heng's rebel army and Chin forces, in anticipation of uniting, proceeded by separate routes to mount an invasion of Sung-controlled territory. By his own hand the Sung emperor ordered Han Shih-chung, then serving as Pacification Commissioner for the area east of the Yangtze River, to cautiously defend his position while making plans to advance and seize the enemy. As the edict's language was bleak and earnest, when he received his instructions Shih-chung was moved to tears and exclaimed, "How can I live when the ruler's worries are so great?" Then he had the army cross the river from their fortified encampment and also ordered Major General Chieh Yüan to defend Kao-yu and await Chin's infantry forces. Meanwhile, he personally led his cavalry forces to temporarily occupy Ta-yi in order to confront the enemy's cavalry. Once there, they cut down the trees to erect palisades and sever the return route.

It happened that Wang Liang-ch'en, a Sung emissary just being dispatched by the Sung emperor to the Chin, was present, so Han Shih-chung had his refectories withdrawn on the pretext that he had received an imperial order to shift camp and defend the estuary. Wang Liang-ch'en then raced off on his mission. When Shih-chung calculated that Wang Liang-ch'en had crossed over the border, he jumped on his horse and ordered the army to "follow where his whip pointed." Thereupon he led the army to reposition at Ta-yi, configuring them into five deployments. He also established ambushes at more than twenty other places, ordering them to arise in a sudden attack when they heard the sound of the drums.

After Wang Liang-ch'en arrived at the Chin encampment the latter inquired about the actions of the Sung armies, to which he replied in detail about all that he had seen. When Che-erh-pei-chin, the Chin commander in chief, heard that Han Shih-chung had withdrawn, he was greatly elated and led his troops to the mouth of the river, about five kilometers from Ta-yi. Moreover, he dispatched a secondary force composed of valiant cavalry under the command of General T'a-pei-yeh to bypass Han Shih-chung's five deployments on the east. Shih-chung then ordered the drums sounded and the troops in concealment raised their flags on all four sides of the enemy. Their flags were soon intermixed with those of the Chin troops as the latter were thrown into confusion, allowing Han's soldiers to successively advance. With their backs to the heights, Han's soldiers wielded long-handled axes that struck the enemy's chests above and chopped at the horses' legs below. In full armor the enemy's cavalrymen fell heavily into the mud. Han Shih-chung then signaled his strong cavalry to trample them from all four sides so that men and horses alike perished. Subsequently they captured T'a-pei-yeh and some two hundred others.[59]

Prisoners

One of the major sources of information has always been prisoners captured either preliminary to battle, often as a result of conscious effort, or incidental to the course of conflict. Although there are numerous problems associated with such potential sources, including deliberate fabrication, self-delusion, and simply inaccurate information derived from a limited perspective, through the techniques advised in the theoretical writings, perhaps buttressed by a general awareness of the principles of evaluating men and motives found in Han Fei-tzu, the Six Secret Teachings, Jen-wu Chih, and similar texts, coupled with duplication, cross-checking, and an occasional defector, vital information could be elicited. The following example of Tzung Tse, a prominent general who lived at the end of the Sung and start of the Southern Sung (A.D. 1060–1128), effectively employing moral persuasion to sway a prisoner into revealing essential details is but one of many successful cases preserved in China's voluminous historical writings:

Wang Ts'e, originally a Liao chieftain, had been actively serving as a Chin general in the upper part of the Yellow River. When Tzung Tse's forces captured him, Tzung untied his bonds, had him seated in the upper part of the hall, and addressed him: "The Khitan and the Sung were originally brother states. Now you have truly insulted my ruler and moreover abandoned your allegiance to your own state. It would be proper to plan together to wipe away this shame." Wang Tse, moved to tears, was willing to die to achieve this end. Tzung then interrogated him about the enemy's vacuities and strengths and obtained complete, detailed information. Thereafter he decided on a plan for a major mobilization that resulted in the Chin forces being defeated and compelled to withdraw from the area.[60]

Part Three

COVERT ACTIVITIES

密 謀 策 劃

8

Systematic Programs and Psychological Warfare

BY THE EARLIEST RECORDED LITERATURE it had become apparent that military measures constituted expensive solutions to problems of state and that other alternatives might prove more efficacious. Particularly as military exercises designed, in part, to confirm each clan member's position and role became less important than the mobilization of citizen populaces and the fielding of mass infantry armies, less disruptive solutions were much to be desired. Although unrecorded, clandestine activities such as bribery, estrangement, and deception no doubt began simply and early. By the Spring and Autumn period typical objectives for the frequently mounted covert operations included sowing dissension, causing misperception, assassinating key personnel, ruining public confidence, and mounting other political measures to subvert enemy governments and undermine their ability to wage war. As theorists began to ponder the nature and implication of such efforts, they naturally envisioned coordinated programs designed to weaken and even topple their enemies, to achieve Sun-tzu's ideal objective of conquering the enemy complete.

Sun-tzu's famous chapter on spies only touched upon the employment of double agents to spread disinformation, but a Warring States work entitled the *Six Secret Teachings* contains two explosive chapters on clandestine operations that were much condemned thereafter for their inhumanity and perverse approach to warfare, one held to be inconsistent with antiquity's great Sages. The first, entitled "Civil Offensive," although presumably providing measures for undermining the power of the dominant Shang, elucidates many techniques of universal validity:

There are twelve measures for civil offensives. First, accord with what he likes in order to accommodate his wishes. He will eventually grow arrogant and invariably mount some perverse affair. If you can appear to follow along, you will certainly be able to eliminate him.

Second, become familiar with those he loves in order to fragment his awesomeness. When men have two different inclinations, their loyalty invariably declines. When his court no longer has any loyal ministers, the state altars will inevitably be endangered.

Third, covertly bribe his assistants, fostering a deep relationship with them. Although they will bodily stand in his court, their emotions will be directed outside it. The state will certainly suffer harm.

Fourth, assist him in his licentiousness and indulgence in music in order to dissipate his will. Make him generous gifts of pearls and jade, and ply him with beautiful women. Speak deferentially, listen respectfully, follow his commands, and accord with him in everything. He will never imagine you might be in conflict with him. Our treacherous measures will then be settled.

Fifth, treat his loyal officials very generously, but reduce the gifts you provide to the ruler. Delay his emissaries, do not listen to their missions. When he eventually dispatches other men, treat them with sincerity; embrace and trust them. The ruler will then again feel you are in harmony with him. If you manage to treat his formerly loyal officials very generously, his state can then be plotted against.

Sixth, make secret alliances with his favored ministers, but visibly keep his less favored outside officials at a distance. His talented people will then be under external influence while enemy states encroach upon his territory. Few states in such a situation have survived.

Seventh, if you want to bind his heart to you, you must offer generous presents. To gather in his assistants, loyal associates, and loved ones, you must secretly show them the gains they can realize by colluding with you. Have them slight their work, and then their preparations will be futile.

Eighth, gift him with great treasures and make plans with him. When the plans are successful and profit him, he will have faith in you because of the profits. This is what is termed "being closely embraced." The result of being closely embraced is that he will inevitably be used by us. When someone rules a state but is externally controlled, his territory will inevitably be defeated.

Ninth, honor him with praise. Do nothing that will cause him personal discomfort. Display the proper respect accruing to a great power, and your obedience will certainly be trusted. Magnify his honor, being the first to gloriously praise him, humbly embellishing him as a Sage. Then his state will suffer great loss!

Tenth, be submissive so that he will trust you and you will thereby learn about his true situation. Accept his ideas and respond to his affairs as if you were twins. Once you have learned everything, subtly gather in his power. Thus when the ultimate day arrives, it will seem as if Heaven itself destroyed him.

Eleventh, block up his access by means of the Tao. Among subordinates there is no one who does not value rank and wealth or hate danger and misfortune. Secretly express great respect toward them, and gradually bestow valuable gifts in order to gather in the more outstanding talents. Accumulate your own resources until they become very substantial, but manifest an external appearance of shortage. Covertly bring in wise knights, and entrust them with planning great strategy. Attract courageous knights and augment their spirit. Even when they are sufficiently rich and honored, continue to increase them. When your faction has been fully established, you will have attained the objective referred to as "blocking his access." If someone has a state but his access is blocked, how can he be considered as having the state?

Twelfth, support his dissolute officials in order to confuse him. Introduce beautiful women and licentious sounds in order to befuddle him. Send him outstanding dogs and horses in order to tire him. From time to time allow him great power in order to entice him to greater arrogance. Then investigate Heaven's signs, and plot with the world against him.

When these twelve measures are fully employed, they will become a military weapon. Thus when, as it is said, one "looks at Heaven above and investigates Earth below" and the proper signs are already visible, attack him.

An example of implementing something like the fifth measure appears in the *Chan-kuo Ts'e:*

The king of Ch'in said to Kan Mao: "The emissaries that Ch'u has dispatched to us are mostly robust persuaders. When we argue, I have frequently found myself confounded. What should I do?"

Kan Mao replied: "Your majesty need not be concerned. When effective emissaries come, you should ignore them, but when timid and weak emissaries come, you should listen to their advice. Then these timid, weak officials will be employed in Ch'u, while the strong will be neglected. Through this method you will control Ch'u."[1]

The second *Six Secret Teachings* chapter, entitled "Three Doubts," expounds the preferred method for undermining enemy rulers, concretely focused in terms of the hated Shang:

King Wu inquired of the T'ai Kung: "I want to attain our aim of overthrowing the Shang, but I have three doubts. I am afraid that our strength will be inadequate to attack the strong, estrange his close supporters within the court, and disperse his people. What should I do?"

The T'ai Kung replied: "Accord with the situation, be very cautious in making plans, and employ your material resources. Now in order to attack the strong, you must nurture them to make them even stronger, and increase them to make them even more extensive. What is too strong will certainly break, what is too extended must have deficiencies. Attack the strong through his strength.[2] Cause the estrangement of his favored officials by using his favorites, and disperse his people by means of the people.

Now in the Tao of planning, thoroughness and secrecy are treasured. You should become involved with him in numerous affairs and ply him with temptations of profit. Conflict will then surely arise.

If you want to cause his close supporters to become estranged from him, you must do it by using what they love, making gifts to those he favors, giving them what they want. Tempt them with what they find profitable, thereby making them ambitious. Those who covet profits will be extremely happy at the prospects, and their remaining doubts will be ended.

Now without doubt the Tao for attacking is to first obfuscate the king's clarity and then attack his strength, destroying his greatness and eliminating the misfortune of the people. Debauch him with beautiful women, entice him with profit. Nurture him with flavors, and provide him with the company of female musicians. Then after you have caused his subordinates to become estranged from him, you must cause the people to grow distant from him while never letting him know your plans. Appear to support him, and draw him into your trap. Don't let him become aware of what is happening, for only then can your plan be successful.

The fourth paragraph of "Civil Offensive" and the last paragraph just cited clearly advocate one of China's favored measures for weakening opponents, whether enemy states or barbarian kingdoms: Entice the ruler and his key advisers with the allure of beauty, and debauch them with scents, music, and sexual delights. Although remarkably obvious and simplistic, it repeatedly proved successful throughout Chinese history (and continues to be widely employed today), particularly among self-indulgent rulers whose arrogance inclined them to neglect the people's welfare and the state's administration, and is therefore accorded a separate chapter later in this section.

The importance of the two *Six Secret Teachings'* chapters to the enterprise of spycraft may be seen in the glowing evaluation of Wang Ming-lo, an experienced high-level Ming dynasty commander who viewed them and Sun-tzu's chapter on "Employing Spies" as the very foundation of spycraft:

All the writings in the "Civil Offensive" chapter of the Martial T'ao within the *Six Secret Teachings* are concerned with concealed plots and secret plans for subjugating enemy forces without engaging in combat. The military esteems the Tao of deception and relies on profits to attain a tactical imbalance of power. Thus the T'ai Kung, who with righteous and benevolent counsel assisted the Chou in realizing the strategic affair of emperorship, put forth the unorthodox and employed agents, actions that might be termed "not shunning anything." I really am amazed that the authors of such secret teachings and strategies managed to be transmitted down with the Six Confucian Classics for more than a thousand years, being preserved like the tortoise and milfoil of the arts of divination. Sun-tzu's discussion of the five types of agents does not exceed the essentials found in twelve paragraphs. Thus agents cannot be abandoned.

Alas, without sagacity one cannot employ spies; without benevolence and righteousness, cannot use them; without subtlety, cannot distill their substance. It is therefore truly hard to speak about spycraft. However, through the employment of spies certain historical rulers exceeded the ordinary, and their fame has thus been inexhaustibly perpetuated. They truly followed the T'ai Kung's and Sun-tzu's bequeathed words.

In summary, when one's wisdom is all-encompassing and the moment for glory arrives, the subtle response cannot be entangled, intentions cannot be fathomed, or measures taken from ghosts and spirits. Subtle, truly subtle! It is truly difficult to speak about agents. Thus it is said, spiritualness and enlightenment lie with men![3]

The other military classics, while failing to emphasize covert actions to this extent, generally advised undertaking a wide range of measures to undermine the enemy, including spreading rumors and manipulating officials. In fact, the *Three Strategies,* which evinces a world vision of Sagely rule, states: "Without stratagems you have no means to resolve suspicions and settle doubts. Without rumor and the unorthodox you have no means to destroy evildoers and stop invaders."[4]

King Kou-chien and the State of Yüeh

Po P'i's corruption (already recounted) just at the end of the Spring and Autumn period dramatically illustrates the fearful impact a single influential adviser in the pay of a foreign state might achieve, especially when manipulating a headstrong, youthful ruler.[5] However, his employment constituted only one aspect, however critical, of an extensive program to debilitate the state of Wu and destroy its ruler, King Fu-ch'ai. The outlines of this famous systematic effort, the process by which it was conceived, and the steps taken to implement it are recounted in a *Wu Yüeh Ch'un-ch'iu* chapter entitled "Kou-chien's Secret Strategy." Although the *Wu Yüeh Ch'un-ch'iu* is a semihistorical work at best, these nine techniques were assiduously studied (and much decried) for nearly two thousand years and therefore merit careful scrutiny.[6] The death struggle between Wu and Yüeh stimulated Wen Chung to formulate a diabolical program:

> In the second month of his tenth year Kou-chien, king of Yüeh, pondered deeply and thought extensively about the insults he had suffered as a result of Wu's invasion, and how he had yet received Heaven's blessings and been restored to Yüeh. His numerous ministers and preceptors had each proposed plans, their words were harmonious and their intentions united. Kou-chien respectfully followed their advice and the state was already rich.
> On the other hand he had not heard any of his friends speak about death-defying action and thought that perhaps his high officials loved their persons and were unwilling to sacrifice their lives. Kou-chien ascended Chien Tower and looked out to see whether his ministers seemed troubled or not. The prime minister Fan Li and the high officials such as Wen Chung and Kou Ju

were all sternly seated in rows. Even though they harbored worries and troubles, none appeared on their countenances. Kouchien then struck the bell to summon a war council and made a covenant with his ministers: "I have been insulted and shamed. Above I have been embarrassed before the king of Chou, below ashamed before the rulers of Chin and Ch'u. Fortunately, through your plans, I managed to return to our state. I have implemented governmental measures, enriched the people, and nurtured officers, but for five years have not heard from any official willing to risk death or any minister who wants to wipe away our enmity. What do I have to do to achieve this?"

All the assembled officials remained silent, none dared reply. Kou-chien looked toward Heaven and sighed: "I have heard that when a ruler is troubled his ministers are disgraced, and when a ruler is disgraced his ministers die. I have personally experienced the misery of being a prisoner, suffered the shame of being incarcerated and broken. I am unable to support myself alone, but must have worthy advisers and entrust power to the benevolent, for only thereafter can we calculate the possibilities for attacking Wu. How is it that ministers and high officials bearing heavy responsibilities are so easily seen but so difficult to employ?"

Chi Yen, a lowly young official seated well in the back, raised his hand, jumped off his mat, and advanced: "Your majesty's words are erroneous. It is not that high officials are easy to see but difficult to employ, but that your majesty is incapable of employing them."

When Kou-chien asked what he meant, Chi Yen replied: "Now official position, riches, money, gold, and rewards are what your majesty disdains. Taking up sharp weapons, treading on naked blades, risking one's life, and flaunting death are what officials value greatly. Now your majesty would exchange the wealth that he disdains for undertaking responsibilities that the officials find heavy. Isn't this perilous?"

Thereupon the king fell silent. With a displeased look and embarrassed countenance he dismissed his assembled officials and had Chi Yen advance in order to ask him, "What are the methods for gaining the hearts of my officials?"

Chi Yen replied: "When the ruler respects benevolence and righteousness, this is the door to control. Officials and the people are the roots of rulership. For opening the door and solidifying the roots nothing surpasses rectifying yourself. The Tao for rectifying yourself is to be cautious about those about you. Associates are the means by which a ruler flourishes or declines. I would like your majesty to wisely select his associates so as to obtain only the worthy. In antiquity the T'ai Kung remonstrated nine times, then fled, eventually suffering from hunger along the Pang-hsi River. The Western Duke [King Wen] employed him and thereby became king of the realm. Kuan Chung was a prisoner from a lost state and had a reputation for avarice. Duke Huan of Ch'i obtained him and became hegemon. Thus the *Tso Chuan* says that 'one who loses officials will perish, and one who gains officials will flourish.' I would like your majesty to carefully examine your associates. Why should you be concerned about your ministers not being employed?"

The king complained: "I employ the worthy and give responsibility to the capable, assigning them each different affairs. I empty my mind of high expectations, hoping to hear about strategies for gaining revenge. At present they all conceal their sounds and hide their forms so that I have not heard any such discussions. Where does my fault lie?"

Chi Yen replied: "Selecting the worthy and successfully employing officials have their individual stages. Dispatch them far off with difficult affairs in order to verify their sincerity, internally advise them of hidden affairs in order to know their trustworthiness. Discuss affairs with them in order to observe their wisdom, get them drunk in order to detect their disorder. Appoint them as emissaries in order to investigate their abilities, display different countenances in order to discern their attitude.[7] Establish them according to their various virtues. Officers will then fully employ their abilities and men exhaust their wisdom. When you know that their wisdom is fully actualized, what worries will my ruler have about his ministers?"

Kou-chien said, "My strategists have exerted a substantial effort, and my men have exhausted their wisdom, but not all the officers have advanced beneficial proposals."

Chi Yen said: "Fan Li is enlightened and understands internal affairs, while Wen Chung is far-sighted and perceives externals. I suggest you invite Wen Chung for a serious discussion because the techniques for attaining kingship and hegemony lie with him."

The king of Yüeh, having invited Wen Chung to an audience, queried him: "Previously, through your advice I escaped from impoverishment and danger. If I would now have you put forth unconstrained calculations for washing away my long-standing enmity, what actions should I undertake?"

Wen Chung said: "I have heard that high-flying birds perish from beautiful food, while the fish found in deep pools yet die from fragrant bait. Now if you want to attack the state of Wu, you must first seek out what they love and participate in what they like, for only then will you be able you achieve it."

Kou-chien said, "How can we determine what people want, even their desires, and control them so that they will perish as a result?"

Wen Chung said: "If you want to repay insults, avenge enmity, destroy the state of Wu, and exterminate your enemies, there are nine techniques. Your majesty should investigate them."

The king of Yüeh replied: "I have been insulted and burdened with worry. Within the court I have been embarrassed before my ministers, outside the state I have been shamed before the feudal lords. My mind is confused and deluded, my spirit empty and vacant. Even though there might be nine such techniques, how could I know about them?"

Wen Chung said: "As for these nine techniques, T'ang of the Shang and Wen of the Chou employed them to become kings, Duke Huan and Duke Mu to become hegemons. With them, attacking cities and seizing towns are as easy as removing one's sandals. I would like you to scrutinize them.

"First, revere Heaven and serve ghosts in order to seek their blessings.

"Second, make generous presents and monetary gifts to the ruler and numerous presents and bribes to please his ministers.

"Third, make the five grains expensive in order to empty their state, take advantage of what the ruler desires in order to weary his people.

"Fourth, present the ruler with beautiful women in order to befuddle his mind and confuse his plans.

"Fifth, send the ruler skilled artisans and excellent materials to stimulate him to undertake palaces and mansions and thereby exhaust their wealth.

"Sixth, dispatch sycophantic ministers, causing the ruler to become easily attacked.

"Seventh, stiffen those ministers who dare to remonstrate, forcing them to commit suicide.

"Eighth, enrich your country and prepare the implements of war.

"Ninth, discipline your soldiers in order to exploit the ruler's perversity.

"Now your majesty should close his mouth and not transmit these nine to anyone. If you preserve them in spirituality, seizing All under Heaven would not prove difficult, so how much less so the state of Wu!"

"Excellent," said the king and then proceeded to implement the first technique. He established the eastern suburb in order to sacrifice to *yang*, calling it the August Duke of the East. He established the western suburb in order to sacrifice to *yin*, calling it the Queen Mother of the West. He sacrificed to the hills and mountains at K'uai-chi and the rivers and marshes at Chiang-chou. After he had served the ghosts and spirits for a year, the state no longer suffered from disasters. The king of Yüeh exclaimed, "How wondrous your techniques. I would like you to discuss the next one."

Wen Chung said: "The king of Wu loves to erect palaces and mansions and employs his workers without respite. Your majesty should select some sacred materials from our famous mountains and present them to the king."

Kou-chien then had more than three thousand woodworkers venture into the mountains to fell trees. After more than a year the unfortunate officers of this army thought about returning home. Everyone harbored rancorous, expectant hearts and went about singing the dirge of the "Tree Guest." One night Heaven gave birth to a pair of sacred trees, each twenty spans around and four hundred feet tall, the *yang* of catalpa, the *yin* of *pien-yu*. The woodworkers then began estimating and calculating, establishing the dimensions with the compass and cord, adjusting the roundness, planing and sanding. They divided the wood into red and green, decorated it with paint, embellished it with white jade disks, engraved and inlaid it with gold, and painted it with images of dragons and snakes.

While the decorations and colors where still new and scintillating, the king had Wen Chung present them all to Fu-ch'ai, king of Wu, saying: "Your servant Kou-chien, dwelling near the East Sea where these materials originate, entrusted me to humbly present them to your majesty. Through your lictors I dared to query your attendants. Based upon your majesty's strength, I dare say they will make somewhat more than a small palace. Therefore, respectfully bowing twice, I present them."

Fu-ch'ai was elated, but Wu Tzu-hsü objected: "Your majesty, do not accept them! In antiquity Chieh erected the Spirit Tower and Chou undertook the Deer Tower. *Yin* and *yang* were no longer in harmony, cold and warmth became unseasonal, and the five grains did not ripen. Heaven sent forth calamity, the people were vacuous, and the state changed, these two kings thereby invoking their own extinction. If your august majesty accepts them, you will certainly be exterminated by the king of Yüeh."

Instead of listening, Fu-ch'ai accepted the materials and erected a tower at Ku-su. It took three years to assemble the materials and five to complete it. From its heights one could see some seventy miles. Men died on the roads, the sound of wailing and crying was unbroken in the lanes and alleys. The people were exhausted and the officials embittered, men had nothing by which to live.

The king of Yüeh said, "This second technique is excellent!"

In his eleventh year the king thought deeply and pondered extensively, wishing only to attack Wu, so he sent for Chi Yen and queried him: "I want to attack Wu but fear we may not be able to destroy it. I would have mobilized the army earlier but wanted to question you about it."

Chi Yen replied: "To mobilize the army and raise troops you must first cultivate the five grains, accumulate silver and gold, fill the storehouses and warehouses, and hone your mailed troops. Now these four require that you first investigate the *ch'i* of Heaven and Earth, make your sources *yin* and *yang*, and become enlightened about solitariness and vacuity. When you have attained a penetrating understanding of survival and extinction, you will be able to analyze the enemy."

Kou-chien said, "Where is the essence of Heaven and Earth, survival and extinction?"

Chi Yen replied: "Through the *ch'i* of Heaven and Earth things live and die, through their sources in *yin* and *yang* they are noble or base. One who is enlightened about the solitary and vacuous knows when they will intersect. One who has fathomed survival and extinction can discriminate the true and false."

Kou-chien said, "What do you mean by death and life, the true and false?"

Chi Yen replied· "In the spring one plants the eight grains, in summer nourishes their growth, in autumn harvests their maturity, in winter stores them away. Now when it is the Heavenly season for birth and one doesn't exert oneself in planting, this is one death. In summer, when things grow, if there are no sprouts, this is a second death. In autumn, when things mature, if there is no accumulation, this is the third death. In winter, when one stores away, if there has been no harvest, this is a fourth death. Even if one possessed the Virtue of Yao or Shun, what could he do?

"Now the seasons of Heaven include birth and striving, aging and completion. When one infrequently contravenes them and their *ch'i* is responsive, when the numbers never lack or are lost, this is the pattern for the first stage of life. Be attentive, carefully investigate, and cautiously remove the weeds among the sprouts. When the weeds are removed and the sprouts flourish, this is the second stage to life. Making preparations in advance so that when events arise one can manage them, no one will evade their taxes, or the people lose their grain, is the third stage to life. When the granaries have already been sealed shut, the old grain replaced by the new, the ruler is at pleasure and the ministers are happy while men and women are faithful, this is the fourth stage to life. As for *yin* and *yang*, the harvest from years designated by *t'ai yin* can be retained for three years. The noble and inferior will be manifest thereby. Now 'solitary' and 'vacuous' refer to the gate of Heaven and door to Earth. Survival and extinction are the ruler's Tao and Power."

Kou-chien said, "How is it that, despite your youth, you are so knowledgeable about things?"

Chi Yen replied, "Whether an official is talented or not is unaffected by age or youth."

The king of Yüeh said, "Your logic is excellent!" Then, looking up, he observed the constellations of Heaven and investigated the astrological configurations, structuring the images of the four seasons to accord with them. Based upon vacuity above he established eight granaries. Following *yin* he stored, observing *yang* he sold grain. After fully implementing this plan for three years the harvest had improved fivefold. Yüeh was glorious and rich. Kou-chien sighed, "This is the basis for hegemony" and thus proclaimed the excellence of Chi Yen's plan.

In his twelfth year Kou-chien addressed Wen Chung: "I have heard that the king of Wu is licentious, loves beauty to the point of confusion, and drinks so heavily that he neglects the management of state affairs. Can we lay some plot to exploit this?"

Wen Chung said: "We can destroy him. Now the king of Wu is licentious and loves beauty, while his chancellor Po P'i flatters him in order to gain control over his heart. If we present beautiful women through Po P'i's intercession, the king will certainly accept them. Your majesty need only select two beautiful women and forward them."

Kou-chien, approving, had his prime minister obtain two women named Hsi Shih and Cheng Tan from Chu-luo-shan and Yü-hsin. He had them adorned with the finest silks, taught manners and bearing, and educated at T'u-ch'eng. After they had been in the capital for three years and their education was complete, he had Fan Li, the prime minister, present them to the king of Wu, saying: "The king of Yüeh, Kou-chien, dares to present these two women. Yüeh is a miserable state and in its present difficulties does not presume to retain them. Therefore the king has ordered your servant Fan Li to present them to your august majesty. I hope he will overlook their rusticity and unattractiveness but accept them for some menial task." The king of Wu, elated, responded, "The fact that Kou-chien has presented these two women is proof of his loyalty to Wu."

Wu Tzu-hsü remonstrated with him: "Your majesty cannot accept them. I have heard that the five colors cause men's eyes to go blind; the five notes, their ears to go deaf. In antiquity Chieh regarded T'ang lightly and was exterminated; Chou thought little of King Wen and perished. If you accept them, your majesty will certainly suffer from calamity.

"I have heard that the king of Yüeh never rolls up the court records but pores over them until the middle of the night. Moreover, he has gathered several tens of thousands of warriors willing to fight to the death. If this man doesn't die first, he will certainly achieve what he desires. The king of Yüeh bears himself with sincerity and practices benevolence. He listens to remonstrance and advances the worthy. If this man doesn't die, he will certainly become famous. The king of Yüeh wears a fur robe in the summer and endures linen in the winter. If this man doesn't die, he will certainly avenge his enmity. I have heard that worthy officials are a state's treasure, beautiful women a state's misfortune. The Hsia perished through Mei Hsi, the Shang through Ta Chi, and the Chou through Pao Ssu." Unwilling to listen, the king of Wu accepted the women. This prompted Kou-chien to exclaim, "How excellent this third technique!"

In his thirteenth year Kou-chien addressed Wen Chung: "All the techniques I have learned from you, the plans you have made, have proven to be appropriate and auspicious. If I want you to again plot against Wu, what would you advise?"

Wen Chung replied: "Your majesty has himself said that Yüeh is minuscule and rustic, our annual harvests not plentiful. I would have your majesty ask them to sell us some grain in order to attain your ambition. If Heaven is about to abandon Wu, their king will certainly assent." The king of Yüeh then dispatched Wen Chung as an emissary to Wu, where he sought an audience with the king through the intercession of Po P'i. He then formally proclaimed: "The state of Yüeh humbles itself before you. The elements of water and heat are out of balance, so the annual harvest has been sparse. The people suffer from hunger and want, the roads are constantly filled with the famished and starving. I would like to request your august majesty to provide us with provisions to be repaid to your great granaries in the coming year. Our only wish is that your august majesty will rescue us from our dire impoverishment."

Fu-ch'ai said: "The king of Yüeh is trustworthy, sincerely preserves the Tao, and is free of disloyal intentions. In their impoverishment he has turned and informed us of his distress. How can I begrudge the expense or be parsimonious with our treasures, snatching away his hopes?"

Wu Tzu-hsü remonstrated: "You cannot! If Wu doesn't have Yüeh, Yüeh will certainly gain control of Wu! When good fortune departs, evil will come. You will nurture invaders who will destroy our state. Granting their request will not bring them closer; not granting it will not cause disaster. Moreover, Yüeh's sagacious minister Fan Li is courageous and excels at plotting. He has certainly disguised their aggressive intentions in order to spy on us and secretly observe us. Kou-chien has dispatched emissaries to request provisions not because their state is poor and the people suffering, but to enter our state and spy on our internal affairs."

Fu-ch'ai said: "I insulted Kou-chien and forced him to submit. I possess his masses. I embraced his altars of state in order to shame him and Kou-chien's spirit submitted. Moreover, he served as a carriage driver and stable hand, something all the feudal lords already know. Now that I have restored him to his state, resurrected his ancestral temple, and revived the altars of state, how would he dare think of turning against me?"

Wu Tzu-hsü said: "I have heard that when a poverty-stricken officer does not find it difficult to repress his inclinations and humble himself before others, he will later have an intimidating appearance. We have now learned that Kou-chien suffers from famine and his people are enduring hardship and destitution. Therefore you can exploit this situation to destroy them. If you do not today employ the Tao of Heaven and accord with the patterns of Earth, but instead ship them provisions, you will solidify your fate. This is like a fox playing among chickens! When the fox humbles himself and the chickens trust him, the fox will gain his ambition and the chickens will certainly die. How can you not be cautious?"

Fu-ch'ai said: "If I provide grain to Kou-chien's state when it suffers from difficulty, this is beneficence flowing out and righteousness accruing. The virtuousness of this course is manifest, so what is there to worry about?"

Wu Tzu-hsü said: "I have heard that a wolf cub still has a wild heart and that great enemies cannot be brought close. Tigers cannot be trusted with edibles or snakes left to fulfill their desires. Today your majesty is about to reduce your state's wealth in order to nourish unsurpassed enmity, to abandon the words of loyal ministers and accord with the wishes of the enemy. I will certainly witness Yüeh destroy Wu, swine and deer amble about the tower at Ku-su, and brambles and thorns fill the palace. I hope your majesty will take a lesson from the affair of King Wu attacking King Chou."

Po P'i, chancellor of Wu, replied from the side: "King Wu was not a true subject of King Chou. He led the feudal lords in an attack against his ruler. Even though he was victorious over the Shang, is he termed 'righteous'?"

Wu Tzu-hsü replied, "King Wu thereby established his fame!"

Chancellor Po P'i then remarked, "I cannot abide a subject exterminating his ruler."

Wu Tzu-hsü said: "One who steals a state is enfeoffed as a feudal lord, one who steals gold is executed. If you would now deprive King Wu of his principles, how would his actions have illuminated virtue in others?"

Chancellor Po P'i retorted: "Tzu-hsü is a subject who only wants to oppose what your majesty wants, to frustrate your majesty's intentions in order to distinguish himself. How is it that your majesty has not recognized his excessiveness?"

Wu Tzu-hsü replied: "Chancellor P'i gratifies your desires in order to ingratiate himself. He previously worked to release Kou-chien from his imprisonment and persuaded you to accept the presentation of two women. He has externally colluded with enemy states and internally deluded his ruler. Your majesty should investigate it, not let yourself be insulted by coteries of menials. You should be like someone bathing an infant—even though they cry, no one listens. Such are the chancellor's words."

The king of Wu said: "Chancellor P'i is someone who never fails to listen to my words. This isn't the way of a loyal, faithful minister but similar to that of sycophants and flatterers."

Chancellor P'i replied: "I have heard that when a neighboring state suffers from distress, one races aid to them from a thousand miles away, for this is the way of a true king. To enfeoff the descendants of a lost state is to continue the achievements of the five hegemons in supporting the remnants of extinction."

King Fu-ch'ai then provided Yüeh with ten thousand bushels of grain and asserted: "In providing this grain to Yüeh, I have acted contrary to the advice of my ministers. After the next full harvest return it to me."

Wen Chung said: "I undertake responsibility for bringing it to Yüeh. We will certainly repay Wu's provisions from the next abundant harvest." When he returned to Yüeh, all the ministers wished him long life and congratulated him. Yüeh then apportioned the grain as a reward to its ministers and the people. The next year Kou-chien had the best grains selected to repay Wu, but secretly had them heated before dispatching them to Wu. They repaid every bushel and moreover had Wen Chung accompany it back to Fu-ch'ai. When Fu-ch'ai saw the size of the grain, he sighed and remarked to Chancellor P'i: "Yüeh is a fertile land, its grains are excellent. We should retain these for planting." Wu subsequently planted the grain from Yüeh, but as the seeds had been killed, it didn't germinate. Wu therefore suffered from a serious famine.

Despite his loyal service over the critical years of struggle with Wu, Wen Chung ironically suffered the fate of all those who served headstrong rulers, being executed when he refused to plan further military actions and otherwise offended Kou-chien. (His end had been foretold by Fan Li, who realized that one could share hardship with Kou-chien, but not success.) The vituperativeness of Kou-chien's final dismissal, while probably fictional, is striking: "We have already employed three of the nine measures contained in your secret plans and strategies for overturning and seizing enemy states to destroy powerful Wu. What I want is for you to employ the remaining six on behalf of my predecessor in the nether world to plot against Wu's former ruler."

Even though this dramatic narrative ventures into the mythical and improbable, it clearly depicts the fundamental intention of sowing dissension and gaining control of Fu-ch'ai essentially through measures such as advocated in the *Six Secret Teachings*. Moreover, it portrays Yüeh's ruthless approach to debilitating and impoverishing the state of Wu itself, not just the ruler and his court, through what might be termed "indirect biological warfare." Unlike earlier in the Spring and Autumn period when states felt compelled to aid their neighbors during times of famine despite considerable tension and enmity between them,[8] Wen Chung conceived and enacted a two-step program to empty Wu's grain reserves and then destroy their next crop, a plot vociferously condemned as heinous and dastardly for two thousand years thereafter, even though it is only hinted at in the more reliable histories. (Others dismiss it simply as the stratagem of a semicivilized peripheral state, as might be expected from men not yet fully versed in righteousness.) Irrespective of the moral dimensions, this program, or at least some of its steps, perhaps paved the way for Yüeh to aggressively exploit King Fu-ch'ai's grandiose schemes and misperceptions and swiftly obliterate the state of Wu itself. This unimaginable reversal of fortunes thus became the basis of history and legend, narrative and romance, creating an indelible impression upon subsequent generations that subversive programs systematically implemented could achieve remarkable results.

Later Contemplations

Wen Chung's program and other materials from the early period prompted the following meditation from Li Ch'uan in the T'ang dynasty in a chapter entitled "Techniques for Secret Plots."

Among the ancients, those who excelled in employing the military invariably emphasized authority over the realm and investigated the thoughts of the feudal lords. One who is not fastidious about the weightiness of tactical power will not know the relative imbalance of the light and heavy, the strong and weak. One who is not particular about probing emotions will not know hidden evils or the transformations of movement and rest. For heaviness nothing is more important than being thoroughly knowledgeable; for probing nothing is more difficult than raising everything. In affairs nothing is more difficult than invariably being successful. A true Sage can undertake these three.

Therefore, military techniques that achieve a hundred victories in a hundred battles are not the height of excellence. Rather, subjugating the enemy's forces without engaging in combat is the pinnacle of excellence. The pinnacle employs plots and plans; the next highest, human affairs; and the lowest undertakes warfare by attacking. Those who employ plots and plans mystify and confuse the enemy's ruler, secretly influence his slanderous ministers to affect his affairs, muddle him with sorcerers and soothsayers, and cause him to respect ghosts and serve spirits. They cause him to indulge in colors and embroidery while cheapening the value he places on grains and foodstuffs, thereby emptying out his granaries and warehouses. They send him beautiful women to unsettle his mind and dispatch skilled carpenters to inveigle him into constructing palaces, rooms, and high towers in order to exhaust the state's wealth and dissipate their strength in labor, thus changing the ruler's nature and inducing licentious practices.

When he has become extravagant, brutal, arrogant, and dissipated, his worthy ministers will bite their tongues, unwilling to provide correctives or support. When he grants overflowing rewards and perverts the punishments, determining them solely by his own happiness or anger, the orders of government will not be implemented. When he believes in divination and looks for ghosts; contravenes the loyal but advances sycophants; publicly holds private audiences but lacks wise men in government; provides positions to those he loves and rank to those without merit; rewards people without achievement but pardons crimes because he is happy and perverts the laws to execute people when he is angry, then although there are laws, the ruler is merely indulging his inclinations and orders are not implemented. When he believes in divination by turtle shell and milfoil casting; when sorcerers and soothsayers, sycophants and slanderers, the strange and skillful, are favored and prevalent within his gates; and whatever he considers correct is actually incorrect, what he terms "incorrect" all correct, a chasm separates the ruler and his ministers.

When you block off the ruler's access to external information and debauch him with licentiousness, attack him with the lure of profits, pleasure him with music, nurture his tastes, and cause him to regard the deceitful as the trustworthy, the trustworthy as deceitful, the loyal as rebellious, and the rebellious as loyal, then those who offer loyal remonstrance will perish while sycophants will be rewarded. When he exiles worthy men to the wilds, retains menial men in official positions, issues urgent orders, and imposes brutal punishments, the people will not sustain his mandate to rule. This is termed "overthrowing the ruler through secret plots without fighting." When the destruction of his state has thus been achieved, if you follow up with troops, the ruler can be captured, his state subjugated, his cities seized, and his masses scattered. Thus King T'ang of the Shang employed this method and King Chieh of the Hsia was deposed; the Chou used it and the last Shang king was killed; Yüeh employed it and the state of Wu was extinguished; Ch'u adopted it and Ch'en and Ts'ai were raised; Lu's three ministerial families followed it and Lu was weakened; Han and Wei employed it and the Eastern Chou cracked.

Even the Confucians say, "One whose forces are large and strong will certainly be victorious; one whose forces are few and weak will certainly perish." For this reason while the ruler of a small state has no hope of becoming hegemon, there is little indication that the king of one capable of fielding ten thousand chariots will be destroyed. However, in antiquity the Hsia was broad, the Shang but narrow, yet the Shang prevailed; later the Shang was great and the Chou small, yet the Chou overthrew them; and finally Yüeh was weak and Wu strong, but Yüeh exterminated them. Thus the strategy for wresting victory without fighting is actually the technique of secretly overturning them, the Tao of night implementation. The Sage is enlightened about the teachings of the martial and civil. He alone sees them clearly, he alone take pleasure in them.[9]

Li Ch'uan thus argued enthusiastically for the importance and necessity of covert actions, justifying them in part as having been historically employed even by the great sages, despite the literati's adamant belief in the dogma of their hegemony having been achieved solely through benevolence and righteousness. Unfortunately his views in the second half of the eighth century were ignored by all but the military writers, who took them very seriously indeed.

Causing consternation in the enemy, the basic thrust of covert programs, is again evident in a chapter entitled "Putting the Enemy in Difficulty" from the Sung dynasty *Hu-ling Ching* that shows theoretical continuity with earlier writings and the timeless applicability of the approach:

When the enemy has planning officers, employ spies to estrange them. When the enemy has accumulated stores, employ covert agents *[hsi jen]* to burn them. Whatever the enemy has planted, cut it down when it ripens. If the enemy has people, forcefully make them prisoners. Secretly bribe the king's favorites to have them send him beautiful women to delude his thoughts, and present excellent dogs and superlative horses in order to incite his mind. Use numerous methods to give him pleasure, and wait until they are suffering consternation without and delusion within, for then he will be remiss in state affairs. Thereafter you can mobilize the army to attack and be successful without laboring. One who excels at employing the military always plots how to put the enemy in difficulty. When the enemy is in difficulty, you will be at ease. When forces at ease strike those in difficulty, what enemy will not be conquered?

Late in the Ming dynasty Chieh Hsüan also contemplated the nature of subversive programs designed to undermine and psychologically impact the enemy, providing two key analyses in his *Ping-fa Pai-yen*. The first defines the character *mu*, which, while translated here as "focus," originally depicted an eye and thus had the primary meaning of "eye" or "eyes." However, in his conception the term obviously entails an extended meaning that on the one hand designates the linchpin of action or center of perception and strategy, on the other perhaps functionally approaches the modern concept of "center of gravity."[10]

Definition: To cover and obfuscate the enemy's enlightenment is termed "focus."

Original Text: What the enemy invariably relies upon for their movement is termed their "focus." You must first observe the location of the enemy's focus and then seize what they rely upon. If the enemy takes their strategists as their focus, concentrate upon expelling them. If they take their enlightened generals as their focus, concentrate upon eliminating them. If they take their intimate, trusted ministers as their focus, you can estrange them. If they take fame and righteousness as their focus, you can destroy them. Extract their roots; strike their strategic points; defeat their secret plans; alienate their reliable allies; strip away their basis; destroy their customary profits. When men have a focus, they are enlightened; in conflict, when they have eyes, they live. Isn't cutting off their lives and destroying their enlightenment the essence of controlling the enemy?

Explanation: Eliminating the enemy's focus is not so easily planned. Until a tree is rotten insects will not live in it. Until the strands snap a rope will not break. If an enemy ruler is free of doubts while his generals are wise, how will rumors succeed in defaming them, how will slanderous agents be able to harm them?

If there is no alternative, eliminating their wise generals has to be the first technique. The wise rely upon the courageous to deploy the army for battle. If there are no warriors capable of penetrating formations and forming an assault front, the wise will find it difficult to implement their plans by themselves. If you can estrange them through covert agents, employ clandestine calculations to beguile them, and multiply the plots and battle plans designed to slay them, you will blunt the sharp edge of their army's front. When the vanes are removed from an arrow, even though the shaft and tip remain it is difficult for the arrow to penetrate deeply. Similarly, even the wisest have little recourse in such circumstances. Thus it may be said that eliminating a state is not as good as eliminating the army's focus.

Less enigmatically, Chieh Hsüan's definition of "noise" directs the strategist's attention to implementing psychologically effective measures to confuse the enemy's analytic skills, coincidentally pointing out the importance of the unrighteous and despised in such work:

Definition: Misleading and confusing the enemy's hearing is termed "noise" [obfuscation].[11]

Explanation: A state beset by treacherous individuals is lost, but when they plague the enemy it is advantageous. In our state Po P'i and Ch'in Hui are brigands, but in the enemy's they are treasures. Rely upon them to confuse the ruler's intelligence, stir up the will of the masses, destroy human relations, and throw the rules and regulations into chaos. When they do not attain their ambitions they grumble uselessly, but if we assist them in gaining their ambitions they will push out everyone who differs with them. Their discourses and discussions are sufficient to confuse and befuddle the worthy and wise, to shake and startle the ordinary and stupid. They can cause the entire populace of a state to be overturned and confused, bereft of any means to serve the ruler. Eventually even the most upright Sages, Worthies, and scholars, as well as the greatest stalwarts and wisest strategists, will abandon their positions and never speak again. Is not such a situation to our state's advantage?

Thus it is better for the enemy to delude themselves rather than for us to delude them. You should especially value the ruler's trusted confidants for nurturing such self-delusion. "Noise" thus has the meaning of deluding someone with the shimmering and sparkling. Reflexively, rulers and ministers should focus upon achieving administrative excellence in order to strengthen the state and preserve uprightness in order to eliminate the disorderly.[12]

Examples: Female musicians and stylish horses were employed by Ch'i to obfuscate K'ang-tzu. Po P'i, Hsi Shih, and Cheng Tan were employed by Yüeh to obfuscate Fu-ch'ai. How can all the cases in which noise caused harm ever be counted? Still, those who come from the enemy are easy to detect, those born within a state hard to prevent.

The thrust of such covert action is to occlude the enemy with a dazzling array of misinformation, distraction, and vices. Therefore the analogy is drawn with noise—the buzzing of insects—that overwhelms the senses and precludes critical focusing, no doubt reflecting many concepts and measures originally formulated in the much excoriated chapter entitled "Civil Offensive" in the *Six Secret Teachings.*

9

Assassination and
Other Techniques

$\mathcal{T}$RADITIONAL CHINA SAW NOT ONLY the widespread practice of assassination, but also its lionization in "The Assassins," a *Shih Chi* chapter depicting five famous assassins.[1] In each case the person was motivated to strike on behalf of someone who had visibly recognized and honored him despite ignominious position, a reaction the cynical will recognize as assiduously cultivated.[2] However, assassins were employed not only in personal vendettas, but also in epoch-making events. For example, the king known as Ho-lü (who presided over Wu's apex and employed the great Sun-tzu just at the end of the Spring and Autumn period) acceded to the throne through the murderous act of Chuan Chu, already related in the historical section on the Spring and Autumn period. Ching K'o's unsuccessful attempt, late in the Warring States period, to stab the king of Ch'in with a dagger originally concealed in a map case represents another state-initiated operation. This readiness to employ covert agents and the determination displayed by the assassins were remembered and emulated throughout Chinese history in both internal intrigues and against external enemies.

Assassination attempts generally relied upon poison and simple strong-arm techniques such as stabbing or multiple attackers. States generally employed swift violence, perhaps for its dramatic decisiveness, while palace intrigues that frequently, but not exclusively, involved women and questions of imperial succession saw a variety of poisons being mixed into strongly flavored foods, such as mushrooms and dates, or hot beverages provided to unsuspecting victims.[3] Poisons being readily available and herbal knowledge commonplace, thwarting such attempts proved difficult. The dynastic histories thus record hundreds of murders, as well as the deaths of numerous food tasters and hapless dogs, all poisoned in the quest for survival. More artistic approaches forced the innocent to commit suicide by constructing elaborate plots and mounting false accusations that exploited the perverse dynamics of court jealousy and hatred, the ruler's insecurity, and ongoing tension between the royal family and court ministers. Many of these remarkable tales are intrinsically fascinating, but as they recount clandestine actions undertaken for internal rather than external objectives, they fall outside the scope of our study.

As reprised in the Spring and Autumn historical section, King Ho-lü found regicide a surprisingly simple, effective method for attaining the throne. Therefore, when he wished to eliminate the residual threat posed by the late ruler's valiant son, he again turned to assassination and his confidant Wu Tzu-hsü in a sorrowful tale that was much remarked thereafter:

Two years after he had killed King Liao, King Ho-lü became troubled that Ch'ing-chi, the king's son, being in a nearby state might unite the feudal lords in an attack upon him. Therefore he spoke with Wu Tzu-hsü: "Formerly you treated me generously by recommending the assassin Chuan Chu. Now that I have learned that prince Ch'ing-chi is plotting with the feudal lords, my food lacks taste and I am unable to sleep peacefully. I would like to entrust this to you."

Wu Tzu-hsü replied: "I was evil and disloyal in planning the death of King Liao with you in my own rooms. I am afraid that eliminating his son will not accord with Heaven's intentions."

Ho-lü retorted: "Anciently, when King Wu of the Chou conducted a campaign of rectification against King Chou of the Shang and thereafter killed Wu Keng, the Chou populace did not display a resentful appearance. Therefore why should Heaven care this time?"

Wu Tzu-hsü replied: "If by thus serving your majesty we unify Wu, what will there be to fear? One man that I have treated well is delicate, but I would like him to participate in these plans."

The king said: "The enemy that worries me has the strength of ten thousand men. How can a delicate man make such plans?"

Wu Tzu-hsü replied, "He plans affairs like a delicate man but has the strength of ten thousand men."

"Who is he?" the king inquired.

Wu Tzu-hsü replied: "His surname is Yao and given name is Li. I previously witnessed his courage."

The king said, "I would like to give a feast for him." Wu Tzu-hsü then went to see Yao Li and said, "The king of Wu has heard of your lofty righteousness and fervently hopes to meet you." So he accompanied Wu Tzu-hsü to see the king. The king asked, "What can you do?"

Yao Li replied: "I am a man from a state a thousand kilometers east of here. I am thin, small, and weak. When I go against the wind I am knocked flat, when the wind is at my back I am pushed down. But if your majesty commands me, how would I dare not exhaust my strength?"

The king of Wu wondered to himself how Wu Tzu-hsü could have introduced this man. After a long silence Yao Li advanced and said: "Your majesty is concerned about Ch'ing-chi. I can kill him."

The king replied: "All the world has heard about Ch'ing-chi's courage. Not one among ten thousand can oppose the strength of his muscles and bones. He can pursue racing animals and his hands snatch flying birds. His bones leap and his flesh soars, his elbows and knees can cover a hundred kilometers. I once chased after him along the Yangtze River but my chariot horses could not catch up to him. I shot at him but he invisibly caught the arrows so that none ever hit their mark. Your strength cannot match his."

Yao Li said, "If your majesty desires it, I can kill him."

The king said, "Ch'ing-chi is perceptive and wise, and even though he is a refugee among the feudal lords, he does not rank below anyone."

Yao Li said: "Your servant has heard that one who rests in the pleasures of his wife and child without fully exerting himself in the service of his ruler's righteous cause is not loyal. Someone who embraces the love of his family without eliminating his ruler's problems is not righteous. I suggest that I flee on the pretense of having committed a criminal offense. I would like your majesty to exterminate my wife and children and chop off my right hand. Ch'ing-chi will then certainly believe me."

The king assented. Yao Li then fled on a pretext of having committed a criminal offense and the king of Wu seized his wife and children, executed them, and then burned their bodies in the marketplace. Yao Li fled out among the feudal lords, where he become known throughout the realm for his protestations of having been wrongfully punished. Eventually he went to Wei, where he sought an audience with Ch'ing-chi, to whom he said: "Ho-lü is completely unprincipled, as your majesty knows. Now he has extinguished my family and burned their bodies in the marketplace. Innocent of any offense, I have been punished. However, I know all the details of Wu's affairs and with your courage King Ho-lü can be captured. Why not go east with me to Wu?"

Since Ch'ing-chi trusted his plans, three months later they proceeded to Wu with selected troops. When they crossed over the Yangtze, Yao Li's strength being small, he sat upwind. Just in the middle of the river, hooking his cap on a spear and then relying upon the power of the wind, he stabbed Ch'ing-chi with it. Ch'ing-chi turned around, grabbed him, dashed his head into the water three times, then held it down on his knee and gaspingly said, "You are the most courageous man in the empire to dare stab me."

His attendants all wanted to kill him but Ch'ing-chi stopped them, saying: "He is one of the realm's courageous officers. How can two such courageous men be slain on a single day?" Thereupon he admonished his attendants to have him returned to Wu in order to be an example of loyalty. Thereupon Ch'ing-chi died.

When Yao Li had crossed over the river to the embankment, stricken with grief he did not stir. The others said, "Sir, why do you not depart?"

Yao Li replied: "Sacrificing my wife and children in order to serve my ruler is not benevolent. Slaying a former ruler's son on behalf of a new lord is not righteous. Overvaluing my death and being unconcerned about righteousness, thereby coveting life and abandoning morality, is not righteous. Marked by these three evils, how might I face the officers of the realm if I remain in the world?"

Having finished his words, he threw himself into the river but Ch'ing-chi's attendants pulled him out before he drowned. Yao Li said, "Do you think I don't want to die?"

They replied, "Sir, do not die in order to await your rewards of rank and salary." However, Yao Li chopped off his hand and feet, fell on his sword, and died.[4]

Even though this must be regarded as a semihistorical account with fabricated dialogue, it depicts the terrible resolve with which assassins historically approached their tasks and was subsequently witnessed in Chinese warrior behavior and among the samurai and ninja in Japan. The *yu-hsia* ("wandering knights") of the late Warring States and thereafter—resolute, often arrogant individuals of no formal rank or status—

exemplified the Chinese fascination with the spirit of martial independence, the refusal to be cowered or flinch in the face of power or insult. Although clearly admired by Ssu-ma Ch'ien (who penned a chapter to memorialize the best of them) and much of the ordinary populace (who willingly shielded them from authorities and flocked to their protection), they were increasingly condemned as Confucian values and the literati's antimartial viewpoint dominated officialdom. Although basically just asocial, the *yu-hsia* and anyone else who would manifest an independent spirit buttressed by martial expertise (in contrast to the simple ideal of a reclusive scholar or Taoist inebriate) were branded as antisocial and therefore criminals to be extirpated. However, evidence from the popular culture provides indications that the common people continued to admire individual strength, decisiveness, and martial virtues, despite their heavy deprecation in the orthodox writings, memorials to the throne, policy debates, and similar records.[5]

The *Shuo Yüan* describes another attempt to end Confucius's dangerous influence as a worthy administrator in the state of Lu. Although it is probably apocryphal, since the *Tso Chuan* does not confirm any aspects of it, nor are the quotations found in any other writing, it had obviously became part of common historical lore by the Han dynasty:

Duke Chien of Chao said: "Chin has Tse Ming and Tu Ch'ou, while Lu has Confucius. If I kill these three men, I can then plot how to seize the realm." He then summoned Tse Ming and Tu Ch'ou, entrusted them with high government positions, and subsequently had them killed. Thereafter he had an emissary go and invite Confucius to come from Lu. En route, when Confucius reached the Yellow River, he approached the water and gazed out at it: "How majestic the water, vast and overflowing. That I will not cross over is fate!"

Tzu Lu hastened forward and inquired, "May I dare ask what you mean?"

Confucius replied: "Now Tse Ming and Tu Ch'ou were Chin's great Worthies. Duke Chien of Chao, having not yet realized his ambition over the realm, consulted with them, then killed them both and personally implemented their policies. I have heard that when unborn infants are murdered and young forests burned down, unicorns do not appear; when marshes are drained to catch fish, dragons will not appear; when nests are overturned and eggs destroyed, phoenix will not soar. I have heard that the true gentlemen regards those who harm his kind seriously."[6]

Through his subterfuge the duke not only deprived Chin of two Worthies, but also acquired vital administrative information. However, by prematurely killing them to ensure they could not be similarly employed by anyone else, he carelessly alerted Confucius to the danger and thus scared him off.

Another compelling depiction of the painful extremes willingly endured by those determined to exact righteous vengeance is found in Ssu-ma Ch'ien's chapter on assassins. However, concise versions of Yü Jang's dramatic story, often with the sequence of events altered, are embedded in such eclectic texts as the *Lü-shih Ch'un-ch'iu* and *Shuo Yüan*. In "Repaying Kindness" the *Shuo Yüan's* narrative unfolds as follows:

Chih Po perished when he fought with the ruler of Chao, the viscount of Hsiang, below Chin-yang.[7] One of Chih Po's ministers, Yü Jang, was so angered by it that his vital energies even affected the viscount's heart. Therefore he blistered his body with lacquer to change his appearance, and swallowed charcoal to alter the sound of his voice. When the viscount of Hsiang was about to go out, Yü Jang feigned being a dead man lying beneath a bridge. However, the viscount's carriage horses, being startled, refused to advance while he also felt his heart stir. When he had his guards look below the bridge they caught Yü Jang. Because he valued Yü's righteousness, he did not have him killed.

Another time, pretending to be a thief by wearing the red jacket of punishment, he entered the palace as a workman to repair the walls. The viscount's heart stirred, so he said, "It must be Yü Jang." After having him seized, he asked: "You initially served the lord of Chung-hang, but when Chih Po slew him, instead of dying for your lord you went on to serve Chih Po. Yet after I killed Chih Po, you lacquered your body to form boils and swallowed charcoal to make yourself hoarse, wanting to kill me. Why is it different from the former case?"[8]

Yü Jang replied: "The lord of Chung-hang treated me as one of the ordinary masses, so I served him in a similar fashion. Chih Po treated me as a minister of his court, so I also continued my employment as a court minister."

The viscount of Hsiang remarked: "Is this not righteousness? You are a resolute officer!" Then he put Yü Jang in his carriage house and abstained from drinking for three days in order to honor him. Knowing the viscount's thoughts, Yü Jang committed suicide.

The *Lü-shih Ch'un-ch'iu* account further illuminates the evolution of his disguise: "Wanting to kill Chao's viscount of Hsiang, Yü Jang shaved his head and eyebrows, mutilated himself as if he had suffered corporal punishment in order to change his appearance, and pretended to be a beggar. In this disguise he went to beg food from his wife, who said, 'Your appearance is not at all like my husband's, so how is it that your voice is so similar?' So then he swallowed charcoal in order to change his sound."[9]

Even the virtuous state of Chou, the final remnant of the glorious Chou dynasty, not only split apart, but also the halves actually became enmired in costly intrigues against each other and resorted to assassination: "During the Warring States period King Wu of Western Chou had an agent assassinate Ling K'uei, a minister in Eastern Chou. Lying down prostrate, Ling ordered his son to immediately weep and cry out, 'Who has stabbed my father?' Hearing this, the assassin believed he was dead and fled. Later, the king of Western Chou, learning that Ling was still alive, assumed the agent had been unfaithful and heavily punished him."[10]

Wang Ch'ung, a Han official, commentator, and professional skeptic active in the first century A.D., analyzed a story current in his time that attributed Ch'in Shih-huang's lingering death to an assassin's blow. Essentially a continuation of Prince Tan's saga (which hastened the extinction of Chao as retold in the Warring States section), the agent was none other than the musician Kao Chien-li, the drinking companion who had played at Ching K'o's ill-fated departure for Ch'in. After some years in hiding as a common servant, he finally betrayed his skill and again became well known:

Traditional works state that Tan, Yen's heir apparent, had the assassin Ching K'o stab the king of Ch'in, but he failed to accomplish his objective and was executed. Somewhat thereafter Kao Chien-li also went to have an audience with the king to perform on the lute. The king of Ch'in was elated but knowing that Kao was formerly a guest of the heir apparent, had him blindfolded before playing his lute. However, prior to coming to court Kao had made his lute heavier by placing lead inside it. Unable to restrain himself during the performance, the king crept forward on his knees. Kao then struck him in the forehead with the lute, seriously wounding the king, who died three months later.

Now to say that Kao Chien-li struck the king with his lute is factual, but to claim that he fell ill and died three months later because he was thus struck is specious because the king in question was the first emperor of Ch'in, Ch'in Shih-huang. It is clear that Yen's heir apparent had Ching K'o attack the first emperor in the latter's twentieth year of rule, but Ch'in Shih-huang killed him. In his twenty-first year the emperor had General Wang Chien attack Yen and bring back the heir apparent's head. In his twenty-fifth year he again attacked Yen and captured the king. Some unknown years thereafter Kao Chien-li struck the emperor with his lute but wasn't accurate and was executed. In his thirty-seventh year the emperor roamed about the realm, visiting various places, before he fell ill and died. He was said to die after another illness, as well as three months after the lute blow, and to have died in different places. However, the common transmission has largely misstated the facts.[11]

Wang Ch'ung's analysis, an example of his critical spirit, also provides evidence of the currency of such stories and the ongoing appreciation of loyalty and devotion.

Although distinct states no longer existed as separate entities to struggle for control of the realm, the political employment of assassins did not cease with the dawn of imperial China because rebel bands, dynastic challengers, and nomadic steppe peoples—against whom every measure, including extravagant bribery, largely failed—plagued the empire. Thus when several of its emissaries to the steppe peoples were slain, the Han readily accepted Fu Chieh-tzu's offer to arrange the impossible assassination of the rebellious leaders:

Chieh-tzu and the officers and troops accompanying him all prepared gold and silks and conspicuously let it be known that they were intended as gifts for foreign states.[12] When they reached Loulan the king did not want to see him, so Chieh-tzu withdrew and made a show of departing, but when he reached the western border of their territory instructed the translator to say: "The Han ambassador, bringing gold and embroidered silks, is traveling about to present gifts to the various states. If your majesty does not come to receive them, I will send them out to the western states." He displayed the gold for the translator to see, who then returned and reported it to the king.

Because he coveted Han goods, the king went to see the ambassador. While Chieh-tzu and the king sat together and drank, Chieh-tzu again displayed the items. They continued drinking until both were drunk, at which time Chieh-tzu informed the king that the emperor had instructed him to personally reward him. The king got up and followed Chieh-tzu into the tent, where two

stalwart officers stabbed him from behind while they spoke together privately. Because their blades penetrated the king's chest,
he died immediately. All his nobles and attendants scattered and
fled.

Chieh-tzu then proclaimed: "The king committed an offense
against the Han, so the emperor dispatched me to come, execute
him, and establish the former heir apparent, who has been a political hostage in the Han. Han troops will shortly arrive, do not dare
move. If you move, we will extinguish your state."[13]

For his extraordinary efforts Chieh-tzu was enfeoffed as lord of Yi-
yang, and his chief assistants were awarded palace guard positions.

A startling example of Han perfidy appears in the *Shih Chi* when
Emperor Wu, the Martial Emperor, who was frequently inclined to
pursue aggressive solutions to the ongoing conflict with the steppe
peoples, agreed to violate the terms of friendly relations in order to
mount an essentially preemptive strike against the Hsiung-nu:

In 135 B.C., at the beginning of Emperor Wu's reign, the Hsiung-
nu came to request the ratification of peaceful relations, a matter
upon which the emperor requested opinions. The Imperial Messenger Wang Hui, a native of Yen who had frequently served as a
border official and was well experienced in barbarian affairs, expressed the following opinion: "Even if the Han concludes a treaty
of friendship with the Hsiung-nu, before many years pass they
will certainly abrogate the agreement. Rather than consenting it
would be better to mobilize troops and suddenly attack them."

Han An-kuo replied: "It is not advantageous for an army to engage in battle a thousand kilometers away. The Hsiung-nu
presently ride swift steppe horses and embody the hearts of wild
animals. They move their forces about and attack as suddenly as
crows, so it would be difficult to wrest control over them. Even if
we were to acquire their territory it would be inadequate to
broaden the Han, even if we wrest control over their masses they
would be insufficient to augment our power. Since remote antiquity they have not been considered civilized men. If our forces
struggle with them for profit some several thousand kilometers
away, the men and horses will be exhausted, and the bastards will
completely seize control over the exhausted remnants. Moreover,
at the end of its flight a bolt from even the strongest crossbow is
unable to pierce thin gauze. When dying down, even the most
brutal wind lacks the power to float goose down. This is not because they were not initially fierce but because their strength de-

clines at the end of their range. Suddenly attacking the Hsiung-nu would not be beneficial. It would be better to conclude an alliance of friendship." Most of the ministers who expressed an opinion accorded with Han An-kuo, so the emperor sanctioned the proposed treaty of friendship.

The next year Nieh Weng-yi, a rich merchant from the city of Ma-yi in Yen-men commandery, submitted a memorial through the auspices of Wang Hui that stated: "The Hsiung-nu initially suggested the establishment of friendly relations. We have now attained a state of friendship and trust along the border so we can manipulate them with the prospect of profits." Accordingly the emperor secretly had Nieh Weng-yi, acting as a Han agent, flee into Hsiung-nu territory, where he tempted the Shan-yü, "I can slay all the high officials in Ma-yi and force the city's surrender, whereupon you may obtain all its goods and riches." The Shan-yü liked the prospects, trusted Nieh, and assented, assuming all was as it seemed.

Nieh then returned to Ma-yi, feigned the murder of the major officials by having some criminals executed, and suspended their heads from the outer walls to show the Shan-yü's observers that he had acted faithfully. He then informed them, "Ma-yi's important officials have all been slain, so you should quickly come down." The Shan-yü then pierced the border barriers and entered Yen-men through Wu-chou, crossing with more than a hundred thousand cavalry.

At this moment the Han forces lying in ambush in the valleys around Ma-yi amounted to more than three hundred thousand soldiers, including cavalrymen, chariots, and logistical support. Li Kuang was general of the elite cavalry; Kung Sun-ho, general of the fleet chariots; Wang Hui, general for the encampments; Li Hsi, general of the quartermaster corps; and Han An-kuo, general of the protective army. The other generals were all subordinate to Han's command. They agreed that as soon as the Shan-yü entered Ma-yi, they would release their own forces. Wang Hui, Li Hsi, and Li Kuang were dispatched as a secondary force to move through Tai-chu and launch a sudden assault on the baggage train.

After the Shan-yü had entered Han territory through the Long Wall at Wu-chou crossing, his forces began pillaging the land, even though still more than a hundred kilometers from Ma-yi. However, he felt it strange that, even though they encountered many herds in the fields, they did not see any people. They therefore attacked a signal tower, captured the commandant for Wu-chou, and interrogated him at knifepoint. The commandant then admitted, "Several hundred thousand Han troops lie in ambush below Ma-yi." Looking about at his staff the Shan-yü exclaimed, "We were almost sold out by the Han!" Then he led his troops in withdrawing. After crossing back over the border he said, "It was the workings of Heaven that we captured this commandant," so he titled him "Heavenly King."

When word of the Shan-yü's retreat reached the Han forces they set out in pursuit, but upon reaching the border realized they could not catch them and therefore abandoned the effort. When Wang Hui learned that the Hsiung-nu were not going to engage the main Han forces in battle, he calculated that by mounting a fast cavalry pursuit to attack their baggage train they would certainly confront elite troops and be defeated, and accordingly concluded it would be best to have his troops stand down. Thus none of the Han generals achieved anything.[14]

A well-orchestrated effort that exploited greed and desire to entice the enemy into essentially a mass assassination, it failed because of gaps in the detailed execution rather than any profound reconnaissance efforts by the Hsiung-nu. Obviously such machinations little enhanced Han-steppe relationships.

The tragic saga of Wu Tzu-hsü, who fled to Wu and became a strategic adviser in his quest to punish the king of Ch'u for killing his father and brother (already reprised in the Spring and Autumn historical section), inspired others to emulate him. One minor official who consciously mimicked him and the acts of the other historical assassins was Su Pu-wei, who lived during the Later Han dynasty. His father died after being imprisoned and brutally interrogated by a political enemy in retaliation for having previously uncovered and reported the latter's corruption. Not satisfied with his death, the hateful Li Hao then even mutilated Su Ch'ien's corpse to exact further revenge. According to the *Hou Han Shu:*

Wearing mourning garb, Su Pu-wei returned to his native village and sacrificed to his father but did not bury him. Looking up to Heaven, he sighed and exclaimed, "Is it only Wu Tzu-hsü who can be a man?" Then he hid his mother away in the mountains of Wu-tu, changed his name, and employed all the family's resources to gather skilled swordsmen. Thereafter he attacked Li Hao between two hills but failed to overcome him.

It happened that Li Hao was transferred to become Minister of Agriculture and the seasonal storehouse for fodder was located in the right capital district below the northern temple wall. Together with his brothers, Su Pu-wei burrowed into the grass to hide, coming out at night to dig a tunnel into Li's residence and sneaking back to sleep by day. They continued in this fashion for a month when they reached Li's sleeping quarters from the side and came out under his bed. It happened that Li Hao was in the privy, so they killed his wife and young son, left a letter, and departed.

Li Hao, startled and terrified, thereafter set thorns out about his rooms and floored up the earthen ground with wooden planks. He also changed his sleeping room nine times every night so that even the members of his family did not know his location. Every time he went out, he carried a sword and pointed halberd and surrounded himself with stalwart guards.

Su Pu-wei knew that Li Hao was prepared so he raced day and night until reaching Li's native district, where he exhumed the body of Li Hao's father, severed the head, and then offered it in sacrifice at his own father's burial, subsequently displaying it on a pole in the marketplace with a sign that read, "The head of Li Hao's father."

Li Hao concealed the episode, not daring to speak of it, and retired from his position to return to his native village, where he personally closed the coffin and covered the grave. After a year of unsuccessfully trying to catch Su Pu-wei his rage so overwhelmed him that he fell ill, choked, and died.[15]

The bizarre exhumation of Li's father's head, a great shame and sacrilege according to traditional Chinese conceptions of rites and propriety, echoes the actions taken by Wu Tzu-hsü when, despite having led Wu to conquer Ch'u, he was unable to directly avenge his father's and brother's deaths at the hands of Ch'u's king. More than five hundred years after his death Wu Tzu-hsü's actions not only were legendary, but also continued to encourage the wronged and oppressed.

In attempting to persuade Yen to give its allegiance to Ch'in, Chang Yi, the famous spokesman for the Horizontal Alliance, unfolded a story of assassination to cast doubt upon Chao's trustworthiness and sincerity:

Among all the states with whom you are closely allied, none is like Chao. Formerly the king of Chao, wanting to annex the minor state of Tai, arranged for his elder sister to marry the king of Tai. Later, when he was to convene with him at the frontier pass at Kou-chu, the king of Chao commanded his craftsmen to cast a bronze wine ladle with an extended handle that could be used to attack someone. Then, just before he went in to drink with the king of Tai, he secretly instructed his cook that when they were flushed from drink and absorbed in pleasure, he should bring in more warm wine but then suddenly swing the ladle around to strike the king of Tai. Accordingly, when they were flushed with wine and had more brought in, the cook advanced with the wine, then swung the ladle about, striking the king in the head so forcefully that his brains covered the ground. When the king of Chao's sister heard about it, she slashed herself with a hairpin pulled from her hair. Thus even today everyone has heard about Hairpin Mountain.[16]

This story, apparently true, illustrates not only the careful planning involved in state-oriented assassinations, but also a unique method. Being famous, it furnishes another example of material subsumed in the mind-set of the period and readily recalled thereafter.

Beauty and Sex

Prompted by an incident in the state of Wei, Confucius exclaimed, "I have never seen anyone who loves virtue as much as he loves beauty!"[17] This famous remark well expresses the strength of sexual appeal and its almost unopposable efficacy in the service of covert operations. Moreover, since "sex" is another fundamental meaning of the character *se*, translated here in accord with the traditional (although not necessarily correct) understanding of "female beauty," sexual connotations are invariably present whenever the character is encountered in discussions focused upon morality and behavior. Confucius may well have meant "sex" rather than the more idealized, morally acceptable "beauty."[18]

The *Book of Odes*, one of the fundamental Confucian classics even though essentially a collection of romantic songs and folk elegies from the early Chou period, opens with a portrait of romantic longing:

> *K'uan k'uan resound the ospreys,*
> *Ensconced on the river mound.*
> *Slender and refined, the alluring girl,*
> *The prince desires her for a mate.*
> *Of variegated length floats the mallow,*
> *Carried left and right by the current.*
> *Slender and refined, the alluring girl,*
> *Awake and asleep he sought her.*
> *He sought her without success,*

Awake and asleep his thoughts dwelled on her,
Long his pondering, interminable his contemplating,
Tossing and turning, bent and unsettled.[19]

Other poems in this work ostensibly praising Virtue and the idealized relationships of ministers and rulers echo these themes from both
the male and female perspectives.[20] Early on the poets and singers
were obviously conscious of the power wielded by desire and its more
romanticized counterpart of love, which made it possible to exploit
natural attractiveness to manipulate men and occasionally women.

   An *Yi Chou-shu* passage traditionally attributed to King Wen, the
great Chou cultural king, sketches the dynamics of human desire. In
admonishing the future King Wu, the actual conqueror of the Shang
dynasty, King Wen stated: "When people are born they have likes and
dislikes. When they gain what they like to some degree, they are
happy; when they obtain what they like in large measure, they are joyful. When they encounter what they dislike to some degree, they become worried; when they are subjected to what they dislike, they feel
grief."[21] Although common sense would dictate this to be so, even the
most transparent of principles eventually requires elucidation for it to
function as a basis for conscious decisionmaking, such as in manipulating people for covert objectives.

   Furthermore, throughout the *Yi Chou-shu* (Lost Books of the Chou)
there is a unifying thread, a recognition that women, being the most
powerful objects of desire, represent both danger and the means for destroying worrisome enemies. Accordingly, King Wen instructed King
Wu not to become arrogant, extravagant, or licentious,[22] while the
text separately notes that "beautiful women destroy a state" and that
"when the ruler monopolizes pleasure, authority passes to the ministers."[23] This being true, it advocates "bending rulers with licentious
music and bribing them with beautiful women,"[24] measures much
employed in the Spring and Autumn period. Thus King Wu's violent
treatment of the Shang king's two concubines (who had already hung
themselves) immediately following the bloody conquest by shooting
their corpses with three arrows each, striking them with a sword, and
then beheading them with an executioner's ax may be understood as
symbolically exorcising the power of sexual desire.[25]

   While sometimes according desires recognition in the classics and
derivative works, such as the *Yi Chou-shu* and *Li Chi*, the Confucians
consistently decried the disruptive power and influence of the desires.
Moreover, virtually every other school of thought from Taoism
through Legalism pondered the nature and dynamics of desire, gener-

ally focusing upon its impact on man's emotional and spiritual life. Although their analyses and conceptions merit several hundred pages, a few pronouncements from the disparate perspectives will indicate the importance attached to the emotional drives whose existence underlay the very possibility of China's two major covert practices—subversion through sexual attraction, discussed in this section, and corruption coupled with estrangement techniques, analyzed in the next.

The *Tao Te Ching*, the definitive Taoist classic traditionally attributed to the semimythical Lao Tan, warns against perturbations induced by the desires with such dire assertions as found in Chapter 12:

> *The five colors cause human eyes to be blind,*
> *The five notes cause human ears to be deaf,*
> *The five tastes cause human mouths to be numb.*

The fairly eclectic *Shuo Yüan* preserves a number of pronouncements from different speakers—some no doubt genuine, others certainly spurious—that indicate what might be termed "the common understanding" and therefore what military and political officials would have taken as fundamental operating assumptions at the end of the Warring States period. For example, Yen-tzu is quoted as saying that "he heard that desire can reverse normality and change nature" and Confucius as observing that "when the average man's emotions follow his desires he is defeated."[26] With desire being so powerful, "it is human nature that everyone wants to excel in virtue, but they are unable to act virtuously because profit defeats them.[27] The tastes and desires cause behavior to fail, they are horses that pursue disaster.[28] Nothing is more poisonous to wisdom than wine; nothing detains affairs more than music; nothing destroys purity more than beauty (sex)."[29] However, Liu Hsiang, compiler of the *Shuo Yüan*, allowed that, even though dynasties perished because of women, they also rose in part because of them.[30]

It was generally accepted that the desires and emotions are innate: "That which first gives birth to man is Heaven, men have nothing to do with it. Heaven causes men to have desires, men cannot keep them from coming. Heaven causes men to have hatreds, men cannot avoid them. Desire and hatred are what is received from Heaven, man cannot have anything to do with it, cannot change them, cannot alter them."[31] And even more ominously, "Heaven gives birth to men and causes them to have greed and desire."[32] In the prevalent view disorder stemmed from external stimuli that drove men to perverse acts in seeking their unbridled fulfillment:

When man is born his body is solid and quiet, only when he responds to outside stimuli does he have wisdom. Something brings
it about. When he follows them without reverting, when he is
controlled by inexhaustible tastes and desires, he will certainly
lose his Heavenly component. Moreover, when his tastes and desires are inexhaustible he will invariably have a greedy, uncouth,
perverse, rebellious, turbulent mind, and perform licentious, lax,
promiscuous, and deceitful actions.[33]

Certainly this constitutes a radically different view from that of the
Taoists who emphasized the natural life force and suppleness of a
child at birth!

Certain observations dominate the extensive passages found in the
Huai-nan Tzu that ponder the desires from an essentially Taoist perspective:

Now music, beauty, the five flavors, valuable and unusual goods
from distant states, and rare and unique items are sufficient to
change the mind and alter the will. The number of things that can
perturb the spirit and stir the blood and *ch'i* cannot be counted.[34]
People have a nature that loves sex so there is the great ceremony
of marriage.[35] In general, what caused rulers to lose their states,
cast away the altars of state, perish at the hands of other men, and
become laughingstocks of the realm has always and invariably
been desire.

Following the final assertion, the text cites five cases in which desire
destructively overwhelmed the powerful, including the "king of the
Hu who dissipated himself in the pleasure of female musicians and
lost his great lands."[36]

Pao P'u-tzu, a Later Han period Taoist adept, as well as administrator and military commander, counseled self-restraint:

What the eyes love should not be followed. What the ear takes
pleasure in should not be accorded with. What the nose likes
should not be trusted. What the mouth enjoys should not be followed. What the mind desires should not be unleashed. Thus
what will confuse the eye will certainly be soft feminine deportment and refined elegance. What will delude the ear will certainly
be beautiful notes and dissipated sounds. What will confuse the
nose will certainly be wondrous fragrances. What will confuse the
mouth will certainly be rare foods and delicacies. What will de-

lude the mind will certainly be power, profit, achievement, and fame.[37]

However, in this same chapter—contrary to normal Taoist inclinations—he expounded upon the dangers of imbibing alcohol, condemning it not only for confusing men, but also for harming them physically and psychologically. (Perhaps the only treatise of its kind, it constitutes an early psychological examination of the effects of alcohol.) Although he adduced several notable figures who destroyed themselves through drunkenness to illustrate his thesis, he uniquely conceded it was not simply the licentious pursuit of beauty that ruined history's despots, but the effects of alcohol that compromised their judgment:

> Now what caused Chieh of the Hsia dynasty, Chou of the Shang, Hsin Ling and Emperor Hui of the Han to dissipate themselves with the licentious sounds of lost states and submerge themselves into a sexual morass sufficient to overturn an entire city stems from alcohol occluding their natures and drunkenness achieving its power. Accordingly, they allowed their emotions to go to extremes and forgot the techniques of cultivating one's person and appearance.[38]

As he elsewhere states, "Human emotion universally loves a rouged face, voluptuous appearance, light bones, and a soft body."[39]

In the Han dynasty Wang Ch'ung, whose fondness for explicating the unusual and debunking the dubious in the *Lun Hing* will be seen shortly, apparently derived an odd theory from a *Tso Chuan* passage. In essence, he asserted that "the exotic gives birth to the beautiful and delightful.[40] Therefore beautiful people are,[41] for the most part, pernicious and evil." He symmetrically concluded that the reverse also holds true: "The strange and unusual always proceed from a love of beauty. In everyone's life poison and harm derive from loving beauty." He thus felt that "loving women brings joy to the heart, but it is difficult to maintain beautiful women.[42] Love of beauty will delude the mind."

Although the original *Tso Chuan* story probably evidences jealousy more than fear, it still embodies an antibeauty viewpoint that is remarkable in having been voiced by a woman:

> Shu Hsiang's mother, being jealous of an extremely beautiful concubine, excluded her from her husband's bed. When her sons advised against this, she retorted: "The deep mountains and great

marshes truly give birth to dragons and serpents. As she is beautiful, I am afraid that she will give birth to a dragon or serpent that will bring misfortune upon you. Our clan is weak, while the state is filled with many favorites. If some perverse individual intervenes, won't it be difficult for you? How would I otherwise begrudge this meeting?" She then arranged for the concubine to visit the duke, resulting in the birth of Shu Hu. Shu Hu proved both handsome and courageous and was thus much favored by Luan Huai-tzu, resulting in their clan being plunged into trouble.[43]

When these fears proved prophetic, Shu Hsiang was implicated and imprisoned. However, after Shu Hu was killed, Hsiang managed to gain his own release and thus escaped capital punishment.

Han Fei-tzu cited a famous case much like the infamous example of Duke Ling of Ch'en to illustrate the power of sex and the consequences of dissipation:

Ts'ui Chü of the state of Ch'i had a beautiful wife with whom Duke Chuang, the ruler, had illicit relations. Therefore the duke frequently went to the Ts'ui family mansion. One day, while en route, one of Ts'ui Chü's retainers led the family forces in an attack on him. The duke managed to reach the interior rooms and offered to divide the state with Ts'ui Chü, but he would not accept. Duke Chuang then raced out and tried to leap over the north wall of the compound but was shot in the thigh by an arrow and fell back. Ts'ui Chü's retainers hacked away at the duke with their halberds until they killed him and then established his younger brother, Duke Ching, as ruler.[44]

Even before Han Fei-tzu's analyses of court dynamics and temptations, a *Chan-kuo Ts'e* persuasion summarized the threats posed by favorites and consorts:

What are referred to as *Sang-yung* are favorites, close attendants, concubines, and beloved youths. They are all capable of exploiting the king's drunkenness and befuddlement to seek what they want. When they succeed in gaining what they want within the palace, outside the great ministers will bend the laws in the court for them. Thus while the sun and moon scintillate outside the palace, the real brigands are present within. People cautiously prepare against those they detest, but misfortune lies in what they love.[45]

Such influences—both male and female—were historically well known, often cited, and therefore frequently suggested. For example, in the initial part of a *Chan-kuo Ts'e* persuasion directed to the king of Ch'in, T'ien Hsin cited a couple of successful examples:

Your servant is afraid that you will be like the lord of Kuo. Once Duke Hsien of Chin wanted to attack Kuo but was troubled by the presence of Chou Chih-ch'iao in Kuo. Hsün Hsi accordingly advised, "The *Book of Chou* states that beautiful women can destroy a tongue so dispatch some female musicians to bring chaos to their government." Chou Chih-ch'iao's remonstrances were then ignored, so when he departed, Chin invaded Kuo and reduced it.

Thereafter the duke wanted to attack the state of Yü but was similarly troubled by the presence of Kung Chih-ch'i. Hsün Hsi again advised, "The *Book of Chou* states that handsome men can destroy the old so send the ruler a handsome young man who has been instructed to revile Kung Chih-ch'i." Kung Chih-ch'i continued to remonstrate but was ignored so he too soon departed. Thereupon Chin attacked Yü and subsequently seized all of it."[46]

However, with martial heroes this ploy did not always succeed, as a T'ang dynasty incident shows:

Han Hung hated Kuang Yen's forceful fighting so he secretly plotted, connived, and was willing to implement every sort of plan against him. Subsequently he scoured the city of Ta-liang until he obtained a beautiful woman, whom he had taught such arts as singing, dancing, and playing musical instruments. Then he had her adorned with jewelry and jade and dressed in the most expensive clothes, expending several hundred million in all. Thereafter he deputed an emissary to escort her to Kuang Yen, hoping that as soon as he saw her he would be stupefied with joy and neglect the affairs of military administration. The emissary therefore forwarded a letter in advance to the fortifications that Kuang Yen was erecting to say: "I have been ordered by my gracious lord, who, respecting your patriotism and becoming concerned that you have long been exposed to the brutalities of military life, wants to send you a courtesan in order to soothe your thoughts during the work of pacification. I respectfully await your orders."

Kuang Yen replied, "As today dusk has nearly fallen, I will accept her tomorrow."

The next morning Kuang Yen held a great feast for his warriors and when the three armies were all assembled had the emissary bring the courtesan in. When she entered, her movement and beauty surpassed all mortals, astonishing the whole assembly. From his seat in the upper hall Kuang Yen addressed the emissary: "Your gracious lord felt pity for my having been away from home so long. Parting with this beautiful courtesan who has just been presented to me would be truly ungracious, yet I have received great beneficence from the state and have sworn not to live under the same sun and moon as these brigands. I have caused several tens of thousands of fighting troops to turn their backs on their wives and families and brave naked blades. How could I find pleasure in a beautiful woman?" As he finished speaking tears caught in his throat, while the soldiers assembled below were all moved to weeping.

Kuang Yen generously rewarded the emissary with rolls of silk, respectfully led the woman off the platform, and addressed the emissary: "Please thank your gracious lord profusely. My heart is loyally fixed upon serving the state until I die." From this time onward the soldier's spirits were greatly stimulated.[47]

Consorts and Concubines

Consorts have historically played an important role throughout Chinese history, whether as active military commanders in the Shang dynasty or more subtly from behind the scenes in the rarefied and constrained atmosphere pervading later dynasties. Apart from simply debauching the ruler or plunging the court into murderous intrigue over issues of power, succession, and displacement, they also wielded influence through proffering advice or dissuading their husbands from contemplated courses of action. Moreover, because they were constantly exposed to the state's most secret affairs, their knowledge was frequently sought by agents trying to learn a ruler's plans and their influence courted in attempts to affect policy. An interesting anecdote in the *Chan-kuo Ts'e* illuminates the potential threat:

Ch'in was a great state and Han only a minor one. Although Han viewed Ch'in with enmity, it manifested an appearance of intimacy. However, they calculated that without additional gold their situation would become hopeless, so they wanted to sell their beautiful palace women. The price was exorbitant so none of the other feudal lords could afford them. Ch'in was willing to purchase them for three thousand catties of gold, which Han could, in turn, employ to serve Ch'in. Contrary to their expectations, Ch'in would of course eventually gain both the women and the gold and the women would inform the king of Ch'in that Han was seriously estranged. From this perspective Han would lose their beautiful palace women and their gold while their estrangement from Ch'in would immediately become increasingly clear. Therefore one of the king's guests remonstrated with him: "It would be better to cease your licentiousness and employ the gold to serve Ch'in. In this way your gold will certainly be adequate and your estrangement from Ch'i will not become apparent. Those who excel at plots do not reveal their internal activities."[48]

During the period of ascendancy when consorts and concubines held a ruler enthralled, they often enjoyed such surpassing credibility that they could easily achieve perverse aims. The following incident, included by Han Fei-tzu in his catalog of dangers besetting rulers, although not an example of a state-mounted covert operation, illustrates the means by which such objectives might be achieved. By adopting it for his discussion of palace dynamics, Han Fei-tzu converted the episode into a lesson for future generations:

The younger brother of King Chuang of Ch'u, known as the Lord of Ch'un-shen, had a beloved consort named Yü. Yü wanted him to abandon his formal wife, by whom he had had a son named Chia, so she wounded herself and then, weeping, showed the wound to Ch'un-shen: "I am extremely blessed to have become your consort. However, accommodating your wife is not the way to serve you, and accommodating you is not the way to serve your wife. It is not that I am disrespectful, but my strength is inadequate to serve two rulers. Since circumstances do not permit accommodating everyone, rather than perish at your wife's hands, I would rather die before my lord. After I have died, if you should again favor anyone among your attendants, I hope your majesty will certainly investigate the circumstances and not be laughed at by the people." Because he trusted her deceitful words, he abandoned his formal wife.

Thereafter Yü wanted to have Chia killed and her own son designated heir apparent. Therefore she ripped her clothes through to her underclothes and then showed them to the ruler, weeping: "I have long been favored by my lord, as Chia must know. Yet today he wanted to rape me, but I fought with him until even my clothes were torn. There is no more unfilial act than this!" Enraged, the lord of Ch'un-shen killed his son. Thus his wife was cast aside because of Yü's deceit and their son was killed. From this we can see that even a father's love for his son can be destroyed.[49]

Among the famous statesmen of the middle Warring States period were Chang Yi, Ch'in's prime minister, and Su Ch'in, a peripatetic persuader who served Yen's interests but also wandered among the feudal lords in Yen's behalf, as already seen in the Warring States section. Chang Yi, whose career as Ch'in's minister began the same year King Huai of Ch'u ascended the throne (328 B.C.), is noted as the progenitor of the so-called Horizontal Alliance—uniting the states in servitude to Ch'in, each motivated by self-interest and survival—and Su Ch'in as the proponent of the Vertical Alliance, which would have preserved all the powerful states by uniting them in opposition to Ch'in in the west. (In fact, according to one dating scheme Su Ch'in succeeded in establishing the Vertical Alliance with King Huai of Ch'u as the coalition head in 318 B.C.) The political machinations of the period and Chang Yi's skills are well portrayed in the following lengthy excerpt from Ch'u's history in the *Shih Chi*, which dramatically concludes with Chang Yi relying upon a consort's influence to save his life:

In 313 B.C. King Hui of Ch'in wanted to attack Ch'i, but Ch'i and Ch'u were united in a troublesome strategic alliance. The king therefore announced Chang Yi's dismissal as prime minister and then dispatched him on a mission south to see King Huai of Ch'u, where he said: "No one pleases our lowly village king more than your majesty, while my fondest wish would be to personally serve as a menial bathroom attendant to your majesty. Moreover, our rustic king detests the king of Ch'i more than anyone, and even I hate him the most. But now that your majesty has concluded a great pact of harmony with him, my miserable king is unable to serve you and I, likewise, unable to act as your insignificant attendant.

"However, if your majesty were to close the passes to Ch'i and sever relations with them, you could have an emissary accompany me west and receive back the six hundred kilometers of territory in Shang-yü previously forfeited to Ch'in. Ch'i would accordingly be weakened. By weakening Ch'i to the north, garnering Ch'in's approbation for virtue in the west, and personally gaining the riches of Shang-yü, you will attain a threefold profit from a single act."

King Huai, greatly pleased, entrusted the seals of a state minister to Chang Yi, feasted him for days on end, and announced to his court, "I will regain the territory of Shang-yü." His ministers all congratulated him, but Ch'en Chen alone mourned his decision. When the king inquired as to the reason, Ch'en replied: "Ch'in treats your majesty respectfully because you have Ch'i's friendship. Now if you sever relations before this land has been received, it will isolate Ch'u. How will Ch'in then regard your solitary state? Moreover, if they first provide the territory and we then sever relations with Ch'i, Ch'in's plan will not work. If you sever relations first and then accost Ch'in for failing to yield the land, you will have been tricked by Chang Yi. If you are tricked by Chang Yi, your majesty will certainly be annoyed. If you become annoyed, you will definitely incur misfortune at Ch'in's hands while having severed relations with Ch'i in the north. When you have aroused Ch'in's displeasure and severed relations with Ch'i, troops from both countries will certainly descend upon us. Therefore I mourn your decision." Instead of heeding his words, King Huai dispatched a general westward to accept the territory.

When Chang Yi returned to Ch'in, he feigned a drunken fall from his carriage and did not appear in court for three months because of the resulting injury. Consequently, Ch'u could not obtain the promised land. King Huai of Ch'u said, "Does Chang Yi think that my actions in breaking relations with Ch'i have been too meager?" Accordingly he dispatched a courageous officer northward to insult the king of Ch'i. Greatly angered, the king of Ch'i broke the emissary's tally in half and reestablished cordial relations with Ch'in. Chang Yi then appeared in Ch'in's court and addressed Ch'u's general, "Why haven't you accepted the land some six kilometers from north to south?"

The general replied, "I was entrusted with a mission to receive six hundred kilometers of terrain; I heard nothing about six kilometers." He hastily returned to Ch'u to report on these developments. King Huai, greatly angered, wanted to mobilize the army and attack Ch'in.

Ch'en Chen again objected: "Attacking Ch'in is hardly a plan. It would be better to bribe them with an important city and join them in attacking Ch'i. Then we shall recoup from Ch'i what we have lost to Ch'in and the state can be preserved. Now that your majesty has already broken relations with Ch'i and would accost Ch'in for tricking you, we will simply bring Ch'i and Ch'in together and summon the realm's forces down upon us. The state will certainly suffer serious harm."

Instead of heeding his advice, King Huai severed all relations with Ch'in and dispatched an army westward to attack them.

Ch'in responded by similarly sending forth troops to strike them. In the spring of the king's seventeenth year [312 B.C.] their armies collided at Tan-yang, where Ch'u was severely defeated, incurred 180,000 casualties, and suffered the capture of its commanding general and some seventy other high-ranking officers. Ch'in thereafter seized the commandery of Han-chung.

The king of Ch'u was so enraged that he mobilized all his troops to strike Ch'in again and subsequently engaged their forces in battle at Lan-t'ien, where his armies were badly defeated. When Han and Wei heard about Ch'u's difficulties, they struck south in an attack that penetrated as far as the city of Teng. When informed of their invasion, King Huai withdrew the army back to the state.

In King Huai's eighteenth year [311 B.C.] Ch'in sent an emissary to reestablish close relations with Ch'u, offering to give back half of Han-chung to make peace. The king of Ch'u said, "I would rather have Chang Yi than land." When Chang Yi heard this he asked leave to go to Ch'u. King Hui said to him: "Ch'u desperately wants to take revenge on you. How will you manage?"

Chang Yi replied: "I am close to the king's attendant, Chin Shang, who in turn has access to Teng Hsiu, the king's favorite consort. King Huai will heed whatever she says. Moreover, my former embassy set up the disavowed agreement to cede Shang-yü and caused the great hatred of the resulting battles between Ch'in and Ch'u. Unless I personally apologize to the king, King Huai will never forget his enmity. Furthermore, as long as your majesty lives Ch'u would never dare seize me. However, if it is to Ch'in's advantage, I am willing to be slain."

Chang Yi then ventured to Ch'u as an official emissary. However, King Huai not only refused to see him, but also imprisoned him, intending to kill him. Chang Yi managed to bribe Chin Shang, who spoke to the king on his behalf: "If you hold Chang Yi, the king of Ch'in will certainly be angry. When the realm then sees that Ch'u lacks Ch'in's support, they will inevitably slight your majesty."

Moreover he advised the king's consort, Teng Hsiu: "Although the king of Ch'in loves Chang Yi very much, our majesty wants to kill him. King Hui is about to offer six districts from the commandery of Shang-yung as a bribe to spare him, as well as beautiful women to serve as the king's concubines, accompanied by excellent singing girls from his own palace. Our king covets land, while the women from Ch'in will certainly be valued, so you will inevitably be neglected. Why not go in and speak with the king?"

Teng Hsiu eventually spoke with the king on Chang Yi's behalf and obtained his release. Thereafter the king treated him well, and Chang Yi in turn advised the king to revolt against the Vertical Alliance directed against Ch'in and join in an alliance of friendship with Ch'in itself.[50]

Exploiting insecurity and jealousy in a powerful ruler's consorts apparently occurred frequently. The *Han Shu* contains a cryptic entry in the basic annals of Han Kao-tsu, the Han dynasty's founding emperor, for his seventh year: "Han Kao-tsu went to P'ing-ch'eng, where he was surrounded by the Hsiung-nu for seven days but, through employing Ch'en P'ing's secret plan, managed to escape."[51] Huan T'an's discussion of Han Kao-tsu's release from the Hsiung-nu siege in his *Hsin Lun* provides evidence that the incident was widely noted in Han literature and served as an example for later generations.[52] Remarkably, he expressed the sort of moral disdain found among the Confucians and literati throughout Chinese history, and his rather deprecatory explanation later became embedded in scholarly commentaries on the episode's *Shih Chi* and *Han Shu* entries:

Someone said: "Ch'en P'ing succeeded in extricating Han Kao-tsu from the siege of P'ing-ch'eng, but the records state the affair was secret so subsequent generations have not succeeded in learning about it. Was it successful because of subtle techniques and transcendent skill and accordingly concealed and hidden without being passed down? Can you, through weighing the factors, penetrate the nature of this affair or not?"

Huan replied "On the contrary, his plan was skimpy, lowly, stupid, and odious; therefore it was concealed and not leaked out. When Han Kao-tsu had been besieged for seven days, Ch'en P'ing went and persuaded Yen-shih, the Shan-yü's consort, to release him. She in turn spoke with the Shan-yü, who sent out Kao-tsu. Accordingly we can deduce the substance of his persuasion. Ch'en P'ing certainly told her that the Han has such surpassingly beautiful women that no one in the world is capable of describing their appearance. Under the difficulty of his present extremity the emperor had already dispatched an emissary to race back, seek out, and obtain them because he wanted to present them to the Shan-yü. Were the Shan-yü to gaze upon these women, he would certainly favor them greatly and love them. When he thus became enamored, Yen-shih would be increasingly estranged from the Shan-yü. Therefore it would be better, before they arrive, to effect the emperor's departure. Once released, he would not forward the women. Yen-shih, a woman marked by an extremely jealous nature, would have certainly detested the prospect of being neglected and wanted to eliminate the possibility. This sort of persuasion is uncouth but effective. When he managed to successfully employ it, Ch'en P'ing wanted to make it seem mysterious and extraordinary, so they concealed it rather than let it leak out."[53]

The chapter on the Hsiung-nu in the *Shih Chi* also records the event, essentially stating that Emperor Kao-tsu, personally leading a large force to repel a major Hsiung-nu incursion, stupidly blundered out into the steppe in the middle of winter. Consequently, when the Hsiung-nu lured him further forward with a feigned retreat, he and his 320,000 men were surrounded by some 400,000 of the enemy at P'ing-ch'eng. Reportedly one-third of his troops suffered from frostbite, and the situation turned desperate because they received no food for seven days. Accordingly, the emperor is said to have dispatched presents to the Shan-yü's consort, thereby convincing her to speak on his behalf. Because the Shan-yü's newly converted Han ally, the great general Han Hsin, had not appeared as agreed—causing the Shan-yü to suspect treachery—he arranged for the emperor and his surviving forces to depart, thus giving the event a rather different cast.

Bribes and Estrangement Techniques

Bribery being the simplest method for affecting another state's political and military activities, dependent solely upon identifying people in a position to influence the ruler or commander, it was much resorted to throughout Chinese history.[54] Several illustrations in the historical section have already indicated its widespread practice even in the Spring and Autumn period, one that proliferated to decimating effect in the Warring States period. Furthermore, during the latter strife-torn era men came to be recognized as essentially creatures of desire, driven to satisfy their needs for food and warmth, stimulated to extreme measures in their quest for profits, as already described in the section on women, sex, and consorts. Therefore every covert program extensively employed bribery as a fundamental method, whether to buy information, influence events, or acquire agents. Even diviners and prognosticators became involved, as this minor incident from the Warring States period illustrates:

The state of Chao seized some territory in Chou where the sacrificial rites were conducted. Deeply troubled, the ruler informed Cheng Ch'ao about it. Cheng responded: "My lord, do not be troubled. Your servant requests the allocation of thirty gold pieces to regain them." The ruler gave them to Cheng, who in turn presented them to Chao's Chief Prognosticator while informing him about the problem of Chou's sacred territory. Somewhat later, when the king of Chao fell ill, he had the Prognosticator divine about his illness. The Grand Prognosticator reprimanded him, "Chou's sacrificial lands are causing this calamity." The king of Chao then returned the lands to Chou.[55]

A second, remarkable example depicts the almost unimaginable consequences realized by Ch'in's plan to vanquish their enemies through a combination of covert action and awesome military force. While self-explanatory, the critical role that King Chien's mother played in Ch'i's government merits note:

King Chien's mother, a woman of great moral character, solicitously served the state of Ch'in and kept faith with the feudal lords. Moreover, although Ch'in unremittingly assaulted the five states of Han, Chao, Wei, Yen, and Ch'u, embroiling them in a struggle to save themselves, King Chien managed to rule for some forty years without ever suffering an invasion because Ch'i was an eastern state situated along the seacoast. When King Chien's mother died, Hou Sheng was appointed as prime minister of Ch'i. Hou not only accepted large payments to act as Ch'in's agent, but also dispatched numerous important guests to Ch'in who were then generously plied with gold. Upon their return to Ch'i they acted as "turned agents" who persuaded the king to abandon the Vertical Alliance [formed by the feudal states to contain Ch'in] and instead politically submit to Ch'in.[56] Furthermore, they successfully advised against preparing the equipment necessary for aggressive warfare or assisting the other five states in a concerted attack on Ch'in.

In consequence, Ch'in succeeded in successively extinguishing the five states. When they had all perished, Ch'in's armies finally entered Lin-tzu, Ch'i's capital, whose populace dared not resist. King Chien subsequently surrendered without fighting and was later transferred to the city of Kung. The state of Ch'i was extinguished [in 221 B.C.] and its territory became merely another Ch'in commandery. The people of Ch'i therefore hated King Chien for not having early on united in a Vertical Alliance with the other states to attack Ch'in, and for listening to the perverse advice of his ministers and honored guests that destroyed the state, and even created songs condemning him. King Chien's employment of foreigners was certainly injudicious.[57]

Bribes were employed not only to subvert other governments, but also to facilitate the execution of estrangement techniques, confirm rumors, cast suspicion, and raise doubts about targeted individuals. This systematic employment of covert agents—identified as turned spies, but not necessarily so—to spread disinformation and create suspicion about effective commanders, as in Wu Tzu-hsü's demise and Yüeh Yi's removal, frequently recurred in the Warring States and subsequent dynasties. Because it was a favored method of both individuals and states, many episodes became well known, thereafter furnishing both examples and a growing knowledge of techniques, comprising a veritable pool of covert wisdom.

The Spring and Autumn historical section includes the story of Confucius being deliberately undermined through the besotting of the ruler with sexual beauty. However, another version of Confucius's departure from Lu suggests that machinations formulated by the famous Yen-tzu—generally regarded as a paragon of Virtue and consummate statesman—played upon the Sage's natural sense of moral superiority, thus directly targeting him rather than the ruler. According to the account found in the *Yen-tzu Ch'un-ch'iu:*

> Confucius was serving as a minister in Lu. Duke Ching, troubled by it, said to Yen-tzu: "The presence of a Sage in a neighboring state causes worry for its enemies. What about Confucius serving as minister in Lu?"
>
> Yen-tzu replied: "My lord, do not be concerned. Lu's ruler is weak, while Confucius is a Sage. You should secretly treat Confucius generously, implying that you will establish him as a minister in Ch'i. Confucius will strongly remonstrate in Lu but not be heeded, and will inevitably become arrogant toward Lu and venture to Ch'i, but then you should not admit him. When he is cut off from Lu and lacks succor in Ch'i, he will be in difficult straits."
>
> After a year Confucius left Lu and went to Ch'i but Duke Ching would not admit him to his court, so he found himself in difficulty between the minor states of Ch'en and Ts'ai.

Commentators have long pointed out that this account is a simple fabrication since Yen-tzu had already died when the events purportedly occurred. However, a product of the early Warring States period, the *Yen-tzu Ch'un-ch'iu* was widely read and generally accorded great respect in later centuries, while the two protagonists were among the most famous men in antiquity, so an important, if specious, lesson was thus established.

Forcing a change in commanders through rumors and disinformation, as in the case of Yüeh Yi, often proved surprisingly easy:

In his fourth year King Ho-lü learned that Ch'u had obtained the Chan-lu sword and became enraged. Subsequently he dispatched Sun-tzu, Wu Tzu-hsü, and Pai Ch'i to attack Ch'u. Wu Tzu-hsü secretly disseminated talk in Ch'u, quoting him as saying, "If Ch'u employs Tzu Ch'i as commanding general, I will surely capture and execute him, whereas if Tzu Ch'ang controls the army I will certainly depart." Ch'u's ruler heard about it and therefore employed Tzu Ch'ang, retiring Tzu Ch'i. Wu's forces then attacked and seized two towns from Ch'u.[58]

At other times a few simple acts could create suspicious circumstances, playing upon the ever-present doubts of disloyalty in the ruler's mind, and achieve the removal of a prominent enemy:

Ch'u's army had advanced into Chou's southern mountains and their commanding general Wu Te was about to expiate Ch'u's pent-up anger upon Chou. Someone said to the ruler of Chou: "Why not have the heir apparent, in command of the army, formally welcome Wu Te at the border while you yourself greet him in the suburbs? Make All under Heaven know that you greatly esteem Wu Te, and ensure that it leaks back to Ch'u that a sacrificial vessel that you presented to Wu Te has a certain name. The king of Ch'u will inevitably importune him for it, but when Wu Te does not produce it he will certainly be found guilty of an offense."[59]

Another Warring States example is furnished by Tsou Chi's successful calumniation of the great strategist T'ien Chi, the statesman who had been responsible for bringing Sun Pin back to Ch'i and played a critical command role in the crucial Warring States battle of Kuei-ling in the mid-fourth century B.C. Although this is an example of internal intrigue, it merits retelling because of its historical prominence and the way Tsou Chi exploited the general credence given to prognostication and omens:

Tsou Chi, Lord of Ch'eng and prime minister of Ch'i, and T'ien Chi, general of the Army, reviled each other. Kung-sun Han addressed Tsou Chi: "Sire, why not plan an attack on Wei for the king? If we are victorious, it will have been due to my lord's plans and you can receive the credit. If we engage in combat and are not victorious, if T'ien Chi has not advanced into battle and perished you can wrangle an accusation of cowardice against him and have him executed."

Tsou Chi agreed, so he persuaded the king to have T'ien Chi attack Wei. In three engagements T'ien Chi emerged victorious three times, so Tsou Chi informed Kung-sun Han. Thereupon Kung-sun Han had a man take ten gold pieces to a diviner in the marketplace and inquire: "I am T'ien Chi's retainer. T'ien Chi engaged in battle three times and was victorious three times. His fame overawes All under Heaven. If he wants to undertake the great affair of usurping the throne, will it be equally auspicious or not?"

The diviner went out and had men detain the person who had requested the divination and then attested to his words before the king. T'ien Chi subsequently fled.[60]

It seems incredible that Tsou Chi's simple ruse might have persuaded anyone that a brilliant, successful general such as T'ien Chi would be so profoundly stupid as to openly make such inquiries. However, several of China's rulers and dynastic founders availed themselves of (or manufactured) prophecies attesting to their "extraordinary" qualities and predestination. Had T'ien Chi actually ordered this inquiry, it might well be understood as a sort of trial balloon, an effort to deliberately stimulate useful rumors, arouse public support, or gauge the extent of potential adherents.

Ch'in's extinction of Chao at the end of the Warring States period was similarly facilitated by bribes employed to cause the dismissal of capable field generals and the substitution of inferior ones. Remarkably, their effort succeeded despite the well-known devastating effects achieved by similar ploys in earlier centuries.

In the seventh year of King Ch'ien's reign in Chao, [229 B.C.], the state of Ch'in had Wang Chien attack the state of Chao. Chao sent Li Mu, Lord of Wu-an, and Ssu-ma Shang to resist them. Ch'in then generously bribed Kuo K'ai, the king's favorite minister, to act as their agent and say that Li Mu and Ssu-ma Shang wanted to revolt. The king of Chao then employed Chao Ts'ung and the Ch'i general Yen Chü to replace Li Mu. However, Li Mu refused to accept his edict, so the king clandestinely dispatched men to capture and execute him and dismiss Ssu-ma Shang. Three months later Wang Chien launched a surprise attack against Chao's forces and inflicted a severe defeat, killing Chao Ts'ung and taking both the king and Yen Chü prisoner. Thereafter he extinguished the state of Chao.[61]

Simply through providing a bribe, Ch'in's juggernaut achieved the unimaginable extinction and annexation of Chao, the linchpin of the northern plains states and last obstacle between itself and Ch'i.

Undoubtedly the most famous, literally epoch-making, example of successfully undermining an important commander occurred during the widespread strife that followed the overthrow of the Ch'in and preceded the founding of the Han dynasty. Shortly after Ch'en P'ing had taken refuge with Liu Pang—the eventual founder of the Han dynasty—and assumed a minor command role, they were cut off by Hsiang Yü's army in the city of Jung-yang. Liu Pang attempted to conclude a peace treaty with his powerful rival Hsiang Yü, even offering to cede considerable territory in exchange, but Hsiang Yü naturally refused, setting the stage for the following meeting between Liu Pang and Ch'en P'ing:

Liu Pang said to Ch'en P'ing: "The whole world is so confused and turbulent, will it ever be settled?"

Ch'en P'ing said: "Hsiang Yü, king of Ch'u, is respectful and loves men, so the incorruptible, constrained, and well-mannered warriors have all given their allegiance to him. But when it comes to doling out rewards for achievement, granting rank and fiefs, he is parsimonious, so they become disaffected. Now you, great king, are haughty and rude, so the incorruptible and constrained do not come. But you, great king, are also generous in enfeoffing men and granting rank, so the unscrupulous, covetous, and shameless give their allegiance to the Han. If you could truly eliminate such shortcomings and garner these strengths, the realm might be settled just like waving a pennant. But my king loves to insult people, so remains unable to gather incorruptible warriors.

"I observe that there is some prospect for throwing Hsiang Yü's camp into confusion. He has only a few highly favored confidants—men like Fan Tseng, Chung Li-mei, Lung Chieh, and Chou Yin-chih. If only you were capable of sacrificing some forty or fifty thousand pieces of gold to employ double agents, we might cause the king and his ministers to become mutually estranged and doubtful. Moreover, Hsiang Yü is plagued by doubt and suspicion and easily believes slanderers, so they will certainly begin killing each other. If you then mobilize your forces and attack, Ch'u's destruction will be inevitable."

As Liu Pang felt this to be true, he provided Ch'en P'ing with forty thousand pieces of gold to dispose of as he wished, never inquiring how. Ch'en P'ing then used most of the gold to loose double agents among Ch'u's forces,[62] spreading talk that Ch'u's generals, such as Chung Li-mei, having achieved great success but not been granted any fiefs or kingships, were inclined to unite with the Han forces, destroy Hsiang Yü, divide his land, and become kings. As expected, Hsiang Yü began to distrust his generals.

When Hsiang Yü had already become doubtful, he dispatched an emissary to Liu Pang. Liu Pang appeared to be preparing a great feast and the best meats had already been brought in when, seeing the emissaries and pretending to be surprised, he exclaimed, "I thought that Fan Tseng had deputed you, but you are Hsiang Yü's emissary," so he had the feast removed and vulgar, common food brought in for Ch'u's ambassador. When the ambassador returned to Ch'u and reported everything to Hsiang Yü, the king became very suspicious of Fan Tseng.

Fan Tseng wanted to urgently assault and subjugate the city of Jung-yang, but Hsing Yü didn't trust him and was unwilling to listen to his strategy. When Fan Tseng heard of Hsiang Yü's doubt he was enraged: "The great affair of emperorship is largely settled! Let my lord finish it himself. I just want my old bones to return home." While en route home, before he had reached P'eng, he was hit in the back with a poison arrow and died. That night Ch'en P'ing then sent two thousand women and children forth from Jung-yang's east gate, and when Ch'u's forces attacked them, Ch'en P'ing and the king fled into the night through the west gate.[63]

Liu Pang was subsequently able to regroup his forces and eventually succeeded in disposing of Hsiang Yü to found the Han dynasty, becoming its first emperor, while the incident thereafter became not only a famous example of the importance and effective employment of clandestine agents in estrangement operations, but also the gist of novels, stories, and romances.

Long after the demise of the Han, the brilliant strategist and spy master Wei Hsiao-kuan mounted a complex ploy that again exploited the power of rumor and prophetic verse and thus illustrates how men came to be condemned because they were mentioned in rumors or sayings. Not only preserved in the standard histories, the incident is also incorporated as the historical illustration for the chapter entitled "Spies" in the *Unorthodox Strategies*.

In the sixth century, during the Northern and Southern Dynasties period, General Wei Hsiao-kuan of the Northern Chou succeeded in defending and protecting the area about Yü-pi through his virtuous actions. Hsiao-kuan excelled in pacifying and governing the people and was able to gain their willing allegiance. All the spies he dispatched into Northern Ch'i fully exhausted their abilities. Hsiao-kuan also bribed many Northern Ch'i citizens with gold for information and reports, and thus knew all about Ch'i's actions and court affairs.

Ch'i's minister Hu Lü-kuang, whose style name was Ming Yüeh [Bright Moon], was worthy and courageous. Hsiao-kuan was deeply troubled about him. Northern Chou's chief of military planning Ch'ü Yen, who was thoroughly versed in milfoil divination, advised Hsiao-kuan, "Next year Ch'i's court will certainly be marked by mutual killing." Thereupon Hsiao-kuan ordered Ch'ü Yen to fabricate a prophetic verse that said, "A 'hundred pints' will fly up to Heaven, a 'bright moon' will shine on Ch'ang-an." At that time a "hundred pints" was equal to a "*hu*," Hu Lü-kuang's surname. Additional verses read, "The high mountain, unpushed, will crumble of itself, the *hu* tree, unsupported, will become established by itself." Hsiao-kuan then ordered several spies to memorize these lines and spread them about Ch'i's capital.

When Tsu Hsiao-cheng, who had recently clashed with Hu Lü-kuang, heard them, he further embellished the lines, and Hu Lü-kuang, known as "Bright Moon," was eventually executed because of it. When Emperor Wu of the Northern Chou learned about Lü-kuang's death, he declared a general amnesty, fully mobilized the army, and subsequently exterminated the Northern Ch'i.

The verses illustrate the nature of Chinese wordplay. In the Northern Chou era a "*hu* " was a large measure for corn and grain equal to "one hundred pints," but was also Hu Lü-kuang's surname, so the "one hundred pints" was immediately understood as referring to him. The "bright moon" of the first couplet, simply being his style name, reinforced the identification. The second couplet turns upon the emperor's surname being "*kao*," translated as "high" in "high mountain," implying that the emperor would perish by himself, while the second half asserts that the "*hu* " tree—a tree name formed by adding a "wood" signifier to the Chinese character identical with Hu Lü-kuang's surname and similarly pronounced—would gain its position even without external support. Naturally the emperor assumed the worst and reacted precipitously, as desired. General Wei Hsiao-kuan thus achieved a lasting historical reputation for his skill in employing secret agents, essentially confirming Sun-tzu's view that "unless someone has the wisdom of a Sage, he cannot use spies; unless he is benevolent and righteous, he cannot employ spies; unless he is subtle and perspicacious, he cannot perceive the substance in intelligence reports."

Finally, during the T'ang dynasty when Liu Shih-jang was about to be appointed as commander in chief for Kuang-chou, he unfortunately was called upon to advise the emperor on basic tactics for containing the Turkish border threat, providing an opinion that ultimately resulted in his death:

Liu replied to the emperor's inquiry: "The southern incursions mounted by the Turks essentially take the road to Ma-yi as their main objective. According to my calculations you should place a wise, courageous general at Kuo-ch'eng, and abundantly supply him with gold and silk. Generously reward anyone who comes to surrender. Furthermore, you should frequently dispatch unorthodox troops to plunder their encampments outside the city and cut down all the standing crops, thereby destroying their livelihood. Within a year they will have nothing to eat and Ma-yi will not even enter into their plans."

Because the emperor didn't have anyone he could entrust with this task, he ordered Liu Shih-chang to race out to oversee the implementation of his plan. Meanwhile, the Turks, fearing his formidable reputation, released double agents to claim that Shih-jang and the khan had been secretly plotting together and were about to mount a revolt. Without investigating, Emperor Kao-tsu had him executed and his family name stricken from the registers. At the beginning of the next reign period a surrendered Turk informed the court that Liu Shih-jang never had any intent to rebel, so his wife and son were restored.[64]

Stealthy Methods

A variety of stealthy methods, such as employed by the "dog thief" already seen in the biography of Hsin-ling Chün, and strong-arm ploys such as the kidnapping of Shih Hui, were commonly employed to achieve clandestine objectives. An early case (680 B.C.), much referred to in subsequent military writings, that clearly became part of the common lore about antiquity saw the first hegemon, Duke Huan of Ch'i, opt to keep faith with a coerced agreement rather than abrogate it, as was clearly his prerogative:

When Duke Chuang was about to meet with Duke Huan, Ts'ao Mei advanced and inquired, "What are your thoughts?" Duke Chuang replied, "It would be better if I were to die." Ts'ao Mei replied, "Then please uphold the role of a ruler while I ask leave to act as a minister."[65] Duke Chuang assented, whereupon they went to meet with Duke Huan.

Duke Chuang ascended the dais with Ts'ao Mei following close behind, sword in hand. Kuan Chung came forward and asked, "What do you seek?"

Ts'ao Mei replied: "Our walls are ruined and our border pressured. Will you plan for it?"

Kuan Chung said, "If so, then what do you want?"

Ts'ao Mei replied, "We would like (the return of) the land on the sunny side of the Wen River."

Kuan Chung said to Duke Huan, "You should allow it." When Duke Huan assented, Ts'ao Mei requested a formal covenant, so Duke Huan descended and swore an oath with them. After the oath Ts'ao Mei threw down his sword and departed. A covenant so coerced could be contravened, but Duke Huan did not deceive him [by doing so]. Ts'ao Mei could also have been regarded as an enemy, but Duke Huan bore him no resentment. Duke Huan's good faith was manifest throughout the realm, commencing from this covenant at K'o.[66]

This episode, reminiscent of Duke Wen of Chin keeping faith by withdrawing the siege of Yüan after three days, no doubt struck the imagination of later listeners because of its improbable nature. Obviously Ts'ao Mei's singular determination, although perhaps formidable, could have been quashed by Kuan Chung or armed attendants who must have been near the dais. Moreover, unlike in the incidents that follow, Ts'ao Mei never directly threatened Duke Huan with harm, perhaps an ameliorating aspect that granted the incident a degree of respectability.

Another famous case arose during the Spring and Autumn period when Ch'u reversed its decision to abandon a lengthy siege of Sung's capital that had been instigated by Sung's execution of a Ch'u emissary. The latter had deliberately violated the state's sovereignty by passing through Sung without proper permission, knowing full well it would result in his death (perhaps making him the first "expendable agent") and provoke Ch'u's vengeance. Sung's situation thus became desperate, forcing them to dispatch Hua Yüan to extort an agreement from Tzu Fan, Ch'u's commander, in an incident that became extremely famous thereafter:

> The people of Sung, being afraid, had Hua Yüan penetrate Ch'u's encampment one night and sit upon Tzu Fan's bed. Rousing him, he said: "My ruler commanded me to report our extremity. In our city the people exchange their children and eat them, then break the bones for faggots. Yet we will not assent to any covenant forced upon us, even though our state be extinguished. However, if you withdraw your forces thirty kilometers, we will obey your orders."
>
> Terrified, Tzu Fan swore an oath with him and subsequently informed the king of Ch'u, with the result that they withdrew the thirty kilometers. With Hua Yüan serving as a hostage, Sung and Ch'u then concluded a peace treaty that stated Sung would not deceive Ch'u or Ch'u harm Sung.[67]

A similar incident that perhaps indicates as much about lax security measures (despite the many admonitions in the military writings and presumably stringent lock-down procedures) as the thief's skills, Ch'u exploited the same technique:

> General Tzu Fa of Ch'u loved to seek out men distinguished by specialized skills. One man in Ch'u who excelled in thievery came to see him and said to his attendants: "I heard that my lord is seeking men skilled in the Tao. I am a thief and would like to offer my skill as one of your followers."
>
> When Tzu Fa heard this, without belting his robe or taking the time to put on his cap, he went out and greeted him with all the proper courtesies. His attendants all remonstrated with him: "A thief is one of the brigands of the realm. Why did you extend such courtesies to him?" He replied, "This isn't something that you would understand."
>
> Not long after this Ch'i mobilized its forces and attacked Ch'u. In command of the army, Tzu Fa went out to resist them but was forced to retreat three times. Ch'u's Worthies and high officials all exhausted their strategies and fully employed their sincerity, but Ch'i's forces grew increasingly stronger. At that moment the market thief came in and respectfully requested that as he had some

minor skill, it ought to be put to use. Tzu Fa agreed and sent him off without asking what he meant.

That night the thief cut down the curtain of Ch'i's commanding general and brought it back to Tzu Fa. The next day Tzu Fa had him return it, saying, "One of our troops, out to gather firewood, found your curtain, which I am returning so that you may conduct your affairs."

The next day the thief went again to steal a pillow that Tzu Fa similarly had returned. The day after the thief went a third time to steal his hairpin, and Tzu Fa once again had it returned. When Ch'i's troops heard about it, they were afraid. Ch'i's commanding general said to his staff, "If we don't leave today, I am afraid the lord of Ch'u will steal my head." Then he faced the army about and left.[68]

Part Four

THEORIES OF EVALUATING AND INTELLIGENCE

識人及資情

10

Basic Theory and Issues

*F*ROM THE WARRING STATES PERIOD onward China almost reli-
giously looked to the past for the wisdom necessary to achieve ideal
government and behavioral patterns to emulate and avoid. Certain
texts, such as the *Ch'un Ch'iu* (due to its presumed editing by Confucius), gradually became canonical, but others, including the *Tso
Chuan, Chan-kuo Ts'e*, and finally the *Shih Chi*, quickly exceeded it
in utility. Efforts were frequently made to deny them to nonofficial
readers and all "barbarians" because of their perceived potential as
subversive handbooks, the very reason many "perverse and devious"
readers found them valuable and interesting. Whether viewed as preserving ideal patterns to consciously emulate or evil techniques to ac-
tualize, they irreversibly became fundamental to China's political culture, with their incidents and anecdotes eventually permeating the
general consciousness.

However, strong disagreement marked Warring States and subsequent debates over the fundamental issues of whether human behavior is consistent and the past germane. The Confucians vehemently
affirmed continuity and relevance as essential points of doctrine, but
the Legalists and an admixture of iconoclasts vociferously argued that
overwhelming changes made the past irrelevant. Such divergence in
essential assumptions directly impacts intelligence activities because
predictive evaluations cannot avoid being based upon past patterns.
Even the *Yi Chou-shu* states: "The Tao for mounting an attack is to invariably obtain advantages of terrain, accord with the season of
Heaven, observe the situation in the present, and examine it with respect to antiquity."[1] Political officials, due to their educational background, were more concerned with this debate over "earlier" versus
"later" kings in the service of the state, but to the extent that military
thinkers mastered general material and were not just specialists in

military matters, they certainly recognized the question and its implications.

By the late Warring States period Confucius's reputation as a transmitter, rather than an innovator, was well established, while the view that antiquity furnished models for study and emulation came to dominate. For example, in arguing against the view that antiquity and his age somehow differed, Hsün-tzu stated:

> The Sage measures things by the things themselves. Thus he evaluates men by men, emotions by emotions, categories of things by their categories, achievement with theory, and observes everything with the Tao. Antiquity and the present are one, their categories do not contravene each other. Even though the time may have been long, they have the same patterns. Thus he can incline to the perverse and twisted and not be deluded, observe intermixed things and not be confused, for he measures them accordingly.[2]

The late Warring States *Lü-shih Ch'un-ch'iu* defined wisdom in terms of a continuity with antiquity: "Wisdom is the means by which one compares the past, views what is far off, and sees what is nearby. The present is to antiquity as antiquity is to later ages. The present is to later ages as the present is to antiquity. Thus if one thoroughly knows the present he can know the past, if he knows the past he can know later ages. Antiquity and the present, earlier and later, are one. Thus the Sage knows a thousand years ahead, a thousand years back."[3]

Tung Chung-shu's influential late second century B.C. treatise, the *Ch'un-ch'iu Fan-lu*, extolled the importance of the *Ch'un Ch'iu*, the chronicles of the Spring and Autumn period, as the paradigm model of the past:

> The ancients had a saying, "If you do not know what is coming, look at what has passed." Now the way the *Ch'un Ch'iu* provides a basis for study is that it takes the past as its Tao and makes the future clear. Moreover, its language embodies the signs of Heaven, and teaches what is difficult to know. For someone incapable of investigating it, it is silent, as if without substance, but for someone able to investigate it, it is all comprehensive.[4] . . .
>
> To observe the movement of things and first become aware of their sprouts, to terminate future chaos, blockage, and harm at the time when they have not yet taken form, this is the intent of the *Ch'un Ch'iu*.[5]

In his thematic compilation titled the *Shuo Yüan*, the famous Liu Hsiang similarly wrote: "A clear mirror is the means to illuminate form, the flow of the past the means to know the present. Now if one knows that evil is the means by which antiquity came to be imperiled and extinguished but doesn't seek out the traces by which they were secure and flourished, then it is no different from running away and seeking to catch someone in front of you."[6] In the Han dynasty Wang Ch'ung claimed that, even though vessels might differ over time, "human nature and behavior are not different. People are not different, nor their desires or inclinations."[7] Thereafter, this was the view commonly embraced.

Although dissenters remained, even a few of the so-called Taoist writings inclined to the view that knowledge can be derived from antiquity and the future predicted from the past. For example, the *Liehtzu* asserts that "the Sage, by looking at what has gone out, knows what is coming back, by observing what has gone before, knows what will come. This is the pattern of his foreknowledge."[8] The *Huai-nan Tzu* echoed it with the view that the Sage investigates what has gone before in order to know future disposition and development.[9] Meanwhile the vociferous countertrends prominent in the late Warring States virtually disappeared after the early Han as their chief proponents—Lord Shang and Han Fei-tzu—were reviled for the influence of their theories in creating and theoretically sustaining the odious Ch'in dynasty and opposing the Confucian views embraced by the literati. However, the *Pao P'u-tzu*, an esoteric Taoist tract, still observed: "In love and hate, likes and dislikes, antiquity and the present are not uniform. Times change, customs alter."[10]

In broadest terms the next most pressing question was whether there would ever be a need for active intelligence gathering when ancient books and records already provided a complete repository of knowledge and the Sage (and by implication the Virtuous ruler, who in theory had no enemies) could know everything without making any external effort. Within the context of a constant tension between those who sought to know and those who presumed to know, the premise of knowing without effort assumed two forms corresponding to the Confucian and Taoist perspectives, although later formulations saw Lao-tzu's original pronouncements adopted by the eclectic writers and officials to justify Confucian views. Both inimically influenced China's attitude toward military preparedness and intelligence over the centuries, often fatally frustrating externally directed efforts against the steppe peoples. In brief, the Confucians felt that all knowledge could be derived from perfect understanding of oneself, whereas the Taoists found that more extensive efforts simply produced lesser returns, reflecting a quietest viewpoint. Their defining passage, parts of which frequently appear in the *Huai-nan Tzu*,[11] including excerpts that will be cited here, recur as Chapter 47 of the received *Tao Te Ching*:

> *Without going out the door he knows All under Heaven,*
> *Without peering out the lattice work sees the Tao of Heaven.*
> *As one goes out further knowledge grows less.*
> *Thus the Sage knows without traveling,*
> *Names things without seeing them,*
> *And achieves without acting.*

The Confucian perspective derives from the image of the Sage rulers of antiquity governing the realm without venturing beyond their courts, expressed in passages such as this one attributed to Confucius: "When you love people then people will love you, but when you hate people then they will hate you. What you know from yourself is the same as what you know from men. What is meant by not venturing beyond the confines of single room and yet knowing all under Heaven just refers to knowing yourself."[12] Naturally the petty-minded stressed the literal interpretation of not venturing to gather information, but there was also a sense that, in the large, major affairs of conflict could be foretold without divination:

> King Wu of the Chou was about to attack King Chou of the Shang, so he summoned the T'ai Kung and inquired, "If I want to know whether we will be victorious before engaging the enemy in battle, know whether it is auspicious without performing divination, whether we can employ men from other states, is there a Tao?"
> The T'ai Kung replied: "There is a Tao. If your majesty gains the allegiance of the people and plans against the unrighteous, you can know that you will be victorious without fighting. If you attack the unworthy with the worthy, then without divining you will know that it is auspicious. When others injure their populaces while we profit them, even though they are not our people we can gain and employ them."[13]

Prejudices, Inclinations, and Interference

Late Warring States and Han writers analyzed and extensively commented upon the actual process of perceiving, understanding, interpreting, and finally deriving knowledge from experience. Their efforts resulted in their insights and historical incidents becoming amalgamated into the amorphous but coherent body of common wisdom seen throughout the eclectic writings, materials certainly known to the military thinkers as well, even though never explicitly incorporated into their texts. The philosopher Hsün-tzu pondered many of these critical issues in a unique chapter entitled "Untangling Obfuscations" that scrutinizes perception and its relationship to understanding, identifying internal disturbances that adversely affect the process itself and thereby induce false impressions and conclusions. In a passage focusing on the critical issue of doubt Hsün-tzu stated:

Whenever making observations, if there are any doubts, the mind will not be settled and external things will not be clear. When thoughts lack clarity, it will not be possible to determine the correct and incorrect. Proceeding in such confusion and murkiness, a person takes a supine rock to be a crouching tiger and standing trees to be people behind him because murkiness has obscured his clarity. When a drunk crosses a hundred-pace-wide channel, he takes it to be a half-pace-wide irrigation ditch. When he crouches down to go out the city gate he takes it to be the small entrance [to the women's quarters]. If you press your eyes and look about, one thing will be seen as two; if you cover your ears and listen, silence will be taken as a great clamor, all because what is grasped has brought confusion to the senses.

Thus, looking down from a mountain top cattle are taken to be sheep, but no shepherd will go down to herd them because distance has obfuscated their size. Looking up from the base of a mountain at the trees at the top, hundred-foot trees seem like chopsticks, but no one who wants chopsticks will ascend the mountain to break them off because the height has obscured their length. When water stirs and reflections shake, people will not use the water to discern beauty and ugliness because it has been darkened. When the blind look up to Heaven and do not see the stars, people will not use their perception to determine whether things exist or not because their employment of vital essence is deluded. Anyone who makes decisions about things at such a time is one of the stupidest people of our age. When the stupid decide things, they take the doubtful to determine the doubtful, so their decisions certainly cannot be accurate. If they are not accurate, how can they avoid error?[14]

Obfuscation has many sources: "What brings about obfuscation? Desires, hatreds, the beginning, the end, the distant, the near, the expansive, the shallow, antiquity, and the present all act as obfuscations. Now the myriad things all differ and thus naturally occlude each other. This is the common worry of mental techniques."[15] Even though everything in the world can, in Hsün-tzu' view, thus cause interference and obfuscation, certain strong emotions were generally recognized as particularly potent. A comprehensive list is provided by the *Lü-shih Ch'un-ch'iu*, which similarly viewed all conceptualizing and emotional activity as a potential source of interference:

> Nobility, riches, eminence, awesomeness, fame, and profit pervert the thoughts. Appearance, actions, colors, the patterns of things, *ch'i*, and thought cause misperceptions in the mind. Hatred, desire, happiness, anger, grief, and joy entangle Virtue. Wisdom, capability, accepting office, leaving office, taking, and abandoning block off the Tao. When these forty-six do not stir in the breast, one will be upright. When upright, tranquil. When tranquil, clear and enlightened. When clear and enlightened, empty. When empty, without acting there is nothing that will not be done.[16]

Hsün-tzu pointed out that strong emotions, such as fear, so thoroughly affect the individual as to dramatically block awareness: "To be externally endangered, yet internally feel no fear has never happened. When the mind is worried and afraid, the mouth might hold the choicest meats yet not know their flavor, the ears hear bells and drums and not know the sound, the eyes see the most majestic sacrificial robes and not recognize their appearance, the body enjoy the lightness and warmth of fine clothes and mats but not know their comfort."[17]

Conversely, when "obsessed" with an activity, when focused upon some objective, the person becomes oblivious to other threats and stimuli: "Among the populace of Ch'i there was one man who wanted to get some gold. Early one morning he put on his clothes and cap and went to a gold shop. He saw someone handling gold coins, so he reached out and snatched them. When the lictors arrested him and tied him up, they asked: 'With all these people here, how is it that you still grabbed the gold?' He replied, 'I never saw the people, I only saw the gold.'"[18]

This, of course, is merely an extreme case of concentration. A more general statement is found in the *Huai-nan Tzu:*

> It is human nature that when the ears and eyes respond to externals and are moved, the mind and intentions know worry and pleasure. The hands and feet brush away gnawing insects and

avoid cold and heat, for these are the ways in which one makes contact with things. If a bee or scorpion stings a finger, the spirit cannot remain placid. When mosquitoes and flies bite the skin, understanding cannot remain calm. Now worry and misfortune also attack the mind. It is not only poisonous stings from bees and scorpions or the grief from mosquitoes and flies that interferes with the desired tranquillity, quietness, vacuity, and emptiness. When the eye is looking at the tip of an autumn hair, the ears will not hear a thunderclap. When the ears are adjusting the sounds of the jade chiming stones, the eyes will not notice even the height of Mount T'ai. Why is this? When you are intent upon the small, the large is forgotten.[19]

The *Lü-shih Ch'un-ch'iu* preserves some incidents that show the effect such "inclinations" or "obfuscations" may have upon the process of evaluating information and turning it into unreliable intelligence, although of course not strictly conceived in such terms:

In our time listeners mostly have that which they incline toward. When their inclinations are many, what they hear will be contrary to reality. What causes numerous inclinations? The chief factors are invariably likes and hatreds. Someone looking out to the east doesn't see the western wall and someone looking at southern villages does not see the northern region because of the direction of their thoughts.

For example, someone who lost a sickle suspected his neighbor's son. When he saw the son walking, it was the walk of someone who had stolen the sickle. Moreover, his facial expressions were those of someone who had stolen the sickle; his speech, actions, and attitude, all of them without exception were those of having stolen the sickle. Later, rummaging in a ravine, the owner found his sickle. The next day when he again saw his neighbor's son, neither his actions nor attitude evidenced having stolen the sickle. His neighbor's son was unchanged, only he had changed. This change was nothing other than having an inclination.[20]

Another simple example with far-reaching implications is found in the *Huai-nan Tzu* as part of its extensive consideration of the process of perceiving and valuing:

In antiquity Hsieh-tzu had an audience with King Hui of Ch'in and the king was pleased with him. He queried T'ang Ku-liang about him, who replied: "Hsieh-tzu is a sophist from east of the

mountains. He thus employed a persuasion on authority in order
to gain a degree of favor with you." The king concealed his anger
and waited for Hsieh-tzu the next day. When he had his audience
the king contradicted him and didn't heed his words. His persuasion hadn't changed, but the listener's perspective was different.[21]

The *Huai-nan Tzu* advocated inner tranquillity to avoid perceptual
and emotional interference, not to perceive reality as such, but because emotions debilitate life's vital spiritual energy.[22] The crux of
this view (which turns upon the concept of *ch'i* already encountered
in the realm of military courage) unfolds in two chapters:

Human nature is settled and tranquil, but tastes and desires confuse it. Now what men receive from Heaven—the ears and eyes
perceiving sound and color, mouth and nose perceiving fragrances
and odors, muscles and skin perceiving cold and heat—their nature is one. Some people penetrate to spiritual enlightenment,
some cannot avoid stupidity and madness. Why is that? The
means they use to control them is different. For this reason spirit
is the original source of knowledge. When the source is clear, then
knowledge will be enlightened.[23]

Now what is the means by which people are able to see so
clearly and hear so precisely; their bodies are capable of rising and
hundred joints bending and stretching; can discern black and
white, see the beautiful and ugly, have the knowledge to distinguish sameness and difference, and be enlightened about right and
wrong? *Ch'i* fills their bodies and spirit brings it about.

How do we know this is so? It is nature human that when
someone is intent upon something the spirit becomes entangled
there. His feet can stumble in pits and his head hit low-hanging
branches and not be aware of it. You can summon him [by wav-
ing], but he can't see it, call him but he can't hear it. Even though
his ears and eyes haven't been abandoned, they cannot respond.
Why? His spirit has lost its preservation. Thus when attention is
directed toward the small, the large is lost; when internally, the
eternal is lost; on the upper, the lower is forgotten; on the left, the
right is forgotten. However, if the *ch'i* fills out everywhere, then
there won't be any place it is not present. For this reason the Sage
esteems vacuity.[24]

The reflective power of water, an image often employed by both
Taoism and Buddhism, was similarly used by the *Huai-nan Tzu* to

concretely portray the situation: "Now if there is a pan of water in the guest hall, it can be left to clear for a day but the reflection of the eyebrows still not be discernible. Stir it but once and even the square and round will not be distinguishable. Human spirit is easily muddied and difficult to clear, just like the pan of water."[25] Therefore, at least theoretically, if perhaps unattainably, achieving proper judgment requires tranquillity and dispassionate objectivity.

Sources and Credibility

Apart from personally generated hindrances to accurately interpreting data, numerous questions arise about the latter's nature, sources, and reliability. Several thinkers examined the phenomena of credibility—one of the requisite traits of any ruler or commander—and how it might be established. For example, late in the Warring States period Han Fei-tzu enunciated a critical principle: "Words act in such a way that their credibility stems from greater numbers. Something untrue, if reported by ten men, is still doubted; by a hundred is taken to be so; and if by a thousand becomes irrefutable."[26] A number of the era's eclectic texts contain well-known stories that illustrate this observation, several turning upon the magic number three. For example, when three people reported the presence of a tiger in the marketplace, despite the absence of real tigers in the area, it was believed.[27] Similarly, when three different people separately ran up to Tseng-tz'u's mother, who was weaving at home, to report her son, already a model of decorum and righteousness and soon to be a famous Confucian scholar, had killed a man, even she eventually succumbed.[28]

Normal human experience, coupled with stories such as these, no doubt prompted the observation that hearsay reports are particularly unreliable: "Now the way words are obtained must be investigated. After several exchanges white becomes black, black becomes white. Therefore if one learns something and analyzes it, it will be fortunate; if not, it would be better not to have learned it."[29] Among the more absurd examples cited by the text is the case of "finding a man when digging a well," contorted from finding someone to dig the well to finding him in the ground when the well was dug!

Although Mencius warned against rulers (and by implication others in power) accepting the unicameral voice of partisan groups in recommending people to office, and others spoke about the dangers of uniformity of view, rulers still failed to maintain the openness required to accept baleful news, a shortsightedness that contributed to Sung's extinction:

Ch'i mounted an attack on Sung, so the king of Sung dispatched an observer to determine how far the invaders had advanced. The emissary returned and reported, "The invaders are nearby and the people of the state are afraid." The king's attendants all said: "This is what is known as meat spontaneously giving rise to worms. Given our strength and the weakness of Ch'i's army, how could this be happening?"

The king of Sung, enraged, had the observer executed, then sent another agent to observe Ch'i's forces who subsequently returned with an identical report. The king of Sung again improperly had him executed. Although this happened three times, he sent yet another scout to make observations. The invaders were quite near, the people of the state were terrified. The observer happened to meet his elder brother, who inquired, "The state being in extreme danger, where are you going?"

The younger brother replied: "I went to observe Ch'i's army for the king. I never expected them to be this close or that the populace would be so afraid. It also worries me personally because when the observers who preceded me reported that Ch'i forces were nearby, they were all executed. If I similarly report the true situation, I will die; if I do not, I must also fear death. What should I do?"

His brother said, "If you report the situation accurately, you will die before the others die and perish before others perish." Therefore he informed the king: "I have no idea where Ch'i's army might be. Moreover, the people are very tranquil." The king was elated and his attendants all said, "The earlier observers were appropriately executed." The king then presented him with generous gifts. Later, when the invaders indeed arrived, the king fled by driving off in a chariot all alone. The observer however became a rich man in another state.

Now ascending a mountain and seeing cattle as sheep and sheep as pigs, even though the nature of cattle is unlike sheep, and that of sheep unlike pigs, stem from the perceiver's circumstances being excessive. To then be angry at the smallness of the cattle and sheep is the greatest madness. To be mad, yet implement rewards and punishments, this is the way the king of Sung was destroyed.[30]

Remarkably, the king of Sung ignored the magic rule of three—the number of emissaries who made identical reports—because he was misled by a coterie of flatters and sycophants who seem to have been remarkably oblivious to their own fates, just as the famous Yen-tzu (seen in the Spring and Autumn historical section) had warned[31] and Han Fei-tzu had particularly emphasized in his many passages devoted to controlling power and ensuring a flow of information. The *Huai-nan Tzu* later admonished: "When listening is lost midst sycophancy and flattery and the eyes in colors, but one wants to have affairs be correct, it is difficult."[32] And even the *Wu-tzu* describes an incident in which Wu Ch'i offers a similar warning:

> Once when Marquis Wu was planning government affairs, none of his numerous ministers could equal him. After dismissing the court he had a happy, self-satisfied look. Wu Ch'i entered and said: "Once in antiquity when King Chuang of Ch'u was planning state affairs, he discovered none of his ministers could equal his talents. After he had dismissed the court he wore a troubled countenance. Duke Shen inquired, 'Why does your lordship have a troubled countenance?' He replied, 'I have heard it said that there is no lack of Sages in the world, and no shortage of Worthies in a state. One who can get them to be his teacher will be a king, while one who has them as his friends can become a hegemon. Now I am not talented, yet none of my ministers can even equal me in ability. Our state of Ch'u is in deep trouble.' This is what the king of Ch'u found troublesome, yet you are pleased by it. I therefore dare to be fearful!" Marquis Wu immediately looked embarrassed.[33]

The speaker or informant's position, entailing personal interests and desires, was also known to affect the veracity and interpretation of the material. Preliminary to the substance of his persuasion, Lou Huan said to the king of Ch'in:

> Have you heard about Kung-p'u Wen-po's mother? He served in the court of Lu, and when he died from illness two women killed themselves in his house. Because his mother didn't weep upon hearing about his death, her maid inquired, "When has there ever been a mother who did not weep over her son's death?"
> His mother replied: "Confucius is a Worthy, but when he was expelled from Lu my son didn't follow him. Yet immediately after his death two women committed suicide over him. Obviously he must have excelled in what he should have been sparing in, and was generous with women."
> Based upon what she said, she was a worthy mother. However, if uttered by his wife, such words wouldn't be anything but jeal-

ousy. Although the words might be identical, when the speaker is different, the mind changes in response.[34]

This was, in effect, how the king of Sung was poisoned to the truth and the underlying psychological mechanism by which King Hui of Ch'in, mentioned previously, was turned against Hsieh-tzu.

Semblances and Doubt

Many Warring States texts comment upon the problems of evaluating men, events, and motives from perceptual evidence alone, making such concerns common thereafter. One particularly well-known concrete image encapsulates the problem: "A madman ran east and his pursuers also ran east. Their running to the east was identical but the reasons they ran that way different. A drowning man sank into the water, his rescuers also entered the water. Their entering the water was the same but their reasons different."[35] More philosophically phrased, "What causes people to be greatly confused and deluded is invariably the mutual resemblance of things. What jade merchants worry about is stone that resembles jade, while those who appraise swords worry that one will look like the famous blade Kan Chiang. What worthy rulers worry about is that the people often hear the disputations of those who seem to have penetrated the Tao."[36] The conclusion inevitably follows that all doubtful semblances must be investigated but with the important qualification, "by the right man."[37]

The problem of semblances raises the question of standards and measures, guidelines for discriminating and judging among possible interpretations. An argument over the critical characteristics in swords that appears in the *Lü-shih Ch'un-ch'iu* has important connotations:

An expert in appraising swords said: "White is the means by which a sword is sturdy, yellow the means by which it is resilient. When yellow and white are intermixed it will be sturdy and resilient, and therefore a good sword."

His critic said: "White is the means by which to make it inflexible, yellow to make it not sturdy, so when yellow and white are intermixed it will neither be sturdy nor resilient. Moreover, when it is soft, it will bend; when sturdy, it will break; so when a sword is breakable and bendable, how can it be an advantageous weapon?"

The nature of the sword has not changed, but one takes it to be good, another to be bad, because theory causes it.[38]

Although a certain degree of unreality has crept in here, the verbal sparring still illustrates the defining impact fundamental theories have in engendering divergent perspectives and providing parameters for evaluation and interpretation. Since similar cases have already been explored in the historical section, one additional example with remarkably different conclusions will suffice to illustrate the growing consciousness of such standards:

King Chuang of Ch'u wanted to attack Ch'en so he dispatched an agent to observe it. The emissary returned and reported, "Ch'en cannot be attacked."

King Chuang asked, "Why not?"

He replied, "Their walls are high, moats deep, food reserves numerous, and the state peaceful."

The king said: "Ch'en can be attacked. Now Ch'en is a small state, yet their reserves are ample. For their reserves to be ample, their taxes and impositions must have been heavy. When military taxes are onerous, the people will resent their ruler. Since their walls are high and moats deep, the people's strength must be exhausted." He mobilized the army and attacked them, subsequently seizing Ch'en.[39]

The Confucians basically evaluated by an ideal of Virtue, righteousness, and benevolent administrative policies; the Legalists, by strictness and effective rewards and punishments; the Taoists, by minimal government measures; and the military theorists, by a balanced view that combined benevolent government with strictness in rewards and severity in punishments. A *Huai-nan Tzu* passage constructed from ancient incidents encapsulates the first two:

Duke P'ing of Chin spoke inappropriately, so his music master struck at him with a lute but merely brushed his lapel, shattering the lute against the wall. The duke's attendants wanted to plaster the wall over to conceal the marks, but Duke P'ing said, "Leave it, for I will take them as a reminder of my error." When Confucius heard about this incident, he remarked, "Duke P'ing wasn't unconcerned about threats to his body, but he wanted to have people come forth and remonstrate." Han Fei-tzu heard about it and said: "Whenever a minister commits an offense that goes unpunished, it opens the way to all transgressions. Because of such practices Duke P'ing never attained hegemony."

One of Mi-tzu's honored guests had a visitor. After observing their interview, upon the visitor's departure Mi-tzu said to his guest: "Your visitor has just three faults. He looked at me and smiled, so he is conceited. He spoke about matters but didn't acknowledge his teacher, which is contrariness. Although his relationship is shallow, his words were deep. This is disorder." Mi-tzu's guest said: "He smiled when he looked upon my lord, an expression of politeness. When he spoke, he didn't allude to his teacher, a sign of penetration. Although the relationship is shallow, he spoke deeply. This is loyalty."

The visitor's appearance remained the same, but one observer regarded him as a superior man, the other a common man. This is due to the observer's perspectives being different. Thus when people agree about their interests and dislikes, their words are seen as loyal and they grow increasingly close, but when they are distant, even excellent plans are doubted. For example, if a mother causes blood to flow down to her son's ear while treating a carbuncle on his head, her behavior would be seen as an expression of love, but if performed by a stepmother would be judged by a passerby as abusive. The nature of the event was unchanged, but the means by which it was judged differed. From the top of a city wall cattle appear like sheep and sheep like pigs because the standpoint is high. If you peer at your reflection in a pan of water your face will be round, but in a cup it will be oval. The shape of your face hasn't changed, the difference in roundness and ovalness being produced by the means employed to peer at it.[40]

Doubt and the Military Perspective

The uncertainty raised by semblances and divergent value schemes, compounded by questions of a reporter's reliability, could lead only to doubt, the anathema of all commanders. Even though doubt would presumably provoke incisive intelligence analysis and prompt effective counterintelligence measures, it equally undermined confidence in the results. The military classics all decried its inimical power to erode confidence and pernicious ability to cause hesitation, dooming armies to defeat. The T'ai Kung said, "Of all the disasters that can befall an army, none surpasses doubt."[41] Wu Ch'i similarly commented, "The greatest harms that can befall the army's employment stem from hesitation, while the disasters that strike an army are born in doubt."[42] Even Hsün-tzu, who disparaged tactics and other realistic measures as mere expediency in comparison with the irresistible power of Virtue, conceded, "When spying on the enemy and observing their changes, you want to be hidden and deep, want to compare extensively and analyze, so that when you meet the enemy in a decisive battle, you will base your strategy on what you are clear about, not what you doubt."[43]

The military writings rarely discuss theoretical issues of intelligence, focusing instead on the problems of gathering information, placing agents, running covert operations, and confirming reports through cross-checking. However, Chieh Hsüan, author of the *Ping-fa Pai-yen*, having lived at the end of the Ming and doubtlessly been exposed to the long heritage of Buddhist, Taoist, and Neoconfucian thought on mind, substance, and principle, devoted two of his definitions to essential intelligence questions. For Chieh Hsüan "doubt" can be a stimulus to certainty, while its problematic aspects should be exploited against the enemy:

Definition: Stirring confusion in the enemy's mind is termed "doubt."

Original Text: Because the military is the Tao of deceit, there will inevitably be doubt. However, one who suffers from unfounded doubt will certainly be defeated.

Explanation: Although doubt is an affliction that besets both ancient and modern armies, it is also the means through which generals and commanders can be effective. Because men obviously have eyes, they cannot avoid seeing things. When they see similitudes, they will be doubtful. Because men certainly have ears, they cannot avoid hearing things. When they hear things that sound like something else, they will be doubtful. Because men clearly have minds, they cannot be without awareness. When they are aware of similitudes, they will be doubtful.[44] Except for the most stupid, who falls into dark obstinacy and insensitivity? Thus it can be said that antiquity and the present suffer the same affliction.

Accordingly, if I have something about which I am doubtful, I proceed to analyze it. I plot affairs myself but decide them with many others, for only then can I destroy the doubtful and gain the useful. Since these doubts originate in wisdom and plans, they cannot be escaped even for an instant, nor can they be taken lightly. You cannot be lax or lethargic in responding to them, or too shallow or hasty in planning. The more you know, the more

doubtful you will become. The more doubtful you are, the more
you will know. If you determine the veracity of your doubts, you
will be victorious; if you fail to determine their veracity, you will
be defeated. Therefore it is said that through doubt generals and
commanders can be effective. Thus the ancient generals excelled
at dispelling their own doubts and stimulating doubts in others.

One example he cites in his definition was the famous Han dynasty
episode in which the vastly outnumbered Li Kuang, isolated in steppe
territory, not only had his troops dismount, but also had them un-
buckle their saddles to convince the Hsiung-nu pursuing him that
they were laying a trap. Chieh thus concluded, "To dispel your own
doubts, use intelligence; to stimulate doubt in others, employ cleverness."

Another important definition focuses on the process of determining
information about the enemy, one Chieh terms "fathoming":

Definition: Applying effort to thoroughly seek out something is
termed "fathoming."

Original Text: When two armies meet, there must be tests,
when two generals are locked in a standoff, there must be fathoming. When you fathom the enemy, you can avoid the substantial
and strike the dispersed. When you detect the enemy fathoming
you, display some shortcoming in order to lead them to your
strength. However, if your own fathoming activity plunges into
the vacuous, it may provide the means for an enemy to deceive
you. Thus although you undertake one analysis, you must be doubly prepared. To anticipate the unforeseen is a complete technique, the Tao of [successful] generals.

Explanation: Surveyors have methods for fathoming heights
and depths, breadth and distance. If one knows the height but not
the distance, or knows the breadth but not the depth, then a single estimation may be employed. But if neither height nor depth,
breadth nor distance is yet known, then a double reckoning is
used. This approach clearly derives from topography. As for estimating the disposition of enemy forces and measuring a general's
wisdom, merely select what is appropriate and use it. The methods of singular and double estimation are simply standards for
surveying.

Examples: Chu Tan lured the enemy forward because he knew
that the Northern Jung could not make estimations and thereby
successfully defeated them three times. Sun Pin decreased the
number of cookstoves over several days, knowing that P'ang

Chüan was capable of calculating the army's strength from them, and subsequently set up his crossbowmen in an ambush at Ma-ling. Thus depending upon whether the enemy is more or less wise, their fathoming efforts will be shallow or deep.

The outcome at Ma-ling furnishes a perfect example of exploiting well-understood evaluative parameters to implement misleading measures and thereby deceive the enemy. Although no doubt detailed in execution, Sun Pin's measures simply enticed P'ang Chüan into an erroneous deduction by presenting easily observable phenomena that confirmed his arrogant preconceptions of Ch'i's cowardice. Because all armies undertake reconnaissance activities, generals must be alert to the danger of drawing fatal conclusions from false phenomena, whether observationally derived, gained through prisoner interrogation, or obtained through one's own spies.

Standards, mentioned in the definition of fathoming, are essential to any thorough, systematic approach to information analysis. The military texts thus contain numerous detailed observations correlated with conceptual inferences derived from categories of terrain, numbers, and character that became the defined standards for understanding enemy behavior and evaluating capabilities. However, even the *Huai-nan Tzu* noted that Sages employ standards: "Now one who relies upon his ears and eyes to hear and see troubles his form but isn't enlightened, one who uses knowledge and thought to govern embitters his mind without achievement. For this reason the Sage unifies his standards for measure and never changes what is appropriate or his constant measures."[45]

Moreover, given that knowledge is extensive but human life short, without learning experientially derived standards, it will be impossible to discern and judge, to make estimations and realize conclusions:

Human knowledge is shallow, while things are always inexhaustibly changing. When someone who previously did not know something now knows it, it is not because they personally experienced it but because they acquired it through learning. Now when things are frequently seen, people recognize them; when affairs are frequently attempted, they become capable of performing them. Through misfortune one learns to make preparations, through difficulty discerns the convenient. Doesn't it require technique to observe the knowledge of a thousand years in a single lifetime through the unchanging theories of the past and present wherein the patterns of the Tao are all fully present? If someone wants to discriminate high and low but cannot, if you teach them to use sighting tubes and the water level, they will be pleased. If they want to distinguish the light and heavy but have no means, if you give them a balance and steelyard, they will be happy. If they want to know the distant and near but cannot, if you teach them the method of the golden eye, they will be elated. So how much the more so knowing how to respond to an amorphous, ever-changing world?[46]

From another perspective this same argument was advanced by Tung Chung-shu for employing the *Ch'un Ch'iu* as the ultimate guide and measure: "The Tao of the *Ch'un Ch'iu* is to honor Heaven and model on antiquity. Even someone with a skillful hand cannot form squares and circles without resorting to the compass and rule. Even those with sensitive ears cannot adjust the five notes without employing the six pitch pipes. Even those with wise minds cannot tranquilize All under Heaven without perusing the former kings. Thus the Tao bequeathed by the former kings is equally the standards and pipes for All under Heaven."[47]

Other Issues and Perceptions

Any reader with even minimal knowledge of contemporary intelligence practices perusing China's philosophical and political works will invariably note perceptive assertions that reflect important issues and illuminate difficulties. However numerous, being scattered and isolated, they represent fleeting insights derived from observing and pondering human experience rather than any systematized, objectively directed consideration. Although innately interesting, a simple enumeration of them for some twenty pages would not prove particularly valuable. Nevertheless, two issues merit at least brief note: the concept of correctness in names and the nature of human activity and inherent biases. The former, eventually dubbed the doctrine of the rectification of names, received its greatest impetus from Confucius's famous statement on government essentials: "Let the ruler be a ruler, the minister a minister, the father a father, and the son a son."[48] Even though much verbiage has been devoted to explicating this brief utterance, it simply means that people should fulfill the duties and obligations of the roles they find thrust upon them by the world at large. More abstractly, names and reality should correspond, so Confucius's prescriptive notion is eventually reversed and etherealized to become an entire doctrine of names needing to be correct for functions to be performed. Other thinkers, ranging from the Taoist and Mohists to such so-called Logicians at Kung-sun Lung-tzu, tackled aspects of the question, but the prevalent view among martial experts and government officials grappling with intelligence issues is perhaps best expressed in the *Lü-shih Ch'un-ch'iu:* "When names are correct there is order, when names are lost there is chaos. Licentious theories cause names to be lost, for when they prevail, the inappropriate is taken as appropriate, the nonexistent as the existent, the incorrect as correct, the correct as incorrect."[49] Obviously the ramifications of misnaming the "weak" or "dispirited" when applied to an enemy could be horrendous.

The second issue, the viability of dissonant information, similarly impacts upon the army's fortunes and the state's survival. As earlier examples have already illustrated, a lack of openness to divergent views, to information that does not confirm predetermined perceptions or, even worse, contravenes the individual's personal interests, tends to result in such information being rejected, whether accurate or not. Consequently, decisions that fail to acknowledge discordant data and disagreeable conclusions invariably prove incorrect. Two proclivities were noted in the philosophical writings. First, men tend to be deeply committed, virtually buried within their own views. Thus Hsün-tzu observed: "When a person has something he has acquired (by dint of effort), he only fears to hear of its negative aspects. Relying upon his own attainment to observe other methods, he only fears to hear about their attractiveness."[50] The *Huai-nan Tzu* similarly noted: "Now men take as worthy what they are pleased with and speak about what they like. Everyone in the world esteems Worthies, some to be ordered, some to be chaotic. It is not that they deceive themselves, but that they seek what agrees with them."[51] Moreover, "man's misfortune is to be obfuscated by some minor aspect and thereby unenlightened about the great patterns."[52] The *Pao P'u-tzu* concurred, stating, "Most men are wise in minor matters but stupid in great ones."[53] An explanation is perhaps found in another *Pao P'u-tzu* statement: "It is normal human nature to esteem the distant and slight the nearby. Trusting their ears and doubting their eyes, this is a misfortune of both antiquity and the present."[54]

Second, there is the problem of background and learning, for without adequate experience, including on the battlefield, the visible may be neither understood nor noticed. People naturally commence from their experience: "Now whenever men undertake affairs, without exception they all start with what they know, order their thoughts, ponder, and calculate, and thereafter dare to decide their plans. That some of them prove profitable, others harmful, is the difference between stupidity and wisdom."[55] This being true, some structuring must occur before the person reaches the stage of minimal wisdom, becomes capable of evaluating and analyzing:

Achievement precedes fame; affairs precede achievement; words precede affairs. If one doesn't know affairs, how can he comprehend words? If he doesn't understand emotions, how can he speak appropriately? Men must have something by which they instruct their minds, only thereafter can they listen to theories. If they do not instruct their minds, they have to train them in studies. If they do not, it has never been the case from antiquity until the present that they could listen to theories.[56]

True in all realms, it would be particularly so in the military sphere, with its mission and specialized knowledge. As the *Lü-shih Ch'un-ch'iu* pointed out: "Knowing that one does not know is best. The misfortune of those who are mistaken is not knowing but thinking that they know. Many things seem to be of the same category but are not, thus they lose their state and destroy their people."[57]

11
Knowing Men

*E*VALUATING MEN AND MOTIVES, crucial to many aspects of intelligence work, has a sophisticated history in traditional China, where enormous time and energy were spent in trying to fathom others, determine the implication of actions, and estimate the likelihood of attacks and subversion. Unfortunately, apart from briefly discussing character flaws in commanders and offering a few cursory thoughts on the qualities required for making appointments, the military writings little ponder the topic. Therefore, to examine the concepts found in general consciousness and elucidate the problems and methods proposed for evaluating men, whether in the abstract or within concrete situations where failure might fate an agent to death, recourse must be to the political and philosophical works from China's intellectually formative Warring States period. Because the factors are many and the concepts extensive, a somewhat lengthy digression is required to adequately delimit the concerns confronting anyone responsible for fathoming character and discerning hidden motives behind often complex facades.

Chih jen, "knowing men," was an all-encompassing term for a concept emphasized in the Warring States period when a state's very survival came to depend upon selecting and employing loyal men of ability. In actuality there were many dimensions to this problematic process, several of which evolved into the distinct traditions of emphasis extensively discussed in the following pages. However, perhaps the most famous element subsumed by the idea of knowing men was the almost mythic act of recognizing the true worth of some lowly, ignominious individual who had been forced to dwell in obscurity until the critical moment. Although the unknown might come from any economic or political level, the lower and more degrading the level was, the more striking the contrast with subsequent events was. Moreover, the act of recognition often created a psychological bond between the two members in a dramatically forged relationship, a felt debt for which the person essentially mortgaged his life and future. Kuan Chung's remarks about why he mourned for Pao Shu-ya vividly illustrates the intensity of this bond: "Those who gave me birth were my parents; he who knew me was Pao Shu-ya. A gentleman will die for one who knows him, so how much more will he feel grief upon his death?"[1] When necessary, these men would repay their benefactors with their very lives, avenge insults, and eliminate threats. Such was the material of stories, several of which are preserved in the *Shih Chi,* particularly in the collected biographies found in the chapter entitled "The Assassins."[2]

Many Sages and wise counselors were similarly discovered in miserable circumstances or among common tradesmen while maintaining the posture of a recluse. According to one of China's best-known stories, the T'ai Kung (whose biography appeared in the initial section) appeared in the peripheral state of Chou virtually out of nowhere after wandering as a commoner for many years; he was discovered while fishing on the banks of the Wei River. His apparent strategic contribution to the Chou's rise and their eventual vanquishing of the Shang impressed upon subsequent generations the importance of knowing men, recognizing talent, and cultivating the skills to evaluate character and intent.

Knowing men was also considered increasingly critical to government and the wielding of power late in the Spring and Autumn period, and to the moral life of Confucians in the Warring States era. By then the wisdom and acumen necessary for selecting men were deemed two of the critical virtues demarking the great Sage rulers of antiquity, the *Shang Shu* even defining the essence of government as knowing men and settling the people.[3] Rulers were responsible for knowing men, whereas their subordinates, who were entrusted with actual administration, had to be knowledgeable about governmental affairs. Thus not only would the realm be well governed, but also the tasks of rulership would become minimal, allowing the monarch to enjoy prosperity and tranquillity.

There was a second tradition probably originating with Confucius that held the *chün-tzu* (perfected man) and anyone else aspiring to the role of the righteous and benevolent should know men, such knowledge being critical to their intercourse with the world. Confucius not only defined knowledge as "knowing men,"[4] but also added, "Do not be concerned you are not known to men, but that you do not know men."[5] Furthermore, the idea that one should associate only with men intent on moral self-cultivation demanded that people be constantly scrutinized to prevent inimical friendships. Conversely, Confucius proclaimed that failing to recognize potential comrades along the path would constitute an equally tragic loss: "Not to speak with someone who may be spoken with is to lose the man. To speak with someone who should not be spoken with is to lose one's words. The wise do not lose men, nor do they lose their words."[6]

The third dominant orientation in evaluating men, one essential to intelligence activities, focused upon discerning thoughts and motives in context. Furthermore, in the attempt to determine what a person might be thinking, what motives his face might conceal, the issues of character and duplicity quickly arose. One of traditional China's major psychological thrusts thus pondered man's ability to create facades to successfully conceal thoughts and character. Two viewpoints received support: Some believed human behavior to be essentially transparent, others that it could easily obscure intentions and motives, making the process of evaluating uncertain even under optimal circumstances. Attempts to fathom character equally stimulated questions about the criteria that might be employed, whether certain characteristics would not invariably prove revealing. Actions and attitudes in intense situations were particularly believed to express mind and mood, especially behavior in the obligatory forms of etiquette and emotions in the rites of marriage, mourning, and other emotionally charged experiences.

A number of analytic approaches evolved, the criteria thus advanced becoming increasingly sophisticated and detailed from the Warring States period through the inception of Ssu-ma Ch'ien's first dynastic history in the Former Han. Although the criteria never remained static, for the purpose of explicating the issues besetting anyone attempting to evaluate men and motives for political or military intelligence purposes in pre-Ch'ing China, our discussion will focus on ideas current in the Han Dynasty, whether incorporated in earlier texts or expressed in the works of the Han period writers. Some differences will be elucidated, but the main references will be to anecdotes and representative material almost certainly known to members of the educated class entrusted with governing and defending the state. (The frequent illiteracy of commanders and generals in the earlier periods did not preclude their acquisition of such knowledge through discussions and oral study, particularly as "books" were mainly bulky bundles of bamboo strips or rolls of silk until the Han, and the traditional method of teaching was verbal.) The philosophic and political works naturally contain the most sophisticated theoretical discussions, as well as innumerable anecdotes and brief characterizations, but extensive developments are also found in the ritual texts, medical writings, and dynastic histories.

Ssu-ma Ch'ien, author of the *Shih Chi* and progenitor of Chinese dynastic historical writing, even created personality archetypes that formed the basis for the classifications underlying many of his individual collected biographies. Remarkably consistent, these archetypes not only could be employed by later readers to recognize people, but also embodied his personal insights and the collective wisdom of his era. The final culmination of this effort was an even more detailed text, Liu Shao's *Jen-wu Chih*,[7] which followed in the tradition of the earlier *"Wen-wang Kuan"* (The Offices of King Wen) chapter of the *Ta-Tai Li-chi*, correlating abilities and offices, a trend that apparently gained strength only in the early Han.[8] Unfortunately, the extensive materials found in the dynastic histories, including the biographies, Ssu-ma Ch'ien's archetypes, and Liu Shao's lengthy work, must be left for another study, even though they clearly express an appreciation of personality types and consistency of tendency within character.

Basic Problems and Questions

Despite his stress upon knowing men, Confucius offered few pronouncements on how to realize this elusive goal beyond implying that good men will practice the virtues he much espoused. When specifically asked how to evaluate men for office and recognize the wise, virtuous, and capable, his answer in the *Analects* was indirect and of little practical value: "If you appoint those you know, will others neglect those whom you do not know?"[9]

Even more fundamental than the problem of method is the question of knowability itself, adverse experience prodding several thinkers to ponder man's opaqueness and openly doubt whether men might really be understood. For example, at the beginning of the Later Han dynasty Yang Hsiung noted that natural phenomena, being visible on a large scale, are easily observed, but good and evil, being basically a question of man's interior, of hidden character and motives, are both difficult to know.[10] Confucius himself shied away from terming individual men "benevolent" or "good" even when their behavior merited praise, being unsure of their true natures.[11] Furthermore, the evaluator's own qualifications frequently prove problematic. According to tradition, the Sages of antiquity, being paragons of talent and ability, had an innate power to fathom men and recognize others marked by similar excellence, causing more than one Warring States author to lament that only men distinguished by extraordinary talent could possibly recognize the merits of the obscure.[12] Accordingly, only through arduous study might a select few, never the ordinary hordes, become adept at knowing others.

The question of knowability tended to be phrased in terms of whether men are transparent or not—whether their behavior, countenance, attitude, clothing, or some other aspect will betray them. Knowability itself can thus be resolved into a brief series of issues: Are men transparent or not? If men are knowable, are there any criteria or methods by which they can be fathomed? What are these criteria or methods? What problems are entailed by perspective? What problems are posed by the talent and moral character of the perceiver? This topic, with its multiple aspects, received considerable discussion in traditional China and was perhaps the object of more psychological speculation than even human nature and the emotions.

Not all their contemplations remained abstract and ethereal. Administrative policies and measures were formulated by Han Fei-tzu and others, while various criteria for selecting men to office, such as found in the "Offices of King Wen," were codified. Even the early medical writings, although approaching the subject from a unified psychophysiological perspective, evolved detailed personality indicators correlated with physique types. Speculation quickly stimulated the development of operational methods and spawned numerous individual applications, resulting in the classic evaluations of Confucius and his original disciples, among others. Clearly the watchword during China's formative intellectual period was "there is nothing harder than knowing men."[13] Moreover, as Shen Chien observed, men also differ with respect to the relative clarity or obviousness of their emotions and character, some appearing very open while yet being secretive, others appearing secretive while yet open.[14] The task was rendered more difficult by the problem of penetrating deceptive facades, an additional complexity beyond the fundamental problem of knowability. Failure to be cognizant of it could result in fatal errors.

There are two basic problems, the first being the questionable correlation between a person's invisible will, intent, thoughts, plans, and emotions and his behavior in the world. The most famous example employed to suggest the difficulty of understanding motives was that of a madman and his pursuers running east, previously noted in the basic intelligence section. The second problem stems from the simple misperceptions that frequently plague even the most common situations. For example, the *Tseng-tzu Chia-yü* records the case of an ill-fated man from Ch'u who covered his mouth whenever he spoke to the king in order to please him, but the king interpreted it as a deliberate insult and had him executed.[15] Motive and perception thus dramatically diverged and the man perished.

Compounding the perplexity, many of the concrete techniques suggested for fathoming men were often attacked as fundamentally deficient. A famous example was Mencius's assertion that he could discern a person's emotional state from the pupil of his eye. However, Wang Ch'ung disputed his claim by asserting that people have predetermined physical dispositions at birth; therefore the pupil, being part of the person's constitution, simply cannot reflect character or mood.[16] Other obvious criteria, such as name, reputation, appearance, words, and behavior, were found to be inconsistent when critically scrutinized.

The mind was therefore frequently said to be difficult to know, hidden and unsusceptible to the usual forms of scrutiny, even in writings stressing the importance of fathoming men and propounding likely methods. For example, the *Lü-shih Ch'un-ch'iu*, which advised looking at the signs visible in the person's countenance, behavior, inclination, and similar aspects, conceded that predicting behavior becomes impossible when the desires are unconstrained: "Affairs follow the mind, the mind follows the desires. In one whose desires have no measure, the mind is without measure. If his mind has no measure, then what he will do cannot be known."[17] Moreover, there are no visible traces to the mind: "Man's mind is hidden and concealed, difficult to see."[18] Accordingly, Confucius was among the first to question whether appearance and behavior truly reflect a man's nature or are merely superficial, socialized manifestations: "Is someone whose discussion is sincere and correct a perfected man? Or is it only a formidable appearance?"[19] To his regret he discovered the inadequacy of such criteria as appearance, language, deportment, and manner.[20]

The military writers, for whom an error in judgment could entail bitter consequences, only infrequently discussed the process of evaluating men. Particularly interesting is an enumeration of fifteen discrepancies in appearance and inner substance attributed to the T'ai Kung:

There are fifteen cases where a knight's external appearance and internal character do not cohere. These are: He appears to be a Worthy but actually is immoral. He seems warm and conscientious but is a thief. His countenance is reverent and respectful but heart is insolent. Externally he is incorruptible and circumspect, but he lacks respect.

He appears perceptive and sharp but lacks such talent. He appears profound but lacks all sincerity. He appears adept at planning but is indecisive. He appears to be decisive and daring but is incapable.

He appears guileless but is not trustworthy. He appears confused and disoriented but on the contrary is loyal and substantial. He appears to engage in specious discourse but is a man of merit and achievement.

He appears courageous but is afraid. He seems severe and re-mote but on the contrary easily befriends men. He appears forbid-ding but on the contrary is quiet and sincere. He appears weak and insubstantial, yet when dispatched outside the state, there is nothing he does not accomplish, no mission that he does not exe-cute successfully.

Those whom the world disdains the Sage values. Ordinary men do not know these things, only great wisdom can discern the edge of these matters. This is because the knight's external appearance and internal character do not visibly cohere.[21]

Finally, Wang Ch'ung noted that since the values normally em-ployed to assess character stress conventional appearance, any man who maintains a facade of virtue and civility will be marked a gentle-man and probably recommended for office, whereas the unconven-tional will simply be neglected.[22] This clearly undermines the reliabil-ity of using appearance, fame, and reputation, a dilemma subsequently considered in detail.

Selecting Men

Apart from the Confucians, who were oriented toward piercing disin-genuous behavior, the main purpose for evaluating men was to select them for appointment to office, employment as personal advisers, and participation in clandestine missions. Several texts warned against al-lowing minor "defects" or character flaws to obscure a man's real worth, advising that few men are so perfectly virtuous as to escape crit-ical scrutiny unscathed. The early *Shang Shu* asserts: "Do not be an-noyed or impatient with the stubborn, do not seek completion in any one individual."[23] The *Huai-nan Tzu* is particularly clear: "It is human nature that everyone has some shortcoming. If overall the person is cor-rect, then even though they may have small faults, they are not enough to be considered an impediment. If in the large they are not correct, then even though someone may have a local reputation for virtue, it is not enough to raise them to major office."[24] Consequently the emphasis should be upon the whole man, upon his general traits rather than some minor point or past error that, even if not precluding future greatness, would in a strict moral context be sufficient cause for rejection. Conse-quently, in a well-known story Duke Huan of Ch'i, the first hegemon, declined to have a man's reputation investigated in his hometown be-cause "if we ask about it, I am afraid that he might have some small faults, and because of these minor transgressions, we would forget the great goodness of the man. This is the way rulers lose the empire's talented officers."[25] This statement was made in the face of a rather decided trend toward evaluating men by their associates, environment, past behavior, families, and hometowns because what a man's behavior revealed in these situations should be the most telling of all.

The question of methods constantly reappeared, with some authors venturing to suggest that objective techniques might be employed. However, favoritism was an obvious obstacle that could easily render any attempt at objectivity invalid. Thus the *Han-shih Wai-chuan* noted:

> When the ruler of men wants to recruit archers who excel at shooting far and striking small targets, he flaunts rank and generous rewards in order to summon them. Within he does not favor his sons or younger brothers; without he does not conceal men from distant quarters, but selects those who can hit the target. Isn't this what is termed "the great Tao"? Even the Sages could not alter it. However, if in wanting to administer the state and govern the people, in seeking ministers, associates, and attendants, the ruler alone is not impartial but only prizes and employs sycophants and his cohorts, isn't this termed "erroneous"?[26]

Similarly, the early military classic entitled the *Ssu-ma Fa* advised seeking out the talented even among the masses rather than confining the search only to men of rank.[27] Thereafter their words and actions should be compared, and if they cohere, these men should be appointed, with subsequent observation being imperative.

Problematic Theory of Transparency

The assumption that men are fundamentally knowable, termed "the theory of transparency" for convenience, holds that the major and minor aspects of human behavior invariably express an individual's true character, motives, and intent. It does not necessarily deny the ability to assume a facade, but it does assert that such fabrications will eventually be pierced by the knowledgeable. Confucius, who made several statements to the contrary that equally raise questions about knowability, also seems to have been a strong proponent of human fathomability: "Look at how someone acts, observe his reasons, and investigate what he rests in. How will the man be concealed?"[28]

Scattered throughout the texts of the Warring States period are concise arguments defending the possibility of determining motives and intentions. Grounded upon analyses of human character and emotions, they represent well-conceived approaches to the question of whether men can be fathomed or not. A passage embedded in the

Huai-nan Tzu stating that from the small and near the distant and large can be determined embodies the most dogmatic assertion of fathomability to be found anywhere, the author being certain that minor, incidental events invariably demark the larger outlines of character.[29] The *Huai-nan Tzu* passage thus evinces a positive commitment, despite an acute consciousness of the problems posed by people feigning emotions and behavior and such negative examples as Kou-chien deceiving Fu-ch'ai. Because of this human ability to manipulate appearance and create self-serving pretenses, officials must develop the skills and acumen necessary to penetrate deliberate facades.[30] Were people simple and transparent, few states would have perished: "If people could be made so that what they harbor within would be what they display without, so that what they harbor within would match what they manifest without as the two halves of a tally do, there wouldn't be any lost states or extinguished bloodlines."[31] The *Huai-nan Tzu* also recognized that the problems entailed by confusing appearances are not confined to the human realm, but also distort the perception of inanimate things in the form of semblances, as previously discussed. However, despite such contradictory observations, the author still considered it basically possible to evaluate men by carefully observing the minuscule and minute.

Mencius believed that the pupil of the eye would naturally reveal a man's inner nature as good or evil: "In the human body nothing surpasses the pupil of the eye in excellence. The pupil of the eye cannot conceal a man's evil. If he is upright within his chest, the pupil of the eye will be bright, but if he is not upright within his chest, the pupil will be dull. If you listen to his words and observe his pupils, how will a man be concealed?"[32] Although a simplistic scheme capable only of affirmation or denial, it still constitutes a strong assertion of transparency. However, he was not alone in suggesting that a person's eyes might unknowingly betray him. Apart from the commonly found assumption that they reflect courage and cowardice, an interesting theory of behavioral discrepancy keyed to the eyes is preserved in a predictive evaluation:

[In 574 B.C.,] when the feudal lords were convened at Chou, Duke Tan Hsiang, observing that Duke Li of Chin looked out far and stepped high, advised the duke of Lu, "Chin will soon suffer from rebellion."

The duke of Lu inquired, "Dare I ask if it will be an act of Heaven or because of men?"

He replied: "I am not a court astrologer, so how would I know the Tao of Heaven? I deduced from the Duke of Chin's manner that he would shortly suffer misfortune.

"Now in the perfected man the eyes determine the intent and the feet follow the eyes. Therefore, when you observe his manner, you can know his mind. When the eyes dwell in what is proper, the feet will appropriately pace it off. However, at this moment the Duke of Chin looks out far and his steps are high, so his eyes are not upon his body and his steps are not in accord with his eyes. His mind definitely has something unusual in it. When the eyes and body are not in accord, how can someone long persist?"[33]

Several examples that attest to the accuracy of concealed motives being deduced from observing someone so self-absorbed in his plans for mounting an attack that he failed to perceive his immediate surroundings appear in the Warring States writings and subsequent dynastic histories.[34] Belief in the eye as an indicator of inner nature was thus not confined to Mencius alone, with one passage even portraying Confucius employing the eyebrows as prime indicators:

Confucius had an interview with a guest. After the guest departed, Yen Yüan commented, "Your guest is benevolent."
Confucius said, "His heart is filled with hatred, but his mouth with excellence. Whether he is benevolent I do not know. His words centered on benevolence."
Yen Yüan flushed with embarrassment. Confucius said, "Even a hundred feet of dirt cannot obscure the brilliance of an excellent piece of jade a foot in length, or a hundred fathoms of water obscure the luster of a superlative pearl one inch in diameter. Now the body, encompassing the mind, provides but an extremely thin concealment. If a man is congenial and good within, his eyebrows and eyelashes will manifest it. If there is some defect within him, his eyebrows and eyelashes will manifest it. If there is some defect within him, his eyebrows and eyelashes will be unable to conceal it."[35]

A verse from the *Book of Odes* then summarized the passage's thrust, expressing complete faith in man's ability to know others:

> The drums and bells are within the palace,
> But their sound is heard without.
> Artifice and deception cannot endure,
> The empty and vacuous cannot be maintained.

The medical writings, much of whose content would be common knowledge, even formulated physiological explanations for the eye's symptomatic sensitivity: "The mind is the concentrated essence of the five viscera, the eye its portal, and the complexion its glow. Thus when a man has virtue, the harmony of his *ch'i* is seen in the eye, whereas when it is lost or he is in sorrow, it is known from his complexion."[36] This passage reflects the concept that men are predisposed to physique, character, and illness at birth, so that a person whose viscera are all correct will normally be good and healthy.[37]

An early, widely accredited passage from the famous *I Ching* advises how a man's composure and attitude will betray his contemplation of evil: "The language of someone about to revolt is ashamed; who has doubts in the depths of his heart, rambling. The language of an auspicious man is sparse; that of the fierce, excessive. The language of one who slanders the good is frivolous; that of one who has lost his principles, contorted."[38] Another section of the *Lü-shih Ch'un-ch'iu* unquestionably asserts that a man's intentions and thoughts can be perceived from his countenance and behavior, that character may even be fathomed without words.[39] In support it cites the case of Confucius understanding a man's intent from his eyes alone and also a number of concrete cases in which the participants, due to a disjunction with the aspects expected within a particular context, are understood to be plotting some treacherous action.

A dramatic example of discerning intentions from countenance and attitude within a political-military context is found in Chih Po's self-destruction, an absorbing historical episode dating from the very beginning of the Warring States period.[40] Shortly after mighty Chin's powerful ministerial families had sundered the state into six segments, Chih Po, head of the most powerful family, coerced the powerful enclaves of Han, Wei, and Chao into a joint action to destroy the Fan and Chung-hang clans and annex their territory, only to then demand that his allies grant him additional land from their own domains. Even though all three states suffered similar coercion, only Han and Wei decided to appease him based on the reasoning seen in Han Kang-tzu's advice to his ruler: "Chih Po's character is to love profit and act recklessly and brutally. If we do not grant what he has requested, he will certainly inflict his army upon Han. By acceding, Chih Po will be inclined to continue his villainy and invariably request territory from some other state. Someone will certainly refuse, and when they do, Chih Po will attack them. In this way we can avoid misfortune and wait for the situation to evolve."

Although all three states developed identical analyses, only Chao had the courage to refuse Chih Po's demands and the foresight to immediately prepare for war, the ruler swiftly ensconcing himself in the bastion of Chin-yang. Chih Po then cowered Han and Wei into joining him in a concerted attack on Chin-yang, offering the additional inducement of equal shares in Chao's territory upon its defeat. After Chin-yang had been flooded and besieged for three years, Chao's hopeless situation prompted the high official Chang Meng-t'an to undertake a secret mission designed to split the besiegers' alliance. The traditional narrative—taken here from the *Han Fei-tzu,* where it illustrates the adverse consequences of becoming greedy and perverse—succinctly shows the clandestine process of subversion and how to both evaluate and misread visible indicators in a concrete context:

Chang Meng-t'an secretly held a meeting with the rulers of Han and Wei and said to them: "I have heard that when the lips are lost, the teeth will feel cold. At present Chih Po is leading you two in an attack that will shortly see Chao perish. However, when we are lost, you will be next."

They replied: "We know it. However, Chih Po's character is brutal and distant. If he discovers we are plotting against him, disaster will certainly result! How can we proceed?"

Chang Meng-t'an replied: "Any plot will proceed from your mouths into my ears alone. No other man will hear of it." The two rulers agreed to turn against Chih Po, set the day, and then dispatched Chang that very night into Chin-yang to report their planned rebellion to his ruler, Chao Hsiang-tzu. When Chao Hsiang-tzu received Chang Meng-t'an, he bowed twice before him, filled with fear and joy.

The morning after reaching an accord with Chang Meng-t'an, the two rulers went to Chih Po's court. Coming out of the headquarters gate, they encountered Chih Kuo, who thought their appearance strange and therefore went in to see Chih Po: "The facial expression on these two rulers indicates they are about to change their allegiance."

Chih Po inquired, "What indicates it?"

"Their movements were bold and attitude arrogant, unlike their previous constraint. It would be best for you to act before them."

Chih Po replied: "I formed a close alliance with these two rulers to destroy Chao and equally divide its territory into three. Because of the basis of our alliance, they would never violate it. Our armies have been exposed here at Chin-yang for three years. Now that we are about to seize it and enjoy the profits, how could they have any intent to betray me? It's certainly not possible, so drop it and don't mention it again."

The next morning the two rulers went to Chi Po's court and again encountered Chih Kuo when they came out of the head-quarters gate. Chih Kuo went in to see Chih Po and reported, "Did you inform them of what I said?"

Chih Po asked, "How did you know it?"

"This morning, when the two rulers came out from your court and saw me, their complexions changed and they glared at me. Without doubt their intentions have changed, so it would be best to kill them."

Chih Po said: "Drop it, do not speak about it again."

Chih Kuo replied: "Impossible, you must kill them. If you cannot kill them, you should draw them closer."

Chih Po asked, "How should I draw them closer?"

Chih Kuo said: "Wei's strategist Chao Chia and Han's strategist Tuan Kuei are both capable of altering their rulers' plans. If you agree to enfeoff each of them with a district of ten thousand households upon Chao's destruction, you will ensure their rulers' intentions remain unchanged."

Chih Po replied: "If we divide Chao into three after destroying it and I further enfeoff each of them with ten thousand households, I will gain very little. It's not possible." When Chih Kuo realized his words would be ignored, he departed from the camp and even changed his clan name to Fu.

On the appointed night Chao's forces slew the troops guarding the dike's embankments and destroyed parts of them so that the water would flood Chih Po's encampment. While Chih Po's army was chaotically trying to rescue themselves from the water's onslaught, Han and Wei's forces mounted a sudden pincer attack from the two wings and Chao Hsiang-tzu led his troops in a frontal assault. They severely defeated Chih Po's army and captured Chih Po himself.[41]

In concluding, Han Fei-tzu cited an opinion already common in his era: "Chih Po perished, his army was destroyed, his state was divided into three, and he became the butt of the realm's laughter. Thus I say that being greedy, perverse, and loving profit are the foundation for extinguishing your state and killing yourself."

This well-known account shows not only how appearance and countenance might effectively be employed within a battlefield context to fathom men and motives, but also how personal beliefs, emotions, and desires can prejudice analysis. Given the three years' suffering already endured by the coalition forces and the uncertainty of successfully mounting a revolt, except in historical hindsight Chih

Po's interpretation was in fact the most probable. However, it would not have been unreasonable to undertake some simple precautions to thwart any possible defection, thereby saving himself from an ignominious death and undying fame as a paradigm of greed and stupidity rather than the glorious name he sought as the founder of a vast, unified empire! Moreover, this episode illustrates the need for vigilance in security measures, for Chang Meng-t'an was able to exit and reenter not only the besieged city, but also the very center of the besiegers' camp and successfully undertake a subversive mission by no doubt exploiting the negligence that usually accompanies "certain" victory.

Another case associated with the legendary Kuan Chung shows the simplistic but effective detection of hidden motives from demeanor and appearance:

When Duke Huan of Ch'i convened the feudal lords, Wei's ruler was tardy. Later Duke Huan held court with Kuan Chung and plotted to attack Wei [for its offensive behavior]. When he retired from court to enter the inner palace, his consort, a princess from Wei, seeing him from afar, descended the hall and bowed repeatedly before him, apologizing for the duke of Wei's offense. Duke Huan said, "I have no issue with Wei, so why are you apologizing?"

She replied: "When I saw you enter the hall, your steps were high and *ch'i* robust, signs that you intend to attack a state. But when you saw me, your appearance changed, evidence that you intend to strike Wei."

The next day when Duke Huan assembled his court, he requested Kuan Chung to come forward. Kuan Chung said, "Have you abandoned the attack on Wei?"

Duke Huan asked, "How did you know?"

Kuan Chung replied: "When you convened the court, you were respectful and your words were slow. When you saw me, you looked embarrassed, so I knew it."

Duke Huan commented: "Excellent! With you to govern external matters and my wife to administer the inner palace, I know I will never become the butt of the realm's laughter."[42]

What Duke Huan thought to conceal and not speak about was detected by Kuan Chung in his appearance and voice and by his wife in his step and intentions. Although Duke Huan did not say anything, it was like the brilliance of a candle in the darkness of night.[43]

Perceiver's Qualifications

The question of individual variation in expressiveness, some people being more direct and open than others—their emotions literally "leaking out"—was occasionally raised in conjunction with assertions of transparency and suggestions of discernible criteria. However, it was little pursued, perhaps because of an abiding concern in the question "Transparent to whom?" Experience apart, since knowledge, intellectual abilities, and moral development are rarely uniform, people similarly differ in their ability to fathom others. Paragons such as Mencius claimed powers that ordinary men might not possess, and although Confucius seems to have been adept at character analysis, his disciples consistently erred and were constantly wondering about the ways in which the Master proceeded, prompting questions about their own moral development. For example, Confucius is often portrayed as having been capable of immediately recognizing another Sage even without speaking to him, quoted in one instance as having said: "Before I saw the man, I knew his inclinations. After I saw the man, his mind and intent were both clear."[44]

Tung Chung-shu asserted that only a Worthy might know another Worthy, and the *Huai-nan Tzu* includes a striking, all-encompassing statement: "From the exterior the sage knows the interior; from what is visible he knows what is hidden."[45] The *Shuo Yüan* even resurrected the eyebrow theme:

The shape of the eyebrows is connected with and expressive of countenance. The tone of the sound is affected and moved by the mind. When Ning Ch'i beat on a cow horn and sang the Song of Shang, Duke Huan heard it and raised him to office. Pao Lung knelt on a rock and recited the ancient texts, and Confucius, hearing him, dismounted from his carriage. Yao and Shun, on seeing each other, did not depart from the shade of the mulberry tree, and when King Wen raised the T'ai Kung, it was not because of having known him for long.

When men of ability see each other, they do not await some test before they know each other. When two gentlemen meet, they do not have to be involved in financial dealings and the division of goods before they know each other's honesty, or face hardship and danger together before they know each other's courage. From the way they decide affairs they can already discern courage, from their taking and yielding can already perceive honesty. Thus when someone sees the tail of a tiger, he already knows it is larger than a fox, and when he sees the tusk of an elephant, knows it is larger than a cow. When one joint is seen a hundred are known. Looking at it in this way, from what can be seen one can fathom what is not yet manifest. Seeing a small joint is decidedly adequate to know the whole body.[46]

Liu Shao later deduced from the limitations of class attraction that only men of the same type, whether Sages or rogues, can truly recognize each other. Thus transparency might be a circumscribed possibility at best, limited to a closed set determined by the perceiver's own character and virtues, clearly problematic in the realm of agent selection, in recognizing potential subversives among the corrupt and willful.

Two or three widely circulated stories give evidence of a common belief in the ability of wise men to fathom character and detect motives and thoughts, even though forced to observe the subjects at some distance through the use of multiple indications and comparative criteria. The most frequently recorded story concerns another incident involving Duke Huan and Hsüan Chung:

Duke Huan and Kuan Chung closed the doors and planned an attack on the state of Chü. Before their plans had been put into action they were already known throughout the state. Duke Huan angrily said to Kuan Chung: "You and I closed the doors and planned an attack on Chü. Although the plan has not yet been put into action, it is known throughout the state. What is the reason for it?"

Kuan Chung said, "There must be a Sage in the state."

Duke Huan said: "So. On that day there was an attendant who in placing the mat and serving the food looked up at us. It must be him." Thereupon he ordered the servers to come again, but not in turn. In a while Tung-kuo Ya arrived. The duke ordered the chief of protocol to bring him forward, seated him in the place of an honored guest, and asked, "Are you the one who spoke about attacking Chü?"

Tung-kuo Ya replied, "Yes."

Duke Huan asked: "I didn't speak publicly about attacking Chü, yet you have. What is the reason for this?"

Tung replied: "I have heard that the perfected man is good at making plans, and the common man is good at figuring them out. I thought it out." The Duke asked, "How did you figure it out?" "Happiness and joy are the appearance of bells and drums. Profundity and quietness are the appearance of mourning attire. Effusive fullness with the fingers and toes moving is the appearance of military affairs. On that day when I saw you two in the tower, your mouths were open and not closed. This was talking about Chü.[47] You raised your hand and pointed, your power will be inflicted on Chü. Moreover I have observed that among the minor feudal lords only Chü is not submissive, so I said you would attack it."

Duke Huan remarked: "Excellent. 'From the minute he hits upon brightness,' this is what the phrase refers to."[48]

The Body as Naturally Expressive

The *Li Chi* and similar texts advance the idea that the sound of the voice and other aspects of the body naturally express human emotions. Because the mind affects the entire body, true emotion has real external counterparts, whereas a feigned exterior is a facade that will lack the depth of actuality and eventually be betrayed by vestiges of actual emotions. The *Huai-nan Tzu* concurred, observing that apparently identical sounds may elicit dramatically different reactions because the nature and intensity of the underlying emotion are different: "The sounds were the same, but the credibility that they were able to elicit was different. This was due to the emotions involved. Thus when the mind is stricken with grief, then the songs are not happy, whereas when the mind is happy, weeping will not be sorrowful."[49] Clearly underlying emotions are thought to be amenable to detection.

However, there is an almost constant dialogue among the various possibilities and positions within the *Li Chi*. The basic idea is one of harmony between form and substance, expression and content. Yet there is the danger posed by the extremes of too great an uncontrolled intensity in the emotions overwhelming the idealized form, or too great a stress upon the form resulting in the absence of real content. Both are emphasized at different times. Consequently, given the perfection of form under the *li*, it would seem that the proper performance would accord with the context and that the absence of substance could not be detected. This is a problem that was neither raised nor even considered during the period.

Finally, there was still another theme associated with the problem of transparency: the difficulty of properly expressing actual emotional substance where attitudes, rather than emotions, were demanded, such as in the performance of filial duties. Even Confucius, who viewed filiality as natural and fundamental, lamented that "it is the appearance that is difficult."[50] According to Hsün-tzu (whose writings were incorporated into the *Li Chi*), society's various roles all have appropriate expressions associated with them.[51] Because producing the expression would be difficult, if it were to constitute the sole measure of emotional appropriateness, many would fail. Tautologically this indicates a lack of proper internal substance, essentially reaffirming the principle of transparency. However, difficulty arises because the behavior evoked by emotional substance may not necessarily cohere with the idealized expression specified by the ritual texts and social convention. Sincere, strenuous efforts to create the proper appearance can then only yield a socially defined facade, leading to numerous secondary and tertiary considerations. Consequently, simply proceeding on the basis of the human body being naturally expressive would not be without problems, though a quasi-belief in transparency based upon it persisted throughout Chinese history.

The Basic Principle

On the premise that all men are fundamentally alike, despite differences in emphasis and development, one fundamental assumption visible throughout the Warring States and subsequent periods was the belief that other people might be fathomed from oneself. Hsün-tzu even ventured to assert that not only are contemporaries identical, but also over the ages human nature and emotions remain alike, contrary to views depicting an ever-changing world.[52] Thus the key injunction was "Measure emotions by emotions, and man by man," meaning "Measure the emotions of others by your own emotions and other people by yourself."[53] Preparation for this commenced with oneself: "If you want to conquer others, you must first conquer yourself. If you want to discuss others, you must first discuss yourself. If you want to know men, you must first know yourself."[54]

The *Mencius*, despite the complete absence of the term "knowing men," contains the best-known example of this concept: Mencius's vaunted ability to penetrate King Hui's mind and perceive his true motives. Being pleased by their discussion, the king commented by citing the famous line from the *Book of Odes* that encapsulates such skills: "The *Book of Odes* states, 'The minds of other men, I am able to measure.' This refers to you, Master."[55] This is a more limited, focused application of the general understanding early exemplified by the Sages who could project from themselves and thereby know other men. Accordingly, Mo-tzu symmetrically suggested that people might learn about themselves by using other men as their mirrors: "In antiquity there was a saying, 'The *chün-tzu* does not use water as a mirror, but finds his mirror in men. Using water as a mirror you will see your countenance, but if you use men, you will see fortune and misfortune.'"[56]

Despite the use of the term "measure" in such passages on evaluating, the modern Western obsession with quantifying personality (on the assumption that quantified measures are both possible and inherently more reliable than dynamic descriptions) never appeared in ancient Chinese thought. Active tests that exploit normal human situations and employ false stimuli were conceived for evaluating character and ability, whereas some traits, such as anger, inherently include a dimension of amplitude. ("See how angry he becomes.") Tangential suggestions along the lines of "measuring" were sometimes made but never realized in either doctrine or practice, even though Mencius also states: "Only after weighing is the weight of things known, only after measuring is their length known. All things are so, the mind especially."[57] Perhaps the closest approach may be found in the *Lü-shih Ch'un-ch'iu*, which compared choosing men with a carpenter's work: "It is like the chief carpenter building a room in the palace. He measures the size and knows the materials required, estimates the effort, and knows the number of men."[58]

Constancy

Another observation fundamental to the project of fathoming men—the essential consistency of human behavior—might be termed "the principle of constancy" for convenience, although it was really an assumption rarely made explicit, except in highly concrete form.[59] Its importance cannot be overestimated, for without the assumption that human behavior is essentially consistent and therefore expressive of core character, projecting future behavior and discerning patterns and personality in current and past actions become impossible. Moreover, because it was popularly believed that facades are difficult to maintain indefinitely, the longer a person evinces a particular behavioral pattern, the more likely it actually manifests his "true" nature. (When this assumption was consciously emphasized in fathoming men, the perceiver apparently became oblivious to certain other problems, such as the effects of environment and the plasticity of human nature. The application of principles in evaluating men was thus selective rather than deliberately exclusive.)

Confucius's evaluation of Yang Hu, a man who had been forced to flee from one state to another because he proved greedy and disloyal each time he acquired power, provides a simple example of projecting behavior on the basis of constancy. Based upon this repeated behavioral pattern, Confucius accurately predicted that Yang Hu would certainly suffer an ignominious end. More generally, Mencius subsequently stated: "A man who ceases his efforts where he should not will abandon them anywhere. A man who is parsimonious with those with whom he should be generous will be parsimonious everywhere."[60] Granting that people generally acquire fixed habits early in life, a man's end may therefore be foreseen by midlife: "Someone who is still disliked at forty years of age will end by being so."[61]

The principle of constancy is also evident in significant situations that require its existence and applicability to be routinely emphasized because the principle underpins any extrapolation of situational dynamics to analogous circumstances. The family was particularly viewed as a proving ground for children and a stage where character might be perceived prior to a person's entrance into society at large. The respectful, fraternal, and, above all, filial person would normally be expected to behave similarly once thrust into the web of real-world relationships. Respect for clan elders and filial behavior toward parents presumably grounded a person's attitude toward his elders and superiors in general, including the ruler, should the respectful person be fortunate enough to attain power and position. Therefore the *Analects* quotes Tzu Yu, one of Confucius's prominent disciples, as saying: "Few men who have been filial and brotherly have ever been inclined to oppose their superiors. No one disinclined to oppose his superiors ever liked to cause rebellion."[62]

Criteria for Evaluating

If the assumption that people may be fathomed is allowed, the immediate problem becomes whether any reliable criteria exist and what they might be. From the early Chou onward it was widely felt that many external signs might indicate a person's character and motives, the most frequently cited including words, actions, desires, countenance, manner, bearing, adherence to the *li* (etiquette or normative forms of behavior), physical features, and the eye. The *Lü-shih Ch'un-ch'iu* even approvingly noted that a few famous men were able to "physiognomize" horses, to detect their inner or true worth by gazing on their exteriors, and men, states, and affairs were thought to be equally amenable to such external scrutiny.[63] Still another view held that a man's character and qualifications could be detected from his works, achievements, and creations,[64] with Wang Ch'ung believing that the writings of unknown scholars could be similarly investigated.[65] Finally there were proponents who extrapolated from exceptional talent (such as singing) because any expert attainment was thought to indicate a man whose overall abilities far exceeded mere singular skills.[66]

The Puzzle of Reputation

Officials selecting men for positions or missions frequently relied upon fame and reputation. Particularly when an individual was closely identified with important deeds, well-known virtuous acts, or other highly visible accomplishments, his talents were felt to surpass the ordinary, his character to have been revealed by his works. Mind and character being intangible, such historical evidence was generally felt to provide incontrovertible evidence. However, doubts were still raised about the validity of fame and reputation, skeptics being troubled by the problem of motivation and the difficulty of distinguishing between actual deeds and mere reputation, especially because rapidly growing reputations were rarely investigated.[67] Moreover, it was well known that fame might be manipulated and a virtuous image deliberately crafted through highly visible acts of sacrifice, daring, or incorruptibility. Many men consciously manipulated their images, and some even died just to create a name for posterity, particularly if they were not as virtuous as those who jumped into rivers or perished in forest fires rather than betray their values. Throughout Chinese history the range of opinion on the possibilities of discerning character thus extended from complete disbelief in the reliability of fame as a valid indication of worth, to complete faith in it as the most reliable indicator. Tempering measures that adjusted for the tendency of stories to become exaggerated and the fanciful to creep in, to distinguish between fame and actual accomplishments, were devised. Even though achievements were considered highly reliable indicators, gaining full knowledge of them was a problem in itself.

Confucius apparently grappled with the problem of reputation, pondering whether there could be any substance to reports of virtue and vice, and decided further investigation would always be required because numerous factors affect public opinion: "When the masses hate someone, you must investigate it. When the masses like someone, you must investigate it."[68] Even the very founders of the Chou dynasty purportedly struggled with this difficulty, according to the *Six Secret Teachings*:

If the ruler takes those that the world commonly praises as being Worthies, and those that they condemn as being worthless, then the larger cliques will advance and the smaller ones will retreat.

In this situation groups of evil individuals will associate together to obscure the Worthy. Loyal subordinates will die even though innocent. And perverse subordinates will obtain rank and position through empty fame. In this way, as turbulence continues to grow in the world, the state cannot avoid danger and destruction.[69]

Although popular opinion might provide an initial basis for consideration, a better indication was felt to be the character of the people making such recommendations: "Tzu Kung inquired, 'What about someone loved by all the people of his village?' Confucius replied, 'It is still insufficient evidence [for goodness].' 'What if all the people of his village hate him?' Confucius replied: 'It is still insufficient evidence [for evil]. It would be preferable that the good people of the village love him and the bad hate him.'"[70]

Mencius, who felt that new appointments naturally disrupt the established social order, displace members of prominent families, offend the ruler's relatives, and raise the lowly over the honorable, continued Confucius's thoughts when queried by a ruler about the problem of reputation and approbation:

When your attendants all say that a man is worthy, it is not yet certain. When your high officials all say that someone is worthy, it is not yet certain. When all the citizens of the state say that someone is worthy, investigate, and if you find him to be worthy, employ him.

When all your attendants say a man is unworthy, it is not yet certain. When all your high officials say that someone is unworthy, it is not yet certain. When all the citizens of the state say someone is unworthy, investigate, and if he is unworthy, dismiss him.[71]

Thus generally the ruler—and by implication anyone else entrusted with responsibility for selecting and tasking men—should not rely upon the uncorroborated judgments of others, but where an opinion is widely held, determine for himself whether a man matches his reputation.

Although most other thinkers gave greater or lesser credence to fame and reputation, many saw at least some likelihood of substance in a good reputation and suggested appropriate techniques for further consideration. For example, the *Ta-Tai Li-chi* concluded that if the people generally approve of some aspects of a man and the reverse, "there must be some substance in it."[72] Parts of the *Hsin Hsü* found public approbation an inadequate recommendation, but also its absence a recommendation against employing someone.⁷³ The *Chung Lun* advocated evaluating the opinion of the masses, never trusting reputation alone, always opting for self-reliance when one's conclusions differ.⁷⁴ However, Shen Chien advocated a middle path—not necessarily relying on others nor oneself, but considering all aspects of the man.⁷⁵ Finally, a section in the *Lü-shih Ch'un-ch'iu* even asserted that words that report past events, particularly the ancient past, are to be doubted—events may be reported out of context, and they should be evaluated with reference to general principles and human emotions to determine whether they are conceivable or not. In this fashion excessive credence will be avoided and the evaluator will be protected from errors.⁷⁶

A number of authors also pointed out that fame, achievements, and the attainment of high office depend upon fate and destiny. Quite simply, without opportunity even the most talented individuals go unnoticed and die forgotten; without ever having been entrusted with power, no man can sufficiently display his character or manifest his abilities. Even Confucians would languish unknown without challenges and the temptations of authority and influence.

Appearance

Appearance, comprising physical characteristics, manner, and bearing, provides another foundation for evaluating. Not easily dismissed, it probably constituted the most frequently employed basis for making judgments in traditional China, just as in the West today. Difficulties were similarly envisioned by a number of thinkers, engendering a general skepticism of the reliability of appearance alone. Again Confucius was among the first to regret having based an evaluation solely upon behavior and manner,⁷⁷ and Mencius found that appearance usually reflects a person's power and position, that people assume airs appropriate to their station and role, complicating the effort to perceive underlying character.⁷⁸ However, unlike the dubious attitude displayed toward words, greater confidence was allotted evaluating by general appearance even though the latter might be a deliberate semblance designed to attain certain ends, merely an external but necessary acquiescence in the real world. Again, appearances that persist were thought more likely to reflect the interior man. A typical middle ground was struck by Hsün-tzu, who believed that an individual's personal habits and choice of clothes would betray his intent.⁷⁹ Therefore, someone who wore antique clothes and visibly preserved ancient ways, rather than succumbing to the customs of a decadent age, would presumably be a conservative scholar bent on maintaining past virtues.[80] (Of course, as Han Fei-tzu frequently noted, such a person might also be an eccentric or someone trying to draw attention to himself as a moral exemplar. Although Hsün-tzu did not mention these possibilities, he obviously was not ignorant of them.) Similarly a man who overstepped the sumptuary regulations to wear the clothing reserved to a higher rank was obviously presumptuous. Should it be the costume of a king or ruler, he could be planning a revolt, as in the following example from the Spring and Autumn period:

> At the assembly of the feudal lords at Kuo, Prince Wei of Ch'u was preceded by two men bearing halberds. Shu-sun Mu-tzu commented, "The prince of Ch'u is splendidly dressed, more like a ruler than a mere high official."
>
> Cheng Tzu-p'i said, "I have doubts about him having two men wielding halberds precede him."
>
> Ts'ai Tzu-chia commented: "Ch'u is a great state, while Prince Wei is its prime minister. Isn't it appropriate that he have two men precede him with halberds?"
>
> Mu-tzu replied: "It should not be so. The emperor has his tiger guards to train people in martial skills. The feudal lords have their clan guards to defend them against disaster and harm. High officials have footmen to undertake affairs. Officers have secondary chariots so that they may race off on missions. Now Prince Wei is merely a high official, yet he wears the clothes of one of the feudal lords, so he must certainly intend to become one. Someone without such ambition wouldn't dare enter among the feudal lords while wearing clothes suitable to their rank.
>
> "Now clothes are the pattern of the mind just as the crack patterns appearing on a turtle shell when you heat the inside for divination. If the prince doesn't become ruler of Ch'u, he will certainly perish. He will not again meet with the feudal lords." Prince Wei indeed rebelled and killed the ruler, replacing him.[81]

Confucius apparently embraced this view because in a discussion with Duke Ai, Confucius projected behavior on the basis of constancy, asserting that people who evince the proper commitments rarely commit evil.[82] (With the choice of the word "rarely" Confucius turned a blind assumption into a more circumscribed means of estimating character, with allowances for exceptions.) When Duke Ai pointedly raised the question whether a person might be known by his clothes, Confucius disallowed the possibility but granted that if a man's clothes and habits were both turned toward antiquity, it might be assumed he would probably not commit evil. However, clothing alone would never be adequate for judging a man as worthy and employing him for a position or on a mission. The topic of appearance thus seems to have occasioned more concrete pronouncements than generalities, including admonitions not to grant credibility to certain types of readily identified people. Two famous illustrations are: "Do not employ clever speakers with ingratiating appearances, who toady and flatter,"[83] and "Clever words and an ingratiating appearance rarely mark the benevolent."[84]

The creation of behavioral facades and deceptive appearances was considered difficult, fraught with a likelihood of self-betrayal. Even though appearances maintained over a period of time acquire reasonable credibility, under stress or temptation people often betray them in the most ordinary details, much as Mencius noted, "A man who loves fame will be capable of yielding a state of a thousand chariots, but if he is not such a man even when he gives up a basket of cooked rice or bowl of bean soup, it will be visible in his appearance."[85]

Apart from facades designed to mislead and misrepresent, there was another difficulty best termed "the problem of semblances," already discussed under basic intelligence. Because semblances prompt erroneous conclusions, even Confucius apparently became perturbed: "I hate weeds, fearing they will be confused with edible sprouts. I hate loquaciousness, fearing it will be confused with sincerity. I hate the sounds of Cheng, fearing that they will bring confusion to pure music. I hate purple, fearing it will be confused with vermilion. I hate the [pedantical] sincerity found in the villages, fearing it will be confused with virtue."[86] In the same vein a man with the appearance of a cultured gentleman might actually lack substance, being all *wen* (cultured form) and little *chih* (substance). This accords with Confucius's early pronouncement regarding the problem of balancing substance and expression: "Substance dominating cultivated form results in barbarism, cultivated form dominating substance results in fastidiousness. Only when substance and cultivated form are harmoniously integrated is someone a perfected man."[87] Only men with expertise such as found among gemologists can distinguish between appearance and reality and discuss the true nature of things, including human character.

Motives, Behavior, and Action

A larger question is posed by whether appearance and behavior can actually be identified with apparent motives and, if so, what means exist for determining the latter. Any solution must resolve the underlying problem that behavior, while appearing identical, may result from different motives: Different paths may lead to the same result, radically different attitudes to the same activity. Somewhat abstractly, Confucius ruefully observed: "Some are born and know things; some study and know them; some learn them through hardship. With regard to their knowing them, it is the same. [As for achievements], some rest in principles and take action; some do things out of a consideration for profit; some do it through coercion. So far as their being successful, it is all one."[88]

The *Huai-nan Tzu* illustrated the existence of varying developmental histories for observable phenomena. For example, by nature the extremely scrupulous never compromise their principles to accept employment under disreputable rulers and therefore, in the absence of inherited wealth, will be found suffering from poverty. However, few are the poor who suffer impoverishment because they refused to accept immoral employment, with its accompanying riches and power. Therefore, concluding that the poor are all scrupulous would be absurd. Similarly, there are many paths to wealth, including inheritance, theft, misuse of power, and honest acquisition through commercial activities, so wealth alone cannot be cited in condemning a man, even under a debauched ruler.[89] Thus from appearance alone a person's actual history and motives cannot be uniquely determined, so character may remain essentially opaque.

A second difficulty suggested by the *Huai-nan Tzu* was the unreliability of singular acts. Single acts of knowledge do not constitute wisdom or one of grief an expression of true sorrow. Any individual instance of behavior may entail remarkably different meanings for the actor and observers and fit into a rather immoral course of action overall. Only repetition, a series of acts along the same path, in the same direction, was thought to convey any real validity. Since any action may have been initiated for many different reasons, the fathoming of character without true knowledge of underlying motives becomes complex, a question resolvable only by time and context. The most dramatic example cited is regicide, normally the most heinous crime imaginable in traditional China. However, a monarch's murder may have been prompted by hatred, greed, political rivalry, desire for power, anger, revenge, or even a belief in having received the Mandate of Heaven.[90]

To distinguish the good from the evil requires standards that can serve as a referent, a value matrix such as furnished by the core beliefs of Confucianism. However, the difficulty of translating abstract virtues into concrete personality traits constitutes another problem. In one rebuttal the Literati in the *Discussions on Salt and Iron* raised the point that without a visibly good man, a Worthy who immediately garners general approbation, the less good and evil cannot be comparatively known.[91] As Lao-tzu pointed out, good and evil are mutually defining concepts, immediately implying that relativity plagues all evaluative processes, obviating the simple adoption of some abstract value system such as Confucianism.

Words, Speech, and Language

A very likely candidate for evaluating a man was thought to be "words," what a man said and how he expressed it, including his writings. Mencius, for example, was confident he could discern the speaker's mind on this basis: "'When his language is prejudiced, I know where he is occluded. When his language is dissolute, I know where he has sunken. When his language is perverse, I know where he has ventured off. When his language is evasive, I know where he is impoverished. Given birth in the mind, they harm the government. Being manifest in government, they cause harm to affairs.'"[92] Mencius's unusual powers presumably derived from an intense moral self-cultivation that somehow laid transparent the motivations of other men. However, closer examination of his criteria indicates but a limited range, all related to moral casts of mind rather than specific motivations. Since Mencius was an acknowledged, as well as self-professed, moral exemplar, his powers were considered exceptional and therefore unattainable to ordinary men immersed in the world of immediacy.

Hsün-tzu felt that from the way a man spoke his progress along the moral way could still be detected, though care had to be exercised in correlating the content of his words with his behavior and appearance. Thus someone who lacked sincerity in speaking about the right subjects—the virtues of old, the rulers of antiquity—wouldn't delight in such topics, evidence that his speech was mere dissembling. In contrast, the perfected man focused his intent upon the Way, put it into practice, and took pleasure in speaking about it, his words, actions, and attitude all cohering.[93] Similarly, when a man surnamed Ying explained why he had not remained with Yang-tzu, a reputed gentleman, he cited a theory that probably enjoyed great credence in the Spring and Autumn and Warring States periods: "Appearance is the flower of emotion, and words are the linchpin of appearance."[94] Words were considered the outward embellishment of the body, whereas the body manifests the inner emotions. Therefore words and appearance, having an inherent relationship, should cohere; consequently, disharmony indicates a facade. Ying further believed that prevarications could not be effectively maintained, eventually disintegrating and betraying the individual's true inner nature.

Confucius was the most famous of those who experienced difficulty in relying upon words to evaluate men, prompting him to rhetorically ask, "If a man's discussions are sincere, does this mean he is a perfected man, or is it only his appearance that is formidable?"[95] He was compelled to conclude: "The virtuous will be sure to speak correctly, but those whose speech is good may not always be virtuous. Men of principle are sure to be bold, but those who are bold may not always be men of principle."[96] By definition, the virtuous are circumspect in speech and dedicated to the Way. However, the class of all good speakers includes the nonvirtuous, those who are wise enough to imitate the traits of the good for ulterior motives, such as personal profit and illicit gain. This leads to the famous corollary already seen: "Clever words and an ingratiating appearance rarely mark benevolence."[97] Moreover, as widely recorded, Confucius felt he had erred in his estimation of Tzu Wu, having discovered him to be asleep during the daytime after previously characterizing him as one of his eloquent disciples.[98] He therefore formulated his well-known operational rule: "The perfected man does not recommend a man because of his words or dismiss words because of the speaker."[99]

Essentially two different dimensions to the problem were thus envisioned. The first was the simple failure of men to live up to their words, sometimes brought about by their cultivating an eloquence that was widely admired and often profitable in itself. The second was the conscious use of deception, of dissembling and advocating something not believed, of deliberately trying to create a distinctive impression because of the common knowledge that men were judged not only by what they say, but also by their sophistication and expressive ability. (The latter constitutes another problem altogether because some people are naturally more talented and therefore enjoy an immediate edge in the world. However, it was little discussed, perhaps because the process of self-cultivation and the study of the classics should lead to a mastery of verbal expression based upon classical models. The embellishment of language, while sometimes evidence of insubstantiality, became commonplace and therefore problematic.[100]) Since persuasion was a profession practiced during the Warring States period and an essential court skill in all eras, the weight attached to words became extremely important. Even though sophists were generally disdained, they still enjoyed wide audiences and found opportunities to be heard, with only Han Fei-tzu advocating draconian methods to make men accountable for their proposals. Consequently, evaluations by words alone were felt to be risky and uncertain, and final reliance never could be placed upon them.[101]

Evaluating by Associates

Without doubt the belief that people might be known by their associates was extremely popular in traditional China, anecdotes and stories illustrating its application being widely scattered throughout the literature. In its simplest form the theory holds that a person's friends, close court associates, and the acquaintances he cultivates, such as recluses and scholars, will all prove revealing.[102] Even though rulers were less often chosen than imposed, the same principles became applicable with the onset of mobility late in the Spring and Autumn period as men began to travel relatively unimpeded to offer their services to willing monarchs. (Rulers might equally be evaluated by their close officers, personal retainers, and officials deputed on foreign missions, as well as by the scholars, magicians, entertainers, and rogues they patronized.[103]) Officials might further be scrutinized by observation of whom they entertained at home and with whom they lodged when abroad.[104]

There was a twofold basis to the theory of association: environmental influence and the tendency of likes to mutually attract and naturally associate, whereas men of dissimilar temperament, tastes, and ideas would not.[105] Numerous thinkers focused upon the theory of association, it was rigorously applied, and the assertion that things, animals, and classes of the same type will naturally respond and associate with each other was frequently seen. The fundamental concept of environmental influence even prompted Confucius to emphasize the need to exercise care in choosing one's dwelling and associates because of their unperceived effects in transforming character and changing customs.[106] Mencius, Hsün-tzu, and, especially, Mo-tzu all stressed the danger of unconscious transformation and the need to consciously select environmental stimuli. Irrespective of a person's initial predisposition, prolonged association with evil inevitably resulted in the person assimilating perverse values and mimicking antisocial behavior, with even good men eventually becoming indistinguishable from their cohorts. Consequently, observing a person's associates predicts future development, as well as indicates current personality and inclinations. Confucius thus felt confident in Tzu Hsia's future because he liked to dwell with those more worthy than himself, whereas he feared for Tzu Kung, who enjoyed persuading the less worthy, thereby exposing himself to their insidious influence.[107]

Sequence and Comparative Criteria

The natural sequence of perceiving others was seen as appearance, words, and, finally, actions or behavior, prompting codified steps to evaluate visitors to a state: "When a man comes from outside the state, irrespective of his route of entrance, if his external appearance and deportment are circumspect, then look into his name. When aware of his name, then check his appearance. Then verify his affairs in order to investigate his virtue. Observe him in externals, and then he will not have any means to put the ruler in difficulty with false virtues and the country will not be misled."[108] Coherence in all aspects suggested that a man's true character had been revealed.

Rather than reliance upon isolated criteria, comparison of indications from different sets of traits was thought to ensure a more accurate evaluation. Although the development of the *li* (normative forms of behavior) marked the pinnacle of structured social behavior, providing a detailed but complex standard for fathoming men, simple discrepancies between words and clothing, clothing and position, or words and behavior would immediately signify a facade or indicate questionable elements in a person's character. Prominently learning from his experience, Confucius regretfully advised: "At first my way with men was to hear their words, and give them credit for their conduct. Now my way is to hear their words and look at their conduct. It is from Yu that I have learned to make this change."[109] Furthermore, in concluding a discussion with Duke Ai, Confucius sounds much like Han Fei-tzu: "The method for choosing men is to observe their words and investigate their actions. Words are the means by which one reveals thoughts and expresses emotions. One who can perform some action can certainly discuss it. Thus first observe their words and then measure their actions. If one employs words to measure actions, then even though a person be evil, he will have no way to avoid revealing his true emotions."[110]

The *Chou Li,* an idealized depiction of Chou administrative structure and rites probably compiled in the early Han, similarly suggested comparing verbal and nonverbal aspects in examining whether a person might be guilty of a crime.[111] The five, all clearly useful for questioning agents and interrogating others, are words (and the language chosen), appearance, the *ch'i* (breathing as normal or not), whether there were any places of doubt (through listening to the sound of his voice), and the eyes, as clear and bright or not. Every aspect should be investigated, and all of them should cohere if the person is both truthful and genuine.[112] In the Han dynasty, even though he accepted the necessity of judging men by their words (on the assumption that a good heart would result in good words), the famous skeptic Wang Ch'ung advanced an even more cautious view. When a man's actions correspond with his words, his family and state should then be investigated. Whether he had previously been successful or not, should all of them still be consistent, he might be considered worthy and appointed to office.[113]

The most thorough, detailed examination might be termed "contextual reference"—comparing the person's name, fame, reputation, position, personal history, character, background, and other manifestations with his environment. Any inappropriate aspect would immediately suggest something amiss, whether in the person's motives or fundamental character. (Again the *li* represent the most precisely developed and defined means for determining the contextual matrix, although common experience furnished more than adequate means and knowledge for examining ordinary people.) This idea appeared in a variety of texts and apparently formed an essential part of the fund of basic knowledge.[114]

Evaluating by Desires

Another train of thought held that a man could be best understood by determining his desires,[115] a method that would immediately facilitate covert intelligence purposes by identifying potential temptations, which are the most effective means for acquiring information and recruiting subversives. Although it requires examining a person's behavior to detect them (and therefore largely represents a variant of the historical approach), evaluating by a man's desires represents a distinctive methodology that utilizes many materials for clues. Being visible in the pleasures and objectives a man pursues, the chief desires are revealed not only in terms of their type and visibility, but also in terms of the degree to which they have been brought under control, mastered as part of a man's self-discipline.[116] Thus the idea that "if you want to know men, then look at their desires" gained great credence, and even the medical writings noted that a man may be known by what he likes and dislikes.[117]

Errors as Expressive of Character

Confucius was among the first to observe that in the cultivation of the moral Way, such as through the study of the classics and other matters, people may err to one-sidedness. Similarly, where emotional substance remains out of balance with constraint or expression, the person may have desirable virtues, yet be criticized for a visible shortcoming. Since these "errors" fall into patterns, it becomes possible to detect underlying virtues from their type and estimate a person's character. The basic premise first appeared in the *Analects:* "A man's transgressions are each indicative of a class. Thus by observing his transgressions the man can be known."[118] Of particular importance would be overdeveloped traits that, in moderation and properly balanced, are admirable, such as respectfulness, generosity, and sternness. (The authors of the military writings were particularly conscious of the potential dangers posed by such unameliorated traits, however outstanding they might ordinarily be considered, and identified them as exploitable flaws in enemy commanders, as will be seen in the military intelligence section.) Confucius in fact identified six inclinations that result in character and behavioral defects:

A love of benevolence without a similar love of study leads to the obfuscation of doltishness. A love of wisdom without a love of study results in the obfuscation of agitation. A love of sincerity (trust) without a love of study results in the obfuscation of precipitousness. A love of straightforwardness without a love of study leads to the obfuscation of bluntness. A love of courage without a love of study leads to the obfuscation of chaos. A love of resoluteness without a love of study leads to the obfuscation of unprincipled behavior.[119]

Scholars immersed in orthodox Confucian studies from the late Warring States onward—increasingly the class from which government administrators originated—were thought to be particularly prone to one-sidedness if they specialized in one of the six classic texts, predisposing them to certain strengths, weaknesses, and methods in grappling with affairs. A passage in Tung Chung-shu's *Ch'un-ch'iu Fan-lu* notes that "the *Book of Odes* and *Book of Documents* order a man's intentions; ritual and music purify his virtuous qualities; and the *I Ching* and *Ch'un Ch'iu* make his knowledge enlightened."[120] More than a century later Yang Hsiung correlated five of the classics with specific subject matter: "The *I Ching* excels in speaking of Heaven; the *Book of Documents*, affairs; the books of ritual, the concrete embodiment of Virtue; the *Book of Odes*, intention; and the *Ch'un Ch'iu*, the patterns of affairs."[121]

Tung Chung-shu similarly elaborated upon the strengths of the individual classics: "The Odes guide the intentions and are thus strong in substance. Ritual governs the constraints and is thus strong in cultivated expression. Music sings of virtue and is thus strong in transforming. The *I Ching* is based on Heaven and Earth and thus strong in the patterns of things. The *Ch'un Ch'iu* discriminates right and wrong and thus is strong in governing." However, the *Li Chi*, the main ritual text, identified certain weaknesses with each of the classics that could prove significant should someone be employed on a sensitive mission or in a critical position.

The Odes teach being congenial and flexible, honest and generous, but have the shortcoming of doltishness. The *Book of Docu-*

ments teaches extensive comprehension and a knowledge of antiquity, but a shortcoming of irrelevance. Music teaches being expansive, relaxed, and peaceful, but a shortcoming of extravagance. The *I Ching* teaches being pure and tranquil, refined and subtle, but a shortcoming of precipitousness. Ritual teaches being reverent and restrained, serious and respectful, but a shortcoming of being vexatious. The *Ch'un Ch'iu* teaches skill in discourse and disputation, but a shortcoming of being chaotic.[122]

Presumably in the recruitment of candidates for subversion or intelligence work only those known not to be inclined to any single one of the classics would be preferable, for only they would have balanced personalities and the necessary self-constraint, just as Tung Chung-shu asserted.

Evaluating Under Stress

Although the assumption of constancy was widely accepted, it was also observed that stressful circumstances elicit unexpected behavior. Moreover, without strong character and great forbearance people eventually succumb to misery and pressure, thereby revealing character flaws likely to reappear whenever under duress.[123] Accordingly, the Confucians and others emphasized that actions witnessed under conditions of deprivation and ignominy have greater validity as indications of character. Especially important would be the attitude displayed in straitened circumstances, for although endurance was necessary, self-restraint alone might be suspect. The true moral exemplar would still manifest equanimity in hardship and tranquillity in poverty, an ideal well represented by Yen Hui, whom Confucius praised by saying: "Worthy indeed was Hui! With only a basket of cooked rice and a gourd of liquid, despite dwelling in a vulgar alley, a misery other men could not endure, his joy was unchanged. Worthy indeed was Hui!"[124] Confucius himself established the basis for this perspective: "Even when I have nothing but coarse grain to eat, water to drink, and simply bend my arm for a pillow, I am still joyful. Unrighteously gained wealth and rank are like floating clouds to me."[125]

Mencius observed that great men frequently endure travails that stimulate and temper them, shaking them out of their comfort and ease,[126] and believed that Heaven would inflict tortuous experiences:

When Heaven is about to entrust a man with great responsibility, it will invariably first subject his mind and intentions to suffering and labor his muscles and bones. It causes his body to be hungry and deprives him of everything. It brings chaos to all his actions and efforts in order to stir his mind and forge his nature, increasing him in all that he is incapable of doing. Men constantly err and only thereafter change; suffer mental distress and consternation of thought and thereafter become creative. Only after things have been attested in appearance and manifested in sound are they understood. Only then is it known that life derives from worry and misfortune, death from security and pleasure.[127]

Other texts express similar ideas, concluding that a personal history of hardship valiantly endured marked strength of character.

Remarkably, riches and honor similarly entail personal temptation, especially for those who indulge long-repressed desires or manifest previously dormant traits after rapidly acquiring wealth. Moreover, suddenly having power and subordinates constitutes a radically different psychological experience, as evidenced by the truism that people tend to arrogance when they acquire power. Tzu Kung thus approved of a man who had resisted it, though Confucius required more: "Tzu Kung asked, 'What do you think about being poor yet not obsequious, rich but not arrogant?' Confucius replied, 'They are acceptable but not as good as being poor yet taking pleasure in the Tao, being rich and loving the forms of propriety.'"[128] In another well-known passage, Confucius added, "People who are not benevolent cannot long endure dwelling in straitened circumstances or extreme enjoyment."[129] Surprisingly, even Han Fei-tzu added some comments in his sections on Lao-tzu: "If the heart that desires profit is not eliminated, it will bring worry to the body. Thus when the Sage's clothes are adequate to ward off the cold and his food sufficient to fill his emptiness, he does not worry. The masses of men are not like this. Whether as great as one of the feudal lords or simply having more than a thousand ounces of gold, their worries over profits are not eliminated. The worry of those who do not know sufficiency never leaves them all their lives."[130]

Never being exposed to the temptations of power denied not only a man any opportunity to make himself famous, but also the world a chance to observe him in a stressful situation. Only in the context of highly visible situations can adequate information be generated: "If the person is honored, see who he introduces; if he is rich, see what assistance he gives to others; if he is of mean condition, see what he does not accept; if he is poor, see what he won't do. From observing these things his character can be known."[131] As summarized in the *Lü-shih Ch'un-ch'iu:* "When a man prospers, see who he treats as a guest. When he has high rank, see who he recommends. When he is rich, see who he supports. When he is poor, see what he will not accept. When he is in a mean condition, see what he will not do."[132]

Active Tests and Trials

The concept of an active test that might reveal flaws under contrived but observable conditions apparently evolved in response to the need to rapidly fathom character and suitability for employment, particularly high office and powerful military positions. Although from early times appointment to office essentially meant embarking upon a lifetime of challenges and evaluations, there was also a notion of a more specific trial, imposed for a limited time. According to the *Shang Shu* and popular tradition, Emperor Yao even subjected the future Sage emperor Shun to scrutiny by marrying his two daughters to him, moral character obviously being more important than talent and ability![133] However, increasingly specific circumstances that focused upon eliciting behavior in stressful situations evolved as the Warring States period progressed.[134] For example, the *Six Secret Teachings* elucidates eight techniques for ascertaining the veracity of apparent characteristics:

First, question them and observe the details of their reply. Second, verbally confound and perplex them and observe how they change. Third, discuss things that you have secretly learned to observe their sincerity. Fourth, clearly and explicitly question them to observe their virtue. Fifth, appoint them to positions of financial responsibility to observe their honesty. Sixth, test them with beautiful women to observe their uprightness. Seventh, confront them with difficulties to observe their courage. Eighth, get them drunk to observe their deportment. When all eight have been fully explored, then the Worthy and unworthy can be distinguished.[135]

Several other texts from the Warring States period contain variations of this same series premised upon the belief that a sequence of circumstances will provide the most illuminating data. The shortest list sought to induce three or four strong emotional states; the most lengthy and time-consuming, perhaps ten. However, methods for stimulating these states were never described, the formula merely asserting, "Anger him" or "Get him drunk," the most easily achieved objectives. The *Huai-nan Tzu* preserves a typically brief set: "Stir him with happiness and pleasure in order to observe what values he maintains. Entrust him with wealth and material goods in order to discern his benevolence. Shake him with fear in order to know his self-restraint. Then his emotional nature will be completely revealed."[136] (This approach assumes transparency of character and further hypothesizes that people will react simply when confronted with such stimuli rather than mounting a deceptive facade.) The idea of providing a person with pleasure, rather easily achieved, obviously reflects Yao's test of Shun.[137] However, causing a person to grieve—which evidently meant placing him in or exposing him to a situation of mourning, not his own, to see if he behaves properly—could be quite difficult short of murdering his friends or someone he loves. Since no methods are ever discussed for inducing the more extreme states, perhaps only the easily achieved temptations of pleasure, profit, and feasting were commonly employed among all those systematically listed.

In many instances the stimuli were no doubt verbal, designed to catch the person in the immediacy of a response. The simplest technique consisted of lying, asserting the opposite of what was actually true or believed, to observe whether they would adhere to their own principles or merely accord with prevailing views.[138] Similarly, failing to reject an idea or subject that should evoke condemnation would be tantamount to accepting evil, implying they sanction and might commit similar acts themselves. No doubt in application the principle was symmetrical: Reacting to the good with distaste and rejection would indicate an immoral bent of character.[139]

Apart from the *Six Secret Teachings*, the most complete sequences for actively creating contexts to elicit primary emotions are found in the *Ta-Tai Li-chi* and the *Lü-shih Ch'un-ch'iu*, both continuations of discussions on passively observing people in varying but normal circumstances. For example, the series found in the latter runs: "Make him happy in order to observe his preservation of principles. Give him pleasure in order to see whether he will abandon restraint. Make him angry to test his restraint. Make him afraid to see where he stands. Put him in grief to see his humaneness. Put him in hardship to see his willpower."[140] A similar sequence is found in the *Ta-Tai Li-chi*:

> Frighten him to see whether he doesn't become afraid. Anger him and observe if he doesn't become disordered. Make him happy and observe if he doesn't become reckless. Send him beautiful women and see if he doesn't overstep proper bounds. Provide him with food and drink and see if he has constancy. Profit him and see if he can be yielding. When he dwells in grief, see if he is correct. When in poverty, see what he will not do. Give him labors to see if he doesn't disturb others.[141]

Under the stimulus of intense emotions strong reactions would normally be expected; only a man of exceptional character would not respond normally, would exhibit self-restraint and control. Consequently the preceding phrasing often employs the term "not" to indicate expectation, with actions contrary to normal vindicating and justifying the individual.

There were a number of other structured tests that were employed, particularly those associated with the major ceremonies of the *li* (rites), such as archery and the village drinking ceremony. Failure to adhere to ritual dictates would immediately indicate either ignorance or the absence of self-restraint, both serious defects.

However, the concept of testing was not confined to evaluating, though the discussion here must necessarily be limited to it. Tests were contrived to fathom motives or states of mind and inclinations, to determine character and evaluate abilities, to test the reliability of what the person proposed or claimed with regard to his actual capabilities, to evaluate the impact of military training, and to determine the effectiveness of rewards and punishments in inculcating desirable values. (Perhaps the most famous example of the latter is found in the *Han Fei-tzu*, which records that the King of Ch'u was persuaded to set his treasury afire to test the men's response.[142]) There is no question that these trials were based upon a body of theory and explicitly conceptualized as tests, specifically designed to produce insights, irrespective of the subject's volitional cooperation.

Similar tests were also adroitly employed in intrigues, the basic procedure being to provoke people into becoming angry or so overwhelmed by hatred that they would recklessly blurt forth clandestine information. (Anger might also be exploited in many other ways, such as by being directed against a target, inducing a desire for revenge, or prompting precipitous action.) Incidents employing this simple mechanism are widely preserved in the literature, particularly the early historical writings and subsequent dynastic histories. A classic example appears in the *Tso Chuan*, where the heir apparent, suspecting he had been set aside, deliberately enraged his father's sister by insulting her, and in her pique she let the truth slip out.[143] In another common scenario the ruler is presented with a set of gifts, all identical with one clear exception, in order to discover the most favored concubine and thus predict the next monarch.[144] Given constancy of human behavior, the ruler would naturally honor his favorite with the best present, and her son would likely be invested as the heir apparent, presuming the monarch continued to be enthralled and befuddled.

Another commonly employed ruse consisted of treating a foreign emissary discourteously in the belief that his reactions would reveal not only his own character and qualifications, but also those of his ruler. The ploy's effectiveness depended upon the principles of association and likes mutually attracting: Worthy rulers will choose capable assistants and attract the Worthy, just as the Worthy will refuse to serve under tyrants and corrupt monarchs. The provocateur must also have a thorough knowledge of the ritual forms normatively governing political intercourse, though other aspects would also be involved and every reaction subject to differing contextual interpretations. For example, indirect insults might provoke only a mild defense, or no visible embarrassment might mark great self-restraint and an exemplary nature, or perhaps (in the absence of shame and moral outrage) an immoral and suspect character. The *Kuan-tzu* offers the following example:

> Ch'u attacked Chü and Lu sent men to seek aid from Ch'i. Duke Huan was about to rescue them, but Kuan Chung said, "Do not rescue them."
> The Duke asked, "Why is that?"
> Kuan Chung said: "I spoke with his ambassador. Three times I insulted his ruler, but his countenance didn't change. Three times I had the officials not perform the rites to their fullest [but he didn't notice]. When we pressed his ambassador, he fought with us as if to the death. The ruler of Chü is a common fellow. Do not rescue him." Duke Huan did not aid him and Chü was lost.[145]

Another popular method was to employ people according to the recommendations they received or the proposals they put forth themselves. (Han Fei-tzu was especially noted for advancing a number of such techniques for mastering the myriad problems involved in evaluating and using men, and he is discussed separately.) Simply put, someone would be entrusted with a duty or mission and his ability evaluated by his performance and the results he achieved. For example, "when someone speaks of courage, test him in the military. If he speaks of knowledge, test him with an office. If he is tested in the military and achieves results, then appoint him; if in office and affairs are well governed, then employ him."[146] Similar examples are found throughout the literature, though being a fairly obvious method, it was not greatly written about.[147]

Physiognomy

Physiognomy enjoyed wide recognition and considerable credibility for more than two thousand years in China, despite being pervaded by a somewhat mystical aura. Even in the Warring States period men became famous for their skill in evaluating character and predicting fate based upon the shape and appearance of a person's face, and some were able to evaluate horses in this fashion. However, a skeptical counter-current suggested that any successful prediction of fate or future great-ness simply resulted from the practitioner's innate astuteness. In fact, when questioned, one famous master revealed that in reality he never employed any techniques from this pseudoscience, but instead simply applied the principle of association to deduce future prospects. For three important classes he studied the following aspects:

> Common men: whether their friends were filial, fraternal, pure, re-spectful, and feared the laws.
> Ministers of state: whether their friends were sincere, trustworthy, and actively performed the good.
> Rulers: whether their ministers were worthy, their assistants loyal; and whether they remonstrated with him.[148]

A person with admirable associates could be expected to prosper, be promoted, or flourish, depending upon his status as a commoner, min-ister, or ruler, respectively. (As this particular story appears in several texts, it represents either a common train of thought or a rationalist attempt to debunk the power and influence of physiognomy.)

Hsün-tzu was among those who denied the effectiveness of this art, believing neither that character can be detected from a person's face nor that appearance is related to mind.[149] (However, he elsewhere indi-cates that the perfected man's expression and bearing mark him as someone who has cultivated the Way.) Remarkably, Wang Ch'ung vouched for the viability of employing bones for physiognomy because he believed an individual's fate to already be predetermined at birth, being manifest equally in his bone structure and the turbidity of his original nature.[150] He therefore concluded that methods for physiog-nomizing both could exist, although only knowledge about the former was common. Any predictive failure stemmed not from inherently flawed premises but from inadequate investigation, and even Confu-cius erred in relying upon such superficial aspects as words and ap-pearance instead of the substantive techniques of physiognomy to evaluate men.[151]

Expressions and Postures

The theory of postures and expression was well developed in Chinese antiquity, with minutely detailed instructions specifying the appear-ance a person should manifest in all of life's situations and stages, whether socially trivial or vitally important. The fundamental psychological thrust of the *li*—the normative forms variously encompassing social etiquette, court behavior, rites, and rituals—was directed toward elucidating forms that should be internalized in preparation for future employment in appropriate circumstances. Although the *Li Chi* and *Ta-Tai Li-chi* preserve critical theories and detailed ritual practices, stories scattered throughout Warring States texts concretely illustrating how the *li* were applied in significant situations provide extensive information about form and behavior. A number of works also dissect appearance and action, expounding upon the ideals they should attain. For example, the *Hsin Shu* enumerates six aspects critical to any civilized man: intent, countenance, perception, speech, stance, and seated posture.[152] The six are further specified for the four primary situations of attending court, performing an ancestral sacrifice, serving in the military, and performing the rites of mourning. They thus provide an immediate contextual matrix for evaluating character, with any deviation clearly revealing character deficiencies and aberrant emotions.

The *Tso Chuan* contains numerous examples of judging people by their performance of the *li*, all founded upon this basic idea that any failure betrays character flaws. Court audiences provide ample opportunities for evaluation:

When Duke Tan Ch'eng held a formal meeting with Han Hsüan-tzu in Ch'i on behalf of the king of Chou, he looked downward and spoke slowly. Afterward Han said: "Tan-tzu will soon die. In court the positions are clearly determined, at convocations there are markers. The upper jacket has its lapels, the sash its knot. In court and at convocations one's words must be audible at all the designated positions in order to illuminate the principles of affairs. The speaker should look between the knot and lapels in order to regulate his own demeanor and countenance. Words are employed to issue commands, whereas the speaker's demeanor and countenance should illustrate them. Any failure in these is a flaw.

The duke is the king's chief official, yet when issuing orders on his behalf at this meeting, he did not look above the sash, nor did his words project beyond a single pace. His countenance did not regulate his demeanor and his words were not illuminating. Not being regulated is irreverent, not being illuminating is disharmonious. He lacks the means to preserve his *ch'i*."[153]

The great ritual text known as the *Li Chi* (compiled in the Early Han) contains a passage explicitly defining the appropriate line of vision for court audiences. In essence, when a court official has an audience with the emperor, his vision should fall between the emperor's sash and lapels; with a state ruler (in the Warring States period), just below the face; and with an official of equal rank, directly upon his face. The text concludes by stating that "whenever the gaze alights above on the face [in an audience with a higher ranking person], it indicates arrogance; when below the sash, it marks sorrow; and if the person peers obliquely, it indicates villainy."[154] Since Duke Tan, as the king's representative, was the highest-ranking official at the meeting, these particular constraints would not apply to him, but to those speaking with him. However, he was still bound to maintain a proper posture, look out correctly, and speak clearly, all of which he failed to do, prompting Han Hsüan-tzu to correctly predict his imminent death.

Among the common deficiencies revealed through such performances are pride and arrogance, often witnessed in a person's clothing and carriage, suggesting an early death;[155] laxity and indifference, indicating inadequate study and self-discipline, a general weakness in temperament and character;[156] and deliberate disregard of the normative forms, proof of a truly perverse character and future trouble.[157] Conversely, expert performance attests to character, poise, and education, to men who have constrained their emotions and curbed their desires, yet allow substance its proper expression at appropriate times.[158]

The rites of mourning for a deceased parent were viewed as the definitive life experience, one in which the mourner would be confronted with the strongest emotional forces marking human existence. For the filial son caught between the raging demands of his inner emotions and the constraints imposed by society, the *li* allowed for a cathartic expression while providing the moderation necessary to prevent the bereaved from being consumed by a grief whose extremity would popularly be regarded as a measure of true filiality. Because of the vital, highly visible role the rites of mourning would play in a person's life and the strong emotional bond expected between parents and children, any lack of emotional intensity or, even more dramatically, unusual or improper emotions would immediately signify a deviant nature and cast suspicion on the mourner's character.

Since the true filial son's grief would not be fully exhausted even during the mourning period, the depth of his emotions would be further attested by his attitude and behavior in the subsequent rites of sacrifice and remembrance. Therefore, the same emotional content, subdued, yet intense, should be visible during their preparation and performance, including the meditative stages preliminary to envisioning his deceased parents. Thus the rites of mourning and the sacrifices to the ancestors were viewed as providing the means to determine a supposedly filial son's actual emotional state. The man of exemplary character would, by definition, necessarily and inevitably be a filial son. He would be moved to grief; his preparation would be meticulous; his performance would be filled with emotion, yet tempered by restraint; and his life would be oriented toward them, letting nothing else interfere with the rites of mourning. (During the rites of mourning he was rather unrealistically expected to withdraw and isolate himself for the twenty-five-month period known as the "three years" mourning.) As the *Analects* succinctly states: "While a man's father is still alive, observe his intent; when his father has died, observe his actions. If he does not change from his father's ways for three years, he may be termed 'filial.'"[159]

Successfully performing the rites of mourning, as all the other rituals, requires thorough knowledge; therefore, failure in any detail may indicate inattentive study or a lack of focus. Condemning an individual for his absent-mindedness in preparing for the ancestral sacrifice was apparently as common for inadequate as for excessive emotional intensity. Confucius thus prophesied that Kung-suo Shih of Lu would perish within three years because he forgot the sacrificial victim.[160] (Since the rite provides the sole means for the filial to express his emotions, forgetting a critical aspect is synonymous with neglecting the rite itself and therefore symptomatic of negligence in such other matters as one's particular duties and responsibilities.) The *Tso Chuan* similarly contains a number of cases in which people are condemned for failing to manifest the proper grief, implying either an absence of sorrow or the presence of some competing emotion. For example, looking pleased (perhaps because of the splendor of the rites or the excellence of the guests) would be a flagrant violation of propriety, an obvious cause for suspicion: "This man did not feel grief while a mourner and amid sorrow had a resplendent appearance. He is what may be termed 'a man without measure.' Rarely does a man without measure not cause misfortune."[161]

Another case with dramatic consequences attests to the validity attributed to such indications: "You must kill him. He feels no sorrow and is very ambitious. He looks about fiercely and raises his feet high, so his thoughts are on something else. If you do not kill him, he will certainly harm you."[162] Finally, in a third incident the mourner displays a startlingly disjointed happiness amid the most sorrowful circumstances, prompting the following analysis:

> The king of Chou will die prematurely! I have heard that men invariably die from what they take pleasure in. At the present time

the king takes pleasure in grief. If he dies because of grief, it cannot be termed "living out his span of years." In a single year the king has suffered two deaths that mandate three-year mourning periods. To feast with guests and request libation vessels at this time of mourning is the extremity of taking pleasure in grief. Moreover, it violates the ritual prescripts, while the submission of such vessels should be to offer congratulations for achievements, not because of mourning.[163]

Although other incidents in the *Tso Chuan* and other works provide similar illustrations,[164] the king of Chou's violation of the ritual prescriptions was particularly heinous because their very genesis was identified with Chou culture!

In detailing the forms of mourning, the traditional ritual works prescribe the expressive modes of behavior, including tones and times for wailing. Even though it was generally accepted that music varied from state to state and the *Huai-nan Tzu* even asserted that the sounds of music in pleasure and that of mourning similarly vary—implying that there is no single correct manifestation of either, and therefore that the measures of grief and joy are less certain and invariable than imagined by the Confucians—the ritualists felt that the tone of the voice in wailing should manifest certain characteristics postulated as being the natural correspondents of that grief.[165] From this it can be inferred that if the sound of the voice fails to manifest real grief, the person cannot be experiencing it, whether because of its simple absence or the presence of some other strong emotion. A famous incident commented upon by Han Fei-tzu and remarked upon by Wang Ch'ung illustrates the concept's application:

> One morning in the state of Cheng when Tzu Ch'an went out and passed the alley where Tung Chiang lived, he heard Tung's wife weeping. He restrained his driver's hand and listened. After a while he dispatched the lictors to seize and interrogate her and subsequently charged her with having murdered her husband. A day later his driver questioned him, "How did you know it?"
>
> Tzu Ch'an replied: "Her voice was fearful.[166] When someone they love first falls ill, people are troubled; when they near death, they become fearful; and after they die, they are struck by grief. She was weeping for her dead husband, but instead of grieving, she was fearful. From this I knew there was some villainy."[167]

Just as the *li*, musical performance was thought to betray the player's intentions to discerning listeners. Numerous examples are

preserved in traditional historical sources, although invariably because of their exceptional nature. Furthermore, even though ordinary
people might be aware of an emotional undercurrent in a performance
or perhaps be affected by the songs chosen, generally the arcane skills
of a Sage were required to fathom true intentions. (The presumption
that the astute listener would be thoroughly familiar with the music
or Odes needs hardly be raised.[168]) Although the many questions entailed by the elaborate theories of musical performance preserved in
the ritual writings are too complex to pursue in this chapter, an example from Ts'ai Yung's career well illustrates how "murderous intent"
was seen:

One day when Ts'ai Yung was in Ch'en-liu, his neighbor invited
him to a feast. By the time he went over, the other guests were already well flushed with wine. Among them was one who was
playing the lute behind a screen, so when Ts'ai reached the gate
he stopped, listened intently, then exclaimed: "Ay! How can he
have invited me for pleasure but have such a murderous intent?"
He then turned about and departed. One of the host's runners
reported it, saying, "Lord Ts'ai came to the door, then left." Because Ts'ai was respected by all the people in the region, the host
quickly raced after him to inquire why he had left, to which Ts'ai
replied truthfully. The lute player said: "When I was plucking the
strings, I saw a praying mantis approaching a chirping cicada. The
cicada was about to fly away but hadn't yet moved, while the
mantis was still rocking back and forth toward it. My heart
jumped, fearing that the mantis would lose it. Could this be the
murderous intent that was expressed in the sound?"
Ts'ai smiled broadly and said, "That certainly would be
enough!"[169]

Possibilities and Problems in Criteria

As discussed previously, the criteria by which people commonly
judged others were fairly simple: Wealth, rank, power, and other visible symbols of success were particularly felt to indicate talent, character, and ability. However, in addition to the inherent problems already
raised, more thoughtful examinations, such as by Wang Ch'ung and
Shen Chien, found them to be unreliable indications of character, often contingent upon capable men fortuitously encountering opportune circumstances.[170] Conversely, people naturally tend to be jealous
of the good and successful, to dislike, slander, and vilify them, causing

them to acquire adverse reputations and be subsequently denied positions.[171] Moreover, highly visible leaders, scholars, and moralists are exposed to public scrutiny, their most minor transgressions being rapidly publicized, while hidden evil remains undetected, lying fallow among the obscure.[172] In addition, should a man's ethics or temperament differ from his superior's, should he fail to be yielding and humbly deferential, he may readily be dismissed, criticism and differences quickly spawning antagonism.[173]

In accord with his penchant for analysis, Wang Ch'ung offered a fairly systematic critique of the criteria conventionally employed for evaluating men, providing many insights of potential utility to the tasks of intelligence work. The more interesting and relevant are summarized here.[174]

Men favored by the ruler may simply be obsequious rather than individuals of character and quality, chosen and retained simply because of their ability to please the ruler.

Generosity and a reputation for practicing the *li* require wealth and may be part of a conscious effort to win the approbation of others.

Successful military command is not a true measure of talent or character because military achievements depend upon craft and strategy.

Being a clever speaker or writer should be a recommendation against someone rather than for him.

Vaunted purity is suspect because a true Worthy should not be totally withdrawn. Moreover, reclusive habits signify failure, rather than virtue, since all men desire wealth and power. The faultless may be men of minor virtue incapable of action.

Being selected for office or position depends upon the criteria employed, high positions often being gained through currying favor.[175]

Being well liked by the people may be the product of conscious policies to please and attract them and stem from exploiting opportunities for developing a base of admirers through congeniality.

Attracting numerous retainers and guests does not signify an admirable person because the individual may simply enjoy assembling people about him or actually be marked by low values that attract dependents. The quality of such retainers is more important than their numbers.

Success in office may be due to winning favor with the ruler, and therefore only apparent, particularly when a man's reputation is

created by the rewards he receives. Success is also a question of
timing.
Recommendations are more indicative of the person making
them than the person being advanced. They also reflect expo-
sure to other people and their attitudes, as receptive to new acquaintances or not.
Being a scholar cannot be construed as a recommendation because
scholars are transmitters, not active agents, and are characterized by personalities that should not be advanced.

The view that officials are talented and scholars useless reflects the
dichotomy between the literati and the realists, though in this case
from the perspective of the people at large. The felt view was that
scholars have limited, useless knowledge, which causes them to remain outside the bureaucracy, whereas men of real talent work within
it. (The *Huai-nan Tzu* noted that an obvious inclination for studying a
subject makes a person neither knowledgeable nor a specialist, so stories to the contrary should be ignored.[176]) Wang Ch'ung sees this as an
error in perception, for in his view scholars are talented, whereas officials by and large have concentrated in a specialized range of texts.
However, officials conform to their age, whereas the scholars maintain their ideals and refuse to compromise, thereby effectively placing
themselves outside the system.[177]
Shen Chien similarly debunked many of the criteria of his era:

Rulers suffer from prejudice and blindness and may fail to employ
qualified people for a variety of reasons, such as being afraid of
them or fearing adverse comparisons. Furthermore, they may
simply accept popular recommendations or select only those
whom they find pleasing and compatible.[178]
Rank reflects fate rather than talent and achievement.[179]
Families do not reveal the character and personalities of individual members (contrary to common view).[180]
The standards of the time are simply inaccurate.[181]

Han Fei-tzu's Views

The ancients were conscious of the effects that perspective has upon
values and valuing, as already noted in the introductory section on basic intelligence. By the Warring States it was also recognized that an
individual's words can be evaluated only by reference to his back-

ground, character, and allegiances. Identical sentences may be interpreted in strikingly different ways, just as actions may be misunderstood and their significance seriously misconstrued. Because worldview and philosophic perspective can dramatically affect behavior and performance, they must be appropriate to administrative position. For example, in Han Fei-tzu's view the Confucians are too ethical for the realities of statecraft and their benevolence will inevitably spawn disaster when, for example, the compassionate heart that Mencius witnessed in King Hsüan of Ch'i proves unable to inflict the punishments necessary to ensure the state's stability.[182] Wielding power requires character and qualifications radically different from mere subservience; therefore candidates with unsuitable traits and tendencies must be eliminated.

Apart from personal relationships and connections, people were primarily selected for office based upon character evaluation, little attention being paid to the specialized requirements of individual positions. However, sections of the *Han Fei-tzu* advance several methods for evaluating men, all of which have already been discussed: projecting on the basis of past behavior and personal history; probing with detailed questions, including misleading stimuli to elicit responses that can be studied and analyzed; and testing within concrete situations. In fact, Han Fei-tzu pointedly denied the possibility of evaluating by appearance alone:

If in forging a sword only the tin employed and the blueness or yellowness of the flames were observed, even the famous blacksmith Ou Chih could not be certain it would be a good sword.[183] But if it can be used to strike geese in the water or sever the heads of horses on land, even the lowliest slave would not doubt its sharpness. If in judging a horse only its mouth is opened to check the teeth and its overall form seen, even Po Lo could not be certain of the horse. But if it is harnessed to a chariot and watched as it runs to the end of a course, the lowliest slave will not doubt its excellence. Similarly, even Confucius was incapable of being certain of a man simply by observing his demeanor and clothing and listening to his language and words. But if he is tested with duties of government and his achievements examined, even an ordinary man will have no doubt about his stupidity or wisdom.[184]

A few of Han Fei-tzu's fundamental observations bear reiteration. First, people can frequently be judged by their facial expressions: "Kung-tzu Chiu being about to revolt, Duke Huan of Ch'i dispatched an agent to watch him. The agent reported: 'He laughs at what is not happy, and sees what is not to be seen. He will certainly revolt.'"[185] Appearances may also be deceiving, particularly when the seemingly inconsequential achieve much,[186] and speech may be deceptive and evoke a spurious response. Naturally such misperceptions turn upon the perceiver's character as much as the speaker's overall image. Han Fei-tzu thus cited, and thereby exploited, Confucius's experience in this regard:

> Tzu Yü had the demeanor of a perfected man, so Confucius expectantly took him as a disciple. However, after a long time together Confucius discovered that his behavior did not match his demeanor. Ts'ai Yü's language was elegant and cultivated, so Confucius expectantly took him as a disciple. However, after some time together he discovered his wisdom did not equal his sophistry. Therefore Confucius said: "Should I select men based on their demeanor? I erred with Tzu Yü. Should I select men by their words? I erred with Ts'ai Yü." Thus despite his wisdom, Confucius has a reputation for failing to grasp the reality.[187]

Han Fei-tzu concludes the passage by citing two famous defeats he attributed to employing men with verbal, rather than martial, skills, including Chao Ma-fu at Ch'ang-p'ing, already seen in the historical section.

Han Fei-tzu also emphasized that the behavior of two individuals, or even of the same individual at different times, although apparently identical in all visible respects, often stems from different motives; therefore, an individual's intent and motivation must be fathomed before an adequate judgment can be made. His analysis integrates two examples:

> T'ien Po-ting liked men of ability and preserved his ruler; Duke Po liked men of ability and created chaos in Ching. Their regard for men of ability was the same, but the reason for it was different. Kung-sun Yu cut off his own feet and was honored for a hundred kilometers, whereas Chien Kou castrated himself and was regarded as a sycophant to Duke Huan. Their self-infliction of punishment was the same, but the reasons were different. Hui-tzu said: "A madman ran east and his pursuers also ran east. Their going east was the same, but the reason they ran east was different." Therefore it is said, "One must thoroughly investigate men performing the same action."[188]

Since appearances may be deceiving, on the assumption that men will eventually betray their actual talents and personalities in the trials of real experience, Han Fei-tzu naturally became a strong proponent of testing.[189]

Han Fei-tzu further noted that when the ruler's attitudes and desires are known, people will deliberately produce behavior that coheres with them.[190] Therefore, when anyone in power evaluates men for a position or mission, his own inclinations and expectations must be concealed, while a constant eye is kept on the motives and outside interests of prospective talents. Negative or misleading stimuli should be exploited to discern whether the individual is honest and sincere or merely seeking personal gain through deception and flattery. Han Fei-tzu thus evolved numerous techniques for comparative observation, the most relevant being visible in the following quotation:

> Compare their words to know if they are sincere, and evaluate them from different perspectives to investigate what they adhere to. Grasp the visible in order to ferret out the unusual. Employ men in single offices so that they may concentrate and become familiar with them. Heavily charge your distant envoys so that they will be frightened. Raise past events in order to comprehend the present. Bring men near to know their inner thoughts, keep them distant to study their outer behavior. Take hold of what you are clear about to probe where you are ignorant. Be deceptive in employing men to thwart dissolute behavior. Deliberately invert words to fathom the doubtful; employ contrary arguments in order to discover secret evil; establish spies in order to reign in the self-reliant; shift men about in order to detect the actions of villains; speak clearly in order to induce error free behavior; be humbly accommodating in order to see who is outspoken and who flatters. Make announcements in order to reach those you have not seen; cause arguments in order to disperse cliques and parties; keep things deeply buried in your mind so that people cannot fathom your happiness and anger; leak out spurious information in order to cause people to change their thinking; categorize semblances and compare them with experience; array errors to be clear about their causes. When you learn of crimes, punish them in order to end the perpetrator's awesomeness; and secretly depute agents to go out from time to time to investigate whether people are sincere or not.[191]

Although Han Fei-tzu felt that the ruler should be formless and inscrutable, deliberately creating artificial situations might also be exploited: "Duke Chao of Han closed his fist and pretended he had lost a fingernail, and was seeking it quite urgently. His attendant thereupon cut off a fingernail and presented it. From this he would see he was not sincere."[192]

Han Fei-tzu also disparaged relying upon constancy of behavior, citing many contrary examples, such as the following:

When Duke Wen of Chin fled outside his state, Chi Cheng carried a pot of food and followed him. However, Chi became confused, lost the way, and was separated from the Duke. Hungry, he wept beside the road. After awaking from his sleep, though famished he still did not dare eat. When Duke Wen returned to Chin, he mobilized his troops and attacked Yüan, conquering and seizing it. Duke Wen said "Someone who lightly endured the misery of starvation while preserving a pot of food for me will never employ Yüan to revolt." He therefore appointed Chi as prefect of Yüan.

When the high official Hun Kan heard about it, he criticized him, saying, "Isn't relying upon him not to revolt because he didn't disturb a pot of food a case of lacking methods?" Thus the enlightened ruler does not rely on others not revolting against him, but relies on it being impossible to rebel. He doesn't rely on someone not deceiving him, but on not being deceivable."[193]

Given that Legalists such as Lord Shang characterized man as motivated by the irrepressible twin desires for life and food, Chi's loyalty would seem to have been well proved. However, Han Fei-tzu found extreme devotion that transcended the bounds of normal human behavior inherently suspicious and clearly assumed that men who violently contravene natural emotional constraints must be driven by abnormal forces and motives. Blind loyalty might be the apparent motivation, but the reality is often otherwise, as in the following classic case where Duke Huan is recorded as questioning the mortally ill Kuan Chung about a possible successor:

"What about Shu-tiao?" inquired the Duke, but Kuan Chung replied: "Not acceptable. To love one's body is universal human nature, but Shu-tiao castrated himself in order to govern the inner palace because he knew you are jealous and love women. If he doesn't love his own body, how will he love you?"

"How about Prince K'ai-feng of Wei?" inquired the Duke, but Kuan Chung replied: "Not possible. The distance between Wei and Ch'i requires less than ten days' travel, yet in order to accommodate you, he has not returned home to see his parents for fifteen years! This is not normal human emotion. If he lacks affection for his parents, how can he possibly feel affection toward you?"

"What about Yi-ya?" inquired the Duke, but Kuan Chung replied: "Not acceptable. He was responsible for the flavors of your dishes and because you had never eaten human flesh cooked his son's head and presented it, something you already know. To love one's son is universal human emotion, but he cooked his son in order to provide you with a savory delicacy. If he did not love his son, how can he love you?"[194]

However, Han Fei-tzu also believed that once the necessary knowledge has been obtained, subject to the usual controls of government and through such methods as "name and responsibility," people can then be employed. In general it becomes a question of applied psychology, of projecting behavior on the basis of past actions and testing expectations against reality.

12

Character, Archetypes, and Typology

*T*HE CLASSIFICATIONS UNDERLYING the collected biographies in Ssu-ma Ch'ien's *Shih Chi* probably represent the fullest, most sophisticated archetypal characterizations found in antiquity. Although he did not explicitly specify the traits composing the various archetypes—they are found only in their embodiment as concrete characters classified under certain rubrics—by a simplified factor analysis the underlying elements may still be winnowed out and shown to be remarkably consistent, as we have already discussed in a separate study.[1] However, the development of personality types (as distinct from the somatotypes that are found in the medical writings) apparently began with the earliest stories of the Sage rulers, for the latter served to integrate a variety of idealized elements. (Their opposites, the depraved and evil rulers who persecuted the innocent and eventually lost their dynastic power to the Sage rulers, correspondingly arose.) With this development the concept of character types, of definite, if simplistic, combinations of character traits, became reality. Evaluating men as marked by certain personality clusters and tendencies then followed, although generally in terms of one or two emotions or desires that predominate and were therefore considered determining elements in a personality.

By the Warring States period the images of the Sage rulers of antiquity were already fully developed, the *Shang Shu* having described Yao as "reverent, intelligent, cultivated, thoughtful, and harmonious. He was completely respectful and capable of yielding."[2] Shun was similarly characterized in the *Shang Shu*.[3] Other writings from the period repeat the story of his ordeals and virtuously portray such other legendary rulers as Yü, King Wen, and the Duke of Chou.[4] Their counterparts, such as the tyrannical Chieh and debauched Chou, are thoroughly vilified, their evil behavior generally being reported with enough concise particulars to clearly establish how they lost the Mandate of Heaven.[5] Although essentially products of the thrust to idealize the Chou and disparage the Shang, these figures were the simplest images found in common awareness.

The *Shang Shu* also contains an enigmatic passage elucidating "Nine Virtues" that, in Wang Ch'ung's view, can somehow be employed to estimate character. (Although he readily admitted the task would be difficult and never provided any actual methods, Wang's recognition of the passage still imparted great import to it.[6]) As recorded in the *Shang Shu* they are composed by a series of paired, often contradictory, traits that largely defy translation: "Genial, yet dignified; pliant, yet upright; substantial, yet reverent; impetuous, yet respectful;[7] abrupt, yet resolute; straightforward, yet mild; terse, yet modest; firm, yet constrained; and strong, yet righteous."[8] In theory, someone who was marked by three of these virtues could serve as a clan or village leader; by six, a high state official; and by nine, ruler of the world.

Depending upon the perceiver's perspective, the concept of character and moral types included an immediate value judgment about worth, employability, and association potential. Despite all the problems and questions already raised, a man found to have embarked along the moral road would normally be a prime candidate for office and friendship, whereas the so-called common or mean fellow would be shunned. Because the emphasis continued to be on character and the moral man, on men with a sense of shame and an orientation to righteousness, abilities were little discussed apart from Han Fei-tzu and Liu Shao somewhat later. However, the writings of the period are replete with specific recommendations on characteristics to be sought in men and traits to be avoided. A man who manifests desirable qualities should be recommended for office and positions of trust; those displaying tendencies associated with trouble or moral deficiencies should not be retained under any circumstances. Somewhere between these two, in a sort of limbo to be evaluated by techniques as best they might, would fall men neither distinguished by prominent attributes nor marred by any glaring defect.

The value matrix for defining these concrete indications was generally a Confucian one, tempered somewhat by the requirements of office. Confucius himself set the tone and often many of the criteria with specific pronouncements in reference to some identifiable person that thereafter became applicable almost as a general rule. Many that do not fall into this category were prompted merely by the particularized experiences of some notable individual, the essence of the situation being distilled and transmitted as abstracted remarks separately from the original context. When taken together, these concrete pronouncements on "other people" constituted a sort of collective wisdom, a compendium of specific insights. Consequently, when a person was labeled with a certain trait that had a recognizable historical identity, the associated material would probably not be far from conscious awareness and the person judged accordingly.

Although much of this material is preserved in the traditional historical writings, the philosophical and political works contain numerous distilled portraits, particularly those built upon trends initiated by Confucius in characterizing his various disciples.[9] In summary, inimical behavioral patterns and personality traits include being flattering and acting obsequiously; being disobedient; being disrespectful; seeking fame irrespective of the cost to one's state and to others; being greedy and covetous, like the evil rulers of old; being ambitious; being domineering; being tough or severe (especially on oneself); being sharp-tongued; seeking office under a poor ruler; liking the small and dangerous; being too puritanical and overly concerned with minor faults; being petty; being ashamed of not being perfect; liking to drink, indulge in sexual pleasures, and other licentious activities; and slandering and demeaning one's own clan. Traits that would disqualify bureaucratic officials are being hard; displaying toughness (as in bravado and misdirected courage); being flowery, all culture or expression, without substance; acting arrogantly; heeding the spirits; becoming easily angered; and lacking Virtue.[10]

There was also a second tendency to classify men into simple categories, such as good or evil, polite or disorderly, arrogant or humble, rich or poor, noble or common, long before the advent of the Chou dynasty and the development of expository written materials. By the end of the Spring and Autumn period Confucius thus elaborated upon his conception of the ideal man (*chün-tzu*, or "perfected man") committed to the moral path of self-cultivation, defined by the practice of such virtues as benevolence and righteousness, and the common or menial man (*hsiao-jen*, or "small man"), marked by the absence of a moral orientation, beset by all of life's cares, and essentially lost amid its struggle.[11] Although not as perverse as true evildoers, their orientation and behavior were governed by simple self-interest, unencumbered by abstract concepts of Virtue that, because of their socioeconomic status, would be unreachable, as Mencius later observed.

With the passing of centuries the conception of ethically defined classes or types of men expanded to include both formal categories and simple characteristics, such as the arrogant and irascible. Classifying someone according to such conceptions would naturally lead to certain behavioral expectations, as well as set the framework for understanding subsequent actions. Even though the details of these characterizations and composite portraits remain unimportant, the existence of this basis for projecting and interpreting is crucial, at least within the framework of intelligence activities. Some idea of their extensiveness may be gained from an explication of the five basic classes of men attributed to Confucius in the *Hsün-tzu:*

Ordinary Man: His mouth cannot speak good words, his mind does not know modesty or to select worthy men and excellent gentlemen to entrust himself to, and so has endless worry. He does not know what aspects of behavior to focus upon, in stopping and acting does not know where to settle. In his daily selection of things he does not know what to value but follows them as if flowing along, not knowing where to return. His five emotions dictate, his mind follows and is destroyed.

Gentleman: Although incapable of fully exhausting the techniques of the Tao, he will certainly accord with them. Even though he is incapable of excellence and goodness in all aspects, he will certainly dwell among them. Accordingly, in his knowledge he doesn't strive for multiplicity but concentrates upon thoroughly examining what he knows. In speech he does not strive for verbosity but concentrates upon examining what is discussed. And in his behavior he does not undertake too much but focuses on thoroughly examining the basis. Thus when his knowledge has solidified, his words convey the discussion, and his actions stem from proper motives, they will be as unchangeable as human nature, fate, and one's skin. Thus riches and nobility will be inadequate to increase him, poverty and lowliness insufficient to reduce him.

Perfected Man: His words are loyal and trustworthy, but his mind does not regard this as virtuous. He embodies righteousness and benevolence, but his appearance does not boast of it. His thoughts and contemplations are enlightened and penetrating, but his language is not contentious, so it seems he can still be reached.

The Worthy: Their actions always accord with proper standards without suffering any injury to their original basis. Their words are sufficient to be taken as a model for All under Heaven, yet are not detrimental to themselves. Even if they possessed the entire realm, they would not accumulate personal wealth; even though their generosity gave everything to the realm, they would not be troubled by poverty.

Great Sage: His wisdom penetrates the Great Tao, he responds to change without being impoverished and is discriminating about the nature of the myriad things. The Great Tao is the means to change and transform the myriad things, whereas their nature is the means to impose patterns on taking or leaving. For this reason his affairs are pervasively discriminated amid Heaven and Earth, clearly investigated in the sun and moon. He unifies the myriad things in the wind and rain. Mysterious and ineffable, his affairs cannot be compassed. Just like the mastery of Heaven his actions cannot be discerned, and in their ignorance the common people do not recognize his proximity.[12]

The last three represent the ideals and were therefore moot, even so-called perfected men and Worthies rarely being seen, despite many highly visible efforts at self-cultivation and perfection. However, the passage does provide a sense of the worldview in the late Warring States period regarding the world of men.[13]

Somatotypes and Character

Among the basic correlates of the five phases are the four compass directions, together with a hypothetical midpoint that lies somewhere in central China. One phase or element is associated with each of the points and further coupled with a large collection of regional characteristics, such as climate, humidity, temperature, predominant food types, and tastes. Because of environmental factors, each region developed a distinctive lifestyle and local specificities in illnesses and treatment. As a result, it was felt that discernible differences also characterized regional behavioral tendencies and personalities, as well as regional physiques, habits, and activities. Although little was said about employing these categories to fathom men, the experienced physician would be expected to recognize them and modify his treatment accordingly, whereas ordinary individuals might have certain expectations based upon a person's regional origins.

The medical writings include another series of types, some parts of which appear in other works, such as the *Huai-nan Tzu* and *Lü-shih Ch'un-ch'iu*. The most extensive of these is a twenty-five-category somatotypology based upon a fivefold variation on the five phases that provides a fairly individualized physical description of each type's outstanding characteristics, basic talents, and possible fate. However, as only the five major categories provide any personality and aptitude information, the fivefold variation within each group has been deleted from the following translation.

Wood Somatotype: They tend to have a greenish cast to their complexion; small heads, with long faces; large shoulders and backs; stand erect; and have small hands and feet. They are very talented but exhaust their minds and have little strength. They worry a lot and fatigue themselves in affairs.

Earth Somatotype: They tend to have a yellow cast to their complexion, round faces and large heads, well-set shoulders, large bellies, attractive thighs and legs, and small hands and feet. The upper and lower parts of their bodies are fleshy and well matched. Their movements are well anchored on the earth, but when they lift their feet, dust floats up. They are tranquil, like to profit others, don't like power and authority, and excel at attracting others.

Fire Somatotype: They tend to have a ruddy cast to their complexion, broad muscles, pointed faces, and small heads. They have substantial shoulders and midsections, but small hands and feet. Their movements are solid, but they sway when anxious. They are full of energy, regard material wealth lightly, trust little, and are frequently worried. They are perspicacious in affairs, and like to give a good appearance. However, they are anxious, have short life spans, and die violently.

Metal Somatotype: They have square faces and tend to have a white cast to their complexion. They have small heads, small shoulders, small abdomens, and small hands and feet, as if the bones were coming out of the heels, and light bones. In personal appearance they are clean and pure. When anxious, sometimes they are quiet, sometimes violent. They are well suited to being minor functionaries.

Water Somatotype: They tend to have a dark cast to their complexion and rough faces. They have large heads, square jaws, small shoulders, a large abdomen, and nimble hands and feet. When they begin to move, they rock from side to side. Their lower backs are long, fully stretched out. They are neither respectful nor fearful, are inclined to cheat and deceive other people, and usually die violent, ignominious deaths.[14]

Yin and *Yang* Somatotypes

A second series of somatotypes is based upon the presence of *yin* and *yang* within the individual. Depending upon the relative balance of the two, there are five basic possibilities: *t'ai-yin, shao-yin, t'ai-yang, shao-yang,* and *yin* and *yang* balanced and in harmony. In the medical text, for each category the personality traits are first explicated and then followed by a discussion of the underlying energetics and a consideration of the implications these phase energetics have for character, illness, and treatment. However, the paragraphs pertaining to physiology and treatment, being irrelevant to concerns of evaluating, have been abridged and the text rearranged for clarity.

T'ai-yin Somatotype: The man of *t'ai-yin* [extreme *yin*] is greedy and inhumane, though appearing humble and congenial. He likes to acquire but hates to expend. His mind harmonizes with others, he doesn't like to move first. He is not concerned with timeliness but follows after others. He has an abundance of *yin* and no *yang*. His *yin* and *yang* are not in harmony. His muscles are relaxed and his skin thick. His appearance is very dark, and he seems thoughtful, with downcast eyes. He approaches deferentially and, although tall and large, is bent over, though not from being a hunchback.

   Shao-yin Somatotype: The man of *shao-yin* [lesser or immature *yin*] is somewhat greedy and has the heart of a thief. When he sees that others have lost something, it's as if he has gotten something. He likes to injure and harm others. When he sees others attaining honors, he turns round and becomes angry. His heart is full of enmity and he has no generosity. He has an abundance of *yin* and a small amount of *yang*. He has a small stomach and large lower belly. His appearance is quiet and furtive, he conceals the heart of a thief. When standing still, his attitude and behavior exude danger. When moving, he seems furtive.

   T'ai-yang Somatotype: The man of *t'ai-yang* [excessive *yang*] is self-satisfied in his normal life. He likes to speak of great matters but lacks ability, and his words are empty. His intentions are widely expressed. In his actions he takes no cognizance of right or wrong. In affairs he always relies upon himself alone and even when matters fail never has any regrets. He has abundant *yang* and no *yin*. His appearance is erect and imposing, and his body is bowed backward.

   Shao-yang Somatotype: The man of *shao-yang* [young *yang*] values self-reliance in his investigations into matters. Even in a very minor post he arrogantly assumes everything he does is appropriate. He likes external activities but not internal attachments. He has an abundance of *yang* and some *yin*. Standing about, he likes to lift his head up, whereas in movement he sways from side to side. He frequently holds his hands behind his back.

   Harmonious Somatotype: The man with *yin* and *yang* in harmony and equilibrium is at peace and tranquil in all aspects of his life, experiencing neither the extremes of fear nor happiness. He flows agreeably with things and does not compete with others. He changes and transforms with the seasons. If honored, he is modest and yielding. Vast, he does not govern, and this is referred to as the apex of governing. His *yin* and *yang ch'i* are in harmony. His appearance is one of satisfaction, flexibility, respect, happiness, friendliness, and clarity. The masses all take him to be a perfected man.[15]

"The Offices of King Wen"

"The Offices of King Wen," found in the *Yi Chou-shu* and *Ta-Tai Li-chi*, texts that probably attained final form in the third century B.C., purportedly records a lecture delivered by King Wen, one of the founders of the great Chou dynasty, to the T'ai-shih on the subject of evaluating, selecting, and employing men.[16] The speaker identified as the king believes that character can be fathomed, that emotions and true personality cannot be concealed. However, while accepting this principle of the transparency of character, he also provides a sophisticated analysis of particular character types, their deliberate facades, and their potential in government. Throughout the lecture, which integrates a wealth of detail, he applies the common knowledge of the Warring States period about human tendencies, coupled with an ideal figure against whom behavior may be appraised. Not content with external evaluations, the speaker also provides psychological principles for evaluating, such as consistency of behavior. The chapter is thus a complete and extensive analytical guidebook for the evaluation and classification of personality and ability and a vast sourcebook on character types of intrinsic value. Prior to Liu Shao's *Jen-wu Chih* there is nothing to compare with it, and it of course merits thorough consideration and study in itself. However, within the context of "knowing men" it is introduced here as a summation and expression of the general approach to evaluating rather than itself being the focus of study (commentary to elucidate the individual sections and passages appears in the notes as appropriate):

King Wen said: "T'ai-shih, you must be cautious and ponder deeply, observe the affairs of the people, investigate and measure their emotions and artifices, make changes in official positions to see their ability to [govern] the people, and array them by their talents and skills. You must be cautious! How can you be careful about those that are not of the right ability? There are seven categories of ability; each category has nine employments; each employment has six indications. The first is observe his sincerity;

the second is test his intentions; the third is look within; the fourth is observe his appearance; the fifth is observe his hidden aspects; the six is estimate his Virtue."

Observe His Sincerity

If he is wealthy and noble,[17] observe his performance of the *li*. If he is poor and in mean condition, observe whether he has Virtue and integrity. If he is heavily favored by the ruler, observe whether he isn't arrogant and extravagant. If he is unknown and in straitened circumstances, observe if he isn't fearful.

Life Stages

If he is young, observe whether he is respectful, likes to study, and can be a proper younger brother. If he is an adult, observe whether he is incorruptible, puts his ambitions into effect, and overcomes his personal desires. If he is old, observe whether he is cautious, exerts himself where he is inadequate, and does not overstep the *li*.

Observe the Person in Relationships

In the relationship of father and son, observe whether the person is a filial son or loving father. In the relationship of elder and younger brother, observe whether the person is harmonious and friendly. In the relationship of ruler and minister, observe whether the minister is loyal and the ruler gracious. In his village and among his associates, observe his faithfulness and sincerity.

Observe Him in Different Contexts

Investigate him in his normal life, and observe his righteousness in measures. Investigate his behavior and grief in mourning, and observe his sincerity and faithfulness. Investigate his social activities, and observe his making of friends. Investigate his making of friends, and observe whether he is responsible and incorruptible.

Actively Test the Person

Test him to observe his trustworthiness. Give him some cues to observe his wisdom. Show him hardship in order to observe his courage. Annoy him with small matters in order to see how he handles it. Immerse him in profit in order to observe whether he isn't greedy. Immerse him in pleasure to observe whether he doesn't become dissolute. Make him happy with things to observe whether he doesn't become frivolous. Make him angry in order to observe his gravity. Make him drunk in order to observe if he doesn't violate propriety. Indulge him in order to observe the mainstays of his character. Keep him at a distance in order to see if he isn't disloyal. Keep him nearby in order to see if he doesn't become too familiar. Sound out his intentions in order to observe his emotions. Try his behavior in order to observe his sincerity. Revisit his minor words to observe his truthfulness. Surreptitiously investigate his behavior in order to observe if it is complete.

This is what is referred to as observing his sincerity.[18]

Testing Intentions

Those who daily improve: Speak with them in order to observe their intentions. Their will is robust and deep; personality broad and pliant; countenance humble without being obsequious; they practice the *li* before other men, but speak after them; and display their own inadequacies.

Those who daily regress: They approach people with arrogant countenances; insult them with haughty attitudes; employ speech to compel others to deem them worthy; conceal their inadequacies and boast of their abilities.

The substantial: Their appearance is straightforward without being insulting; their words upright and unselfish; they don't adorn their good points, or conceal their evil ones; they don't cover over their errors.

The insubstantial: Their countenance is a facade of friendliness; their words are clever and artful; they gloss over their base inclinations; they exert themselves in establishing minor acts of trust, and employ reason to their own ends.

Men of equanimity and perseverance: If you make them happy or angry with external things, their countenances will not betray any changes; if you annoy them, their intentions will remain unaffected; if you speak with them about great profits, their minds will not change; if you frighten them with majesty, their spirits will not be humbled.

The vulgar and artificial: If you make them happy or angry with external things, their changes will easily be known; if you annoy them, their intentions will be ungoverned; if you display profits to them, they will be easily changed; if you frighten them with majesty, they will easily be scared.

The thoughtful: Threaten them with external things and they will decide with alacrity; startle them with sudden affairs and they can take the full measure of them; even without studying, they can bc discriminating.

Dolts: It is difficult to entrust any affairs to them or to speak with them about anything. They know things as if they could never be shaken from them; in difficulty they do not know how to proceed; they lack discrimination; and they bring about their own worries.

The pure and decisive: Confront them with matters, they will not be worried; oppose them with sudden affairs, they will not be afraid. They are resolute in establishing righteousness; approached with material goods or beautiful women, they remain unaffected.

The weak-willed: They are easily moved by words and cannot maintain a steadfast will. Although they mentally affirm something, they are incapable of decisively putting it into practice.

The tranquil: Agreeing with them will not make them happy, grabbing them not make them angry. Deeply quiet and of few words, they are contemplative and yet humble in appearance.

Jealous slanderers: They are discriminating in language but do not put the Tao into practice. Even when a state is well ordered, they are among the first to be in difficulty. They follow their own inclinations and are unyielding, vehement in the pursuit of their interests.

Men of controlled intent: They are able to distinguish the minute and quiet; they measure and investigate matters, and thus can exhaust them.

Loquacious slanderers: They employ clever words, have a specious appearance, display a superficial respect for others, and all take nothing to be something.

Look at the Interior

If there is sincerity within,[19] it will be manifest without. One takes what is manifest to estimate what is concealed, what is small to estimate the large, and the sounds to know the *ch'i*.

At the origin, *ch'i* gave birth to things. When things came alive, they had sound. Among sounds there are the hard and the soft, the murky and the clear, the good and the evil. They are all expressed in the sound.

If the mental *ch'i* is flowery and expansive, then the sound is flowing and dispersed. If the mental state is congenial and trustworthy, then the sound is congenial and measured. If the mental state is vulgar and perverse, then the sound is hoarse and ugly. If the mental state is generous and mild, then the sound is mild and attractive.

The *ch'i* of trustworthiness is correct and placid. The *ch'i* of righteousness is always relaxed. The *ch'i* of knowledge is complete. The *ch'i* of courage is strong and straightforward.

Listen to his sound; determine his *ch'i*; examine what a person does; observe its basis; look into what they rest in; and estimate the future from the past, the invisible by what is manifest, and the large by the small.

Emotions and Their Manifestations

Man has five emotions:[20] happy, angry, desirous, fearful, and anxious. When the *ch'i* of happiness accumulates within, even if one wishes to conceal it, the signs of happiness will certainly be manifest. When the *ch'i* of anger accumulates within, even if one wishes to conceal it, the signs of anger will certainly be manifest. When the *ch'i* of desire accumulates within, even if one wishes to conceal it, the signs of the desires will certainly be manifest. When the *ch'i* of fear accumulates within, even if one wishes to conceal it, the signs of fear will certainly be manifest. When the *ch'i* of worry and sorrow accumulates within, even if one wishes to conceal it, the signs of worry and sorrow will certainly be manifest. When any of these five *ch'i* is truly present within, they will be expressed externally. People's emotions cannot be concealed.

The appearance of happiness is of bubbling forth. The appearance of anger is aroused and insulting. The appearance of desire is expectation with pleasure. The appearance of fear is as if being pressed down. The appearance of worry and sorrow is exhausted and silent.

True wisdom will certainly have the appearance of inexhaustibility. True humaneness will certainly have the appearance of should-be-respected. True courage will certainly have the appearance of being difficult to frighten. True loyalty will certainly have the appearance of being approachable. True purity will certainly have the appearance of being difficult to tarnish. True tranquillity will certainly have the appearance of can-be-trusted.

The appearance of true substance is luminously solid and peaceful, the appearance of artifice is confused, turbulent, and vexed. Even though one wished to conceal it within, the appearance will not listen. Even though one changes it, it can be known. This is referred to as observing the appearance.

Observe What Is Concealed

The people have *yin* and *yang* aspects.[21] There are many who conceal their emotions, who adorn themselves with artifice in order
to seek fame. There are those who hide in humanness and substance, in knowledge and principle, in culture and art, in purity
and courage, in loyalty and filiality, and in friendship. Such cases
must be investigated.

Those who hide in benevolence and worthiness: They make minor gifts but expect large returns; they yield but little, yet like
great projects. Their words are circumspect and taken to have substance. They feign love and it is taken to be loyalty. Their faces
are congenial and appearance compassionate. They feign the constraints in order to display them to others. They act deliberately
in order to forge their names.

Those who hide in knowledge and principles: They investigate
old transgressions thinking to know men. When people are successful, they are envious and deprecate their shortcomings. If
their plans fall short, they feign not being willing to talk about
them. If they are inadequate within, they feign having an excess.
Thus they know how to move men. They follow themselves
without ever yielding. They never complete their words, and no
one knows their true emotions.

Those who hide in culture and art: They move people with
empty phrases, and set out things without ever coming to the end.
If you ask them about something, they do not reply but feign having inexhaustible knowledge, manifesting an appearance of having an excess. They pretend to have realized the Tao but follow
only themselves in employing it. If affairs turn difficult, they
make them seem deep.

Those who hide in purity and courage: Their words bespeak integrity so that they may be taken as their character. Their arrogance and harshness are taken as courage. Within they are afraid,
without they are braggarts. They respectfully repeat their words
in order to deceive others.

Those who hide in loyalty and filiality: They are fond of telling
other people about how they serve their parents. They repeatedly
speak of their labors and fatigue, forcing the proper facial expressions of respectfulness and love, adorning their visible efforts, and
thus they attain their fame. However, while their names are
raised without, internally it is not so. They flaunt their filial reputations in order to profit. Whatever they do to publicize their
names is solely for self-benefit.

Those who hide in friendship: They employ secret means to gain fame, form cliques with others for the purpose of mutual praise, and make it clear that they know Worthies who can attest to their character. When they associate with others who are different, it will be that the association is of greater benefit to them. Even though they are happy with someone, they will not approach them. Even if they get close to someone, in actuality they do not accept them or feel happiness or loyalty. However, they feign satisfaction and loyalty in front of others, their appearance overcoming any lack of substance.

Estimating Virtue

When words and actions are not of the same category, end and beginning contrary to each other, *yin* and *yang* conquer in turn, and the exterior and interior do not cohere, when even their behavior manifests artificial constraints and visible virtue, it is said not to be true substance.

Those with humane hearts: Their words are extremely loyal and actions are very even. Their thoughts are free of selfishness. In assisting others, they do not exceed what is necessary. They are loyal and congenial. Although imposing, they set people at ease.

Those with expansive knowledge: Although matters change, they can control them. If something is good, they can speak of it to others. Burdened with poverty they can prosper. They dedicate themselves to establishing the Tao and are able to attain their objectives.

The circumspect and good: They speak little but put it into action. They are respectful, frugal, and compliant. They have knowledge but do not flaunt it. They aid others but do not consider it to be great virtue.

The congenial and trustworthy: Minor words suddenly spoken long ago are still viable. Their private, unseen actions are directed solely toward their goodness, not overcoming others. Although others be gone, they act as if they were still present.

Men of Virtue: Although they have rank, wealth, and honor, they are respectful and frugal, and capable of assisting others. Even when their lands are large and subjects numerous, when they are stern and majestic, they still adhere to the *li* and are not arrogant.

Men who preserve principles: If they dwell obscurely in poverty, they are unafraid, whereas if they enjoy luxury, they do not go to excess. Though they labor hard, they do not change. Whether happy or angry, they do not lose their self-constraint.

The proper and upright: They are firm and upright, and do not toady to others. They are scrupulous, pure, and not violent. They stand strongly in the Tao and are not self-oriented.

The pensive: Upright and quiet, they await orders. If not summoned, they do not go; if not queried, do not speak. Their words do not surpass their actions, and their actions do not transgress the Tao.

The truly filial: They serve their parents with sincere love and happily respect them. They exhaust their strength, but not merely with a respectful countenance designed to overcome others or to attain a name that they do so.

True friends: Their inclinations are in harmony, and they are united in the Tao. They share each other's worries and take responsibility for their hardships. Their actions are loyal and trustworthy, they have no doubts about each other. Whether in straitened circumstances or far apart, they do not abandon each other.

Position seekers: Their attitude and words can penetrate and make people very happy. They can advance or retreat with skill, so they are very skillful with people. They can quickly become familiar with people, yet may easily turn against them.

Greedy, rough fellows: They ply people with food and drink in order to draw close to them, and use gifts and bribes to attract associates. They will unite with others for profit, employ name and reputation for gain, and rely on secretly exploiting material things.

The artificial and deceitful: They never decide anything substantial, their words never express the matter. They minimize their own inadequacies and make plans unceasingly.

Those who lack sincere intent: Their words and behavior are always changing, their manner wanton and frivolous. For them good and evil are not constant, their behavior and personality have no coherence.

The vain and boastful: They have little knowledge and cannot decide great matters. They have little ability and cannot attain great achievements. They focus on minor matters and do not know about great affairs. They are extremely changeable and very selfish.

Those skillful at achieving fame: They offer corrective remonstrance but inappropriately. They implement the Tao but do not delight in it.

Thus those who like to find difficulty when they encounter some matter are not constant. Those who rely on the spirits are not benevolent. Those who seek only superficial fame are not sincere. Those who put on an appearance are not showing their true emotions. Those who hide in the constraints are not equanimous. Those who are very self-centered are not righteous. Those who exaggerate are seldom trustworthy.

T'ai-shih! Extrapolate past words in order to estimate future actions. Listen to what people say to scrutinize their past actions. Observe their *yang* [visible aspects] in order to examine into their *yin* [hidden natures]. Investigate them internally in order to appraise them externally. Accordingly, those who conceal their emotions can be known; those who feign not having any emotions can be discerned; men of substance and sincerity who dwell in the good can be found; and the loyal, benevolent, constrained, and righteous will be seen.

Alas, you must be cautious! How can you be careful of those who are not of the right mind? How can you be careful of those who are not the right men? Men have six indications. When these six have been completely investigated, then observe the nine employments.

The Nine Employments

Imperturbable, benevolent, and thoughtful: in charge of governing the state and leading the people.[22]

Loving, beneficent, and principled: heads of villages and towns, govern fathers and sons.

Straightforward, industrious, truly upright: oversee government offices, evaluate officials as good or not.

Respectful, straightforward, investigate what they hear: in charge of criminal and legal cases, act as liaisons for the ruler.

Can manage affairs, upright, incorruptible: in charge of the treasury, administer income and expenditures.

Careful in investigations, incorrupt and pure: in charge of dividing wealth, handling goods, and making rewards.

Like to make plans and know men: govern difficult lands and be in charge of the artisans.

Sensitive and perceptive: administer the feudal lords and take care of state guests.

Firm, resolute, self-reliant in decisionmaking: be in charge of the army and patrol the border.

In accord with their talents you should employ them. This is what is referred to as "employing ability."

When the nine employments have been investigated, then entrust men according to the seven categories. The first states that for a state use men of noble rank. The second, for villages use the true. The third, for offices use leaders. The fourth, for students use teachers. The fifth, for clans use the clan heads. The sixth, for the families use the heads. The seventh, for teachers use Worthies.[23]

13
Intelligence
Applications

MANY CHAPTERS IN THE PHILOSOPHICAL writings contain passages of utility and importance to anyone entrusted with the tasks of intelligence gathering, operations, and analysis, but only Han Fei-tzu extensively addressed the critical issues of power and control in dedicated sections. Known in the West in recent centuries as China's Machiavelli, Han Fei-tzu not only observed and described the psychological dynamics of hierarchically structured human interactions, but also offered methods for controlling others through their inclinations and desires, which Li Ch'uan adopted among his techniques for interrogating and appraising. Before briefly studying his most famous chapter—one cited in virtually every modern Chinese book on plans, strategies, spying, controlling, and even combative business practices—we should note his citation of Kuan Chung's warning about the dangers of court subversion and the common practice of "inner court officials spying out the ruler's emotions in order to inform those outside for their own benefit."[1] An example of how this might be implemented appears in the following mid-fourth century B.C. incident:

Chao had an emissary seek troops from Han through the intercession of Shen-tzu, the prime minister, because they were about to attack Wei. Shen-tzu wanted to speak to the ruler about it but feared he would be suspected of acting in the interests of a foreign state. However, if he failed to communicate their request, he was afraid of offending Chao. Therefore Shen-tzu first had two of the ruler's favorites test the duke while he observed his reactions and countenance, only thereafter broaching the subject. Thus he was able to learn the ruler's intentions and also achieve Chao's purpose.[2]

Although Han Fei-tzu's infamous chapter of nefarious techniques, entitled "Eight Villains," undertakes an incisive analysis of the ways in which rulers may be manipulated (prepared for the latter's benefit), it was thereafter regarded as a handbook of techniques universally applicable against powerful people irrespective of their actual rank or position. Virtually all the modern Chinese works that discuss intrigue and methods for controlling men focus upon it, even though it was much condemned by the Confucian literati throughout the centuries whenever not simply or deliberately ignored. Although the core methods fully accord with the simplistic premises of exploiting the ruler's desire for riches, power, and sex previously witnessed, many other subtle and sophisticated techniques are identified. The chapter commences with Han Fei-tzu noting that "there are eight techniques that subordinates follow to achieve perverse objectives," although in most instances "subordinates" or "ministers" can be understood as men in general and their targets as the rich and powerful rather than just the ruler:

First, exploiting those who share the ruler's bed—noble consorts, beloved youths, favored concubines, and nymphomaniacs who can delude the ruler. Taking advantage of his moments at pleasure and exploiting the time when he is drunken and satiated, they press their own desires, a technique that ensures they will be heeded. Other men then bribe these members of the inner palace with gold and jade to have them delude the ruler.[3]

Second, exploiting his attendants—actors and jesters, comedians and dwarfs, all those who are close and familiar, who concur even before the ruler indicates his wishes and assent before he commands them, always anticipating his intentions. Observing his face and peering at his countenance, they precede him in realizing his intent. They advance and withdraw in unison, reacting and replying with identical language in a single chorus in order to affect the ruler's mind. Other men then provide these inner court members with gold, jade, curios, and rarities and act illegally outside it in order to transform the ruler through them.

Third, exploiting the elder generation—princes of collateral lines and those whom the ruler loves within his own family, as well as great ministers and court officials with whom the ruler evaluates plans. When they all exhaust their strength in fully discussing a topic, the ruler will invariably heed them. Other men provide these collateral family members with music and women and gather in the great ministers and court officers with words and speech. They arrange to have them propose affairs that, when achieved, result in higher ranks and increased compensation, and thus encourage their minds.

Fourth, nurturing misfortune—rulers take pleasure in splendid palaces, towers, and pools, and love to adorn themselves with beautiful women, dogs, and horses in order to bring joy to their hearts. These are calamities for rulers. Their subordinates exhaust the people's strength in these beautiful palaces, towers, and pools, and redouble the taxes and impositions in order to grace them with beautiful women, dogs, and horses, thereby pleasuring their hearts and bringing turbulence to their minds. By following what the ruler desires, they establish their own profit in their midst.

Fifth, cultivating the people—by dispersing public funds in order to please the people and performing minor acts of generosity in order to gain the hundred surnames, bringing it about that everyone in the court, market, and villages is encouraged to praise them. They thus eclipse the ruler and achieve what they desire.

Sixth, exploiting eloquent behavior—the ruler, being insulated from conversation and isolated from discussions, is easily swayed by the eloquent speech of sophists. Other men therefore seek out sophists among the feudal lords and nurture eloquent speakers within their states, employing them to dispute on their behalf. They embellish their words and hold forth eloquently, showing the ruler advantageous circumstances and frightening him with misfortune and harm. They flourish vacuous language and destroy the ruler.

Sixth, awesomeness and strength—rulers assume the officials and hundred surnames create their authority and strength. Those that the officials and hundred surnames regard as excellent the ruler does as well, those that they do not regard as good the ruler does not either.[4] Other men assemble sword-bearing retainers and nurture death-defying warriors in order to flaunt their awesomeness and make it clear that their partisans will profit and enemies perish. They thus frighten the officials and hundred surnames and secure their personal desires.

Seventh, the Four Quarters—rulers whose states are small serve large states, whose armies are weak fear strong armies. Whatever large states want, small states must yield. Wherever strong forces are applied, weak armies must submit. Their subordinates double the taxes and impositions, exhaust the treasuries and warehouses, and empty out the state in serving these large states while also exploiting their own resulting awesomeness to control the ruler. The most extreme raise the army in order to provoke an accumulation of troops along the border and control exactions within the state, while the least frequently bring in ambassadors from great states in order to shake the ruler and cause him to be fearful.

Another chapter entitled "Ten Errors" discusses tendencies commonly found among rulers that lead to their destruction and may therefore be profitably exploited, often as previously outlined, such as being obsessed with profit, indulging in music, and losing oneself in sexual pleasure. However, one section known as "The Difficulties of Persuasion" ventures even farther into the detailed psychology of affecting powerful individuals, not just through their vices and inclinations, but through the very techniques employed in speaking to them, in manipulating and cajoling them through ostensibly disinterested proposals and admonitions. Virtually all the techniques explicated in this unique chapter can be abstracted from the initial context—exercising one's persuasion upon a ruler—and applied to any situation where the speaker seeks some objective, whether the target holds a high rank and exercises power or not.[5] Such has been the practice and thrust of modern books oriented to business, management, plots, and schemes in China, not to mention traditional thinkers interested in subversive operations and clandestine conversions.

The difficulty in persuading others doesn't lie in having the knowledge to affect them, the disputational skills to illuminate one's ideas, or the daring to venture widely and exhaust one's views. Rather, the difficulty in persuading others lies in knowing their minds and crafting arguments that conform to them.

If they are motivated by lofty reputation but you discuss abundant profits, you will be seen as vulgar, treated humbly and disdainfully, and certainly cast far away. If they are motivated by abundant profits but you discuss ways to achieve a lofty reputation, you will be seen as mindless and unrealistic, and will certainly not be accepted. If they are secretly motivated by abundant profits while conspicuously claiming to be interested in achieving a lofty reputation and you discuss name and reputation, they will visibly accept you but actually be distant. However, if you discuss abundant profits, they will secretly employ your words but visibly cast you aside. These must be investigated.

Affairs achieve success through secrecy; discussions that leak them out will fail. It is not necessary that others allow something to be leaked out, for if your words touch upon some concealed matter, you will be endangered. If they conspicuously undertake some project while actually seeking to achieve something very different, should you happen to know not only what they purport to be undertaking but also what they are actually doing, you will be endangered. If you devise some extraordinary plan that gains acceptance but is guessed by some perspicacious outsider who then divulges it to the world at large, it will certainly appear that you revealed it, and you will be endangered.

If you do not yet generously enjoy someone's confidence and beneficence, yet have exhausted your profundity, should your advice be successfully employed, you will be shunned, but if it is not employed and they moreover suffer some reversal, you will be doubted and endangered.

If someone powerful shows the beginnings of misbehavior and you discourse upon ritual and righteousness in order to illuminate their flaws, you will be endangered. If someone powerful acquires a plan and wants to claim the resulting achievements for themselves, should they realize you know it, you will be endangered.

If you coerce people to either undertake or cease something that they cannot, you will be endangered.

If you speak with people about great men, they will assume you are disparaging them. If you speak with them about common men, they will assume you are currying favor. If you discuss what they love, they will assume you are trying to exploit their inclinations; if you discuss what they hate, they will assume you are testing them.

If you are direct and sparse in your discussions, they will assume you are ignorant and treat you as blundering, but if you discourse eloquently in both breadth and detail, they will assume you are loquacious and jumbled. If you focus on the essentials in outlining your ideas, they will assume you are timid and inadequately express your subject, but if you contemplate them from every aspect, they will assume you are rustic but conceited. You must be aware of these difficulties.[6]

The essence of persuading others lies in knowing how to magnify aspects the person boasts about and eliminate those he is ashamed of. If they feel urgently about something, you should strongly encourage it in terms of its public benefits and righteousness. If their intentions are vile but cannot be abandoned, you should embellish the attractive aspects and hardly speak about not doing them. If they have admirable aims in mind but are incapable of actually realizing them, you should raise the negative aspects of such aims and point out the bad points, making much of not doing them.

If they want to boast of their wisdom and talents, then bring up some distinct but similar affairs and provide numerous steps so that they become material for their discussions with you. Then you can feign ignorance while still introducing your knowledge.

If you want your words to be accepted and preserved, you must embellish and clearly expound them while also subtly showing that they coincide with the listeners' selfish aims. If you want to expound against dangerous and harmful matters, you must conspicuously make their destructive and chastising aspects visible while also subtly showing that they entail personal harm as well.

Praise others who act similarly, acclaim as extraordinary any affairs coinciding with their plans. Identical defects should be energetically shrugged off as innocuous, common defeats dismissed as entailing no loss. If the listeners believe themselves powerful, do not cramp them by revisiting past difficulties. If they view themselves as courageous and decisive, do not provoke them with their failures. If they regard themselves as wise strategists, do not subvert them with their defeats.

If you eliminate all antagonisms from your core ideas and rid your language of all irritants, you will be able to fully exploit your wisdom and sophistry. This is the Tao for becoming intimate with people, winning their confidence, and fully exhausting your persuasion unquestioned.

Interestingly, Hsün-tzu (Han Fei-tzu's own teacher) offered an appraisal of five types of ministers that, although somewhat simplistic and certainly defined against the basic values of Confucianism, broadly characterized the nature of most officials and thus identified those marked by tendencies that might be exploited for covert purposes. Although certain traits are isolated, it is the general concept that is important.

Nominal Ministers: Internally they are incapable of unifying the state's populace, externally unable to keep hardship away. They do not attract the allegiance of the hundred surnames. The feudal lords do not trust them, but with artful and clever ways and obsequious speech they excel at gaining the ruler's favor.

Grasping Ministers: Above they are not loyal to the ruler, below they excel at gaining the approbation of the people. They have no concern for the public good or effecting righteousness, but form cliques and parties in order to delude the ruler. They concentrate upon selfish planning.

Meritorious Ministers: Internally they are capable of unifying the state's populace, externally they keep hardship distant. The people give their allegiance to them and officials trust them. Above they are loyal to the ruler, below they love the hundred surnames untiringly.

Sagacious Ministers: Above they are able to make the ruler honored, below they can love the people. Their administrative orders transform the people, being a model followed just like a shadow. They respond to sudden change and master transformation as sensitively as an echo responding to its sound. From categories and associations they realize ways to contend with the extraordinary, completing every affair and governing the [Heavenly] emblems.[7]

Obviously the first two categories represent attractive targets for recruiting informants and subversives, preying upon their self-interest and fundamental disloyalty.

Li Ch'uan's famous T'ang dynasty military classic, the *T'ai-pai Yin-ching*,[8] probably composed in the latter part of the eighth century, contains two chapters that rigorously apply many of the principles already seen, as well as provide evidence that troubling issues of evaluation and fathoming had not been dismissed from consciousness. Although not directed toward selecting spies, his chapter on analyzing men through their general appearance, appropriately entitled "Scrutinizing Men," illustrates another approach to selecting and employing men, including generals and agents. Although not as extreme an approach as physiognomy, which enjoyed great popularity and became more detailed with the passing of centuries, it represents a shift in that direction and no doubt reflects the general approach seen in Liu Shao's *Jen-wu Chih* characterizations. Particularly important is Li Ch'uan's clear statement of the transparency principle— "observing their exterior is sufficient to know their interior"—commencing the chapter:

As for men, observing their exterior is sufficient to know their interior. The seven orifices of the head are the gates and doors to the five viscera. Thus all the aspects of the head and the prominence of the forehead, nose, and chin define the face's features. The appearance of wisdom or stupidity, courage or fear is expressed by a single inch of eyes. From the indications of Heaven and markings of wealth they are separated into noble and ignoble, poor and rich.

Now if you want to entrust a general with command, first observe his facial appearance and afterward know his mind. The method for determining an abundance of spirit: His facial expression is grave and dignified; he is marked by integrity and energy;

his intentions are unaffected by the pleasures of music or the allure of sex; his principles of self-cultivation are unchanged by
prosperity or adversity. This is termed "an abundance of spirit."

The method for determining a corpuscular abundance: The top
of the head is abundant and broad; the belly, thick; the nose,
straight but rounded at the end; the mouth, square and protrud-
ing; the chin and forehead closing toward each other; high cheek-
bones and ears; excessively corpulent; coarse bones that, however,
are not visible; eyebrows and eyes bright and clear; hands and feet
fresh red. When he looks down on inferiors, he seems tall, but
compared to the great he is solitary and small. This is termed "an
abundance of physique."

An abundance of heart: He conceals the evil in others and raises
their good points, puts himself last and others first, does not deprecate others in order to make himself seem worthy, or endanger
other men to make himself secure. He performs unseen acts of
Virtue, always preserves loyalty and sincerity, is liberal and mag-
nanimous, unconcerned by petty morality. This is an abundance
of heart.

The three portraits strongly echo the "Offices of King Wen" and per-
haps reflect the concepts of Virtue found in the characterizations of
Confucius's disciples, as well as the famous "Nine Virtues" of the
Shang Shu.

Although the chapter entitled "Numerous Methods for Probing the
Mind" focuses upon evaluating and controlling men in general,[9] the
passages also make up a primer on controlling spies and were subsequently quoted in this application:

In antiquity neighboring states could see each other's signal fires
and hear the sounds of each other's chickens and dogs, but their
footsteps never encroached upon each other's borders or the
tracks of their wagons meet a thousand kilometers away. They
preserved life through the Tao, tranquilized their bodies with
Virtue, and the people took pleasure in their dwellings. Later,
when the winds of degeneracy arose, purity and simplicity dispersed. Authority and wisdom were employed, prevarication and
artifice were born. Neighboring states used spies in their intercourse with each other, the Vertical and Horizontal Alliances employed forceful persuaders. The state of Hsü cleaved to benevolence and righteousness, but its altars were laid waste, the state of
Lu esteemed Confucianism and Mohism, but their ancestral temples were destroyed.[10]

Unless you penetrate the mysterious and know the subtle, you will not be able to resist your enemies. Unless you exert your mind and trouble your thoughts, you will not be able to penetrate the source of affairs. Unless you can always distinguish the real and false, you will not be able to achieve fame. If you are not perspicacious about talent, you will not be able to employ the military. If you cannot discern loyalty and disloyalty, you will never be able to judge men. For this reason Master Kuei-ku secretly composed his chapters on verbal persuasion, instigation, and disputation to instruct the famous Warring States strategists Su Ch'in and Chang Yi, who then wandered among the six states, probed the minds of the feudal lords, and implemented his techniques.

In general, to employ the techniques of mental probing, begin by intermixing and inclusively speaking about the Tao, Virtue, benevolence, righteousness, the rites, music, loyalty, trust, the *Book of Odes,* the *Book of Documents,* the *Tso Chuan,* the philosophers, histories, plots and stratagems, successes and failures. Settle the subject's mind; tranquilize his intentions; spy out his emotions, what he loves and hates, likes and dislikes. Employ his desires to attack him. Secretly ponder but outwardly express something different in order to approach him with specious words while he responds sincerely. Then compare his mind and his appearance, listen to his sounds, and investigate his words. If his speech does not cohere with them, turn about and seek out the truth. When he has truly been forced to respond, you will have fathomed his mind. Then turn again to strike at his meaning, and if query and response have no gap, if they cohere tightly, bind him closely, do not let him reverse anything, like Yang Yu grasping his bow or Feng Meng taking up an arrow, never missing in a hundred shots. Just as snares and traps are set to catch fish or rabbits, once the prey have been trapped, even though they bang about, they merely get hung up in the netting and none escape.

Now to probe the mind of the benevolent, you must employ sincerity, not wealth. To probe the heart of a courageous warrior, you must employ righteousness, not fear. To probe the mind of a wise officer, you must employ loyalty, not deceit. To probe the mind of a stupid man, you must use obscurity, not brightness. To probe the mind of a menial man, you must employ fear, not ordinary virtue. To probe the mind of the greedy, you must employ bribes, not integrity.

Now when you speak with the wise, you should rely on erudition because wisdom has limits, whereas erudition has none. Therefore the wise will not be able to fathom such breadth.

When you speak with the erudite, rely upon disputation. The erudite take antiquity as their teachers, but disputation responds to the present, so the erudite are unable to respond to such facileness.

When you speak with the noble, rely upon political power, for although the noble have high position, they are controlled through power. Even position cannot stop power.

When you speak with the wealthy, rely upon things. When the rich accumulate wealth, they can acquire treasures, but even their wealth proves inadequate to acquire great treasures.

When you speak with the poor, rely upon profits. The poor suffer from want and impoverishment while great profits can provide abundant aid. The impoverished lack the means to provide aid of any magnitude.

When you speak with the lowly, rely upon deference because the lowly rank below other men. By deferring to them, the lowly will not be able to speak about humbleness.

When you speak with the courageous, rely upon daring because the courageous dare to be firm and resolute. Then the courageous will not be able to monopolize firmness.

When you speak with the stupid, rely upon sharpness because the stupid are simple and substantial, while sharpness is brilliant and enlightened. Then the stupid will not be able to investigate the intelligent.

These eight are all founded upon their similarity in the Tao but differ in their final expression. By employing the Tao of what people want to hear but making the end expression different, even though they listen, they will fail to understand.[11] In this fashion they are unable to fathom the shallow or deep. Thus I am able to go out where there is no chink and enter where there is no gate. I can go alone and come alone, sometimes horizontally, sometimes vertically. It is just like bending dry grass over—if I bend it eastward, it goes east; westward, it goes west—or like stopping up the river's current so that when the dam is broken, it flows, but when obstructed, it ceases. What worry is there that a plan will not be followed?

Now the Tao esteems controlling men, not being controlled by men. Those who control others take hold of authority, those who are controlled by others comply with their commands. The technique for controlling others is to avoid strength and attack weakness while displaying your own strength and concealing your shortcomings. Thus when animals move, they first strike with their claws and teeth; when birds move, they will invariably employ their beaks and talons; when insects and snakes move, they will always employ poison; and when shelled creatures move, they use their shells for protection. Since all the wild creatures employ their strengths to wrest control over other animals, how much more so the wise?[12]

Now if people like to discuss the Tao and Virtue, you must break them with benevolence and righteousness. Those who like to speak about the ways of Confucianism and Mohism must be controlled with theories of the Horizontal and Vertical Alliances. Those who like to speak about laws and regulations must be suppressed with techniques and authority. You must exploit their beginnings, accord with their conclusions, destroy their teeth, and force their horns down, never letting them escape your control. Thereafter gradually speak about either gleeful or depressing affairs to make them happy or trouble their hearts, causing their spirits to be unable to act as masters of their minds. Discussions focused on longevity, tranquillity, pleasure, riches, nobility, honor, glory, music, and sex are joyful. Death, perishing, depression, misfortune, poverty, mean condition, bitterness, insults, punishment, execution, and fines all involve words concerned with mourning. When you speak to the noble with such words of mourning, they will grieve, whereas if you speak to the lowly about gleeful affairs, they will be pleased. Take command of their minds, respond to their thoughts, sometimes auspiciously, sometimes balefully, in order to effect a response in their intentions.[13] Their emotions will change within, their appearance will alter without. Constantly observe their external manifestations in order to discern what they conceal, for this is termed "the technique for fathoming the hidden and probing the mind." Even though one possesses the Tao of the former kings, the methods of the Sages and the Wise, without this technique even they would be inadequate to achieve the objective of hegemony over the realm.

Although clearly reflecting both lessons and techniques derived from Han Fei-tzu's chapters, Li Ch'uan's approach might well be characterized as more aggressive, unrelenting, even brutal, assaulting the target both directly and indirectly to simultaneously fathom and convert, to both structure and control.

14

Political Intelligence

*D*URING THE SPRING AND AUTUMN and Warring States periods, when a state's very existence depended upon anticipating and fathoming one's enemies, political consciousness and its derivative, intelligence, permeated every realm. This produced a diffuse, generally high level of common knowledge—accurate or not—about political events, terrain characteristics, and "national character" that functioned as the basis for more concrete, data-driven analyses in the immediacy of a crisis. Evidence for this at the end of the Spring and Autumn period may be seen in the way even Confucius suited his teachings to particularized political situations:

> Tzu Kung said: "Duke Yeh of Ching inquired about government and you said, 'Government consists in treating those close by well and attracting the distant.'[1] Duke Ai of Lu inquired about government and you said, 'Government lies in controlling your ministers.'[2] Duke Ching of Ch'i asked about government and you said, 'Government lies in constraining one's expenditures.' Three rulers inquired about government and your reply differed each time. Do governments differ?"
>
> Confucius replied: "Now Ching's territory is broad but its capital narrow and the people have wills that are difficult to govern, so I said, 'Government consists in treating those close by well and attracting the distant.' Duke Ai of Lu has three ministers who internally form cliques to delude him and externally obstruct the visits of foreign diplomats in order to occlude his enlightenment, so I said, 'Government lies in controlling your ministers.' Duke Ching of Ch'i is extravagant in building towers and dissipates himself in parks and gardens. He is constricted by the pleasures of his five senses, and in one morning awarded a hundred chariots each to three families. Thus I said, 'Government lies in constrain-

ing one's expenditures.' Looking into what these three rulers desire, can their governments be identical!?"³

Three categories of material provide sources for studying China's
traditional practices in gathering and analyzing what might be broadly
defined as political information: historical works, the writings of
philosophic and political thinkers, and the extant military texts.
Moreover, the numerous "case studies" found embedded in works
such as the *Tso Chuan* and the *Twenty-five Dynastic Histories* are particularly valuable because they provide parameters whose reliability
has been attested, inaccurate evaluations simply never being perpetuated except when leading to horrendous defeats. However, political
analyses of other states, whether examinations of actual states or
merely abstract lists of strengths and weaknesses for conducting such
evaluations, are virtually absent from the military writings. Among
the massive *Seven Military Classics* only selected passages in the
Three Strategies, "Honoring the Worthy" in the *Six Secret Teachings*,
and "Evaluating the Enemy" in the *Wu-tzu* provide useful observations. Because the post-Han tactical writings focus on terrain, enemy
strength, and other military issues, they are similarly silent, except for
an occasional observation or two simply repeated from the classics.
However, in the Spring and Autumn and Warring States periods—
when China consisted of states much like Europe at the turn of the
twentieth century—political intelligence was much valued, and undertaken ultimately for military purposes, including thwarting the enemy's plans, as Sun-tzu advocated.

Historical Episodes and Their Significance

One of the fundamental assumptions underpinning virtually every political evaluation in the early Chou period was that the presence of
"Worthies" in any government—men of great talent and, more important, surpassing moral self-cultivation—was essentially an ironclad
guarantee of the ruler's excellence and government's stability. Although this should already be apparent from the passages reprised in
the historical sections, a series of illustrations from well-known texts,
often integrated within chapters attempting to adduce sufficient examples to "prove" a political or philosophical point, will further define the essential principle in its concrete variations and surprising
complexity when other factors intervene. The first example, from the
Shuo Yüan, describes a typical political mission undertaken to ascertain the viability of military attack. The actual evaluation focuses on

government, rather than military, readiness, showing the two were regarded as inherently one prior to actual battlefield confrontations:

> Wanting to attack Chin, King Chuang [reigned 613–591 B.C.] of Ch'u dispatched Chu Yin to conduct observations there. Upon his return Chuo reported: "They cannot be attacked. Worry besets the ruler while the people enjoy pleasure. Moreover, they have a worthy minister, Ch'en Chü." A year later the king again dispatched Chuo to conduct similar observations and he returned with his conclusion: "They can be attacked. Ch'en Chü has died, there are many sycophants and toadies in the court, and the ruler loves pleasure and has abandoned the proper forms of behavior. The people below are endangered and angry at the ruler. Upper and lower are thus estranged, so if you attack the state, the people will rebel." King Chuang followed his advice, the result being as predicted.[4]

The absence of a single Worthy apparently freed the ruler to indulge his latent desires, propelling the state into an easily exploited catastrophic situation.

A Spring and Autumn observational mission cited in the same *Shuo Yüan* chapter shows how the emissary's conclusions might also be applied reflexively:[5]

> Duke P'ing of Chin [reigned 557–532 B.C.] dispatched Shu Hsiang on a friendly mission of inquiry to the state of Wu, where the people of Wu dragged a boat across land to meet him. On the left of it were five hundred men, on the right five hundred. They wore embroidered leopard coats and brocaded fox jackets. Shu Hsiang returned to Chin and reported this to Duke P'ing, who said: "Wu will certainly perish! Do they respect boats or people?"
>
> Shu Hsiang replied: "Your majesty is presently constructing the Chih-ti tower, so how will you be able to send forth a thousand soldiers? Will you set out your bells and drums in formation? When the feudal lords hear about your majesty, they will ask, 'Does he respect towers or people?' You only differ in what you value." Thereupon the duke ceased the tower's construction.

As previously seen, near the end of the Spring and Autumn period Confucius's presence became an important sign of moral excellence, or at least apparent revival:

> Chao Chien-tzu, being about to mount a sudden attack on Wei, had Shih An go to observe them. He left in January and returned in June. Chien-tzu asked, "Why did it take so long?"

Shih An replied: "Planning to gain some advantage but instead suffering harm stems from not investigating properly. Right now Chü Po-yü is prime minister and Shih Yü is assisting him. Confucius is a guest, while Tzu Kung implements orders before the ruler and is much listened to. The *I Ching* states, 'He disperses the gathered herd, primordial auspiciousness!' This dispersing refers to the presence of Worthies, whereas the herd refers to the masses. The primordial is the beginning of good fortune. 'Dispersing the herd, primordial good fortune' means there are numerous worthy associates." Chien-tzu stayed his army and made no further movement.[6]

Shu Hsiang's citation of the *I Ching* illustrates how the text was often employed, not to mention contorted, to buttress arguments, even though the original—the hexagram *Huan*—is not particularly auspicious.[7]

Another example from late in the Spring and Autumn period of an emissary gathering information to determine whether a state might be attacked again finds the presence of a benevolent, exemplary official a sufficient deterrent:

Ch'u dispatched Shih Yin-ch'ih as an emissary to Sung, where the prime minister, Tzu Han, feasted him. The walls of the house south of Tzu Han's mansion stuck out precipitously and were not straight, while the water channel for the house of the left passed through his mansion. Shih Yin-ch'ih queried Tzu Han as to the reason for these oddities, who replied: "The dwelling to the south is the home of shoemakers. I was going to move them, but his father said, 'We have been earning our livelihood from shoes for three generations. If you now move us, those people in Sung who wish to buy shoes will not know our location and we will starve. I hope that the prime minister will be concerned that we will not eat.' This is the reason for his walls being like this. The house to the west lies on higher terrain than my mansion, which is lower. To have the water channel pass through it is advantageous, so I did not prohibit it."

When Shih Yin-ch'ih returned to Ch'u, the king was just about to mobilize the army to attack Sung. Shih advised against it, saying: "Sung cannot yet be attacked. Their ruler is worthy, the prime minister benevolent. The Worthy can win the people, the benevolent can employ them. If Ch'u attacks, will we not fail and be laughed at by everyone?" For this reason the king abandoned their attack on Sung and struck Cheng instead.

When Confucius heard about this incident, he said: "Cultivating oneself in the upper chambers of the court and thereby thwarting attacks a thousand kilometers off, doesn't this refer to Tzu Han?" Sung lies amid three great states of ten thousand chariots each, but during Tzu Han's era none of them made any incursions, while the borders benefited on all four sides. He served as prime minister to Dukes P'ing, Yüan, and Ching, and to the end of his life didn't he truly maintain his benevolence and the constraints of moral behavior! Thus the achievements of benevolence and constraint are great.[8]

Other factors had to be pondered when evaluating enemy states, including their material prosperity and control of the populace. Under the old system of imperial inspections that reportedly occurred either every five or twelve years, certain aspects of state government and behavior were examined to determine whether the ruler should be censured or rewarded. This *Shuo Yüan* recounting, although a later idealization, reflects the values felt to be important in the Warring States, even examining the material goods available and the songs (or Odes) of the state:

In the spring the Son of Heaven examined the planting and supplemented what was insufficient. In the fall he examined the harvests, assisting those in need. Circuits of inspection were made every five years, going east in the second month as far as the eastern peaks where a wooden pyre would be burnt in respect to the spirits of the mountains and rivers. He would interview the feudal lords and ask about anyone a hundred years old. He would order the Grand Tutor to have the state's Odes performed in order to observe their customs and direct that goods be brought in from the markets to discover what the people liked and disliked, to see if they were licentious and dissolute. He ordered the performance of their rites and examined the calendar and days set for fundamental activities; unified the laws, rites, music, and regulations; and corrected the sumptuary restrictions. Anyone who failed to respect the spirits of the mountains and rivers and offer sacrifice to them was deemed irreverent and accordingly demoted. Anyone whose ancestral temples were marked by contention was deemed unfilial and their lands were reduced. Anyone who benefited the people had their lands increased.

When he entered the borders, those who were opening unused lands, who respected the old and honored worthies, were congratulated and had their lands increased. However, if he entered their borders and found that the fields were becoming overgrown, they neglected their elderly, lost their Worthies, and arrogant and oppressive men were on the throne, they were fined and their lands reduced. If they failed to attend court after their ranks had been reduced, their lands were reduced again. A third time and the six armies were sent forth to rectify them. In the fifth month of an inspection year the emperor made a circuit to the south, venturing as far as the southern peaks, where he repeated the same ceremonies as in the east. In the eighth month he traveled to the west as far as the western peaks and again repeated the same ceremonies, and in the eleventh month went to the north and performed the same ceremonies.

Tan Hsiang's mission, previously translated in the Spring and Autumn section, provides another concrete illustration of emphasizing the vital activities of agriculture and public works, communal efforts essential to the state's economic and military survival, in evaluating.

The presence of Worthies was not unequivocally felt to be a valid indication of a state's strength, as the views of Han Fei-tzu and Huai Nan-tzu will show. Moreover, conflict between embarrassment at serving the unrighteous during an age of corruption and decline and compassionate impulses to aid the people and reform the government frequently perturbed the Worthy. Although many became recluses or exiles, others embraced the view that the misdeeds and perversity of others cannot contaminate anyone who perfects himself. Thus care had to be exercised in assessing the motivations of highly visible moral paragons and determining whether they were merely "window dressing" or actually able to affect the government. A story found in the eclectic *Lü-shih Ch'un-ch'iu* indicates the values an official might employ in deciding whether to undertake administrative responsibilities in a state:

Pai Kuei of Wei went to the state of Chung-shan, where the king wanted to retain him, but he forcefully declined, ascended his carriage, and went off. Then he ventured to Ch'i, where the king also wanted to retain and employ him, but he again declined and departed. Someone asked him why he had not remained in either state, to which he replied: "Both of them are about to perish. They show all five signs that I once learned indicate exhaustion."

"What are these five exhaustions?"

He replied: "When certainty does not exist, credibility is exhausted. When praise is absent, fame is exhausted. When there is no love, intimacy is exhausted. When travelers lack provisions and inhabitants lack food, resources are exhausted. When they can employ neither men nor themselves, achievements are exhausted. When a state has these five, without good luck they will certainly perish. Chung-shan and Ch'i are both in this situation."[9]

Pai Kuei apparently made these astute observations in the very last years of the fourth century B.C. Shortly thereafter Chung-shan was in fact exterminated, and little more than a decade later Yen, under Yüeh Yi's command, overran Ch'i and nearly extinguished it before Yüeh Yi was foolishly recalled (as seen in the introductory section on the history of the Warring States period).

Pai Kuei was not the only official capable of deciding that Chung-shan was about to perish:

Chin's Grand Historian, observing the state's chaos, the duke's arrogance, and his lack of virtue and righteousness, took the state's records and went to Chou. Duke Wei saw him in audience and inquired, "Among the states under Heaven, who will perish first?" He replied, "Chin will perish first."

Duke Wei asked for an explanation, to which the Grand Historian replied: "I did not dare speak out honestly, so I showed the duke some extraordinary phenomenal events. I said that the revolutions of the stars and planets were not correct, to which he inquired, 'Why is it so?' I showed him that affairs in the human realm were mostly unrighteous, that the common people bore him great enmity, to which he asked, 'What harm is there in this?' I showed him that neighboring states were not submissive, that the Worthy and good were not allying themselves with the state, to which he inquired, 'What disadvantage is there in this?' Since he does not know how states are preserved or perish, your servant says Chin will perish first." After three years Chin did in fact perish.[10]

Duke Wei again saw the Grand Historian in audience and inquired, "Who will follow?" "Chung-shan will be next." The duke inquired about the reason, to which he replied: "When Heaven gave birth to men, it caused them to have distinctions. Such distinctions constitute man's righteousness, the way in which men are distinguished from the animals, and why rulers and subjects, the positions of superior and inferior, were established. The custom in Chung-shan is to take day as night, while night continues day, and men and women licentiously intermix without cessation. They are promiscuous, confused, besotted with pleasure, and enamored of singing mournful tunes, yet the ruler does not know that it is evil, that this is the style of a lost state. Therefore I say that Chung-shan will be next." After two years Chung-shan indeed perished.

Duke Wei again interviewed the Grand Historian and asked, "Who will follow?" The Grand Historian did not reply. The duke persisted, so he finally said, "You will." Terrified, Duke Wei sought out the state's elders, ceremoniously brought in two famous Worthies, and added two others to sharply remonstrate with him about his transgressions. He dispensed with thirty-nine onerous laws and then informed the Grand Historian of his actions.

The latter observed: "The state will survive until the end of your life. Your subject has heard that when a state is about to flourish, Heaven will send worthy men and others who will sharply remonstrate, but when a state is about to perish, Heaven sends sycophants and men who bring chaos."[11] After Duke Wei died, his body went uninterred for nine months. Chou then split into two.[12]

Someone holding the post of Grand Historian, familiar with the state's history, as well as that of neighboring states, would presumably be well qualified to discern trends inimical to survival. Although he clearly deemed the absence of worthy men paramount, debauched extravagance, such as marked the demise of the Hsia and Shang, was viewed as a prominent, irrefutable indicator throughout Chinese history, particularly when day and night were inverted. Consequently, in accord with such foresight two ancient historians were also portrayed as abandoning their governments in incidents that not only illustrate the important role of defectors and the sort of critical information they might convey, but also essentially justify such betrayals in terms of a greater righteousness:

Near the end of the Hsia dynasty the *T'ai-shih-ling* Chung Ku, settling the laws, registers, and seals of state out before him, wept because King Chieh had become extremely deluded, perverse, and brutal. Therefore Chung Ku took them and fled to the state of Shang. King T'ang of Shang, elated, announced to the feudal lords: "The king of the Hsia has abandoned the Tao, is brutal and oppressive to the people, steals their fathers and brothers, shames his meritorious officials, slights good and worthy men, casts aside the righteous, and listens to sycophants. The masses are stirred to resentment, and his ministers who uphold the laws have fled of their own accord to Shang!"

Centuries later, Shang's *Nei-shih*, Hsiang-chi, saw that King Chou was becoming increasingly confused and deluded, so fled to the state of Chou with their records and canons of state. King Wu, greatly elated, said to the feudal lords: "The king of the Shang is very confused, and has sunk into debauchery. He keeps Chi-tzu distant but brings women and menials near. His consort Tan Yi controls the government, rewards and punishments are implemented without principle, they do not employ the method of laws, and they have executed three famous Worthies, although innocent of any crime. The people are very disaffected, the ministers who uphold the laws have fled to Chou."[13]

In both cases essential documents, such as population registers and vital information about cities and towns, were furnished to a more righteous leader. Presumably military, as well as administrative, information was thereby acquired, although adherence to the canons of morality should have precluded the defectors acting inimically to the interests of one state. However, their mere defection confirmed the premise that the departure of Worthies marked a doomed state.

Remarkably, despite living in an age of disorder, the literati deemphasized the martial in comparison with civil righteousness, and their viewpoint severely affected the analytic process, as the following episode indicates:

Wu Chi-tzu traveled to Chin and, upon entering their borders, exclaimed, "Alas, this is a brutal state!" When he entered the capital he exclaimed, "Ah, this is a state whose strength is exhausted!" When he entered the court he remarked, "This is a chaotic state!" His followers inquired, "Since you have just recently crossed the borders, how can you identify these characteristics without any doubt?"

Wu Chi-tzu replied: "When I entered the borders, I saw that the fields had become overgrown with tall weeds and were not being maintained. From this I knew that the government was brutal. When I entered the capital, I observed that their new dwellings were rustic but the old ones beautiful, that the new walls were low but the old ones high, from which I knew that the strength of the people is exhausted.[14] When I stood in their court, I noticed that the ruler merely looked on without making any inquiries, while his ministers excelled at attacking each other, yet offered no remonstrance. From this I knew that the state had fallen into chaos.

The reason Ch'i is not as well ordered as Lu is that the T'ai Kung was not as worthy as Ch'in Po, the Duke of Chou's son. Three years after both of them had been enfeoffed and begun ruling their states, the T'ai Kung went to court to have an audience. The Duke of Chou asked, "What do you consider important in governing?" He replied, "Honoring the worthy, giving priority to the distant and putting relatives second, putting righteousness first and benevolence second." These are the signs of a hegemon, so the Duke of Chou said, "Your influence will extend down five generations." Five years after they were both enfeoffed, Ch'in Po came to the court for an audience and the Duke of Chou similarly asked what he considered the most difficult aspect of governing. Ch'in Po replied, "Being intimate with one's relatives, putting those within first and those outside second, placing benevolence first and righteousness second." These are the signs of true kingship, so the Duke of Chou said, "Lu's influence will extend ten generations." Thus Lu has the trappings of kingly rule and benevolence is emphasized, but Ch'i has a hegemon's heritage, a martial administration. That Ch'i is not equal to Lu stems from the T'ai Kung not having been as worthy as Ch'in Po.[15]

The impact of this deprecatory attitude toward martial values exerted a monumental, highly subversive impact on China over the millennia, causing it to underestimate the capabilities and endurance of more warlike peoples, including the Ch'in in the Warring States period and the steppe peoples throughout the imperial age.

Since the ruling clan would ultimately set the state's style and administration, its vulnerability might be determined by examining the ruler's tastes and behavior:

Having destroyed Yüeh, King Fu-ch'ai of Wu was about to attack Ch'en. Ch'u's high officials, afraid, all said: "Previously King Ho-lü, being able to well employ his masses, badly defeated us at Po-chü. Now we have learned that Fu-ch'ai is even more fierce."

Tzu Hsi said: "Too bad you cannot act together more often. There is nothing to fear from Wu. Previously King Ho-lü never enjoyed two flavors in his dishes, arrayed double mats in his dwelling, or chose things requiring great expenditures. Whenever the state suffered from disaster or his relatives from want, he supplied their needs. When commanding the army, he never ate until more than half the men had received hot food. Whatever he enjoyed the troops did also. For this reason the people never felt tired and knew that if they died, they would not be abandoned in the wilds. However, today King Fu-ch'ai must have towers and pools constructed wherever he stops, and concubines and female attendants to wait upon him in his lodgings. Whatever he desires during his daily travels must be completed at once. Whatever amusements he wishes to pursue must be followed, so rarities and curios are gathered for him. King Fu-ch'ai will first defeat himself, so how will be able to defeat us?"[16]

King Ho-lü's selfless behavior when in command of the army well cohered with the ideals advanced in such subsequent military classics as the *Wu-tzu*, which felt that the ideal commander shared every hardship with his men and led by personal example rather than simply remaining aloof in remote comfort.

Veteran diplomats attained great skill in contextually discerning motivation, critical to avoid being blindly manipulated to another state's advantage. The *Han Fei-tzu* preserves numerous examples of such skill in evaluating foreign rulers:

> When Ch'i attacked Sung, Sung dispatched Tsang Sun-tzu south to beg assistance from Ch'u. The king of Ch'u, greatly elated, agreed to provide it and was very encouraging. Much troubled, Tsang returned to Sung. En route his driver asked, "You gained what you sought, so why do you have a troubled countenance?"
>
> Tsang replied: "Sung is small state and Ch'i a large one. Offending a large state while rescuing a small one is something that rulers worry about, yet the king of Ch'u was elated. He must want to stiffen our resolve, for if we strongly resist, Ch'i will be enervated to Ch'u's advantage." Following his return to Sung, Ch'i went on to seize five cities, but Ch'u's rescue forces never arrived.[17]

Furthermore, valuable intelligence was also derived by astutely interpreting concrete observations:

> King Chao of Ch'in [reigned 306–251 B.C.], in the midst of holding court, sighed and said: "Ch'u's swords are extremely sharp, but their entertainers are rustic. When swords are sharp, warriors are mostly impetuous and courageous, and when their entertainers are rustic, their thoughts are far-reaching. I am afraid that Ch'u is plotting against us." This is termed "thinking about misfortune during times of blessing, and not forgetting disaster during times of security," so it is appropriate that he attained the rank of hegemon.[18]

Observations of the ruler, the state's conditions, and the presence or absence of worthy officials and advisers thus formed the basis for assessing the enemy's condition and capabilities, according to early historical writings.

Political Evaluation in the Military Writings

Information about the enemy, however acquired, remains useless without a set of parameters or beliefs by which to interpret it. Although several philosophically distinct approaches to statecraft contended for dominance over the centuries, China's central government and administrative apparatus were largely marked by severe policies derived mainly from Legalism conjoined with an ostensibly Confucian outlook. Even though the military writers embraced similar views—emphasizing the people's welfare, including low taxes, combined with strict organization and a draconian legal edifice—they all discerned certain particulars in character evaluation, administrative overview, government effectiveness, population disaffection, and signs of chaos and deprivation that marked weaknesses in the enemy. The most detailed series is preserved in the *Three Strategies,* perhaps reflecting the rise and precipitous demise of the Ch'in dynasty, as well as the general heritage of the Warring States. Some are quoted from earlier works, long lost; others are apparently original with the author. As they are important for any understanding of the evaluative process and were well noted by later authors, a few examples may suffice to indicate their nature and range:

> When a ruler's actions are cruelly violent, his subordinates will be hasty to implement harsh measures. When the taxes are onerous, impositions numerous, and fines and punishments endless while the people mutually injure and steal from each other, this is referred to as a "lost state."
>
> When the secretly greedy display an external appearance of incorruptibility; prevarication and praise can gain fame; bureaucrats steal from the state to distribute their own beneficence, causing confusion in the ranks; and people adorn themselves and feign the proper countenance in order to attain high office, this is referred to as "the beginning of thievery."
>
> If administrative officials form parties and cliques, each advancing those with whom they are familiar; the state summons and appoints the evil and corrupt, while insulting and repressing the benevolent and Worthy; officials turn their backs on the state and establish their personal interests; and men of equal rank disparage each other, this is termed "the source of chaos."
>
> When strong clans assemble the evil, people without position are honored, and there are none who are not shaken by their majesty; when these practices proliferate and are intertwined, they cultivate an image of Virtue, establishing it through public

beneficence, and they snatch the authority belonging to those in official positions; when they insult the people below them and within the state there is clamoring and backbiting, while the ministers conceal themselves and remain silent, this is "causing chaos at the root."

Generation after generation they act treacherously, encroaching upon and stealing district offices. In advancing and retiring they seek only their own convenience, and they forge and distort documents, thereby endangering the ruler. They are referred to as "the state's treacherous ones."

When the officials are many but the people few; there is no distinction between the honored and lowly; the strong and weak insult each other; and no one observes the prohibitions or adheres to the laws, then these effects will extend to the ruler, and the state will reap the misfortune.

When the ruler regards the good as good but doesn't advance them, while he hates the evil but doesn't dismiss them; when the Worthy are hidden and covered, while the unworthy hold positions, then the state will suffer harm.

When the branches [the ruler's relative] and leaves [the powerful families] are strong and large, forming parties and occupying positions of authority, so that the lowly and mean insult the honored, growing more powerful with the passing of time, while the ruler cannot bear to dismiss them, then the state will suffer defeat from it.

When deceitful ministers hold superior positions, the entire army will be clamoring and contentious. They rely on their awesomeness to grant personal favors and act in a manner that offends the masses. Advancement and dismissal lack any basis, the evil are not dismissed, and men seek gain with any appearance possible. They monopolize appointments for themselves and in advancements and dismissals boast of their own merits. They slander and vilify those of great Virtue and make false accusations against the meritorious. Whether good or evil, all are treated the same by them. They gather and detain the affairs of government so that commands and orders are not put into effect. They create a harsh government, changing the ways of antiquity and altering what was common practice. When the ruler employs such wanton characters, he will certainly suffer disaster and calamity.

When evil men of courage praise each other, they obfuscate the ruler's wisdom. When both criticism and praise arise together, they stop up the ruler's wisdom. When each person praises those he favors, the ruler loses the loyal.

Accordingly if the ruler investigates unusual words, he will discover their beginnings. If he engages scholars and Worthies, then evil men of courage will withdraw. If the ruler appoints virtuous men of experience and age, the myriad affairs will be well managed. If he respectfully invites the recluses and hidden scholars to take positions, the officers will then fulfill their functions. If plans extend to the firewood carriers, achievements will be predictable. If he does not lose the minds of the people, his Virtue will flourish.[19]

Common problems identified in "Honoring the Worthy," a chapter of the *Six Secret Teachings*, equally serve as criteria for evaluating states that are being undermined by their own, self-serving people:

There are six thieves. First, if the ruler's subordinates build large palaces and mansions, pools and terraces, and amble about enjoying the pleasures of scenery and female musicians, it will injure the king's Virtue.

Second, when the people are not engaged in agriculture and sericulture, but instead give rein to their tempers and travel about as bravados, disdaining and transgressing the laws and prohibitions, not following the instructions of the officials, it harms the king's transforming influence.

Third, when officials form cliques and parties, obfuscating the Worthy and wise, obstructing the ruler's clarity, it injures the king's authority.

Fourth, when the knights are contrary-minded and conspicuously display "high moral standards," taking such behavior to be powerful expressions of their *ch'i,* and have private relationships with other feudal lords, slighting their own ruler, it injures the king's awesomeness.

Fifth, when subordinates disdain titles and positions, are contemptuous of the administrators, and are ashamed to face hardship for their ruler, it injures the efforts of meritorious subordinates.

Sixth, when the strong clans encroach upon others, seizing what they want, insulting and ridiculing the poor and weak, it injures the work of the common people.

There are seven harms. First, men without knowledge or strategic planning ability are generously rewarded and honored with rank. Therefore the strong and courageous who regard war lightly take their chances in the field. The king must be careful not to employ them as generals.

Second, they have reputation but lack substance. What they say is constantly shifting. They conceal the good and point out deficiencies. They view advancement and dismissal as a question of skill. The king should be careful not to make plans with them.

Third, they make their appearance simple, wear ugly clothes, speak about actionless action in order to seek fame, and talk about nondesire in order to gain profit. They are artificial men, and the king should be careful not to bring them near.

Fourth, they wear strange caps and belts, and their clothes are overflowing. They listen widely to the disputations of others and speak speciously about unrealistic ideas, displaying them as a sort of personal adornment. They dwell in poverty and live in tranquillity, deprecating the customs of the world. They are cunning people, and the king should be careful not to favor them.

Fifth, with slander, obsequiousness, and pandering they seek office and rank. They are courageous and daring, treating death lightly, out of their greed for salary and position. They are not concerned with major affairs, but move solely out of avarice. With lofty talk and specious discussions they please the ruler. The king should be careful not to employ them.

Sixth, they have buildings elaborately carved and inlaid. They promote artifice and flowery adornment to the injury of agriculture. They must be prohibited.

Seventh, they create magical formulas and weird techniques, practice sorcery and witchcraft, advance unorthodox ways, and circulate inauspicious sayings, confusing and befuddling the good people. The king must stop them.

Many of these practices appear among the criteria identified by Warring States thinkers as marks of a doomed state. The diabolical encouragement of extensive building projects was a hallmark of covert programs designed to subvert enemy states by exhausting their people and resources.

Political Intelligence in the Philosophical and Political Writings

The political and philosophical writings of the Warring States period, such as the *Hsün-tzu* and *Huai-nan Tzu*,[20] preserve a few contemporary analyses of the extant states and the criteria by which they were judged. Hsün-tzu, despite his fervent belief in the efficacy of Virtue, formulated realistic measures for evaluating the strength and weakness of enemy states. Two passages particularly illuminate his criteria and conclusions:

To determine whether a state is well governed or in turmoil, virtuous or not, simply observing the border will immediately provide evidence. Strict, frequent border patrols and very thorough customs examinations are already evidence of a state in turmoil. After entering the border, weed-choked fields and exposed city walls are already evidence of a greedy ruler. If you observe that the nobles in court are not morally superior, the administrators capable, or the ruler's trusted attendants sincere, this is already evidence of an ignorant ruler. If it is the habit of the ruler, prime minister, court officials, and lictors to precisely calculate and thoroughly investigate all expenditures or exchanges of wealth and goods while their performance of the customary rites is lax and negligent, this is already evidence of an insulted state.

However, if the farmers take pleasure in their fields, the soldiers are comfortable in difficulty, the hundred officials love the laws, the court esteems the customary rites, and the high ministers consult together harmoniously, this is a well-governed state. When you observe the honored nobles in their court are morally superior, the administrators capable, and trusted attendants sincere, this is an enlightened ruler.

Now when it is the habit of the ruler, ministers, and hundred officials to be generous whenever there is any expenditure or exchange of wealth, but diligent and thorough in the performance of the customary rites, this is a glorious state. When there are Worthies of equal distinction and the ruler's relatives are honored first; when capabilities are comparable and old friends are first appointed to office; and among the hundred officials the impure are all transformed to cultivate themselves, the ruthless to be ingenuous, and the crafty to be sincere, these are the accomplishments of an enlightened ruler.

There is evidence for observing whether a state is strong or weak, rich or poor. When the ruler does not esteem the customary rites; does not love the people; his measures are not believed; his praise and rewards do not penetrate; or the generals are incompetent, the army will be weak.

When the ruler is enthralled with great projects or loves profits; when the high officials, artisans, and merchants are numerous; or the state lacks regulations or fixed measures, the state will be impoverished. When the people are poor, the ruler will be impoverished. When the people are rich, the ruler will be wealthy. Thus fields and rural areas are the foundation of wealth, walled enclosures and storehouses the end. Thus when the fields are going to ruin but the warehouses replete, when the common people are empty but the storehouses full, it is referred to as "a stumbling state." Anyone who attacks the foundation and exhausts the sources, uniting them in end pursuits, will lack a flow of wealth. When the ruler and his ministers do not recognize this as evil, the state's overturn and extinction will just be a matter of time. Being sustained by the state, yet lacking enough to adorn the body is termed "the height of greed," the epitome of stupid rulership. Thus they seek wealth but lose their states, seek profit but endanger their lives. In antiquity there were ten thousand states, today there are only several tens, all lost in the same way, for no other reason.[21]

Hsün-tzu's surprisingly candid observations following his visit to Ch'in, a state whose style and measures were ever after vociferously condemned by the Confucians, reveal much about its strengths and Hsün-tzu's own astuteness:

Ch'in's barriers and passes are solidly defended, while the overall configuration of terrain facilitates defense. Its mountain forests and river valleys are spectacular and numerous profits are derived from their natural resources. This is terrain conducive to victory.

Entering their borders and observing their style of life and customs, I found that the hundred surnames were straightforward, their music neither licentious nor muddy. Their clothes were not provocative, while they deeply feared and obeyed the officials. They are like an ancient people.

The hundred capital officials were all serious and reserved, reverent and respectful, loyal, trustworthy, and honest. They are the officials of antiquity.

While in Ch'in I noted that when the high officials left their residences they went to their government offices, and when they left their government offices they returned home without undertaking private affairs. They neither formed cliques nor joined in parties. Properly reserved, they all were marked by penetrating wisdom and public spirit. These are the high officials of ancient times.

I observed that when the court listened to the hundred affairs and rendered decisions their implementation was never delayed, yet they were still and reserved as if no one were governing. This is the style of an ancient court. That they have been victorious for four generations is no accident but a question of their measures. This is what I saw.[22]

Despite his almost enthusiastic approbation, Hsün-tzu couldn't resist commenting that since the state lacked Confucian Worthies, it could never aspire to true kingship!

A century later, in a chapter discussing the impact of regional characteristics in engendering various philosophic schools, the eclectic *Huai-nan Tzu* described several states, including Ch'in:

Ch'i's territory backs the ocean to the east and takes the Yellow River as a defensive barrier to the north. The land is constricted and its agricultural fields few, but the people are very wise and clever.

Han is one of Chin's segmented states. The soil is rocky and the people treacherous, and they are pinched between two great states. Chin's old ceremonial usages have not yet been extinguished, whereas Han's new laws have already been issued. The orders of its former ruler have not yet been rescinded, but those of the present rulers have already been sent down. The old and new are at odds, the former and latter mutually destructive. The hundred officials are rebellious and in turmoil, not knowing what to employ.

Ch'in may be characterized as having the avariciousness of a wolf. Their strength is great, they have little regard for righteousness, and they pursue profit. They can be awed with punishments but cannot be transformed through goodness. They can be motivated with rewards but cannot be threatened with names. The state backs difficult terrain and is belted by the Yellow River. Their four passes constitute a bulwark, the land is advantageous, and the configuration of terrain is conducive to defense. Their harvests and stores are extremely plentiful.

No one looking toward Ch'in from the open terrain of the northern plains—where cities such as Ta-liang (present-day Kaifeng) were exposed on all four sides to raiders and invaders—failed to be impressed by their inherent strategic advantages. Not only did Ch'in occupy a virtually unassailable mountainous bastion, but it also lay on the periphery of the older, "more civilized" states and thus enjoyed the isolation provided by remoteness, coupled with the twin stimuli of civilization in the east and more warlike, nomadic peoples to the west, just as the Chou before them when the Ch'in were considered semi-barbarians.

At the end of the Warring States period, Hsün-tzu's disciple Han Fei-tzu envisioned the ideal state as governed by a strong ruler buttressed by an efficient, obedient administration that acted in a realm free of distracting, inimical values. Thus his signs of incipient disorder—essentially inherent tendencies to destruction—are elaborated in paragraphs that often condemn the presence and activity of so-called scholars and Worthies, the Confucian epitome of administrative excellence:

Its scholars praise the Tao of the former kings so as to rely on righteousness and benevolence, and flourish their manners and adorn themselves with sophistry in order to cast doubt upon the regulations of the present age, causing the ruler's mind to become indecisive.

Those fond of disputation create false assumptions, rely upon artifice, and exploit external power in order to achieve their private purposes to the state's disadvantage.

Those who bear swords assemble their own bands, establish their own code of behavior, and manifest their names while transgressing the government's prohibitions.

Those who are troubled by the prospect of serving in the state's defense seek collective refuge at the gates of the powerful and expend their wealth to employ the intercession of influential men to avoid the sweaty labors of military service.

Their merchants and artisans laboriously create outlandish vessels and hoard useless resources, accumulating things to await the period when they may acquire the farmers' profits.

These five are the state's parasites. Rulers who do not eradicate these five pernicious peoples, who do not nurture resolute officials, should not be surprised when their states suffer destruction and their courts are reduced.[23]

In a second passage Han Fei-tzu detailed additional parasites (although not so termed) that adversely affect a state, making it vulnerable to attack and collapse:

Anyone who arranges personal benefits for old friends is said not to abandon them. Anyone who distributes the state's resources to others is termed "a benevolent man." Anyone who disdains salary and esteems himself is termed "a superior man." Anyone who bends the laws in order to embrace his intimates is termed "a man of principle." Anyone who abandons official position to indulge in close personal relationships is called "a bravo." Anyone who departs from the world and hides away from the ruler is said to be lofty and unsullied. Anyone who is argumentative and contentious, who violates the government's orders, is said to be a resolute talent. Anyone who dispenses personal largess in order to gain the allegiance of the masses is said to have gained the people.

Those who do not abandon their friends will be corrupt as officials. Where the benevolent are present, the state's resources will be diminished. Where there are perfected men, it will be difficult employ the people. Where there are men of principle, the laws and regulations will crumble. Where there are bravos, officials will be despised. Where there are lofty and unsullied men, the people will not serve the government. Where there are resolute talents, orders will not be implemented. Where there are those who gain the allegiance of the masses, the ruler will be orphaned. These eight are what the people praise but constitute great defeats for the ruler. If a ruler fails to investigate what is profitable and harmful to the altars of state, but instead employs those whom the common people praise, it will be impossible for him to avoid entangling the state in danger and ruin.[24]

A third, powerful series of values inimical to the state's survival is elaborated in a chapter entitled "Deceitful Employments":

Now the ruler is concerned that those below him obey his orders, but the honest, upright, pure, and trustworthy who exert their minds but are cautious in speech are termed "rustic." Those who sternly uphold the laws and obey all the aspects of the regulations are termed "stupid." Those who respect the ruler and fear punishment are termed "fearful." Those who speak at appropriate times and whose actions suit the situation are said to be ordinary. Those who are free from duplicity, do not pursue unorthodox studies, obey the lictors, and follow their instructions are said to be uncouth. Those who are difficult to employ are termed "upright." Those difficult to reward are termed "pure." Those who are difficult to restrain are termed "robust." Those who do not obey orders are termed "courageous." Those who do not profit their superiors are termed "unsullied." Those who are generous, beneficent, and virtuous are termed "benevolent." Those who are important and haughty are termed "elders." Those whose personal schools attract many pupils are termed "teachers of disciples." Those who are tranquil, remote, and dwell quietly are termed "thinkers."

Those who diminish others to pursue profit are termed "clever." Those who slander, vituperate, and are indecisive are termed "wise." Those who put others first and themselves second, who designate appellations and speak about loving All under Heaven, are referred to as Sages. Those who speak about the great and surpassing, things that cannot be used, whose actions are contrary to the norms of society, are termed "great men." Those who despise rank and salary, who do not obey their superiors, are termed "heroes."

When the lower ranks become soaked in these beliefs, internally it will make the people chaotic, externally it will prevent them from being employed by the state. The ruler ought to prohibit their desires and extinguish their traces, but if instead of stopping them follows and esteems them as the means to govern, he merely teaches the lower ranks to bring chaos to the upper ones![25]

The idea that dissolute rulers bring disaster upon themselves existed continually from antiquity, early focusing upon the much propagandized examples of Chieh and Chou, vile despots who perpetuated day and night and, according to the *Book of Documents*, even had boats run on land. A premise found throughout the Confucian school, it was especially developed by Mencius, who strongly condemned licentious extravagance as the ruination of states. However, the *Ch'un-ch'iu Fan-lu* composed by Tung Chung-shu in the Former Han dynasty correlated such excesses with the phase of earth and the associated season of midsummer, when agricultural matters should be coming to fruition:

If the ruler loves ease and dissipation; is licentious; his consorts and concubines exceed the normal measure; he offends his relatives; insults his brothers; deceives and ensnares the common people; creates great pleasure towers; and has the five colors scintillate throughout his court while carvings and inlays abound in his palaces, then the people will suffer jaundice and pellagra and their tongues will be parched with pain. If the disaster extends to earth, then the five grains will not mature and there will be brutal oppressions and unlawful executions. If the disaster extends to the hairless mammals so that they will not reproduce, the people will turn rebellious and leave, Sages and Worthies will depart.[26]

Other series of interest are found in the *Lü-shih Ch'un-ch'iu* and the *Pao P'u-tzu*, particularly the chapter entitled "Chün Tao."[27]

The *Han Fei-tzu* incorporates numerous historical episodes and anecdotes in proof of the author's contentions, including a mission that apparently took place about 306 or 305 B.C. that concretely illustrates Han Fei-tzu's view that, rather than aiding a state, those bent on moral self-cultivation actually destroy it when the ruler succumbs to the view that such superiority will power his state:

> Duke Wu-ling of Chao dispatched Li Ts'u to observe whether Chung-shan might be attacked or not. Li Ts'u returned and reported: "Chung-shan can be attacked. If you do not hurry, you will lag behind Ch'i and Yen."
>
> Duke Wu-ling inquired, "Why can they be attacked?"
>
> Li Ts'u replied: "The ruler loves the recluses dwelling amid the mountain caves. Many times while I was there, he went out in an uncovered carriage to visit with scholars living in impoverished villages and humble lanes, and also treated the lowest ranking of men as his equals hundreds of times."
>
> Duke Wu-ling said: "From what you have said, he must be a worthy ruler, so how can he be attacked?"
>
> Li Ts'u responded: "Not so. When he treats recluses with distinction and brings them to court, his military officers will be lax in their deployments. When a ruler honors scholars and humbles himself to extend positions in his court to them, the farmers will grow remiss in the fields. When warriors are unmotivated in battle, the army grows weak. When farmers become dilatory in their fields, the state grows impoverished. Since no impoverished state has ever fielded an army weaker than its enemies and survived, isn't it appropriate to attack it?"
>
> Duke Wu-ling assented, mobilized his troops, and attacked Chung-shan, eventually extinguishing it.[28]

Han Fei-tzu of course cited this example not only because the criteria applied to evaluate the state coheres with his own viewpoint, but also because the analysis proved accurate and the resulting military action had the major historical consequence of Chung-shan being defeated and annexed in 295 B.C. by Wu-ling's successor.

Han Fei-tzu was not the only thinker to actively decry the value of virtuous advisers and postulate dramatically different criteria for evaluating states. For example, on the premise that only power affects customs, the *Huai-nan Tzu* examined the characteristics of well-governed states and chaotic states:

> Most of those dwelling under Heaven are dazzled by fame and reputation, few investigate the reality behind them. For this reason recluses are honored with praise and itinerant persuaders are distin-

guished by their sophistry. But if one investigates why they are honored and distinguished, it is for no other reason than that the ruler is not enlightened about the techniques for distinguishing benefit and harm, and takes those that the masses speak about as worthy.

The well-governed state is not thus. Those who speak about affairs must fully adhere to the laws, and those who would implement them must be governed by offices. The ruler takes hold of names in order to hold them responsible for actuality. Ministers preserve their duties in order to attain merit. Words do not succeed in exceeding substance; actions do not overstep the regulations; all the ministers offer their services together to the ruler, like the spokes of a wheel converging; none dares to monopolize the ruler's power. Affairs not falling within the regulations and laws but of possible benefit to the state and administration are invariably evaluated through extensive comparative procedures and secretly investigated to determine whom they will benefit. Moreover, all aspects must be questioned in order to investigate the transformations. There is no inclination to one corner, no formation of cliques over one issue, so the middle is established and the movements benefit all within the seas. The ministers are all impartial and upright, none dares act perversely. The hundred offices report on their affairs, focusing upon achieving the ruler's benefit. The ruler is perspicacious and enlightened above; the officials exert their energies below; all traces of licentiousness and perversity are obliterated; the accomplishments of the common people daily advance. For this reason the courageous fully exhaust their strength in the military.

A disordered state is not thus. Those whom the masses praise are rewarded despite lacking merit, officials are executed despite being innocent. The ruler is ignorant and unenlightened above, the ministers form cliques and are disloyal. Those who can speak and discourse indulge in sophistry, those who cultivate their behavior compete in augmenting themselves. When the ruler above issues an order, they join together in opposing it; what the laws and edicts would prohibit, they violate with perversity. The wise concentrate upon artifice and prevarication, the courageous focus upon fighting and conflict. The great ministers monopolize authority; lesser officials seize power; cliques and parties manipulate the ruler. Even though the state still seems to exist, the ancients would say it is already lost.[29]

In accord with its overall perspective, the *Huai-nan Tzu* even contains an anecdote that discovers the greatest Sage being one who is in fact advocating inaction:

When Chü Po-yü was serving as prime minister in Wei, Tzu Kung went to see him and inquired,[30] "How does one govern a state?" He replied, "One governs by not governing."

Chao Yang, chancellor in Chin, wanted to attack Wei, so he dispatched Shih Hsia to go and observe them. Shih returned and reported: "Chü Po-yü is prime minister, so we cannot attack them yet. Moreover, their passes and valleys are solidly defended, so we could not overcome them."[31]

Thus rather than Confucian values or Han Fei-tzu's strict but activist regime, the virtue of governing through inaction (presented by employing Tzu Kung as a foil) is viewed as the ideal way to ensure a strong state—virtually the military theorists' concept of not interfering or overlaboring the people carried to its final, generally considered Taoist, extreme.

In this same chapter, the *Huai-nan Tzu* further explicated the indications marking a lost state in an age of decline, emphasizing the people's welfare:

On the day that the ruler comes to possess the riches of the realm and occupy the seat of power, he begins to exhaust the people's energies in satisfying the pleasures of his ears and eyes. His mind is focused solely upon his palaces and pleasure towers, pools and gardens, fierce animals and bears, objects of pleasure and rarities. For this reason the impoverished people do not even have winnowed husks to eat while tigers and bears enjoy fresh grass and grain. The common people lack even short coats to keep them warm, but all within the palace wear the finest silks. The ruler fervently pursues useless achievements, throughout the land the common people are worn out with grief. Thus the ruler causes All under Heaven to fail to rest in their natures.

Signs of a Doomed State

"Doomed states"—states whose pervasive internal corruption, weakness, and disorder obviated hope of revival and made them easy prey for external forces—came to virtually make up a special category within the political writings. Assessments naturally turned upon the parameters chosen by those viewing the situation, but with a number of surprising traits and expanded situations. Since intelligence insights usually stem from details rather than grandiose schemes and sweeping evaluations, several concrete examples merit contemplation. To begin, when queried how states lose the allegiance of their people and then perish, Yen-tzu enumerated a range of inimical behaviors observed in rulers:

When the state is impoverished but the ruler likes to boast; his wisdom is meager but he likes to rely upon himself; he is estranged from the noble and lowly; the great ministers neglect the rites; he inclines to flatterers and sycophants while slighting worthy men; takes pleasure in being rude and uncouth and in manipulating the common people; the state lacks constant laws; the people lack pattern and order; he takes those skilled in sophistry as wise, those harsh to the people as loyal; he is constantly inebriated and forgets the state; loves the army and forgets the populace; is strict about punishment and execution, but slow in bestowing rewards; takes pleasure in other people's grief and finds profit in their hardship; his virtue is insufficient to embrace the people and his government inadequate to nourish them; rewards insufficient to stimulate them to goodness and punishments inadequate to prevent evil—this is the behavior of a doomed state.[32]

In another purportedly Spring and Autumn conversation, Yen-tzu undertook a comparative analysis of Chü and Lu to determine which would perish first:

The menial people of Chü are constantly changing but do not really transform. They are greedy and love artifice, esteem courage, and deprecate benevolence. In martial matters their warriors are fervent but their anger is quickly spent. For this reason the upper ranks are unable to nurture the lower and the lower ranks unable to serve the upper. When upper and lower ranks are mutually unable to receive what is appropriate, the great body of government is lost. Thus Chü will perish first.

Lu's ruler and ministers still love acting righteously, so the lower ranks are solidly settled and little heard of. For this reason the upper ranks are able to nurture the lower ones, and the lower ones able to serve the upper; therefore upper and lower mutually receive what is appropriate and the great body of government is preserved. Lu can yet survive for a long time, but there is also one difficulty. A state so small that a pheasant could easily fly across it, the ruler still styles himself a "duke" and ranks among the feudal lords. Lu is close to Ch'i but seeks to be intimate with Chin. To be unwilling to act submissively to nearby Ch'i while looking out hopefully to distant Chin is the way for insignificant Lu to extinguish itself.[33]

Eventually both states perished, with Chü becoming part of Ch'i and Lu being annexed by Ch'u.

One of the fragmented texts recovered in 1971 from a Former Han dynasty tomb is a dialogue between the king of Wu—presumably Ho-lü—and Sun-tzu on the factors from which the dissolution of Chin might be predicted:

The king of Wu asked Sun-tzu: "When the six generals divide up and occupy Chin's territory, who will perish first? Who will be solid and successful?"

Sun-tzu said, "The Fan and Chung-hang clans will be the first to perish."

"Who will be next?"

"The Chih clan will be next."

"Who will be next?"

"The Han and Wei will be next. The Chao have not lost their ancient laws, so the state of Chin will revert to them."

The king of Wu asked, "May I hear the explanation?"

Sun-tzu said: "Yes. The Fan and Chung-hang clans, in regulating their fields, take 80 paces as the length and 160 paces as the breadth, and impose taxes of one-fifth of the produce on them. The fields under administration are narrow, the warriors attached to the fields numerous. Because they impose a tax of one-fifth, the ducal house is rich. The ducal house is rich, the attached warriors are numerous. The ruler is arrogant, the ministers extravagant. They hope for achievement and frequently engage in warfare. Thus I say they will perish first.

The Chih, in regulating their fields, take 90 paces as the length and 180 paces as the breadth, and impose taxes of one-fifth on them. The fields under administration are narrow, the attached warriors numerous. Because they impose a tax of one-fifth, the ducal house is rich. The ducal house is rich, the attached warriors numerous. The ruler is arrogant, the ministers extravagant. They hope for achievement and frequently engage in warfare. Thus the Chih will be next after the Fan and Chung-hang.

The Han and Wei, in regulating their fields, take 100 paces for the length and 200 paces for the breadth, and impose taxes of one-fifth on them. The lands under administration are narrow, the attached warriors are numerous. Taxing them at one-fifth, the ducal house is rich. The ruler is arrogant, the ministers extravagant.

They hope for achievement and frequently engage in warfare. Thus I say Han and Wei will be next after the Chih. The Chao, in regulating their fields, take 120 paces for the length and 240 paces for the breadth. The duke does not impose any taxes on them. The ducal house is poor, their attached warriors few. The ruler is frugal, the ministers respectful, and they thereby govern a rich populace. Thus I say it is a solid state. The state of Chin will revert to them."

The king of Wu said: "Excellent. The Tao of the true king must be to generously love his people."[34]

The following list from the *Yi Chou-shu*—a Warring States compilation that apparently preserves some core material from the early Chou period—enumerates ten "promiscuities," or licentious practices, that destroy the virtues and values necessary to effectively govern and may therefore be seen as symptomatic of a state in terminal decline:

First, promiscuous government destroys a state. When actions do not accord with the seasons, the people are not preserved.

Second, licentious inclinations destroy righteousness. When edicts do not accord with what is right, the people will not be in harmony.

Third, promiscuous music destroys virtue. When the Virtue of government is not pure, the people will lose their essential nature.

Fourth, promiscuous actions destroy the sense of shame. When shame is inadequate, the people will not yield.

Fifth, promiscuity in the inner court destroys the rites. When the rites are not unified, the people will not be cooperative.

Sixth, promiscuity in colors destroys the gradations of clothing. When clothing does not accord with sumptuary regulations, the people will not be obedient.

Seventh, promiscuous writing destroys the classics. When the classics are no longer taken as the model for teaching, the people will not be humane.

Eighth, promiscuous employment of authority destroys the models of old. When the practices of old are not taken as models for government offices, the people will lack laws.

Ninth, promiscuous goods destroy the performance of duties, so orders will not be recognized in the hundred offices.

Tenth, promiscuous artifice destroys fundamental use. When use becomes insufficient, none of the hundred intentions will ever be achieved.[35]

In identifying these core weaknesses in the process of governing and the ruler's leadership, the text clearly reflects a Confucian perspective, consistent with its overall advocacy of Virtue and social order rather than strict laws and punishments.

The most extensive compilation of behavioral and governmental practices that may be viewed as foretelling collapse or at least the possibility of successfully attacking an enemy state appears in the *Han Fei-tzu*. However, as Han Fei-tzu himself asserts, these factors are merely predispositions and thus not certain to lead to ruin. Additional external factors, analogous to heavy rain beating on a weakened wall, are needed to precipitate an actual collapse. In other words, military strikes or covert actions to subvert the state should readily prove successful. Naturally most of his indications are symptomatic of the ruler not being in complete command, the state not being well administered or ordered, or distracting influences and contending power centers being present rather than failures in the Confucian ideals of benevolence, righteousness, and the people's welfare.

Whenever the state is small but the ruler's clan large, the ruler's authority light but that of his ministers heavy, the state can be destroyed.

If the ruler disregards the laws and prohibitions to concentrate upon strategies and plots, allows the state to go to ruin while depending upon foreign support, the state can be destroyed.

If the ministers believe in classical studies, the ruling clan members love sophistry, merchants accumulate wealth outside the state, and the ordinary people are not submissive, the state can be destroyed.

If the ruler loves palaces, pleasure towers, and pools; devotes himself to amusing himself with carriages, clothes, and curiosities; exhausts the people in outdoor projects; and wastes the state's resources and wealth, the state can be destroyed.

If the ruler is obsessed with astrological concerns in his daily activities, enthusiastically serves the ghosts and spirits, believes in divination by the turtle shell and milfoil stalks, and loves the rites of sacrifice, the state can be destroyed.

If the ruler heeds advice only from men of rank rather than verifying it with other sources and relies upon one man as his gate, the state can be destroyed.

If official positions can be gained through influence and rank and salary through bribes, the state can be destroyed.

If the ruler thinks slowly without accomplishing anything and is too flexible to make many decisions so that neither good nor evil is settled nor any standpoint established, the state can be destroyed.

If the ruler is insatiably greedy and always wants to grab whatever profits are about, he can be destroyed.

If the ruler takes pleasure in promiscuously imposing punishments without regard to the laws, loves sophists without considering their utility, and indulges in literary flourishes without being concerned about achievements, the state can be destroyed.

If the ruler is shallow and easily fathomed; leaks out the state's affairs, keeping nothing secret; and is unable to preserve secrecy but conveys the speech of various ministers to each other, the state can be destroyed.

If the ruler treats remonstrators perversely and loves to vanquish them, is unconcerned with the fate of the state, and lightly trusts in himself, the state can be destroyed.

If the ruler relies upon the support of allies but insults nearby states, depends upon the strong and great for rescue but insults the states pressing upon him, the state can be destroyed.

If foreign visitors and itinerant persuaders who have ample funds outside the state clandestinely observe the state's plans and estimations while also becoming involved in the people's affairs below, the state can be destroyed.

If the people do not trust the prime minister and subordinates do not obey their superiors, but the ruler loves them and is unwilling to dismiss them, the state can be destroyed.

If the ruler doesn't employ outstanding native talent but instead seeks officers outside it, does not promote men according to their accomplishments but likes to advance and dismiss them according to their reputations, so that foreign born officials eclipse the long-serving veterans, the state can be destroyed.

When the ruler slights his eldest son and all his offspring contend for influence, or the ruler dies before the appointment of an heir apparent, the state can be destroyed.

If the ruler is careless but never has regrets, the state is in chaos but he sees himself doing well, and without calculating the state's resources he snubs nearby enemies, the state can be destroyed.

If the ruler is not humble although the state is small, he doesn't respect the powerful even though the state's strength is minimal, and he is impolite and insulting to large neighbors, the state can be destroyed.

If after the heir apparent has already been designated, the ruler marries a woman from a powerful enemy state, the heir apparent will be endangered. In this situation the ministers will be troubled by the changes. When they are troubled by such changes, the state can be destroyed.

If the ruler, being timid and fearful, mounts only a weak defense; although events can be foreseen, his mind is too weak and pliant; and he knows what ought to be done, but even after making a decision still does not take action, the state can be destroyed.

If when the ruler has ventured outside the state a new one is enthroned, or before the heir apparent has returned from serving as a hostage in another state a new heir apparent is designated, the state will be beset by disloyalty. When a state suffers disloyalty, it can be destroyed.

If the ruler humiliates his chief ministers yet keeps them near, punishes and mutilates common people yet perversely employs them, so that these people all harbor rancor and mull over their shame, yet he continues these practices, it will produce murderous brigands. When brigands are spawned, the state can be destroyed.

If the chief ministers are doubly powerful and their relatives are numerous and strong, if they form cliques within the court and seek foreign support without in order to compete for influence and power, the state can be destroyed.

If the ruler heeds the words of his maidservants and concubines, employs the knowledge of his beloved companions, while both inside and outside the court there are grief and misery, yet he repeatedly acts without regard to the laws, the state can be destroyed.

If the ruler is insulting to the chief ministers and discourteous to his uncles, imposes onerous labor services on the common people, and executes and exterminates the innocent, the state can be destroyed.

If the ruler loves to use his knowledge to alter the laws, constantly manipulates public matters for his personal benefit, alters and changes the regulations and prohibitions, and frequently issues all sorts of directives, the state can be destroyed.

If a state lacks bastions of terrain, the exterior and interior walls are in ruins, accumulated stores are nonexistent, resources are few, and equipment for mounting a defense lacking, yet the ruler carelessly launches attacks against other states, the state can be destroyed.

If successive generations fail to achieve longevity, several rulers dying in succession, so that mere youths occupy the throne and the chief ministers monopolize power, establishing cliques with the participation of foreign guests, and they have sacrificed territory several times in order to sustain foreign alliances, the state can be destroyed.

If the heir apparent is honored and highly esteemed, his supporters being numerous and strong, and he has established personal relationships with several powerful states so that his awesomeness and power are fully complete early on, the state can be destroyed.

If the ruler's intellect is narrow but heart hasty, he is impetuous and acts carelessly, and never ponders the consequences when he become angry, the state can be destroyed.

If the ruler frequently gets angry and loves to employ the army, slights instructions in the fundamentals of agriculture and treats military attacks lightly, the state can be destroyed.

If the noble ministers are jealous of each other, the chief ministers overly powerful, and they all rely upon enemy states abroad while putting the common people into strictures at home in order to attack their enemies, but the ruler does not execute them, the state can be destroyed.

If the ruler is unworthy but the collateral houses virtuous, the heir apparent is demeaned and his brothers feisty, the officials weak and the populace bold, the state is fierce. A fierce state can be destroyed.

If the ruler harbors anger but doesn't express it, suspends punishments and puts off executions, causing the court to secretly hate him and grow increasingly fearful without knowing their fate over a long time, the state can be destroyed.

If when sending the army forth on campaign, the commanding general's mandate is too sweeping or those entrusted with border defenses are so honored that they can monopolize the army's authority and issue orders without recourse to the ruler, the state can be destroyed.

If the queen is involved in illicit affairs, the ruler's mother cultivates immoral relationships, the inner palace and the court are mutually involved with each other, and proper distinctions between the sexes no longer observed, this is termed "a state with two rulers." Such a state is doomed to perish.

If the queen is demeaned but concubines honored, the heir apparent lowly but the other sons esteemed, the prime minister's household lightly regarded but the inner palace functionaries honored, the inner palace and outer court contravene each other. A state whose inner palace and outer court contravene each other is doomed to perish.

If the chief ministers are very honored while their cliques are so extensive and powerful that they can obstruct and impede the ruler's decisionmaking and exercise the authority of government, the state can be destroyed.

If functionaries from the powerful families are employed in the government but descendants of military officials are not, those who excel in benefiting their villages are promoted but old officials long in government offices are dismissed, and the ruler esteems personal action but deprecates public achievement, the state can be destroyed.

If the royal house is impoverished but the ministerial families are wealthy, the families on the state's registers are poor but aliens residing there wealthy, farmers and soldiers are in straits but merchants profiting, the state can be destroyed.

If the ruler perceives great profits but does not pursue them, learns about incipient misfortune but does not make preparations, is lax and makes little effort in matters of battle and defense, but focuses upon adorning himself with benevolence and righteousness, the state can be destroyed.

If the ruler does not fulfill his filial obligations to his royal ancestors in governing the state but only worries about pleasing his mother, thus fulfilling the filial behavior of a common man, and is unconcerned with the altars of state, instead intent on obeying his mother's commands so that women control the state and eunuchs administer its affairs, the state can be destroyed.

If the ruler's speech is clever but he does not adhere to the laws, he is wise but lacks techniques for control and administration, he is multitalented but doesn't administer affairs in accord with the regulations, the state can be destroyed.

If those he favors advance while old ministers withdraw, the unworthy handle affairs while the Worthy and good submerge themselves, those without merit are honored while the industrious suffer and are demeaned, these subordinates will bear resentment toward the ruler. When subordinates are resentful, the state can be destroyed.

When the emoluments and positions of the ruler's clan and high ministers exceed their achievements, their insignia and attire encroach upon the gradations of rank, and their palaces and allowances become excessive, but the ruler does not prohibit such extravagance, then the hearts of his ministers will be insatiable. When their hearts are filled with unfulfilled desires, the state can be destroyed.

If the royal clan members and marriage-related families who dwell among the common people behave brutally and perversely toward their neighbors, the state can be destroyed.[36]

Steppe and Border Peoples

From the breakdown of Chou authority even prior to the Spring and Autumn period through to the end of the Warring States, China consisted of states—often European-sized countries—which of necessity had to direct intelligence-gathering activities against each other. However, with their unification under the Ch'in and subsequent imperial dynasties, the situation was dramatically transformed, the only enemies suddenly becoming internal factions, disaffected royal clan members, divisive segments of the populace, and highly elusive steppe peoples. Intelligence efforts toward the latter require a separate study during the imperial period, but it can be noted that the gathering of information and development of profiles had already begun in the early Chou. Ch'in, Ch'u, Wu, and Yüeh had in fact been "barbarian" regions until being gradually acculturated and becoming integral players in the so-called Hwa-Hsia (Chinese) cultural and political sphere formerly identified solely with the Chou ruling house and its subject states. Information about them was first gathered in the Shang and became part of everyday political dialogue during the Warring States, but contact with more remote peoples, as well as the descendants of tribes that had troubled even the earliest Sage emperors, such as the Eastern Yi, produced increasing numbers of profiles. Many of those recorded in the *Shih Chi* contain basic information that was gathered through diplomatic and trade missions and then subsequently expanded and altered in later dynastic histories. For example, in a lengthy *Shih Chi* chapter recording historical events that occurred among the "Foreign Peoples," profiles such as the following are found:

The remote ancestors of the Hsiung-nu were descendants of the Hsia known as the Ch'un-wei. Before the Sage emperors T'ang and Yü they were known as the Mountain Jung, the Hsien-yün, and the Hsün-chu and dwelled among the northern barbarians, shifting their abode in pursuit of their herding activities. The majority of their animals are horses, cattle, and sheep, but they occasionally rear camels, donkeys, mules, and three different breeds of swift horses. They move about in pursuit of water and grass, and although having neither cities nor fortifications, nor engaging in farming, they still have allotted territories. They do not have writing or documents, but make agreements verbally. Male children are able to ride sheep, hold a bow, and shoot birds and rats. Young men shoot foxes and rabbits for food. Their warriors are all strong enough to pull a bow and be armored cavalrymen.

In ordinary times it is their custom to practice herding and hunting and capture animals as their occupation, but in times of military crisis they are practiced in martial arts and aggressive attacks, for this is their Heavenly nature. Their long-range weapons are the bow and arrow, their close weapons the knife and truncheon. When it is advantageous, they will advance; when disadvantageous, they will withdraw, never finding it shameful to retreat. They are solely concerned with profit, not with ceremony or righteousness. From the ruler on down they all eat the flesh of animals, make clothes from their hides, and wear fur coats. The strong eat the best, most appealing food, the old what is left over. They esteem youth and strength, disdain age and weakness. When a father dies, the son will marry his widows; when a brother dies, the remaining brothers his wives. In their customs they have names but no surnames or avoidance.[37]

The Hsiung-nu were a focal subject in the heated discussion of Han barbarian policy marking the great debate that occurred in 81 B.C. Known as the *Discussions on Salt and Iron (Yen-tieh Lun)*, this debate was so titled because it was ostensibly convened to argue the appropriateness of the state monopolies of salt and iron. The positions taken by the literati and the officials, although derived from presumably common knowledge, evidence radically different perspectives and interpretations:

The High Officials said: "The Hsiung-nu lack the defenses of city walls and stoutness of moats, the use of long pointed halberds and strong crossbows, and accumulated stores in granaries and warehouses. The ruler lacks righteousness and laws, the people civility and order. Ruler and minister slight each other, upper and lower ranks have no ceremony between them. They braid willow to make frames for their dwellings and use felt for the covering. They have plain crescent bows and use bone arrowheads. Their horses do not eat grain. Internally their preparations are inadequate to be a cause for concern, externally their rites are not worth noting.

"China is the heart of All under Heaven where worthy officers gather, the rites and righteousness accumulate, and wealth and commerce are nurtured. Now if the wise plot against the stupid and the righteous attack the unrighteous, it will be like the leaves falling from the trees after an autumnal frost. The *Ch'un Ch'iu* states, 'Duke Huan simply expelled the Jung and Ti.' How much more so one who has all the strength under Heaven?"

The Literati: "The Hsiung-nu do not embellish their chariots or vessels with silver and gold, threads and lacquer. They are plainly made and concentrate upon sturdiness. Their materials lack fancy colors, their clothes the various distinctions of collars and sleeves. They simply concentrate upon making them complete. The men do not pursue the artifice and skill of inlaying and engraving, or the labor of constructing palaces and city walls. The women make no contribution to embroidery or other dissipated skills, or the work of fine silk weaving. Their affairs are simplified and utilitarian, easily finished, difficult to cause distress.

"Even though they do not have long pointed halberds or strong crossbows, they have barbarian horses and good bows. Families have allotted preparations, men their employment. If one morning there is a military crisis, they stretch their bows and mount their horses. Although they do not seem to accumulate resources, their provisions are adequate to sustain them for several tens of days. They rely upon the mountains and valleys as their fortifications and the rivers and grasslands as their granaries and storehouses. Their laws are concise but easy to understand, what is sought easily satisfied. Therefore their punishments are minimal and rarely violated. They signal with a pennant and orders are followed. They slight the customary rites but are sincere in trust, they are uncultured but astute in affairs. Although they do not have books on the rites and righteousness, with carved bones and rolled up wooden slips, the hundred officials have a means to record their actions, superiors and inferior to employ each other.

When our ministers make plans for the district governments, they similarly speak about how easily affairs will be achieved, but in actuality they always turn out to be difficult. Thus Ch'in wanted to expel the Hsiung-nu but instead was ruined itself. Accordingly, military weapons are inauspicious implements and cannot be lightly employed.[38] Will it be only one dynasty that assumed the strong were weak and the existent to have perished?"[39]

Even though the accuracy of their perceptions remains to be ascertained, for the most part they were observationally derived and no doubt reasonably reliable, especially as intelligence failures might be expected more in fathoming intent and behavior than in perceiving the easily visible material aspects of nomadic civilizations.

A slightly later but still typical analysis found in the chapter on the Eastern Yi peoples in the history of the Later Han preserves intriguing notes on unusual weapons that should have greatly troubled any commander facing the Pa-lou in the field.

> The Pa-lou dwell in the ancient state of Su-chen. Their territory lies more than a thousand kilometers northeast of Fu-yü and has its eastern border along the shores of the great sea. To the south it is contiguous with Pei-yao-chü, to the north extends out to unknown regions. The land is marked by numerous mountains and ravines. The appearance of the people is like the Fu-yü, but their languages are completely different.
> They have the five grains and hemp cloth, produce garnets and good sables. They do not have rulers or elders, but each encampment has its own great men. They live amid the mountain forests where the earth's atmosphere is extremely cold. They usually dwell in caves, valuing depth, with the largest reaching down nine ladders. They like to raise pigs and eat the meat, as well as make clothes from the hides. In the winter they smear pig fat on their skins several layers thick in order to ward off the wind and cold. In the summer they go about naked except for a loincloth front and rear.
> The people are smelly, dirty, and impure, and put their outhouses in the middle of their settlements. Ever since the rise of the Han they have been subordinate to the Fu-yü. Although their numbers are few, they are mostly courageous and strong. They dwell among the mountains and ravines and so excel at shooting that they can hit a man in the eye with an arrow. Their bows are four feet long with the strength of a crossbow. Their arrows are made from Hu wood, one foot eight inches long, with bluestone arrowheads on which they spread poison. A man hit by such an arrow will die. They are facile in the use of boats and like to make raids and plunder, so the abutting states are afraid and worried, but their troops cannot subdue them. All the Eastern Yi peoples eat with platters and dishes, only the Pa-lou do not follow this habit. Their customs lack any fixed patterns whatsoever.[40]

The Pa-lou description indicates the widespread knowledge and application of indigenous poisons in warfare, particularly among steppe peoples. (Such practices are virtually unmentioned in traditional Chinese warfare except in an assassination context.) Although felt to be uncouth and uncivilized, the steppe peoples clearly had mastered the mobile tactics of guerrilla warfare and were thus able to exploit the natural advantages of difficult terrain to thwart protagonists.

.

Part Five

MILITARY INTELLIGENCE

軍　情

15

Field Intelligence

*P*OLITICAL AND GENERAL ISSUES of military capability and intentions having been determined, the next concern would be acquiring focal intelligence of actual field forces embarked upon campaigns, mounting invasions, or preparing for immediate battles. That reconnaissance patrols, direct observers, lookouts, and agents were employed to acquire information about the enemy and determine their position need hardly be mentioned. Of far greater interest is the overall approach and criteria by which opposing forces were evaluated and the decisions that might be derived from processed data, such as the number of men or the commander's character. In order to exploit any weaknesses, basic information had to be developed about the enemy's physical condition, logistics, morale, officers, secondary forces, deployment, defenses, and probable intentions. Chinese intelligence operations traditionally emphasized three factors: morale, configurations of terrain, and the enemy commander's personality and skills.

The *Six Secret Teachings* clearly states that "the technique for military conquest is to carefully investigate the enemy's intentions and quickly take advantage of them, launching a sudden attack where unexpected."[1] Sun-tzu earlier defined the parameters for such evaluative thrusts in the initial chapters of the *Art of War* with a series of pronouncements, many of which have already been noted in earlier sections. Because military theorists evolved a wide range of tactics to cope with the three main possibilities of being outnumbered, facing equal strength, and outnumbering the enemy,[2] determining the enemy's actual strength was naturally important, although never paramount. Sun-tzu advised: "After estimating the advantages in accord with what you have heard, put it into effect with strategic power supplemented by field tactics that respond to external factors. As for strategic power, it is controlling the tactical imbalance of power in accord with the gains to be realized."[3]

Four of Sun-tzu's seven critical factors focus upon military questions: "Which general has greater ability? Who has gained the advantages of Heaven and Earth? Whose forces are stronger? Whose officers and troops are better trained?"[4] Moreover, he demarked five indices of success:

There are five factors from which victory can be known: One who knows when he can fight and when he cannot fight will be victorious. One who recognizes how to employ large and small numbers will be victorious. One whose upper and lower ranks have the same desires will be victorious. One who, fully prepared, awaits the unprepared will be victorious. One whose general is capable and not interfered with by the ruler will be victorious. These five are the Tao for knowing victory.[5]

Sun-tzu's pronouncements, even though premised upon centuries of intelligence activity, essentially initiated the systematic effort to conceptualize military intelligence objectives, format operations, and consciously exploit the material thus acquired.

Concept of Timeliness

The concept of timeliness appears throughout the writings of the Warring States period, nonmilitary as well as military, evidence that it was paramount in determining an action's feasibility. For example, in the *Six Secret Teachings* the T'ai Kung advised King Wen:

Do not dig valleys deeper to increase hills. Do not abandon the foundation to govern the branches. When the sun is at midday you should dry things. If you grasp a knife you must cut. If you hold an ax you must attack.

If at the height of the day you do not dry things in the sun, this is termed "losing the time." If you grasp a knife but do not cut anything, you will lose the moment for profits. If you hold an ax but do not attack bandits will come.

If trickling streams are not blocked, they will become great rivers. If you do not extinguish the smallest flames, what will you do about a great conflagration? If you do not eliminate the two-leaf sapling, how will you use your ax when the tree has grown?[6]

Remarkably, similar thoughts are expressed in Chapters 63 and 64 of the *Tao Te Ching:*[7]

Plot against the difficult while it remains easy,
Act against the great while it is still minute.
Difficult affairs throughout the realm invariably commence with
the easy,
Great affairs throughout the realm inevitably commence with the
small.
For this reason the Sage never acts against the great and is thus
able to complete greatness.
What is tranquil remains easily grasped,
What has not yet betrayed signs is easy to plot against.
The brittle is easily split,
The minute is easily scattered.
Act upon them before they attain being,
Control them before they become chaotic.
Trees that require both arms to embrace
Are born from insignificant saplings.
A nine story tower commences with a little accumulated earth,
A journey of a thousand kilometers begins beneath one's feet.

The proto-Taoist *Lieh-tzu*, attributed to the late Warring States, also took as one of its essential themes the need to discern the proper moment because times differ and carefully planned actions may suddenly become inappropriate. In the Later Han an esoteric work entitled the *Pao P'u-tzu*, authored by an experienced military commander and Taoist adept, even contains a section entitled "The Difficulties of Timing" that may be distilled as "It's not speaking that is difficult, but talking about the time that is hard."

Agriculturally based societies could not ignore the pressing need to organize and undertake timely efforts throughout the year in order to ensure that crops were planted, the basic infrastructure of dikes and roads maintained, and preparations made against natural and military disasters. In all these activities one inescapable, operative principle prevailed: Acting in accord with the seasons will bring prosperity; going contrary to them, only misery. This idea predominates in the late Warring States *Lü-shih Ch'un-ch'iu*, a massive thematic compilation whose initial chapters include an extensive, detailed calendar of correspondences, seasonal changes, requisite actions, and symbolical undertakings. According to the *Lü-shih Ch'un-ch'iu*, wisdom is one of the four critical factors of military knowledge. Wisdom, in turn, is "knowing the transformations of time. If you know the transformations of time, you will know the changes of the vacuous and substantial, flourishing and decline, the measures of advancing and retreating, far and near, releasing and uniting."[8] The *Lü-shih Ch'un-ch'iu*,

Chuang-tzu, and *Wu-tzu* all recognize the idea of a subtle moment when incipient affairs rise, termed *chi* in Chinese,[9] a technical concept especially applicable in military intelligence. Determining it requires the fullest knowledge possible of general trends, such as the seasons and regional disturbances, and specifics, such as the details of the enemy's plans or actions. As the *Yi Chou-shu* states, "Employing the military lies in knowing the time."[10] More aggressively framed, knowledge must be timely, acquired expeditiously, and exploited ruthlessly, whether in diplomatic or military affairs, such as by thwarting an enemy's alliances or shattering a temporary river dam and thereby drowning a negligent enemy force in midcrossing.[11] Thus the great strategist Sun Pin observed: "When the army sees the good but is dilatory; when the time comes but it is doubtful; when it expels perversity but is unable to dwell in the results, this is the Tao of stopping. If you implement the Tao of stopping, then even Heaven and Earth will not be able to make you flourish."[12]

Observation and Reconnaissance

All the military theorists made extensive reconnaissance efforts incumbent upon commanders at all levels. However, the earliest recorded incident of a ruler (synonymous with commander in chief) personally undertaking this responsibility appears in an incident dated to 717 B.C. According to the *Tso Chuan*, when Duke Yin of Lu was criticized by his ministers for planning to "shoot fish" in the area of T'ang, he retorted that he wanted to "gain an understanding of the terrain," presumably to assess border defenses because of ongoing tensions with other states.[13] Another king in the Warring States period took even more dramatic action in an episode that coincidentally shows the effectiveness of disguise and the ability of emissaries to penetrate other states and gather information:

> After ordering his son to assume administrative control of Chao, around 298 B.C. King Hui of Chao, personally wearing the garb of the Hu nomadic people, led his warriors and officials out into the northwest to invade Hu territory, intending moreover to move due south from Yün-chung and Chiu-yüan and unexpectedly attack Ch'in. Accordingly he pretended to be a Hu emissary and thus entered Ch'in.
>
> Although the king of Ch'in didn't recognize him, he felt it strange that he appeared so powerful and noted that his attitude certainly was not that of a mere minister. Accordingly, the king

had someone pursue him, but King Hui had already escaped by racing out through the pass. When they inquired and discovered that it was King Hui of Chao, the populace was astonished. King Hui succeeded in entering Ch'in because he had wanted to personally ascertain the terrain's configuration and thus observe what sort of man the king of Ch'in might be.[14]

King Hui subsequently led successful military expeditions out into these territories.

Han Shih-chung (1089–1151), a famous Southern Sung general who futilely opposed appeasing the northern barbarian forces, was similarly motivated to undertake his own observations of the enemy:

Liu Chung had occupied Mount Pai-mien with several tens of thousands of troops, the palisades around their encampments even being within sight of each other. When Han Shih-chung first arrived in the area, he wanted to quickly mount a surprise attack. However, Meng Yü, the regional Pacification Commissioner, would not permit it. Han Shih-chung then said: "For the military strategist advantage and disadvantage are a matter of thoroughness in planning, something that those in central government administration would not understand! Please allow me to report back in half a month." He proceeded to erect fortifications opposite all the enemy's encampments and then sat around playing chess and holding drinking feasts, solidly ensconced within his walls. No one could understand it.

One evening Han Shih-chung and Su Ke rode together into the enemy's camp. When the perimeter guards challenged them, Shih-chung responded with the password he had previously secured. After looking all about their encampments, they departed. Elated, Shih-chung exclaimed, "This is a gift from Heaven!" That very night he had two thousand elite troops establish an ambush on Mount Pai-mien and then led his generals in a penetrating assault upon Liu's encampments. Just when the enemy's troops were responding to the attack, Han's concealed forces raced into the central army's position where they seized the watchtowers, emplaced their own flags, and then began yelling like thunder. Looking back, the rebel troops became frightened and crumbled. Han Shih-chung then led his generals and troops in a pincer attack, severely defeated the enemy, and beheaded Liu Chung. Honan was thus pacified.[15]

Not only actual commanders felt the pressing need for forward observers, security patrols, reconnaissance scouts, various agents, and spies, but also the theoretical writings all emphasized the employment of forward scouts. Apart from Sun-tzu's initial emphasis upon securing precise knowledge of the enemy and terrain through various means, including local guides, the T'ai Kung stated:

> In general, when you venture deep beyond the enemy's borders, you must investigate the configuration and strategic advantages of the terrain and concentrate upon seeking out and improving the advantages. Rely upon mountains, forests, ravines, rivers, streams, woods, and trees to secure defense. Carefully guard passes and bridges, and moreover be certain you know the advantages of terrain conveyed by the various cities, towns, hills, and funeral mounds. In this way the army will be solidly entrenched. The enemy will not be able to sever our supply routes, or be able to occupy positions cutting across our front and rear.
>
> Now the rule for commanding an army is always to first dispatch scouts far forward so that when you are two hundred kilometers from the enemy, you will already know their location. If the strategic configuration of the terrain is not advantageous, then use the Martial Attack chariots to form a mobile rampart and advance. Also establish two rearguard armies to the rear, the further one a hundred kilometers away, the nearer fifty kilometers away. Thus, when there is a sudden alarm or urgent situation, both front and rear will know about it, and the Three Armies will always be able to complete their deployment into a solid formation, never suffering any destruction or harm.[16]

Chu-ko Liang even condemned as "worm infested" any army whose reconnaissance scouts were not thorough or whose forward observers failed to properly maintain the various signals and fires that would indicate an enemy advance.[17]

In the T'ang dynasty Li Ch'uan, following in the tradition of the *Wu-tzu* and *Six Secret Teachings,* discussed the qualifications required for field personnel, together with the commander's intelligence responsibilities:

> When someone unites the masses of six armies and commands a force of a million men but instead of having a selected front employs all his troops indiscriminately, the wisest will lack the means to implement their plans, the sophists to exercise their persuasion, the courageous to rouse their daring, and the strong to show off their robustness. This is no different from advancing alone out onto the central plains—how could anyone achieve vic-

tory in battle? Thus Sun-tzu said, "An army that lacks a selected front is called routed."[18]

Now one selects officers with rewards, and through rewards ensures their advancing. One employs officers through punishment, for punishment makes them wary of retreating. In antiquity those who excelled at selecting officers posted a list of rewards at the Central Army's gate that ran as follows:

Those who ponder deeply and develop plans and strategies, who surpass the norm, will be assigned the highest rewards and decorously called "Wise and Capable Officers."

Those who can speak fluently about Horizontal Alliances, discuss the principles of the Vertical Alliance, excel at verbal rebuttals and instigating and settling disputes, and are able to alter people's natures and seize their minds, will be assigned the highest rewards and decorously called "Disputatious and Persuasive Officers."

Those who can obtain information about private discussions between rulers and ministers, the nature and circumstances of audiences and court visits, will be assigned the highest rewards and decorously termed "Agents and Spies."

Those who know the mountains and rivers, water and grasses, way stations and lodgings, roads and lanes, direct and indirect routes, will be assigned the highest rewards and decorously called "Local Guidance Officers."

Those who fashion the five weapons, the implements for assault and defense, unorthodox changes, deceit and disgrace, will be assigned the highest rewards, treated generously and termed "Officers of Skill and Artifice."

Those who can pull a five-picul bow; whose arrows pierce several layers of armor; can easily wield halberds, spears, swords, and pointed halberds; can attack a rhinoceros on land and seize great turtles in water; facilely take prisoners; capture flags; and collect the enemy's drums, will be assigned the highest rewards, well treated, and called "Fierce and Resolute Officers."

Those who can quickly mount and race a horse, jump over and circumvent walls and fortifications, and enter and leave encampments without any trace will be assigned the highest rewards, gathered together, and termed "Energetic, Nimble Officers."

Those who can race out and back three hundred kilometers before nightfall will be assigned the highest rewards, collected together, and termed "Officers with Fleet Feet."

Those whose strength is great enough to lift 630 catties and carry them fifty paces will be assigned the highest rewards and gathered together. Those who can lift 240 catties will be assigned the next highest reward and gathered together. They will all be termed "Officers of Great Strength."

Those well-versed in the five elements and three phases, who can speak voluminously about the Tao of Heaven, *yin* and *yang*, feign and dissemble, will be assigned the lowest rewards, preserved, and termed "Officers of Techniques and Skill."

Now in employing these ten types of officers, you must fully exhaust their talents and entrust them according to the Tao. For planning employ Wise and Capable Officers; for discussions, employ the Disputatious and Persuasive Officers. To separate the intimate and estrange the close, employ Agents and Spies. To deeply penetrate the territory of the feudal lords, employ Local Guidance Officers. To create the five weapons, employ the Officers of Skill and Artifice. To destroy enemy fronts, capture prisoners, defend dangerous locations, and attack the strong, employ the Fierce and Resolute Officers. To confuse the stupid and muddle the moronic, employ Officers of Technique and Skill.

This is termed "the Tao for entrusting responsibility to talent," the technique for selecting officers. Those descendants of the Three Sage Emperors and Five Hegemons who realized this Tao flourished, those who lost it perished. The Tao of flourishing and perishing does not lie in the ruler's brilliance and cultural attainments, but in selecting the capable and appropriately exploiting their talents.[19]

The attack on "brilliance and cultural attainments" in the last sentence is but another salvo in the unremitting conflict between the literati, who esteemed the power of the civil, and the military officials burdened with the awesome martial responsibility of preserving the state from external threats.

During the early years of the Southern Sung after the emperor had been forced into the south, Hua Yüeh (who was actually banished for his outspoken opposition to barbarian appeasement) similarly decried the government's deliberate laxity in investigating and preparing against border incursions:

I have heard that an army having scouts and agents is like a human body having ears and eyes. When the eyes and ears are incomplete, the person is handicapped, but when scouts and agents are not established, the army itself is crippled. My deafness and blindness only handicaps my four limbs, but blindness and deafness in the army cause incalculable handicaps. Thus when reconnaissance officers are not strict, wise men say the army lacks ears and eyes.

Only when the army can precede others in acting can it seize their minds. Enemy provocateurs gaining undetected entrance to your encampment and troops penetrating your walls, resulting in the unbroken battle sounds of pipes and drums, both stem from the army lacking its own scouts and agents.

Since the establishment of the present peace the court hates to hear about developments along the border; therefore, generals and commanders fail to buy agents and spies. If they improve the defenses in the absence of incidents, they are said to be provoking border clashes, whereas if they speak about deployments and strategic power when incidents arise, they are said to be divulging information about military essentials.

In recent years those occupying the rank of general have all been ordinary, undistinguished officers. Among them all, from the highest imperial official on down, including the commanding generals of our field armies, I have yet to hear of anyone able to seek out agents and spies, to gather up what has been missed and thus assist what is merely heard about, to employ what is termed "the method of scouts and agents."

What is vision when border patrols are not strict and stations not established; when rewards are not bestowed to sustain their hearts, or gold or silk to stimulate fortitude in the officer's spirit? Those who learn of affairs achieve no merit, those who misperceive them no punishment. Thus officers do not go out beyond the border, spies do not enter the enemy's encampment. Although the opposing armies may be separated by only a river and can look across at each other as if in the same encampment, the smoke from their fires colliding in the air above, no one knows how many troops are in the enemy's camp. Even though they hear each other's chickens and dogs at dawn and dusk, no one knows the fullness or emptiness of enemy states, the so-called names and surnames of the villain's generals, their level of skill, whether their strategic power is poised to advance or not, and whether they are courageous or fearful, probably regarding these as if they were matters of a different era.

When they dare to look out across at the enemy, they only learn a minute portion of the situation. Thus it is hardly surprising that they perish and are defeated. Only through establishing watch stations, summoning and enlisting agents and spies, and establishing communications with distant outposts will our border troops be free from difficulties and gain respite. Then, should incidents arise, they will not be distressed. This is termed "the method of scouts and agents."[20]

Not only a perspicacious condemnation of the practices of his age, his admonition repeatedly went unheeded in subsequent centuries, despite the great military compendium known as the *Wu-ching Tsung-yao* having thoroughly discussed the qualifications and active employment of reconnaissance scouts nearly two centuries earlier.

The late Ming dynasty *Ping-fa Pai-yen*, written during the depressing onslaught of the Manchus by the heroic Chieh Hsüan, concludes the thread of theoretical assertions on the pressing need for knowledge of the enemy:

Definition: Skillfully employing one's ears and eyes is termed "knowledge."

Original Text: The first is called penetrators, the second spies, the third observers, and the fourth villagers [local guides]. Agents who penetrate enemy territory know the enemy's plans and plots; spies *[tie]* know the enemy's vacuities [gaps] and strengths; observers know the enemy's movement and rest, going forth or standing down; villagers know the mountains, rivers, and roads in the enemy's state. When you know the enemy's plans, you know what to destroy. When you know the enemy's strengths and vacuities, you know where to suddenly strike. When you know the enemy's movement and rest, going forth and standing down, you know what can be exploited; when you know the mountains, rivers, and roads, you know where to move.

Explanation: If you can successfully penetrate, spy out, observe, and attain local guidance, it is all because the state has worms. If this is not the case, then its generals are incapable. Or again, because the army is filled with resentment. When worms arise in the state, then more enter from outside, for this is a natural pattern. Thus if you wish to know another man's state, you must first know the state's worms.[21]

Under the rubric for "advancing" Chieh stressed the importance of reconnaissance scouts and various forward agents by selectively enumerating the potential dangers an advancing army might encounter:

Definition: To penetrate where one intends to go is termed "advancing."

Original Text: When traversing constricted terrain, you should consider the possibility of ambushes; when fording rivers, your only worry is sudden inundation. When setting out at daybreak be fearful of explosive attack, when halting at night be wary of baseless disturbances. When supplies may be easily cut off, form closely connected columns, where hasty advance is difficult, roll up your baggage and advance.[22] If you do not take defensive precautions over one segment, you will be lost over the distance of the advance. First sketch out the configuration of terrain in order to observe its major strategic features, then seek out some natives in order to investigate it in minute detail. Concentrate upon finding out and knowing each and every marshy wood and mountain torrent, for only thereafter can you advance the army.

Explanation: When the army moves forward, you must have maps and natives in order to prepare for careful examination. Moreover, you should have reconnaissance patrols and roving scouts on the perimeter in order to defend against the unexpected. [When in movement,] make the army heavy with the power of formations, be selective about the forces by employing defensive generals, supplement them with a covering army, constrain them with the two wings, and continue them with a strong rearguard. Even when passing through ravines and narrows, you cannot proceed in disorderly fashion, even when on level ground, you cannot abandon these preparations. Be cautious in sustaining the effort and there will be few instances of obstruction.

Active Probing Measures

Despite the employment of spies, reconnaissance efforts, and other observational clues, a general confronted by opposing forces might still be unsure of many aspects, including the configuration of terrain, the enemy's strength and component forces, the condition of the enemy's soldiers, and the commander's character and abilities. Consequently, the only alternative to simply blundering forward with a haphazard plan based upon partial intelligence, perhaps buttressed by experience, would be to actively probe the enemy, to test their defenses and responses with a heavy reconnaissance patrol or light cavalry company and thereby detect weaknesses, gaps, and possible patterns of response, always assuming the enemy commander had not anticipated these probes and prestructured a misleading response. By the end of the Spring and Autumn period active probing was apparently an essential part of military operations, critical to the project of intelligence gathering. Two early military writings, the *Ssu-ma Fa* and the *Wu-tzu*, defined the classic method that commanders studied and emulated on through the Ming:

In general, in warfare employ large and small numbers to observe their tactical variations; advance and retreat to probe the solidity of their defenses. Endanger them to observe their fears. Be tranquil to observe if they become lax. Move to observe if they have doubts. Mount a surprise attack and observe their discipline.
Mount a sudden strike on their doubts. Attack their haste. Force them to constrict their deployment. Launch a sudden strike against their order. Take advantage of their failure to avoid harm. Obstruct their strategy. Seize their thoughts. Capitalize on their fears.[23]

Marquis Wu asked, "When our two armies are confronting each other but I don't know their general, if I want to fathom him, what methods are there?"

Wu-tzu replied: "Order some courageous men from the lower ranks to lead some light shock troops to test him. When the enemy respond, they should concentrate on running off instead of trying to gain some objective. Then analyze the enemy's advance, whether their actions, such as sitting and standing, are in unison and their organization well preserved. Whether when they pursue your retreat they feign being unable to catch you, or when they perceive easy gain they pretend not to realize it. A commander like this may be termed 'a wise general.' Do not engage him in battle.

"If their troops approach yelling and screaming, their flags and pennants in confusion, while some of their units move of their own accord and others stop, some weapons held vertically, others horizontally—if they pursue our retreating troops as if they are afraid they won't reach us, or seeing advantage are afraid of not gaining it, this marks a stupid general. Even if his troops are numerous they can be taken."[24]

Sun-tzu also believed in actively probing the enemy and was equally followed by Sun Pin in this regard:

Critically analyze them to know the estimations for gain and loss. Stimulate them to know the patterns of their movement and stopping. Determine their disposition of force to know the tenable and fatal terrain. Probe them to know where they have an excess, where an insufficiency.[25]

— — —

King Wei of Ch'i, inquiring about employing the military, said to Sun Pin, "If two armies confront each other, their two generals looking across at each other, with both of them being solid and secure so that neither side dares to move first, what should be done?"

Sun Pin replied: "Employ some light troops to test them, commanded by some lowly but courageous officer. Focus on fleeing, do not strive for victory. Deploy your forces in concealment in order to abruptly assault their flanks. This is termed 'the Great Attainment.'"[26]

General Field Assessments

The character, quality, and other aspects of an opposing force—apart from the detailed question of the commander's character and qualifications, discussed subsequently—may be determined in large part from direct observation. Accordingly, beginning with the Spring and Autumn period perceptive thinkers isolated certain behavioral gestalts as predictive; once the enemy was appropriately categorized, specific conclusions and potential paths of action immediately followed. Again, Sun-tzu's concise observations anchored the practice, although later elaborations expanded them greatly. Among the most interesting might be the following from "Maneuvering the Army":[27]

If an enemy in close proximity remains quiet, they are relying on their tactical occupation of ravines. If while far off they challenge you to battle, they want you to advance because they occupy easy terrain to their advantage.

If large numbers of trees move, the enemy are approaching. If there are many visible obstacles in the heavy grass, it is to make you suspicious. If the birds take flight, there is an ambush. If the animals are afraid, enemy forces are mounting a sudden attack.

Those who stand about leaning on their weapons are hungry. If those who draw water drink first, they are thirsty. When they see potential gain but do not know whether to advance, they are tired.

Where birds congregate it is empty. If the enemy cries out at night, they are afraid. If the army is turbulent, the general lacks severity. If their flags and pennants move about, they are in chaos. If the officers are angry, they are exhausted.

If they kill their horses and eat the meat, the army lacks grain. If they hang up their cooking utensils and do not return to camp, they are an exhausted invader.

One whose troops repeatedly congregate in small groups here and there, whispering together, has lost the masses. One who frequently grants rewards is in deep distress. One who frequently imposes punishments is in great difficulty. One who is at first excessively brutal and then fears the masses is the pinnacle of stupidity.

One who has emissaries come forth with offerings wants to rest for a while.

If their troops are aroused and approach our forces, only to maintain their positions without engaging in battle or breaking off the confrontation, you must carefully investigate it.

The great general Wu Ch'i similarly arrayed some basic observations for Marquis Wu, translating circumstances and behavior into tactical possibilities:

Marquis Wu inquired: "From external observation of the enemy I would like to know their internal character, from studying their advance know at what point they will stop, in order to determine victory and defeat. May I hear about this?"

Wu Ch'i replied: "If the enemy approaches in reckless disarray, unthinking; if their flags and banners are confused and in disorder; and if the men and horses frequently look about, then one unit can attack ten of theirs, invariably causing them to be helpless.

"If the feudal lords have not yet assembled; ruler and ministers are not yet in agreement; ditches and embankments not yet complete; prohibitions and orders not yet issued; and the Three Armies clamoring, wanting to advance but being unable to, wanting to retreat but not daring to—then you can attack with half the enemy's force, and never lose in a hundred encounters. . . .

"In general when evaluating the enemy there are eight conditions under which one engages in battle without performing divination.

"First, in violent winds and extreme cold they arise early and are on the march while barely awake, breaking ice to cross streams, unfearing of any hardship.

"Second, in the burning heat of midsummer they arise late and without delay press forward in haste, through hunger and thirst, concentrating on attaining far-off objectives.

"Third, the army has been out in the field for an extended period; their food supplies are exhausted; the hundred surnames are resentful and angry; and numerous baleful portents have arisen, with the superior officers being unable to quash their effects.

"Fourth, the army's resources have already been exhausted; firewood and hay are scarce; the weather frequently cloudy and rainy; and even if they wanted to plunder for supplies, there is nowhere to go.

"Fifth, the number mobilized is not large; the terrain and water not advantageous; the men and horses both sick and worn out; and no assistance comes from their allies.

"Sixth, the road is far and the sun setting; the officers and men have labored long and are fearful. They are tired and have not eaten; having cast aside their armor, they are resting.

"Seventh, the generals are weak; the officials irresponsible; the officers and troops are not solid; the Three Armies are frequently frightened; and the forces lack any assistance.

"Eighth, their formations are not yet settled; their encampment not yet finished; or they are traversing dangerous territory and narrow defiles, half concealed and half exposed.

"In these eight conditions attack them without any doubts.

"There are six circumstances in which, without performing divination, you should avoid conflict.

"First, the land is broad and vast, the people wealthy and numerous.

"Second, the government loves the people, the ruler's beneficence extends and flows to all of them.

"Third, rewards are trusted, punishments are based upon investigation, and both are invariably implemented in a timely fashion.

"Fourth, people are ranked according to their military accomplishments, they award official positions to the Worthy and employ the able.

"Fifth, their forces are massive and their weapons and armor are all first rate.

"Sixth, they have the assistance of all their neighbors and the support of a powerful state.

"In general in these situations you are not a match for the enemy, so without doubt avoid them. This is what is meant by 'seeing possibility and advancing, knowing difficulty and withdrawing.'"28

The immediate leap from certain conditions to the judgment that an enemy might be attacked—an assessment obviously based upon experience, upon discerning a functionally debilitating trait—marks the Chinese theoretical approach to warfare and will again be seen in the tactical principles rigorously correlated with certain classifications of terrain. The symmetrical provision of conditions that are conducive or

Field Intelligence

detrimental to attack reflects the categorical methodology of paired analysis and is similarly found in many other writers, such as Sun Pin's analysis of cities that may or may not be attacked, essentially continuing the idea of classifying potential targets as "go/no go."

Sun Pin similarly compiled a list of critical weaknesses that might be detected in an approaching army in a chapter entitled "The General's Losses":

First, if he has lost the means for going and coming, he can be defeated.

Second, if he gathers together turbulent people and immediately employs them, if he stops retreating troops and immediately engages in battle with them, or if he lacks resources but acts as if he has resources, then he can be defeated.

Third, if he constantly wrangles over right and wrong and in planning affairs is argumentative and disputatious, he can be defeated.

Fourth, if his commands are not implemented, the masses not unified, he can be defeated.

Fifth, if his subordinates are not submissive and the masses not employable, he can be defeated.

Sixth, if the people regard the army with bitterness, he can be defeated.

Seventh, if the army is "old," he can be defeated.

Eighth, if the army is thinking about home, he can be defeated.

Ninth, if the soldiers are deserting, he can be defeated.

Eleventh, if the army has been frightened several times, he can be defeated.

Twelfth, if the soldiers' route requires difficult marching and the masses suffer, he can be defeated.

Thirteenth, if the army is focusing upon ravines and strongpoints and the masses are fatigued, he can be defeated.

Fourteenth, if he engages in battle but is unprepared, he can be defeated.

Fifteenth, if the sun is setting and the road is far while the masses are dispirited, he can be defeated.

Seventeenth, if the masses are afraid, he can be defeated.

Eighteenth, if commands are frequently changed and the masses are furtive, he can be defeated.

Nineteenth, if the army is disintegrating while the masses do not regard their generals and officials as capable, he can be defeated.

Twentieth, if they have been lucky several times and the masses are indolent, he can be defeated.

Twenty-first, if he has numerous doubts so the masses are doubtful, he can be defeated.

Twenty-second, if he hates to hear about his excesses, he can be defeated.

Twenty-third, if he appoints the incapable, he can be defeated.

Twenty-fourth, if their *ch'i* [spirit] has been injured from being long exposed on campaign, he can be defeated.

Twenty-fifth, if their minds are divided at the appointed time for battle, he can be defeated.

Twenty-sixth, if he relies upon the enemy becoming dispirited, he can be defeated.

Twenty-seventh, if he focuses upon harming others and relies upon ambushes and deceit, he can be defeated.

Twenty-ninth, if he deprecates the troops and the minds of the masses are hateful, he can be defeated.

Thirtieth, if he is unable to successfully deploy his forces while the route out is constricted, he can be defeated.

Thirty-first, if in the army's forward ranks are soldiers from the rear ranks and they are not coordinated and unified with the forward deployment, he can be defeated.

Thirty-second, if in engaging in battle, he is concerned about the front and the rear is therefore empty; or concerned about the rear, the front is empty; or concerned about the left, the right is empty; or concerned about the right, the left is empty, his engaging in battle being filled with worry, he can be defeated.[29]

The *Six Secret Teachings* also preserves extensive material of this type, critical to assessing the prospects for victory and predicting enemy behavior. The chapter entitled "Empty Fortifications" opens with a general statement of the need for accurate observation before arraying some concrete clues:

A general must know the Tao of Heaven above, the advantages of Earth below, and human affairs in the middle. He should mount high and look out far in order to see the enemy's changes and movements. Observe their fortifications, and then you will know whether they are empty or full. Observe their officers and troops, and then you will know whether they are coming or going.

Listen to see if their drums are silent, if their bells make no sound. Look to see whether there are many birds flying above the fortifications, if they weren't startled into flight. If there aren't any vapors overhead, you will certainly know the enemy has tricked you with dummies.

If enemy forces precipitously go off but not very far, and then return before assuming proper formation, they are using their officers and men too quickly. When they act too quickly, the forward and rear are unable to maintain good order. When they cannot maintain good order, the entire battle disposition will be in chaos. In such circumstances quickly dispatch troops to attack them. If you use a small number to strike a large force, they will certainly be defeated.

No doubt these simplified recommendations were based upon battlefield experience, for similar examples may be found in the historical writings from the ancient period. For example, after the battle between Chin and Ch'i recounted earlier, Ch'i's clandestine nighttime withdrawal was deduced from three sounds: the "happy chirping" of the birds, indicating a vacant terrain; groups of horses on the move; and the presence of birds just above the fortifications.[30]

Li Ch'uan, one of China's foremost military theoreticians, contemplated these issues in more abstract terms, focusing on the dynamic dichotomy of form and spirit:

When armies are mobilized they have form and spirit. Flags and pennants, weapons and armor are their visible form; wisdom, plots, plans, and affairs are matters of spirit. Being victorious in battle and successful in attacks is a matter of form, but the army's employment lies with spirit. Vacuity and fullness, change and transformation are accomplishments of spirit, but their achievement lies in form. Form is coarse but spirit subtle. Form without definitive characteristics cannot be mirrored, spirit free of affairs cannot be investigated. When form appears confused, external manifestations become delusory; when spirit is secretive and self-contained, affairs are internalized. Within these shapes spirit remains unseen; within self-contained spirit, affairs avoid discernment. Accordingly, ponder the following:

Dragging firewood to raise dust gives the appearance of numerous troops. Reducing the number of cookstoves and extinguishing fires give the appearance of fewness.[31] Being courageous but not firm, initially opposing an enemy only to quickly run off, are the shape of retreat. Posting scouts in critical locations throughout the mountains and marshes gives evidence of an advance. Oiled tents and pennon-topped screens are manifestations of strength.

Fallen flags and silent drums, the loneliness of desolation, are the shape of weakness.

Thus it is said that an army's form may be likened to a potter pulling clay or a smith forging metal. They make squares or circles, bells or sacrificial vessels. Metal and earth have no fixed nature, they acquire names through workmanship. Combat deployments have no inherent power, they assume their shape depending upon the enemy. "Thus the pinnacle of military deployment approaches the formless." When this is achieved, agents and spies will be unable to find a chink, the wisest strategists unable to plot against it.[32] [As Sun-tzu said:] "In accord with the enemy's disposition measures that achieve victory are imposed on the troops, but the troops are unable to fathom them. Men all know the disposition by which we attain victory, but no one knows the configuration through which we control victory." Form that does not proceed from spirit is unable to change and transform; spirit not based upon the enemy is unable to create wise plans. Thus water configures its form in accord with the terrain, the army controls its victory in accord with the enemy.[33]

Since an army's organization, discipline, and command are all reflected in their flags and drums, the latter immediately provide clues for evaluating enemy forces and estimating the possibilities for victory. For example, the *Six Secret Teachings* preserves an assessment based upon the flags and drums in combination with more conventional factors:

When the Three Armies are well ordered; the deployment's strategic configuration of power solid, with deep moats and high ramparts, and they also enjoy the advantage of high winds and heavy rain; the army is untroubled; the signal flags and pennants point to the front; the sound of the gongs and bells rises up and is clear; and the sound of the small and large drums clearly rises—these are indications of the armies having obtained spiritual, enlightened assistance, foretelling a great victory.

When their formations are not solid; their flags and pennants confused and entangled with each other; they go contrary to the advantages of high wind and heavy rain; their officers and troops are terrified; their war horses have been frightened and run off; their military chariots have broken axles; the sound of their gongs and bells sinks down and is murky; the sound of their drums is wet and damp—these are indications foretelling a great defeat.

In a famous dictum Sun-tzu enjoined, "Do not intercept well-ordered flags; do not attack well-regulated formations."[34]

However, in contrast to feigned disorder, true confusion and chaos are an invitation to victory and a sign that even numerically superior forces can be successfully attacked, as Wu Ch'i observed in two well-known passages:

> If their troops approach yelling and screaming, their flags and pennants in confusion, while some of their units move of their own accord and others stop, some weapons held vertically, others horizontally—if they pursue our retreating troops as if they are afraid they will not reach us, or seeing advantage are afraid of not gaining it, this marks a stupid general. Even if his troops are numerous, they can be taken. . . .
>
> If the enemy approaches in reckless disarray, unthinking; if their flags and banners are confused and in disorder; and if their men and horses frequently look about, then one unit can attack ten of theirs, invariably causing them to be helpless.[35]

A retreating force presents the commander with a particularly complex dilemma because failing to exploit the victory allows an already vanquished enemy time and opportunity to regroup and perhaps counterattack, but overzealous pursuit might disorder one's own forces, making them vulnerable to a counterattack or ambush. Moreover, feigned retreats designed to induce such disorder always being a possibility, they were already much pondered in such classic writings as the *Ssu-ma Fa* and *Wu-tzu* and remained a critical concern throughout China's military history. Accordingly, it fell to commanders to decipher whether they were witnessing real enemy retreats or mere lures. The Northern Sung *Hu-ling Ching* summarized the parameters for such judgments in a chapter entitled "Pursuit of the Enemy":

> When an enemy flees during an engagement, there are five situations in which you can pursue them.
>
> First, when their fighting spirit has abated.
>
> Second, when their infantry and cavalry have scattered chaotically, many of the fleeing soldiers stumble and fall, and they do not reform their units.
>
> Third, when they run off to their native villages or race to their fortifications.
>
> Fourth, when their supplies and mailed troops are dispersed without being reassembled.
>
> Fifth, when their commanding general has already died.
>
> There are six situations in which you cannot pursue them.

First, even though they are defeated, if their fighting spirit has not abated.

Second, if the water in old streams and irrigation channels that the enemy have already crossed over suddenly stops flowing.

Third, when the ranks and formations of a defeated, fleeing enemy are not particular disordered.

Fourth, if in fleeing, the officials and officers are not really stumbling or falling nor are their infantry and cavalry intermixed.

Fifth, if in fleeing, they lack an escape route while mountains and valleys lie in all directions about them.[36]

Sixth, the road is exhausted and their food used up, yet their officials and officers have not scattered very much.

When the enemy can be pursued, you should urgently pursue them. When the enemy should not be pursued, you should solidify your walls and observe them until there is some change in the relative advantages and disadvantages. Wait to advance until the moment when raising your forces will prove advantageous and damage their retreat.

By the Northern Sung dynasty Hsü Tung (976–1018) was thus able to effectively gather numerous individual pronouncements on assessing enemy strength, organization, intentions, condition, and vulnerability and integrate them into several categories, prefaced by some preliminary observations, in his *Hu-ling Ching*.[37] Moreover, at this time the *Seven Military Classics*, although not yet formally collected into one integrated volume, were well known and commentaries on Sun-tzu's *Art of War* were flourishing. Because he had the writings of the great Li Ch'uan and employed his insights extensively, Hsü Tung's chapters may be viewed as the culmination of the tradition, as will become clear as the following selections unfold. The first, entitled "Five Vital Points," expands the concept of a vital point *(chi)*, the subtle crux or moment when (as already discussed) incipient change can be actualized, where minimal forces can have maximum effect. The idea, although found in philosophical writings such as the *Chuang-tzu* as well, was perhaps first fully enunciated in the *Wu-tzu*:

In general, warfare has four vital points: *ch'i*, terrain, affairs, and strength. When the masses of the Three Armies, the million soldiers of the forces, are strategically deployed in appropriate formations according to varying degrees of strength by one man, this is termed the "vital point of *ch'i*."

When the road is narrow and the way perilous, when famous mountains present great obstacles, and if ten men defend a place a thousand cannot pass, this is termed a "vital point of earth."

Being good at controlling clandestine operatives, with a few light troops harassing the enemy, causing them to scatter, and forcing rulers and ministers to feel mutual annoyance, higher and lower ranks to reproach each other, this is termed the "vital point of affairs."

When the chariots have solid axles and secure pins, the boats well-suited rudders and oars, the officers are thoroughly familiar with the fighting formations, and the horses practiced in pursuit and maneuvers, this is termed the "vital point of strength."[38]

Hsü Tung transformed Wu Ch'i's four vital points into five, two of which focus on intelligence operations:

Military affairs have five vital points: the first is terrain; the second, affairs; the third, strategic power; the fourth, advantage; and the fifth, spiritualness.

When in arraying your encampments and deploying into formation, you occupy the strategic points first and thus compel the enemy to advance against the advantages conferred by your strategic power, this is termed the "vital point of terrain."

If you carefully ferret out the enemy's affairs and then exploit this knowledge to deceive the enemy by apparently acting in accord with their expectations without allowing them to realize it, this is referred to as the "vital point of affairs."

When you can excite the spirit [ch'i] of ten men so that they may be employed as if they were a hundred, and similarly a hundred as if they were a thousand, so that the awesomeness of your army's name and its ch'i resounds like thunder and whoever opposes you will be destroyed, this is termed the "vital point of strategic power."

When provisions and fodder have been massively accumulated, the men and horses well trained, and supply routes to the enemy's borders are everywhere open and advantageous, this is termed the "vital point of advantage."

When the enemy successfully estimates your strength to the front but miscalculates about the rear, or proves accurate when far off but fails when you are near, while they are unable to determine the nature and direction of your actions, this is termed the "vital point of spirituality."

Anyone who employed the army in accord with these five points in reacting to their enemies never proved incapable of assaulting cities and occupying territory.[39]

Once defined, Hsü Tung's critical points may be employed to evaluate enemy forces by their coherence or deviation:

Those who employ their officers and troops without timely constraints can be attacked.[40] Those whose soldiers and horses miss the proper time for eating can be attacked. Those who establish encampments on terrain that lacks convenient access can be attacked. Those who are noisy and clamoring when deploying into formation, who do not stop when constrained, can be attacked. Those whose fortified encampments lack deep springs or streams can be attacked. Those who cannot avoid moving on inauspicious days and baleful lunar phases can be attacked. Those whose generals argue over their achievements can be attacked. Those who expel their planning officers can be attacked. Those whose officials are resentful and high officers angry can be attacked. Those whose soldiers do not appropriately respond to challenges can be attacked.

If you are able to observe any of these ten, attack without doubt. Sun-tzu said, "Observe them to know their patterns of movement and stopping."[41] This is what he meant. If you are unable to observe the enemy's nature and situation, yet recklessly engage in battle, it is termed "offering your troops to the enemy."[42]

Just as Wu Ch'i listed favorable and unfavorable circumstances for attacking an enemy, Hsü Tung enumerated ten exploitable conditions and five negative situations. Those listed in "Ten Possible Attacks" focus on the enemy's beliefs, morale, organization, and unity:

First, an enemy that believes in ghosts and frequently prays must be harboring doubts and fears because they are incapable of properly employing men.

Second, the enemy concentrates upon seasonal concordances, selecting appropriate geomantic positions, and observing cloud phenomena without concerning themselves with topographical characteristics, such as difficult or easy, or carefully examining whether they are acting in accord with or contrary to human hearts.[43]

Third, when halting, the enemy is obsessed with advantages of terrain but unable to maintain proper order, ensure adherence to commands, or impose strict precautions among the troops.

Fourth, the army's troops are constantly moving and shifting about whether in camp or deployed in formation. They are mostly afraid and doubtful.

Fifth, the commander's announcements lack substance, affairs are designed to profit him, the officials are annoyed, and the officers are angry.

Sixth, the generals and officials are dissipated and dilatory.
Seventh, the terrain on which they have established their encampment lacks defensible terrain in all four directions.
Eighth, the general treats his subordinates unceremoniously.
Ninth, rewards and punishments have been overturned.
Tenth, their generals and officers are mostly light.
However, if you want to launch a sudden attack against them, you must first have your spies *[hsi jen]* secretly ferret out their actual conditions in order to exploit them. Only then will your attacks invariably strike home. It would also be appropriate for your own forces to regard these ten as a warning.[44]

Corresponding to conditions susceptible to attack are five whose problematic aspects suggest the enemy are trying to deceive your reconnaissance agents and lure your forces into a trap:

First, when your two armies are separated by some kilometers and you observe that the enemy are tired, weak, negligent, and lazy, their commands and orders not being respected, you may therefore conclude the enemy are vulnerable to attack. However, if you do not yet know the terrain's configuration or the enemy's disposition of power—whether there are stagnant expanses of water or treacherous marshes, the roads twist and turn back upon themselves, the heights and lowlands mutually recede into each other, or the degree of forestation and heavy vegetation—you should respond as if the enemy is deliberately manifesting weakness while concealing strength, displaying laxity while hiding good order, showing a lack of planning while concealing wisdom, and showing being far off while their core forces are nearby. When they act thus without retreating for a long time, they must be executing an unorthodox strategy.

Second, when the engagement has neither been long nor have the enemy's forces sustained significant damage, yet they abandon their drums and flags to hurriedly race off, do not pursue them, for there are certainly forces concealed in ambush.

Third, when prisoners taken by the enemy suddenly escape and return with information about the enemy's activities or we capture enemy prisoners who similarly tell us about the enemy's activities, these are both enemy plots. Do not trust such reports.

Fourth, when the enemy's forces, exploiting their strategic power, drum the advance and press forward to assault us, encourage your troops to maintain a solid defense and await them. Engaging in battle with soldiers exploiting their strategic power, whose morale is awesome and spirit exhilarated, is not advantageous.

Fifth, if the enemy establishes their formations without regard to being on fatal terrain while their drums and flags are well ordered and constrained.[45]

The third item attests to the common employment of disinformation through priming prisoners who are then allowed to escape and suddenly capturing prisoners who willingly offer information, methods espoused by many of the later military theorists.

A long-range method for assessing an enemy's strength and determining their basic movements was observing the dust clouds raised by their activities. Although no doubt summarizing common knowledge at the end of the Spring and Autumn period, Sun-tzu drew attention to its potential with the first theoretical discussion: "If dust rises high up in a sharply defined column, chariots are coming. If it is low and broad, the infantry is advancing. If it is dispersed in thin shafts, they are gathering firewood. If it is sparse, coming and going, they are encamping."[46]

Hsü Tung, being an ardent student of Sun-tzu, expanded his correlations to subsume the new force components of the cavalry and the evolution of maneuver and unorthodox tactics over the centuries to systematically derive fundamental intelligence about the enemy. His *Hu-ling Ching* chapter entitled "Analyzing Dust" provides the most sophisticated and comprehensive example of this observational science.

When the enemy first approaches, if the dust rises in streams but is dispersed, they are dragging brushwood. If it rises up likes ears of grain and jumps about chaotically, chariots are coming. If the dust is thick and heavy, swirling and turbulent as it rises up, cavalry are coming. If it is low and broad, spreading and diffuse as it rises, infantry are advancing.

When the army is small and the dust is scattered and chaotic, it means the units are not closely ordered. If the troops are numerous but the dust clear, it means the units are well ordered and the general's commands systematic. If dust arises to the front and rear, left and right, it means they are employing their troops without any consistent method.

When the army moves and the dust rises in streaks without dispersing, or when the army halts and the dust also stops, it is because the general's awesomeness and virtue have caused the units to be strictly ordered. If when they encamp or set out their deployments dust rises up and flies off, mount defenses against those places where it originated because enemy forces will certainly be approaching in ambush there. Observing the enemy through rising dust is thus a technique for estimating the enemy's forces and seizing victory.

Although a number of military formations—such as square, round, goose, eagle, and elongated—were frequently discussed and presumably employed by the classic writers, including Sun-tzu and Sun Pin, reconnaissance observations always tended to focus upon how the enemy exploited the configuration of terrain and whether the process of deploying their troops was orderly or haphazard. In "Analyzing Enemy Formations" Hsü Tung moves from the simple elongated formation to two common types of terrain—tenable and mountainous:

When the enemy's deployment is somewhat elongated and marked by a thin center, from a firm position opposing their flanks our elite forces should first forcefully penetrate the enemy's heart. When their strength wanes, increase the number of soldiers advancing against them. Wait for the enemy to initiate some minor movement on the flanks to rescue the center, and then withdraw your assault troops and reestablish the solidity of your formations. Wait until their deployments again begin to shift, then signal your flanking troops to take advantage of it.

If the enemy deploys well-ordered, apparently unified units on fatal terrain, their commander is worthy and the troops picked, so you cannot launch an attack against them. However, if their flags move about chaotically, the commander is stupid and incapable of selecting advantageous terrain, causing uneasiness in their units. You can therefore press them and then launch an assault that will certainly prove victorious.

However, if they deploy on tenable ground where it is convenient for the men and horses to enter and exit, their lines are strictly ordered, their flags and pennants like a picture, and their drums and gongs respond to the measures without any clamoring or shouting, their commanding general is executing preplanned tactics and excels at gaining advantages of terrain, so you cannot carelessly attack. Conversely, if they deploy on tenable ground but their orders are not strict, their formations undisciplined, and their advancing and retreating disordered, it indicates that internally the general is incapable of understanding military administration, and externally cannot select advantageous terrain. The minds of the officers and troops will certainly not be stalwart, so by unleashing some troops to mount a sudden strike, you will certainly be victorious.

If the enemy deploys where there are mountains to both sides but cannot fully occupy the valley, you can attack them. Anyone who arrays his formations but is incapable of according with the strategic advantages of the terrain can be attacked. Thus among those who excel in warfare there were none who did not follow these indications to analyze the possibilities of victory and defeat.

Every encampment represented both a threat and a target of opportunity, depending upon the commander's skill in selecting the terrain and organizing his defensive forces. Surprise was generally considered essential to any assault, but observational analysis might reveal fatal weaknesses that might easily be exploited:

When the supply routes into the enemy's encampment are not convenient, it will be advantageous to mount a sustained defense. When the enemy has encamped on high, dry terrain but not concerned themselves with the advantages of water supplied from a spring, you can wait them out because the men and horses will grow thirsty after some time. If the encampment benefits from springs but the terrain is wet, they can be pressed. If the configuration of terrain about their encampment is not conducive to entering and exiting, you can attack them. If their encampment is large and spread out while the number of troops is few, you can assault them. But if their encampment has a tight perimeter with numerous troops, you cannot take them lightly. If their perimeter defenses are not uniform, attack their gaps. If the enemy's encampment has convenient access in all directions and benefits from ample water and grass, they cannot be taken lightly. This is the method for analyzing enemy encampments.[47]

The existence of such fundamental knowledge about enemy behavior and principles for evaluating never guaranteed that such hard-won perceptions would be exploited. For example, in the Sung dynasty Liu K'ai's astute deductions were thoroughly frustrated:

As the emperor had just ordered a major campaign of rectification in the north, Liu K'ai's company was employed in forwarding provisions to the army. When the imperial forces were about to reach Chuo-chou, a Khitan leader in command of ten thousand cavalry came up and engaged Mi Hsin, Liu's commander, in a standoff. Somewhat thereafter the Khitan leader dispatched an emissary to pretend to discuss terms of surrender. Liu K'ai said to Mi Hsin: "The *Art of War* states, 'One who requests peace without conditions has a plot.' They certainly have some secret plot. If you urgently attack them, we will certainly be victorious." However, Mi Hsin was doubtful and indecisive. Two days later the rebels again brought their troops up and sought to provoke an engagement. Observers later learned that the Khitan had, in fact, run out of arrows and been awaiting resupply from Yu-chou.[48]

This passage incidentally provides evidence that military officials were well versed in the *Art of War* but had not necessarily memorized it exactly because the closest statement to be found therein advises that "one who has emissaries come forth with offerings wants to rest for a while."[49]

However well conceived and experientially based Sun-tzu's and Wu-tzu's methods, with the passing of centuries their tactics became increasingly well known and could therefore be balked by knowledgeable commanders anticipating the enemy's actions based upon the situation's parameters. Thus in the Sung dynasty—although certainly earlier in practice—Hsü Tung strongly advocated operating contrary to normal expectations, exploiting the predictable range of interpretations to achieve the surprise necessary for decisive victory, thereby frustrating the enemy's intelligence and planning cycle. "Contrary Employment of Ancient Methods" takes as its basis several detailed statements found in Sun-tzu's *Art of War* and Wu Ch'i's observations in the *Wu-tzu:*

One who studies ancient tactics and employs the army in accord with their methods is no different from someone who glues up the tuning stops and yet tries to play a zither. I have never heard of anyone being successful. The acumen of strategists lies in penetrating the subtle amid unfolding change and discerning the concordant and contrary. Now whenever mobilizing the army, you must first employ spies to investigate whether the enemy's commanding general is talented or not. If instead of implementing tactics, he merely relies on courage to employ the army, you can resort to ancient methods to conquer him. However, if the commanding general excels in employing ancient tactics, you should use tactics that contradict the ancient methods to defeat him.

Now in the army's unorthodox employment nothing is more unorthodox than establishing ambushes. Furthermore, in the unorthodoxy of establishing ambushes, nothing is more unorthodox than new wisdom. However, it is not that this new wisdom fails to take antiquity as its teacher, but that it contravenes it. When the ancients analyzed an approaching enemy, before the fronts engaged in battle they first provoked them with some lower-ranking but courageous men to observe whether the commands conveyed by their signal flags and drums were unified or disordered; whether their officers and horses were strong or weak; whether their deployments were distorted or correct; whether their subformations were strictly ordered or chaotic; and whether their speech was clamoring or subdued, in order to determine whether they could be victorious or not. Thus the ancient tactics state: "If their troops approach yelling and screaming, their flags and pennants in confusion, while some of their units move of their own accord and others stop, some weapons held vertically, others horizontally—if they pursue our retreating troops as if they are afraid they will not reach us, or seeing advantage are afraid of not gaining it, this certainly marks a general without tactics. Even if his troops are numerous they can be taken."[50] Although the ancients achieved success in this way, if someone analyzes us and we apparently act in accord with such analyses, we can deploy troops in ambush to await them. Manifest some false appearance, wait for them to send forth their troops, and then spring your ambush to attack them.

The ancient manuals state: "Those who stand about leaning on their weapons are hungry. Those who draw water and drink first are thirsty. Those who see potential gain but do not advance are tired. If the army is turbulent, the general lacks severity. Those whose flags move about are in chaos. Those whose officers are resentful are tired. If they hang up their cooking utensils and do not return to camp, they are an exhausted invader. One whose troops repeatedly congregate in small groups here and there, whispering together, has lost the masses.[51] Those who frequently look about have lost their unit integrity. One who has emissaries come forth with offerings wants to rest for a while." The ancients analyzed men in this fashion, but today it is different. Armies presently segment off elite, spirited warriors and officers to establish ambushes at strategic choke points, then have their tired and wounded act hungry and thirsty, or pretend they have lost their unitary organization, or frequently move their flags about. They startle and perturb their troops a few times, or have their officers talk clamorously, all in order to respond as predicted by the enemy's analysis. If they suddenly send their army forth to attack you, secretly spring your preestablished ambushes and unexpectedly strike them.

[Wu-tzu's] ancient methods state: "When the enemy has just arrived and their battle formations are not yet properly deployed, they can be attacked. When they have traveled a great distance and the rearguard has not yet had time to rest, they can be attacked. When they are crossing ridges or traversing ravines, half concealed, half exposed, they can be attacked. When fording rivers and only half of them have crossed, they can be attacked. On narrow and confined roads they can be attacked. If their flags and banners move about chaotically, they can be attacked. When their formations frequently move about, they can be attacked."[52] However, in our case this isn't true. When we haven't fully deployed into our final disposition, we can establish ambushes on the four sides. When traveling a great distance without resting, we can establish ambushes in the middle. We can also establish ambushes when half hidden and half exposed on mountain ridges, in long forests, and along sandy valleys. When fording a river, even with half still not yet across, we can establish ambushes along the banks and ridges. Along narrow and confined roads we can establish ambushes both ahead and behind. When our flags chaotically move about and our formations frequently shift, we can establish ambushes both to the fore and rear.

When a defeated enemy flees but the army dares not offer pursuit, it is to prevent being ambushed. [Sun-tzu's] ancient methods state: "When birds take flight, there is an ambush. If large numbers of trees move, the enemy are approaching."[53] However, it's not invariably the case that there is an ambush or troops coming. Perhaps they want to create a feigned army. If we have already fled, we can order many old and weak soldiers to shake numerous trees, startle birds into flight, and create similar phenomena. The *Art of War* states: "One who seeks peace without setting any prior conditions is executing a stratagem. One whose troops half advance and half retreat is enticing you." This also stemmed from large armies sneaking away but, fearing pursuers to the rear, establishing such techniques to cause doubt.

When analyzing an enemy based upon their manifestations, give great thought to contravening the methods of the ancients. Make them numerous and employ them among men. Thus tactics are like a wagon carrying goods: The wagon's movement depends upon the wheels turning, but the direction as north, south, east, west proceeds from man. Thus it is clear that ancient tactics cannot be taken up and employed.

Hsü Tung's chapters clearly provide a late Sung perspective on the realities of military combat in an uncertain age of warfare, and the chapter thus preserves a final, sophisticated approach to exploiting anticipated enemy intelligence analyses. However, he uncritically ignores Sun-tzu's discussions on the formless and unorthodox, especially as encapsulated in "Strategic Military Power," which stress them as the foundation for mystifying the enemy, as well as other classical writers, such as Li Wei-kung, who extensively analyzed the inherent relationship between expectation and the unorthodox. Certainly Sun-tzu never intended his tactical principles to be taken as definitive or single-mindedly empl)yed, for he clearly stated: "A victorious battle strategy is not repeated, the configurations of response are inexhaustible."[54]

The Role and Importance of *Ch'i*

In the *Questions and Replies* the second T'ang emperor is quoted as stating he evaluates others by using himself as a reference point: "When I was about to engage in battle, I first evaluated the enemy's mind by comparing it with my mind to determine who was more thoroughly prepared. Only after that could I know his situation. To evaluate the enemy's *ch'i*, I compared it with our own to determine who was more controlled. Only then could I know myself. For this reason, 'know them and know yourself' is the great essence of the military strategists."[55] The emperor's statement briefly refers to the question of the enemy's *ch'i* (or spirit), the critical component in the Chinese psychology of warfare that was the subject of extensive writing and theorizing. In essence, it was vital to determine the enemy's psychological energy, manipulate the situation to exploit any weakness or dissipation, and compel their forces into enervating and demoralizing activities before engaging in battle. Among intelligence objectives, it ranked paramount with troop strength and the enemy's commander and could never be neglected.

The first historical passage to raise the concept of *ch'i* in a military context is a *Tso Chuan* entry for a seventh century B C. event that prompted discussion for millennia thereafter, even being adopted in the late Sung to illustrate *ch'i*'s psychodynamics:

> During the Spring and Autumn period, the state of Ch'i attacked the state of Lü. Duke Chuang, commanding Lü's forces, was about to commit the army to battle when Ts'ao Kuei requested permission to join him. The Duke had him ride in his chariot and went into battle at Ch'ang-shao. The duke was about to have the drums sound the advance when Ts'ao Kuei said to him, "Not yet." Ch'i sounded their drums three times then Ts'ao said, "Now." They

beat the drums and engaged in combat, and Ch'i's army was severely defeated.

The duke inquired why Ts'ao Kuei had delayed the drums. Ts'ao replied: "Combat is a matter of courageous *ch'i*. A single drumming arouses the soldiers' *ch'i*, with a second it abates, and with a third it is exhausted. They were exhausted while we were vigorous, so we conquered them."[56]

The military thinkers, who well understood the difficulty of compelling men to engage in combat, identified *ch'i* as the psychophysical component whose surge made violent actions possible. Sun-tzu was perhaps the first to recognize and describe the critical role of spirit and courage in battle, but the other *Seven Military Classics* and some of the early philosophical writings similarly pondered ways to nurture and manipulate a true combative spirit. Among the philosophers Mencius also gained fame for cultivating his "overflowing *ch'i*," although his conception differed significantly from that of the martial theorists.[57]

The concept of *ch'i*—essentially the vital energy of life—is integral to many fields of Chinese thought, ranging from metaphysics to medicine, science to religion. A traditional view envisions the character as originally representing fragrant vapors rising from steaming rice; therefore *ch'i* symbolizes nourishment in every sense. (The modern character is written with a component that means "rice.") However, the actual origins are obscure and a matter of much speculation that looks to such natural phenomena as vapors and clouds for possible images. The character itself seems to have appeared late in the Spring and Autumn, becoming frequent only in the Warring States period.

The early *Ssu-ma Fa* preserves a succinct analysis of the role of *ch'i* in soldiers: "In general, in battle one endures through strength, and gains victory through spirit. One can endure with a solid defense, but will achieve victory through being endangered. When the heart's foundation is solid, a new surge of *ch'i* will bring victory. With armor one is secure; with weapons one attains victory. When men have their minds set on victory, all they see is the enemy. When men have their minds filled with fear, all they see is their fear."[58] Men oblivious to death and committed to victory fight courageously, becoming extremely powerful in comparison to reluctant soldiers hoping to avoid wounds and death. Wu Ch'i embodied this insight with an image that greatly impacted the popular mind ever after: "I have heard that men have strengths and weaknesses, that their *ch'i* flourishes and ebbs. Now if there is a murderous villain hidden in the woods, even though a thousand men pursue him, they all look around like owls and glance about like wolves. Why? They are afraid that violence will erupt and harm them personally. Thus one man oblivious to life and death can frighten a thousand."[59]

The late Warring States *Wei Liao-tzu* transposed the image into the ordinary life experience of the populous marketplace: "If a warrior wields a sword to strike people in the marketplace, among ten thousand people there will not be anyone who doesn't avoid him. If I say it's not that only one man is courageous, but that the ten thousand are unlike him, what is the reason? Being committed to dying and being committed to seeking life are not comparable."[60]

Sun-tzu analyzed the importance of recognizing and exploiting the enemy's *ch'i* state in a famous passage widely known from the Warring States on: "The *ch'i* of the Three Armies can be snatched away; the commanding general's mind can be seized. For this reason in the morning their *ch'i* is ardent; during the day their *ch'i* becomes indolent; at dusk their *ch'i* is exhausted. Thus one who excels at employing the army avoids their ardent *ch'i* and strikes when it is indolent or exhausted. This is the way to manipulate *ch'i*." However, Sun-tzu's passage—his only direct comment upon *ch'i*, even though the entire *Art of War* may be seen as directed toward recognizing and manipulating it—was often misinterpreted as simply meaning attacks should be made only late in the day, prompting the following T'ang dynasty discussion on the extended meaning and implications of his analysis:

T'ang T'ai-tsung said: "Sun-tzu spoke about strategies by which the *ch'i* of the Three Armies may be snatched away: 'In the morning their *ch'i* is ardent; during the day their *ch'i* becomes indolent; and at dusk their *ch'i* is exhausted. One who excels at employing the army avoids their ardent *ch'i* and strikes when it is indolent or exhausted.' How is this?"

Li Ching said: "Whoever has life and a natural endowment of blood, if they die without a second thought when the drums are sounded to do battle, it is the *ch'i* that causes it to be so. Thus methods for employing the army require first investigating our own officers and troops, stimulating our *ch'i* for victory, and only then attacking the enemy. Among Wu Ch'i's four vital points, the vital point of *ch'i* is foremost. There is no other Tao. If you can cause your men to want to fight themselves, no one will be able to oppose their ardor.

"What Sun-tzu meant by the *ch'i* being ardent in the morning is not limited to those hours alone. He used the beginning and end of the day as an analogy. In general, if the drum has been sounded three times but the enemy's *ch'i* has neither declined nor become depleted, then how can you cause it to invariably become indolent or exhausted? Probably those who study the text merely recite the empty words and are misled by the enemy. If one could enlighten them with the principles for snatching away the *ch'i*, the army could be entrusted to them."[61]

The tactical discussion found in "Spirit in Warfare" from the *Hundred Unorthodox Strategies* provides a characterization of *ch'i* dynamics:

The means by which the commanding general wages warfare is his soldiers; the means by which the soldiers engage in combat is their *ch'i*. The means by which *ch'i* proves victorious is the beating of the war drums. Since the drums are capable of inciting the *ch'i* of the officers and troops, they should not be incessantly employed. If employed too many times, the soldiers' *ch'i* will easily decline. Similarly, they cannot be employed when too far away from the enemy. If too far, the soldier's strength will easily be exhausted. You must estimate when the enemy will be within sixty or seventy paces and then beat the drums to signal the officers and troops to advance into combat. If the enemy's *ch'i* abates while yours surges, their defeat will be certain. A tactical principle from the *Wei Liao-tzu* states, "When their *ch'i* is substantial they will fight; when their *ch'i* has been snatched away they will run off."[62]

This brief analysis opens and closes by essentially splitting an observation from the *Wei Liao-tzu*: "Now the means by which the general fights is the people; the means by which the people fight is their *ch'i*. When their *ch'i* is substantial they will fight; when their *ch'i* has been snatched away they will run off."

The core insight found throughout such passages is the need to avoid stimulating the army's *ch'i* too early, causing it to fruitlessly peak and then diminish. As Wu Ch'i said, *ch'i* ebbs and flourishes, and success in combat depends upon it reaching a zenith just at the moment of battle. The Chinese military writings thus emphasize measures to manipulate the enemy until they become physically and emotionally exhausted, until their spirit or "will to fight" so severely diminishes that victory becomes certain. When men are well trained, rested, properly fed, clothed, and equipped, if their spirits are roused, they will fight vigorously. However, if physical or material conditions have blunted their spirit, if there is any imbalance in the relationship between command and troops, or if for any reason they have lost their motivation, they will be defeated.

Correlatively, the commanding general must avoid the enemy when their spirits are strong, such as early in the day, and exploit any opportunity presented by their diminishment, attacking when they no longer have any inclination to fight, such as when about to return to camp. Prolonged warfare can lead only to enervation; therefore, careful planning to guarantee the swift execution of campaign strategy is paramount. Certain situations—such as being thrust onto fatal terrain where a desperate battle must be fought—are conducive to eliciting the army's greatest efforts. Others are debilitating, dangerous, even fatal, and must be scrupulously avoided.

Sun Pin's *Military Methods* also contains an important chapter on *ch'i*, the first part of which describes the process of attaining the requisite levels as the time for battle approaches: "When you form the army and assemble the masses, concentrate upon stimulating their *ch'i*. When you again decamp and reassemble the army, concentrate upon ordering the soldiers and sharpening their *ch'i*. When you approach the border and draw near the enemy, concentrate upon honing their *ch'i*. When the day for battle has been set, concentrate upon making their *ch'i* decisive. When the day for battle is at hand, concentrate upon expanding their *ch'i*."[63]

Given the gravity of psychologically preparing for battle, a lack of similar commitment in an enemy would immediately become obvious, indicated by external signs such as noted by the *Wei Liao-tzu:* "One who occupies ravines lacks the mind to do battle. One who lightly provokes a battle lacks fullness of *ch'i*. One who is belligerent in battle lacks soldiers capable of victory."

In Sun-tzu's view the special case of hopeless circumstances, rather than causing the soldiers to despair, can be exploited to elicit an ultimate effort once the soldiers resign or even commit themselves to certain death. The psychological difficulty of course lies in convincing them there is no hope of survival without provoking the loss of their will to fight (as frequently happened throughout history). Although many military writers remarked upon the psychology of spirit, or *ch'i*, in desperate battles, Sun-tzu was probably the first to consciously articulate it as an operational principle. In the *Art of War* he states:

Cast them into positions from which there is nowhere to go and they will die without retreating. If there is no escape from death, the officers and soldiers will fully exhaust their strength.

When the soldiers and officers have penetrated deeply into enemy territory they will cling together. When there is no alternative they will fight. Cast them into hopeless situations and they will be preserved; have them penetrate fatal terrain and they will live. Only after the masses have penetrated dangerous terrain will they be able to craft victory out of defeat.

For this reason even though the soldiers are not instructed, they are prepared; without seeking it, their cooperation is obtained; without covenants they are close together; without orders being issued, they are reliable. Prohibit omens, eliminate doubt so that they will die without other thoughts. Thus it is the nature of the army to defend when encircled, to fight fervently when unavoidable, and to follow orders when compelled by circumstances.[64]

Whenever fatal terrain is encountered or an enemy is surrounded, allowances must similarly be made for a possible resurgence in the enemy's spirit and then suddenly encountering fierce opposition.

Although many of the specific traits observed in enemy armies enumerated by the various writers are obviously indications of the army's *ch'i*, the most comprehensive and focused chapter appears in the *Six Secret Teachings*. Entitled "The Army's Indications," it interprets their *ch'i* in terms of discipline and mental state, translating those indications into predispositions for victory or defeat:

King Wu asked the T'ai Kung: "Before engaging in battle, I want to first know the enemy's strengths and weaknesses, to foresee indications of victory or defeat. How can this be done?"

The T'ai Kung replied: "Indications of victory or defeat will be first manifest in their spirit *[ch'i]*. The enlightened general will investigate them, for they will be evidenced in the men.

"Clearly observe the enemy's coming and going, advancing and withdrawing. Investigate their movements and periods at rest, whether they speak about portents, what the officers and troops report. If the Three Armies are exhilarated; the officers and troops fear the laws; respect the general's commands; rejoice with each other in destroying the enemy; boast to each other about their courage and ferocity; and praise each other for their awesomeness and martial demeanor—these are indications of a strong enemy.

"If the Three Armies have been startled a number of times, the officers and troops no longer maintaining good order; they terrify each other with stories about the enemy's strength; they speak to each other about the disadvantages; they anxiously look about at each other, listening carefully; they talk incessantly of ill omens, a myriad mouths confusing each other; they fear neither laws nor orders, and do not regard their general seriously—these are indications of weakness.

"When the Three Armies are well ordered; the deployment's strategic configuration of power solid, with deep moats and high ramparts; and moreover they enjoy the advantages of high winds and heavy rain, while the army is untroubled the signal flags and pennants point to the front; the sound of the gongs and bells rises up and is clear; and the sound of the small and large drums clearly rises—these are indications of having obtained spiritual, enlightened assistance, foretelling a great victory.

"When their formations are not solid; their flags and pennants confused and entangled with each other; they go contrary to the advantages of high wind and heavy rain; their officers and troops are terrified; and their *ch'i* broken while they are not unified; their war horses have been frightened and run off; their military chariots have broken axles; the sound of their gongs and bells sinks down and is murky; the sound of their drums is wet and damp— these are indications foretelling a great defeat."

Commanders

As warfare evolved and campaign armies exceeded one hundred thousand men early in the Warring States period, field commanders assumed ever greater importance in any evaluative scheme. Sun-tzu early asserted that character flaws would readily doom an army to defeat: "The general is the supporting pillar of state. If his talents are all-encompassing, the state will invariably be strong. If the supporting pillar is marked by fissures, the state will invariably grow weak."[65] Consequently, all the military writers, but especially Sun-tzu, Sun Pin, and the T'ai Kung, devoted extensive passages to enumerating the field commander's requisite characteristics—mainly focusing upon courage, wisdom, righteousness, benevolence, and credibility—and discussed such exploitable flaws as short-sightedness, arrogance, and a tendency to become easily angered.[66] Sun-tzu began the tradition of not just isolating flaws and correlating them with probable consequences, but also identifying techniques for exploiting them: "Generals have five dangerous character traits. One committed to dying can be slain. One committed to living can be captured. One easily angered and hasty to act can be insulted. One obsessed with being scrupulous and untainted can be shamed. One who loves the people can be troubled."[67]

Roughly a century later Wu Ch'i amplified Sun-tzu's views in a chapter that integrated command considerations with the army's behavioral characteristics:

In general the essentials of battle are as follows: You must first attempt to divine the enemy's general and evaluate his talent. In accord with the situation exploit the strategic imbalance of power, for then you will not labor but still achieve results.

A commanding general who is stupid and trusting can be deceived and entrapped. One who is greedy and unconcerned about reputation can be given gifts and bribed. One who easily changes his mind and lacks real plans can be labored and distressed.

If the upper ranks are wealthy and arrogant, while the lower ranks are poor and resentful, they can be separated and divided. If their advancing and withdrawing are often marked by doubt and the troops have no one to rely on, they can be shocked into running off. If the officers despise their commanding general and are intent on returning home, by blocking off the easy roads and leaving the treacherous ones open, they can be attacked and captured.

If the terrain over which they advance is easy, but the road for withdrawal difficult, they can be forced to come forward. If the way to advance is difficult, but the road for retreating easy, they can be pressed and attacked.

If they encamp on low wetlands, where there is no way for the water to drain off, if heavy rain should fall several times, they can be flooded and drowned. If they make camp in a wild marsh or fields dense with a heavy tangle of grass and stalks, should violent winds frequently arise, you can burn the fields and destroy them. If they remain encamped for a long time, the generals and officers growing lax and lazy, the army becoming unprepared, you can sneak up and spring a surprise attack.[68]

The expansive correlations embedded in a pivotal chapter of the *Six Secret Teachings* provide a basis for fathoming men and concocting plans:

What we refer to as the five talents are courage, wisdom, benevolence, trustworthiness, and loyalty. If he is courageous he cannot be overwhelmed. If he is wise he cannot be forced into turmoil. If he is benevolent he will love his men. If he is trustworthy he will not be deceitful. If he is loyal he will not be of two minds.

What are referred to as the ten errors are as follows: being courageous and treating death lightly; being hasty and impatient; being greedy and loving profit; being benevolent but unable to inflict suffering; being wise but afraid; being trustworthy and liking to trust others; being scrupulous and incorruptible but not loving men; being wise but indecisive; being resolute and self-reliant; and being fearful while liking to entrust responsibility to other men.

One who is courageous and treats death lightly can be destroyed by violence. One who is hasty and impatient can be destroyed by persistence. One who is greedy and loves profit can be bribed. One who is benevolent but unable to inflict suffering can be worn down. One who is wise but fearful can be distressed. One who is trustworthy and likes to trust others can be deceived. One who is scrupulous and incorruptible but does not love men can be insulted. One who is wise but indecisive can be suddenly attacked. One who is resolute and self-reliant can be confounded by events. One who is fearful and likes to entrust responsibility to others can be tricked.[69]

The recently recovered *Military Methods* devotes two of its later chapters to flaws in the commander's character and in the army itself. The first list, from "The General's Defeats," originally enumerated twenty defects, of which sixteen have survived two millennia underground: "First, he is incapable but believes himself to be capable. Second, arrogance. Third, greedy for position. Fourth, greedy for wealth. Sixth, light. Seventh, obtuse. Eighth, has little courage. Ninth, courageous but weak. Tenth, has little credibility. Fourteenth, rarely decisive. Fifteenth, slow. Sixteenth, indolent. Seventeenth, oppressive. Eighteenth, brutal. Nineteenth, selfish. Twentieth, induces confusion." Sun Pin concluded by noting that "when his defects are numerous, his losses will be many."

The Northern Sung *Hu-ling Ching* also pointed out ways to exploit discernible traits:

Before your two armies have clashed, observe the enemy's condition and situation, for then the general's talents and inclinations can be discerned. The ferocious who treat death lightly can be provoked and ambushed. The wise but slow can be pressed. Those who react rapidly but not wisely to critical events can be enticed. Those who react slowly but wisely to critical events can be resisted. The boastful can be isolated. Those who trust others can be deceived, those who do not can be estranged. The stubborn, perverse, and self-reliant can be suddenly attacked. Those who love others can be insulted. The greedy can be bribed. The rustic can be snatched. The incorruptible can be contaminated. The pure and aloof can be insulted. Those who fear ghosts and spirits can be scared. The timid who excel in using men can be deceived. When generals have any of these fifteen characteristics, attack them without doubt.[70]

The process of discerning character deficiencies was not merely passive, but included battlefield feints and probes mounted by reconnaissance forces to ferret out an enemy commander's capabilities and weaknesses. Since battlefield observations frequently failed to provide sufficient data for evaluation, critical information about character and propensities also had to be gained through spies and defectors.[71]

16

Classifications
of Terrain

T HE CONCEPT OF REGIONALISM probably predates the Shang dynasty, originating whenever people first traveled beyond the nuclear area of Chinese culture and confronted startling differences in terrain and vegetation. Since the population centers were scattered throughout the Yellow River valley and out onto the northern plains area, mountains would be found in many directions, while to the north and west lay the steppe, a region too dry to sustain agriculture. South across the Yangtze River existed a wetter, warmer region where rice, rather than millet or wheat, was cultivated. (Throughout subsequent history the difference between the northern wheat-based food culture with pasta, steamed breads, and dumplings was popularly contrasted with the south, which emphasized rice.) Further distinctions were quickly noted among China's diverse regions, including barbarian and other remote areas, such as hot Szechwan, where radically different customs and impenetrable languages predominated. Even in the Spring and Autumn period the newly powerful states of Wu, Yüeh, and Ch'u were treated as uncivilized because of their uncouth clothing and strange practices, such as tattooing, and long after their "sinicization" were still regarded as uncultured areas where miscreants and political offenders might be banished.

With the inception of the doctrines of *yin* and *yang* and the five phases in the Warring States period—two fundamental concepts of Chinese protoscience used to classify and interpret phenomenal occurrences and their patterns—the five phases quickly became organizing rubrics for the cycles of seasonal activity, directions of the earth, and important regional differences. Their fullest expression occurs in eclectic texts compiled around the end of the Warring States period, as well as the early medical writings, which correlate them with physiological aspects, visceral functions, the famous channels empirically employed for acupuncture, herbal and mineral materials, bodily types, personalities, emotions, and even individual traits, such as courage, as already seen. Concepts of regionalism invariably entailed political and projective implications because the different states, being sited in geographically distinct regions, were expected to manifest different temperaments, tastes, and behavioral tendencies, such as being easily angered. Such thinking was equally reflected in Wu Ch'i's and Hsün-tzu's characterizations of the fighting tendencies of different states already noted in the Warring States historical section. Although never specifically employed in the military writings,[1] these concepts were so powerful and prevalent, constituting an essential part of the literate person's worldview, that their principles and assumptions unavoidably influenced the tactical theorists and their expectations when, for example, traveling or campaigning in the west, a region associated with fall, death, and the element metal. They also influenced accounts of barbarian areas preserved in the historical writings, some of which were reprised in the section on political intelligence; others will be noted again in passages from the *Wu-ching Tsung-yao* on regional traits and customs.[2]

The earliest expression of regional theory has traditionally been attributed to the *Shang Shu*, which purportedly chronicles China's ancient history, although it largely consists of formal speeches on Virtue and details of government apparently delivered on important political occasions. The classic asserts that the great Yü, one of China's mythical cultural heroes, delineated China's nine regions as part of his efforts to tame the floodwaters that previously inundated China, and characterizes them in terms of soil type, field productivity, and inhabitants such as "wild people dressed in skins." Much of this sort of information, coupled with fanciful myths, commonsense observations, and astute detail, eventually found its way into the *Classic of Mountains and Seas (Shan Hai Ching)*, probably compiled late in the Warring States period. Some of the information is simplistic, such as might immediately be imagined or deduced (correctly or not) about the Amazon or Australia from so-called common knowledge without actual experience. However, other passages evidence unique points derivable only from close observation, even if subsequently embellished and transformed.

A scheme found in the *Shang Shu* subsequently proved fundamental to conceptualizing and organizing information into a series of concentric realms centered on the king that radiate out to subsume the feudal lords, dependent states, and barbarian peoples. However, the latter were generally considered too remote to be fully incorporated into the administrative order and were therefore exempt from sending tribute, although still expected to acknowledge the emperor and China's greatness as the center of the known realm.[3] From the Han dynasty on imperial Chinese dynasties similarly sought to structure their diplomatic relations and impose obligations of recognition on the outer barbarian areas in this way, but with all the feudal lands having been integrated into China itself, the concept lost its functional validity except in formally differentiating China from increasingly barbarous terrain. However, in the early Chou period the idealized concept of mounting imperial inspections to procure information and manifest the ruler's awesomeness at fixed intervals determined solely by the region's distance from the capital was at its apex. Essentially discontinued from the Spring and Autumn onward, the *Chou Li* still incorporated the concept into its schematized portrait of Chou rites.

Topography and Configurations of Terrain

The recognition that topography is fundamental to military tactics, the classification of terrain types, and the association of basic tactical principles with particular terrains may all be attributed to Sun-tzu. Even though a cursory examination of the *Tso Chuan* indicates that effective commanders had long been implementing terrain-based tactics, and certain land configurations, such as sinkholes, were known to present fatal obstacles, Sun-tzu was the first theorist to develop and systematically correlate a coherent body of operational principles with particularized terrains. Thereafter one of the defining thrusts of Chinese intelligence practice and field theory was identifying discrete terrain features and formulating tactics for their exploitation. In this regard the *Art of War* influenced all the later military writings, including several chapters found in the comprehensive late Warring States *Six Secret Teachings* and the insightful *Hu-ling Ching*.

In the very first chapter of the *Art of War* Sun-tzu included terrain (Earth) among warfare's five major factors, providing a limited definition of "Earth": "Earth encompasses far or near, difficult or easy, expansive or confined, fatal or tenable terrain." Therefore, determining who has gained the advantages of terrain offers a valuable indicator when calculating the probable victor in any encounter, and underpins another fundamental Chinese concept, that of *shih*, or strategic configuration of power.[4] Moreover, everything depends upon terrain because "terrain gives birth to measurement," leading in turn to calculating the forces required to achieve victory and envisioning their configuration: "Terrain gives birth to measurement; measurement produces the estimation of forces. Estimation of forces gives rise to calculating the numbers of men. Calculating the numbers of men gives rise to weighing strength. Weighing strength gives birth to victory. Military intelligence thus consists not only of knowledge of the enemy, but also of the topography of the invasion route, the time of the engagement, and the physical characteristics of the battleground."[5]

Although there have been reasonable suggestions that analysts in Sun-tzu's time employed some sort of tally board in the general assessment process, perhaps allotting a number of points represented by sticks or tallies to various categories, the actual method remains unknown. However, in addition to these boards and, subsequently, maps, which were extensively employed beginning with the Warring States period, three-dimensional strategic portrayals were also made, similar to the sand tables used in military intelligence until their recent displacement by computer graphics. The first recorded incident, illustrating the importance placed upon topography and the categories of terrain, is preserved in the historical records dating to A.D. 32, when general Ma Yüan, frustrated by Emperor Kuang-wu's indecision, illustrated the enemy's bottled up positions among the surrounding hills with kernels of rice mounded appropriately on a table.[6]

Nine terrains are frequently associated with Sun-tzu because that is the number described in a chapter with the same name. However, the *Art of War* actually discusses some twenty distinct configurations of terrain and further identifies several deadly land formations, such as Heaven's Well. Commanders contemplating forward movement, assaults upon an entrenched enemy, or any sort of tactical maneuvering ignored such terrains at their peril, just as they neglected the effects of simple grades, sand, wet ground, and other factors that exhaust an army only at great cost. Accordingly, Sun-tzu not only advocated avoiding such conditions—while exploiting them whenever possible—but also insisted that "local guides," one of his five categories of agent, be employed to develop concrete knowledge of the land, as already noted.

Sun-tzu analyzed terrain configurations in three chapters: "Nine Changes," "Configurations of Terrain," and "Nine Terrains." Although many of his well-known nine terrains are identically described, minor variations mark the two key sequences and several other configurations of importance. In "Configurations of Terrain" Sun-tzu begins, "The major configurations of terrain are accessible, suspended, stalemated, constricted, precipitous, and expansive," whereas in "Nine Terrains" he states, "There is dispersive terrain, light terrain, contentious terrain, traversable terrain, focal terrain, heavy terrain, entrapping terrain, encircled terrain, and fatal terrain."

This suggests either that the concepts were still in flux or that the text has been corrupted and essential materials lost. However, since the sequence found in "Nine Terrains" describes an army acting as an invader, the slight differences may derive from operational tactics for general combat verses those appropriately implemented on enemy territory.[7] In any event, in "Configurations of Terrain" Sun-tzu states: "Configuration of terrain is an aid to the army. Analyzing the enemy, taking control of victory, estimating ravines and defiles, the distant and near, is the Tao of the superior general. One who knows these and employs them in combat will certainly be victorious. One who does not know these or employ them in combat will certainly be defeated." More importantly, he also asserted, "There is terrain for which one does not contend."

Sun-tzu's descriptions, being laconic indications of mere essentials, may be explicated by comparatively integrating all the material pertaining to any single category. Discrepancies in the suggested tactics and terms employed for a single description thus become immediately apparent, but so do the dimensions of his characterizations. Based upon the three chapters just mentioned, the major categories with their defining attributes thus produce the following characterizations, with the generally superior definitions found in "Nine Terrains" preceding material from the other two chapters:

When the feudal lords fight in their own territory it is dispersive terrain.[8] On dispersive terrain do not engage the enemy. The Tao of the invader is that when the troops have penetrated deeply, they will be unified, but where only shallowly, they will be inclined to scatter. On dispersive terrain I unify their will.

When they enter someone else's territory, but not deeply, it is light terrain.[9] On light terrain do not stop. The Tao of the invader is that when you have penetrated only shallowly, it is light terrain. On light terrain I have them group together.

If when we occupy it, it will be advantageous to us, whereas if they occupy it, it will be advantageous to them, it is contentious terrain.[10] On contentious terrain do not attack. On contentious terrain I race our rear elements forward.

If it is not advantageous for us to go forth or advantageous for the enemy to come forward, it is termed "stalemated."[11] In a stalemated configuration, even though the enemy tries to entice us with profit, we do not go forth. Withdraw our forces and depart. If we strike them when half the enemy has come forth, it will be advantageous.

When we can go and they can also come, it is traversable terrain.[12] On traversable terrain do not allow your forces to become isolated. On traversable terrain I focus on defense. If we can go forth and the enemy can also advance, it is termed "accessible." In an accessible configuration first occupy the heights and *yang* side, and improve the routes for transporting provisions. Then when we engage in battle it will be advantageous.

As for expansive configurations, if our strategic power is equal, it will be difficult to provoke them into combat. Engaging in combat will not be advantageous.

Land of the feudal lords surrounded on three sides such that whoever arrives first will gain the masses of All under Heaven is focal terrain.[13] On focal terrain unite and form alliances with nearby feudal lords. The Tao of the invader is that when the four sides are open to others, it is focal terrain. On focal terrain I solidify our alliances. Unite with your allies on focal terrain.

If we can go forth but it will be difficult to return, it is termed "suspended." In a suspended configuration, if they are unprepared, go forth and conquer them. If the enemy is prepared and we sally forth without being victorious, it will be difficult to turn back and is not advantageous.

The Tao of the invader is that when the army has left the state, crossed the enemy's border, and is on campaign, it is isolated terrain. Do not remain on isolated terrain.

When one penetrates deeply into enemy territory, bypassing numerous cities, it is heavy terrain.[14] On heavy terrain plunder for provisions. The Tao of the invader is that when you have advanced deeply, it is heavy terrain. On heavy terrain I ensure a continuous supply of provisions.

As for precipitous configurations,[15] if we occupy them, we must hold the heights and *yang* sides to await the enemy. If the enemy occupies them first, withdraw our forces and depart. Do not follow them.

Where there are mountains and forests, ravines and defiles, wetlands and marshes, wherever the road is difficult to negotiate, it is entrapping terrain.[16] On entrapping terrain move through quickly. On entrapping terrain I speedily advance along the roads. Do not encamp on entrapping terrain.

As for constricted configurations, if we occupy them first, we must fully deploy throughout them in order to await the enemy.[17] If the enemy occupies them first and fully deploys in them, do not follow them in. If they do not fully deploy in them, then follow them in.

Where the entrance is constricted, the return is circuitous, and with a small number they can strike our masses, it is encircled terrain.[18] On encircled terrain use strategy. The Tao of the invader is that when you have strongholds behind you and constrictions before you, it is encircled terrain. On encircled terrain I obstruct any openings.[19] It is the nature of the army to defend when encircled. Make strategic plans for encircled terrain.

Where if one fights with intensity he will survive but if he does not fight with intensity he will perish, it is fatal terrain.[20] On fatal terrain engage in battle. If there is no place to go, it is fatal terrain.[21] On fatal terrain I show them that we will not live. It is the nature of the army to fight fervently when unavoidable, to follow orders when compelled by circumstances. On fatal terrain you must do battle.

Scattered throughout the *Art of War*, but especially in "Maneuvering the Army," are numerous other important pronouncements on terrain-related issues, and crucial identifications of recurring features correlated with suggested tactics and operational principles. Three of the most significant, much explored in later writings (such as the *Hu-ling Ching*), are fatal terrain, tenable terrain, and maneuvering the army across unfamiliar ground. Only a few pertain to problems posed by rivers and water obstacles, no doubt reflecting an early heritage of plains warfare. (As the scope of conflict expanded, the problems entailed by fording rivers, crossing wetlands, and negotiating lakes grew enormously, stimulating the development of naval forces in the southeast. Accordingly, the later military classics address these concerns more extensively.) According to Sun-tzu:

As for deploying the army and fathoming the enemy: To cross mountains follow the valleys, search out tenable ground, and occupy the heights. If the enemy holds the heights, do not climb up to engage them in battle. This is the way to deploy an army in the mountains.[22]

After crossing rivers, you must distance yourself from them. If the enemy is fording a river to advance, do not confront them in the water. When half their forces have crossed, it will be advantageous to strike them. If you want to engage the enemy in battle, do not array your forces near the river to confront the invader, but look for tenable ground and occupy the heights. Do not confront the current's flow.[23] This is the way to deploy the army where there are rivers.

When you cross salt marshes and wetlands, concentrate on quickly getting away from them; do not remain. If you engage in battle in marshes or wetlands, you must stay in areas with marsh grass and keep groves of trees at your back. This is the way to deploy the army in marshes and wetlands.[24]

On level plains deploy on easy terrain with the right flank positioned with high ground to the rear,[25] fatal terrain to the fore, and tenable terrain to the rear. This is the way to deploy on the plains.

These four deployments, advantageous to the army, are the means by which the Yellow Emperor conquered the four emperors.

Now the army likes heights and abhors low areas, esteems the sunny *[yang]* and disdains the shady *[yin]*. It nourishes life and occupies the substantial.[26] An army that avoids the hundred illnesses is said to be certain of victory.

Where there are hills and embankments you must occupy the *yang* side, keeping them to the right rear. This is to the army's advantage and exploits the natural assistance of the terrain.

When it rains upstream, foam appears.[27] If you want to cross over, wait until it settles.

You must quickly get away from deadly configurations of terrain such as precipitous gorges with mountain torrents, Heaven's Well, Heaven's Jail, Heaven's Net, Heaven's Pit, and Heaven's Fissure.[28] Do not approach them. When we keep them at a distance, the enemy is forced to approach them. When we face them, the enemy is compelled to have them at their rear.

When on the flanks the army encounters ravines and defiles, wetlands with reeds and tall grass, mountain forests or areas with heavy, entangled undergrowth, you must thoroughly search them because they are places where an ambush or spies would be concealed.

The later military writings, beginning with Sun Pin's *Military Methods* and the *Six Secret Teachings* in the Warring States period, essentially accepted Sun-tzu's categories as definitive, but of course expanded, reoriented, and elaborated them, particularly emphasizing the broad but critical distinction of tenable and fatal terrains.

In the *Military Methods* Sun Pin, who presumably received intensive instruction in the family school of tactics, clearly adopted most of Sun-tzu's categories, although without the systematization of the famous nine terrains. For example, the deadly terrains he enumerates are all familiar: Heaven's Well, Heaven's Jail, Heaven's Net, Heaven's Fissure, and Heaven's Pit. However, he emphasizes a number of "entrapping terrains" that retard the army's progress and convert even the most spirited aggressors into vulnerable targets: gorges with streams, valleys, river areas, marshes, wetlands, and salt flats. Moreover, as the scope of warfare expanded into the wetter, peripheral regions during the Warring States period, water hazards became particularly troublesome, so Sun Pin advised against going contrary to the current's flow or being caught while fording rivers. *Yin* and *yang* classifiers were applied to mountains, formations, and seasonal indicators, and five-phase categorizations similarly employed, generally phrased in terms of conquest relationships, for such objectives as soil classification. Ground unable to sustain life, including incinerated areas, should be avoided whatever the season or location.

More important is Sun Pin's general principle that the commanding general must investigate the terrain, become thoroughly familiar with it, and actively exploit the topography to emplace his troops and defeat the enemy. When the advantages of terrain are realized, the troops will naturally be inclined to fight. The enemy should be targeted on deadly ground after being forced onto it, while easy terrain can be exploited only when a commander enjoys a decisive superiority in numbers or mobile elements. Correspondingly, constricted terrain and ravines should be fully utilized to control and vanquish the enemy. They provide the means not only for the few to attack the many, but also for the concealment of troops in ambush. With appropriate fortifications erected across the mouth, including interconnected chariots deployed with shields to fill the voids, they become strongholds not easily assaulted.

From an intelligence standpoint, conceptually the most important chapter in the *Military Methods* is entitled "Treasures of Terrain":

As for the Tao of terrain, *yang* constitutes the exterior, *yin* constitutes the interior. The direct constitutes the warp, techniques constitute the woof. When the woof and the warp have been realized, deployments will not be confused. The direct traverses land where vegetation thrives; techniques take advantage of where the foliage is half dead.

As for the field of battle, the sun is the essence, but the eight winds that arise must not be forgotten. Crossing rivers, confronting hills, going contrary to the current's flow, occupying killing ground, and confronting masses of trees—all these that I have just mentioned, in all five one will not be victorious.

A mountain on which one deploys on the south side is a tenable mountain; a mountain on which one deploys on the eastern side is a fatal mountain.

Water that flows to the east is life-sustaining water; water that flows to the north is deadly water. Water that does not flow is death.

The conquest relationship of the five types of terrain is as follows: mountains conquer high hills; high hills conquer hills; hills conquer irregular mounds; irregular mounds conquer forests and plains.

The conquest relationship of five types of grasses is as follows: profusion of hedges, thorny brambles, cane, reeds, and sedge grass.

The conquest relationship of the five soils is as follows: blue conquers yellow; yellow conquers black; black conquers red; red conquers white; white conquers blue.

Five types of terrain are conducive to defeat: gorges with streams, valleys, river areas, marshes, and salt flats.

The five killing grounds are Heaven's Well, Heaven's Jail, Heaven's Net, Heaven's Fissure, and Heaven's Pit. These five graves are killing grounds. Do not occupy them, do not remain on them.

In the spring do not descend; in fall do not ascend. Neither the army nor any formation should attack to the front right. Establish your perimeter to the right; do not establish your perimeter to the left.

This chapter clearly discusses configurations of terrain best avoided while making some general observations about the respective values of various physical aspects. Many of the concrete contents are identical with those raised in Sun-tzu's *Art of War* and may also be found scattered throughout the *Seven Military Classics.* Clearly every strategist and commander had to be cognizant of such dangers, as well as the principles for exploiting them, and direct efforts to discovering them appropriately, particularly "terrains conducive to defeat" and "killing grounds."[29]

The remaining paragraphs array heights, grasses, and soils in sequences based upon relative conquest power. Heights may be understood simply in terms of greater heights being strategically superior to lesser ones, whereas the grasses are ranked according to their strength and ability to act as obstacles sufficient to impede an advancing force. However, the five soils are characterized in terms of one of the conquest cycles found within the theory of five-phase correlative thought. (Unfortunately, even though the sentence is perfectly intelligible, the underlying meaning and implications remain to be understood, and are the subject of extensive arguments that cannot be considered here. Whether Sun Pin truly believed in their efficacy or merely included them for theoretical purposes, or whether they are simply later accretions remains to be studied.[30])

"Offices, I" enumerates a series of thirty-one disparate pronouncements upon concrete tactical principles, some situationally derived, others related to circumstances of terrain. Among the most important for terrain-based military intelligence considerations are the following:

When attacking mountain cliffs, employ Arrayed Walls. On open terrain employ a square formation. When you confront heights and deploy your forces, employ a piercing formation.

For ravines employ a circular formation. When engaged in combat on easy terrain, to effect a martial retreat employ your soldiers in a rearguard action. When the enemy is bottled up in a ravine, release the mouth in order to entice them farther away.

Amid grasses and heavy vegetation use *yang* [visible] pennants. To create awesomeness, deploy with mountains as the right wing. When the road is thorny and heavily overgrown, use a zig-zag advance. In ravines and gullies use intermixed elements.

When circumventing mountains and forests, use segmented units in succession. Attacking state capitals and towns with water will prove effective. Descending dragons [hidden power] and deployed ambushes are the means by which to fight in the mountains.

Preventive ditches and concentrated formations are the means by which to engage [a superior enemy in battle] with a few troops. The Floating Marsh Formation and flank attacks are the means by which to fight an enemy on a confined road. [The various units] moving in turn is the means by which to pass over bridges.

Nearly half the chapters incorporated in the *Six Secret Teachings*, a far-ranging theoretical work probably compiled within a century of Sun Pin's death, if not earlier, advance concrete tactical solutions for problematic circumstances, all based upon knowledge of the enemy, many correlated with specific terrains. For example, "Certain Escape" commences with the following query and response:

King Wu said: "In front of us lies a large body of water, or broad moat, or deep water hole that we want to cross. However, we do not have equipment such as boats and oars. What should we do?"

The T'ai Kung said: "Large bodies of water, broad moats, and deep water holes are usually not defended by the enemy. If they are able to defend them, their troops will certainly be few. In such situations you should use the Flying River with winches and also the Heavenly Huang to cross the army over. Our courageous, strong, skilled soldiers should move where we indicate, rushing into the enemy, breaking up their formations, all fighting to the death.

In "Planning for the Army" the key features of terrain encountered by the invading army are deep streams, large river valleys, ravines, and defiles, with the complication that a sudden downpour inundates the army in the midst of crossing them.[31] In contrast, rather than water the danger that must be confronted in "Incendiary Warfare" is conflagration, the enemy having taken advantage of windy conditions to set the dry deep grass and heavy undergrowth afire. (Even though the T'ai Kung suggests a desperate tactic, one of the main lessons of the *Six Secret Teachings* is the need to gain the advance knowledge that will prevent becoming entrapped on such terrain.) Mountainous terrain is similarly pondered, with the description found in "Crow and Cloud Formation in the Mountains" no doubt typical of territory in the arid northwest: "high mountains with large flat rock outcropping, on top of which are numerous peaks, all devoid of grass and trees." Forests and valleys complete the list, with material from the former being incorporated in the *Wu-ching Tsung-yao* passages that are translated here.[32]

The concluding section of the *Six Secret Teachings* preserves extremely valuable material about the three component forces of chariots, cavalry, and infantry, including a chapter on their respective strengths and equivalents, essentially explicating the statement that "the infantry values knowing changes and movement; the chariots value knowing the terrain's configuration; the cavalry values knowing the side roads and unorthodox Tao." Thus "Battle Chariots" delineates ten types of terrain that are considered fatal for employing chariots:

If after advancing there is no way to withdraw, this is fatal terrain for chariots.

Passing beyond narrow defiles to pursue the enemy some distance, this is terrain that will exhaust the chariots.

When the land in front makes advancing easy, while that to the rear is treacherous, this is terrain that will cause hardship for the chariots.

Penetrating into narrow and obstructed areas from which escape will be difficult, this is terrain on which the chariots may be cut off.

If the land is collapsing, sinking, and marshy, with black mud sticking to everything, this is terrain that will labor the chariots.

To the left is precipitous while to the right is easy, with high mounds and sharp hills. This is terrain contrary to the use of chariots.

Luxuriant grass runs through the fields, and there are deep watery channels throughout. This is terrain that thwarts the use of chariots.

When the chariots are few in number, the land easy, and one is not confronted by enemy infantry, this is terrain on which the chariots may be defeated.

To the rear are water-filled ravines and ditches, to the left deep water, and to the right steep hills. This is terrain upon which chariots are destroyed.

It has been raining day and night for more than ten days without stopping. The roads have collapsed so that it's not possible to advance or to escape to the rear. This is terrain that will sink the chariots.

These ten are deadly terrain for chariots. Thus, they are the means by which the stupid general will be captured, and the wise general will be able to escape.

The chapter then proceeds to analyze what it terms "eight conditions of terrain conducive to victory." However, none of the eight is inherently related to configurations or conditions of terrain, all of them being general indications of weakness in the enemy and are therefore discussed in the section on generally evaluating enemy armies.

"Cavalry in Battle" focuses upon ten conducive and nine inimical conditions for employing the cavalry. Only two of the conducive circumstances ponder the impact of terrain: "When the enemy, although lacking the advantages of ravines and defiles for securing their defenses, have penetrated deeply and ranged widely into distant territory, if we sever their supply lines they will certainly be hungry. When the land is level and easy and we see enemy cavalry approaching from all four sides, if we have our chariots and cavalry strike into them, they will certainly become disordered." In contrast, seven of the nine inimical conditions are correlated specific circumstances of terrain:

When we go forward but there is no road back, we enter but there is no way out, this is referred to as "penetrating a Heavenly Well," "being buried in an Earthly Cave." This is fatal terrain for the cavalry.

When the way by which we enter is constricted but the way out is distant, their weak forces can attack our strong ones, and their few can attack our many, this is terrain on which the cavalry will be exterminated.

When there are great mountain torrents, deep valleys, tall luxuriant grass, forests, and trees, these are conditions that will exhaust the cavalry.

When there is water on the left and right, while ahead are large hills and to the rear high mountains, and the Three Armies are fighting between the bodies of water while the enemy occupies both the interior and exterior ground, this is terrain that means great difficulty for the cavalry.

When the enemy has cut off our supply lines and if we advance we will not have any route by which to return, this is troublesome terrain for the cavalry.

When we are sinking into marshy ground while advancing and retreating must both be through quagmires, this is worrisome terrain for the cavalry.

When on the left there are deep water sluices, and on the right there are gullies and hillocks, but below the heights the ground appears level, good terrain for advancing, retreating, and enticing an enemy, this terrain is a pitfall for the cavalry.

The conclusion reiterates the dual nature of such conditions: "These nine constitute fatal terrain for cavalry, the means by which the enlightened general will keep the enemy far off and escape while the ignorant general will be entrapped and defeated."

The final chapter focuses on the infantry, which by then had become massive and unwieldy, numbered in the hundred-thousands. Apart from the types of terrain that must be exploited, the chapter makes the interesting and historically important assumption that infantry forces could withstand both chariots and cavalry:

When infantry engage in battle with chariots and cavalry, they must rely on hills and mounds, ravines and defiles. The long weapons and strong crossbows should occupy the fore, the short weapons and weak crossbows should occupy the rear, firing and resting in turn. Even if large numbers of the enemy's chariots and cavalry should arrive, they must maintain a solid formation and fight intensely while skilled soldiers and strong crossbowmen prepare against attacks from the rear.

To be effective, the commander would of course have to know, from reconnaissance or spies, the composition of the enemy's forces and the probable component spearheading the attack, as well as the configuration of the surrounding terrain, so that he might emplace his infantry appropriately.

A battle that developed during the Later Han as government forces sought to contain the Yellow Turban uprising illustrates how knowledge of topographical features might be exploited while coincidentally showing the continuity and application of classic military thought. Whereas Sun-tzu devoted a chapter to incendiary attacks and the T'ai Kung discussed defensive measures, Sun Pin detailed the method and its applicability:

The tactics for incendiary warfare: If the enemy is downwind in an area abundant with dry grass where the soldiers of their Three Armies would not have anywhere to escape, then you can mount an incendiary attack. When there is a frigid fierce wind, abundant vegetation and undergrowth, and firewood and grass already piled up while their earthworks have not yet been prepared, in such circumstances you can mount an incendiary attack. Use the flames to confuse them, loose arrows like rain. Beat the drums and set up a clamor to motivate your soldiers. Assist the attack with strategic power. These are the tactics for incendiary warfare.[33]

As portrayed in the *Hou Han Shu,* Huang-fu Sung was an astute student:

After Chu Chün was defeated by the [Yellow Turban forces] under the rebel leader Po Ts'ai, Huang-fu Sung advanced and secured Ch'ang-sheh. Po Ts'ai then led a large number of troops to besiege the city. Because Sung's troops were few, he summoned the army's officers and said: "The military Tao lies in unorthodox changes, not in numbers. It happens the brigands have built their encampment with straw, so it will be easy to launch an incendiary attack by exploiting the wind. If we set them afire at night, they will certainly be thrown into chaos. If we then send our soldiers forth to suddenly strike them, engaging them from all four sides, we can repeat T'ien Tan's achievements."

That night a strong wind arose, so Sung had his soldiers ascend the city walls with burning torches and had his elite soldiers secretly work their way out through the siege lines to set fire to the enemy's encampment from outside with a great yell. Those on the wall responded by raising their burning torches. Sung then drummed a rapid assault into the enemy's deployment. Terrified, the brigands ran off in chaos. It happened that Ts'ao Ts'ao, who had been dispatched by the emperor, arrived and united with Chu

Chün and Huang-fu Sung to severely vanquish Po Ts'ai's forces, killing several tens of thousands.[34]

The simple knowledge that the enemy had encamped in grassy areas and stupidly utilized the readily available straw for building their shelters allowed Sung to exploit the wind and surprise in an incendiary attack that well duplicated Sun Pin's tactical advice.

Configurations of Terrain in the *Hu-ling Ching*

The Northern Sung *Hu-ling Ching* contains several important chapters that commence with Sun-tzu's concepts and definitions but then provide updated explications based upon two additional millennia of warfare experience. The first, "Analyzing Terrain," tackles six fundamental configurations. With Sun-tzu's original material identified for convenience, it runs:

In order to employ the six methods for terrain, one must analyze their configurations and strategic advantages. The six are accessible, suspended, stalemated, constricted, precipitous, and expansive.

Accessible Terrain: [Sun-tzu said,] "If we can go forth and the enemy can also advance, it is termed 'accessible.'" When on accessible terrain it will be advantageous to occupy the heights and await the enemy. Open supply routes to the rear, and prepare defenses along the less visible roads to prevent any unseen advances by the enemy. Then if you engage in battle, it will be advantageous.[35]

Suspended Terrain: [Sun-tzu said,] "If we can go forth but it will be difficult to return, it is termed 'suspended.'" When occupying suspended terrain, first carefully determine whether the enemy is unprepared; then establish ambushes to sever their supply routes; after which it will be advantageous to engage them. If the enemy is prepared and you sally forth, you will trip yourself up.

Stalemated Terrain: [Sun-tzu said,] "If it is not advantageous for us to go forth or advantageous for the enemy to come forward, it is termed 'stalemated.'" When [both sides are] occupying stalemated terrain, if the enemy withdraws their troops, it is to entice you. Do not attack, for it will be advantageous to wait until they launch an assault to strike them.

Constricted Terrain: A defensible position at the mouth of a mountain valley or the gorge marking the intersection between two steep hills is termed "constricted."[36] If you occupy constricted terrain first, you should set out your encampments and improve your deployments to await the enemy, precluding any worry about sudden onslaughts. When the enemy occupies such terrain first, if they fully deploy throughout it wait them out. To attack a less than full deployment it is advantageous to approach by another route.

Precipitous Terrain: Occupying heights while awaiting those below, dwelling in security while awaiting the endangered, is termed "precipitous." If you are first to occupy precipitous terrain, it will be advantageous to engage in battle. If the enemy occupies it first, halt your troops, retreat, and then determine what might be advantageous.

Expansive Terrain: When your fortified encampment is far from the enemy's fortifications, it is termed "expansive." If the enemy tries to provoke you into battle without first advancing, even if you engage them do not advance as they will certainly have established ambushes there. Similarly, if they withdraw without engaging in battle, you cannot pursue them; such pursuit would not be advantageous.

When the ancients said that advantages of terrain are the real treasures in military tactics, this is what they meant.

As already seen, Sun-tzu also posited two fundamental categories— tenable and fatal terrain—that are the focus of the following two *Hu-ling Ching* chapters. In essence, tenable terrain refers to any ground whose configuration does not doom an army occupying it to defeat, but it also encompasses areas where troops can safely find grass, firewood, and water, as Sun Pin subsequently emphasized.

Tenable terrain refers to the absence of fatal terrain to the front and rear, left and right, so that the supply routes and both advancing and retreating are all unobstructed. Accordingly, tacticians assert that tenable terrain is advantageous.

There are six possible employments.

First, a cutoff force has deeply penetrated enemy territory.

Second, the horses are selected and the men stalwart, and they are well practiced in the strategic advantages of deployments.

Third, the general's orders are enlightened and strict.

Fourth, the forces are strong, while the enemy is weak.

Fifth, the commanding general's style emphasizes beneficence and trust, and the officials and officers all follow him.

Sixth, the officials and officers take pleasure in warfare.

However, there are three cases in which tenable terrain cannot be employed.

First, the officers and troops are thinking of their families.

Second, since there are no advantages in front to entice them, the officers and troops hope to withdraw.

Third, advancing will be disadvantageous and retreating advantageous.

Can the advantages and disadvantages of tenable terrain not be analyzed?[37]

The importance of the army's *ch'i*, although not specifically referred to by this term, is apparent in several of the circumstances listed here. Most of them have previously been seen in one or another list of traits that can or cannot be attacked, whereas the first of the three conditions disfavoring the employment of tenable terrain is clearly Sun-tzu's "dispersive terrain."

Paradoxically, fatal terrain—dangerous ground that virtually fates an army to extinction—can be exploited to generate a zealous commitment in the men, a resolute will to fight to the death, as first discussed by Sun-tzu and much theorized about thereafter. (The choice had to be deliberately made and preceded by certain acts to create the proper psychological response to avoid merely engendering defeatism and despair. Several chapters of the late Sung *Hundred Unorthodox Strategies* focus upon this process, closely following in the footsteps of the definitive *Military Methods* chapter entitled "Expanding *Ch'i*," which delineates the psychological stages for nurturing the army's *ch'i* or fighting morale, as discussed earlier.[38])

Fatal terrain is characterized by mountains to the rear, rivers to the front, and all the supply and escape routes cut off. Although fatal terrain is said to be the bane of tacticians, there are four circumstances in which it can be employed for battle.

First, when the general's beneficence and awesomeness have not yet been made manifest, the officials and officers not yet fully submissive.

Second, the soldiers are a match for the enemy so that if you fight vigorously it will be advantageous, but being afraid to fight will prove disadvantageous. It will be necessary to force the officials and troops to fight to the death.

Third, when pressed by the enemy and the provisions and fodder are nearly exhausted.

Fourth, the forward army has already been destroyed, but the rear army is still solid.

There are also three circumstances in which fatal terrain should not be employed for battle.

First, the enemy is numerous while you are few.

Second, the advantages and disadvantages have not yet been estimated, while the troops have to be compelled to act strongly.

Third, indecision.

Mountains and Rivers

Warfare in China originated mostly in the northern plains area, but by the Spring and Autumn period had already engulfed most of the territory encompassed by modern China, with its wide diversity of terrains and features. Mountains and rivers, two obvious, often almost insurmountable obstacles, entailed different dangers and tactical opportunities and were thus already much discussed by Sun-tzu's era, even if not extensively by Sun-tzu himself. The evolution of cavalry and mass infantry forces further increased their strategic importance, heightening the threat they posed to operational plans, no doubt prompting Hsü Tung to comment on them both:

When the power of a mountain looms close by, do not encamp for fear of ambushes at the side. When a mountain has a depression in the middle with forests surrounding it, do not encamp for fear of ambushes from all four sides. Roads that meander through mountains cannot be recklessly traversed for fear of ambushes lying ahead. Quickly distance yourself from mountains that lie to your rear, and urgently post a rearguard for fear that the enemy will cut you off.

When there are mountains to the front and rear, left and right, and you are ensconced in their midst, carefully investigate all the minor roads and by-paths and guard them with troops. Moreover, whenever there are ridges and forested wilds nearby, if you occupy them to wage battle you can establish ambushes. In urgent situations you can hide in them, or when defending them, gather firewood. Someone capable of knowing the advantages and disadvantages of mountain forests will rarely fail to be victorious.[39]

China's great rivers not only frequently defied attempts to cross them, but also inundated the land with floods in the spring and times of disorder, such as when the dikes were inadequately maintained or deliberately broken to thwart advancing enemies.[40] The many ordinary and secondary rivers, even though less difficult to ford or cross by small boats and makeshift, often highly imaginative rafts, provided entrenched enemies with natural defenses whose flowing waters could blunt the most determined assaults, creating killing fields for their skilled bowmen and crossbowmen. Sun-tzu and Sun Pin both discussed the hazards of fighting near rivers—some of which are mentioned previously—and China's early history is replete with examples of thwarting enemy crossings by first damming the water upstream, then releasing it when the enemy became exposed, as well as diverting streams to inundate enemy positions.[41]

However, sometimes simple ignorance, contrary to Sun-tzu's warnings, unexpectedly resulted in self-decimating effects, as this anecdote employed by the *Lü-shih Ch'un-ch'iu* indicates: "Ching wanted to launch a surprise attack against Sung, so they had scouts first chart the depth of the Yung River. Unknown to them, the river suddenly surged higher so that when they employed their charts to ford it at night, more than a thousand men drowned and the army was so panicked that it destroyed their own encampment."[42]

Local guides, if reliable, could provide the best information, even when merely being insightful rather than informative:

> Ch'i ordered General Chang-tzu to attack the state of Ching in alliance with Han and Wei. Ching ordered T'ang Mieh to assume command of their response. The two armies engaged in a standoff for six months without engaging in combat. Ch'i then ordered Chou Ts'ui to press Chang-tzu to urgently engage in battle. His language was extremely harsh, so Chang-tzu replied, "Kill me, remove me, exterminate my family, all these the king can do to me, but make me fight when we cannot, or make me not fight when we can, this the king cannot obtain."
>
> Subsequently the two forces deployed opposite each other on either side of the Tz'u River. Chang-tzu ordered his men to see whether the water could be crossed, but Ching's archers shot at them, so they couldn't get near the river. Someone cutting grass along the banks informed Ch'i's scouts that "it's easy to learn the depth of the water. Wherever Ching's forces mount a strong defense will all be shallow places, whereas anywhere weakly defended will be deep." The scouts brought him to see Chang-tzu. Elated, Chang-tzu then trained his soldiers to launch a sudden night attack against any places that Ching strongly defended, and they indeed killed T'ang Mieh. Chang-tzu can be said to have truly known the basic duties of a general.[43]

This incident coincidentally illustrates the growing professionalism of commanders in the Warring States and their adherence to Sun-tzu's fiat that a field commander, once on campaign, had to act independently in determining when and where to fight, and disregard any political interference.

Rivers also offered transport opportunities and much-needed water, the very life of the army if disease vectors and poisons might be avoided.

> Whenever encamping the army, if the river's flow is clear, this is the best drinking water. When its flow is yellow and turbid with sand, this is the next best. When it flows black, this is the least acceptable drinking water. However, if the river's flow should cease, then do not drink it. If the river flows past the enemy's position upstream, do not drink it. If the river's flow occasionally has black streams in the midst, marking poison, do not drink it or death will result. If the river is filled with debris and refuse, do not drink it or illness will result. When there are corpses or the bodies of animals in the river, do not drink it. If there is no potable water, you should dig a well at the side of the river because the army must have water whenever it encamps, even if only temporarily.
>
> If your troops are about to ford a river that sometimes flows quite full and sometimes diminishes, do not cross because some sort of temporary sandbag dam has certainly been erected upstream as part of an unorthodox strategy. Where the water stops stick close to the roads along the embankment for fear of sinking into marshy terrain. When a river in the enemy's strategic area is unguarded by armored soldiers, you still should not immediately ford it, but have your light troops conduct a reconnaissance of the nearby mountains and ravines for fear of ambushes secreted there. When you want to seize the enemy's strength, first seize their water supply. To accomplish this, nothing is better than gaining control of the river upstream![44]

Historically, armies often lost more men to illness than to the battlefield, prompting Sun-tzu to declare: "An army that avoids the hundred illnesses is said to be certain of victory."[45] Discovering and ensuring potable water thus being vital, Sun Pin observed: "If an army drinks from flowing water, it is water that will sustain life and they cannot be attacked. If an army drinks stagnant water, it is water that will result in death and they can be attacked."[46]

Hsü Tung's Contrary Practices

Since the literature on topographical configurations with correlated tactical principles became readily available and was carefully studied with the passage of time, however meritorious Sun-tzu's and Wu-tzu's ancient methods, their well-known tactics could be balked by knowledgeable commanders. Thus in the Sung dynasty—although certainly earlier in practice—in his *Hu-ling Ching* Hsü Tung strongly advocated operating contrary to normal expectations, exploiting the enemy's normal range of interpretations to achieve the surprise necessary for decisive victory. His "Contrary Employment of Ancient Methods" has already been reviewed earlier in this section; the incisive "Contrary Employment of Terrain Configurations" that follows takes as its basis detailed statements found in Sun-tzu's *Art of War* and Wu Ch'i's observations in the *Wu-tzu* (all identified in quotation marks). His assessments quickly refute conventional wisdom, probe for psychological factors, and then situationally justify the suggested tactics, thus providing an illustration of surpassing expertise in the practice of categorical analysis, the foundation of Chinese military intelligence.

The *Art of War* states, "On dispersive terrain do not engage the enemy." Dispersive terrain is land within your own borders. The officers and troops are concerned about their families, their thoughts are not unified, so you cannot engage in battle.

It also states, "On light terrain stop."[47] When you enter the enemy's territory but only shallowly, the thoughts of the officers and troops are not yet solidified. You cannot advance against the enemy because you need to first solidify their hearts.

"On contentious terrain do not attack." Mountain valleys and the mouths of constricted ravines where the weak can vanquish the strong constitute terrain where a small number of troops can successfully strike a large number.

"On traversable terrain do not allow your forces to become isolated." Since both sides can advance and retreat you cannot sever it with troops.[48]

"On focal terrain unite and form alliances." As there are roads coming and going, you can form alliances with the feudal lords.

"On heavy terrain plunder for provisions." When you have deeply penetrated into the enemy's territory, the thoughts of the officers and troops will already be solid and unified, so you can plunder for material resources.

"On encircled terrain use strategy." The officers and troops are put in difficulty by constricted terrain. When your army is too weak to fight but extensive delay will mean your provisions will run out and be cut off, you must employ stratagems in order to resolve the difficulty.

"On fatal terrain engage in battle." When you find yourself with high mountains in front and a large river to the rear; your supply lines cut; and neither advancing nor retreating, or even undertaking defensive preparations, advantageous, you are on "fatal terrain."

If the topography compels you to employ these eight ancient methods for exploiting the terrain to wage battle, then do so, but if not, then act contrary to their methods. What do I mean by going contrary to them? If the enemy's masses have deeply penetrated your territory but their encampment's fortifications are incomplete, their fodder and provisions limited, and their defenses not advantageous, how can you not engage them in battle just because you are on dispersive terrain? You must constrain the men with the will to fight to the death. Make it clear that those who retreat in fear will certainly be executed, whereas those who capture enemy soldiers will be rewarded. Set standing orders among all the officers that when the battle is joined anyone who looks back should be beheaded, while anyone whose eyes are not fixed when approaching the enemy or whose own units shift about will also be beheaded. Similarly behead those with worried countenances, who stumble or fall, who look about with eyes askance, leave behind their weapons, or whose drums and gongs do not respond to the measures. Anyone who kills an enemy soldier will be generously rewarded. In this way you can utilize dispersive terrain.

When you enter the enemy's territory only shallowly, if the terrain is difficult, you should occupy it and provoke battle, but if it is level, then defend it and respond to the enemy's actions. If you are concerned about the minds of the officers and troops not being unified, select difficult terrain that lacks escape in any direction, strictly order the units, severely impose disciplinary measures, and compel every man to fight for himself. Such is the employment of light terrain.

If the enemy occupies mountain valleys and precipitous terrain first, they will constrict your power. You should respond by ensconcing the army in a large encampment with broad deployments and concentrating upon attacking their negligence. Secretly give an appearance of lax security, of allowing the enemy to discern your tactics, so that your plans will seem to leak out and thus make the enemy prepare to the fore. Then clandestinely dispatch elite troops, men with the courage to fight to the death, to infiltrate through by-paths to assault their supply lines and pound their rear. Along these by-paths there will certainly be numerous ravines and gullies, as well as areas with steep cliffs and precipices, so put up ladders and hang bamboo ropes to climb them. There may also be deep pools that can be crossed with large pottery jars. When you perceive the enemy being disrupted within, respond by sending elite troops forth from the encampment, thereby attacking them from both within and without. This is the way to employ contentious terrain.

When the roads intersect so that you can go forth but they can also come up, it will be advantageous to establish ambushes and advance into battle. Once combat commences, feign flight. Wait until more than half the pursuing enemy have passed before raising the signal for an ambush and suddenly striking into them, and also turn your retreating forces about in response. This is the way to utilize traversable terrain.

If the terrain on which you are temporarily encamped is accessible from all four directions, you must select your closest and most courageous associates to command the infantry and cavalry units entrusted with defending the four roads. Employ them in accord with the number available, so that even though there is no response from your allies, you will be able to utilize focal terrain.

Once your troops have arrived at the enemy's border, you should employ any accompanying defensive equipment to provide security at appropriate times. If not, then destroy it. You must have your subordinate commanders bring in whatever resources and provisions they capture for the enjoyment of the soldiers, thereby also denying it to the enemy.[49] Why must you enter heavy terrain before you can begin plundering? Plundering materials from the enemy should not just be a utilization of heavy terrain.

Whenever a large army is about to move, you should analyze its strengths and weaknesses, observe the clouds and vapors [ch'i] about it, investigate whether the configurations of terrain are conducive or inimical, examine whether the hearts of the soldiers are willing or rebellious, and thereafter mobilize your forces.[50] The *Art of War* states: "Critically analyze them to know the estimations for gain and loss. Observe them to know the patterns of their movement and stopping."[51] Thus in the Tao of success or failure, advantage lies in advance knowledge. Excellence means planning a victorious strategy before victory has been achieved and being cautious about losses before they have materialized.

Take, for example, the danger of fatal terrain. If you begin planning in the army, you will certainly suffer when responding to stratagems. But if you can reverse this lateness and attain advance knowledge, you will definitely escape from the misfortunes of encircled terrain. Now lofty mountains, expansive marshes, constricted ravines, precipitous cliffs, wetlands, and minor routes that are suddenly cut off, terrains where there are no escape routes, are of the greatest benefit to wise strategists in their planning. You should unexpectedly impede invading enemies and then suddenly strike them from behind. In the past commanders such as T'ien Tan and Yang Pan employed blazing horses and cattle to mount unorthodox assaults that rushed into the enemy. Others awaited the dusk of night to create false insignia and then launch a penetrating assault that exploited the resulting intermixture with previously recognized enemy units. Battles such as these must be engaged with the objective of fighting to the death; otherwise, should the enemy grow stronger and your reserves never arrive, you will encounter the difficulty Li Ling faced when all his bows were broken and his arrows used up.

When the battle is most intense and the army's strength exhausted, when disaster looms imminently, anyone able to exhaust their knowledge and employ stratagems that effect a myriad inexhaustible changes will never have to worry about being on fatal terrain. Sun-tzu said: "In combat value advantages of terrain." Yet such advantages cannot have a single use, for only in the actual moment can their employment be discerned. Furthermore, the army values employing change. One who cannot employ the army with such changes will find advantages of terrain to be of no benefit.

The *Wu-ching Tsung-yao*

Completed slightly more than two decades after Hsü Tung's death, the great Sung military encyclopedia *Wu-ching Tsung-yao* was compiled as a compendium of current military knowledge. A careful reading indicates that hardly a sentence is original with the authors, although the source of much material is not always immediately evident because, except in some extremely famous cases such as the *Art of War*, the materials lack any attribution or identification. However, it remains a significant work because it preserves many passages otherwise lost and reflects the method of comprehensive inclusion that maintained the currency of ancient doctrines and attested to their validity, despite Hsü Tung's previously cited views and the likely practice of astute commanders in his and later eras. The "Miscellaneous Discussion of Combat Terrains" section ("Tsa-shu Chan-ti") essentially adopts Ho Yen-hsi's commentary from the *Art of War* as its prefatory remarks for a systematic review of Sun-tzu's configurations of terrain, completing each entry with relevant dialogues wherein the king of Wu apparently questions Sun-tzu about appropriate tactics.[52] (These dialogues, drawn from the chapters on the nine configurations in the military section of the *T'ung Tien* compiled by Tu Yu in the eighth century A.D., were traditionally thought to comprise material preserved from the eighty-two-chapter version of the *Art of War* apparently still extant in the Han dynasty. However, if not a post-Han forgery, at least parts were certainly revised after the Warring States period because cavalry is mentioned prominently.[53]) As well as providing a contemporary record of the integrated approach of terrain analysis correlated with tactical implications, being an imperially sponsored project completed in A.D. 1043, the *Wu-ching Tsung-yao* chapters assumed a disproportionately important role in the Chinese military tradition thereafter.

The Tao for deploying the army includes advantages of terrain. If we occupy conquest terrain first the enemy will not be able to control us, but if the enemy occupies it first we will not be able to control them. When selecting terrain for deploying the army, if you are unable to realize advantages and avoid harm, it is the same as racing a mass of a million and casting them onto fatal ground. This would not be a disaster from Heaven but the commanding general's error. The *Art of War* states: "Configuration of terrain is an aid to the army. Analyzing the enemy, taking control of victory, estimating ravines and defiles, the distant and near, above and below, is the Tao of the general." In discussing this Sun-tzu said: "The nine transformations of terrain, the advantages deriving from contraction and expansion, and the patterns of human emotion must be investigated. Thus it is the nature of the army to defend when encircled, to fight when unavoidable, and to follow orders when compelled. For this reason one who does not know the plans of the feudal lords cannot forge preparatory alliances. One who does not know the topography of mountains and forests, ravines and defiles, wetlands and marshes, cannot maneuver the army. One who does not employ local guides cannot secure advantages of terrain. One who does not know any one of these four or five cannot command the army of a hegemon or true king."

This apparently speaks about the advantages of the nine terrains.⁵⁴ If someone who does not know one of them is not an appointee for a hegemon or king, how much more so anyone ignorant of them all? For this reason the basic method for controlling the army is to esteem heights and disdain low ground, for by gaining a strategic advantage through their occupation it will be easy to control others. Thus because Ch'in enjoyed the solidity of the Yao-han pass, even though the six feudal lords knocked on the pass to assault it, without Ch'in perturbing itself at all the armies of the feudal lords were already in difficulty. Moreover, Ch'in's territory was not as wide as Wu's or Ch'u's or its soldiers as fierce as Yen's or Chao's, but they were able to be victorious because their terrain had ravines and solidity. Their strategic power might be compared with setting up a vase and their defenses thus enjoyed an advantage of a hundred to two. Shouldn't we focus on this? Accordingly, we have now written a section on configurations of terrain.

Dispersive Terrain

When the officers and troops rely upon it, cherishing affection for their wives and children, so that in combat they scatter and run off, it is termed "dispersive terrain." One opinion is that when the terrain lacks any constraints, allowing the officers and troops to easily scatter and desert, anyone occupying it cannot drum an advance into combat. It is also said that when the terrain remains flat far out in all four directions and lacks strategic points, the officers and troops will not be determined and so easily scatter and depart. Therefore it is called dispersive terrain. The *Art of War* states: "When the feudal lords fight in their own territory, it is dispersive terrain. On dispersive terrain do not engage the enemy." It also states: "On dispersive terrain I unify their will."

The king of Wu asked Sun-tzu: "On dispersive terrain the officers and troops are thinking of their families. As we cannot engage in battle with them, we must solidly defend our positions and not go forth. If the enemy attacks our cities and fortifications, plunders our fields, prevents us from gathering firewood, blocks our major roads, and awaits our emptiness and depletion to urgently attack, what should we do?"

Sun-tzu replied: "When the enemy has deeply penetrated our capital region and numerous fortified towns, their officers and men regard the army as their family, are focused in their intentions, and slight the enemy. On the contrary our troops are in their native state; they feel secure on their territory and embrace life. Therefore in battle formation they are not firm, when they engage in battle they are not victorious. We should assemble the people and gather the masses; collect the foodstuffs, livestock, and cloth; defend the walled cities and prepare to defend the passes; and dispatch light troops to sever their supply routes. If they are not able to provoke us into battle, their provisions fail to arrive, and there's nothing in the countryside that they can plunder, their Three Armies will be in difficulty. If we exploit the situation to entice them, we can be successful.

"If we want to engage in battle in the countryside, we must rely upon the strategic configuration of power. Utilize ravines to establish ambushes. Lacking ravines, we must conceal ourselves in the weather, darkness, dusk, and fog, going forth where they will not expect it, suddenly striking their indolent forces. Then we will achieve results."

Light Terrain

Where strongly inclined to withdraw. When you have entered enemy territory but not yet penetrated deeply so that advancing and retreating are both easy, you cannot halt or rest. The general cannot frequently stir or labor the men. The *Art of War* states: "When you enter someone else's territory but not deeply, it is light terrain. On light terrain do not stop." And also "on light terrain I have them group together."

The king of Wu asked Sun-tzu: "Suppose we have reached light terrain and have just entered the enemy's borders. Our officers and men are thinking of turning back. It's hard to advance but easy to withdraw. We do not yet have ravines and defiles behind us and the Three Armies are fearful. The commanding general wants to advance, the officers and troops want to retreat, so above and below are of different minds. The enemy is defending their walled cities and fortifications, putting their chariots and cavalry in good order. Some occupy positions to our fore, others strike our rear. What should we do?"

Sun-tzu replied: "When we have reached light terrain, the officers and men are not yet focused because their task is entering the border, not waging battle. Do not approach their famous cities or traverse their major roads. Feign doubt, pretend confusion. Show them that we are about to depart. Then initially select elite cavalry to silently enter their territory and plunder their cattle, horses, and other domestic animals. When the Three Armies observe that they were able to advance, they will not be afraid. Divide our elite soldiers and have them secretly prepare ambushes. Should the enemy come up, strike without hesitation; if they do not come up, then abandon the ambushes and depart."

He also said: "Suppose the army has entered the enemy's borders. The enemy solidifies his fortifications without engaging in battle. Our officers and troops are thinking of returning home, but even if we want to retreat it will also be difficult. This is referred to as 'light terrain.' We should select elite cavalry to establish ambushes on the strategic roads. When we withdraw, the enemy will pursue us; when they come up, quickly strike them."

Contentious Terrain

Facile, advantageous terrain such that whoever first occupies it will emerge victorious. For this reason one struggles for it. The *Art of War* states: "If when we occupy it, it will be advantageous to us, whereas if they occupy it, it will be advantageous to them, it is contentious terrain." And, "on contentious terrain do not attack. On contentious terrain I race our rear elements forward."

The king of Wu asked Sun-tzu: "On contentious terrain suppose the enemy arrives first, occupies the strategic positions, and holds the advantageous ones with selected troops and well-trained soldiers. Some of them go forth, others assume defensive positions against our unorthodox tactics. What should we do?"

Sun-tzu replied: "The rule for fighting on contentious terrain is that one who yields will gain, whereas one who fights will lose. If the enemy has gained a position, be careful not to attack it. Draw him away by pretending to go off. Set up flags, beat the drums, and move swiftly toward what he loves. Drag wood to raise clouds of dust, befuddle his ears and eyes. Divide up our superior troops, secretly placing them in ambush. The enemy will certainly come forth to rescue the endangered target. What others want we will give them; what they abandon we will take. That is the Tao for fighting for land they occupy first.

"If we arrive first and the enemy uses this tactic, select fierce troops to solidly defend our position. Have our light troops pursue the enemy's feigned departure, splitting some off to set up ambushes in the ravines and defiles. If the enemy turns about to fight, the troops on the flanks in ambush should rise up. This is the Tao for achieving complete victory."

Traversable Terrain

Level plains open to communication. [Ho T'ing-hsi] says it can be employed for forming alliances but cannot be blocked off or severed. Severing it will leave crevices.[55] It is also said that when communications penetrate far out in all four directions, they cannot be severed. The *Art of War* states: "When we can go forth and they can also come forth, it is traversable terrain," and "on traversable terrain do not allow your forces to become isolated. On traversable terrain I focus on defense."

The king of Wu asked Sun-tzu: "If on traversable terrain where movement is easy we are about to isolate the enemy and want to ensure they cannot advance, we must order our cities along the border to improve their defensive preparations, thoroughly sever all open roads, and secure the blockades at the passes. Suppose we have not planned for it beforehand while the enemy has already made such preparations. They will be able to advance, but we will not be able to go forth. If our numbers are moreover equal, what then?"

Sun-tzu replied: "Since we cannot go forth but they can come up,[56] we should split off some troops and conceal them. Our defenders should appear at ease and lax. Display incapability and the enemy will definitely arrive. Establish ambushes, conceal ourselves in the grass, and go forth where he doesn't expect it. Then we can be successful."

Focal Terrain

Land that occupies an important intersection and controls several roads so that the masses must follow whoever first occupies it. Therefore by gaining it you will be secure; losing it will be endangered. The *Art of War* states: "Land of the feudal lords surrounded on three sides such that whoever arrives first will gain the masses of All under Heaven is focal terrain. On focal terrain unite and form alliances with nearby feudal lords. On focal terrain I solidify our alliances."

The king of Wu asked Sun-tzu: "On focal terrain one values being first. If the road is far and we mobilize after the enemy, even though we race our chariots and gallop our horses, we will not be able to arrive first. What then?"

Sun-tzu replied: "Focal terrain is territory bordered by three states with roads open in the four directions. If we and the enemy oppose each other while on the side there are other states, then one who would be referred to as 'first' must dispatch polite emissaries with generous gifts to make alliances with the neighboring states. Establish friendly relations with them and secure their favor. Then even though our troops arrive after the enemy, the masses will already be allied with us.[57] We will have the support of the masses, while the enemy will have lost its partisans. The armies of the feudal states, like the horns of an ox, thundering their drums will attack en masse. The enemy will be startled and terrified, and no one will know what they ought to do."

Heavy Terrain

When you have deeply penetrated the enemy's territory and it is difficult to supply provisions from your state, if the officers and troops do not plunder, what can they get? The *Art of War* states: "When one penetrates deeply into enemy territory so that it is difficult to turn back,[58] bypassing numerous cities, it is heavy terrain. On heavy terrain by plundering I ensure a continuous supply of provisions." Moreover, "the Tao of the guest [invader] is that when the troops have penetrated deeply, they will be unified and the host will not be victorious.[59] If you forage in the fertile countryside, the Three Armies will have enough to eat. If you carefully nurture them and do not overly labor them, their *ch'i* will be united and their strength will be at maximum. When you mobilize the army, your strategic plans must be unfathomable. Cast them into position from which there is nowhere to go and they will die without retreating. If there is no escape from death the officers and soldiers will fully exhaust their strength. When the soldiers and officers have penetrated deeply they will be unafraid. When there is nowhere to go they will be solid, when they penetrate deeply they will cling together. When there is no alternative, they will fight. For this reason even though the soldiers are not instructed, they are prepared; without seeking it their cooperation is obtained; without covenants they are close together; without issuing orders they are reliable. Prohibit omens, eliminate doubt so that they will die without other thoughts. [If our soldiers] do not have excessive wealth, it is not because they detest material goods. If they do not live long lives, it is not because they abhor longevity. On the day that the orders are issued, the tears of the soldiers who are sitting will soak their sleeves, while the tears of those lying down will roll down their cheeks. However, if you throw them into a hopeless situation, they will have the courage of Chuan Chu or Ts'ao Kuei."

The king of Wu asked Sun-tzu: "Suppose we have led the troops deep into heavy terrain, bypassing a great many places so that our supply routes are cut off or blocked. Suppose we want to return home but cannot get past their strategic configuration of power. If we want to forage on the enemy's land and maintain our troops without loss, what should we do?"

Sun-tzu replied: "Whenever we occupy heavy terrain, the officers and troops will readily be courageous. If the supply routes are no longer open, we must plunder to extend our provisions. Whatever grain or cloth the lower ranks obtain must all be forwarded to the top, with those who collect the most being rewarded. Then the warriors will no longer think about returning home.

"If you want to turn about and go forth, urgently make defensive preparations. Deepen the moats and raise the ramparts, showing the enemy our determination to remain indefinitely. The enemy will suspect we have an open route somewhere and will remove themselves from the critical roads. Then we can order our light chariots to sally forth silently, the dust flying up, using the cattle and horses as bait. If the enemy goes forth, beat the drums and follow them. Prior to this secretly conceal some warriors in ambush, setting the time with them so that our forces within and without can launch a coordinated attack. The enemy's defeat can then be known."

Entrapping Terrain

Terrain with little solidity so that neither fortifications nor moats can be constructed. The *Art of War* states: "When maneuvering where there are mountains and forests, ravines and defiles, wetlands and marshes, wherever the road is difficult to negotiate, it is entrapping terrain. On entrapping terrain I advance along the roads."[60]

The king of Wu asked Sun-tzu: "Suppose we enter entrapping terrain—mountains, rivers, ravines, and defiles. The road is difficult to follow, while we have been on the move for a long time and the troops are tired. The enemy lies before us and is ambushing our rear. Their encampment occupies a position to the left while they defend against our right. Their superior chariots and skilled cavalry are pressing us on a constricted road. What then?"

Sun-tzu replied: "First have the light chariots advance about ten kilometers so that they and the enemy are observing each other. When our main army has reached their ravines and defiles, deploy some to go to the left, others to the right, while the commanding general conducts observations in all directions. Select vacuities and seize them, then have all our forces converge together on the road, stopping only when tired."

Encircled Terrain

When the entrance is constricted and precipitous, the route back circuitous, and advancing and retreating disconnected, even though one has masses of troops, what use are they? However, through unorthodox tactics and changes this terrain can be followed. The *Art of War* states: "Where the entrance is constricted, the return is circuitous, and with a small number they can strike our masses, it is encircled terrain." Moreover, "when you have strongholds behind you and constrictions before you, it is encircled terrain. On encircled terrain use strategy. On encircled terrain I obstruct any openings."

The king of Wu asked Sun-tzu: "Suppose we have entered encircled terrain so that before us there is a strong enemy and to our rear precipitous and difficult ground. The enemy have severed our supply lines and are taking advantage of our moving disposition. If they beat their drums and yell but do not advance in order to observe our capability, what should we do?"

Sun-tzu replied: "On encircled terrain it is appropriate to block up all the openings, showing the troops that there is nowhere to go. Then they will regard the army as their family, the multitude will be of one mind, and the strength of the Three Armies will be united. Furthermore, steam food for several days, thereafter not displaying any fire or smoke, thus creating the appearance of decay, confusion, paucity of numbers, and weakness. When the enemy see this, their battle preparations will certainly be light.

"Incite our officers and troops with exhortations, arousing their anger. When you assume formation, deploy our superior troops in ambush in the ravines and defiles to the left and right. Beat the drums and go forth. If the enemy opposes us fervently, strike them, concentrating on breaking through. Fight in the front, consolidate in the rear, and set out our flanks to the left and right [in a pincer movement]."

The king of Wu again asked: "Suppose the enemy is surrounded by our forces. They lie in ambush and make deep plans. They display enticements to us, they tire us with their pennants, moving all about as if in confusion. We do not know how to deal with this. What should we do?"

Sun-tzu replied: "Have a thousand men take up pennants, divide and block off the strategic roads. Have our light troops advance and try to provoke the enemy. Deploy our battle arrays, but do not press them. Intercept them, but do not go off. This is the art of defeating stratagems."

Fatal Terrain

Is where if you fight fervently perhaps you will survive, but if you just assume a defensive posture will die. The *Art of War* states: "Where if one fights with intensity he will survive but if he does not fight with intensity he will perish, it is fatal terrain. On fatal terrain I show them that we will not live." Also, "on fatal terrain engage in battle." Cast them onto fatal terrain, "for only thereafter will they penetrate the enemy's territory, only thereafter will the host's masses be thrown into danger and our troops be able to wrest victory from defeat."

The king of Wu asked Sun-tzu: "Suppose our army has gone out beyond the borders and our forces are arrayed in front of the enemy. The enemy's forces arrive in great number, encircling us several layers deep. We want to suddenly burst out, but all four sides are blocked. If we want to encourage our officers and incite our masses of troops to have them risk their lives and crush the encirclement, how should we do it?"[61]

Sun-tzu replied: "Make the moats deeper and the ramparts higher, showing that we are making preparations to defend our position. Be quiet and still, without moving, to conceal our capability. Announce orders to the Three Armies to feign hopelessness. Kill the cattle and burn the supply wagons to feast our warriors. Burn all the provisions, fill in the wells, level the stoves, cut off your hair, cast aside your caps, completely eliminate all thoughts of life, and have no further plans. When the officers are determined to die, then have them polish their armor and sharpen their blades. When their *ch'i* has been united and their strength as one, some should attack the two flanks with thundering hearts and yelling fervently.[62] The enemy will also become frightened, and no one will know how to withstand us. Elite troops and detached units should urgently attack their rear. This is the Tao by which to lose the road and seek life. Thus it is said that 'one who is in difficulty but doesn't make plans is impoverished; one who is impoverished and doesn't fight is lost.'"

The king of Wu also asked, "What if we surround the enemy?" Sun-tzu replied: "Mountain peaks and valley confines that are difficult to traverse are referred to as the 'means to impoverish invaders.' The method for attacking them is to set our troops in ambush in dark and concealed places. Open a road for the enemy to depart, show them a path for flight. When they are seeking life and escaping from death, they certainly won't have any will to fight. Then we can strike them and even if they are numerous, they will certainly be destroyed."

The *Art of War* also states: "If the enemy is on fatal terrain, the *ch'i* of their officers and troops will be courageous. If we want to strike them, the strategy is to seemingly accord with them and not resist. Secretly guard against their advantageous positions, but you must allow them an escape route. Employ elite cavalry to segment off and block the strategic roads, employ light troops to advance and entice them. Deploy but do not engage in battle, this is the way to defeat their strategy."[63]

Six Configurations

Accessible Configuration

Where either side can get there first and whoever arrives first will await the enemy. The *Art of War* states: "If we can go forth and the enemy can also advance, it is termed 'accessible.'" When occupying accessible terrain, "first occupy the heights and *yang* [sunny] side. If you improve the roads for transporting provisions, when you engage in battle you will be victorious."

Suspended Configuration

If you go forth you will not be victorious, whereas returning will also be difficult. The *Art of War* states: "If we can go forth but it will be difficult to return, it is termed 'suspended.' If the enemy is unprepared, go forth and conquer them. If the enemy is prepared and we sally forth without being victorious, it will be difficult to turn back and is not advantageous."

Stalemated Configuration

Stalemated configuration is broken off and constricted but simultaneously sustains both sides. Because both sides are being sustained it will not be advantageous to go forth first. The *Art of War* states: "If it is not advantageous for us to go forth or advantageous for the enemy to come forward,[64] it is termed 'stalemated.' In a stalemated configuration, even though the enemy puts us in difficulty and presses us,[65] we do not go forth. Withdraw our forces and depart. If we strike them when half their forces have come forth, it will be advantageous."

Constricted Configuration

In a constricted configuration, if the enemy defends the narrows first, we depart. If they do not defend them, we follow them in. The *Art of War* states: "As for constricted configurations, if we occupy them first, we must fully deploy throughout them in order to await the enemy. If the enemy occupies them first and fully deploys in them, do not follow them in. If they do not fully deploy in them, then follow them in."

Precipitous Configuration

As for precipitous configurations, you should occupy the ravines and defiles but cannot arrive after others. The *Art of War* states: "As for precipitous configurations, if we occupy them, we must hold the heights and *yang* sides to await the enemy. If the enemy occupies them first, withdraw our forces and depart. Do not follow them."

Expansive Configuration

When you engage with an equally powerful enemy so that victory and defeat cannot be known. The *Art of War* states: "As for expansive configurations, if our strategic power is equal, it will be difficult to provoke them into combat. Engaging in combat will not be advantageous."

Miscellaneous Discussion of Combat Terrain

The *Art of War* states: "As for deploying the army and fathoming the enemy, to cross mountains follow the valleys, search out tenable ground, and occupy the heights.[66] [If the enemy holds the heights] do not climb up to engage them in battle. This is the way to deploy an army in the mountains." This teaches mountain warfare.

[The *Art of War* states]: "After crossing rivers, you must distance yourself from them. If the guest is fording a river to advance, do not confront them in the water. When half their forces have crossed, it will be advantageous to strike them. If you want to engage the enemy in battle, do not array your forces near the river to confront the invader, but look for tenable ground and occupy the heights. Do not confront the current's flow. This is the way to deploy the army where there are rivers."

[The *Art of War* states]: "On level plains deploy the army on easy terrain with the right flank positioned with high ground to the rear, fatal terrain to the fore, and tenable terrain to the rear. This is the way to deploy on level plains."

[The *Art of War* states]: "When you cross salt marshes and wetlands, concentrate on quickly getting away from them, do not remain. If you engage in battle in marshes or wetlands, you must stay in areas with marsh grass and keep groves of trees at your back. This is the way to deploy the army in marshes and wetlands."

[The *Art of War* states]: "These four regulations for the army are the means by which the Yellow Emperor conquered the four emperors."

The king of Wu asked Sun-tzu:[67] "The enemy is securely holding the mountains and ravines, occupying all the advantageous positions. Their provisions are also sufficient. Even though we challenge them, they do not come forth. They take advantage of cracks in our defenses to raid and plunder. What should we do?"

Sun-tzu said: "Segment and deploy our forces to defend the strategic points; exercise vigilance in preparations; do not be indolent. Deeply investigate their true situation, secretly await their laxity. Entice them with profit, prevent them from gathering firewood. When they have not gained anything in a long time, they will inevitably change by themselves. Wait until they leave their strongholds, seize what they love. Even though the enemy forcibly occupies precipitous passes, we will still be able to destroy them."

Moreover, Marquis Wu of Wei asked Wu Ch'i:[68] "On the left and right are high mountains, while the land is extremely narrow and confined. If when we meet the enemy we dare not attack them, yet cannot escape, what shall we do?"

Wu Ch'i replied: "This is referred to as 'valley warfare.' Even if your troops are numerous, they are useless. Summon your talented officers to confront the enemy, the nimble footed and sharpest weapons to be at the forefront. Divide your chariots and array your cavalry, concealing them on all four sides several kilometers apart so that they will not show their weapons. The enemy will certainly assume a solid defensive formation, not daring to either advance or retreat. Thereupon display your flags and array your banners, withdraw outside the mountains, and encamp. The enemy will invariably be frightened, and your chariots and cavalry should then harass them, not permitting them any rest."

"If the enemy mounts a stout defense, urgently deploy agents and spies, observe their changes and confusion, then suddenly attack them. If they contract, you can overturn them and be victorious. In general, soldiers employed in valley warfare must be skilled at establishing ambushes. Select fierce, elite troops to act as a vanguard, array strong crossbowmen [behind them], then the short weapons. Fight courageously and quickly press the battle."

Moreover, select soldiers who are light of foot; pick out bypaths; ascend the heights and make observations on the enemy's troops below; and then engage in battle. Set up numerous flags and drums on the heights in order to shake them. If you suddenly encounter the enemy in a mountain gorge, then urgently beat the drums and shout, first causing them to be startled into confusion, then uniting through unorthodox changes to suddenly strike them.

If we have led troops deep into the territory of the feudal lords, where they encounter a large forest that we share with the enemy in a standoff, it is termed "forest warfare."[69] Have our Three Armies divide into the assault formation. Improve the positions the troops occupy, and station the archers and crossbowmen outside, with those carrying spear-tipped halberds and shields inside. Cut down and clear away the grass and trees, and extensively broaden the passages in order to facilitate our deployment onto the battle site. Set our pennants and flags out on high, and carefully encourage the Three Armies without letting the enemy know our true situation. Then suddenly form our spearbearers and crossbowmen into squads of five. If the woods are not dense, cavalry can be used in support. Fight when it is advantageous, halt when it is not. If we encounter woods that are dense with numerous ravines and defiles, deploy our forces in the Assault Formation in order to be thoroughly prepared both front and rear. If we fight and rest in turn, the enemy can certainly be driven off.

Another method for forest warfare is spread out the flags and pennants during the daytime, multiply the fires and drums at night, and employ short weapons. Skill will lie in unorthodox ambushes, some sprung from the front, others raised in the rear. Place strong crossbows in the middle of the left and right flanks. It will be advantageous to defend the ravines and halt.

When Han Kao-tsu initiated his sudden strike against Mao Tun, Mao Tun concealed his elite warriors and displayed only emaciated and weak ones.[70] When Kao-tsu reached P'ing-ch'eng but before his infantry had fully arrived, Mao Tun released some three hundred thousand elite forces that besieged the emperor for seven days on Pai-teng Mountain. Although this is a historical experience, in recent ages the unorthodox strategies of barbarian armies have not gone beyond such measures, something enlightened generals successfully fathom but stupid ones fall into.

At the same time their tactical skills differ from those of our Central State [China]. They can ascend and descend mountain slopes, go in and out along mountain streams, something that China's horses cannot match. For racing along precipitous roads that wind about hills and shooting their bows, China's cavalry is not as good as theirs. In exhausting themselves in wind and rain and being untroubled despite hunger and thirst, China's soldiers are unlike them. These are skills in which barbarian invaders excel.

But out on the easy terrain of the plains, if we employ light chariots or a surprise cavalry attack, the barbarian's masses will be easily thrown into confusion. Barbarians bows are not a match for our strong crossbows for distant, dispersed shooting, nor their weapons for our long halberds. Barbarians soldiers cannot oppose our stout armor, sharp blades, intermixed long and short weapons, crossbow guerrilla tactics, or orderly vanguard formations. Their leather shields and wooden bucklers cannot withstand the hail of arrows loosed by our skilled archers as they travel uniform paths to the target. Dismounted, fighting on the ground with swords, clashing back and forth, their infantry skills are not a match for ours. These are the skills in which China excels.

If we analyze it on this basis, barbarians excel in three skills and China five. Earlier ages calculated five barbarians were required to match one Han soldier. These days, even though they have managed to learn some of our techniques, three are still required to confront one of our soldiers. This is largely because of our advantageous weapons and the fact that barbarians are skilled in cavalry methods, not infantry fighting. China's infantry have strong crossbows and sharp-edged axes that are sufficient to resist them, but we Chinese are not a match for them because our people are accustomed to tranquillity and lack their ability to tolerate suffering out in the frost, snow, and grassless lands of sand. Furthermore, it is their nature not to be good at attacking or to long sustain an assault. Their sole advantage lies in sudden penetrating assaults. Therefore generals in former generations controlled them with unorthodox measures but were unable to pursue them to fight.

The nature of the Jung barbarians in the south is agile, cruel, hateful, and angry. They take pleasure in being thieves and brigands but cannot sustain their power. Their weapons are simply various types of spears and javelins, flying and ringed knives, and wooden crossbows. They so excel at making poisoned arrows that anyone hit by them will scream loudly and die after a couple of nights. They take advantage of the mountains and obstacles of rivers and rely upon the ravines. In times of crisis they sneak away and lay ambushes, but when it is calm they plunder and forage. When moving by boat, they can cross most of the rivers, when traveling on land, they can enter all the ravines and defiles, what we cannot do. To attack them, it is advantageous to exploit level terrain and employ unorthodox strategies, enticing their soldiers forward and then springing elite troops from concealed ambush to capture them. There are many methods for luring them in, such as releasing turned agents to go and speak about great riches, so that when we summon their ambassadors they will fall into our trap.

Now the Chinese people dwell in buildings, cook their food, and wear clothes of silk and other fine materials. However, in the north the killing cold of fall comes early, hands and feet crack, so we are unable to cross the Han River. In the southern region of licentious heat there are narrow ravines with poisons whose peaks cannot be scaled. If we defend the border there with soldiers from the Central State, then ten men will not even be able to match one. In antiquity they thus had the various barbarians attack each other so that their strengths were appropriately matched. In this way people outside the passes were summoned and brought in to be employed in combat. They opened lands in order to feed them and provided generous rewards in order to stimulate them. They sought to nurture a character for warfare and accumulate skill in galloping and shooting. They minimized district expenses in order to provide for their labors. They released agents and spies with generous bribes to attract their powerful clans and chiefs and sent them to attack the north. They reaped a tenfold benefit from employing them thus. Therefore Wu Ch'i, an excellent general of antiquity, also frequently discussed the character of the six states.[71]

Local Customs

The peoples' customs in the outer states and five regions of our great China all have natures that cannot be changed.[72] They are hard or soft, slow or fast, have different sacrifices and vessels, diverse regulations and clothing, all appropriately. Thus in the wilds of the northern frontier regions where *yin* accumulates they eat meat and drink fermented milk, and their skin is dense so that they can endure the cold. But in the humid semitropical south of constant *yang* the people's skin is open so that they can tolerate the heat. This is their Heavenly given nature. When the famous generals of antiquity received an order to attack one of these states, they would invariably calculate the strength and weakness of their customs and capabilities, and always attacked shortcomings with strength. They analyzed what they liked and employed it to entice them, determined what they hated and exploited it to attack them.

For the most part the nature of the northern Ti is similar to those of the Western Jung. Their warriors are all strong enough to pull a bow and be armored cavalrymen. In ordinary times it is their custom to practice herding and hunting and capturing animals as their occupation, but in times of military crisis they are practiced in martial assaults and make it their affair to invade and attack us. Their long-range weapons are the bow and arrow, close weapons the knife and short spear. When it is advantageous, they advance; when disadvantageous, withdraw. They never find it shameful to retreat as long as it is profitable.[73]

The method for suddenly attacking them is to hide troops in ambush along the ravines and other concealed terrain or occupy thick woods with tangled vegetation. Select elite soldiers and sharp weapons, with a thousand men to a unit. Near each strategic point where you have established ambushes employ fierce but not stalwart-looking troops, and follow up with some weak troops who will pretend the situation has become untenable. Use several hundred to a thousand men to abandon your visible positions. The barbarians will certainly be greedy for what they might capture, so if you wait until they are competing with each other to advance to spring your ambushes and suddenly strike them, you will certainly be victorious.

However, we Chinese do not excel in mounting great, pitched, all-or-nothing battles with them out on the open plains or in the wilds. Moreover, their skill is with ordinary bows and arrows, whereas we ought to press them with our strong crossbows. Thus in the Warring States period the method for combat stated: "Have some courageous but not resolute men test the invaders but then quickly depart, setting up three ambushes to await them. If the barbarians lightly advance without good order, if they are greedy and disharmonious, if they do not yield when victorious or rescue each other when in defeat, then those in front, when they see some rewards, will certainly strive to advance. When they advance and then encounter an ambush, they will certainly run off quickly. Since those in the rear will not rescue them, they will be disjointed." This is already a method for testing them.[74]

The barbarians are also accustomed to enticing armies. They displayed emaciated regiments in order to bring the enemy to them, so it is important to closely observe them. Thus whenever employing the army, Han Kao-tsu valued heights and detested lowlands, esteemed the sunny [yang] and disdained the shady [yin]. He nurtured life and dwelled in the substantial. Life is yang, so when one nurtures oneself in yang, his ch'i will be victorious. The heights are substantial, so when Han Kao-tsu occupied the heights, the low wetlands were kept distant and the hundred illnesses did not arise. Men were settled in their employment. This was to the advantage of the army, and the assistance of the terrain.[75]

The Art of War speaks of precipitous gorges with mountain torrents, Heaven's Well, Heaven's Jail, Heaven's Net, Heaven's Pit, and Heaven's Fissure. These six are referred to as the "six harms." When you encounter them, quickly depart, do not approach them. What is termed "a precipitous gorge" is mountainous land with a deep river valley. Heaven's Well is a natural depression in which excessive water can accumulate. Heaven's Net is a mountainous gorge with a stream with the sides so narrow that it becomes land where men could be caught in a net. Heaven's Jail is where the forest is dark and overgrown, land where tangled vegetation is deep and expansive. Heaven's Pit is land where the escape road is muddy and neither men nor horses can traverse it. Heaven's Fissure is where the terrain is mostly watery ditches and pits, land where one sinks into watery gravel. Always have our army keep them at a distance, but force the enemy to approach them. We face them, the enemy has them at their back. [Sun-tzu said]: "When an army on campaign encounters ravines and defiles, wetlands with reeds and tall grass, mountain forests or areas with heavy, entangled undergrowth, you must thoroughly search them because they are places where an ambush or spies would be concealed. Thus when the army advances, there are roads on which one does not attack, terrain for which one does not contend." He referred to these sorts of terrain.[76]

Now when sending the army forth there are the distinctions of host and guest, and in employing the army there is infantry and cavalry. Since there are already such differences, every terrain cannot be advantageous. Thus Ch'ao Ts'uo said:[77] "Where there are moats fifteen feet deep, water that will sink chariots, or grass and trees, it is terrain for infantry." Here chariots and cavalry will not even enjoy a two to one force advantage. Dirt-covered hills, interconnected rolling ridges, level plains, and broad expanses of wilderness are terrain for chariots and cavalry. Here ten infantry-men cannot match a single cavalryman.

Where there are flattened mountaintops far apart with a river valley between them where one must look up high and can approach below, this is terrain for bows and crossbows. A hundred close-range weapons will not match one bow.

Where two forces are closely deployed with level terrain and shallow grass between them across which they can advance and withdraw, this is terrain for employing long halberds. Here three swords and shields will not match one halberd.

Tangled overgrowth, bamboo clumps, heavy grass, and areas where dense leaves interconnect to shade and cover everything are terrain for spears and truncheons. Here two long weapons will not match a single one of them.

Winding roads where ambushes might be set and ravines and constrictions where attacks can occur are terrain for swords and shields. Here three bows or crossbows will not match one of them.

The *Art of War* states:[78] "Wherever you can look out, whether across divided valleys or over rivers, you can employ bows and arrows. In heavy vegetation and dense grass you can exploit wind and fire. If to the left and right are both high mountains, then elongate your flanks and advance. If the terrain is high to the rear but low in front, use a fierce assault and advance. When traversing wetlands and marshes, put your companies in order and quickly pass through. When occupying level inland terrain, keep fatal terrain to the fore and tenable terrain to the rear. On hills or rises you must occupy the *yang* side and keep them to the right rear. On embankments you must occupy the *yin* side and keep them to the left front." In this way the commanding general must investigate these principles and comprehend them in his mind first.

If their men are zealous in combat and practiced in weapons but slight their general and disdain their salaries while their officers have no commitment to die, they are ordered but not usable. Focus on the tactics for this situation: If they deploy in limited force, press them; if their masses come forth, resist them; if they depart, pursue them in order to wear out their army, for then they can be defeated. This is termed "investigating the distresses of human nature."

Moreover, analyze the losses marking their state's administration and control them in accord with their distress. Then we will gain an advantage, they will suffer a disadvantage, and we will easily act strongly. The *Ssu-ma Fa* states: "Men from each quarter have their own nature, character changes from region to region."[79] This speaks about the men of the four quarters. Human nature includes the hard and soft, stupid and wise, all different. "Through instruction they come to have regional habits, the customs of each state thus being different." This speaks about the military strength of the four quarters.

The west and north are conducive to soldiers and horses, the east and south have the convenience of boats and oars. The west and north are cold and miserable and lack copper and iron, whereas the east and south are hot and humid, their bows and crossbows rot away. The middle terrain [of the Central State] has the five weapons in abundance and various trees and is conducive to bows and horses, boats and oars. These are their appropriate differences. Thus "the state of Yen lacks armor, Ch'in lacks bamboo shafts for their weapons, while the Hu lack bows and chariots." This speaks about the strength of customs.

Sun-tzu said: "Evaluate comparatively through estimations and seek out their true nature. Which ruler has the Tao? Which general has greater ability?" This also means that we must first determine our relative strengths. Otherwise, anyone who doesn't know this but still employs the military will be like a blind man without direction and will be overturned in no time at all.[80]

Evaluating and Targeting Cities

China early on developed densely populated administrative centers that became the focus of economic, as well as military, activities and thus prime targets whether a campaign army was simply bent upon defeating the enemy or capturing power centers and annexing territory. However, as early as the Shang dynasty the technique of rammed-earth wall building had been perfected, resulting in the classic combination of deep moats fronting massive walls often thirty feet in height and thickness. In Sun-tzu's era, roughly the end of the Spring and Autumn period, siege technology was just beginning to evolve, so cities represented formidable targets that required a vast expenditure of time and effort to capture or reduce. Moreover, inspired defenders could easily decimate any impatient attackers who chose to mount a premature assault. Even though cities were the military and economic centers of the surrounding area, they had not evolved into critical targets, and could easily be bypassed as armies moved through reasonably open countryside. Accordingly, Sun-tzu decried protracted sieges and discouraged precipitous urban assaults by classifying them as the lowest form of warfare, rather than dogmatically asserting they should never be undertaken:

> The tactic of attacking fortified cities is adopted only when unavoidable. Preparing large movable protective shields, armored assault wagons, and other equipment and devices will require three months. Building earthworks will require another three months to complete. If the general cannot overcome his impatience, but instead launches an assault wherein his men swarm over the walls like ants, he will kill one-third of his officers and troops and the city will still not be taken. This is the disaster that results from attacking fortified cities.[81]

Modern Western professional military publications have frequently but incorrectly simplified Sun-tzu's admonitions to "Do not attack cities" or "Avoid urban warfare." However, a slightly earlier passage reconfirms that, rather than simply condemning such attacks outright, Sun-tzu advocated the considered implementation of more effective tactics: "The highest realization of warfare is to attack the enemy's plans; next is to attack their alliances; and the lowest is to attack their fortified cities." Furthermore, tomb fragments recovered with Sun Pin's *Military Methods* that may have been an integral part of Sun-tzu's *Art of War* further explicate his view:

> As for fortified cities that are not assaulted: We estimate that our strength is sufficient to seize it. If we seize it, it will not be of any advantage to the fore; if we gain it, we will not be able to protect it to the rear. If our strength equals theirs, the city certainly will not be taken. If when we gain the advantage of a forward position the city will then surrender by itself, whereas if we do not gain such advantages the city will not cause harm to the rear—in such cases, even though the city can be assaulted, do not assault it.[82]

Sun-tzu thus emphasized calculating the potential net gain and employing methods other than frontal assaults, such as drawing the enemy out so that they will be compelled to fight on more advantageous terrain.

Sun Pin's dual categorization of "male" and "female" cities in the middle of the Warring States period is generally contrasted with Sun-tzu's reluctance to assault fortified cities and interpreted as reflecting the growth of cities as economic and strategic centers, as well as the evolution of effective siege techniques and weaponry, such as the catapult.[83] Unlike the Spring and Autumn era, when campaign armies could move relatively unhindered through the sparsely populated open countryside, in the middle Warring States period they could be thwarted by the heavily fortified strongholds that had concurrently assumed much greater military and economic value. Among these cities the strategically weaker ones, which he classified as female, could be attacked, whereas the stronger, or male, ones should be avoided. (However, Sun Pin never explicitly stated that female cities should invariably be attacked or designated them as more than preferred targets.) His classificatory principles in the chapter entitled "Male and Female Cities" appear to be simply topographical, although other situations similarly categorized for their attack potential (deleted here) were also intermixed.[84]

A city that lies amid small marshes, lacks high mountains and notable valleys, but has moderate-sized mounds about its four quarters is a male city that cannot be attacked.

If before a city there is a notable valley while it has a high mountain behind it, it is a male city and cannot be attacked.

If the terrain within a city is high while it falls away outside it, it is a male city and cannot be attacked.

A city with moderate-sized mounds within is a male city that cannot be attacked.

A city with a notable valley behind it that lacks high mountains to its left and right is a vacuous city and can be attacked.

A city that lies amid vast marshes and lacks notable valleys and moderate-sized mounds is a female city that can be attacked.

A city that lies between high mountains and lacks notable valleys and moderate-sized mounds is a female city that can be attacked.

If there is a high mountain in front of a city and a notable valley behind it, while before it the ground ascends and to the rear it descends, it is a female city and can be attacked.

The *Wei Liao-tzu*, a military classic probably composed a century after Sun Pin's death, discussed the economic importance of city markets for sustaining the armed forces and noted that "land is the means for nourishing the populace; fortified cities the means for defending the land; and combat the means for defending the cities." Accordingly, the author advocated making cities a primary objective, particularly if "the cities are large and the land narrow":

> When the troops have assembled at the enemy's border and the general has arrived, the army should penetrate deeply into their territory, sever their roads, and occupy their large cities and large towns. Have the troops ascend the walls and press the enemy into endangered positions. Have the several units of men and women each press the enemy in accord with the configuration of the terrain and attack any strategic barriers. If you occupy the terrain around a city or town and sever the various roads about it, follow up by attacking the city itself.

According to the *Wei Liao-tzu*, determining whether to besiege or assault a city is simply part of an overall strategic assessment, a basic intelligence operation:

> Attack a country according to its changes. Display riches in order to observe their poverty. Display exhaustion in order to observe their illness. If the ruler is immoral and the people disaffected, one has a basis for attack.
>   In general, whenever about to mobilize the army, you must first investigate the strategic balance of power both within and without the borders in order to calculate whether to mount a campaign. You must know whether the army is well prepared or suffers from inadequacies; whether there is a surplus or shortage of provisions. You must determine the routes for advancing and returning. Only thereafter can you mobilize the army to attack the chaotic and be certain of being able to enter their state.
>   If the territory is vast but the cities small, you must first occupy their land. If the cities are large but the land narrow, you must first attack their cities. If the country is vast and the populace few, isolate their strategic points. If the land is confined but the people numerous, construct high mounds in order to overlook them. Do not destroy their material profits or seize the people's agricultural seasons. Be magnanimous toward their government officials, stabilize the people's occupations, and provide relief for their impoverished, for then your Virtue will be sufficient to overspread All under Heaven.[85]

Other passages in the *Wei Liao-tzu* identify several factors that make cities vulnerable:

When the general is light, the fortifications low, and the people's minds unstable, the masses can be attacked. If the general is weighty and the fortifications are high but the masses are afraid, they can be encircled. In general, whenever you encircle someone, you must provide them with a prospect for some minor advantage, causing them to become weaker day by day. Then the defenders will be forced to reduce their rations until they have nothing to eat.

When their masses fight with each other at night, they are terrified. If the masses avoid their work, they have become disaffected. If they just wait for others to come and rescue them and when the time for battle arrives they are tense, they have all lost their will and are dispirited. Dispirit defeats an army, distorted plans defeat a state.[86] . . .

If the enemy's generals and armies are unable to believe in each other, the officers and troops unable to be in harmony, and there are those unaffected by punishments, we will defeat them. Before the rescue party has arrived the city will have already surrendered.

If fords and bridges have not yet been constructed, strategic barriers not yet repaired, dangerous points in the city walls not yet fortified, and the iron caltrops not yet set out, then even though they have a fortified city, they do not have any defense!

If the troops from distant forts have not yet entered the city or the border guards and forces in other states yet returned, then even though they have men, they do not have any men! If the six domesticated animals have not yet been herded in, the five grains not yet harvested, the wealth and materials for use not yet collected, then even though they have resources, they do not have any resources! Now when a city is empty and void and its resources are exhausted, we should take advantage of this vacuity to attack them.[87]

The *Wei Liao-tzu* also contains extensive passages on the nature of sieges and fortified defenses, including a brief analysis of the defender's psychology, that merit examining because their thorough implementation precludes an easy, even successful, assault:

In general, when the defenders go forth, if they do not occupy the outer walls of the cities or the borderlands, and when they retreat do not establish watchtowers and barricades for the purpose of defensive warfare, they do not excel at defense. The valiant heroes and brave stalwarts, sturdy armor and sharp weapons, powerful crossbows and strong arrows should all be within the outer walls, and then all the grain stored outside in the earthen cellars and granaries collected and the buildings outside the outer walls broken down and brought into the fortifications. This will force the attackers to expend ten or a hundred times the energy, whereas the defenders will not expend half theirs. The enemy aggressors will be harmed greatly, yet generals through the ages have not known this.

If a wall is ten thousand feet long, then ten thousand men should defend it. The moats should be deep and wide, the walls solid and thick, the soldiers and people prepared, firewood and foodstuffs provided, the crossbows stout and arrows strong, the spears and halberds well suited. This is the method for making defense solid.

If the attackers are not less than a mass of at least a hundred thousand while the defenders have an army outside that will certainly come to the rescue, it is a city that must be defended. If there is no external army to inevitably rescue them, then it isn't a city that must be defended.

Now if the walls are solid and rescue certain, then even stupid men and ignorant women will all, without exception, protect the walls, exhausting their resources and blood for them. For a city to withstand a siege for a year, the strength of the defenders should exceed that of the attackers, and the strength of the rescue force exceed that of the defenders.

Now if the walls are solid but rescue uncertain, then the stupid men and ignorant women, all without exception, will defend the parapets, but they will weep. This is normal human emotion. Even if you then open the grain reserves in order to relieve and pacify them, you cannot stop it. You must incite the valiant heroes and brave stalwarts with their sturdy armor, sharp weapons, strong crossbows, and stout arrows to exert their strength together in the front, and the young, weak, crippled, and ill to exert their strength together in the rear.[88]

Throughout the Warring States period siege warfare rapidly evolved, producing specialized techniques, machines, and subversive methods, making it possible to subjugate cities far more expeditiously, sometimes even in days. The *Six Secret Teachings* describes some tactics for besieging cities that emphasize the role of intelligence. For example, when confronted with a double-pronged night attack from both outside and inside the siege lines, the T'ai Kung predicated the tactical response upon thorough knowledge of the situation: "In this case you should divide your forces into three armies. Be careful to evaluate the terrain's configuration and then strategically emplace them. You must know in detail the location of the enemy's second army, as well as their large cities and secondary fortifications. Leave them a passage in order to entice them to flee. Pay attention to all the preparations, not neglecting anything."[89] Another chapter elucidates an unusual technique for determining a city's vulnerability based upon observations of the *ch'i* in its environs, which will be discussed in the final section on portents.

The preceding materials clearly witness a historical progression from Sun-tzu through Sun Pin to Wei Liao-tzu, from viewing assaults on cities as the lowest tactical option to emphasizing the need to defend and attack them as the highest. After the establishment of the Ch'in dynasty and the elimination of conflict between the distinct political entities known as states, the military horizon shifted to ongoing conflict with steppe peoples interspersed with the fragmenting battles of periodic dynastic strife. Although some cities were encountered in the Han's far-ranging campaigns, the efforts to contain, even vanquish, the steppe peoples were little concerned with city assaults because of the seasonal movements and absence of permanent fortifications around even their largest population centers. However, during the repeated, interminable wars that marked China's history from its imperial inception, the question was no longer whether to attack the cities, but how and when. Some reluctance is still seen in the later military writings because they continued to be under the theoretical influence of earlier concepts and sieges still required enormous effort, but generals would rarely bypass such valuable and powerful targets, and the techniques of siegecraft accordingly receive considerable space in the great military compendiums.

The late Sung *Hundred Unorthodox Strategies* contains two tactical lessons that reflect the parameters for evaluating cities as targets of opportunity. The first, "Slowness in Warfare," surprisingly advises mounting a siege preliminary to an assault despite the presence of strong fortifications: "In general, assaulting fortified enemy cities is the lowest form of strategy, to be undertaken only when there is no alternative. However, if their walls are high and their moats deep, their people many and supplies few, while there is no prospect of external rescue and you can thoroughly entangle and take the city, then it will be advantageous. A tactical principle from the *Art of War* states: 'Their slowness is like the forest.'"

Two factors predispose the city to a siege and eventual assault: The large occupation force lacks sufficient supplies to withstand a long siege and has no hope of rescue. Therefore, the siege need not be prolonged and as the fortifications are basically good—high walls and deep moats—once taken, will prove highly defensible. In contrast, the situation in the next chapter, "Quickness in Warfare," assumes the opposite: ample food, few men to resist, and the danger of external forces attacking from without if the siege is prolonged. Thus, in the former case the attackers can afford to wait for the besieged to grow weaker, but in the latter they must act quickly to achieve their tactical objectives: "Whenever attacking an encircled town, if the enemy's supplies are ample but their men few while they have a prospect for external aid, you must quickly assault them and then you will be victorious. A tactical principle states: 'The army values spiritual speed.'"

Undertaking a prolonged siege, rather than mounting a swift assault, is thus judged inadvisable because the defenders have ample food supplies and strong prospects for being rescued by a formidable external force. Should the latter arrive, the attackers would be exposed to a crushing external assault combined with a simultaneous interior counterattack by highly motivated defenders, just as the T'ai Kung pondered previously. As the *Six Secret Teachings* states, "Being as swift as a flying arrow and attacking as suddenly as the release of a crossbow are the means by which to destroy brilliant plans." Clearly, numerous factors, including the spirit and resolve of the defenders, still had to be weighed whether one is considering a siege or an assault, or undertaking a sustained defense against siege, which is somewhat less discussed, except in the *Wei Liao-tzu*, and equally requires adequate information about the enemy's forces, position, and intentions.

Part Six

PROGNOSTICATION, DIVINATION, AND NONHUMAN FACTORS

占 卜 及 徵 兆

17

Historical Practices
and Their Rejection

*P*LASTROMANCY AND THE SHANG DYNASTY ruling house were
so intertwined as to be indivisible, current knowledge of the Shang essentially being derived from the hundreds of thousands of turtle plas-
trons and ox bones used in scapulimancy, supplemented with other archaeological evidence. The ruler questioned the spirits on numerous
topics regarding administration, sacrifices, rituals, and personal affairs, including his own health, but especially military actions and
campaigns. The hope was expressed that a specific campaign, undertaken on a certain day or within a specified time period, would prove
successful, and confirmation was then sought from the spirits, perhaps in a sort of normative mode rather than simple inquiry.[1] This tradition continued into the Chou, although much deemphasized because the Chou proclaimed they had inherited the Mandate of
Heaven, and from examples in the *Tso Chuan* the tradition may also
be seen in the Spring and Autumn period, as rulers in the individual
states sought to determine the auspiciousness of contemplated military actions.[2] For this purpose both the turtle and the *I Ching*—divination by milfoil stalks—were used, with the former being given preference for serious affairs of state, although the latter became more
popular with the passing of time.[3]

A very early example of employing the *I Ching,* presumably dating
from the Spring and Autumn period, is preserved in the *Tso Chuan* entry for Duke Hsi's fifteenth year (645 B.C.):

> The Earl of Ch'in was about to invade the state of Chin. Tu Fu,
> the official prognosticator, cast the milfoil stalks and pronounced:

"It is auspicious. If you cross over the Yellow River, the marquis' chariot forces will be defeated."

When the earl interrogated him further, Tu Fu responded: "It is really very auspicious! After defeating them three times you will invariably capture Chin's ruler. The hexagram that has been cast is called '*Ku*.' A verse states, 'A thousand chariots are three times repulsed; what remains to be captured after three repellings is a male fox.' This fox, found in the hexagram *Ku*, must be the ruler. The lower trigram symbolizes the wind, whereas the upper trigram symbolizes mountains. The time of year is now termed 'autumn.' We will drop their fruit and seize their material wealth. This is the way we will conquer. When their fruit has dropped and their material wealth has been lost, on what might they rely to withstand defeat?"[4]

In this case Tu Fu's interpretation turned upon the idea of the wind, symbolized by the lower trigram in the *I Ching* hexagram (identified with Ch'in's forces), blowing destructively up over the mountain above, causing the fruit or substance of the enemy's strength to drop and their material wealth—possibly the trees on the mountainside—to be taken. As predicted, the subsequent engagement resulted in three consecutive defeats for Chin.

Another example preserved in the *Shuo Yüan* dating back to the Spring and Autumn period illustrates how dreams and divination might be employed to produce conjoined prognostications. Prior to the battle of Ch'eng-p'u, Duke Wen (who appeared in the historical section) observed troubling celestial phenomena and experienced an odd dream that he felt presaged a baleful outcome, but an alternative interpretation was quickly offered:

Duke Wen addressed Chiu Fan: "When I wanted to perform divination by the turtle shell and heated it [to induce cracks], the fire went out. Moreover, we confront the year star while they have it at their backs. A comet [broom star] is also visible in the sky whose position is such that they hold the handle while we grasp the tail [brush]. In addition, I dreamed that I fought with the king of Ch'u, who was on top while I was beneath him. I do not want to engage in battle. What do you think?"

Chiu Fan replied: "The fire going out when you performed plastromantic divination indicates that Ch'u's army will be extinguished. Confronting the year star while they back it means they will go off while we will follow them. As for them grasping the handle of the comet while we hold the tail, if they were engaged in sweeping with a broom, it would be to their advantage, but for attacking, it is to ours. As for my lord's dream about wrestling with the king of Ch'u with him on top and you below, you look up to Heaven while the king of Ch'u bears the responsibility for his offenses. Moreover, we act as leader of the alliance with Sung and Wei while Ch'i and Ch'in also support us. We accord with the Tao of Heaven, so based just upon human endeavor, we should be victorious."[5]

Separately the *Shuo Yüan* notes that "ominous phenomena are the way Heaven warns the son of Heaven and the feudal lords, while nightmares are the way it warns officers and officials."[6]

Even in the interlude between the Spring and Autumn and Warring States periods the great general Wu Ch'i assumed that divination would be performed to confirm the prospects for success, the advisability of undertaking a campaign, or even the permissibility of a specific attack. The first chapter of the *Wu-tzu* states:

There are four disharmonies. If there is disharmony in the state, you cannot put the army into the field. If there is disharmony within the army, you cannot deploy into formations. If you lack harmony within the formations, you cannot advance into battle. If you lack cohesion during the conduct of the battle, you cannot score a decisive victory. For this reason when a ruler who has comprehended the Tao is about to employ his people, he will first bring them into harmony and only thereafter embark on great affairs. He will not dare rely solely upon his own plans, but will certainly announce them formally in the ancestral temple, divine their prospects by the great turtle shell, and seek their confirmation in the Heavens and seasons. Only if they are all auspicious will he proceed to mobilize the army.[7]

Accordingly, even when Wu Ch'i identified situations in which victory should invariably follow, he felt compelled to preface them as "not requiring divination," saying, "In general, when evaluating the enemy there are eight conditions under which one engages in battle without performing divination." Conversely, situations too disadvantageous to contemplate required active means of avoidance: "There are six circumstances in which, without performing divination, you should avoid conflict."[8]

Perceiving the critical moment and acting appropriately were dominant concerns among inhabitants of the late Warring States period. The *I Ching*, although perhaps developed in part to resolve the interpretive difficulties posed by the sometimes bizarre crack patterns in turtle shells, provided a method for generating consistent phenomenal signs and a handbook for fathoming them. However, achieving true insight remained problematic, eventually prompting the creation of other, more accessible works in the same genre, such as the *Ling Ch'i Ching*.[9] (Even though the *I Ching* frequently conceptualizes in terms of military images, its explanations often refer to military events, and it was consulted before battles as early as the Spring and Autumn period, it apparently had no direct influence upon pre-T'ang military writings.) The employment of prognosticatory phenomena, whether in seeking to harmonize with the universal flux or fathom concrete situations, continued throughout the Warring States period. Thus the *Six Secret Teachings*, representative of middle Warring States thought, includes three astrologers on the command staff, holding them responsible for "the stars and calendar; observing the wind and *ch'i*; predicting auspicious days and times; investigating signs and phenomena; verifying disasters and abnormalities; and knowing Heaven's mind with regard to the moment for completion or abandonment."[10]

At the same time the Warring States period saw increasingly common opposition to divination, omen-taking, and other practices among the military writers, even as these practices apparently continued to flourish and evolve. Accordingly the *Three Strategies*, probably composed at the very end of the Warring States or slightly thereafter, characterized states that relied upon divination as likely targets for easy conquest.[11] The slightly earlier *Wei Liao-tzu* opens with a much-quoted passage condemning such beliefs:

> King Hui of Liang inquired of Wei Liao-tzu, "Is it true that the Yellow Emperor, through punishments and Virtue, achieved a hundred victories without a defeat?"
>
> Wei Liao-tzu replied: "Punishment was employed to attack, Virtue was employed to preserve. This is not what is referred to as 'Heavenly Offices, auspicious hours and days, *yin* and *yang*, facing toward and turning your back to.' The Yellow Emperor's victories were a matter of human effort, that's all. Why was that?
>
> "Now if there is a fortified city and one attacks it from the east and west but cannot take it, and attacks from the south and north but cannot take it, can it be that all four directions failed to accord with an auspicious moment that could be exploited? If you still cannot take it, it is because the walls are high, the moats deep, the weapons and implements fully prepared, the materials and grains accumulated in great quantities, and their valiant soldiers unified in their plans. If the wall is low, the moats shallow,

and the defenses weak, then it can be taken. From this perspective, 'moments,' 'seasons,' and 'Heavenly Offices' are not as important as human effort.

"According to the *Heavenly Offices*, 'Deploying troops with water to the rear is referred to as "isolated terrain." Deploying troops facing a long ridge is termed "abandoning the army."' When King Wu attacked King Chou of the Shang, he deployed his troops with the Chi River behind him, facing a mountain slope. With 22,500 men he attacked King Chou's hundreds of thousands and destroyed the Shang dynasty. Yet had not King Chou deployed in accord with the Heavenly Offices?

"The Ch'u general Kung-tzu Hsin was about to engage Ch'i in battle. At that time a comet appeared with its tail over Ch'i. According to such beliefs, wherever the tail pointed would be victorious and they could not be attacked. Kung-tzu Hsin said: 'What does a comet know? Those who fight according to the comet will certainly be overturned and conquered.' On the morrow he engaged Ch'i and greatly defeated them. The Yellow Emperor said, 'Putting spirits and ghosts first is not as good as first investigating my own knowledge.' This means that the Heavenly Offices are nothing but human effort."[12]

A chapter somewhat later in the text reprises the common practices of the time and reiterates the author's deprecatory view:

Generals of the present generation investigate "singular days" and "empty mornings," divine about Hsien-ch'ih, interpret "full" and "disastrous" days, accord with turtle shell augury, look for the auspicious and baleful, and observe the changes of the planets, constellations, and winds, wanting to thereby gain victory and establish their success. I view this as very difficult!

Now the commanding general is not governed by Heaven above, or controlled by Earth below, or governed by men in the middle. Thus weapons are evil implements. Conflict is a contrary virtue. The post of general is an office of death. Thus only when it cannot be avoided does one employ them. There is no Heaven above, no Earth below, no ruler to the rear, and no enemy in the front. The unified army of one man is like the wolf and tiger, like the wind and rain, like thunder and lightning. Shaking and mysterious, All under Heaven are terrified by it.

The army that would be victorious is like water. Now water is the softest and weakest of things, but whatever it collides with, such as hills and mounds, will be collapsed by it for no other rea-

son than its nature is concentrated and its attack is totally committed. Now if someone has the sharpness of the famous sword
Mo Yeh, the toughness of rhinoceros hide for armor, the masses of
the Three Armies, and orthodox and unorthodox methods, then
under All Heaven no one can withstand him in battle.

Thus it is said that if you raise the Worthy and employ the talented, even if the hour and day are not auspicious, your affairs
will still be advantageous. If you make the laws clear and are cautious about orders, without divining with the turtle shell or milfoil you will obtain propitious results. If you honor achievement
and nurture effort, without praying you will obtain good fortune.
It is also said that "the seasons of Heaven are not as good as advantages of Earth; the advantages of Earth are not as good as harmony among men." The Sages of antiquity stressed human effort,
that's all.[13]

The great T'ang general Li Ching believed that even when the Chou
was mounting its final attack against the Shang, a humanistic orientation prevailed:

The T'ai-tsung said: "T'ien Tan entrusted their fate to the super-
natural and destroyed Yen, whereas the T'ai Kung burned the milfoil and turtle shells yet went on to exterminate King Chou. How
is it that these two affairs are contradictory?"[14]

Li Ching said: "Their subtle motives were the same. One went
contrary to such practices and seized the enemy, one accorded
with them and implemented his plans.

"In antiquity, when the T'ai Kung was assisting King Wu, they
reached Mu-yeh, where they encountered thunder and rain. The
flags and drums were broken or destroyed. San Yi-sheng wanted to
divine for an auspicious response before moving. This then is a
case where, because of doubts and fear within the army, he felt
they must rely upon divination to inquire of the spirits. But the
T'ai Kung believed that rotted grass and dried up bones were not
worth asking. Moreover, in the case of a subject attacking his
ruler, how could there be a second chance?[15]

"Now I observe that San I-sheng expressed his motives at the
beginning, but the T'ai Kung attained his subsequently. Even
though one was contrary to and the other in accord with divinatory practices, their reasons were identical. When I previously
stated these techniques should not be abandoned, it was largely to
preserve the vital point of *ch'i* before affairs have begun to mani-

fest themselves. As for their being successful, it was a matter of human effort, that's all."[16]

The *Wei Liao-tzu* contains an interesting passage that essentially comments upon this event:

When King Wu attacked King Chou, the army forded the Yellow River at Meng Chin. On the right was the king's pennant, on the left the ax of punishment, together with three hundred warriors committed to die and thirty thousand fighting men. King Chou's formation deployed several hundred thousand men, with Fei Liao and O Lai personally leading the halberdiers and ax-bearers. Their lines stretched across a hundred kilometers. King Wu did not exhaust the warriors or people, the soldiers did not bloody their blades, but they conquered the Shang dynasty and executed King Chou.[17] There was nothing auspicious or abnormal; it was merely a case of perfecting oneself, or not perfecting oneself, in human affairs.

Even though divinatory practices persisted unabated throughout China's history, Li Ching cynically voiced the ultimate rationale for visibly continuing them while maintaining an attitude of disbelief:

The T'ai-tsung asked, "Can the divination practices of *yin* and *yang* be abandoned?"
Li Ching said: "They cannot. The military is the Tao of deceit, so if we apparently put faith in *yin* and *yang* divination practices, we can manipulate the greedy and stupid. They cannot be abandoned."
The T'ai-tsung said: "You once said that selecting astrologically auspicious seasons and days are not methods of enlightened generals. Ignorant generals adhere to them, so it seems appropriate to abandon them."
Li Ching said: "King Chou perished on a day designated as *chia-tzu*, King Wu flourished on the same day. According to the astrologically auspicious seasons and days, *chia-tzu* is the first day. The Shang were in chaos, the Chou were well governed. Flourishing and perishing are different in this case. Moreover, Emperor Wu of the Sung mobilized his troops on a 'going to perish day.' The army's officers all felt it to be impermissible, but the emperor said, 'I will go forth and he will perish.' Indeed, he conquered them.

"Speaking with reference to these cases, it is clear that the practices can be abandoned. However, when T'ien Tan was surrounded by Yen, Tan ordered a man to impersonate a spirit. He bowed and prayed to him, and the spirit said Yen could be destroyed. Tan thereupon used fire-oxen to go forth and attack Yen, greatly destroying them. This is the deceitful Tao of military thinkers. The selection of astrologically auspicious seasons and days is similar to this."[18]

Li Ching advocated similar measures to obscure the designations for formations and thereby keep people mystified:

The T'ai-tsung said: "The four animal formations also have the notes *shang*, *yü*, *wei*, and *chiao* to symbolize them. What is the reason for this?"
Li Ching replied: "It is the Tao of deceit. By preserving them, one is able to dispense with them. If you dispense with them and do not employ them, deceitfulness will grow ever greater. The ancients obscured the names of the four formations with those of the four animals, together with the designations of Heaven, Earth, wind, and clouds, and moreover added the notes and associated phases of *shang* and metal, *yü* and water, *wei* and fire, *chiao* and wood. This was the cleverness of the ancient military strategists. If you preserve them, deceitfulness will not increase further. If you abandon them, how can the greedy and stupid be employed?"[19]

From the late Warring States period when the practice of consulting omens was strongly condemned by the *Wei Liao-tzu*, despite a widespread fascination with anticipatory phenomena, military thought witnessed a theoretical bifurcation into contradictory orientations. However, even though some military texts (such as the *Wei Liao-tzu* and *Questions and Replies*) completely eschew divinatory practices, a vast literature devoted to their methods and measures simultaneously evolved, with material from both traditions being encompassed, if not exactly integrated, from Li Ch'uan's T'ang dynasty *T'ai-pai Yin-ching* through such Sung dynasty works as the *Hu-ling Ching* and *Wu-ching Tsung-yao*. Even the *Ping-fa Pai-yen*, dating from the transition period between the Ming and Ch'ing, while emphasizing natural phenomena, still grudgingly granted theoretical credibility to such methods under its definition of Heaven:

Definition: Being able to observe the phenomena of clouds is referred to as "Heaven."

Original Text: When strong winds blow, be careful about whirl-winds. When the myriad stars move about, it will be rainy and wet. When clouds and fog converge from all directions, be wary of ambushes and surprise attacks. When there are violent winds and heavy rain, rumbling of thunder and lightning intertwined, quickly prepare your strong crossbowmen and cautiously guard against sudden attacks by the enemy. Those who excel in employing such circumstances will never fail to exploit an opportunity, those who excel at defense will never fail to respond to changes. Heaven always lies with men, but only the wise are able to rely on it to seize victory. What further evidence does one need to seek?

Examples: Farmers recognize the signs of clearing and rain, boatmen know the direction of the wind. What need is there for them to read different books or grasp other interpretations? They gain experience through their affairs and verify their observations through constant discussion. Their eyes see phenomena and their minds absorb them. If they can be focused, how much more so the wise who have penetrated the mysteries of yin and yang and the five phases; who synthesize the entirety of sounds, appearances, vapors, and flavors; who have extensive comprehension of the books on the vast night skies; who are practiced in the arts of divination, calculation, and phenomenal observation? With one look they recognize auspicious omens and ill portents, with one silent glance comprehend misfortune and blessings, good fortune and calamity. Few are the human affairs and season of Heaven that can be simply pondered out. Therefore, one who knows Heaven becomes wise, one who knows Heaven is knowledgeable. To attain victory through relying upon Heaven is spiritual!

Examples: Tactical methods that prove victorious in the darkness of night are the pinnacle of subtle essence. Thus darkness and light, wind and rain depend upon Heaven; flat land and ravines, broad and constricted terrain depend upon Earth; segmenting and reuniting, advancing and retreating depend upon men.

Prognosticatory Systems in Military Practice

Although Chinese military intelligence, no doubt largely in response to Sun-tzu's emphasis upon acquiring knowledge through human agency, was firmly grounded in human effort and realistic practices, the countercurrent of belief that envisioned a useful resource in various divinatory and prognosticatory practices continued to flourish.

Numerous methods derived from astonishingly complex theories evolved by the T'ang dynasty, requiring arcane skills, intricate observations, and extensive knowledge. Their prevalence may be deduced from the lengthy sections devoted to them in the major military writings of the Sung dynasty: some 45 percent of the *Hu-ling Ching's* 430 pages, many of them expansions of material found in the *T'ai-pai Yin-ching;* 15 percent of the 2,340 pages in the lengthy *Wu-ching Tsung-yao*, an encyclopedia of military knowledge compiled in the mid-eleventh century, just a few decades after the *Hu-ling Ching;* and four of the ten volumes in the massive *Wu-pei Chih* completed in the last decades of the Ming dynasty. (That the voluminous works on prognostication and divination outside the military tradition also contain materials with martial implications hardly needs mention.)

The military writings organize this vast material to reflect the requirements of military intelligence. Certain conditions or circumstances therefore recur, with observations being systematically interpreted by various methods formulated according to the theories and premises of the distinct systems. The topics commonly found in the T'ang and Sung military texts include selecting an appropriate day for initiating a campaign, predicting victory or defeat, determining the basic advisability of engaging an enemy, fathoming enemy commanders, determining an emissary's credibility, predicting the existence of ambushes, discerning the enemy's location, fathoming where to encamp, determining whether to assume the tactical role of a guest or host, warning of as yet unseen threats, and deciding when to dispatch spies and agents.

Several prominent systems employ various combinations of the stars, Chinese zodiac, and sequential series known as the "Ten Stems and Twelve Branches" (for Heaven and Earth, respectively) that, when paired in an ongoing cycle, provide the sixty designations for the days in the traditional calendrical science that still underlies contemporary lunar calendars. For example, in the *Hu-ling Ching* chapter on determining an auspicious day for sending the army forth, this cycle of sixty is employed to designate certain days—such as the "Nine Uglies" and "Six Impoverishments"—falling in various lunar months on which the commencement of military activities should definitely be avoided. (Other inimical days include those when the phases of the moon are unstable—the end and beginning of the moon's cycle, a reflection of *yin*'s activity—and therefore deadly, as well as numerical combinations that presage calamity.) Unifying them all is the general principle that "on days when Heaven's *ch'i* is severed, you cannot send the army forth or launch an attack."[20] Theories based upon the five phases, *yin* and *yang*, and even the sixty-four hexagrams of the *I*

Ching—abstracted from their original context and converted into time and space markers with an intrinsic hierarchical order and inherent, dynamic interrelationships—similarly provide the foundation for single theories and complex hybrid systems.[21]

Other celestial phenomena of importance include the type and orientation of rainbows; the direction, type, ferocity, and duration of the wind; the nature and activity of innumerable stars, as well as their positions in various constellations and the zodiac, and important conjunctions; comets, meteors, and shooting stars; the sun and moon's characteristics, position, and eclipse activity; the general appearance of the sky; rain; and various seasonal activities and discordances. Finally, as will be seen in the extensive case studies that follow, the practice of watching the subtle vapors known as *ch'i* and their more visible manifestation, the clouds, engendered hundreds of detailed observations with correlated implications, including victory and defeat.

The evolution of these complex systems invariably strikes most modern readers, including those who evince a belief in Western astrology, as astonishing, and their persistence in China's highly rational, experientially derived military literature as incomprehensible, even if they were never as bizarre as certain Roman practices or as localized as the Delphic Oracle. Although it *appears* that this literature, being bereft of any scientific basis or empirical validity, was largely irrelevant to actual battlefield command from the late Warring States on, the degree to which such methods were recognized and employed remains to be studied. However, anyone who has ever been confronted by major events, suffered from uncertainty, or foundered in doubt over actions and their probable results can well understand the anxiety of commanders entrusted with responsibility for the army's fate and the very existence of the state, as well as their quest for any indication of the correct path. Contemporary Western military literature on commanders employing intuitive (otherwise termed "experientially based" or "enlightened insight") aspects of decisionmaking abilities, despite the plethora of data and ever-increasing real-time micromanagement of the battlefield, even though couched in "rational" terms, perhaps veers not too distantly from the unconscious recognition of battlefield factors vaguely expressible in terms of mood, context, abnormalities, or miasmic *ch'i*. The accumulation, classification, and codification of particularized experiences, although theoretically verifiable in subsequent concrete events, thus furnished another informational dimension for military intelligence efforts.

Even though certainly disbelieved by military commanders in the details, visible omens were generally given credence, especially by ordinary soldiers (prompting concern about defusing the impact of these omens and preventing their occurrence),[22] and they were certainly an integral part of the mind-set and cultural heritage. Just as the most modern, rational citizens of scientific culture may be taken aback by strange phenomena or perturbed by unusual phenomena, commanders could not help musing on forthcoming events as the day broke, and they perceived colors and shapes among the clouds forming over the enemy, in the *ch'i* rising from their encampment, strange configurations of stars, or a halo around the moon. Although many military writings still voiced caveats about the need to train, prepare, and fight well—thereby vitiating any baleful predictions—this undercurrent could never be eradicated.

The strength of widespread belief in the validity of predictive phenomena may be seen in two Han dynasty examples. Once the Ch'in reunified China, the government's focal military concern became the danger posed by the nomadic border peoples. An indication of how portents might be exploited within this redefined orientation appears in a memorial presented by the famous Han dynasty general Chao Ch'ung-kuo, who was active during Emperor Wu-ti's aggressively martial reign and successfully specialized in border affairs: "Just now the five main stars are emerging in the east, which presages great advantages for China and great defeats for the barbarian peoples. T'ai-pai is high in the sky, so daring to lead troops deep into enemy territory and engage in battle will be auspicious, but not daring to do so will be baleful. If our generals urgently strike, by relying on the advantages of Heaven to execute the unrighteous, the realm will be preserved and there will not be any future doubts."[23] He subsequently received permission to take action against the Hsien-ling and succeeded in vanquishing them.[24]

The debilitating effect of omens and portents was much warned against in the military writings, leading to psychological countermeasures. Conversely, when an ill omen was seen, learning of its effects upon the enemy and exploiting them could prove advantageous, as General Tung Chuo proved in the Later Han dynasty when he served as one of the commanders of some one hundred thousand infantry and cavalry dispatched to crush a barbarian force.[25] They were standing off against the enemy after an indecisive engagement in the eleventh month when "that night there was a meteor like a flame whose light stretched out a hundred feet, illuminating both camps so that the horses and donkeys all whinnied and brayed. The barbarians, feeling it was inauspicious, wanted to return to their stronghold of Chin-ch'eng. When Chung Chuo learned of it, he was elated. The next day he launched a coordinated attack with the other commanders that severely defeated the enemy, killing several thousand of them."[26]

Dust, Smoke, and Atmospheric Manifestations

To study, even in brief, each of the representative systems of belief would require a lengthy, complex work clearly tangential to any focus upon military intelligence activities. However, China has a unique tradition of antique origin of watching clouds, smoke, earthly vapors, dust, mist, and other atmospheric phenomena forming, floating, and dispersing for indications about current and future events. Although often explained in terms of *ch'i*—the vital pneuma of life (including breath) that empowers everything and was later understood as the indefinable substance that constitutes all matter—and much intertwined with *ch'i* prognostication from the Han dynasty on, the traditions were originally distinct. In fact, as we argue elsewhere in detail, there is a sort of continuum ranging from observationally based phenomena, such as the dust column from a chariot advance, through indications of life in an encampment, to clouds and vapors. Even while "rationalists" were railing against divination techniques, official credence was often granted to complex *ch'i* practices that ranged from imperially sanctioned efforts to determine the first stirrings of seasonal *ch'i*, and thus fine-tune the calendar, to simple musings on the battlefield.[27] Even though they may be disparaged today, in numerous variations they were long regarded as an integral part of the arsenal for gathering information and predicting military events and therefore merit analysis as a case study.[28]

In the *Art of War* Sun-tzu included field guidelines that provide evidence that tactical information was derived from dust observations at least as far back as the Spring and Autumn period: "If dust rises high up in a sharply defined column, chariots are coming. If it is low and broad, the infantry is advancing. If it is dispersed in thin shafts, they are gathering firewood. If it is sparse, coming and going, they are encamping." However, in a lengthy chapter already reprised here,[29] after similarly arraying various phenomena that might be employed to fathom the enemy, the T'ai Kung concluded with a paragraph that ventures into the realm of *ch'i* phenomena:

In general, when you attack city walls or surround towns, if the color of their *ch'i* is like dead ashes, the city can be slaughtered. If the city's *ch'i* drifts out to the north, the city can be conquered. If the *ch'i* goes out and drifts to the west, the city can be forced to surrender. If the *ch'i* goes out and drifts to the south, it cannot be taken. If the *ch'i* goes out and drifts to the east, the city cannot be attacked. If the *ch'i* goes out but then drifts back in, the city's ruler has already fled. If the *ch'i* goes out and overspreads our army, the soldiers will surely fall ill. If the *ch'i* goes out and dust rises up without any direction, the army will have to be employed for a long time. If you have attacked a walled city or surrounded a town for more than ten days without thunder or rain, you must hastily abandon it, for the city must have a source of great assistance. These are the means by which to know that you can attack and then go on to mount the attack, or that you should not attack and therefore stop.[30]

Another chapter in the *Six Secret Teachings* preserves an active process already grown antique by the Warring States period:

King Wu asked the T'ai Kung, "From the sound of the pitch pipes can we know the fluctuations of the Three Armies, foretell victory and defeat?"

The T'ai Kung said: "Your question is profound indeed! Now there are twelve pipes, with five major notes: *kung, shang, chiao, cheng,* and *yü.* These are the true, orthodox sounds, unchanged for over ten thousand generations.

"The spirits of the five phases are constants of the Tao. Metal, wood, water, fire, and earth, each according to their conquest relationship, can be employed to attack the enemy. In antiquity, during the period of the Three Sage Emperors they used the nature of vacuity and nonaction to govern the hard and strong. They did not have characters for writing; everything proceeded from the five phases. The Tao of the five phases is the naturalness of Heaven and Earth. The division into the six *chia* is a realization of marvelous and subtle spirit.

"Their method was, when the day had been clear and calm, without any clouds, wind, or rain, to send light cavalry out in the middle of the night to approach the enemy's fortifications. Stopping about nine hundred paces away they would all lift their pipes to their ears and then yell out to startle the enemy. There would be a very small, subtle sound that would respond in the pitch pipes.

"If the *chiao* note responded among the pipes, it indicated a white tiger. If the *cheng* note responded in the pipes, it indicated the Mysterious Military. If the *shang* note responded in the pipes, it indicated the Vermilion Bird. If the *yü* note responded in the pipes, it indicated the Hooked Formation. If none of the five notes responded in the pipes, it was *kung,* signifying a Green Dragon.

"These signs of the five phases are evidence to assist in the conquest, the subtle moments of success and defeat."[31]

In addition to the response generated by their probing, certain external indications aided the process:

These subtle, mysterious notes all have external indications. When the enemy has been startled into movement, listen for them. If you hear the sound of the *pao* drum, then it is *chiao*. If you see the flash of lights from a fire, then it is *cheng*. If you hear the sounds of bronze and iron, of spears and halberds, then it is *shang*. If you hear the sound of people sighing, it is *yü*. If all is silent, without any sound, then it is *kung*. These five are the signs of sound and appearance."[32]

The *Shih Chi, Han Shu,* and *Sui Shu* treatises on astronomy and astrology composed from the Han through the T'ang contain numerous passages correlating observable phenomena with prognosticatory interpretations, including many with military implications. Not only are comets, scintillating stars, and the appearance of constellations extensively discussed, but also certain cloud formations and their movement. Some sound almost like those found in the *Six Secret Teachings* or even Sun-tzu's observations on dust, except that they lack any physical or causal earthly correlate. One particularly interesting series associates the appearance of the *ch'i* with the army's component forces:

The *ch'i* indicating infantry forces is white; that for earthly achievements yellow. The *ch'i* indicating chariot forces ascends and descends, moving about and then congealing. The *ch'i* indicating cavalry forces is low and widespread, that for infantry forces concentrated. When the front is low but the rear high forces are urgently moving, when the front is square and high while the rear is angular and low the forces are withdrawing. If the *ch'i* is tranquil, their movement is leisurely; if the front is high and the rear low, they will turn back without halting. When two constellations of *ch'i* encounter each other, the forces [indicated by the] lower one will conquer those signified by the higher, those indicated by the angular will conquer those symbolized by the square.[33]

Similar indications, including predictions about the auspiciousness of engaging in battle or the size of unknown forces yet to appear, are provided by cloud formations, especially those suggesting animals and earthly phenomena, all of which became more prevalent with the appearance of the T'ang and Sung dynasty military texts that followed.[34]

Ch'i Theory and Representative Selections

Despite philosophical interpretations and extensive theorizing, *ch'i*'s exact nature remains elusive, conveying diverse meanings in different contexts. In its metaphysical guise, as the essential constituent of the universe and all its particulars, it may be considered the substance of objects as realized, with the *li*—patterns or principles—furnishing the defining form. However, more commonly it was early imaged as the vapors clearly visible rising from cooking food, especially rice (and thus written with the character for rice within it), ephemerally visible before vanishing as wisps in the air. (Another common tradition envisioned it as the vital breath of life, visible in a man's winter breath.) In the military writings *ch'i* clearly refers to something at least vaguely substantial, tenuously existent, visible only to practiced eyes in the most subtle cases but to everyone in its densest concentration. Although always entailing a metaphysical aspect, it included the vapors or mists rising above a lake or early morning field, those visible over an army, and the panoply of colors in an imperceptibly moisture-laden sky.

A basic statement in the *T'ai-pai Yin-ching* chapter entitled "Fathoming Cloud *Ch'i*" sets *ch'i* theory within the context of portent concepts while clearly indicating its dynamic relationship with clouds: "When Heaven and Earth mutually respond, *yin* and *yang* mutually interact, it is termed *ch'i.* When *ch'i* accumulates over a long time, it becomes clouds. In all cases things attain form below and *ch'i* responds above. Thus it is said, 'By fathoming the *ch'i,* one will know affairs; by looking at the *ch'i,* know people.'" The late Sung dynasty *Hu-ling Ching* adds: "Wherever there are more than a hundred men, the *ch'i* of victory or defeat will be concretely visible. Those who accord with it will flourish, those who contravene it will perish. Heaven and Earth do not speak, so auspiciousness and balefulness must be fathomed through symbols. Unusual *ch'i* invariably entails disaster and change."[35] As the representative selections will show, unusual *ch'i* might range from the extremely simple with direct consequences— such as a reddish diffusion in the sky presaging great bloodshed—to the most intricate and complex, including dragons playing and headless dead men.

Cloud Ch'i Above Cities

A chapter entitled "Cloud *Ch'i* Above Cities" in the *Hu-ling Ching* continues Sun Pin's effort to characterize cities as susceptible to attack or not, echoing the T'ai Kung's early *ch'i* indices:[36]

Whether you want to advance your army and attack a city or the enemy is coming forth to besiege you, you should investigate the auspiciousness and balefulness of the clouds and *ch'i*. If the *ch'i* above a city or encampment is like men in squads of five and ten with folded hands and bowed heads, their army is willing to surrender. If the cloud *ch'i* is yellow above and white below, it is termed "excellent *ch'i*." Any army that it approaches wants to negotiate peace.

If the *ch'i* within a city is like a white flag, you cannot seize it. If yellow clouds approach a city, it will have cause for celebration. If green color *ch'i* is like a cow's head butting a man, the people within the city cannot be slain. If the *ch'i* in the city emerges from the eastern quarter and its color is yellow, it indicates Heaven's Ax and the city cannot be attacked. Anyone who attacks it will suffer great misfortune.

If the *ch'i* above a city is like fiery smoke that divides and bubbles up, it signifies that they want to sally forth and fight. Their *ch'i* cannot be attacked. If multiple colors emerge one by one and are unconstrained, you cannot slay them. If red or black *ch'i* shaped like a pestle extends out from inside the city, the troops within it will suddenly sally forth and it presages a great victory.

If the cloud *ch'i* above a city divides to form the appearance of two spikes of fire, you cannot attack. If it mistily surrounds a city but doesn't enter, troops outside will not succeed in entering.

Whenever attacking a city or strongpoint, if variegated *ch'i* goes in and out of your army, it is *ch'i* that foretells victory. Carefully prepare for it.

If when attacking a city red *ch'i* hovers over it and yellow *ch'i* surrounds it on all four sides, the commanding general will die and the city will surrender. If the *ch'i* above a city is red like flying birds, by urgently striking, you can immediately destroy it. If the *ch'i* goes out of the city, the populace wants to sneak out and disperse and lacks the will to fight. Quickly attack them.

If the *ch'i* is like dead ashes and overspreads the city and strongpoints, the officers and troops are ill and the city can be slaughtered.

If there is not any cloud *ch'i* above the city, there is dissension among the officers and troops. If the red *ch'i* above a city is like a mass of men with their heads facing down, below there will be many dead and wounded. If white *ch'i* surrounds a city and enters it, by urgently attacking, you can seize it. If the white *ch'i* gleams like a long sword more than a hundred staffs long that rises up above the enemy and stretches over the city, anyone who attacks will suffer disaster. The city cannot be slain, but within eighty-one days you can effect a subversive response.

If black clouds with yellow fringes rise up high, stretching out and solidifying in front of their formation, arrayed as if kneeling or crouching, linked together like men in groups of three and five, with heads bowed and hands folded above the encampment or deployment, they will certainly surrender. If the cloud *ch'i* is like chickens, pheasants, or running rabbits, brigands will come to attack your forces, so you must urgently prepare.

If three or five streamers of cloud *ch'i* stretch across to form a deployment with stripes like tigers, any army it approaches will certainly seize fortifications and kill generals, so if you see it, you must attack them. If the clouds are like dragons moving over the city, there will be a great flood.

Now the *ch'i* for victory or defeat above a city are such. If it indicates victory for the enemy, you cannot attack, but if defeat for them, you should attack. When victory lies over you, then it will be advantageous to send forth the army and advance to attack. When defeat is indicated over you, you should solidify your walls, clear the fields, and strictly defend them. All cloud *ch'i* manifests the mind of Heaven and Earth, so how can you not be cautious?

Evaluating Generals

One of the chief concerns of military intelligence was learning the identity and characteristics of opposing generals so that flaws might be exploited and tactics conceived. Therefore virtually all the military texts that contain prognosticatory material devote often lengthy sections to generals' *ch'i* indications. Although the information thus gleaned—primarily whether the general is fierce or timid, ruthless or stupid—is limited, it might still be acted upon to save the army from an unexpected defeat. The two selections that follow indicate the detailed historical progression from Li Ch'uan's T'ang dynasty *T'ai-pai Yin-ching* to the Sung dynasty *Hu-ling Ching* and *Wu-ching Tsung-yao*.

"Ch'i of Fierce Generals" (T'ai-pai Yin-ching)

A fierce general's *ch'i* is like a dragon or tiger in the mood for killing. When a fierce general is about to move, his *ch'i* will first be manifest. If this sort of *ch'i* is seen without any general taking action, it presages brutal forces arising.

A fierce general's *ch'i* is like smoke and fog, fulminating up like the light from a fire illuminating the night. A fierce general's location will have reddish white *ch'i* surrounding it. A fierce general's *ch'i* is like a mountain forest, like woods of bamboo. Its appearance is like a purple canopy or a gate tower with black above and red below, or like a pennant, a taut bow, or dust soaring high with a sharp head and wide base.

When two armies oppose each other, if the *ch'i* above the enemy's encampment is like a granary or pure white so that the sun is seen even more clearly, these are all the *ch'i* of a fierce general who cannot be suddenly attacked.

If the *ch'i* above the enemy's encampment is yellow white and glistening, the general has awesome virtue and cannot be attacked. If the *ch'i* is greenish white and high, the general is very courageous. If before a great battle it is white and low to the front but green and high to the rear, the general is afraid but the officers courageous. If it's voluminous to the front but pauce to the rear, the lieutenant generals are afraid and unenlightened.

If the *ch'i* above the enemy is black with red in the middle and lies to the front, the general is perspicacious and ruthless and cannot be withstood.

If the *ch'i* above the enemy is green and widely dispersed, the general is afraid. However, if the *ch'i* above the enemy's army gradually assumes a form like a mountain in the clouds, the general has secret plots and cannot be attacked. If this happens above your army, by quickly attacking, you will gain a great victory.

If the *ch'i* above the enemy's army is like great snake moving toward a person, it is the *ch'i* of a fierce general and cannot be opposed. If it occurs above your army, by quickly engaging in battle you will achieve a great victory.

"Cloud Ch'i of Generals" (Hu-ling Ching)

Whether an enemy's commanding general is worthy or stupid can be learned through cloud *ch'i* prognostication.[37] Now if the clouds above an army are green with some red and interiors of yellow white and do not disperse from morning to night, the ruler is weak, the ministers strong, and the commanding general arrogant and dissipated. Their rules and commands are overturned, so you should urgently attack them.

If the clouds above the army are confused and muddy, the ruler and generals are unenlightened and the good and Worthy do not associate with them.

If the *ch'i* above the army is like a scaly dragon, the commanding general's spirit is dissipated and turbulent, so they can be suddenly attacked.

If green clouds emerge after sunset in the west to spiral up to Heaven and it doesn't rain for ten days, the commanding general will lose his position after being strong for three years. But if green clouds change to red, it presages a great defeat.

If the green *ch'i* above the army gradually turns black, the commanding general will die.

If the clouds are yellow white and glistening, the general has awesome virtue.

If the *ch'i* above the army, just like clouds, changes to form the shape of mountains, the general has profound knowledge.

If the outside of the clouds is black but inside red, lying toward the front of the army, or when two armies are opposing each other the clouds are like state granaries or the red *ch'i* is like a mountain, in all three cases the general is ferocious, perspicacious, strong, and courageous.

If the clouds above the army connect with Heaven, the general is wise.

If the clouds are like dragons or tigers in the mood for killing, or like fire and smoke swirling, or like firelight scintillating and changing, or like the trees in a forest or lofty heights, or like dust low in the sky with a large head, or purplish black shaped like a gate tower, or like purple powder floating down, or like a dragon roaming about a black mist, or like the sun and moon with red *ch'i* arising and surrounding them, or shaped like a door with the upper part black and bottom part red, or like a black flag, or shaped like a bow, or wiggling about like scaly dragons and snakes—these thirteen are the *ch'i* of a fierce general.

If the cloud *ch'i* is green and widely dispersed, the general is timid and weak. Or if the front is large and rear small, the general is not enlightened. Or if it is black edged with white *ch'i*, the general is afraid and lacks plans. In this case you can trick him into movement, delude him with affairs, make him fearful with awesomeness, or press him with strength and be decisively victorious.

"Cloud Ch'i Prognostication" (Wu-ching Tsung-yao)

Ch'i Symbolism for Generals: If the general's *ch'i* extends up to Heaven, it indicates a fierce general of many strategies. The *ch'i* of a fierce general is like a dragon. If two armies deploy opposite each other, if his *ch'i* appears above, the general is fierce and sharp. If it is like a tiger in the mood for killing, it indicates a fierce general about to move. If there is redness amid the tiger *ch'i*, it signifies brutal forces arising. Auspiciousness and balefulness are determined by the sun and stars. Moreover, a fierce general's *ch'i* has the appearance of fire and smoke, mountain forests and woods of bamboo, or purplish black, or black above and red below. Or like a black flag, or a tautbow or crossbow. Or like dust with the head sharp and the base large, ensconced over the encampment, fortifications, or army. These are all the *ch'i* of a fierce general.

If the *ch'i* above an army is like round and square granaries, increasingly clear in the daylight, this is the *ch'i* of a fierce general who cannot be attacked.

If the *ch'i* above the army is yellow white and turns to become misty, the general has superlative plans and cannot be attacked.

If the *ch'i* is greenish white and high, the general is courageous.

If during a great battle you observe that the *ch'i* to the front is white but green and high to the rear, the general is weak but the officers strong, but if the front is large and rear small, the general is afraid.

If the enemy's *ch'i* is black above and red below and lies to the front, the general is perspicacious and ruthless and cannot be opposed.

When the *ch'i* is clear and widely dispersed, the general is timid and weak.

If the *ch'i* slowly appears over the army and gradually changes like clouds to form an appearance like mountains, the general has profound plans and cannot be attacked. If this happens above your army, if you fully engage in battle, you will gain a great victory.

If the *ch'i* above the enemy is like a giant snake facing a man, the fierce general's *ch'i* cannot be withstood. However, if it is above our army, engaging in battle will certainly prove victorious.

If red *ch'i* above the army connects with Heaven, there must be a worthy general in its midst.

Victory and Defeat

Fathoming enemy generals represents but one aspect of observing and evaluating the portents associated with an opposing army to determine the prospects for victory and defeat. Extensive materials were formulated on precisely this focal topic, which, if at all accurate, would obviate the need for much intelligence gathering, analysis, and assessment! The two chapters translated here from the *Hu-ling Ching* well represent the intricate observations and complex assessments found in this tradition.

"Cloud Ch'i of Victorious Armies"

When occupying an encampment or deploying into formation, if purplish *ch'i* emanates above your army, it is an omen of great fortuitousness. On that day there will be a celebration.

If the *ch'i* above your army appears as if overflowing a dike with the front being red and the rear white, it is the *ch'i* of victory, so it will be advantageous to advance the army and mount a sudden attack. But if it is over the enemy, they will be victorious.

If the *ch'i* over an army condenses to form stationary clouds in the midst of the sky, solid and unchanging, it is called "firm *ch'i*." If it is above the enemy, then do not attack.

If the cloud *ch'i* over your army forms into a low squatting shape, it is termed "Heaven's Majesty." It would be appropriate to employ picked troops to form a solid front and gradually advance into combat.

If the cloud *ch'i* above the army is like a fancy canopy that moves first or cloud *ch'i* that is red above but black below approaches the army, they are comparatively stronger. However, in the end you can destroy the strong. The small will be able to suddenly strike the large, winning great victories in major engagements and small victories in minor ones.

If the cloud *ch'i* is like a black man among red clouds, it is referred to as "victorious *ch'i*." If the *ch'i* is like young boys in groups of five and ten, red in the middle, and lies to the fore, it is the *ch'i* of a strong army.

If the cloud *ch'i* is like mountainside forests or white *ch'i* divided and glistening like multiple stories edged with red in the sky, or the cloud *ch'i* is scintillating like the glow of a fire or surging up like fire and smoke on a mountain, or if the cloud *ch'i* is like twin mountain peaks jumbled like smoking grass, these are all signs of [the army] having obtained Heaven's strategic power.

If the cloud *ch'i* congeals white, then displays five colors, or cloud *ch'i* forms groups of five and ten like red birds squatting in black *ch'i*, or the *ch'i* is like black smoke, or the cloud *ch'i* is like a horse with its head high and tail hanging down, or the cloud *ch'i* is like a man wielding an ax toward the enemy, or the cloud *ch'i* is like two groups in training, in these ten cases the *ch'i* indicates a strong army.[38] If it hovers over the enemy, you should avoid them; if over your army, wherever it indicates you will be victorious.

If the cloud *ch'i* is yellow white, thick, moist, and heavy, or if the cloud *ch'i* moves and expands like three pieces of black silk with the front large and rear narrow, or when the army moves on campaign in its midst there are clouds like gamecocks, red and white succeeding each other amid the *ch'i*, or above the deployment there is five-colored *ch'i* that connects with Heaven or in the soaring cloud *ch'i* there is a man dressed in black in a red cloud, or if yellow *ch'i* traverses the sky, these five indicate troops responding to Heaven's will. Attacking them would be very inauspicious.

If the *ch'i* above the army is like a snake raising its head toward the enemy, or if red and yellow *ch'i* shields the sky, or the cloud *ch'i* is like the sun and moon with red *ch'i* surrounding them, or the cloud *ch'i* is like the glow of the sun's halo, or the *ch'i* gathers and congeals without dispersing, or red clouds like dragons and variegated colors luxuriously striking Heaven, or clouds swirling about to form patterns, shaped like phoenixes, or cloud *ch'i* moist and glittering like a city gate secreted amid white clouds, or clouds that internally divide into red and yellow, these nine are the victorious *ch'i* of a strong army, also said to the *ch'i* of a king's army. When cloud *ch'i* like this accumulates above your army, go forth and mount a sudden attack on the enemy. But if it assembles above the enemy, then absolutely do not make any wanton moves. Moreover, if it hovers above your army while the *ch'i* over the enemy's army is normal, it presages victory.

Cloud Ch'i of Defeated Armies

If the *ch'i* above an army is like dead ashes, a horse's liver, bent cover, herd of sheep, frightened deer, or black *ch'i* like a man's hands,[39] they are all indications of defeat.

If black *ch'i* like a crumbling mountain follows an army, the army will be defeated and the general will die. If it follows you, you should avoid conflict.

If cloud *ch'i* of white and yellow intermixed appears several nights in succession, a surprise attack will scatter the enemy's army and throw them into confusion. Suddenly striking will prove auspicious.

If the *ch'i* over the army is low, they will be defeated in every encounter. If it emanates from the east, then there will be profound disaster. If the cloud *ch'i* has five colors but has not settled in the north, east, south, or west, the army will be defeated. If red *ch'i* gloriously flares up to Heaven, the commanding general will die and the troops will crumble in disorder.

If there is black *ch'i* like cows and horses gradually emerging from the fog in the form of an army, it is called the "Heavenly Dog." It will feed on blood below, so you must encamp far off to avoid it.

If cloud *ch'i* overspreads the road, obfuscating the daylight with darkness, it is an omen of imminent defeat. There isn't time for food to cook; quickly avoid it.

If the cloud *ch'i* is green or in pieces like a shattered tile, any army it approaches will be defeated. If the cloud *ch'i* is red or white like a person's head, or someone crawling on the ground with his head down, any army it approaches will be defeated and the blood will flow for a hundred kilometers. If it approaches us and we want to propitiate it, moving far away to another location would be auspicious. If you stimulate the spirit of the men to soar up, you can attain good fortune.

If the cloud *ch'i* is like a river breaking through an embankment, it is an omen of the officers and squads breaking down.

If after the enemy general has secreted troops to make a sudden attack against us, the cloud *ch'i* at night extends out like a rope hanging down, whichever army it approaches will be defeated.

If in the middle of the night the cloud *ch'i* is dense and black, there are numerous secret plots. Both bluish white and greenish black are omens of reversal and calamity. Black clouds like rotating wagon wheels entering the army mean that low-ranking people are plotting against you. You should urgently investigate and prepare against them. Wherever the cloud *ch'i* is shaped like a dog, there will be great bloodshed below.

If the cloud *ch'i* is black with yellow above, the officers and troops are afraid and there are internal plots of rebellion. Black clouds like pennants streaming amid the *ch'i*, or red *ch'i* like blood or birds flying amid black *ch'i* are all omens of defeat.

Black [cloud *ch'i*] intermixed and shattered like a bunch of pigs or a herd of cows and horses or like a flock of frightened birds are all omens of defeat.

If the cloud *ch'i* is like floating dust, dispersing everywhere, the officers and troops are planning a revolt. If it is red like the fierce flames of a fire rising up to illuminate Heaven, it indicates a great defeat and bloodshed. If red clouds are like people, in groups of two and three, some walking, some sitting, brutal forces will soon arrive.

If the cloud *ch'i* is like the smoke from fresh grass burning, any army it approaches will suffer a great defeat. If in the middle of the night the cloud *ch'i* is dense and black, there are many secret plots. If the color is bluish white or greenish black, it presages rebellion.

If the *ch'i* is like the smoke from fresh grass burning, any army it approaches, even though their front be courageous, will see the rear withdraw of their own accord. If you can wait a month or year to suddenly attack, you can be victorious.

If red cloud *ch'i* is very full or like a suspended cover, the army will fall into turbulence by itself. If red clouds are forming an eyebrow-like formation with increasingly large sharp ends, there will be a great battle and much bloodshed. Whoever moves first will be defeated.

When the cloud *ch'i* is like suspended clothes, it is the omen of defeat.

If the cloud *ch'i* is like a turning front, it is an omen of defeat.

If both armies have deployed and the enemy's soldiers completely lack any *ch'i*, by suddenly striking, you can destroy them.

If both armies have deployed against each other and the *ch'i* over the enemy reaches up to Heaven as if in a formation, this is termed "a transverse sea of *ch'i*." If you forcefully attack, you can destroy them.

If the two armies are deployed against each other and you see that above their army there is a man illuminated by fire, this means they have lost the mind of the commanding general. If you attack, they will be defeated.

If the cloud *ch'i* is like a flock of birds chaotically flying about, it is an omen of defeat. If the cloud *ch'i* is fuzzy like a tiger's tail hanging down over the army, the army wants to surrender. Otherwise, some villains intend to mount a response for the enemy.

If the two armies are deployed within ten kilometers, if you see the *ch'i* above their army is both white and high while to the rear are green clouds, it is an omen of imminent defeat. You should quickly beat the advance and strike them.

If the cloud *ch'i* is greenish black, it is an omen of defeat.

If the cloud *ch'i* is like a row of walking cows, a drum chariot, a group of snakes chaotically proceeding, or blacks clouds like a man leading a cow, all these are omens of defeat.

If the clouds are like a ruined house, the army will be defeated and the general will die.

If among gray clouds there are deep black clouds glinting in the west like stars, this is termed "the *ch'i* of a defeated army." The army will suffer a great disaster.

546   Historical Practices and Their Rejection

Now whenever a commander moves troops, Heaven will inform men about forthcoming defeat and victory with *ch'i*. However, anyone who enjoys victorious *ch'i* cannot simply rely on it, but should order the army and rectify its essence, ponder their plans, make their orders strict, and rectify their rewards and punishments. Then they will accord with Heaven and Earth's blessings. Anyone who relies on correct victorious *ch'i* without ordering the army's administration, who is dissipated and lazy will be defeated. In this way they can convert victory into defeat. Similarly, how can anyone who encounters the *ch'i* of defeat invariably be defeated? By strictly enforcing their instructions, cautiously employing their wisdom in making plans, upbraiding themselves, accepting that the guilt lies with them, and reverently according with Heaven's missive, they can change defeat into victory. Shouldn't a commanding general who has not received any indication of defeat or victory establish policies to cultivate his virtue?

The admonitions in the final paragraph, although often found in passages warning generals who hold a clear strategic superiority not to become lax, are unusual within prognosticatory sections and bear noting as evidence that false confidence was to be allayed.

Ch'i and Counterintelligence

Prognosticatory theory also had applications in the realm of counterintelligence, guidelines being formulated for employing a complex star system to evaluate the credibility of emissaries and the existence of secret plots.[40] The *T'ai-pai Yin-ching* also contains a brief chapter that focuses on *ch'i* phenomena warning of subversive activities:[41]

If the *ch'i* is white and in a clump of lines, coming forth, moving to and fro, appearing like a deployment, men from other states will be coming to hatch plots against you.[42] You should not hastily respond, but observe where they go, follow, attack them, and gain the advantage.

If black *ch'i* like a screen emerges from the encampment, black above and yellow below, the enemy will come as if to seek battle but not sincerely. The truth will be the opposite of what they say. For the next seven days you must be alert. Being prepared would be auspicious.

If black *ch'i* approaches your army like a chariot wheel turning, the enemy is plotting to stir up chaos and conspiring with minor ministers from your state, so you should investigate it.

If black *ch'i* comes on like someone leading an animal or a deployment whose front is strong, there are secret plots.

If the sky is sunk in darkness without any rain so that during the day the sun is not visible or the stars or moon at night for more than three days, there is a secret plot. The commanding general should take precautions against his attendants.

If it is gray for ten days in succession, turbulent winds arise from all four quarters, and it wants to rain but doesn't, it is called "Nebulous." It means a minister is plotting against the ruler.

If the sky is so deeply *yin* [dark] that the sun and moon have no light and clouds shield them but it does not rain, both the ruler and ministers have secret plots, but if two armies are opposite each other, both have secret plots. If it is clear in the daytime but dark at night, ministers are plotting against the ruler; if it is gray in the daytime but clear at night, the ruler is plotting against his ministers.

Notes

Insofar as this is a work intended for general readers, as well as sinologists, an abbreviated form of reference for Chinese source materials has been employed throughout the notes, citing by chapter name rather than page number in any particular edition. In addition to being common Chinese practice, we believe it is justified by the ready availability of modern paperbacks and popular editions of most of the ancient writings cited and translated in *The Tao of Spycraft*. The modern proliferation of variant versions clearly obviates the traditional practice of referring to the great classic collections found only in a few libraries or particular editions, except in the case of rare books or more specialized annotated texts such as Ch'en Ch'i-yu's *Han Fei-tzu*. Through the use of chapter or similar names, readers with various modern typeset editions— for whom *chüan* and page references would be frustratingly useless—can easily locate the relevant passages within the short chapters.

References to the various volumes in the *Seven Military Classics* (whose chapter titles are provided in English) are to our translation published by Westview Press (1993). Titles apart from the *Wu-tzu* and *Wei Liao-tzu* are abbreviated as follows:

Art of War	*Sun-tzu's Art of War*
Ssu-ma Fa	*The Methods of the Ssu-ma*
Questions and Replies	*Questions and Replies between T'ang T'ai-tsung and Li Wei-kung*
Three Strategies	*Three Strategies of Huang Shih-kung*
Six Secret Teachings	*T'ai Kung's Six Secret Teachings*

The single-volume *Art of War* with expanded discussion and historical analysis available from Westview Press (1994) may also be consulted for more extensive contextual material as indicated. Finally, references to Sun Pin's *Military Methods* are to our translation published by Westview (1995).

Chapter 1

1. Certain principles and historical cases rapidly became canonical, almost defining the mind-set, and continue to be immediately brought to mind whenever the subject is raised. For example, see "Ho wei 'yung Chien'? T'a tsai chün-shih-shang yu ho tso-yung?" in *Chung-kuo Ku-tai Chün-shih San-pai-t'i* (Shanghai: Ku-chi Ch'u-pan-she, 1989), pp. 447–449.

2. Wu was taught by the duke of Shen, an exile from Ch'u via Chin, as discussed in the Spring and Autumn historical section that follows.

3. For convenience, the *Tso Chuan* quote has been provided in interpretive summary.

4. "T'u-fan, Shang," *ChiuT'ang-shu.*

5. "Hsüan Yüan Liu-wang," *Han Shu.* Note the emphasis upon geographical knowledge.

6. Duke Ai, 1st year (494 B.C.). The critical sentence and most of the story also appear in the traditional commentary to the *Bamboo Annals;* the main entry states that Ju-ai attacked and killed Chiao, the man who had slain Shao-k'ang's father (*Chu-shu chi-nien pu-cheng,* 1:12b). Other popular accounts suggest that he also dispatched his eldest son to two small foreign states that, based upon their reports, he subsequently attacked and exterminated. The account being some fifteen hundred years after the event, its validity remains highly questionable.

7. "Employing Spies," *Art of War.*

8. A discussion of terms appears in the Spring and Autumn section that follows.

9. "Shen-ta Lan," *Lü-shih Ch'un-ch'iu.*

10. For this he is frequently compared with the Duke of Chou, who acted as regent to King Wu's son until relinquishing power when the latter had sufficiently matured.

11. Similarly, the claim was made—only to be vehemently repressed—that the Duke of Chou had also usurped the throne rather than simply serving as regent by proxy.

12. For example, *Huai-nan Tzu,* chaps. 1, 9, 11, 13, 19, 20; *Han Fei-tzu,* chaps., 14, 17, 18, 19, 36, 37, 44, 50; *Pao P'u-tzu,* chaps. 7, 8, 22; *Yen-t'ieh Lun,* chaps. 2 (acts as a cook), 7, 11, 14, 18, 20, 51; *Kuei Ku-tzu,* chap. 6.

13. "T'ai-tsu Hsün," *Huai-nan Tzu. Mencius,* VIB6, also notes that Yi Yin went to T'ang and Chieh five times each.

14. *Mencius,* VA7.

15. "Wu Tu."

16. "Liu Yeh," *Jen-wu Chih.*

17. "Jang Wang," *Chuang-tzu.* A translation may be found in Burton Watson, *The Complete Works of Chuang-tzu* (New York: Columbia University Press, 1968), p. 320.

18. The T'ai Kung's biography is found in the *Shih Chi* chapter reprising the history of the state of Ch'i, to which he was appointed first king by the victorious Chou dynasty. An extensive discussion of his possible role, incorporating a translation of his biography, may be found in our translation of the *Six Secret Teachings* in the *Seven Military Classics of Ancient China* or the introduction to the Shambhala edition of the *Six Secret Teachings.*

19. The *Six Secret Teachings,* a remarkable work of strategy and tactics dating from the middle to late Warring States period, is the most comprehensive of the so-called *Seven Military Classics* collected and made canonical in the Sung dynasty. Although the *Six Secret Teachings* never enjoyed the respect accorded Sun-tzu's *Art of War* by nonmilitary thinkers in China and

also suffered disparagement by effete bureaucrats who found it unthinkable that one of China's greatest figures was apparently a political realist, as well as a military sage, real commanders and those interested in preserving the state amid the turmoil that repeatedly engulfed it over the centuries valued the *Six Secret Teachings* greatly and profitably employed its teachings. The most extensive of the classic writings, it explores numerous fundamental topics from an essentially humanistic, Taoistically oriented perspective while also providing a compendium of useful, frequently unorthodox tactics for concrete application. Interspersed among its pages may be found many of man's most pressing concerns, including social organization, development of Virtue, creation of a productive society, and the role of the military. Throughout, the essential vision is one of maneuver warfare—battlefield encounters designed to minimize losses while still retaining the martial spirit and capability to prevail in perhaps history's most turbulent era, the Warring States.

20. This battle is extensively discussed in introductory material to our translations of the *Six Secret Teachings*.

21. This was an approach similarly exploited by the PRC in the 1950s and 1960s.

22. "Feng-mou chieh." Commentators date these reports as either one or eight years prior to the victorious attack on the Shang. See, for example, Huang Huai-hsin, ed., *Yi Chou-shu Hui-chiao Chi-chu* (Shanghai: Shanghai Ku-chi, 1995), pp. 313–314.

23. "Shen-ta-lan," *Lü-shih Ch'un-ch'iu*. The passage goes on to describe King Wu's sincerity in upholding the date he swore with the feudal lords and also informing a neglected minister of Yin.

24. The employment of women, the fundamental response in antiquity, should be particularly noted.

25. And largely found in the compilation *Kuo-yü*, fabricated then but attributed to the Spring and Autumn period.

26. See *Analects*, V:4a.

27. *Analects*, XIX:22.

28. *Analects*, I:10. The wording is slightly different. Note how information can be garnered through congeniality and inquisitiveness, a point not lost on later thinkers.

29. *Analects*, I:15. The sequence of the items is, however, reversed.

30. The numbers of chariots are anachronistic.

31. This is a rather surprising comment given that all the historical records portray him as oblivious to any threat from the king of Yüeh. (Their conflict is discussed in several other contexts in the remainder of our study.)

32. Po P'i, as will be seen later, was actually under Yüeh's control.

33. Yüeh was especially known for its swords, so such a gift would have been quite special.

34. The lengthy, dramatic conflict between Wu and Yüeh is discussed in detail in the historical introduction to our translation of the *Art of War*.

Chapter 2

1. See, for example, Duke Ting, 12th year; and Duke Ai, 7th year, *Tso Chuan.*

2. Karlgren, GSR 812l.

3. See, for example, Duke Min, 1st year; and Duke Hsi, 19th and 24th years.

4. GSR 553h.

5. GSR 158i.

6. Neither of them is so employed in the *Tso Chuan,* but *k'uei* does appear in this meaning in the *Kung Yang Chuan.*

7. GSR 633j, given as meaning "to spy." The locus classicus is the *Tso Chuan.*

8. Duke Huan, 12th year.

9. Duke Chuang, 28th year.

10. In contrast, T'ien Tan deliberately attracted birds to imply spiritual powers in the famous tactics witnessed at the siege of Chi-mo, where he engineered a breakout by loosing fire-oxen, a battle discussed in detail in our forthcoming *History of Warfare in China: The Ancient Period.*

11. Duke Ai, 11th year. However, he may have been a reconnaissance scout.

12. He did this because he undoubtedly expected to be enfeoffed in Chin and perhaps to develop a base from which he could retake the throne of Ch'u. His actions coincidentally illustrate the major role defectors and exiles played in the ancient period.

13. Duke Ai, 16th year.

14. Duke Hsüan, 8th year.

15. See Yang Po-chün, *Ch'un-ch'iu Tso-chuan Chu* (Peking: Chung-hua Shu-chü, 1981), 2:696.

16. The covert agents who undertook such tasks and the technique as well were classified as *li chien,* "estrangement agents." (See the theory section for a full discussion and numerous examples.) Even as late as the Ming-Ch'ing transition, in his brief work *Ping Mou* Wei Hsi emphasized the estrangement role of *hsien (chien)* and the covert agent nature of *tie.*

17. GSR 191h.

18. Duke Chuang, 8th year. Note that this is a case of employing disaffected women who attained their positions through sexual attraction to gain illicit ends. Numerous such cases will be cited here and in the section on covert operations.

19. Duke Hsiang, 4th year.

20. See, for example, Duke Ch'eng, 18th year; and Duke Hsiang, 25th year.

21. "Tao-ying Hsün," *Huai-nan-tzu.* The original *Tso Chuan* account for Duke Hsi's 33rd year (627 B.C.) is comparatively terse; later versions found embedded in various Han dynasty works expand the story and exploit it to illustrate philosophical or political points, thereby giving the historical events renewed currency and import.

22. Duke Ch'eng, 17th year.

23. "T'an Kung, Hsia," *Li Chi.*

24. Duke Min, 1st year, *Tso Chuan.*

25. One ancient Chinese calendar has been preserved in the *Lü-shih Ch'un-ch'iu* and *Li Chi;* contemporary almanacs still contain extensive information based upon the twenty-four seasonal periods and lunar data. Tan's series of celestial observations essentially corresponds to a three-month progression through the fall.

26. The *Chou Li* enumerates several other officials who probably performed intelligence-gathering duties because of their extensive contacts with foreign officials, although at somewhat less prestigious levels. For example, the *Ssu-yi*, who was in charge of foreign contacts; the *Hsing-fu*, a sort of a junior *Hsing-jen* who served as an aide to the *Hsing-jen* and seems to have been stuck with all the miserable jobs; the *Hsing-hsü*, who handled foreign ambassadors from the barbarian states and oversaw communications between their envoys and the Chou king; and the *Chang-k'o*, who was entrusted with "handling guests" but seems to have supervised the meal service.

An article analyzing a wide variety of official Ch'in seals presently preserved in a regional collection includes one for a *Ch'in-hsing*, the *Hsing-jen's* title when his position was renamed late in the Ch'in. (Although the title was again revised during the Han, it is no longer of interest because China's political terrain had vastly altered.) Other posts of note with likely information-gathering responsibility represented by these seals include the *tien-song*, a lesser official in charge of relations with submissive barbarian peoples, and various messengers responsible for communications. (See Chou Shao-lu, Lu Tung-chih, and T'ang Yi, "Ch'in-tai feng-ni te chung-ta fa-hsien," *K'ao-ku Wen-wu* 1 [1997]:37ff.)

27. Numerous examples of this mundane usage occur throughout the period. See, for example, Duke Hsüan, 12th year, in a military context; Duke Ch'eng, 13th year; Duke Hsiang, 8th, 21st, and 24th years; and Duke Chao, 18th year.

28. Duke Wen, 14th year. This is confirmed by a discussion in the *Kuo-yü* ("Chou-yü, Chung") for King Chien's 8th year (577 B.C.) as to whether to accord an envoy from Lu the full ceremonies dictated for a *Hsing-jen* since his mission seemed less than official in conception.

29. The *Tso Chuan's* account of the battle of Yen-ling, including this incident, appears as the conclusion to this section on the Spring and Autumn period, and will also be extensively discussed in our forthcoming *History of Warfare in China: The Ancient Period.*

30. A similar case with a contrary outcome arose in Duke Wen's 12th year when an officer from Ch'in taunted Chin's army. Since he spoke incoherently and his eyes darted all about, it was correctly concluded that Ch'in would withdraw during the night.

31. For example, see Duke Chao, 23rd year, when Chin seized the *Hsing-jen* from Lu, resulting in complex political ramifications.

32. The episode began late in Duke Hsiang's 11th year and concluded early in his 13th year.

33. Duke Hsiang, 18th year. The *Ku Liang* notes his seizure was due to enmity toward his superiors.

34. Duke Chao, 23rd year.

35. Duke Huan, 9th year.

36. Duke Chao, 8th year.

37. Duke Ting, 7th year. (This makes Pei one of history's first "dead agents.")

38. Duke Ai, 12th year.

39. Duke Hsiang, 11th year.

40. Duke Hsiang, 26th year. The *Hsing-jen* was sometimes instructed to deliver verbatim messages, as well as written missives. (See also Duke Chao, 6th year.)

41. Duke Wen, 4th year. For a similar case, see Duke Hsiang, 4th year.

42. Duke Ch'eng, 7th year; noted again under Duke Hsing, 26th year.

43. Duke Ting, 4th year. (Further discussion of Wu Tzu-hsü's historical role will be found in the sections on assassins and coordinated covert programs. His full biography will be found in the introduction to our translation of Suntzu's classic *Art of War*.)

44. *Analects*, XIV:8. (This ability even resulted in his name being cited in connection with the definition of *Hsing-jen* in several dictionaries.)

45. This enigmatic statement is understood by all the commentators and essentially confirmed by what follows in the passage. It of course suggests he insisted upon holding serious discussions of military policy in total secrecy, out in the wilds, away from prying eyes and well-stretched ears.

46. Duke Hsiang, 31st year.

47. See also Duke Chao, 1st year; and Duke Hsiang, 29th year, when he served as an envoy to a funeral. An anecdote in the *Yen-tzu Ch'un-ch'iu* ("Nei-p'ien Tsa-hsia") shows the king of Wu testing Yen-tzu, who was visiting in his capacity as Ch'i's *Hsing-jen*, by having him inappropriately summoned to an audience with the "Son of Heaven." The ruse failed because he struck a baffled pose until after the third summons, when he expressed astonishment at having somehow lost his way and wandered into the court of an emperor rather than a king.

48. *Han-shih wai-chuan, chüan* 6. A nearly identical passage is found in the opening paragraphs of the *Shuo Yüan*.

49. Duke Hsüan, 3rd year, *Tso Chuan*.

50. Several occurrences refer to shepherding; others employ the term as a verb, one case of which is understood as meaning "to investigate" (speaking about an official responsible for "stemming brutality." See "Ch'iu-kuan Ssu-kuan").

51. "T'ien-kuan Chung-tsai," *Chou-li.*

52. "Ch'un-kuan Tzung-po," *Chou-li.*

53. "Hsia-kuan Ssu-ma-hsia," *Chou-li.*

54. Duke Huan, 5th year.

55. Duke Chuang, 10th year.

56. Duke Hsi, 15th year. Note the emphasis already being placed on elite fighters and psychological factors.

57. Wu Ch'i's contributions to intelligence theory will be discussed in the theory section, and are reprised in full in our translation of the *Seven Military Classics of Ancient China*.

58. Duke Hsi, 30th year.

59. Ibid. The term *chien* here clearly means "to spy" (despite tendencies of translators to understand it as "to exploit") because the redundant clause that follows reiterates the fact of the attack.

60. Duke Hsi, 33rd year.

61. Duke Wen, 17th year.

62. See, for example, Duke Hsüan, 13th year, wherein Hsien Ku invited the Red Ti to invade Chin, further compounding Chin's problems of internecine strife among their powerful families. (Such factionally prompted alliances contributed greatly to China's turmoil in the centuries following the Han's collapse.)

63. The first noted betrayal of a state's military plans is recorded for 658 B.C. when "an officer of Ch'i, for the first time, leaked the army's plans at Tuo-yü" (Duke Hsi, 2nd year, *Tso Chuan*).

64. Duke Ai, 8th year. The mat-maker clearly falls within Sun-tzu's concept of "local guides."

65. Duke Chao, 19th year, *Tso Chuan*.

66. Although this persuasion evidences Warring States characteristics, it may have some factual basis and certainly coheres with what would have been required in the circumstances.

67. This is exactly the sort of instruction that Sun-tzu identified with fighting on fatal terrain, eliciting the ultimate effort from the troops. (See, for example, "Nine Terrains," *Art of War*. Several examples are also found in the *Unorthodox Strategies*.)

68. Duke Hsiang, 26th year, *Tso Chuan*.

69. Duke Ch'eng, 7th year.

70. Duke Chao, 28th year.

71. This is, of course, the same state of Ch'en as in Tan Hsiang's earlier observations, and in fact it is Duke Ling who is murdered and Ch'en extinguished.

72. Duke Hsüan, 9th year.

73. Ibid.

74. Duke Hsüan, 11th year.

75. Duke Ch'eng, 2nd year. It would also make it seem that he had mounted the attack merely to satisfy his own lusts.

76. Duke Ch'eng, 7th year.

77. The event would appear to be a fabrication of the Warring States period, projected back to around 498 B.C., but it is reported in numerous sources thereafter.

78. "Kong-tzu Shih-chia," *Shih Chi*.

79. *Analects*, XVIII:4. (Rulers and powerful nobles enjoyed sexual liaisons with such musicians and kept astounding numbers of favorites and serving girls, in addition to a formal wife and officially recognized concubines of various rank.)

80. These two techniques are found in the T'ai Kung's "Civil Offensive," a chapter from the *Six Secret Teachings* that is abstracted and discussed in the theoretical section.

81. Commentators to Han Fei-tzu's chapter entitled "Ten Errors" point out that the king failed to shift their encampment as seasonally appropriate, resulting in half their horses and cattle perishing.

82. "Ch'in Pen-chi," *Shih Chi*.

83. See "Ten Errors." It also appears in *Han-shih Wai-chuan, chüan* 9; and "Fan-chih," *Shuo Yüan*.

84. "Kui-chih-lun."

85. Hsi Kung, 33rd year, *Tso Chuan*.

86. "Wu Tzu-hsü Lieh-chuan," *Shih Chi*.

87. Hsi Kung, 24th year, *Tso Chuan*.

88. Also note Duke Ting, 5th year, *Tso Chuan*, when the king has a man assassinate Tzu Ch'ao in Ch'u.

89. He had been killed by a boatman, a prisoner from Yüeh, when he inspected the boats (Duke Hsiang, 29th year).

90. Duke Ting, 10th year.

91. "Wang Liao shih Kung-tzu Kuang."

92. Duke Chuang, 12th year, *Tso Chuan*.

93. Duke Wen, 12th year.

94. Duke Wen, 13th year, *Tso Chuan*.

95. See Yang Po-chün's comments based on recently recovered Ma-wang-tui slips, *Ch'un-ch'iu Tso-chuan Chu*, 2:595–596.

96. "Chin Shih-chia," *Shih Chi*. (The episode is also noted in "Chou Pen-chi." Shih Hui also appears as Sui Hui, for unknown reasons.)

97. "Ch'i T'ai Kung Shih-chia," *Shih Chi*.

98. Although the text doesn't specify, they may have been disguised as women. This would not be completely abnormal, for other instances of men disguising themselves as women to either gain surreptitious access to the women's apartments for licentious reasons or to carry out murderous acts are recorded.

99. See the records for Duke Hsiang, 23rd year, for the military events; and the 22nd year for his arrival in Ch'i and the outrage his presence evoked, as seen in the *Shih Chi* account.

100. Additional examples of stealthy methods will be found in the last part of the third section, on covert activities.

101. Duke Hsiang, 10th year, *Tso Chuan*.

102. Duke Chao, 4th year, *Tso Chuan*.

103. The term employed is *tie*, normally "spy" but here "reconnaissance troops."

104. Duke Ch'eng, 16th year, *Tso Chuan*.

105. Insofar as the *Tso Chuan* apparently reflects a Warring States perspective, these essential formulations may well be anachronistic projections.

Chapter 3

1. The Battle of Ma-ling is extensively analyzed in the historical introduction to our translation of Sun Pin's *Military Methods*.

2. The actual impact of Sun-tzu's writings and thought remains to be determined, turning upon the pivotal question of the availability of his writings and whether his disciples actively disseminated his teachings or if the teachings remained a family school of tactics down through his famous descendant, the great Ch'i tactician Sun Pin, in the mid-fourth century.

3. As many commentators have pointed out, these two events actually occurred a decade before Fan Sui went to Ch'in in 265 B.C.

4. "Wei Kung-tzu Lieh-chuan," *Shih Chi.*

5. See Yang K'uan, *Chan-kuo Shih,* rev. ed. (Shanghai: Jen-min Ch'u-pan-she, 1979), pp. 342–343. In two pages of dense notes Yang provides an extensive discussion of the thorny problem of Su Ch'in's dates and the resulting confusion with his two brothers, concluding that he was active during King Min's reign in Ch'i, roughly 300 to 284 B.C., being an honored minister in Ch'i near the end of his reign.

6. This is summarized in "Yen Chao-kung Shih-chia," *Shih Chi,* as well: "Su Ch'in had illicit relations with the king's mother and, fearing execution, persuaded the king to employ him in Ch'i as a 'turned agent' with the intention of plunging Ch'i into chaos." This was certainly a case of a true "double agent."

7. Takigawa Kametaro, *Shiki Kaichū Kōshō* (Taipei: I-wen Yin-shu-kuan, 1972), p. 884, doubts that he lived into King Min's reign, implying he actually died while Yi was still on throne in Yen, perhaps having been discovered after only two years in Ch'i. However, as already noted, Yang K'uan, based on recently discovered tomb materials, concludes the records support the traditional account (*Chan-kuo Shih,* p. 343).

8. This was an ambitious aspect of the era's covert programs, such as previously advocated by Wen Chung at the end of the Spring and Autumn period against Wu and seen again in Han's attempt to exhaust Ch'in in canal building, found subsequently. (Wen Chung's covert program, purportedly preserved in the Han dynasty *Wu Yüeh Ch'un-ch'iu,* is fully translated in the section on systematic covert programs.)

9. "Su Ch'in Lieh-chuan," *Shih Chi.*

10. "The Treatise on the Yellow River and Canals." A translation of the complete treatise may be found in Burton Watson, *Records of the Grand Historian of China* (New York: Columbia University Press, 1961), 2:70–78.

11. "Lien P'o Lin Hsiang-ju Lieh-chuan," *Shih Chi.*

12. The incident, which appears in chapter 35, "Mountains," is fully translated in our *Unorthodox Strategies.*

13. The identification of cavalry at this early date bears noting. Although cavalry apparently originated in Chao, the actual date is uncertain.

14. This is perhaps a serious underestimate, certainly increasing rapidly.

15. Throughout, the figures for chariots seem far too low since several states supposedly possessed ten thousand chariots early in the Warring States period, and battlefield commitments of several thousand per state are noted in major battles. However, these figures are taken verbatim from the *Chan-kuo Ts'e.*

16. Theories of regional character evolved during the period as well, often organized around concepts of the five phases, associating the north with cold,

harshness, and endurance. Hsün-tzu, a late Warring States Confucian philosopher who believed man to be innately selfish and conflict to be inherent to society, addressed both military and civil problems from a more realistic viewpoint than the earlier Confucians and exerted considerable influence on subsequent governmental thought and over pivotal figures.

17. The Three Chin are Han, Wei, and Chao.

18. "Evaluating the Enemy."

19. The system of battlefield rewards and punishments thus emphasized individual performance to the detriment of the army's performance as a whole. This encouraged warriors, rather than soldiers, men who fought individually with a view to their own profit largely unconcerned with the overall progress of the battle.

20. These tests were singular, not simultaneous, with the last being directed toward mobility and endurance under load. They no doubt reflect Wei's heritage, for tests of this type were strongly advocated by the famous general Wu Ch'i, who successfully commanded the western region in Wei, frequently defeating Ch'in, for many years early in the fourth century B.C. Appropriate criteria and the importance of selected troops are discussed in the first two chapters of the *Wu-tzu*.

21. Among the recently recovered tomb texts, a fragment entitled "The King of Wu's Questions" (translated in the intelligence section) apparently preserves Sun-tzu's analysis of the tax structure of the various clan lands in Chin (which had not yet split asunder) and their associated martial prospects. At that time he estimated the taxes as one-fifth of a family's income.

22. This of course follows Lord Shang's draconian conception.

23. Hsün-tzu's grudging acknowledgment of Ch'in's remarkable success, despite their perverse methods, will be further discussed in the sections on political and military intelligence.

24. See the introduction to the *Wei Liao-tzu* in the *Seven Military Classics*, p. 231.

25. "Li Ssu Lieh-chuan," *Shih Chi*. The king referred to in the passage is the eventual unifier of all China, the first emperor of the Ch'in dynasty, Ch'in Shih-huang.

26. "Chin-yü, 3," *Chan-kuo Ts'e*.

27. "Chin-yü, 4," *Chan-kuo Ts'e*. Note that Li Mu's spies, already mentioned, failed to protect him from covert enemies.

28. The turned agents are really traitors who act as agents for an enemy state, Sun-tzu's "internal agents" rather than double agents.

29. "Chao-yü," *Chan-kuo Ts'e*.

30. "Yen Chao-kung Shih-chia," *Shih Chi*.

31. This criticism is reminiscent of those leveled at Patton and anyone else who outstripped their lines of support in World War II and throughout history. Although current terminology would view the issue as one of "synchronization," the crux is seizing penetration opportunities versus the danger of becoming isolated and enveloped.

32. His reluctance well accords with Sun-tzu's famous admonition to avoid urban assaults whenever possible.

33. "Chou-chi, 4," *Tzu-chih T'ung-chien.*

34. T'ien Tan also proved highly capable in manipulating Yen into provoking his own warriors, raising their *ch'i,* determination, and resolve.

35. "Yüeh Yi Lieh-chuan," *Shih Chi.*

36. This battle, its recorded sources, and the political circumstances surrounding it are fully discussed in our forthcoming *History of Warfare in China: The Ancient Period.*

37. "T'ien Tan Lieh-chuan," *Shih Chi.*

38. Figures from this period are difficult to accurately evaluate. Although traditional sources seem to be filled with exaggerations, they may be less inaccurate than thought. Certainly both sides fielded several hundred thousand men, and the number of men from Chao slaughtered at Ch'ang-p'ing is reported as 450,000 or 485,000 in various sources. Recent archaeological evidence indicates that a great battle was fought there, and states of the period were certainly capable of mobilizing a very high percentage of their male population, particularly when threatened with extinction. (This battle is extensively discussed in our forthcoming *History of Warfare in China: The Ancient Period.*)

39. Pai Ch'i's biography in the *Shih Chi* notes that "Ch'in's prime minister, the marquis of Ying, moreover dispatched men to distribute a thousand catties of gold around Chao to have 'turned agents' spread the rumor that the only thing Ch'in feared was that Chao She would become commander."

40. "Lien P'o Lin Hsiang-ju Lieh-chuan," *Shih Chi.*

41. A similar account of these events with additional details of the battles themselves, told from Ch'in's point of view, appears in the combined biographies of Pai Ch'i and Wang Chien, *chüan* 73 of the *Shih Chi.* (Also see *Shih Chi, chüan* 79, the biography of Fan Chu.)

42. A second example of exploiting the era's belief in divination, perhaps prompted by knowledge of this incident, appears in the covert section.

43. "Ch'i-yü, 1," *Chan-kuo Ts'e.*

44. Equally important with singular talent and remarkable character was dedication, the focused effort that resulted in particularized expertise and became the foundation for the martial arts practices that proliferated in later centuries. Astute leaders proved their ability to "know men" through recognizing and exploiting such individuals.

45. "Meng-ch'ang Chün Lieh-chuan," *Shih Chi.*

46. "Wei Kung-tzu Lieh-chuan," *Shih Chi.*

47. This is a very odd name indeed, meaning "one who despises Chin" or a "rustic of Chin."

48. This is a famous phrase attributed to Sun-tzu, but widely found.

49. Although listed in the *Han Shu* bibliography, the work is now lost.

50. Here the term is *fan chien,* possibly "doubled spies" but more likely just "agents."

51. This was an essential aspect of the traditional practice of "knowing men" that will be discussed in the section on evaluating men.

52. "Ts'u K'o," *Shih Chi.* A complete translation may be found in Burton Watson, *Records of the Grand Historian, Qin Dynasty* (New York: Columbia

University Press, 1993), pp. 167–178; and the *Chan-kuo Ts'e* version ("Yen, 3") in J. I. Crump, *Chan-kuo Ts'e* (London: Oxford University Press, 1970), pp. 553–561.

53. Ts'ao Mei's coercion of an agreement from Duke Huan is reprised in the covert section.

54. Although the prince's intention had been to extort an agreement, Ching Ko's actions were too precipitous for anything but assassination—contrary to his dying claims—as many commentators have subsequently noted.

Chapter 4

1. Debate rages over whether the *Art of War* was actually composed by Sun-tzu at the end of the sixth century B.C., written by his disciples shortly after his death, or compiled from oral teachings somewhere about the end of the fifth century B.C. (For a brief discussion, see the introduction to our *Art of War*.)

2. Recourse to the ancestral temple for councils of war had the additional value of entrusting the decision to the ancestral spirits, essentially receiving their sanctification and psychologically shifting the responsibility to them in the event of failure.

3. See D. C. Lau, "Some Notes on the Sun Tzu," *BSOAS* 28 (1965):331–332. A highly simplified example of employing chopsticks to visibly count off advantages and disadvantages, no doubt in the same mode, appears in Li Sheng's analysis of the strategic situation for Liu Pang during the last years of the struggle to establish the Han ("Chang, Ch'en, Wang, Chou Chuan," *Han Shu*).

4. According to Michael Handel, "Intelligence in Historical Perspective," in *Go Spy the Land*, ed. Keith Nielson and B.J.C. McKercher (Westport, Conn.: Praeger, 1992), pp. 179–180, Sun-tzu was "the first to explicitly discuss the role of what is today termed net assessment."

5. "Incendiary Attacks," *Art of War*.

6. "Initial Estimations," *Art of War*. The famous *Huai-nan Tzu* military chapter reiterates the temple calculation theme several centuries later.

7. A paraphrase from "Opening Instructions" in the *Six Secret Teachings* that discusses the appropriate time for the Chou to revolt against the hated Shang: "If there are no ill omens in the Tao of Heaven, you cannot initiate the movement to revolt. If there are no misfortunes in the Tao of Man, your planning cannot precede them."

8. The choice of "symptoms" reflects the military theorists' (as well as Mencius's and other later Confucians') concern with benevolent government, economic prosperity, and programs that do not impoverish or exhaust the people. For example, see "Affairs of State," *Six Secret Teachings*.

9. Again this echoes "Opening Instructions" from the *Six Secret Teachings*: "You must look at the Shang king's *yang* aspects [his government], and moreover his *yin* side [personal deportment], and only then will you know his mind. You must look at his external activities, and moreover his internal ones, and only then will you know his thoughts."

10. "Initial Estimations," *Art of War*.

11. "Military Disposition," *Art of War.*
12. "Ch'üan-mou," *Shuo Yüan.* Note that the term translated as "factors" is *ch'ou* (Matthews 1323), which fundamentally means "to calculate," as well as a "tally," such as employed for making these net assessments.
13. "Ch'üan-mou," *Shuo Yüan.*
14. "T'an-ts'ung," *Shuo Yüan.*
15. "Determining Rank," *Ssu-ma Fa.*
16. "The Tao of the General," *Wu-tzu.* In "Responding to Change" Wu Ch'i also states, "If the enemy has fortified their defenses in order to solidify their troops, quickly dispatch spies in order to observe their plans."
17. He is even cited in the *Encyclopedia Britannica.* The question of the *Art of War*'s composition date and whether the chapter on spycraft was an integral part of the original text of course affects the assignment of priorities. Even though the chapter is consistent with his theoretical conceptions and emphasis, three questions arise. First, when was the *Art of War* actually composed—at the end of the sixth century B.C., by Sun-tzu himself, prior to assuming his famous (if questioned) role in Wu, or by his disciples or later members of his school, perhaps at the end of the fifth century B.C.? Second, was chapter 13 on spies part of the original text, or was it appended later in the Warring States? Third, is it by the same author as the other chapters? In terms of context, all the types of spies Sun-tzu discusses existed in the Spring and Autumn period—even expendable ones—but their real proliferation came in the Warring States, possibly in small part the result of Sun-tzu's conceptualizations. Even though too tangential to undertake here, the problem clearly merits further research.
18. "Nine Terrains."
19. "Employing Spies."
20. "Configurations of Terrain."
21. "Seven Standards."
22. Ibid. In the Three Kingdoms period Chu-ko Liang similarly stated, "Those who excel at combat invariably first investigate the enemy's situation and thereafter make their plans" ("Chi Shih," *Chu-ko Chung-wu-hou Wen-chi*).
23. "Ping-lüeh-hsün."
24. *Li Wei-kung Ping-fa.*
25. "Spies in Warfare."
26. "Spies," *T'ou-pi Fu-t'an, chüan* 5.
27. "The Enemy's Situation," *T'ou-pi Fu-t'an, chüan* 5.
28. "Employing Spies."
29. See, for example, Handel, "Intelligence in Historical Perspective," pp. 180ff.

Chapter 5

1. *Li Wei-kung Ping-fa.*
2. This is not the case in the *Chou Li. Tie* is not used there either, so it is probably an error for *mou,* "to plot" or "to plan."

3. This occurred in A.D. 29, during the Later Han dynasty. (See "Compulsion," *Unorthodox Strategies*, for a more detailed version.)
4. These are almost exactly Sun-tzu's words throughout, except for the elision of one clause.
5. "Five Agents."
6. We are emending *t'ien* to *jen*, as the former is clearly erroneous here.
7. This differs from Sun-tzu's concept because the agents are not deliberately sacrificed.
8. Tu Mu's commentary.
9. *Mencius*, IIIA3, quoting Yang Hu in a somewhat distorted context!
10. "The Unorthodox Army," *Six Secret Teachings*.
11. Note that credence is basically accorded these methods; the problem lies in their opacity and difficulty, not premises or theory.
12. This occurred at the battle of Yen-ling, already reprised in the Spring and Autumn section.
13. So he claims really double agents, rather than just internal agents, spreading disinformation.
14. The extant texts of the *T'ai-pai Yin-ching*, translated separately, contain only two types of roving agents. Whether the *Yin-ching* has suffered condensation (Shih Tzu-mei had a copy with three types) or is simply misquoted, dividing the two into three, is unknown.
15. This incident provides the historical illustration for "Snow," *Unorthodox Strategies*.
16. Duke Hsüan, 15th year, *Tso Chuan*.
17. The next section, to the end of the paragraph, is supplemented from "Huai-yin-hou Lieh-chuan," *Shih Chi, chüan* 92.
18. "Li Sheng, Lu Chia Lieh-chuan," *Shih Chi, chüan* 97. For another translation, see Burton Watson, "The Biographies of Li Yi-chi and Lu Chia," in *Records of the Historian* (New York: Columbia University Press, 1961), 1:269–274. Li Sheng's death marks the dramatic conclusion to the episode and thus imprints it upon historical memory. However, this did not prevent others from questioning his demise thereafter.
19. "Tung Chou," *Chan-kuo Ts'e*.
20. "Shu-shu 13," *San-kuo-chih, chüan* 43.
21. "Chou-yü," *Chan-kuo Ts'e*.

Chapter 6

1. *Questions and Replies*, Book II. The boat analogy also appears in a parallel passage in Li Ching's *Li Wei-kung Ping-fa*, and Li Ching's conclusions are paraphrased in the anonymous Ming Dynasty, "Spies," *Ts'ao-lu Ching-lüeh*.
2. "Spies," *T'ou-pi Fu-t'an, chüan* 5.
3. Never specifically mentioned in this context, but fundamental to the military writings, was the belief that warfare, being the greatest affair of state, could not be undertaken for emotional reasons. Therefore, the evaluation of acquired material should not be prejudiced by optimism, emotional tendencies, or personal desires.

4. "Middle Strategy," *Three Strategies*. The conclusion should also be noted.

5. "Controlling the Army," *Chu-ko Chung-wu-hou Wen-chi.*

6. "Chien-tie."

7. "Hsiao K'uang." In the T'ang dynasty a rebel commander employed a puppet show that he dispatched in advance into unconquered areas to ferret out the people's inclinations and fathom the local political situation (*Chiu T'ang-shu, chüan* 177).

8. "Spies." Even the initial chapter of the *Six Secret Teachings* emphasizes the need for material incentives with an analogy of bait and fishing.

9. "Employing Spies."

10. *Li Wei-kung Ping-fa.* The passage echoes some of the T'ai Kung's methods in "Civil Offensive," *Six Secret Teachings*, discussed in the section on systematic programs.

11. *Li Wei-kung Ping-fa.*

12. "Local Guides," *T'ai-pai Yin-ching.*

13. *Hou* (observer), a character not often seen, although more common in the military writings, is certainly deputed by the king to make clandestine observations.

14. In traditional China the number three seems to have been almost magical in attesting to the veracity of an event, as will be discussed in the section on basic intelligence.

15. "Ch'i-yü, 1," *Chan-kuo Ts'e.*

16. The character for control originally meant "to drive a chariot."

17. For "exhaust themselves" some editions have "love men."

18. "Jen Yung," *Hu-ling Ching.*

19. Such "bravos" were often identified with outlaw bands, especially during times of turmoil and hardship.

20. "Hao-chieh wei Chien."

21. The echoes are chilling.

22. The *Hu-ling Ching* is found as a separate text and preserved in the *Wu-pei Chih*. There are some problems with textual variation and corruption for this chapter, much of which reflects the T'ai Kung's "Civil Offensive."

23. The word is *fan chien*, which by this time simply designates "spy."

Chapter 7

1. "The Army's Strategic Power."

2. "Vacuity and Substance," *Art of War.*

3. "Nine Terrains," *Art of War.*

4. "Vacuity and Substance," *Art of War.*

5. "Military Discussions," *Wei Liao-tzu.*

6. "Superior Strategy," *Three Strategies.*

7. "Ping-lüeh-hsün."

8. Examples of fathoming men from afar based upon their appearance and demeanor will be found in the section on evaluating men.

9. Compare the terms employed in "King's Wings," *Six Secret Teachings.*

10. "Chen Chien"

11. "T'an Ts'ung." In "Chiang T'i," *Ch'ang-tuan Ching,* it states: "When the general's plans leak out, the army will lack strategic power; when internal affairs can be spied out from outside, the resulting disaster will be uncontrollable."

12. "Tactical Balance of Power in Warfare."

13. "Nine Terrains," *Art of War.*

14. "The Source of Offices," *Wei Liao-tzu.*

15. The traditional function of "feathers and wings," according to the late Warring States *Six Secret Teachings,* was "to flourish the name and fame of the army, shake distant lands with its image, and move all within the four borders in order to weaken the enemy's spirit" ("The King's Wings").

16. "Orders for Segmenting and Blocking Off Terrain," *Wei Liao-tzu.* In "Army Orders, II" forward reconnaissance forces are also entrusted with a mandate to control the terrain and prevent anyone from moving in or through the area of forward advance.

17. "Wang Lou." Similar pronouncements are found in the roughly contemporaneous *Wu-ching Tsung-yao,* such as in "Chih-hou T'ing-wang."

18. "Yu Yi." Similar methods are found in "T'an Ma" and "Hsing Feng," *Wu-ching Tsung-yao.*

19. See, for example, "Severed Routes."

20. The *Wu-ching Tsung-yao* chapter entitled "Ch'uan-hsin Pei" discusses such methods as splitting coins and other objects in half, as well as multiple use tallies.

21. "Secret Tallies."

22. Ibid. The severe penalty for discussing them, even within the camp, should be noted.

23. Ibid.

24. David Kahn, *The Codebreakers,* rev. ed. (New York: Scribner, 1996), pp. 73–74. Remarkably, Kahn also notes the existence of this *Wu-ching Tsung-yao* section, but questions whether it or similar systems were much employed.

25. The construction, staffing, and employment of beacons to report border incursions and similar events with fires, smoke, and other visible signals are described in "Feng Huo," *Wu-ching Tsung-yao.*

26. Although the Western military tradition is hardly bereft of the theory and practice of deception, in recent centuries it seems to have not only been disdained but also vociferously rejected with the coincident condemnation of the "morally deficient" Chinese approach to warfare. However, closer examination reveals the systematic employment of deception from Greek and Roman times right through the twentieth century, particularly by Britain and Russia in the last world war. (For an insightful overview of Western practices, see James F. Dunnigan and Alfred A. Nofi, *Victory and Deceit* [New York: William Morrow, 1995]; for Russian methods, see David Glantz, *Soviet Military Deception in the Second World War* [London: Frank Cass, 1989].)

27. "Li, Lu, Chu, Liu, Shu, Sun Chuan," *Han Shu, chüan* 43.

28. Perhaps these were straw dummies, perhaps just nonfighters from the baggage train.

29. Duke Hsiang, 18th year.

30. The battle of Ma-ling and the earlier battle at Kuei-ling are analyzed in detail in the historical introduction to our translation of Sun Pin's *Military Methods.*

31. For further discussion, see "The Weak," *Unorthodox Strategies.* (The battle of Ma-ling is discussed in the chapter entitled "Knowledge," as well as in the introduction to our translation of the *Military Methods.*)

32. "Offices, I," *Military Methods.*

33. See, for example, the *Six Secret Teachings* chapters "Divided Valleys," "Forest Warfare," and "Crow and Cloud Formations in the Mountains."

34. "The Cavalry in Battle." Book I of the *Questions and Replies* discusses the tactical utility of interchanging the uniforms of barbarian and Chinese troops.

35. "Movement and Rest."

36. "Planning for the Army."

37. "Preparation of Strategic Power."

38. "Initial Estimations," *Art of War.*

39. "The Tao of the Military," *Six Secret Teachings.*

40. A famous quote from "Initial Estimations," *Art of War.*

41. This echoes "Vacuity and Substance," *Art of War.*

42. "Initial Estimations," *Art of War.*

43. "Nine Changes," *Art of War.*

44. "Nine Terrains," *Art of War.*

45. Sun-tzu's objectives in "Military Combat."

46. "Great Appendix," *Yi Ching.*

47. "Submerged Plans."

48. The word here is *chan,* meaning through reconnaissance scouts, clandestinely.

49. "Strategic Military Power," *Art of War.*

50. This statement is not found in the present *Six Secret Teachings* but certainly echoes Sun-tzu's sentiments in "Military Disposition," *Art of War.*

51. "Strategic Military Power," *Art of War.*

52. This is no doubt a quote from "The Unorthodox Army," *Six Secret Teachings.* However, the original differs in having "divide" rather than "extend."

53. "Submerged Changes."

54. This basically echoes Sun-tzu's concept of compelling others, not being compelled by them.

55. "Tsa-shih," *Hsin Hsü.*

56. "Wei-yü, 4," *Chan-kuo Ts'e.*

57. *Li Wei-kung Ping-fa, chüan* 1.

58. "Yüeh Fei," *Sung Shih, chüan* 365.

59. "Han Shih-chung," *Sung Shih, chüan* 364.

60. "Tzung Tse, Chao Ting," *Sung Shih.*

Chapter 8

1. "Chin-yü, 2."

2. These are all tactics that clearly reflect Taoist thought. (For a discussion, see the introduction to our translation of the *Six Secret Teachings.*)

3. "Chi Chien-tie Shuo," *Teng-t'an Pi-chiu.*

4. "Inferior Strategy," *Three Strategies of Huang Shih-kung.*

5. "Wu Tzu-hsü Lieh-chuan," *Shih Chi.* The complete biography, together with an analysis of the political and military conflicts between Wu and Ch'u, may be found in the introduction to our single-volume *Art of War.*

6. This somewhat fictionalized account of the dramatic conflict between the two states of Wu and Yüeh was probably written in the first century A.D. Even though the reliability of its dialogues is very questionable, the author may well have had access to oral transmission and records no longer extant and was thoroughly knowledgeable about the area.

7. This standard series of techniques for evaluating men will be discussed in the section on knowing men.

8. For example, during the reign of Duke Wen, Chin provided aid to Ch'in.

9. *T'ai-pai Yin-ching.*

10. The definition remains problematic, particularly as it runs contrary to the idea of "darkness" or "obfuscation" that might be expected from "covering the enemy's enlightenment," and there may well be difficulties with the text that fortunately do not detract from the concept's importance as explicated.

11. The character *ying* (Morohashi 4462), rarely used, is defined as the "sound of animals." Note that the "Original Text" for this entry has been lost.

12. This, of course, echoes his various definitions seen in the section on deception.

Chapter 9

1. The chapter has been translated by Burton Watson and is included in his compendium *Records of the Historian* (New York: Columbia University Press, 1969). However, traditional elitist prejudices apparently prevented later writers from emulating it in the so-called official dynastic histories.

2. For a discussion of the psychological impact of the Chinese practice termed "knowing men," see our earlier work by the same name or the forthcoming revision.

3. Jujubes, for example, were a much-favored medium for administering poisons ("Yu Hui," *Shih-shuo Hsin-yü*).

4. "Ho-lü Nei-chuan," *Wu-Yüeh Ch'un-ch'iu, chüan* 4, abridged, leaving out his confrontation with a stalwart who had battled a river spirit over the death of his horses.

5. The prevalence of admiration for martial values in the common culture will be discussed at length in our forthcoming *History of Warfare in China.* Essentially, most of China's historical records, such as the official dynastic histories, were composed by literati deeply imbued with a "civic" orientation that stressed nonviolence, the reign of Virtue over power. This has led to nu-

merous assertions that China lacked a martial tradition, that the civil controlled the martial, and that the people disdained strongmen, bravados, fighters, and similar miscreants. However, China's history is one of almost incessant warfare, and when the civil dominated the martial, it often undermined any hope of survival. Popular culture clearly diverged from the literati's value scheme, flocking to such individuals as the *yu-hsia* and openly applauding the strong. Thus, although virtue is much spoken about and expected to carry the ruler to tranquil governance of the realm, even the court itself seethed with intrigue and recourse was easily had to murder and assassination without any moral compunction whatsoever. Those who would boldly throw away their lives and all that men value to revenge a wrong or save the state were heroes, whatever actions they might endure or take. (The *Shih Chi*'s chapter on the *yu-hsia* [*chüan* 124] has been translated by Burton Watson as "The Biographies of the Wandering Knights," in *Records of the Grand Historian of China* [New York: Columbia University Press, 1961], vol. 2, whereas the *yu-hsia* have been studied by James Liu, *The Chinese Knight-Errant* [Chicago: University of Chicago Press, 1967].)

6. "Ch'üan Mou."

7. Even though actually falling in the interval between the Spring and Autumn and the Warring States periods, Chih Po's Greek-like tale of hubris is also recounted at length in the *Chan-kuo Ts'e* and may be found in J. I. Crump's translation by the same title (Oxford: Oxford University Press, 1970). Portions relating to his demise will also be found in the section on evaluating men.

8. In the *Lü-shih Ch'un-ch'iu* version a friend makes this inquiry.

9. "Shih-chün-lan," *Lü-shih Ch'un-ch'iu*. The event also receives mention in three other chapters; the sequence differs greatly from that found in the *Shih Chi* chapter on assassins.

10. "K'ai Ch'un," *Lü-shih Ch'un-ch'iu*.

11. "Shu Hsü," *Lun Heng*.

12. This shows that they expected spies to be about even in the Han itself, especially in the regions near the border, and make reports.

13. "Fu Ch'ang, Cheng Kan, Ch'en Tuan," *Han Shu*.

14. "Han Ch'ang-ju Lieh-chuan." Another account is found in the chapter on the Hsiung-nu. The Hsiung-nu chapter in the *Shih Chi* portrays the sequence as evolving more gradually, with Nieh first acting as a trader, under the emperor's instructions, then enticing them with the betrayal of Ma-yi. Moreover, the emperor apparently instigates the plan, no suggestion being recorded of it originating with Nieh. The commandant simply betrays the Han plot when about to be slain of his own accord, rather than as the result of forcible questioning. Of course, the Shan-yü seized him to learn exactly why circumstances seemed so suspicious and thus obtained his own "native guide," even if by coercion. For further information, see Watson's translations of these two chapters in *Records of the Historian*, "Han Ch'ang-ju" and "The Account of the Hsiung-nu."

15. "Kuo Tu, Kong Chang, Lian Wang, Su Yang, Chia Lu."

16. "Yen-yü, 1," *Chan-kuo Ts'e*.

17. This is found in Confucius's biography in the *Shih Chi* and twice in the *Analects*, IX:18, XV:13. (Chapter 15 being a late chapter, the sentence was clearly viewed as important.)

18. Even the pedant Mencius saw sex as innate, as seen from the opening paragraphs of Book V.

19. *Shih Ching*, Mao 1.

20. See, especially, Mao 143, describing male longing.

21. "Wen-cho-chieh."

22. "Wen-ch'uan-chieh."

23. "Shih-chi-chieh."

24. "Ta Ming-wu."

25. "K'o-Yin-chieh."

26. "Tsa Yen," *Shuo Yüan*. (In a fabricated chapter of the *Kung-tzu Chia-yü* entitled "Li Yün," Confucius even speaks fluently and at length [in contrast to his "discussions" in the *Analects* and even the *Li Chi*] about the seven emotions [which include the desires] as innate.)

27. "Kuei Te," *Shuo Yüan*.

28. "Ching Shen," *Shuo Yüan*. The tastes and desires are coupled with "slander and flattery" in their ability to confuse the upright mind.

29. Ibid.

30. *Hsin Hsü, chüan* 1. A man's commitment to the world was even thought to be confirmed by his continuing interest in women. Therefore, in the Three Kingdoms period Ssu-ma Yü once noted that Hsieh An, a famous recluse, would probably reappear because he constantly had a courtesan with him and couldn't avoid being troubled by the world's anxieties ("Shih Chien," *Shih-shuo Hsin-yü*).

31. "Chung-Hsia-chi," *Lü-shih Ch'un-ch'iu*.

32. "Chung-Ch'un-chi," *Lü-shih Ch'un-ch'iu*.

33. "Chung-Hsia-chi," *Lü-shih Ch'un-ch'iu*. Hsün-tzu framed the principle of external stimuli stimulating the desires that is no doubt being followed in this passage. The psychology of self-control gave rise to the theory of the *li*, the rites and ceremonies governing social life that, when internalized, become the forms and possibility for a sort of transcendent freedom. (For an extensive discussion, see Ralph Sawyer, *Psycho-emotional Conceptualization and Expression in the Li Chi* [Taipei: Kaofeng, 1978].)

34. "Pen-ching-shun."

35. "T'ai-tsu-shun."

36. "Ching-shen-shun." The "king of Hu" refers to the Jung ruler Duke Mu subverted, already recounted in the historical section.

37. "Wai-p'ien, Chiu-ch'eng," *Pao P'u-tzu*. According to Han Fei-tzu, even the great Lao Tan adopted a similar practice: "Lao Tan was the epitome of purity and vacuity. Yet he would not dare gaze at what he desired in order to prevent his mind from becoming perturbed."

38. Ibid.

39. "Pien Wen," *Pao P'u-tzu*.

40. The character *yao* is difficult to translate here, but can mean "beauty," as well as "strange."

41. This characterization includes men as well.

42. The term he employs is *ch'u*, "to rear," just like domesticated animals!

43. Duke Hsiang, 21st year, *Tso Chuan*. Wang Ch'ung's version is nearly identical.

44. "Chien Chieh-shih Ch'en," *Han Fei-tzu*.

45. "Chao-yü, 4," *Chan-kuo Ts'e*.

46. "Ch'in-yü, 1," *Chan-kuo Ts'e*.

47. *Chiu T'ang-shu, chüan* 161.

48. "Han-yü, 3," *Chan-kuo Ts'e*.

49. "Chien-chieh Sha-chün." The episodic story of Duke Wen's trials and wandering before he finally ascended Chin's throne even includes his stepmother's attempt to frame him for trying to poison his father to ensure her own son's succession. A very dramatic story, it readily became the stuff of romantic legends and provided a lesson for later generations seeking instant solutions for difficult situations.

50. "Ch'u Shih-chia," *Shih Chi*. (The dates cited are much disputed and are included merely to provide a chronological sense of the events.)

51. "Hsiung-nu Lieh-chuan," *Shih Chi, chüan* 110. (The chapter has been translated in full by Watson, "The Account of the Hsiung-nu.") A similar but slightly longer entry appears in Ch'en P'ing's biography in the *Shih Chi, chüan* 56. Some commentaries to the *Han Shu* suggest that Ch'en P'ing had pictures painted of these idealized women to create a stronger impression. (Ch'en P'ing was the famous strategist who estranged Fan Tseng from Hsiang Yü with unfounded rumors of duplicity and is remembered as the progenitor of other ruses and deceptions.) The background to this incident has already been recounted in the section on concealment and deception.

52. Huan Tan's discussion is noted by Dubs in a footnote to the Kao-tsu entry. See Homer H. Dubs, trans., *The History of the Former Han Dynasty* (Baltimore: Waverly Press, 1938), p. 117.

53. *Hsin Lun.*

54. Chu-ko Liang even recommended it as the policy of choice against the Eastern Yi, a barbarian people he characterized as "having few rites and little righteousness" and being susceptible to estrangement techniques based upon bribery preliminary "to enticing them with Virtue and attacking them with power" ("Tung Yi," *Chu-ko Chung-wu-hou Wen-chi*).

55. "Tung Chou," *Chan-kuo Ts'e*.

56. The term employed is "turned agent," but again they are simply agents, traitors who have turned against their own state.

57. "T'ien-ching Chung-wan Shih-chia," *Shih Chi*.

58. "Ho-lü Nei-chuan, 4," *Wu-Yüeh Ch'un-ch'iu*.

59. "Chou-yü," *Chan-kuo Ts'e*.

60. "Ch'i-yü, 1," *Chan-kuo Ts'e*.

61. "L'ien P'o Lin Hsiang-ju Lieh-chuan," *Shih Chi. Fan chien* is again the term, but he was merely a traitor, contrary to Sun-tzu's definition.

62. Although termed "double" or "turned agents," they were probably just agents in the Han's employ.

63. "Ch'en Yung-hsiang Shih-chia," *Shih Chi*.

64. "Hou Chün-chi, Chang Liang, Hsüeh Wan-ch'e," *Chiu T'ang-shu.*
65. This is an ironic request because his contemplated actions would violate all the forms and proprieties of a minister serving at a formal convocation.
66. Duke Chuang, 13th year, *Ku-liang Chuan.*
67. Duke Hsüan, 15th year, *Tso Chuan.*
68. "Tao-ying Hsün," *Huai-nan Tzu.*

Chapter 10

1. "Shao-ming Wu-chieh." To evaluate men and behavior, consistency of course must be assumed.
2. "Fei Hsiang," *Hsün-tzu.*
3. "Chung-tung Chi."
4. "Ching Hua."
5. "Jen Yi Fa," *Ch'un-ch'iu Fan-lu.*
6. "Tsun Hsien," *Shuo Yüan.*
7. "Ch'i Shih," *Lun Heng.*
8. "Shuo Fu."
9. "Miu-ch'eng Hsün."
10. "Chuo Ts'ai," *Pao P'u-tzu.*
11. See, for example, "Tao Ying Hsün."
12. "Cheng Li," *Shuo Yüan.* Naturally the Sage is capable of knowing himself; otherwise he wouldn't be a Sage. However, most rulers fell far beneath the ideal. As Han Fei-tzu stated in his commentary upon Lao-tzu ("Yü Lao"), "The difficulty of knowing does not lie in seeing other men but in seeing oneself."
13. "Chih Wu," *Shuo Yüan.* The concept of the virtuous being able to invariably triumph without combat, strongly identified with Mencius, plagued China's military preparedness for millennia and obstructed efforts to resist and subdue external, more warlike steppe peoples such as the Mongols and Manchus thereafter.
14. "Chieh-pi," *Hsün-tzu.* As the *Ping-fa Pai-yen* states in its definition of emptiness: "When the mind has no errors to obstruct it, it is termed 'emptiness.'" However, the definition is more tactically than psychologically oriented, focusing on deluding the enemy through their preconceptions. Thus it states, "When the enemy has extensive plans and we are able to balk them, their wisdom will fail."
15. "Chieh Pi," *Hsün-tzu.* The *Huai-nan Tzu* defined technique as "when you see the foundation and know the ends, observe indications of going and see the return, grasp one and respond to the myriad, take hold of the essential and control the details, this is called 'technique'" ("Jen-hsien Hsün").
16. "Ssu-hsün Lun," *Lü-shih Ch'un-ch'iu.*
17. "Cheng Ming," *Hsün-tzu.*
18. "Hsien-shih Lan," *Lü-shih Ch'un-ch'iu.*

19. "Shu-chen Hsün."

20. "Yu-shih Lan," *Lü-shih Ch'un-ch'iu.* The ax story is also found in "Shuo Fu," *Lieh-tzu.*

21. "Hsiu-wu Hsün." This text is also found in "Hsien-shih Lan," *Lü-shih Ch'un-ch'iu.*

22. This is no doubt based upon chapter 12 of the *Tao Te Ching*, which states that input from the senses overwhelms the sensory organs.

23. "Shu-jen Hsün."

24. "Yüan Tao Hsün."

25. "Shu-chen-hsün."

26. "Pa Ching," *Han Fei-tzu.*

27. "Tsa Shih, 2," *Hsin Hsü.*

28. Ibid.

29. "Shen-hsing Lun," *Lü-shih Ch'un-ch'iu.*

30. "Kuei-chih Lun," *Lü-shih Ch'un-ch'iu.* (Sung's story is much discussed in the literature, and the historical section has already recounted other aspects of it.)

31. "Nei-p'ien wen-hsia." Interestingly, Yen-tzu found that when the ruler was too severe, he would equally not hear any criticism or ill news ("Nei-p'ien Chien-hsia").

32. "Ch'i-ssu Hsün."

33. "Planning for the State."

34. "P'ing-yüan Chün, Yü Ch'ing Lieh-chuan," *Shih Chi.*

35. "Shuo-shan Hsün," *Huai-nan Tzu.* The question of evaluating men is discussed separately.

36. "Shen-hsing Lan," *Lü-shih Ch'un-ch'iu.* A similar point is made in the *Huai-nan Tzu* in a passage that employs the identical images of jade and another famous sword, noting that only an expert can distinguish them ("Fan-lun Hsün").

37. Ibid.

38. "Ssu-hsün-lun," *Lü-shih Ch'un-ch'iu.* The colors no doubt refer to the copper and tin employed in alloying bronze.

39. "Ch'üan Mou," *Shuo Yüan.* An almost identical, probably original, version appears in "Ssu-hsün-lun," the *Lü-shih Ch'un-ch'iu.* King Chuang was one of the five hegemons; the attack took place in 597 B.C.

40. "Ch'i-ssu Hsün," *Huai-nan Tzu.* (The lute incident has been partially reconstructed from an earlier passage.)

41. "The Army's Strategic Power," *Six Secret Teachings.* See also "Doubt and Timeliness," *Art of the Warrior.*

42. "Controlling the Army," *Wu-tzu.* The *Yi Chou-shu* ("Wu-chi Chieh") also observes that "one who assumes power but is doubtful will never escape disaster."

43. "Yi Ping."

44. A more extreme expression deduces that the eyes and ears simply cannot be relied upon, although not in the same sense as in some eras of the Western philosophical tradition. (See, for example, "Shen-fen Lan," *Lü-shih Ch'un-ch'iu.*) This is also the thrust of Taoist transcendent knowledge.

45. "Yüan Tao Hsün."
46. "T'ai-tsu Hsün."
47. "Ch'u Chuang Wang," *Ch'un-Ch'iu Fan-lu.*
48. *Analects,* XII:11.
49. "Hsien-shih Lan."
50. "Chieh Pi," *Hsün-tzu.* The *Pao P'u-tzu* notes that people who espouse different views, who follow their own paths, are mistrusted and doubted by others ("Wei Chih").
51. "Miao-ch'eng Hsün," *Huai-nan Tzu.*
52. "Chieh Pi," *Hsün-tzu.*
53. "Tao Yi," *Pao P'u-tzu.*
54. "Kuang P'i," *Pao P'u-tzu.*
55. "Jen-hsien Hsün," *Huai-nan Tzu.*
56. "Yu-shih Lan," *Lü-shih Ch'un-ch'iu.*
57. "Ssu-shun Lun." This certainly echoes a fundamental *Tao Te Ching* insight (chap. 71), although commentators also see it as referring to Confucius's pronouncement on knowing (*Analects,* II:17). The passage ends by noting that great wisdom and little wisdom are distinct, a concept probably derived from Chuang-tzu.

Chapter 11

1. "Fu En," *Shuo Yüan.*
2. The tradition of knowing men, although pronounced and dramatic, has occasioned little scholarly interest apart from Eric Henry, "The Motif of Recognition in Early China," *Harvard Journal of Asiatic Studies* 47, no. 1 (1987):5–30; and our early work, *Knowing Men* (Taipei; Kaofeng, 1979), in revision for reissue.
3. "Kao-yao Mo," *Shang Shu.* The "Doctrine of the Mean" similarly notes the ruler must "know men."
4. *Analects,* XII:22.
5. *Analects,* I:16.
6. *Analects,* XV:7.
7. This text is available in John Shryock's classic translation, *The Study of Human Abilities* (New Haven: American Oriental Society, 1937).
8. The "Wen-wang Kuan" is translated later in this chapter. A chapter in the Later Han *Pao P'u-tzu* entitled "Hang-p'in" also enumerates dozens of character types, with a brief phrase describing their dominant traits.
9. *Analects,* XIII:2. Note that in a dialogue with Duke Ai ("Ssu Tai," *Ta-Tai Li-chi*) Confucius suggested observing the people at large, for the Worthy will clearly stand out, just as a tiger in the depths. In later texts Confucius is also quoted as advising Duke Ai against employing three types of men: the close-mouthed, the strong, and the sharp-tongued ("Ai Kung," *Hsün-tzu;* and "Tsun Hsien," *Shuo Yüan*), or the strong, the flatterer, and the loquacious (*Han-shih Wai-chuan, chüan* 4).

10. "Wen Shen," *Fa-yen.*
11. *Analects,* V:5, V:8, V:19, XIV:1.
12. See, for example, "Shen-ying Lan," *Lü-shih Ch'un-ch'iu,* where Confucius speaks about men who have the skill to "know words."
13. "Jen Shin," *Lü-shih Ch'un-ch'iu;* "Wei Chiang-chün Wen-tzu," *Ta-Tai Li-chi.*
14. "Tsa Yen," *Shen Chien.* Also note "Shih Fan," *Feng-su T'ung-yi.*
15. "Wen Chien." Another interesting example is found in "Yü Ho," the *Lü-shih Ch'un-ch'iu.*
16. "Pen Hsing," *Lun Heng.*
17. "Kuan Piao," *Lü-shih Ch'un-ch'iu.* In this regard the Sage is envisioned as capable of fathoming a person's actual intent rather than simply watching his activities.
18. "Kuan Piao," *Lü-shih Ch'un-ch'iu.*
19. *Analects,* XI:20.
20. "Wu-ti Te," *K'ung-tzu Chia-yü.*
21. "Selecting Generals," *Six Secret Teachings.*
22. "Lei Hai," *Lun Heng.* Wang Ch'ung observed that the evil can still create a reputation for goodness.
23. "Chün Ch'en." The object of such forbearance was probably the conquered Hsia people, but the saying is frequently cited out of context.
24. "Fan Lun."
25. "Tsa Shih, 5," *Hsin Hsü.*
26. *Chüan* 4. This text is also found in *Hsün-tzu* ("Chün Tao"), which is probably the original source.
27. "Ting Chüeh" ("Determining Rank"), *Ssu-ma Fa.*
28. *Analects,* II:10.
29. "Jen Hsien." A man who shows sympathy for a horse would be expected to be benevolent.
30. "Jen Hsien," *Huai-nan Tzu.*
31. Ibid.
32. *Mencius,* IVA15. (The last line deliberately repeats Confucius's earlier assertion.) Note that the *Ling-shu* ("Shih Ch'uan") also states that the eye expresses courage.
33. "Wu-hsing Chih," *Han Shu,* cited by the author as coming from *Shih Chi,* but probably originally from "Chou-yü, Hsia," *Kuo-yü.*
34. Han Fei-tzu even cites the case of a prince so intent on plotting a revolution to gain revenge for his father's death that he didn't realize his chin was leaning on the point of his staff and bleeding from being punctured ("Yü Lao").
35. *Han-shih Wai-chuan, chüan* 4.
36. "Chieh-ching Wei-lun," *Su-wen.*
37. "Pen Ts'ang," *Ling-shu.*
38. "Hsi Tz'u," *I Ching.*
39. "Ching Lun."
40. The episode is found in the records for both Chao and Wei in the *Chan-kuo Ts'e,* as well as in various forms in the *Shih Chi* (historical houses of Han, Chao, and Wei), the *Huai-nan Tzu* ("Chien Hsün"), *Shuo Yüan* ("Ch'üan

Mou"), and other parts of the *Han Fei-tzu* ("Shuo Lin, Shang" and "Nan San"). It ranks among the most famous Warring States stories, well known through the centuries.

41. "Shih Kuo."

42. This is an ironic comment because of the ignominious death he later suffered, having ignored Kuan Chung's dying words on selecting a successor.

43. "Shen-ying Lan," *Lü-shih Ch'un-ch'iu.*

44. "Ching Yü," *Lü-shih Ch'un-ch'iu.* (The passage of course entails vestiges of the mystic tone of the "knower," the man who can know without visible signs and actual behavior.)

45. "Shuo Shan."

46. "Tsun Hsien," *Shuo Yüan.*

47. This is, in part, a pun on the construction of the Chinese character for Chü, which consists of two mouths stacked one over the other underneath the signifier for grass.

48. "Shao Wen," *Kuan-tzu.* This is also found in "Chih Shih," *Lun Heng;* "Chung Yen," *Lü-shih Ch'un-ch'iu;* "Ch'üan Mou," *Shuo Yüan;* and *Han-shih Wai-chuan, chüan* 4.

49. "Miu Ch'eng." This reflects the common view that sounds and tones express underlying emotion, even if unintentionally, and have a significant effect on the listener. Therefore even the songs of a state allow it to be evaluated for a sort of national temper and character.

50. *Analects*, II:8 (also note II:7).

51. "Fei Shih-erh-tzu," *Hsün-tzu.*

52. "Fei Hsiang," *Hsün-tzu.*

53. Ibid. His train of thought was also incorporated by the *Han-shih Wai-chuan.*

54. "Hsien Chi," *Lü-shih Ch'un-ch'iu.* Sun-tzu, more than two centuries earlier, had expressed the similar sentiment that one must know the enemy and oneself.

55. *Mencius*, IA7. The king confesses he did not understand his own motives in sparing an ox from being sacrificed. (Legge's classic translation unjustifiably introduces the phrase "by reflection.") Tung Chung-shu also cites this verse as an example of the principle of association, concluding that "exhaustively looking at a person's exterior one can see the interior" ("Yü Pei," *Ch'un-Ch'iu Fan-lu*).

56. "Fei Kung, Chung," *Mo-tzu.*

57. *Mencius*, IA7. The *Ho Kuan-tzu*, in introducing the set of standard criteria employed for evaluating men in varying circumstances, also speaks of "measuring men."

58. "Chih Tu." The idea is advanced here and in one or two other texts (such as "Tsun Hsien," *Shuo Yüan*) that men such as the T'ai Kung and Yi Yin must be recognized in their situations and then appropriately employed based upon an estimation of their abilities if the ruler is to attain ultimate status as a hegemon.

59. Wang Ch'ung ponders it as the basis for asserting behavior can be fathomed, citing the "Offices of King Wen" (translated at the end of this section). See "Ta Ning," *Lun Heng.*

60. *Mencius*, VIIA44.
61. *Analects*, XVII:26. (This is the traditionally sanctioned understanding of the sentence, but it might be translated as "Someone who still displays evil at forty years of age will end by being so.")
62. *Analects*, I:2.
63. "Kuan Piao," *Lü-shih Ch'un-ch'iu*. Also note "Tao Ying," the *Huai-nan Tzu*.
64. *Chung-lun*, A:9a; *Analects*, II:10.
65. "Shu Chieh," *Lun Heng*.
66. See, for example, "Tsa Shih, 5," *Hsin Hsü*.
67. "Chu Shu," *Huai-nan Tzu*.
68. *Analects*, XV:27.
69. "Advancing the Worthy."
70. *Analects*, XIII:24.
71. *Mencius*, IB7.
72. "Ssu Tai."
73. "Tsa Shih, 1."
74. A9b, B19b–21b.
75. "Ch'ien T'an" and "Chung Kuei," *Ch'ien-fu Lun-chien*.
76. "Ch'a Ch'uan," *Lü-shih Ch'un-ch'iu*.
77. "Tzu Lu Ch'u-chien" and "Wu-ti Te," *K'ung-tzu Chia-yü*. Also note "Wu-ti Te," *Ta-Tai Li-chi*; and "Tsa Shih, 4," *Hsin Hsü*.
78. *Mencius*, VIIA36.
79. "Ai Kung," *Hsün-tzu*.
80. "Lu-yü, Hsia," *Kuo-yü*.
81. "Lu-yü, Hsia," *Kuo-yü*.
82. "Ai-kung Wen Wu-yi," *Ta-Tai Li-chi*.
83. "Ch'iung Ming," *Shang Shu*.
84. *Analects*, I:3.
85. *Mencius*, VIIB12.
86. *Mencius*, VIIB37. (This essentially combines two passages from the *Analects*, XVII:13 and XVII:18.)
87. *Analects*, VI:16.
88. "Ai-kung Wen Cheng," *K'ung-tzu Chia-yü*. (Compare "Hsiao Chih," *Fa Yen*.)
89. "Shuo Lin." (This is contrary to later Confucian attitudes, which condemned any successful person serving in a debauched state.)
90. Ibid.
91. "Lun Fei."
92. *Mencius*, IIA2.
93. "Fei Hsiang," *Hsün-tzu*. Also note "Li Yi," *Yen-t'ieh Lun*, which likens raising men to selecting a horse by its hair.
94. "Chou-yü, Shang," *Kuo-yü*.
95. *Analects*, XI:20.
96. *Analects*, XIV:5.
97. *Analects*, I:3, XVII:17.
98. *Analects*, V:9; "Tzu Lu Ch'u-chien" and "Wu-ti Te," *K'ung-tzu Chia-yü*; *Analects*, XI:2.

99. *Analects*, XV:22.

100. "Jui Liang-fu," *Yi Chou-shu*.

101. "Wu-ti Te," *Ta-Tai Li-chi*; "Nei-ch'u-shuo Shang, Ch'i-shu," *Han Fei-tzu* (through listening the wise and stupid cannot be distinguished); and "Jui Liang-fu," *Yi Chou-shu*.

102. "Wu Pen," *Lü-shih Ch'un-ch'iu*; "Ta Lüeh" and "Hsing Eh," *Hsün-tzu*; "Feng Shih" and "Tsa Yen," *Shuo Yüan*; "T'ai-tsu Hsün," *Huai-nan Tzu*; and "Shih Kuo," *Han Fei-tzu*.

103. "Hsing Eh," *Hsün-tzu*.

104. *Mencius*, VA8; "Chih Kung," *Shuo Yüan*; and "Ta Lun," *Yen-t'ieh Lun*.

105. "Cheng Ming," *Hsün-tzu*; *T'ai-hsüan Ching* (Ch'ü tetragram); and "Yü Pei" and the important "T'ung-lei Hsiang-tung," *Ch'un-Ch'iu Fan-lu*.

106. This thought pervades the *K'ung-tzu Chia-yü*, a work that presumably preserves the Master's teachings. (Note that in the *Shuo Yüan* ["Tsa Yen"] Confucius observes that someone entering a strongly smelling environment quickly becomes accustomed to the odors and no longer notices them.)

107. "Liu Pen," *K'ung-tzu Chia-yü*.

108. "Wen Ti," *K'ung-tzu Chia-yü*. The *Han-shih Wai-chuan* (chüan 2) similarly notes the sequence by which people see and evaluate the powerful: from far to near, appearance, voice, and then actual behavior.

109. *Analects*, V:9.

110. "Tsun Hsien," *Shuo Yüan*.

111. "Ch'iu-kuan Shih-k'ou," *Chou Li*.

112. Note that the *Ta-Tai Li-chi* ("Ts'eng-tzu Li-shih") and *Tseng-tzu Chia-yü* ("Li-shih") compare words and eyes.

113. "Ting Hsien," *Lun Heng*. (Compare "Ch'ien T'an," "Chung Kuei," "Shih Kung," and "Chiao Chi," *Ch'ien-fu Lun-chien*.)

114. See, for example, "Ching Yü," *Lü-shih Ch'un-ch'iu*; and "Fei Shih-erh-tzu," *Hsün-tzu*.

115. See, for example, "Chu Shu," *Huai-nan Tzu*; and "Tzu Lu Ch'u-chien," *K'ung-tzu Chia-yü*.

116. "Miu Ch'eng," *Huai-nan Tzu*.

117. "Shih Ch'uan," *Ling Shu*.

118. *Analects*, IV:7. Also note "Kuo Yü," *Feng-su T'ung-yi*.

119. *Analects*, XVII:8. The term "obfuscation" was later employed by Hsün-tzu in a similar manner in his famous chapter "Explaining Obfuscations." In an interesting *Hsün-tzu* passage Confucius is quoted as discussing some counterbalances to unstructured substance that turn the individual into a virtual paragon: "One who is artful but loves measure will certainly constrain himself; who is courageous and loves to unite with others will be victorious; who is wise but loves modesty will be come a Worthy" ("Chung-ni").

120. "Yü Pei," *Ch'un-Ch'iu Fan-lu*.

121. "Kua Chien," *Fa-yen*.

122. "Ching Chieh," *Li Chi*.

123. See, for example, "Ta Ning," *Lun Heng*.

124. *Analects*, VI:9. Also note I:15.

125. *Analects*, VII:15.

126. *Mencius*, VIB15.
127. *Mencius*, VIB15. Also note VIIA18.
128. *Analects*, I:15.
129. *Analects*, IV:2. Mencius.of course concurred, and the Confucian school adopted it as a fundamental belief.
130. "Chieh Lao," *Han Fei-tzu*.
131. "Ch'en Shu," *Shuo Yüan*.
132. "Lun Jen," *Lü-shih Ch'un-ch'iu*. Such series are extremely common. See, for example, "Ting Hsien," *Lun Heng*; *Ho Kuan-tzu*; "Fan Lun," *Huai-nan Tzu*; and *Han-shih Wai-chuan* (*chüan* 3) where Li K'o's criteria for evaluating men run: "When at rest see whom they are intimate with; when rich, see whom they associate with; when successful, see whom they recommend; when impoverished, see what they will not do; when lowly, see what they will not take. These five are sufficient to observe men."
133. "Yao Tien," *Shang Shu*. The story is widely found, such as in Mencius, and *Lü-shih Ch'un-ch'iu* ("Yu Tu").
134. The concept of a test or probationary period is found throughout Warring States texts, including, for example, "Ching-kung Wen Te-hsien chih Tao," *Yen-tzu Ch'un-ch'iu*; "Ssu Tai," *Ta-Tai Li-chi*; "Wu-yi Chieh," *K'ung-tzu Chia-yü*; and "Yao Tien," *Shang Shu*.
135. "Selecting Generals."
136. "Fan Lun," *Huai-nan Tzu*.
137. For another example, see "Ch'au Shih," *Ta-Tai Li-chi*.
138. "Pa Ching," *Han Fei-tzu*.
139. "Tseng-tzu Li-shih," *Ta-Tai Li-chi*; and "Li Shih," *Tseng-tzu Chia-yü*.
140. "Lun Jen," *Lü-shih Ch'un-ch'iu*.
141. "Tseng-tzu Li-shih," *Ta-Tai Li-chi*. This text is also found in "Li Shih," *Tseng-tzu Chia-yü*. Another series designed to determine ability appears in Hsün-tzu's chapter "Chün Tao."
142. "Nei-ch'u-shuo Shang, Ch'i-shu," *Han Fei-tzu*.
143. Duke Wen, 1st year, *Tso Chuan*.
144. See, for example, "Ch'i, 3" and Ch'u, 4," *Chan-kuo Ts'e*; and "Wai-ch'u-shuo, Yu-shang," *Han Fei-tzu*.
145. "Shuo Wen." Yen-tzu's thwarting of such a test is discussed in the political intelligence section, and another interesting example is seen in Shen Sheng's response, "Chin-yü, 1," *Kuo-yü*.
146. "Ming-fa Chieh," *Kuan-tzu*.
147. See, for example, Duke Ch'eng, 17th year, *Tso Chuan*; "Wu-yi Chieh," *K'ung-tzu Chia-yü*; "Ch'au Shih," *Ta-Tai Li-chi*; and "Ch'u Hsia," *Yen-t'ieh Lun*.
148. "Kuei Tang," *Lü-shih Ch'un-ch'iu*. This incident is also found in such other texts as *Han-shih Wai-chuan*, chüan 9; Duke Hsi, 23rd year, *Tso Chuan*; and "Tsa Shih, 5," *Hsin Hsü*.
149. "Fei Shih-erh-tzu," *Hsün-tzu*.
150. "Ku Hsiang," *Lun Heng*. A similar idea is found in "Hsiang Lieh," *Ch'ien-fu Lun-chien*.
151. "Ku Hsiang," *Lun Heng*.

152. "Jung Ching," *Hsin Shu.*

153. Duke Chao, 11th year, *Tso Chuan.*

154. "Ch'ü Li, Hsia," *Li Chi.*

155. Duke Hsiang, 28th year, *Tso Chuan;* Duke Hsi, 31st year; Duke Wen, 9th year; Duke Wen, 15th year; and Duke Ch'eng, 13th year.

156. Duke Hsi, 12th year, *Tso Chuan.*

157. *Tso Chuan.*

158. Duke Wen, 18th year, *Tso Chuan;* and Duke Hsi, 27th year.

159. *Analects*, I:11.

160. "Hao Sheng," *K'ung-tzu Chia-yü.* Also in "Ch'üan Mou," *Shuo Yüan.*

161. Duke Hsiang, 31st year, *Tso Chuan.*

162. Duke Hsiang, 30th year, *Tso Chuan.*

163. Duke Chao, 15th year, *Tso Chuan.* (For another example, see Duke Hsiang, 31st year.)

164. See Duke Hsiang, 19th year, *Tso Chuan*, where the absence of grief indicates he has lost his foundation; and Duke Chao, 11th year, where the mourner lacks sorrow, steps high, and looks fierce.

165. "Hsin Wu," *Huai-nan Tzu.*

166. The *Lun Heng* has "her voice was unmoved."

167. "Nan San," *Han Fei-tzu;* and "Fei Han," *Lun Heng.*

168. A striking example of evaluating intent by the Odes appears in Duke Hsiang, 16th year, *Tso Chuan.*

169. A prominent official of many skills, including mathematics, astronomy, and music, during Wang Mang's reign and the first years of the Later Han dynasty, he enjoys a biography in the *Hou Han Shu* ("Ts'ai Yung Lieh-chuan").

170. See, for example, "Ming Lu," *Lun Heng;* and "Chih Shih," *Lü-shih Ch'un-ch'iu.*

171. "Ting Hsien" and "Lei Hai," *Lun Heng;* "Hsien Nan," *Ch'ien-fu Lun-chien.* (Purity itself seems to spawn antagonism.)

172. "Lei Hai," *Lun Heng;* and *Analects*, XIX:21.

173. "Lei Hai," *Lun Heng.*

174. Abstracted from "Ting Hsien," *Lun Heng.*

175. Note also "Lun Jung" and "Ch'ien T'an," *Ch'ien-fu Lun-chien.* An additional complication, raised by Wang Ch'ung (in "Liang Chih"), is that two men performing the same job do not imply equal talent. For example, Confucius and an ordinary man might both hold the same administrative position.

176. "Shuo Shan."

177. "Ch'eng Ts'ai" and "Shu Chieh," *Lun Heng.*

178. "Hsien Nan," "Ch'ien T'an," and "Chung Kuei," *Ch'ien-fu Lun-chien.*

179. "Pen Cheng," *Ch'ien-fu Lun-chien.*

180. "Lun Jung," *Ch'ien-fu Lun-chien.*

181. Ibid.

182. "Nei-ch'u-shuo Shang, Ch'i-shu," *Han Fei-tzu.* (The famous Mencian passage appears in IA7.)

183. There were actually many tests and indications for forging China's superlative swords, some of them preserved in the work on technology known as the *T'ien-kung K'ai-wu.*

184. "Hsien Hsüeh," *Han Fei-tzu.*

185. "Shuo Lin, Hsia." *Han Fei-tzu.* (This is another example of employing spies to watch political enemies.)

186. "Wai-ch'u Shuo, Tso-hsia," *Han Fei-tzu.*

187. "Hsien Hsüeh," *Han Fei-tzu.* The examples are drawn from the *Analects.*

188. "Shuo Lin, Shang," *Han Fei-tzu.*

189. "Nei-ch'u-shuo Shang, Ch'i-shu" and "Pa Shuo," *Han Fei-tzu.*

190. "Wen Pien," *Han Fei-tzu.* Han Fei-tzu was particularly known for his analysis of penchants and inclinations, and suggested methods for exploiting them, which will be discussed at the end of the section.

191. "Pa Ching," *Han Fei-tzu.* Many of these techniques are also found in Han dynasty texts such as the *Ch'un-Ch'iu Fan-lu* ("Li Yüan-shan") and later adopted by Li Ch'uan in his *T'ai-pai Yin-ching* and perhaps derive from the mysterious figure known as Kuei Ku-tzu, whose apocryphal book advances methods for confounding and probing other people. Unfortunately, space does not permit an examination of Kuei Ku-tzu's abstruse techniques, though they are incorporated by dozens of modern popular Chinese works.

Several of the clauses are a matter of considerable disagreement, as the extensive commentaries in Ch'en Ch'i-yu, *Han Fei-tzu Chi-shih* (Taipei: Shih-chieh Shu-chü, 1972), 2:1017–1025, indicate.

192. "Nei-ch'u-shuo, Shang: Ch'i Shu," *Han Fei-tzu.* A similar ploy precedes it.

193. "Wai-ch'u shuo, Tso-hsia," *Han Fei-tzu.*

194. "Shih Kuo," *Han Fei-tzu.* As is well known, Duke Huan failed to heed his advice and died ignominiously, despite his great stature and power, not long thereafter, a victim of their treachery.

Chapter 12

1. *Knowing Men* (Taipei: Kaofeng, 1979).

2. "Yao Tien," *Shang Shu.*

3. Ibid.

4. See, for example, "Ch'i Shu," *Huai-nan Tzu;* "San-tai Kai Chih-wen," *Ch'ien-fu Lun-chien;* and *Han-shih Wai-chuan, chüan* 7.

5. "Ta Yü Mo," *Shang Shu;* and "Shen-ta Lan," *Lü-shih Ch'un-ch'iu.*

6. "Ta Ning," *Lun Heng.*

7. This phrase is normally translated, despite an apparently different meaning, as "aptness for government combined with reverence," which is based upon somehow contorting the character *luan* (signifying chaos, turbulence, disorder in its primary meaning) to mean "to govern" or "put in order."

8. "Kao-yao Mo." Some of the pairs are, based upon normal readings, inherently contradictory, leading to imaginative explanations and alternative readings. (James Legge's classic translation of the *Shu Ching* [1865], as well as Bernhard Karlgren, *The Book of Documents, BMFEA* 22 [1950]:8, may be consulted for traditional renderings.)

9. His characterizations are apparently preserved in *Kung-tzu Chia-yü; Ts'eng-tzu Chia-yü;* and *Ta-Tai Li-chi.*

10. Extensive discussion of the disciples' characterizations will be found in *Knowing Men.*

11. The dozens of passages defining their respective attributes in the *Analects* and their subsequent elaboration by Mencius and especially Hsün-tzu may easily be consulted for specifics.

12. "Ai Kung," *Hsün-tzu.* Being found in a late Warring States work, the passage has only nominal connections with Confucius. (There is another passage attributed to Confucius in the *Han-shih Wai-chuan* in which he essentially berates the five classes of "gentlemen" found in his time who abuse their position and privileges rather than pursue self-cultivation and the Way [*chüan* 2].)

13. The *Shuo Yüan* arrays two sets of six ideal and pernicious ministers in "Ch'en Shu." Although largely stereotypes, certain characteristics and practices are distinguishable.

14. "Yin-yang Erh-shih-wu Jen," *Ling Shu.*

15. "T'ung T'ien," *Ling Shu.*

16. There are some important discrepancies in the two versions, including whether King Wen instructs the T'ai-shih (synonymous with the T'ai Kung, as in the *Six Secret Teachings*), or it is the Duke of Chou instructing King Wen (highly unlikely). The translation that follows is based upon the somewhat more expansive "Wen-Wang Kuan-jen" chapter in the *Ta-Tai Li-chi,* emended slightly where characters seem obviously incorrect from the "Kuan-jen" version preserved in the *Yi Chou-shu.* Because of the extensive use of adjectives, often puzzling, to characterize various types of individuals, extensive recourse was also made to the notes found in two contemporary editions: Kao Ming, *Ta-Tai Li-chi chin-chu chin-yi* (Taipei: Shang-wu Shu-chü, 1975); and Li Hsüeh-ch'in, *Yi-Chou-shu hui-chiao chi-chu* (Shanghai: Shanghai Ku-chi ch'u-pan-she, 1994).

17. The basis for the criteria that follow is human tendencies prevalent in less than ideal circumstances. The noble and wealthy usually become arrogant and ignore the *li,* the poor tend to be forced into illegal actions, the favored become haughty and exploit their positions, and the unknown, who have failed to realize their ambitions, generally become anxious. Maintaining proper behavior under such stressful situations provides a strong indication of character and virtue.

18. This concludes the first section of material that emphasizes internal and external coherence and the discernment of true emotions and commitments within a variety of contexts. The last part of this section provides techniques and suggestions for actively probing and testing a person to discover his hidden aspects. Even though King Wen had faith in the principle of transparency, he provided methods for actively setting up stimuli to elicit reactions that might then be judged for internal coherence, as well as appraised against external standards. The tests include providing major temptations based upon man's powerful, often overwhelming desires for wealth and beauty, situations such as rejection and favor in which undesirable emotional reactions might appear, and false clues or suggestions.

19. This brief section is essentially an explicit assertion of the transparency of character followed by a set of illustrative examples correlating the sound of the voice with internal mental states on the premise that through them the person's psychological state may be fathomed. (Throughout the term *ch'i*, basically synonymous with psychic energy and spirit, is employed in a quasi-technical sense.)

20. This section begins with a strong assertion of essential transparency based on the assumption that affective states will invariably be visible in the individual's manners, appearance, and physique and therefore that internal states can be fathomed and people evaluated.

21. King Wen begins by pointing out that people attempt to conceal their emotions and true personalities, and he goes on to indicate some character types and the ploys they use to consciously manipulate their images in order to gain fame as a particularly virtuous type of person while masking their true nature.

22. The king enumerates nine employments, following which the text repeats them, correlated with appropriate official duties. (The redundancy has been eliminated.)

23. The section closes with the king charging his officials to conscientiously perform their duties and warning that "bringing confusion to the laws" and other failures would be punished without pardon. In comparison with the six indications, and to a lesser extent, the nine employments, the seven categories consist of titles and only the broadest indication of positions. Perhaps much material has been lost, or perhaps King Wen never expanded upon this classification. Equally likely, the emphasis naturally fell upon evaluating personality and talent, and therefore the six indications are extensive and detailed.

Chapter 13

1. "Wai-ch'u-shuo Yu-shang," *Han Fei-tzu.* Some commentators take "outside" as referring to foreign states, which is certainly true in other passages and contexts, but is less likely here as they profit from such information from the outer officials and powerful families.

2. "Nei-ch'u-shuo, Shang," *Han Fei-tzu.*

3. This is, of course, the old idea of consorts, previously seen, but codified.

4. This is a practice strongly warned against by many writers from Mencius through the T'ai Kung, as already seen in the section on judging by fame, reputation, and approbation.

5. The translation adopts a more general rubric for the "target," even though the original intent was specifically rulers in the Warring States period.

6. Another chapter entitled "Difficulty in Words" ("Nan Yen") discusses how various types of presentation, phrasing, and choice of topics lead to misperceiving the speaker's intent, attainments, and character.

7. "Ch'en Tao," *Hsün-tzu,* slightly abridged and rearranged for convenience.

8. The *T'ai-pai* in the title refers to Venus, the "star" designated by metal in the five-phase system—metal (as in weapons) of course being associated with

the west, fall, oncoming cold, and death. The *yin* (of *yin* and *yang*) is understood as referring to the arts of darkness—death and killing—but is also said to mean "hidden," resulting in the translation of *Hidden Classic.*

9. "Shu yu t'an-hsin."

10. This first chapter essentially reprises the fall from natural harmony theory identified with Taoism that clearly influenced some of the military writings as well.

11. Essentially lead them on by similarity of view or approach, but then—to their surprise—confound them.

12. This passage is somewhat puzzling insofar as Master Kuei-ku (Kuei-ku Tzu) and much military thought stressed deceit and misdirection, especially initially concealing strength. Of course there was always a conceptual strain that emphasized the psychological impact of awesomeness.

13. Some texts have "delude" rather than "respond." Response is preferable, as translated.

Chapter 14

1. Also found in *Analects,* XIII:16.

2. Also found in "Chung-shu" and "Ai-kung Wen," *Li Chi.*

3. "Cheng Li," *Shuo Yüan.*

4. "Feng Shih."

5. Ibid.

6. "Shih Chün," *Lü-shih Ch'un-ch'iu.* Also found in "Feng Shih," *Shuo Yüan,* with slight changes suggesting the *Lü-shih Ch'un-ch'iu* version is original.

7. Rather problematically, the passage would require the *I Ching* to have been in existence at this time.

8. "Serving the Ruler," *Lü-shih Ch'un-ch'iu.*

9. "Shih Lan," *Lü-shih Ch'un-ch'iu.* Also found in "Ch'üan Mou," *Shuo Yüan.*

10. Chin was rent asunder by its ministerial families, rather than destroyed, in 434 B.C.

11. *Hsün-tzu* made a similar observation but emphasized the act of changing itself, coming to appreciate Worthies, noting that when a state is about to rise, it will invariably esteem teachers and learning, and thus laws and measures will be preserved, but when it is about to perish, the opposite will be true ("Ta-lüeh," *Hsün-tzu*).

12. "Ch'üan Mou," *Shuo Yüan.*

13. "Hsien-shih-lan," *Lü-shih Ch'un-ch'iu.*

14. Of course, from another perspective it might be argued that dissipation and excess characterized the earlier period, frugality and security the later, which is why intelligence analysis remains an art rather than a science.

15. "Cheng Li."

16. "Ch'üan Mou," *Shuo Yüan.* The original is found in Duke Ai, 1st year, *Tso Chuan.*

17. "Shuo-lin, Shang."

18. "Chih Wu," *Shuo Yüan.*

19. A similar range of criteria may be derived from the lengthy *Kuan-tzu* chapter entitled "Eight Observations," which analyzes the strengths and style of a state.

20. Later writers, such as Chu Hsi, were uninterested in the topic, perhaps because they confronted a very different political world.

21. "Fu Kuo."

22. "Chiang Kuo."

23. "Wu Ku."

24. "Pa Shuo," *Han Fei-tzu.*

25. "Kuei Shih."

26. "Wu-hsing Shun-ni."

27. "Li-su-lan." For a translation of "Chün Tao," see Jay Sailey, *The Master Who Embraces Simplicity* (San Francisco: Chinese Materials Center, 1978), esp. pp. 57–60.

28. "Wai-ch'u-shuo, Tso-shang."

29. "Chu-shu Hsün."

30. This is the same Tzu Kung already encountered in the introductory historical material.

31. "Chu-shu-hsün."

32. "Nei-p'ien Wen-shang," *Yen-tzu Ch'un-ch'iu.*

33. Ibid.

34. This entire dialogue has been previously translated in our *Art of War,* which may be consulted for appropriate notes.

35. "Ta Wu-k'ai," *Yi Chou-shu.* An interesting list of ten practices, aptly called Ten Defeats, is found in "Feng-pao-chieh." Another section of the *Yi Chou-shu* also notes that when a ruler loves wealth and treasure, it facilitates the acquisition of power by the perverse, and that one immersed in pleasure will lose his power to his ministers ("Shih-chi Chieh").

36. "Precursors to Extinction," *Han Fei-tzu.*

37. "Hsiung-nu Lieh-chuan," *Shih Chi.*

38. This sentence, a quote from the *Tao Te Ching,* is frequently found in military and political writings discussing—usually opposing—military action.

39. "Lun Kung," *Yen-t'ieh Lun.*

40. "Tung Yi Lieh-chuan," *Hou Han Shu.*

Chapter 15

1. "The Tao of the Military," *Six Secret Teachings.*

2. These have been extensively analyzed in our various books, including *Unorthodox Strategies* and *Complete Art of War.*

3. "Initial Estimations," *Art of War.*

4. Ibid.

5. Ibid.

6. "Preserving the State's Territory."

7. For a discussion, see the introduction to our translation *The Six Secret Teachings on the Way of Strategy* (Boston: Shambhala, 1997).

8. "Chüeh Sheng."

9. GSR 547C.

10. "Wang-p'ei Chieh."

11. See, for example, "Shih-jung Lun," part 4, "Jen-ti," *Lü-shih Ch'un-ch'iu.* The concept will be reexamined later in this section in conjunction with the *Hu-ling Ching.*

12. "The Army's Losses," *Military Methods.*

13. Duke Yin, 5th year. Some commentators suggest that this was only an excuse to go fishing, but later military writers see it as foresighted "walking of the terrain."

14. "Chao Shih-chia," *Shih Chi.*

15. "Han Shih-chung," *Sung Shu.*

16. "Severed Routes." In other chapters he also emphasizes the need to know the enemy's location at all times (chap. 45) and constantly observe them (chap. 44).

17. "The Army's Worms," *Chu-ko Liang Wu-hou Wen-chi.*

18. "Configurations of Terrain," but the intent is different.

19. "Selecting Officers," *T'ai-pai Yin-ching.*

20. "Scouts and Agents," *Ts'ui-wei Pei-cheng Lu.*

21. The very first example the author cites is that of the infamous Po P'i.

22. Reading "roll up" in concord with Sun-tzu, rather than "slowly" found in an alternate text, since slowness may be fatal on constricted terrain.

23. "Employing Masses," *Ssu-ma Fa.*

24. "The Tao of the General," *Wu-tzu.*

25. "Vacuity and Substance," *Art of War.* Book II of the T'ang dynasty *Questions and Replies* refers to Sun-tzu's approach, providing evidence of the tradition's continuity.

26. "The Questions of King Wei," *Military Methods.* (This is essentially Wu Ch'i's method.)

27. Many of Sun-tzu's basic observations are cited and integrated into the military writings through the Ch'ing dynasty, including Chu-ko Liang's collected works.

28. "Evaluating the Enemy *(Liao Ti)*," *Wu-tzu.* His observations are fully incorporated in the *Wu-ching Tsung-yao* chapter "Ch'a Ti-hsing."

29. The 10th, 16th, and 20th items have been lost.

30. Duke Hsiang, 18th year, *Tso Chuan.*

31. The same things were done at Sun Pin's famous victory at Ma-ling.

32. This closely paraphrases Sun-tzu but is not exact. (This whole final paragraph elaborates a section of Sun-tzu's "Vacuity and Substance," including the exact sentences that follow.)

33. "Ping-hsing," *T'ai-pai Yin-ching.* The last paragraph is almost identical with the concluding section of "Vacuity and Substance," substituting "flow" for "form."

34. "Military Combat."

35. "Evaluating the Enemy." A similar passage appears in the "Tao of the General," and is quoted in "Liao Ti-chiang," *Wu-ching Tsung-yao.*

36. Because they are on "fatal terrain," they would seem to have no alternative to standing and fighting. However, the author might equally be pointing out the danger of such forces exploiting the advantages of constricted terrain, entrapping and slaying any enemy troops that pursue them in.

37. The *Wu-ching Tsung-yao,* compiled slightly later, also contains a lengthy section that provides historical illustrations for many of the conditions and situations. (See *Hou-chi, chüan* 11.)

38. "The Tao of the General."

39. "Wu Chi," *Hu-ling Ching.* (Also see "Ping Chi.")

40. Sun-tzu mentioned constraints, but Wu-tzu explicated them in "Controlling the Army."

41. The original, in "Vacuity and Substance," has "stimulate them" rather than "observe them," thus an active probe rather than mere passive observation.

42. "Observing the Enemy."

43. Note that he isn't condemning these practices, just their emphasis to the exclusion of fundamental, human-focused measures.

44. "Shih K'o-chi," *Hu-ling Ching,* slightly rearranged for clarity.

45. "Five Conditions That Should Not Be Attacked," *Hu-ling Ching.*

46. "Maneuvering the Army." This will be further discussed in the final section on omens.

47. "Analyzing Enemy Encampments."

48. "Wen Yüan, 2," *Sung Shih, chüan* 440.

49. "Maneuvering the Army."

50. "The Tao of the General," *Wu-tzu.* Hsü Tung's remarks about various phenomena all derive from this chapter and the previous one entitled "Evaluating the Enemy."

51. All the examples to this point are from Sun-tzu's chapter entitled "Maneuvering the Army"; "The Army's Indications," *Six Secret Teachings,* is similar.

52. These observations are taken mainly from "Evaluating the Enemy," *Wu-tzu.*

53. "Maneuvering the Army."

54. "Vacuity and Substance."

55. *Questions and Replies,* Book III. The *Mencius* also remarks upon a similar procedure in a well-known passage in the first chapter.

56. "Spirit in Warfare," *Hundred Unorthodox Strategies.* Written in the Warring States period, the *Tso Chuan* entry may simply reflect Warring States conceptions projected backward.

57. *Mencius,* IIA2. The definitions, dimensions, and dynamics of *ch'i* are quite complex, entailing both metaphysical and psychological aspects. This extremely important concept still lacks a serious monograph in English, although it is touched upon in a number of places in Joseph Needham's multivolume *Science and Civilisation in China;* and a few monographs have appeared in Japanese and Chinese.

58. "Strict Positions."

59. "Stimulating the Officers."

60. "Discussion of Regulations." There is, of course, a distinction between being oblivious to life and death and being committed to dying in the fight.

61. *Questions and Replies*, Book III. Nominally attributed to Li Ching, the text's actual relationship to the T'ang period is somewhat murky.

62. "Spirit in Warfare," *Hundred Unorthodox Strategies*.

63. "Expanding *Ch'i*."

64. "Nine Terrains." Several chapters in the *Hundred Unorthodox Strategies* discuss the question of "fatal terrain" and eliciting the ultimate effort from the troops.

65. "Planning Offensives," *Art of War*.

66. For example, in "Initial Estimations" Sun-tzu states, "The general encompasses wisdom, credibility, benevolence, courage, and strictness."

67. "Nine Changes," *Art of War*.

68. "The Tao of the General," *Wu-tzu*. Most of the observations on generals are incorporated in the *Wu-ching Tsung-yao* section entitled "Liao Ti-chiang."

69. "A Discussion of Generals." Although similar materials are found throughout the military writings, the formulations in the *Six Secret Teachings* remain the most detailed and comprehensive.

70. "Observing the Enemy," *Hu-ling Ching*.

71. A number of military writings identify similar strengths and weaknesses in commanders, such as *Chu-ko Chung-wen-hou Wen-chi* ("Ch'ing Shih"), as well as the military sections of the *Ch'ang-tuan Ching* ("Chiang Ti"). More general assessments of position-correlated strengths and weaknesses are delineated by two sections of the *Jen-wu Chih*, "San Tu" and "Ts'ai Li."

Chapter 16

1. The exception is in prognostication texts. Sun-tzu employs the five colors, tastes, and sounds in an analogy in "Strategic Military Power" but without any reference to the five phases. Sun Pin apparently exploits their inherent conquest relationships in the enigmatic chapter entitled "Treasures of Terrain," but again without explicitly mentioning the concept.

2. The topic, as many others, clearly requires a dedicated volume or two. To date the best and practically only coverage remains Joseph Needham's explorations, with charts, in volume 2 of *Science and Civilisation in China, History of Scientific Thought* (Cambridge: Cambridge University Press, 1968).

3. See *Shang Shu*, the Books of Yao and Shun.

4. For a discussion of *shih*, see the introduction to our *Art of War* translation. Originally it probably entailed the concept of positional advantage coupled with power to signify the strategic advantage enjoyed by an army, but eventually it came to designate strategic power in general. However, *shih* is not something that might be observed in itself, but instead resolves in, and is evidenced by, its components—position, configuration of terrain, number of troops, discipline, spirit, and so forth, all key indicators enumerated by these observational check lists.

5. "Military Disposition," *Art of War*.

6. See Li Kang, "Chung-kuo ku-dai-shih shei shou chuang-yung sha-p'an ts'o ping-lai fen-hsi ti-ch'ing te," in *Chung-kuo Ku-dai Chün-shih San-pai-t'i* (Shanghai: Shanghai Ku-chi, 1987), p. 43. The incident is preserved in Ma Yüan's biography in the *Hou Han Shu*.

7. This explanation, perhaps plausible, was advanced by the modern military historian General Wei Ju-lin. See his *Sun-tzu Chin-chu Chin-yi* (Taipei: Shang-wu Yin-shu-kuan, 1972), pp. 222–224.

8. The commentators generally understand dispersive as referring to the tendency of the men while fighting in their native states to be thinking of their homes and families and inclined to return. Consequently, they are neither unified nor aroused to a fighting spirit, contrary to Western conceptions that men will fight most vigorously in defense of their immediate homes.

9. Apparently the soldiers still do not regard the enterprise too seriously and continue to think about home and family. Because it remains relatively easy to withdraw but dangerous to forge ahead, it is termed "light" terrain.

10. This is ground for which one contends, therefore "contentious" terrain.

11. "Stalemated" describes the tactical situation, although the exact character is *chih*, "branch" or "to support." Both sides are supported, so they are in a stalemate. Many commentators suggest a lengthy standoff.

12. This is also termed "accessible terrain." The army's movement is unhampered.

13. Presumably this is territory in which major roads intersect and is accessible to great powers on various sides. (The characters literally mean "terrain where highways intersect"; therefore, narrowly defined it would be land that is accessible from several directions over prepared roads.) Its occupation is the key to controlling vast territory.

14. This term contrasts with "light terrain," the severity of their situation now being apparent to the soldiers. Their minds are unified, their courage united.

15. "Precipitous" invokes the image of steep mountain gorges or ravines, "ravines" being the translation in other contexts. It is difficult terrain to traverse; therefore, occupying the heights is paramount.

16. "Entrapping terrain" is traditionally understood as low-lying ground, perhaps surrounded by hills or mountains, and characterized by bodies of water such as marshes or swamps. It is thought to be land that can be inundated, by heavy rains or by the breaking of restraining banks (as was done in China in World War II), and consequently involves heavy slogging for the chariots and men. However, there is considerable disagreement as to its defining characteristics.

17. "Constricted" configurations are generally described as extensive mountain valleys. Others also identify them with river or lake crossings.

18. The term for "encircled" is normally translated as "besieged" in other contexts. The emphasis here is on the necessity to pass through a narrow opening or along a narrow passage that constrains the flow of men and materials and thereby makes them vulnerable to even a small force.

19. In the original *Wu-ching Ch'i-shu* edition Liu Yin explains this as meaning that the general closes off any openings deliberately offered by the enemy to lure his forces out of their encirclement. Leaving such an opening was a

common way to keep the defenders from mounting a last-ditch, pitched defense. (Both the *Six Secret Teachings* and the *Wei Liao-tzu* discuss this technique.)

20. Sun-tzu consistently advocates exploiting the "ground of death" because when troops are deployed on it, the situation forces them to fight valiantly. Most commentators think it would be terrain with solid obstacles to the front—such as mountains—and water to the rear, preventing a withdrawal.

21. The tomb text differs somewhat: "If you have strongholds behind you and the enemy before you, it is fatal terrain. If there is no place to go, it is exhausted terrain."

22. The *Six Secret Teachings* analyzes the tactics for mountain warfare in a number of places and focuses on them in such chapters as the "Crow and Cloud Formations in the Mountains." The other military classics also discuss such terrain considerations, but are less focused.

23. This is understood as meaning that armies should not assume positions downstream from an enemy because of the potential danger of being inundated by suddenly released floodwaters or felled by drinking water drawn from a poisoned river.

24. The problems posed by wetlands and marshy terrain (also termed "entrapping" terrain) must have been well known to every military commander, and they are duly noted in virtually all the military writings, including Sun Pin's *Military Methods*. For example, see "Responding to Change," *Wu-tzu*; and "Crow and Cloud Formation in the Marshes" and "Battle Chariots," *Six Secret Teachings*.

25. Presumably, this is terrain that is easy for chariots to negotiate and for supply wagons to cross.

26. Life-supporting terrain is obviously ground that has sunlight, grass for the animals, brush and trees for firewood, and, especially, potable water.

27. Chu Chün points out that observing the presence of bubbles or foam on the river, which indicates rain upstream, exemplifies Sun-tzu's approach to analyzing and fathoming the enemy and battlefield situations. From the bubbles one can deduce that it has rained and can anticipate a surge in the river's flow and level. Such a surge could prove disastrous for an army encamped too close to the shore or caught suddenly in midstream. See his *Sun-tzu Ping-fa Shih-yi* (Peking: Hai-ch'ao Ch'u-pan-she, 1990), p. 137.

28. Heaven's Well is so named because it is a significant depression, such as a valley, surrounded on four sides by hills or mountains. It is dangerous because the runoff of rainwater from unexpected storms can inundate the lowlands. Heaven's Jail is a valley with steep hills or mountains on three sides. Forces that carelessly enter it can easily be bottled up, unable to ascend the sides to escape. Heaven's Net refers to any area of extensive, dense growth—including heavy forests or dense vegetation (such as junglelike growth of underbrush and vines) that will obstruct the passage of vehicles or entangle men. Heaven's Pit refers to an area characterized by soft, probably muddy terrain, perhaps marked by wetlands, that will mire both men and vehicles. Heaven's Fissure refers to terrain that suggests a fissure in the earth. Therefore, it en-

compasses long, narrow passages constrained by hills or forests from which an enemy might advantageously dominate the passage.

29. In "Eight Formations" he clearly states: "On both difficult and easy terrain you must know the tenable and fatal ground. Occupy tenable ground and attack the enemy on fatal ground." Ravines ranked paramount among the terrain that cause difficulty ("The Questions of King Wei").

30. Extensive discussion of all these questions together with sentence notes will be found in our translation of the *Military Methods*.

31. Being confronted by a wide river is also pondered in "Crow and Cloud Formation in the Marshes."

32. In "Divided Valleys" the enemy is encountered in the midst of a steep valley, with movement being constrained by a river to the right and mountains to the left.

33. "Ten Deployments," *Military Methods*.

34. "Huang-fu Sung, Chu Chün Lieh-chuan."

35. His description is almost exactly the same as Sun-tzu's, with the addition of preparing defenses on less visible roads to prevent an unseen advance by the enemy. (It might also mean "preventing spies from obtaining access.")

36. This is clearly not Sun-tzu's definition, but is somewhat more dramatic.

37. "Tenable Terrain." See, for example, "Treasures of Terrain," *Military Methods*.

38. "Fatal Terrain," *Hu-ling Ching*.

39. "Analyzing Mountains," *Hu-ling Ching*.

40. The difficulty in crossing rivers and the degree of exhaustion that would result may be seen in Sun Pin's assessment that "an army that is encamping after being on the march without avoiding notable rivers, whose *ch'i* has been harmed and determination weakened, can be attacked" ("Male and Female Cities," *Military Methods*).

41. For an example, see the historical illustration to "Rivers," *Unorthodox Strategies*.

42. "Shen-ta-lan."

43. "Ssu-hsun-lun," *Lü-shih Ch'un-ch'iu*.

44. "Analyzing Rivers," *Hu-ling Ching*.

45. "Maneuvering the Army," *Art of War*.

46. "Male and Female Cities," *Military Methods*.

47. This clearly contradicts the extant *Art of War*, which states, "On light terrain do not stop." Since the sentence clearly appears thus from the *Seven Military Classics* editions onward, and no doubt earlier as evidenced by the first commentaries (which much of his passage also draws upon), his reversal is highly puzzling. However, all the editions consulted write it thus.

48. This is exactly Tu Yu's commentary. Hsü quotes the commentaries very extensively here, intermixing them with the original *Art of War* text.

49. This is in accord with Sun-tzu's dictum in "Military Combat."

50. Although said about the enemy's forces, it is equally applicable to one's own in line with the principle of knowing the enemy and knowing yourself.

51. "Vacuity and Substance." The original has "stimulate them" for "observe them."

52. The text always has Wu-tzu as the speaker rather than the king of Wu, but the two were not contemporaries. Unless viewed as a deliberately fictional dialogue, the king of Wu should be understood as the actual speaker.

53. They also appear as part of Ho Yen-hsi's commentary in the Ten Commentaries edition of the *Art of War*. Unfortunately, Ho is otherwise unknown, although he probably lived around the end of the T'ang and certainly before the eleventh century. One line of thought sees these dialogues as having been passed down by Ts'ao Ts'ao, the first commentator on the *Art of War*, who is much reviled for radically editing the extant Han dynasty text to produce the present thirteen-chapter version. Despite historical references to Sun-tzu having presented a thirteen-chapter book to the king of Wu, the tradition of an eighty-two-chapter version—based upon a Han dynasty bibliographic entry—continues until today, where new claims of having recovered it are being made. (The entire *T'ung Tien* section is translated in our *Art of War*.)

54. Note that he uses terrains and configurations separately.

55. This is a different interpretation from those that emphasize not allowing troops to become broken off, isolated.

56. Supplementing "not," which has been lost.

57. The *T'ung Tien* has the following additional sentences: "With picked soldiers and well-trained troops they will block off the advantageous positions and occupy them. They will sustain our military affairs and make our provisions substantial. Order our chariots and cavalry to go in and out with an attitude of respectful anticipation."

58. This phrase is found in the *Art of War*.

59. The last clause does not appear in the *Art of War*.

60. The idea of "speedily" has been lost.

61. Situations such as this are the subject of several chapters in the *Six Secret Teachings*.

62. The *T'ung Tien* has "thundering the drums."

63. The text is corrupt but also differs from Ho's original commentary and the *T'ung Tien*, which runs: "Sever their supply routes. If you are afraid that they have unorthodox troops concealed that have not been observed, have our bowmen and crossbowmen guard against their positions."

64. Restoring "not," which has dropped out.

65. "Tries to entice us with profit" has dropped out.

66. This entire section is largely from Sun-tzu's chapter entitled "Maneuvering the Army."

67. *T'ung Tien*, chüan 159.

68. "Responding to Change," *Wu-tzu*.

69. This paragraph is essentially a condensation of "Forest Warfare," *Six Secret Teachings*.

70. This is discussed in the section on counterintelligence.

71. The section concludes by quoting in full Wu Ch'i's characterization of the spirit and martial practices of the various states already reprised in the historical section on the Warring States. (Many of the sentences describing the barbarians in this passage are taken verbatim from *chüan* 49 of the *Han Shu*, which has already been provided in translation.)

72. "Our Great China" was literally the Central State or Kingdom as it came to be popularly translated, but "China" for convenience.

73. This description of their warriors to this point all comes, with only slight variations, from the *Shih Chi* antique chapter on the Hsiung-nu already quoted in the political intelligence section.

74. This paragraph incorrectly attributes the method to the Warring States period when in fact this is the tactical advice offered for confronting the Jung in one of the first battles in the *Tso Chuan*, recorded for Duke Yin's 9th year, 713 B.C., right at the beginning of the Spring and Autumn period. Wu Ch'i later adopted this method, but it became famous in itself, even contributing a well-known dictionary entry for "three ambushes" (*san fu*).

75. This is essentially a paraphrase of Sun-tzu's "Maneuvering the Army."

76. The author apparently treats most of the paragraphs as quotes from Sun-tzu ("Maneuvering the Army"), as all but the last one essentially are, and then appends his comment. However, it is a loose construction at best. (Also note how the compilation moves from subject to subject simply on the turn of a keyword.)

77. His observations are found in a memorial preserved in the *Han Shu*, thus showing the wide variety of sources employed by the text. (He actually cites some military writings similar to the *Six Secret Teachings*.)

78. The first four sentences are not in the *Art of War* as such, but the later ones are derived from it.

79. This and the following quotation are from "Strict Positions."

80. Despite being such a significant undertaking, the compendium lacks the flow and well-integrated (or thought out) quality of Tu Yu's *T'ung Tien*, from which it borrows extensively. Often a pastiche of rather disjointed sentences that betray the compilers' (predominately scholars rather than military men?) cut-and-paste mentality, it frequently revises or misquotes original works and suffers from numerous miscopied and missing characters. The translation emends or supplements where necessary from the original texts when identifiable, any significant changes being indicated in the notes.

81. "Planning Offensives," *Art of War*. Incredible motivation was of course required to elicit such performances from the men. Even the late Sung *Hundred Unorthodox Strategies* cites this situation as exemplifying the need for rewards in a chapter entitled "Rewards in Warfare": "In general, if despite high walls, deep moats, and a hail of stones and arrows the officers and troops are to compete with each other to ascend the walls, or when the naked blades first clash they are to contend with each other in rushing forth, they must be enticed with heavy rewards. Then every enemy will be conquered. A tactical principle from the *Three Strategies* states: 'Beneath heavy rewards there will certainly be courageous fellows.'"

82. In "Nine Changes" the traditional text simply asserts, "There are fortified cities that are not assaulted." The tomb fragments include this, as well as the passage translated here.

83. For a comprehensive discussion of the evolving tactics and technology of sieges and countersieges, see Robin D.S. Yates, "Early Poliorcetics: The Mo-

hists to the Sung," in Joseph Needleman, *Science and Civilisation in China* (Cambridge: Cambridge University Press, 1994), 5:6:30.

84. A discussion of the theory behind these classifications may be found in our translation of the *Military Methods*.

85. "Military Instructions, II."

86. Ibid.

87. "Tactical Balance of Power in Attacks."

88. "Tactical Balance of Power in Defense."

89. "Occupying Enemy Territory."

Chapter 17

1. These were originally thought to be simple queries about whether an act would be auspicious, but the current view is that the ruler believed he could influence the state of affairs. See, for example, David N. Keightley, *Sources of Shang History* (Berkeley and Los Angeles: University of California Press, 1978), p. 33; and Paul Serruys, "Studies in the Language of the Shang Oracle Inscriptions," *T'oung Pao* 40, nos. 1–3 (1974):25–28.

2. The *Shuo Yüan* preserves an interesting example of a leader being forewarned of a military attack through plastromancy. In this incident Hsien Chen, who had distinguished himself at the battle of Ch'eng-p'u, for his own purposes persuaded Duke Hsiang of Chin to attack Ch'in, but the latter became aware of Chin's approaching army through routine divination, which coincidentally indicated it would be auspicious to attack the invaders, a tactic that was successfully executed ("Ching Shen").

3. For an overview, see Michael Loewe, "Divination by Shells, Bones, and Stalks," in *Divination, Mythology, and Monarchy in Han China* (Cambridge: Cambridge University Press, 1994). The *Shang Shu* discusses the relative importance of the types of divination for state purposes, giving slight preference to the turtle over the newer milfoil, but even greater import to the opinions of men. It also notes that there are other basic forms of verification for courses of activity that largely relate to proper seasonable activity, with extremes being omens of inimical courses. (See "Hung Fan" and "Ta Yü Mo.")

4. For a discussion of the *I Ching*'s role in the *Tso Chuan*, see Kidder Smith, "*Zhouyi* Interpretation from Accounts in the *Zuochuan*," *HJAS* 49, no. 2 (1989):421–463.

5. "Ch'üan Mou," *Shuo Yüan*.

6. "Ching Shen." Dreams were another important source of information about the future—worthy of a chapter in themselves—but had to be interpreted before being of any value. Remarkably, divination by the *I Ching* was often employed to provide critical clues necessary for complete insight.

7. "Planning for the State," *Wu-tzu*.

8. "Evaluating the Enemy," *Wu-tzu*.

9. Although clearly intended for individual use, the *Ling Ch'i Ching* contains a number of military images and prognostications. (For further discus-

sion, see the introductory material to our translation [Boston: Shambhala, 1995].)

10. "The King's Wings," *Six Secret Teachings*. Extensive material on interpreting the significance of comets, scintillating stars, the varying appearance of stars and constellations, and other observable phenomena are preserved in a number of military works and in the treatises on astronomy in the early histories.

11. "Middle Strategy." A similar view appears in the *Hu-ling Ching*. (The *Three Strategies* also states, "Prohibit mediums and shamans from divining about the army's good or bad fortune on behalf of the officials and officers.")

12. "Heavenly Offices."

13. "Martial Plans," *Wei Liao-tzu*.

14. T'ien Tan, whose was previously mentioned in conjunction with Yüeh Yi, is discussed in our forthcoming *History of Warfare in China: The Ancient Period*.

15. The T'ai Kung's biography in the *Shih Chi* relates his effort to stiffen the troops when the omens for attacking the Shang proved inauspicious and heavy wind and rain, both ill portents, arose at the critical moment. To justify his disregard for such overwhelmingly baleful signs, he claimed that the overthrow of the ruling house could hardly produce favorable indications. This may be understood as referring to the moment of action, rather than the enterprise in general, because in "Opening Instructions" he stresses that revolutionary activity cannot be undertaken on personal responsibility alone: "If there are no ill omens in the Tao of Heaven, you cannot initiate the movement to revolt. If there are no misfortunes in the Tao of Man, your planning cannot precede them. You must first see Heavenly signs and moreover witness human misfortune; only thereafter can you make plans." His emphasis upon relieving the suffering of the people, the sole justification in the view of Confucians such as Mencius and most of the military writers, stands forth clearly.

16. *Questions and Replies*, Book III.

17. These comments essentially embody the "Virtue triumphant" approach to warfare, which dogmatically asserted that the ancient Sages always conquered through Virtue, without bloodshed, despite evidence to the contrary. Mencius was a chief proponent of this view, and its inclusion in the *Wei Liao-tzu*, a harsh military work, is both remarkable and puzzling.

18. *Questions and Replies*, Book III.

19. Ibid., Book II.

20. "Ch'u-chün Jih," *Hu-ling Ching*.

21. Over the centuries several well-known arrangements for the sixty-four hexagrams evolved that, once codified, permitted their employment in both abstract and concrete ways.

22. Eliminating doubt among the troops and defusing inimical influences that might undermine their spirit and confidence, such as unexplained portents and omens, were paramount concerns for military commanders and thus the subject of numerous passages and injunctions throughout the military writings.

23. "Chao Ch'ung-kuo, Hsin Ch'ing-chi," *Han Shu.*

24. Chao's tactics are reprised as the historical illustration for chapter 92 of the *Unorthodox Strategies.*

25. "Tung Chuo Lieh-chuan," *Hou Han Shu.*

26. Individuals, as well as armies, also profited from intelligence gleaned from knowledge and skill in these practices. At the end of the Former Han Jen Wen-kung, a noted practitioner of esoteric methods, escaped the violence spawned in Wang Mang's era by foretelling its arising and moving into the hills with his family ("Fang-shih Lieh-chuan"). Perhaps not coincidentally, he earlier had served as a spy along the provincial borders to secretly investigate the strategic situation.

27. For a discussion of the practice of determining seasonal progressions by watching for a *ch'i* response amid the ashes of appropriate pitch pipes, see Huang Yi-long and Chang Chih-ch'eng, "The Evolution and Decline of the Ancient Practice of Watching for the Ethers," *Chinese Science* no. 13 (1996):82–106.

28. Derke Bodde broached the subject in 1959 with his article "The Chinese Cosmic Magic Known as Watching for the Ethers," reprinted in *Essays on Chinese Civilization* (Princeton: Princeton University Press, 1981), pp. 351–372. A.S.P. Hulsewe added further information two decades later with "Watching the Vapours: An Ancient Chinese Technique of Prognostication," *Nachrichten* 125 (1979):40–49. Recently Michael Loewe expanded the discussion with a series of interesting articles on it and other aspects of divination— such as "the oracles of the clouds and winds"—conveniently gathered in *Divination, Mythology, and Monarchy in Han China* (Cambridge: Cambridge University Press, 1994). Unfortunately, even though all three provide examples of military cases from the general literature, especially the dynastic histories, little use has been made of the military literature itself. Two articles in Chinese also provide useful discussions: Ho Kuan-hu, "Hsien-Ch'in Liang-Han Chan-hou Yün-ch'i chih Chu-tso Shu-lüeh," *Chung-kuo-shih Yen-chiu* 1 (1988):133–139; and Ch'en P'an, "Ying-ch'ao Tun-huang Hsieh-pen Chan-yün-ch'i-shu Ts'an-chüan Chieh-t'i," *BIHP* 50, no. 1 (March 1979):1–27.

29. See the section entitled "General Field Assessments."

30. "The Army's Indications."

31. "The Five Notes."

32. Ibid.

33. "The Book of Heavenly Offices," *Shih Chi.* Hulsewe discusses this passage and others, and provides examples of actual military incidents employing them, in "Watching the Vapours."

34. In *Divination, Mythology, and Monarchy,* Loewe provides some examples of military prognostication from cloud formations based upon recently recovered texts and also incidents of wind interpretation in a military context.

35. "Yün Ch'i T'ung-lun" (General Discussion of Cloud *Ch'i*).

36. Distinctions in the text among clouds, *ch'i,* and cloud *ch'i*—whatever their essence and phenomenal correlates—are maintained in the translation.

37. "Chiang-chün Yün-ch'i."

38. There are not exactly ten, just as thirteen earlier was puzzling. Perhaps it is a character error for six, or perhaps material has been lost.

39. Some texts say a headless dead man.

40. "Shih Lai Hsü-shih Chan," *Wu-ching Tsung-yao.*

41. "Yin-mou Ch'i" (*Ch'i* of Secret Plots).

42. This might also be understood as "emissaries from other states coming to make plans with you," but the conclusion—assassinating them—would be inappropriate to Li Ch'uan's moral orientation.

Index